ESSENTIALS OF

Business Research Methods

SECOND EDITION

Therese,

Glad to have you in the DBA program. Hope you find my new book useful in your research and classes.

Joe Hair
February 2011

ESSENTIALS OF
Business
Research
Methods

SECOND EDITION

Joseph F. Hair Jr. • Mary Wolfinbarger Celsi

Arthur H. Money • Phillip Samouel • Michael J. Page

M.E.Sharpe
Armonk, New York
London, England

Library of Congress Cataloging-in-Publication Data

Essentials of business research methods / by Joseph F. Hair Jr. ... [et al.]. — 2nd ed.
  p. cm.
 Includes bibliographical references and index.
 ISBN 978-0-7656-2631-8 (pbk. : alk. paper)
 1. Business—Research. I. Hair, Joseph F.

 HD30.4.E86 2011
 650.072--dc22   2010022588

Printed in the United States of America

The paper used in this publication meets the minimum requirements of
American National Standard for Information Sciences
Permanence of Paper for Printed Library Materials,
ANSI Z 39.48-1984.

IBT (p)   10   9   8   7   6   5   4   3   2   1

Brief Table of Contents

PREFACE   xv

PART I. INTRODUCTION

1. Business Research for the Twenty-First Century   3
2. Overview of the Research Process   27
3. Ethics in Business Research   52

PART II. BEGINNING THE RESEARCH PROCESS

4. Defining the Research Problem and Reviewing the Literature   81
5. The Nature and Sources of Secondary Business Data   110
6. Conceptualization and Research Design   133

PART III. SAMPLING AND DATA COLLECTION

7. Sampling Approaches and Considerations   163
8. Methods of Collecting Primary Data   185
9. Measurement and Scaling   209
10. Questionnaire Design   247

PART IV. ANALYSIS AND INTERPRETATION OF DATA

11. Basic Data Analysis for Qualitative Research   275
12. Basic Data Analysis for Quantitative Research   294
13. Testing Hypotheses in Quantitative Research   320
14. Examining Relationships Using Correlation and Regression   348
15. Other Multivariate Techniques   385

PART V. COMMUNICATING THE RESULTS

16. Reporting and Presenting Research   425

GLOSSARY   443
INDEX   461
ABOUT THE AUTHORS   475

v

Detailed Table of Contents

PREFACE   XV

PART I. INTRODUCTION   1

1. BUSINESS RESEARCH FOR THE TWENTY-FIRST CENTURY   3
Learning Outcomes   3
Business Research Defined   4
    A Truth-Seeking Function   4
Elements of Business Research   5
What Do Business Researchers Study?   6
Trends Impacting Business Research   9
    Expanding Market Freedom   9
    International Research   10
    Relationship Marketing   11
    The Information Revolution   12
The Manager-Researcher Relationship   19
    Who Performs Business Research?   19
Continuing Case Study: Samouel's and Gino's Restaurants   20
Continuing Case: Samouel's Greek Cuisine   21
Summary   22

2. OVERVIEW OF THE RESEARCH PROCESS   27
Learning Outcomes   27
The Business Research Process   27
    Phase I: Formulation   28
    Phase II: Execution   31
    Phase III: Analytical   32
Theory and Business Research   33
    The Fuel for Research   33

Continuing Case: Samouel's Greek Cuisine—Do Lower Prices
  Result in Higher Sales?   34
The Practicality of Theory   35
The Scientific Method and Business Research   37
  Rigor of Science   40
  The Pragmatics of Business   40
Research Proposals   40
  Structure of a Research Proposal   41
Continuing Case: Samouel's Greek Cuisine—Is Theory Useful
  in Business Research?   45
Summary   49

3. ETHICS IN BUSINESS RESEARCH   52
Learning Outcomes   52
Business Ethics Defined   52
Relevance of Business Ethics   53
Ethical Obligations of the Researcher   55
  Before the Research Project   55
  During and After the Research   57
Ethical Obligations of the Client   64
  Before the Research   64
  During and After the Research   64
Ethical Obligations of Research Participants   65
  Voluntary Participation   65
  Faithful Participation   66
  Honesty   66
  Privacy   66
Implications of Unethical Actions   66
Access to Respondents: Strategies and Tactics   69
Issues in Obtaining Access   69
  Barriers to Access   71
Continuing Case: Samouel's Greek Cuisine   74
Summary   74

PART II. BEGINNING THE RESEARCH PROCESS   79

4. DEFINING THE RESEARCH PROBLEM AND REVIEWING THE LITERATURE   81
Learning Outcomes   81
Characteristics of a Quality Research Topic   82
Converting Research Ideas into Research Questions and Objectives   85
  The Role of Theory in Research   88
Preparing a Literature Review   89
Contributions of the Literature Review   93
  Defining the Research Problem   93
  Background Information   94

Research Questions and Hypotheses   95
Methodology   95
Interpretation   96
Literature Sources   96
Books   97
Journals and Conference Proceedings   97
Government and Industry   98
Theses and Dissertations   98
Electronic Databases   98
Internet Searches   99
Planning the Literature Search   99
Writing a Literature Review   100
Confirming Research Questions with the Literature Review   102
Continuing Case: Samouel's Greek Cuisine—Developing Research
   Questions and Objectives   105
Summary   106

5. The Nature and Sources of Secondary Business Data   110
Learning Outcomes   110
Secondary Business Data Defined   111
Sources and Types of Secondary Business Data   111
Locating Secondary Business Data   114
Advantages and Disadvantages of Secondary Data   119
Advantages of Secondary Data   119
Evaluating Secondary Sources   120
Disadvantages of Secondary Data   122
Evaluating the Quality of Secondary Business Data   124
Evaluating the Source   124
Evaluating the Research Design   124
Evaluating Data Collection Methods   125
Ethical Issues Related to the Use of Secondary Data   127
Continuing Case: Using Secondary Data with Samouel's Restaurant   128
Summary   128

6. Conceptualization and Research Design   133
Learning Outcomes   133
Developing a Conceptual Model   133
Identifying Variables and Constructs   134
Preparing a Conceptual Model   139
Basic Research Designs   144
Qualitative Versus Quantitative Approaches   145
Three Types of Research Designs   147
Using Several Research Designs   155
Continuing Case: Samouel's Greek Cuisine   156
Summary   157

PART III. SAMPLING AND DATA COLLECTION 161

7. SAMPLING APPROACHES AND CONSIDERATIONS 163
Learning Outcomes 163
Sampling 164
The Sampling Process 165
  Defining the Target Population 165
  Choosing the Sampling Frame 166
  Selecting the Sampling Method 167
  Probability Sampling 168
Continuing Case: Samouel's Greek Cuisine—Which Is Better,
  Proportionately or Disproportionately Stratified Samples? 172
Continuing Case: Samouel's Greek Cuisine—Cluster Sampling
  of Restaurant Customers 174
  Nonprobability Sampling 174
Determining Sample Size 176
  Sampling from a Large Population 176
  Sampling from a Small Population 179
Implementing the Sampling Plan 180
Continuing Case: Samouel's Greek Cuisine—Which Sampling Method
  Is Best? 182
Summary 182

8. METHODS OF COLLECTING PRIMARY DATA 185
Learning Outcomes 185
Data Collection Methods 185
Qualitative Data Collection 186
  Observation 186
  Ethnographic Research 188
  Content Analysis 189
  Interviews 190
Quantitative Data Collection 197
  Self-Completion Surveys 198
  Interviewer-Completed Surveys 203
  Observation 204
Continuing Case: Samouel's Greek Cuisine—Choosing the Best
  Data Collection Method 204
Summary 204

9. MEASUREMENT AND SCALING 209
Learning Outcomes 209
What Is a Concept? 209
Measurement in Business Research 210
  Measurement Difficulties 211
How to Measure Concepts 214

Types of Scales   215
    Nominal Scale   215
    Ordinal Scale   216
    Interval Scale   219
    Ratio Scale   220
Frequently Used Measurement Scales   221
    Metric Scales   221
    Nonmetric Scales   227
Practical Decisions When Developing Scales   230
    Number of Scale Categories   230
    Number of Items in Measuring a Concept   230
    Odd or Even Number of Categories   231
    Balanced or Unbalanced Scales   231
    Forced or Nonforced Choice   231
    Category Labels for Scales   232
Criteria for Assessing Measurement Scales   232
    Reliability   233
Continuing Case: Samouel's Greek Cuisine—Using SPSS to
    Calculate Cronbach's Alpha   237
    Validity   238
How to Develop a Scale   240
Summary   241

10. QUESTIONNAIRE DESIGN   247
    Learning Outcomes   247
    Questionnaires   247
    Steps in the Questionnaire Design Process   249
        Initial Considerations   252
        Clarification of Concepts   254
        Determining Question Types, Format, and Sequence   254
        Preparing and Presenting Good Questions   262
        Preparing Clear Instructions   266
        Pretesting the Questionnaire   267
        Administering the Questionnaire   268
    Continuing Case: Evaluating the Samouel's and Gino's Customer Survey
        Questionnaires   269
    Summary   269

PART IV. ANALYSIS AND INTERPRETATION OF DATA   273

11. BASIC DATA ANALYSIS FOR QUALITATIVE RESEARCH   275
    Learning Outcomes   275
    Understanding Qualitative Research   275
    Qualitative Research Approaches   276
    Managing Qualitative Data   278

Analyzing Qualitative Data 281
Data Reduction 282
Data Display 283
Drawing and Verifying Conclusions 286
Assessing Credibility 287
Continuing Case: Samouel's Greek Cuisine—The Role of Qualitative
Research 289
Summary 290

12. BASIC DATA ANALYSIS FOR QUANTITATIVE RESEARCH 294
Learning Outcomes 294
Analyzing Quantitative Data 295
Data Preparation 295
Data Analysis Using Descriptive Statistics 299
The Frequency Distribution 300
Histograms 302
Bar Charts 306
Pie Charts 306
The Normal Distribution 308
Measures of Central Tendency 310
Examples of Measures of Central Tendency 311
Measures of Dispersion 312
Examples of Measures of Dispersion 315
Outliers 315
Continuing Case: Samouel's Greek Cuisine—Using Descriptive Statistics
with the Restaurant Employee Survey 317
Summary 317

13. TESTING HYPOTHESES IN QUANTITATIVE RESEARCH 320
Learning Outcomes 320
Understanding Hypothesized Relationships 321
Sample Statistics Versus Population Parameters 321
Type I and Type II Errors 323
Hypothesis Testing 325
Choosing the Appropriate Statistical Technique 325
Other Considerations in Hypothesis Testing 326
Single Group Hypothesis Testing 327
Multiple Group Hypothesis Testing 330
ANOVA (Analysis of Variance) 336
Factorial Design: Two-Way ANOVA 340
Multivariate Analysis of Variance (MANOVA) 343
Continuing Case: Samouel's Greek Cuisine—Developing Relationships
and Testing Hypotheses 344
Summary 345

14. Examining Relationships Using Correlation and Regression 348
Learning Outcomes 348
Types of Relationships Between Variables 348
   Presence 349
   Nature of Relationships 349
   Direction 349
   Strength of Association 350
Variable Relationships and Covariation 350
Correlation Analysis 352
   An Example of Pearson Bivariate Correlation 353
   Practical Significance of the Correlation Coefficient 355
   Measurement Scales and Correlation 355
   An Example of the Spearman Rank Order Correlation 356
Statistical Techniques and Data Analysis 358
Regression Analysis 361
   An Example of Bivariate Regression 363
Multiple Regression Analysis 366
   Statistical Versus Practical Significance 368
   An Example of Multiple Regression 369
   Multicollinearity and Multiple Regression 374
   An Example of Multicollinearity 374
Advanced Topics in Multiple Regression 377
   The Role of Dummy Variables in Regression 377
   An Example of Dummy Variables 378
Summary 381

15. Other Multivariate Techniques 385
Learning Outcomes 385
Exploratory Factor Analysis 386
   Deriving Factors 388
   Number of Factors 392
Interpreting Factors 394
   An Example of Factor Analysis 395
   Cluster Analysis 399
   Deriving Clusters 400
   Phase I 401
   Phase II 404
   Phase III 404
   An Example of Cluster Analysis 405
   Multiple Discriminant Analysis 408
   An Example of Discriminant Analysis 415
   Stepwise Discriminant Analysis 418
Summary 419

PART V. COMMUNICATING THE RESULTS 423

16. REPORTING AND PRESENTING RESEARCH 425
Learning Outcomes 425
Written and Oral Communications 426
 Audience Sophistication 426
 Written Communication 426
Research Proposals 428
The Written Research Report 429
 An Outline of an Applied Business Research Report 430
 An Outline of a Basic Research Report 434
Oral Presentations 436
 Considering the Audience 436
 Presentation Format 437
 Presentation Dos and Don'ts 437
Summary 439

GLOSSARY 443
INDEX 461
ABOUT THE AUTHORS 475

Preface

Business research in a knowledge-based, global economy presents many challenges for managers. Businesses are challenged to be more decisive and offer higher-quality products and services, and they must do so with fewer people at lower costs. This means modern business managers must make more decisions in a shorter period of time, and those decisions must be better. Fortunately, the tools and technologies available to business professionals have expanded dramatically. Computing power, storage capacity, and software expertise no longer represent significant barriers to processing information. The speed and memory of personal computers have been doubling every eighteen months while prices have been dropping. Windows-based and other user-friendly interfaces have brought sophisticated data analysis software packages into the "click-and-point" and "drag-and-drop" era, greatly reducing the need for specialized computer skills to utilize otherwise complex statistical software packages. Now, even "unsophisticated" users can analyze large quantities of complex data with relative ease. The knowledge that emerges from application of these new tools and technologies contributes to better decision making.

Research turns information into knowledge. Better business knowledge is essential to improved decision making. This book is about making better decisions by using knowledge that only research can create. The book places minimal emphasis on statistical theory and maximum effort in providing basic skills covering a wide range of potential business research applications. By using the concepts and principles presented in this book, the reader will be better able to cope with the fast-paced decision-making environment of business today and tomorrow.

MANAGERS NEED BUSINESS RESEARCH SKILLS

The amount of information available for decision making has exploded in recent years, and it will continue to do so. Until recently, much information just disappeared. Either it was not collected or it was discarded, often because there was no cost-effective way of keeping it. Today information is collected and stored in data warehouses, and it is available to be mined for improved decision making. Sometimes the information can be analyzed and understood with simple analytical tools. Other times, turning it into business intelligence requires more complex approaches. In this book, we cover the simple as well as some of the more complex tools in an easily understood manner. Without knowledge of these business research tools, managers and entrepreneurs simply cannot benefit from the intelligence emerging from this expanded database of information.

Most business research texts are long and take an encyclopedic approach. This book covers the important topics in a concise manner and focuses on the essentials of business research for managers. It includes coverage of the increasing role of knowledge management as well as how to conduct information-gathering activities more effectively in a rapidly changing business environment. The fundamentals of business research, such as research design, use of qualitative and quantitative data, and sampling and questionnaire design, are presented in a highly readable format. Illustrations are used in conjunction with many practical examples to highlight significant points.

A Business Research Dashboard feature provides applied examples of actual research problems and current issues. Some Business Research Dashboard examples summarize actual research studies. Others describe Web sites that help researchers analyze qualitative data, locate sources of secondary data, or design better survey questionnaires. Case studies involving applications of research approaches are also included as well as instructions on how to use statistical software to analyze data. With more than 100 Business Research Dashboard examples, the text material is truly brought to life! In addition to the Business Research Dashboard examples, we give Internet applications/questions at the end of each chapter that provide interactive exercises for students as well as discussion questions that pose analytical issues going beyond just repeating topics covered in the chapters. Finally, each chapter has an ethical dilemma case to stimulate thinking on and understanding of ethics-related topics.

The book is based on the need of managers to make better decisions. Thus, research is couched in the greater decision-making context. Because managers increasingly must make decisions based on almost unlimited information in data warehouses, we provide more coverage of data analysis techniques in this book than do other texts. We recognize that most managers and business students will not be data analysts. But an understanding of data analysis techniques will help them to better utilize the increasing amounts of information they will be expected to apply in decision making. Our straightforward, hands-on approach makes the book particularly successful with advanced undergraduates in all business disciplines and graduate business students, both in traditional and executive programs. The book will also serve as an effective reference guide for advanced users, including basic researchers and beginning doctoral students.

Changes in the business environment have created opportunities as well as uncertainty, and they make the role of business research even more important in improving decision making. For example, information technology has made more accurate financial forecasting possible, has improved employee productivity, and enables more information to be collected and stored at a reasonable price. Knowledge is power, but managers must convert the increasing amount of information into knowledge before its power can be tapped. Businesses that are best able to harness this power will be those that are successful in the long run. Hence, a main focus of the book is the collection, evaluation, understanding, and use of information from the manager's perspective.

EXCELLENT PEDAGOGY

Our pedagogy has been developed from many years of conducting and teaching business research. To bring the concepts to life and make the text more interesting, we focus on a single case throughout the book. Phil Samouel is a restaurant entrepreneur in New York City. His Greek restaurant competes with Gino's Italian Ristorante. Phil hires a business research consultant to help him, and the case study is used to illustrate the principles of business research throughout the book. The consultant has recommended two surveys, one of customers and the other of Phil's employees. Both questionnaires are included in the text, and two databases from the results of the surveys are used to demonstrate the data analysis techniques. A sample report of the surveys' initial findings is available on our Web site (www.mesharpe-student.com). Exercises at the end of the chapters provide an opportunity for students to further examine the findings of the two surveys and to use them in preparing a more comprehensive report on the restaurant case study. Electronic copies of the questionnaires and databases are available on our Web site.

The running case study makes it easy for readers to become familiar with the Samouel's Greek Cuisine case and refer to it in each chapter. For example, we refer to the case when we discuss research design alternatives as well as when evaluating different sampling approaches. The thinking behind the employee questionnaire is provided in the measurement and scaling chapter, and the rationale for the customer survey questionnaire is reviewed in the questionnaire design chapter. In all the data analysis chapters we use the case study data to illustrate SPSS, Excel, and the various statistical techniques. A copy of the research proposal given to Phil Samouel is provided in chapter 2, and a summary of the research report is on our Web site, at www.mesharpe-student.com. Focusing on a single case study throughout the book enables readers to more easily understand the benefits and pitfalls of using research to improve business decision making.

The book's coverage of quantitative data analysis is more extensive and much easier to understand than that in other texts. Step-by-step instructions are included on how to use SPSS to execute data analysis for all statistical techniques. In selected instances similar information is provided for Excel. This enables instructors to spend much less time teaching students how to use the software. It also saves time later by providing a handy reference for students if they forget how to use the software. For instructors who want to cover more advanced statistical techniques (e.g., multivariate data analysis), our book is the only one that addresses this topic. Thus, the approach of our book is much more balanced between qualitative and quantitative than are other books.

ORGANIZATION OF THE BOOK

The text and all major supplements are organized around the learning objectives given at the beginning of each chapter. Instead of a single summary of the chapter, there are summaries accompanying each learning objective. This organizational approach makes the book especially readable for students and readily useful for instructors. In short, it delivers value for both students and teachers.

The organization of the book follows the logic of the business research process. It is organized into five parts. Part 1 introduces the reader to business research, emerging trends, the research process, and the role of ethics. Part 2 provides an overview of how to begin the business research process, from defining the problem to conceptualization and research design. Part 3 covers data collection, including sampling, measurement, and questionnaire design. In Part 4 we examine data analysis and interpretation for both qualitative and quantitative research. Part 5 focuses on writing reports and presenting research findings.

COMPREHENSIVE INSTRUCTOR AND STUDENT RESOURCES

The book includes an extensive set of resources for instructors and students. For instructors, there is a test bank providing a wide variety of questions on all the major concepts in the book. The instructor's manual includes lecture outlines, answers to end-of-chapter questions, and teaching notes for the exercises. Each chapter has twenty to thirty PowerPoint slides summarizing and illustrating the key concepts. Two data sets for the restaurant case in both SPSS and Excel format are provided for instructors to use in teaching quantitative analysis and for students to learn the software and concepts. Additional end-of-chapter assignments give the user an opportunity to experience a wide range of analytical applications using the data sets. This eliminates the need for instructors and students to hunt for data demonstrating business research concepts and techniques.

M.E. Sharpe's instructor's Web site (www.mesharpe-instructor.com) includes a wide array of supplementary materials for instructors to incorporate into their teaching. In addition to electronic copies of all instructor's teaching support materials, copies of sample questionnaires used in research projects are provided on the Web site, answers to frequently asked questions related to business research, and copies of the data sets. In short, it is, we believe, one of the most comprehensive Web sites of any business research book.

ACKNOWLEDGMENTS

Among the many people to mention, we thank, first, our families and colleagues for encouraging us to write the book and for their support and comments throughout the process of bringing it to completion. Second, at M.E. Sharpe, we thank Harry Briggs, our executive editor, Elizabeth Granda, associate editor, and Angela Piliouras, our production editor. Finally, we owe a debt of gratitude to our students, who inspired us to write this book. Their questions and comments helped us to know which important topics to cover and how to cover them. We also offer gratitude to our teachers, who inspired us to a lifelong mission of learning and sharing knowledge. Our hope is that this book will be of particular help to students as they apply themselves to the study of business research and data analysis and, more generally, pursue their own careers and goals.

Joe Hair, Kennesaw State University, USA
Mary Wolfinbarger, California State University, Long Beach, USA
Arthur Money, Henley Business School, UK
Phillip Samouel, Kingston University, UK
Mike Page, Bentley University, USA

Part I

Introduction

1 | Business Research for the Twenty-First Century

LEARNING OUTCOMES

1. Provide an introduction to modern-day business research
2. Define business research and the people who use it
3. Discuss recent business trends and how they affect business research
4. Examine research-related technologies
5. Introduce the continuing case used throughout the text

Research is a discerning pursuit of the truth. Those who do research are looking for answers. In our everyday lives, we all play the role of researcher. A trip to the theater is rarely undertaken without some period of discernment. During this process, prospective theater patrons first determine what type of movie would best fit their present desire. They may form a preliminary opinion of several movies based on previous knowledge of the actors and directors involved. Is *The Mystery of the Blue Dog Café* worth seeing? Media sources, previews, and input from personal acquaintances often provide information to answer this question. Thereafter, if a prospective theater patron is reasonably confident about their conclusion, a decision is made. This simple illustration contains some of the basic elements of business research. Good decision making depends on conducting research that will result in accurately predicting an outcome of importance, in this case enjoyment of *The Mystery of the Blue Dog Café*.

Although formal research training is relatively new to the business world, business research is perhaps as old as commerce itself. International commerce expanded rapidly with the rise of Phoenician traders during the early classical period, about 500 B.C.[1] Investors in trading expeditions soon realized it was too risky to simply load ships with surplus goods and sail from port to port until a buyer was found. So they began to gather information about how goods might be altered to appeal to specific markets. With this information, merchants made strategic decisions involving product

3

differentiation and market segmentation. Merchants discovered the existence of price and quality segments. Wine from the countries of Thaos and Chios was highly sought after in some markets. Thasian and Chiot wine sold for as much as one drachma per liter compared to one fourth that for other wines. Winemakers from southern Italy performed research while peddling their own goods on the seas and attempted to capitalize on this new intelligence. While they were unable to match the quality of Thasian or Chiot wines, they appealed to these markets by making imitations of higher-quality wines. Consequently, research may have led to the first product knockoffs.[2]

Research also proved a key to success in selling crockery (dinnerware or china). Corinthians lost out to the Athenians in serving the early Etruscan market for crockery. The Athenians produced a style known as Tyrrhenian. Tyrrhenian crockery more closely matched Etruscan taste. It was "cheap and gaudy . . . and often carried mock inscriptions, presumably to impress Etruscans who would not have been able to read."[3] Perhaps Tyrrhenian crockery was the pink flamingo of its time. There seems to be little doubt, therefore, that the products were produced with a specific market in mind based on information gathered from the market.

Increasing literacy, the industrial revolution, continued advances in transportation, the advent of various forms of computing, and the general expansion of commerce worldwide have changed the way research is done. Frederick Taylor used early motion picture technology to film workers and demonstrate how they could improve their productivity. Similarly, General Electric was among the first companies to use consumer research to design new products.

Today, there are thousands of companies whose primary activity involves providing research services that help businesses answer key strategic, tactical, and operational questions. Research has become much more formal and technical. But its purpose remains much the same as inquiries undertaken by those Phoenician merchants. How do I find the answers to improve my performance and make life better for customers, employees, and owners? Business research is designed to answer these questions.

BUSINESS RESEARCH DEFINED

Business research includes several interrelated components. The most important are described in the following sections.

A TRUTH-SEEKING FUNCTION

We begin with a simple definition of science as systematic truth seeking. **Science** seeks to explain the world as it really is. Real-world, or physical, scientists seek the truth about the world's physical realities. Chemists deal with chemical phenomena, biologists with biological phenomena, and so forth. Social scientists, such as psychologists and sociologists, seek to describe and predict the realities of individual human behavior and the interactions of humans in a society. Business researchers are generally social scientists, because most business problems and opportunities involve people.

Like all scientists, **business researchers** pursue the truth about business phenomena. The essence of business is people serving people through participation in a value-creating process with exchange at its core. This includes all the support systems necessary to facilitate the process. **Business research** seeks to predict and explain phenomena that, taken together, constitute the ever-changing business environment. Thus, business research is a truth-seeking function that gathers, analyzes, interprets, and reports information so that business decision makers become more effective.

ELEMENTS OF BUSINESS RESEARCH

The scope of business research is broad, and the types of phenomena business researchers study are expanding rapidly. Time and motion studies are relatively infrequent today, although they were essential in the development of scientific business management. Instead, business researchers may study employee productivity as a function of a communication channel's richness or how purchasing patterns have changed because of the Internet. Thus, business research is truly dynamic in that researchers are constantly studying new issues with new tools. Below is a list of key elements of business research.

1. Business research involves the study of a wide range of phenomena, such as:
   a. People, including employees, customers, supervisors, managers, and policy makers
   b. Systems or groups of people, including strategic business units, offices, factory labor, management groups, boards of directors, managing directors, market segments, cultures, subcultures, corporate cultures, communities, companies, and industries
   c. The interaction of people with systems, including accounting or audit systems, legal systems, management practices, compensation systems, manufacturing systems, production processes, and financial systems
2. Business research can be formal. Researchers may undertake systematic and sometimes exhaustive projects aimed at answering very specific questions. As an illustration, Toyota was interested in knowing the effects of one-price retailing, where, in auto purchases, car prices are not subject to negotiation. It tested the idea in several countries. Customers in Montreal, Canada, for example, generally preferred the one-price system by about two to one.[4] But the effects of one-price retailing may extend beyond customers to Toyota's dealer network and employees. Thus, Toyota could also research the effects of one-price retailing on its dealer network and employees. Carefully researching the impact of the pricing strategy in several countries among customers, dealer networks, and employees results in a fairly comprehensive study. Toyota's research project is a good example of a one-shot research project. **One-shot research projects** are performed to address a single issue at a specific time.
3. Business research can be informal. Restaurant owners or managers often spend a portion of each night circulating through the dining room. They stop at each

table and ask, "How is everything?" The information they receive helps to identify patterns and improve decision making for enhancing the restaurant experience of their customers. While this sort of research is easy for small ventures, it's more of a challenge for larger firms. New technologies are creating ways, however, where informal feedback can be entered into databases by frontline employees who receive the information from customers. E-mail, social networking sites, and blogs can also provide informal feedback for larger firms. Informal research is often ongoing. This means it is performed constantly and not directed toward any specific issue.

4. Good research is replicable. A goal of scientific research is to be as objective as possible. When research is objective, it is generally **replicable**, meaning that another researcher could produce the same results using the identical procedures employed by the original researcher. An example is the research done by Pepsi as part of its advertising and promotion approach for the Pepsi Challenge that was later replicated by Coca-Cola. The Pepsi Challenge was a promotion in which consumers were intercepted in a supermarket, allowed to taste two unidentified colas, and given a six-pack of the one they preferred. Pepsi routinely televised these consumer taste tests on live television. More people chose Pepsi in the Pepsi Challenge. Coca-Cola, questioning the authenticity of this research, conducted its own taste challenges but kept them out of the public eye. Coca-Cola's research confirmed the Pepsi Challenge results. Thus, the Pepsi Challenge research was replicable.

5. Good research should provide more benefit than it costs. Ultimately, this is of primary importance in determining if the research was worthwhile. Management should not conduct a $100,000 research project to make a $25,000 decision. Many decisions are made with little or no research because they do not involve a lot of risk. Other times, research is designed and executed in a manner that limits its costs so they do not exceed the potential benefits of the decision.

Business research is scientific inquiry. But the terminology of business research differs depending on what motivates a particular study. **Applied business research** is motivated by an attempt to solve a particular problem faced by a particular organization. For example, Coca-Cola may want to know why Pepsi is gaining market share in Paris. **Basic business research** is motivated by a desire to better understand some business phenomenon as it applies to an entire industry or business in general. For example, why are people drinking more bottled water and less cola? Applied business research helps decision makers make specific decisions bound by time and an organization. Basic research helps develop theory that attempts to describe and predict business events so that all business decision makers can benefit. Exhibit 1.1 compares applied and basic business research.

WHAT DO BUSINESS RESEARCHERS STUDY?

The boundaries of business research today are nearly limitless. Business research is intended to result in better decision making. Business decisions often involve all

Exhibit 1.1

Examples of Applied and Basic Business Research

Applied research issues	Basic research issues
What is the effect on Samsung's DVD market share of adding digital audio and photo managing features?	How does technological turbulence affect business performance?
How will stocking wines from a new French vineyard in Languedoc-Roussillon affect the profitability of Albertsons supermarkets?	What factors relate to consumer satisfaction with and loyalty to a supermarket?
How would imposing reduced working hours rather than downsizing affect employee morale at Ford Motor Company?	Are staff reductions or furloughs more likely to affect employee morale?
Can using prospective employee psychological profiles reduce turnover at McDonald's?	What psychological factors predict reduced turnover in service occupations?

aspects of business. Therefore, it should be no surprise that business research involves all aspects and all functions of business.

Marketing managers are often interested in new product development, effectiveness of promotional efforts, brand image, customer satisfaction, and brand and product positioning, for instance. Most consumers can recall times when they have responded to some type of customer-satisfaction study. This information is vital for strategic decisions. Which strategic actions should the firm take? Should it diversify or stay entrenched as a specialist within a niche market? Business researchers contribute significantly to these decisions, as exemplified in the Global Effie Awards, which recognize effective and creative marketing campaigns that have been proven in multiple markets worldwide.

For manufacturing firms, efficient and effective production processes are essential if customers are to realize product quality and satisfaction. Business research is often tasked with identifying processes that create the optimal amount of product and service quality. Further, because employees are ultimately responsible for quality production, a great deal of research is directed at understanding employee job satisfaction, employee performance, and employee turnover. In the United Kingdom, research indicates that firms incur $8,000 a year in additional costs for every employee quitting their job.[5] Similarly, U.S. firms estimate average turnover costs at $10,000 or more for each employee that leaves.[6] Thus, turnover receives a great deal of attention from researchers and decision makers.

Strategic and tactical decisions often involve capital investment. Online grocers did not enjoy the early success many experts predicted. One reason industry analysts gave is that online grocers underestimated the required capital intensity. One key to their eventual survival is selecting the best way to obtain this capital. Business research on financing alternatives could help answer this question. Exhibit 1.2 illustrates some of the business research implications that might be involved in an entrepreneurial venture in the online grocery industry.

Accounting rules also present a need for research. Different accounting procedures

Exhibit 1.2

Business Research Applications for a Start-Up Venture in Online Grocery Sales

Decision involved	Research topic	Implications
What type of capital resources should be used?	Identify the financial and risk implications associated with the various options.	Online grocers are highly capital intensive. The result is cash starvation during the early months of operation.
What markets should we serve?	Identify the potential profitability of potential markets.	Online grocers must identify markets with high volume potential relative to a small service area.
What product assortments should be emphasized?	Identify the shopping value associated with product acquisition of various types.	Online grocers must determine the products for which customers believe physical product interaction is a value-added process.
What type of personnel should be involved in operations?	Identify the impact of outsourcing on perceived service quality.	Online grocers may find it more cost-effective to outsource certain operational components, including product delivery.
How should customers be attracted?	Identify the potential response rate from the different options for inducing trial.	Customer acquisition costs are extremely high for new online retailers. Therefore, successful online grocers will need to be efficient in attracting customers.

bring with them different financial implications. It is clear that both Grant Thornton International and Deloitte Touche Tohmatsu should have more closely examined the accounting procedures used at Parmalat, the Italian-based multinational company.[7] Similarly, Arthur Andersen and several financial institutions should have looked more closely at Enron's accounting practices. So decisions must be researched for potential tax implications as well as for their impact on product and strategic business unit (SBU) financial performance.

Industries change, but the research process remains much the same. Research has always been a search for truthful explanations and accurate predictions. The tools researchers use, however, have changed and will continue to do so. **Information-only businesses** are those that exchange information or information-related services, such as distribution and storage, for a fee. As information-only products become an ever-increasing part of the economy, it will be interesting to see what new tools, if any, may be needed. Information-only businesses are a major part of e-commerce. They include relatively small companies that, for example, provide details related to third-party, mortgage, or life-insurance products for small, owner-managed businesses. But they also include large companies such as Yahoo! and Google as well as specialized firms such as Kieskeurig (www.kieskeurig.nl), which provides price information on thousands of products at the click of a mouse.

Several aspects of information-only businesses present a challenge for business researchers. Researchers have identified attributes of information-only products that affect pricing strategies. **Stickiness** is how much it costs to transfer a given unit of information to an information seeker.[8] Stickiness is higher when information is costly to acquire, transfer, and use. Stickiness affects pricing strategies for information-only businesses. For example, what is the best way to determine the price of information-only products when the cost to transfer such products is practically zero? Should price be determined by a buyer's willingness to pay instead of being based on cost.[9] The low transfer cost of many information-only products clearly has implications for the way pricing studies are conducted. With information-only products, greater emphasis is placed on protecting intellectual property rights. This means researchers must help to define the boundaries of infringement and thus contribute to establishing legal protection for information-only companies.

What types of businesses benefit from research? All types of businesses can benefit from research. Large and small businesses can answer key questions about markets and about their own internal work environments.[10] Many low-technology firms use research. For example, hotels and restaurants frequently collect information on satisfaction and lodging and dining-out patterns to enable them to better serve their customers. The new, ever-growing class of highly skilled, highly educated entrepreneurs also understands the key to success is being able to identify new ways to provide customers with enduring and satisfying bundles of benefits.[11] Clearly, research has played a key role in technological development as it has addressed many topics related to the adoption of new technologies.

Business research is no longer confined to for-profit businesses. Nonprofit institutions have also found research useful in addressing questions related to the core client segments they serve. As an example, the Catholic Church has found research useful in addressing questions related to recruiting clergy and increasing fund-raising activities without sacrificing spirituality.[12] Thus, far from being exclusive to a small set of large companies, research can benefit all types of businesses.

TRENDS IMPACTING BUSINESS RESEARCH

Recent business trends have affected business research in many ways. They have helped shape the types of research performed, the way research is conducted, and the phenomena that are studied; they have also highlighted the importance of research in business decision making. Among the more important trends impacting business research are expanding market freedom, globalization, relationship marketing, and the information revolution.

EXPANDING MARKET FREEDOM

Since the removal of the Berlin Wall in November 1989, free markets have emerged in many formerly closed markets. Prior to this many managers in the former Soviet Union were not motivated to develop or acquire research capabilities because consumers represented a captive audience, except for the black market.[13] There was little job mobility, so there was little incentive to study the internal, organizational workings of a firm. Little advantage could be gained from the added intelligence that research could bring.

As free and competitive markets emerged, companies became motivated to answer questions about the types of products and services customers wanted. One result has been a greater emphasis on product quality, which requires input from both customers and employees. The Volga, perhaps the best-known Russian automobile, has a long and infamous history as a symbol of the poor product quality that epitomized Soviet industry. More recently, Gorkovsky Avtomobilny Zavod (GAZ), the Russian manufacturer of the Volga, used research input to expand its product line and market share. GAZ assessed market trends, then entered the minivan market with the Gazelle, and it has penetrated markets in Iraq, Hungary, and even the United States![14]

Russian managers have also had to learn to deal with free labor markets. Job satisfaction in Russia remains low. In fact, many skilled Russian workers have been attracted to the West by better working conditions.[15] Since Russian labor markets have traditionally been understudied,[16] business research may provide gains to managers that are even greater than those resulting from similar studies in developed economies. As firms benefit from improved decision making, research becomes an essential part of effective decision making.

INTERNATIONAL RESEARCH

Business research today is truly an international endeavor. Firms around the globe now perform business research to improve their decision making. This research influences decisions often involving unfamiliar cultures. For example, foreign-acquisition decisions can be made with much more certainty when the competitive and economic market structures are known. Similar to the Volga, the Czech Skoda also had a reputation for poor quality. After its initial introduction to the United Kingdom, 98 percent of British consumers rated it as a low-quality, low-end product. After Volkswagen acquired Skoda, however, business research was used to improve product quality and design promotional campaigns using humor to counter the negative image. Through careful consumer profiling, Skoda currently targets consumers who are deemed rational rather than emotional in their decision making. The result has been a dramatically increased response to direct marketing appeals and sales increases exceeding 20 percent.[17]

Globalization means business research must take an international focus.[18] Difficult managerial decisions involving consumers and employees in a foreign culture are made even more difficult by an array of communication barriers, both verbal and nonverbal. These decisions require research regarding cultural differences which includes, for example, the ability to translate meaning from one language into another.

The Internet has led many businesses to consider the world their market. But to reach the global marketplace, a company's Web site must be available in multiple languages. In such a case, translational equivalence becomes essential. **Translational equivalence** means text can be translated from one language to another and back into the original language with no distortion in meaning. Exhibit 1.3 provides examples of translational inequivalence.

Exhibit 1.3

Research Could Prevent Errors Like These

Description of situation	Intended meaning (Product name/slogan)	Interpreted meaning
English name of a U.S. product and its German interpretation	Clairol Mist Stick	Piece of manure
English name of a U.S. product and its Spanish interpretation	Matador (AMC auto)	Killer auto
Japanese interpretation of English name	Guess jeans	Vulgar/low-class/ugly jeans
German interpretation of English name	Puffs tissue	Whorehouse tissue
German interpretation of product term	Credit card	Guilt card
Japanese interpreter's translation from Japanese into English to be sold in China	Antifreeze	Hot piss spray
Japanese interpreter's translation from Japanese into English to be sold in China	Ready-to-eat pancakes	Strawberry crap dessert

Sources: Thomas T. Semon, "Cutting Corners in Language Risky Business," *Marketing News*, 35 (April 23, 2001), 9; Andy Cohen, "What You Didn't Learn in Marketing 101," *Sales and Marketing Management*, 150 (February 1998), 22–25; Greg Steinmetz, "Germans Finally Open Their Wallets to Credit Cards but Aren't Hooked Yet," *Wall Street Journal* (April 6, 1997), A14; Shelly Reese, "Culture Shock," *Marketing Tools*, 5 (May 1998), 44–49.

Beyond mere translational equivalence,[19] researchers must investigate Internet usage patterns and the technical details of browsers and computers that businesses rely on to display their Web sites. The world's languages make use of a variety of writing systems. Many computer system configurations are unable to properly translate into certain scripts. Without the proper hardware and software, for instance, a Russian Web page could end up looking like Chinese!

Issues such as these are sure to arise as businesses cross international boundaries. Research designed to bring about understanding of both the languages and cultural dimensions of doing business is more cost-effective than paying for a serious linguistic or cultural mistake.

RELATIONSHIP MARKETING

Business has entered the **relationship marketing** era. Relationship marketing emphasizes long-term interactions between a business and its stakeholders. It seeks to identify mutually beneficial exchanges where both the firm and the stakeholder (i.e., customer, shareholder, or employee) maximize value. The emergence of relationship marketing is changing research in terms of whom and what is studied.

An important aspect of relationship marketing is the realization a firm cannot be everything to everybody. That is, firms have to recognize that not every customer, employee, or shareholder provide a good match for a long-term relationship. Frederick Reichheld encourages firms to be "picky" and choose relationship partners carefully.[20] Otherwise, limited resources could be spent on unprofitable customers.

Successful companies have loyal customers, loyal employees, and loyal stake-holders.[21] Relationship marketing has placed an increased emphasis on the study of loyalty-related factors. Employee loyalty issues such as turnover and organizational commitment have received a great deal of attention from researchers because of their relationship to firm performance.[22] Turnover represents the average tenure of an employee and relates to the replacement rate needed to maintain production. Organizational commitment is the degree to which an employee identifies with the goals and values of a firm.[23] When employees are highly committed they exhibit high loyalty. Knowledge of the factors associated with decreased turnover and increased commitment improves the likelihood of organizational success.

Researchers now extend the idea of loyalty to customer and shareholder populations. New concepts such as customer share and customer churn are increasingly studied. **Customer share** is the proportion of resources a customer spends with one firm in a given competitor set.[24] For example, a customer who goes to McDonald's five out of ten times when buying fast food would have a customer share of about 50 percent. **Customer churn** is the annual turnover rate of customers. Wireless telephone companies use research to reduce customer churn because it averages about 30 percent annually and is very costly. Businesses also research **customer commitment**, the degree to which customers identify with the values of a firm. They have learned that, like loyal employees, customers are willing to sacrifice to maintain valuable relationships.[25] None of these areas was researched as recently as twenty years ago.

Similarly, companies have begun placing greater emphasis on relationships with employees. The dramatic increase in dual-income families has meant greater stress on employees as their free time has shrunk. As a result, employers have had to pay attention to life outside the workplace in an effort to maintain workplace cohesiveness. Research has led to a number of innovative programs designed to help employees cope with routine aspects of everyday life. Child-care support is just one of the innovative workplace ideas stemming from this work.

THE INFORMATION REVOLUTION

The information age has facilitated many research processes. Technological advances in computing and electronic storage have dramatically increased research efficiency. This has happened in a very short period of time. For example, most individuals reading this book were born before the widespread diffusion of desktop personal computers. Likewise, most readers of this book have never heard of a card reader. A **card reader** enabled an analyst to feed data into a computer using elongated cardboard index cards. Different data values were represented by punching patterns of holes in the card. Thus, it wasn't unusual for a researcher to carry around stacks of thousands of cards. One stack contained the data while the other contained the computer program intended to analyze the data, assuming there were no errors in the pattern of holes. Typically the researcher would place the cards in a card reader and then go for an extended lunch. It might take hours for the mainframe computer to process the program. Upon returning from lunch, the analyst would obtain a printout that contained either the results or, more commonly for first-time runs, an error message.

Cards had to be guarded with great care. A dropped stack of cards caused more than a few broken hearts for researchers. Now the data contained in the thousands of cards can be stored on a single USB stick. Moreover, the data is likely placed in a file in real-time programs used by researchers who simply point and click, relying on the computer to run even the most advanced statistical programs in a fraction of a second.

Just as certainly as the card reader is now obsolete, more new technologies will emerge that will make our current methods of data input, storage, and analysis obsolete. Following are several information-technology developments that are affecting business decision making and research:

Electronic Communication

E-mail and technologies such as video conferencing and voice over IP (VoIP) are examples of **electronic communication** methods. These methods and others have replaced the telephone and traditional snail mail for many types of business communication, including matters directly related to research. Questionnaires are now routinely administered by providing a link in an e-mail directing the respondent to a hosted Web site. Chapter 8 contains a more complete description of the technological advances in data collection. Electronic communication is also impacting other developments, examples of which follow.

Networking

Networking refers to computers connected to one another through various servers. The Internet connects your computer to nearly every other computer in the world. From a business perspective, networking allows greater communication and data transfer between interested parties. In many cases, networking allows for real-time information transfer from markets to the analyst. FedEx and UPS both provide real-time 24-7 information transfer that enables customers to track shipments. Firms use **intranets** as well. These are networks that rely on Internet technology to link computers internally in a single organization. For example, a researcher who needs sales and profit data for the last twenty quarters can tap into a company's financial records directly and retrieve the desired information. No paperwork is necessary and no delay occurs while waiting for the accounting department to process the request!

A company can expand its intranet network so that suppliers and vendors also have access to the network. This capability allows for automated purchase systems and increased manufacturing flexibility. Intranet technology has been advantageous to Budweiser in reducing its procurement costs, managing its inventories, and shortening its cycle times by introducing an "extranet," or private network, connecting the company's central database to its customers, suppliers, and salespeople.

Data Warehouses

Company information is now stored and cataloged in an electronic format in **data warehouses**. Twenty years ago, data may have been stored on computer cards or magnetic tape, but generally it would have been accessed through paper reports generated by a computer program. Today, these electronic data warehouses replace other, more costly approaches to storing data. For example, the cost of storing one megabyte of information in 1992 was about $15, but today it is only a penny.

Some research tasks have been made infinitely easier through the availability of off-the-shelf data. **Off-the-shelf data** is readily available information compiled and sold by content-provision companies. For example, an analyst researching several different locations for a new branch office within the United States or overseas can likely access all the needed statistical data without ever leaving the office. Census data are cataloged electronically and is accessible in numerous formats through the Web site of the U.S. Census Bureau (www.census.gov). Previously, researchers had to go to a local or national government agency library, find the correct volumes and tables, then manually transfer the numbers into a usable format. A laborious process that may have taken days or weeks has been reduced to hours. Likewise, retail site location research projects that would have taken weeks previously are now automated through the use of **geographic information systems (GIS)**. GIS systems can create, within a few minutes, numerous maps that overlay information from census data inventories on top of satellite photo imagery. For example, GIS systems can identify the locations of households with income profiles between $75,000 and $125,000 and with two teenage children at home.

Numerous industry statistics are now available electronically. In the past, for example, global wholesalers and retailers anxiously awaited national monthly or quarterly reports giving trade turnover statistics that they then needed to integrate. Now they are readily available in various convenient downloadable formats.

Organizational Learning

Motivated by the low cost of electronically storing information and a desire to better understand multiple relationships, many organizations have developed formal systems aimed at recording all important events in a database. The resulting database is an electronic representation of **organizational memory**. Some input into these systems is automated. Information from routine financial and market reports, for instance, is fed automatically into a database. Other information, such as a list of effective employee motivational tools, must be input through a special report. The result is an internal data warehouse. **Organizational learning** can be defined as the internalization of both external and internal information for use as an input to decision making. Within a few short years, organizational learning has taken on a central role in the selection of business strategies aimed at improving firm performance.[26]

One relatively new organizational learning tool is **data mining**. Data mining refers to electronically mining data warehouses for information identifying ways to improve organizational performance. Data mining is not performed with a pick or a shovel. Rather, the analytical tools are statistical **algorithms** that automatically analyze potential patterns in data stored in the electronic warehouse.

Data mining represents "knowledge discovery in databases," or KDD.[27] The KDD process involves the following steps:

1. Establishing access to relevant data
2. Selecting the set of events (data) to be analyzed
3. Cleaning the data so it is understood by the algorithm
4. Developing and using rules for selecting interesting relationships
5. Developing a report of relationships that may affect firm performance

Data mining began with the early advent of significant computing power in the 1960s. Researchers developed **Automatic Interaction Detection (AID)** software that considered possible relationships between all pairs of quantified data within a data set.[28] During the 1960s, a mainframe computer took hours to analyze all potential relationships between a dozen or so variables. For example, a data set with twenty-four variables requires 16,777,216, 224 computations. Today, sophisticated data-mining tools use more powerful statistical procedures. Tools like data mining enable variables to be analyzed more than two at a time and in greater number. If we analyzed twenty-four variables in all possible three-way comparisons, 282,429,536,481 computations would be required. We won't even attempt to demonstrate what would be required with more variables and more combinations! But modern computing power enables even these types of analyses to be performed with a desktop or laptop computer in seconds. As a result, researchers have much greater power to find information that could improve business performance.

An interesting, perhaps disturbing, example of data mining is its use by state and national tax departments. Tax authorities use data mining to identify patterns in income tax returns that may signal a high potential for unreported (and therefore untaxed) income. Attention is then focused on auditing the identified individuals and companies. Similarly, companies can use data-mining research to identify potentially profitable customers, more effective employees, and attractive investments, for example. More recently, researchers have been combining data mining with traditional research tools, including survey research, to further improve the value of database technology in decision making.[29]

The Business Research Dashboard (see page 16) illustrates how Pfizer is successfully using data mining of its past clinical trials.

Satellite Technology

Business research even extends beyond the Earth. Many companies are gathering and analyzing information obtained from Global Positioning System (GPS) devices. GPS allows real-time tracking of movement. For example, delivery companies can equip trucks with a GPS system. Every move the truck makes is monitored by a signal sent from a GPS device on the truck to a satellite, which is then sent to a company computer. Researchers can analyze these patterns to increase the efficiency of the delivery system.[30] Similarly, rent-a-car companies are placing GPS devices on their cars. With this, customers enjoy the benefits of electronic directions. In return the companies know exactly how their customers use their cars. This may enable better services and pricing alternatives. Some research firms have hired people to wear a pocket-size GPS while shopping. This enables the researchers to examine mall and

---

■———Business Research Dashboard———■
Learning from the Past

Pfizer is increasing its efforts to get more from its clinical trial data. The company has moved away from the tradition of filing away clinical trials once a drug has been submitted for approval. Whether or not the drug is approved for a particular application, Pfizer now adds the clinical test results to an active database that is available for continued data mining by its scientists and statisticians.

According to the Mani Lakshminarayanan, a director and statistical scientist at Pfizer, the company is seeking to extract as much as possible from its clinical trials. Exploratory analysis of clinical trial data helps identify specific or unknown patterns of potential relevance for future studies.

Pfizer uses secondary data from clinical studies for numerous reasons that include but are not limited to (1) helping design new studies by providing additional information on sample size and target population, (2) supporting bridging studies when the company has approval in one national jurisdiction and wishes to apply for a license in another, (3) supporting its capacity to undertake confirmatory and extension studies sometime during the patent life of the drug to explore further opportunities, and (4) undertaking finer segmentation and looking for correlated effects in targeted ethnic or age-specific populations.

Data-mining techniques are being applied to clinical research trial data in other situations. Pharmacovigilance is a field built on data mining of large volumes of interconnected data to investigate the safety of drugs after they come to market. Data may be combined from various sources, including the Food and Drug Administration, the European Medicines Agency, and the World Health Organization. Advocates of pharmacovigilance believe that data mining can greatly increase drug safety, because the effects on patient subpopulations can be analyzed and the integrity of clinical investigations can be assessed. Data-mining techniques can be used to examine multiple studies for drug interaction or safety issues that may impact a particular genetically defined group.

Sources: http://www.bio-itworld.com/newsitems/2006/february/02-23-06-news-pfizer; Hermann Mucke, "Data Mining in Drug Development and Translational Medicine," *Insight Pharma Reports*, July 2009, http://www.insightpharmareports.com/reports_report.aspx.aspx?id=93404&r=7167, accessed December 21, 2009.

---

store traffic patterns precisely. Information like this can be useful in determining how much rent a potential retail location could get. The Business Research Dashboard (see facing page) further discusses GPS applications.

The information age has transformed modern economies. Researchers are expected and able to be more productive than they were a generation ago. Likewise, decision makers have more relevant information available to use as input for strategic and tactical decision making. Exhibit 1.4 summarizes several implications of the information age for business research.

Interestingly, some individuals have begun asking whether technology has advanced beyond our desire and ability to take advantage of it. How many people really need 2.5 gigahertz of processing speed? This doubtfulness may be partly to blame for the technology industry's performance slump in recent years.[31] Exhibit 1.5 lets you test your technology IQ and see how you are adapting to the technology explosion.

■————**Business Research Dashboard**————■
Global Big Brother System?

Are there ethical dimensions of location tracking as a research tool? The exceedingly extensive mobile telephone system has resulted in the development of a number of products that enable companies to use GPS (Global Positioning System) and mobile phone technology to track vehicles and report their location down to the street level. The extent of mobile phone coverage facilitates systems being able to combine GPS technology with telecommunications equipment to achieve real-time tracking, because vehicles can be kept connected to the Internet continuously. This enables fleet managers to monitor driver behavior on the road and to establish whether a driver leaves his or her route for non-business-related purposes.

Insurance companies also use GPS technology for research purposes so that they can consider greater degrees of stratification in insurance policy pricing. As an illustration, Progressive Insurance offers drastically reduced rates for some customers and increased rates for others based on driving performance as monitored by GPS systems. Drive less and you pay less. Drive within the speed limit and you pay less. Some consumer advocates argue that this level of monitoring is a violation of an individual's right to privacy.

Sources: Annette Cardwell, "Building a Better Speed Trap," *Smart Business*, 14 (December/January 2002), 28; Ira Carnahan, "Insurance by the Minute," *Forbes*, 166 (December 11, 2000), 86; and http://www.environmental-studies.de/GPS/gps.html, accessed November 2009.

Exhibit 1.4

How the Information Age Is Affecting Researchers and Decision Makers

Matter matters less	Company value is increasingly found in intangible, or "soft," assets. In the new economy, knowledge is the key to success. Information-only products account for a significant portion of the economy. Therefore, researchers are required to process more and produce better information and intelligence.
Distance matters less	Many employees can perform their work from remote locations beyond the traditional workplace. Customers can shop from anywhere, including an airplane, their office, and, believe it or not, their car! Researchers can conduct Delphi interviews (a type of expert-opinion polling) with top executives from every continent in the world simultaneously.
Time matters more	Given the new world of twenty-four-hour-a-day instantaneous connections, the pressure to react quickly has increased enormously. Business customers are demanding reduced cycle times. Cycle time is the amount of time consumed between the point when an order is placed with a supplying company and the time when the benefits are realized. Thus, those companies that can reduce response time will benefit greatly. Researchers must continually trade off the demand for quick results with the desire for meaningful results.

(continued)

Exhibit 1.4 *(continued)*

Customization matters more	Research, including database technologies, makes it easier for companies to customize products. This is especially true for information-only products. Therefore, the need for companies to have a better and deeper understanding of their customers is greater than ever
People matter more	Convenient worldwide communication has continued to shift the power away from the top of the organizational chart. Purchasers can compare prices for products among hundreds of competing sellers with the click of a mouse. Employees can offer their skills to hundreds of potential employers in a similar manner. Traders have similar access to worldwide investment opportunities. Therefore, businesses that treat customers, employees, and shareholders with true empathy and respect will maintain a unique and sustainable point of differentiation. Again, this increases the need for research into the processes by which these stakeholders receive value from their relationships. High-tech solutions should also be "high touch," meaning the human element is most important.

Exhibit 1.5

Test Your Technology IQ

Can you match the acronyms and terms on the left with the descriptions on the right? All of these may have a significant impact on business-research processes.

Acronym	Definition	Implication
1. PUSH	a. Enables real-time voice, video, and data transfer by continually reallocating unused bandwidth.	Improved and faster electronic communication.
2. SMART	b. Monitors software usage among all computers on a network.	Usage patterns can be tracked and product improvements can be made with increased efficiency.
3. ATM	c. A technology that automatically delivers customized information to a person via a browser interface	Researchers have greater access to more relevant information in less time.
4. ASP	d. A document transfer and preparation system that allows the user to focus on the logical structure of a message rather than the format codes.	More efficient information processing.
5. LATEX	e. A technology in which a microprocessor resides on a personalized card (the size of a credit card). Information can be exchanged with computer interfaces by reading the card.	Researchers can track behavior more closely and accurately making it possible for decision makers to better customize solutions.
6. Crypto rage	f. The anger associated with computer hackers' attempts to breach computer security or infect systems with computer viruses (not a new heavy metal rock group).	System security should be a high priority.
7. PATROL	g. Secure, remote hosting of complex database software that enables more companies affordable access to sophisticated tracking and information gathering.	Better access to information for researchers and decision makers in a wider variety of firms.

Answers: 1-c, 2-e, 3-a (asynchronous transfer mode), 4-g (application service provider), 5-d (Lamport, Tex.), 6-f, 7-b; http://www.technology.com/encyclopedia, accessed June 20, 2010.

THE MANAGER-RESEARCHER RELATIONSHIP

Effective decision making requires that both managers (decision makers) and researchers perform their respective roles responsibly and ethically. Ethics in the researcher-manager relationship means each party treats the other honestly and fairly. In addition, the researcher should realize that a breach in professional ethics harms the entire research industry. Conflict between the decision maker and the researcher (even when they are one and the same person) is inevitable. The decision maker wants to spend minimal money, utilize minimal human resources, and get an error-free answer immediately. The researcher realizes that implementing research designs can be expensive, involves substantial time and labor resources, can be time-consuming, and is never error-free. Somewhere in between, there needs to be a reasonable compromise.

WHO PERFORMS BUSINESS RESEARCH?

The business researcher becomes formally involved in the decision-making process once a decision maker, who may be either an entrepreneur or a manager, recognizes a need for new information. The researcher's role is to fill this need. Decision makers use researchers who are either employed by the same firm or part of an external consulting agency. Researchers not employed within a firm are **outside research consultants**. Research decisions involve varying degrees of complexity and internal complications. Consequently, from time to time even firms that have in-house research departments may outsource a research project to an external firm. The following describes several situations that make hiring an outside research consultant advantageous over doing the research in-house.

1. An outside research consultant may have special expertise or capabilities. For example, a U.S. firm wishing to begin operations and marketing in Germany might hire a German research firm to investigate potential locations, employee behaviors, and market receptivity. Similarly, would you like to find out about some aspect of the business environment in Japan? International Business Research and Access Japan are two companies that provide specialized Japanese business research. A research firm may even be able to do the project more quickly and cheaply when it has the corresponding degree of specialized skills and technology.

2. An outside research firm can conduct and interpret research more objectively. The outside firm is not influenced by the corporate culture or worldview. Therefore, when a decision is likely to evoke intense emotions among different factions of the company, an outside firm may be a good idea. Otherwise, the in-house researcher could present results that will anger somebody with whom the researcher may have to continue to work in the future. In some cases, the researcher may present research that suggests some manager's brainchild project is a bad idea. The outside consultant can present such results and then return to the safety of a different company.

3. The outside firm may provide fresh insight into a problem. Particularly when employees within the firm have been unsuccessful in understanding the problem, an outside firm may offer fresh insight and new approaches.

Likewise, there are reasons why internal (in-house) researchers may be advantageous.

1. Generally, in-house researchers can provide information more quickly than an outside agency. One reason is they are part of the same corporate culture and require far less time to gain an understanding of the decision issue. They already possess a great deal of the knowledge that an outside researcher would have to spend time acquiring.

2. A company's employees are more likely to collaborate with in-house researchers. A member of an outside consulting team may be viewed as a threat. In addition, employees with whom the researcher needs to collaborate may know him or her well. Thus, there is a certain amount of trust in the relationship that is difficult for an outside agency to duplicate.

3. The in-house researchers can often do the research for less money. External consultants can be very expensive. Consultants may charge hourly rates of $200 or more for research work. The one exception is when the research requires a specialized skill or access that a consulting firm may already possess and that would be expensive to obtain otherwise.

4. In-house researchers may be better able to follow up on a research project. One project often spawns the need for others. If a small follow-up study is needed, in-house researchers can begin the work right away. An outside consulting agent can also do a follow-up study, but, at the very least, a new contract may have to be negotiated.

In discussing the ethical obligations of researchers and decision makers further in Chapter 3, our comments generally pertain to both in-house researchers and outside consultants.

CONTINUING CASE STUDY: SAMOUEL'S AND GINO'S RESTAURANTS

To illustrate business research principles and concepts, we have prepared a case study that will be used throughout all the chapters in the book. The case study is about two restaurants in New York City that are competitors. One of the restaurants is Samouel's Greek Cuisine. The other is Gino's Ristorante, a southern Italian restaurant located about a block away. Both restaurants cater to the upscale crowd for lunch and dinner. We refer to the case study in discussing the various research topics, and specific exercises related to the case are placed at the end of every chapter. For example, Phil Samouel hired a research company to conduct interviews with both his customers and Gino's customers. Results of the surveys will help him prepare a business plan. In Chapter 2 we provide a copy of a research proposal given to Phil so he could decide if the value of the research project justified its cost. When we discuss sampling in Chapter 7 we evaluate different sampling approaches and point out why the research company recommended exit interviews. Similarly, copies of the questionnaires used to collect primary data are shown in Chapters 9 and 10 to illustrate measurement and questionnaire design principles. In all the data analysis chapters we use the case study data to illustrate statistical software and the various statistical techniques for analyzing data. Finally, a summary of the research report provided to Phil Samouel is included in Chapter 16. The focus on a single case study of a typical business research problem will enable you to more easily understand the benefits and pitfalls of using research to improve business decision making.

■————Business Research Dashboard————■
Conducting Global Research

Among the biggest challenges in conducting business research internationally is deciding which data collection technique to use. Traditionally, telephone surveys have been effective regardless of where they are administered, but Internet surveys are becoming popular in many countries. Some business researchers believe in-person interviews are best for the South American and Asian markets. Since business contacts in South America are much more social in nature, conventional wisdom says the research method you use should be too. In-person interviews are viewed as more social than an impersonal telephone call. For Asian markets, in-person interviews are often suggested because they allow the researcher to show proper respect for respondents.

In designing questionnaires for global markets, the introduction and purpose of the survey should be described more fully than in the United States. Respondents outside the United States are often more inquisitive and require a higher degree of formality than Americans. For example, a survey that requires fifteen minutes to complete in the United States may take up to forty minutes in Germany because German respondents like to talk more and the language is less concise than English. The longer response time adds to the cost of the research.

The major stumbling block with most international research is translation. Keep in mind that if you are researching five markets with five different languages, the questionnaire must state exactly the same question in the same place for each of those markets. Otherwise, you could tabulate the different sets of responses and end up with little useful information.

Should research firms be hired in the country where the research is being done, or in the country where the research buyer is located? Even if the surveys are translated perfectly, are there other factors that could prevent research findings between countries from being comparable? Can you think of other issues that might be encountered in international marketing research?

Sources: C. Samuel Craig and Susan P. Douglas, *International Marketing Research*, 3rd ed. (London: Wiley, 2005); and Chris Van Derveer, "Demystifying International Industrial Marketing Research," *Quirk's Marketing Research Review* (April 1996): 28, 35.

CONTINUING CASE: SAMOUEL'S GREEK CUISINE

Samouel's Greek Cuisine restaurant is located in New York City. Phillip Samouel, owner of the restaurant, is a successful manager and businessman. He came to New York about fifteen years ago and has owned several other businesses but is relatively new to the restaurant industry. He and his brother opened the restaurant about four years ago. The decor and menu are similar to those of a restaurant they remember from their early days in Greece. The concept of the restaurant was to feature traditional dishes with the freshest ingredients, an informal and festive atmosphere, and a friendly and knowledgeable staff. In making the initial decision to open the restaurant, Phil and his brother talked with several friends but did not conduct a formal feasibility study. Also, they chose the location based on the fact that a restaurant had previously been in operation there and the cost of renovation would therefore be much less than if they had selected a location of another type of business.

(continued)

About two blocks from Samouel's location is an Italian restaurant owned and managed by Gino. Gino's Italian Ristorante has been open at its current location for about ten years and has a southern Italian menu. Gino and his family emigrated from Sicily and started the restaurant. His mother runs the kitchen using family recipes gathered over the years and makes sure the food is properly prepared.

When Phil and his family were starting their restaurant, their background research suggested that many restaurants collect information on the characteristics of their customers, such as that listed below:

- Age
- Income
- Where customers live and work
- Ethnic background
- Gender
- How often they eat out, for lunch, for dinner
- How much they typically spend when they eat out
- Kinds of food they eat most often when dining out
- The kind of atmosphere that is most appealing

They have been so busy since starting the restaurant that there has been no time to collect any of this data.

Last week when Phil Samouel was passing by Gino's, he noticed a crowd of customers waiting to be seated. He believes Gino's is his major competitor because both restaurants cater to the same lunch and dinner clientele. This started him thinking about the competitive positioning of his restaurant relative to Gino's. Phil's opinion is that Gino's has the advantage of being located in a higher traffic area with greater visibility, and that the length of time Gino's has been in business has resulted in a larger, more loyal customer base. In addition, Phil and his brother believe that Gino's is able to charge higher prices without sacrificing business. Phil's informal research has shown that the entrées at Gino's are all $14 to $15, whereas his entrees are $10 to $11. Satisfied customers may be willing to reward the restaurant by paying higher prices and are likely to be more frequent patrons.

1. Is a research project needed? If yes, what kind of project?
2. What areas should the research focus on?

Note: This case appears in every chapter of the book. It is used to illustrate business research concepts covered in the chapter.

Summary

Provide an Orientation to Modern-Day Business Research

Businesspeople have been doing research for millennia. It's as old as international trade itself. The formal study of business research is relatively young. The need for business research increases as firms realize more opportunities, in the form of increased trade, or more competition. These conditions create an environment in which a business stands a chance of benefiting from well-made decisions.

DEFINE BUSINESS RESEARCH AND THE PEOPLE WHO USE IT

Business researchers try to accurately determine the truth about business-related phenomena. Business research is a truth-seeking function responsible for gathering, analyzing, interpreting, and reporting information so that business decision makers become more effective. There are few limits to what a business researcher might be asked to study. The work could involve any business discipline and affect tactical or strategic business decisions. All organizations, profit and nonprofit, big or small, that manage employees, study systems, or market to customers are potential users of business research.

DISCUSS RECENT BUSINESS TRENDS AND HOW THEY AFFECT BUSINESS RESEARCH

Several trends are affecting business research. These include relationship marketing, which has brought new concepts and a greater need to integrate research studies across multiple stakeholder groups; the globalization of business, which requires researchers to study previously unfamiliar cultures; and the information revolution, which provides researchers easier access to greater volumes of data. These trends are increasing the importance of business research.

EXAMINE RESEARCH-RELATED TECHNOLOGIES

Technology is affecting the way business research is conducted. Data warehousing provides the researcher with off-the-shelf data, saving enormous amounts of time and avoiding expensive data collection in many situations. Researchers' ability to network via the Internet and intranets allows information to be shared more readily. These tools have made the researcher more productive.

INTRODUCE THE CONTINUING CASE USED THROUGHOUT THE TEXT

The book has a case study that is used in all the chapters to help you apply the concepts to a realistic situation. The case is Samouel's Greek Cuisine and it focuses on how the owner, Phil Samouel, can improve his business. His direct competitor is Gino's Italian Ristorante. Gino is more successful for a variety of reasons, and your task is to help Phil Samouel identify his problems and develop solutions to improve his operations. In order to do that, you will need to evaluate both secondary and primary data to have a complete understanding of the restaurant's situation. You will also have to comment on research designs, sampling, and questionnaires, as well as use statistical software to analyze data and develop appropriate strategies.

ETHICAL DILEMMA

NRG, an online music retailer, places a cookie on its customers' computers in order to identify customers whenever they log on to the company's Web site. The cookie allows NRG to maintain a database containing its customers' names, addresses, e-mail information, purchasing histories, and credit card numbers. The technology even allows NRG to track its customers' visits to other Web sites. NRG analyzes this information internally to make product, inventory, and promotional decisions.

After a favorable article about NRG appears in a leading business publication, the marketing director of another company who is interested in targeting its customer base contacts NRG. Instead of paying a business research firm to help it identify the online shopping habits of its target audience, the company asks NRG if it would be willing to sell its information.

What do you think NRG should do? If you would like more background information to help you answer this question, refer to Chapter 3, which covers business ethics.

REVIEW QUESTIONS

1. How was research related to business strategies in the early classical period, some 2,500 years ago?
2. What is business research?
3. List and briefly describe trends affecting business research.
4. What is data mining? How is it related to a data warehouse?
5. Should a business do its research in-house or pay an outside agency to do it?

DISCUSSION AND APPLICATION ACTIVITIES

1. How has the computer, since its emergence in the 1940s, affected the field of business research?
2. Suppose a university has student records in a database that include demographic, lifestyle, and attitudinal data that students volunteered while attending the college. The records also include information on student course work and grades. Data is maintained in the database for both students who graduate and those who do not. If alumni agree to fill out surveys about their current jobs and salaries, that information is added to the data set and matched with the existing data. How could the university use this database? Does the database represent a threat to student privacy? Why or why not?
3. Suppose you wished to start a venture involving the manufacture of portable fax machines in Poland for export to the United States. List at least five areas in which business research could provide information allowing for better decision making as you begin this venture.
4. Suppose a company wished to do a research project testing whether a level of management could be removed from the organization without any serious negative consequences. Should this project be conducted by in-house researchers or by outside consultants?

INTERNET ACTIVITIES

1. Using the Web search engines Google and Yahoo! conduct a search with the key words "business research." Prepare a brief report telling what you found and how the results differed between the two search engines.

2. The Roper Center, at the University of Connecticut, has one of the largest collections of public opinion data in the world. Its Web site (http://www.ropercenter.uconn.edu) has the results of many surveys. Identify two articles or studies related to business research and prepare a report on what you learned.

3. The European Commission monitors the evolution of public opinion within member states and publishes its findings online through its Eurobarometer surveys (http://ec.europa.eu/public_opinion/index_en.htm).Read an article from the site. Is the information interesting? Would it be useful to business decision makers? Why or why not?

4. Go to http://www.employeeopinionsurvey.com. Which services are available at this Web site? If you were a business wishing to survey your employees, would you consider hiring this firm? Why or why not?

NOTES

1. Terence R. Nevett and Lisa Nevett, "The Origins of Marketing: Evidence from Classical and Early Hellenistic Greece (500–30 B.C.)," *Research in Marketing*, 6 (1994), 3–12.

2. V.R. Grace, *Amphoras and the Ancient Wine Trade* (Princeton N.J.: American School of Classical Studies at Athens, 1961).

3. Nevett and Nevett, "Origins of Marketing," 9.

4. Robert Gibbens, "Toyota Extends One-Price Retailing: Montreal Now, Vancouver and Toronto to Follow," *National Post* (January 22, 2002), FP3.

5. Zoe Roberts, "UK Businesses Sustain Their Highest Labour Turnover Costs," *People Management*, 7 (October 11, 2001), 11.

6. "Please Don't Go," *CFO*, 14 (May 1998), 23.

7. Cohn, Laura, and Gail Edmondson, "How Parmalat Went Sour," *Business Week Online*, January 12, 2004. http://www.businessweek.com/magazine/content/04-2, accessed August 2010.

8. Erich von Hippel, "Economics of Product Development by Users: The Impact of 'Sticky' Local Information," *Management Science*, 44, 5 (1998), 629–644.

9. George S. Nezlek and Gezinus J. Hidding, "An Investigation into the Differences in the Business Practices of Information Industries," *Human Systems Management*, 20, 2 (2001), 71–82.

10. Helen Lingard, "The Effect of First Aid Training on Objective Safety Behaviour in Australian Small Business Construction Firms," *Construction Management and Economics*, 19 (October 2001), 611–619.

11. William A. Sahlman, "The New Economy Is Stronger Than You Think!" *Harvard Business Review*, 77 (November/December 1999), 99–107.

12. "Keep Faith First, Fund-Raising Will Follow," *Fund Raising Management*, 26 (November 1995), 48.

13. Anne Papmehl, "Russia Has Emerged as an Enticing Business Market," *CMA Management*, 75 (November 2001), 50–51.

14. "Russia Begins Selling Cars in the U.S.," *Eastern Economist Daily*, October 12, 2000, Globe-Newswire; "GAZ to Open Office in Hungary," March 30, 2000, MTI (Hungarian news agency).

15. William Glantz, "Gorbachev Touts Russian Workers," *Washington Times* (April 25, 2001), B8.

16. Mitch Griffin, Barry J. Babin, and Doan Modianos, "Shopping Values of Russian Consumers: The Impact of Habituation in a Developing Economy," *Journal of Retailing*, 76 (Spring 2000), 20–53.

17. Diana James, "Skoda Is Taken from Trash to Treasure," *Marketing News*, 36 (February 18, 2002), 4–5.

18. Ernest Hall, "Broadening the View of Corporate Diversification: An International Perspective," *International Journal of Organizational Analysis*, 7 (January 1999), 25–54.

19. Jagdip Singh, "Measurement Issues in Cross-National Research," *Journal of International Business*, 26, 3 (1995), 597–619; Jan-Benedict, E.M. Steenkamp and Hans Baumgartner, "Assessing Measurement Invariance in Cross-National Research," *Journal of Consumer Research*, 25 (June 1998), 78–90.

20. Frederick F. Reichheld, "Lead for Loyalty," *Harvard Business Review*, 79 (July/August 2001), 76–84.

21. Ibid.

22. J.E. Mathieu and D.M. Zajac, "A Review and Meta-Analysis of the Antecedents and Consequences of Organizational Commitment," *Psychological Bulletin*, 108 (September 1990), 171–195.

23. Arnon E. Reichers, "A Review and Reconceptualization of Organizational Commitment," *Academy of Management Review*, 10, 3 (1985), 465–475.

24. Barry J. Babin and Jill P. Attaway, "Atmospheric Affect as a Tool for Creating Value and Gaining Share of Customer," *Journal of Business Research*, 49 (August 2000), 91–101.

25. David I. Gilliland and Daniel C. Bello, "Two Sides to Attitudinal Commitment: The Effect of Calculative and Loyalty Commitment on Enforcement Mechanisms in Distribution Channels," *Journal of the Academy of Marketing Science*, 30 (Winter 2002), 24–43.

26. Graham Hooley, Gordon Greenley, John Fahy, and John Cadogan, "Market-Focused Resources, Competitive Positioning and Firm Performance," *Journal of Marketing Management*, 17 (2001), 503–520; Anil Menon, Sundar G. Bharadwaj, Phani Tej Adidam, and Steven W. Edison, "Antecedents and Consequences of Marketing Strategy Making: A Model and Test," *Journal of Marketing*, 63 (April 1999), 18–40; Anne S. Minor, Paula Bassoff, and Christine Moorman, "Organizational Improvisation and Learning: A Field Study," *Administrative Science Quarterly*, 46 (June 2001), 304–337.

27. Edward Rigdon, "Data Mining Gains New Respectability," *Marketing News*, 6 (January 6, 1997), 8.

28. Terrence E. O'Brien and Paul E. Durfee, "Classification Tree Software," *Marketing Research*, 6 (Summer 1994), 36–40.

29. Michael S. Morgan, "Research Boosts Database's Power," *Marketing News*, 9 (October 8, 2000), 16.

30. "Customer Tracking Pays Off," *Security: For Buyers of Products, Systems and Services*, 35 (August 1998), 79.

31. Paul McDougall, "Intel's Got the Speed: Do Customers Need It?" *InformationWeek*, http://www .informationweek.com/news/showArticle.jhtml?articleID=6506072, accessed September 2009.

2 | Overview of the Research Process

LEARNING OUTCOMES

1. Describe the phases of the business research process
2. Understand theory and how it is used in business research
3. Explain how the scientific method improves business research
4. Contrast the rigor of science with the pragmatics of business
5. Understand the role and importance of research proposals

Business students often struggle with starting a research project because they do not know how things like questionnaires and data analyses eventually produce results, or how to use survey findings to develop meaningful conclusions. But experienced researchers have the benefit of prior knowledge of the research issues as well as the tools to do the job. This chapter tries to answer the question, where do I start? We begin with an overview of the basic business research process.

THE BUSINESS RESEARCH PROCESS

The **business research process** provides a roadmap with directions for conducting a business research project. Generally, three phases are involved: formulation, execution, and analysis. Each is summarized in Exhibit 2.1. Each of the three phases includes several steps. But business research studies are not as orderly and sequenced as it may appear from this diagram. Studies sometimes skip steps because they are not necessary for a particular research design, and the steps are not always followed in the given sequence. Indeed, it is quite common to move through the process, encounter some kind of obstacle, and have to go back up to an earlier step and modify the initial research plan. The process is thus best used as a guide to understanding where to start, what to consider and agree on as you move forward, and where you can expect to be when the research is complete.

Exhibit 2.1 **The Basic Business Research Project**

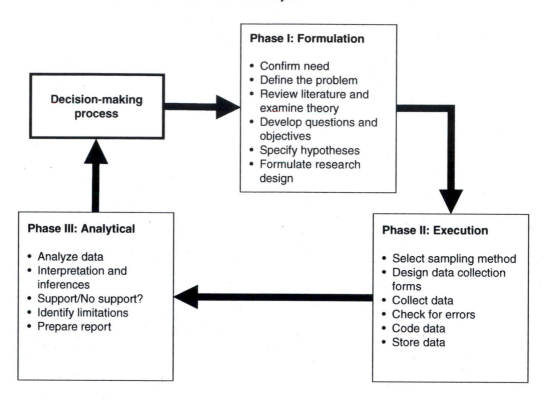

PHASE I: FORMULATION

The **formulation phase** involves defining the substance and process of the research. This phase is very much like creating a recipe. The creation of a research design, like that of a recipe, involves combining ingredients that will eventually produce the desired result. A step-by-step set of instructions is provided with any recipe, and this is the process through which the separate ingredients are made into an edible solution. A similar process is followed in business research.

The first task in the formulation phase is to confirm the need for the research. Business research is needed when managers must make decisions but do not have enough information to do so. Determining if enough information is available is based on whether additional information can be collected quickly enough to help, at a price within the firm's budget, and if it will substantially reduce the risk associated with making a decision based on the existing information. If the answer is yes to all three questions, then business research is needed.

The second task is to define the problem. This is perhaps the most important task because an incorrectly defined problem will mean the research is of no value. A problem is any situation where a gap exists between the actual state and the desired one. But a problem does not necessarily mean that something is seriously wrong. Instead,

---

■————**Business Research Dashboard**————■
How Should Tesco Define Its Problem?

Tesco, the United Kingdom's dominant supermarket chain, has decided to use its highly successful intelligence-driven retailing system as a way to move into the very competitive U.S. food market. It will position itself head-to-head against retail powerhouses Walmart and Costco. With over half its retail operations outside the United Kingdom, Tesco has decided to set up shop on the U.S. West Coast with a convenience-store format. The company's chief executive says, "We have been watching the U.S. market for many years, but never thought we had the right approach and format for the American consumer. We could have gone in before, but our new format is tailored to the U.S. and brings something original."

As Tesco enters the U.S. food market, how would you define its research problem as it attempts to develop the best strategy?

Sources: "British Invasion: The Tesco Test," *Corante*, February 9, 2006, http://customer.corante.com/archives/2006/02/09/british_invasion_the_tesco_test.php; Parija Bhatnagar, "Wal-Mart, Kroger, Safeway Better Watch Out: The British Are Coming!" *CNN Money*, February 27, 2006, http://money.cnn.com/2006/02/24/news/companies/tesco_us/index.htm; and Aisha Labi, "The Virtual Grocer," *Time Europe*, 156, 18 (October 30, 2000), http://www.time.com/time/europe/magazine/2000/1030/tesco.html, accessed November 2009.

---

it could be an opportunity to improve an existing situation. Thus, problem definitions can include both existing problems in the current situation as well as the opportunity to pursue a more favorable situation in the future. You will learn more about defining the research problem in Chapter 4. Looking at the Business Research Dashboard, reflect on how you would define the research problem facing Tesco.

Problems are identified and defined in a logical manner. Both organizational and environmental changes may prompt the desire to identify problems and opportunities. For example, a manager might be concerned because sales of a particular product are down, or because the cost of carrying inventory has increased. Or, a manager might notice important changes that could signal new opportunities. For example, marketing managers may note frequent business press attention to the emergence of digital environments such as Second Life, where consumers adopt avatars and personas and buy virtual products and services, and feel a need to conduct research to see if there are advertising and marketing opportunities for their businesses in these new environments. When a problem is recognized, a manager undertakes preliminary data collection. Managers often use informal interviews, both unstructured and structured, to get an idea or feel for what is happening.

The nature of the problem is confirmed when the third task of the formulation phase is undertaken, examination of the literature and relevant theories. The **literature review** is a comprehensive examination of the published and unpublished work from secondary data sources in the areas related to the problem. Literature reviews are used to learn what others have found in previous research on similar problems, to avoid mistakes they may have made and to identify any emerging trends. For example, if your business problem is low morale among employees, clearly you would want to determine what factors have caused low morale in other businesses, particularly those in your industry. Finally, any relevant theories can be used to specify hypotheses for testing. Reviewing the literature is covered in Chapter 4.

Some examples of business problems that could benefit from research include:

- How do price and quality rate on customers' evaluations of products?
- Is the effect of participative budgeting on performance moderated by control systems?
- Does improved automation lead to greater asset investment per dollar of output?
- Has the new packaging affected the sales of the product?
- To what extent does the organizational structure and type of information system account for the variance in the effectiveness of managerial decision making?
- Will global expansion result in an improvement in the firm's image and value?
- What are the effects of downsizing on long-run growth?
- What are the components of quality of life?
- What factors should be considered in creating a data warehouse for the firm?

As you can see, business problems like those listed above affect all aspects of a firm's operations.

The fourth task in the formulation phase is to specify research questions and objectives. This involves redefining the initial business problem in scientific terms. For example, assume the branded fashion clothing chain Gap (www.gap.com) is concerned about its overall image among retail customers. As initially defined, the research problem is, Do marketing strategies need to be changed to improve customer satisfaction? But after further examination and a review of published research, the following questions arise:

- What is the customer awareness level of Gap stores compared to that for its major competitors?
- What factors are important in selecting a retail store that offers fashionable, high-quality products at affordable prices?
- What is the current image of Gap stores?
- Which companies are its major competitors and what is their image?
- What is the demographic profile of Gap customers compared to that of customers of its major competitors?

Translating the problem into specific questions enables managers and researchers to specify research objectives, hypotheses for testing, and information needs, and ultimately to determine the appropriate research design.

Obtaining information to answer specific research questions may involve collecting data. But before collecting new data the researcher should determine if relevant data has already been gathered, perhaps for a purpose other than the research at hand. This type of data is referred to as secondary data. Government agencies, commercial research firms, universities, trade groups, and others collect and report tremendous amounts of information every year. Some of the information is free, in other cases it must be purchased. The Internet has emerged as a means of easily locating secondary data from anywhere in the world. We discuss the role and importance of secondary data in Chapter 5.

The final task of the formulation phase is research design. To complete this task, the researcher considers what information is needed to satisfy the research objectives, the type of data-collection approach, sampling, when the research findings are needed, the budget, and so forth. The three types of research designs are exploratory, descriptive, and causal. They are discussed in Chapter 6.

PHASE II: EXECUTION

After formulating the research, the **execution phase** begins. Here the researcher actively gathers information from the appropriate sources. The information is then checked for errors, coded, and stored in a way that allows it to be analyzed quickly and conveniently.

Before collecting data, the researcher must first decide on the sampling design. The sampling design process involves answering the following questions:

- Should a sample or a census be used?
- If a sample, which sampling method is best?
- How large a sample is necessary?

In answering these questions, the researcher must always consider ways of minimizing error that could occur because of the sampling process. Sampling is covered in Chapter 7.

Data collection is an important task in the research process. It is also often among the most costly components of the research process. The type of data collection that is suitable depends on the questions being asked. Data collection involves either observation or surveys. Sometimes interviewers are involved, other times not. For example, interviewers are not involved when respondents complete a survey questionnaire on their own or when a computer is used to record data on click-through sequences on a Web site. Information on behavior, attitudes, beliefs, lifestyle, expectations, perceptions, and similar characteristics is collected in this phase. Once collected, the data is analyzed and becomes the basis for improved decision making. Chapter 8 identifies the various approaches to collecting data, both qualitative and quantitative, and summarizes the advantages and disadvantages of each.

To properly collect data, researchers must have valid and reliable data-collection forms. These forms are used to ask and record information gathered during business research. The forms must include the right questions in the correct sequence to ensure the research findings are valid and reliable. To ensure data-collection forms collect reliable and valid data they are always pretested. Measurement and scaling are covered in Chapter 9 and questionnaire design in Chapter 10.

There are many opportunities for errors to occur in data collection. These errors are called nonsampling errors because they arise from sources other than the sampling process. Once data has been collected the first step is to check it for errors. There may be missing data or responses that suggest the person who completed the questionnaire either did not understand it or was not properly following instructions. Other errors may be the result of inadequate interviewer training. Errors can never be totally eliminated, but good researchers anticipate potential problems and design controls to minimize them.

Along with checking for errors and inconsistencies, researchers doing quantitative research must code the data and create the data file. With quantitative studies answers to many of the questions are often precoded. That is, there are structured responses, and the respondent simply checks a number or letter associated with a particular response. In contrast, with qualitative studies the researcher examines the data both during and after collection looking for commonalities or patterns. In some instances, the researcher prepares a written description of these patterns without formally coding the data. In others, the researcher codes the answers to qualitative questions and uses software to aid the process of examining the findings.

Data preparation for qualitative research is discussed in Chapter 11 and for quantitative research in Chapter 12.

PHASE III: ANALYTICAL

The third phase is analytical. In the **analytical phase**, the data is analyzed. If the research involves hypothesized relationships, they are tested and either supported or not supported based on comparing the actual study outcome with the outcome predicted in the formulation phase. Results are examined to provide answers to the key research questions. A report is prepared to communicate the results to the appropriate audiences. The decision maker can then take actions based on better knowledge of the situation.

The first task in the analytical phase is to select and apply a method for analyzing the data. The method of analysis depends on whether you have conducted a qualitative or quantitative study. With qualitative studies, the process involves identifying categories or themes for your data, assigning findings to the appropriate category, specifying relationships, and in some instances testing hypotheses. These tasks are discussed in Chapter 11. In contrast, quantitative studies generally tabulate and report the data in diagrams and charts. For example, your results may show that males consume more Guinness beer and females prefer white wine. Other times the data is examined to identify relationships and test hypotheses. For example, you may apply a statistical tool and learn that older workers are more concerned about being laid off by their company than are younger workers. You will learn data analysis for quantitative studies in Chapters 13, 14, and 15. To make learning data analysis easier, we refer to the continuing case of Samouel's Greek Cuisine.

The last task in the business research process is preparing the report. The report is an important component of the research process because it communicates the results of your research project. The research report summarizes the findings for all the questions posed in the project. It also briefly states the limitations of the research so individuals using the findings will understand how much they can rely on the study in making decisions. Chapter 16 tells you how to prepare an effective report. It also provides suggestions for effectively presenting the research findings.

THEORY AND BUSINESS RESEARCH

Theory refers to a set of systematically related statements including some law-like generalizations that can be tested empirically.[1] A specific theory is a proposed explanation for some event. Sometimes theories have been confirmed by past research. Other times they are proposed theories with either limited or no validation. **Law-like generalizations** are expectations of what will happen under specified circumstances, thus allowing for predictions about reality.

Competition is an example of a theory in business strategy. The theory of competition predicts that firms within an industry that are able to differentiate themselves over time gain a competitive advantage. A key law-like generalization related to the theory of competition is that differentiation is a competitive advantage that enables firms to charge higher prices.[2] Basic business research is still testing this generalization empirically, and the notion is generally supported. Management strategy at Macy's has led to a commitment to a relatively highly trained workforce. This point of difference makes customers more willing to pay a higher price than they might elsewhere. Managers and researchers evaluate theories based on how well they predict outcomes.

Researchers develop theory based on the accumulated body of previous research. Therefore, a researcher will seek previously reported studies involving similar phenomena. Applied business researchers also rely on the history of a particular company to help develop a set of expectations in a given research situation. Without theory, the formulation stage becomes more difficult because business researchers cannot set boundaries on the study situation. When existing theory is not particularly helpful in understanding a research problem, qualitative research may be used to generate a new theory or to revise an existing one.

THE FUEL FOR RESEARCH

Theories provide key inputs into the research process. Business theories explain and predict business phenomena. Decision makers want to know the likelihood these explanations and predictions are accurate. Thus, theory helps shape the research questions and specific predictions as expressed in hypotheses. Research projects then validate or invalidate these predictions.

Problems can arise, however, when theories are incomplete. Consider, for example, a theory of the relationship between advertising and sales. Given the key nature of this relationship to business success and the variety of research questions that might be influenced by this theory, much research is affected by it.

What do you think is the relationship between advertising and sales? Does advertising cause sales? There may be a good reason to expect it to do so. Thus, a theoretical explanation can be developed, as the following example shows.

> Increased advertising means more people will know about a business. Knowledge precedes desire, and therefore advertising will eventually increase sales.

To this day, however, the advertising-sales relationship is an unsettled issue despite many, many studies of this topic. Some research counters the logic of the previous example, claiming that sales cause advertising: managers often set advertising budgets as a percentage of product sales. Therefore, products that have higher sales have larger advertising budgets. Thus, past sales often determine advertising spending.

Since advertising is a critical business variable, many researchers have attempted to develop a theory explaining how sales and advertising are interrelated. Like most theories, this one contains gaps. For example, as mentioned, there is uncertainty whether sales cause advertising or advertising causes sales. This and similar gaps motivate further research.

Normative business decision rules are often theory based. Such **normative decision rules** suggest what individuals should do when faced with a situation described by a theory. An example of a normative decision rule from economic theory is one indicating that prices should be raised when demand is stronger than supply. The continuing case of Phil Samouel, owner of Samouel's Greek Cuisine, describes a business decision made according to a theory-based generalization.

CONTINUING CASE: SAMOUEL'S GREEK CUISINE
Do Lower Prices Result in Higher Sales?

Phil Samouel has been conducting some informal research about Gino's Italian Ristorante. By standing across the street several days and observing Gino's customer levels during the middle of the day, he has learned that Gino's Ristorante does more lunch business than he does. To better understand why Gino's lunch business is bigger, he goes to the restaurant with some friends and they eat lunch. While there, he discovers Gino's has a separate lunch menu and the prices are much lower than the dinner prices. Samouel then does some background research on restaurant operations and finds support for the generalization that lower lunch prices lead to higher lunchtime volume. As a result, Samouel decides to follow the normative rule that a restaurant's lunch prices should be lower than its dinner prices. He then prepares a separate lunch menu with lower prices in an effort to improve his business.

Are there other generalizations about restaurant operations you can think of that Phil should examine to improve his business?

Behavioral learning theory provides managers with normative decision rules related to the amount and timing of employee compensation. However, behavioral learning theory contains many gaps. According to behavioral learning theory, changes in behavior are brought about through conditioning, which provides reinforcement or rewards for desirable behavior. But it isn't necessarily clear why behavioral patterns change as a result of conditioning. Does an employee gain new knowledge as the result of the training provided by conditioning and then use this knowledge to rationally perform the desired behavior? Or, are the changes more instinctive, like the conditioned responses observed in animals? After all, circus animals can be trained to perform a variety of tricks if a food reward is associated with the desired response. Employees can be trained, too, but they generally do not react as a circus animal does to a reward such as food. Do employees use some type of higher (cognitive) learning? If so, managers can place a greater emphasis on process training and engage employees' cognitive reasoning skills. If not, employee behavior would best be controlled by rewarding desired outcomes and providing disincentives (punishment) for undesirable outcomes. Researchers are motivated to close these theoretical gaps so that they can provide managers with better normative decision rules. In this way, theory provides fuel for research.

THE PRACTICALITY OF THEORY

It has been said that "nothing is more practical than a good theory."[3] An opposing view is sometimes voiced by business: "Your explanation is too theoretical; give us something we can use!" Obviously, there are differences of opinion on the benefits of theory. Let's look at the role theory plays in the decision-making and research processes.

When taking their car to a mechanic people often describe symptoms of a problem by trying to duplicate the sound the car is producing. If a car owner doesn't include a sound when describing the problem, the mechanic may ask, "What does it sound like?" Why is sound so important in such cases? It's because sound enables the mechanic to develop a theory about what is wrong with the car. The mechanic does this by integrating the new information about the sound with previous automotive knowledge that he has developed into a theory about the connection between automobile sounds and car problems. Using this theory, the number of parts that must be checked can be narrowed down to a manageable number. Without some type of theory, the mechanic might as well begin checking parts in alphabetical order.

This analogy illustrates one of the key roles of theory. Theory points us in a direction that is likely to produce valuable results quickly. This is important to phase I of the research process because most of the research steps will follow naturally from the theory. In particular, theory is valuable because it suggests what the researcher needs to measure for obtaining useful results.

A great deal of research is aimed at developing descriptive theories of business, the marketplace, and customer practices. **Descriptive theory** is just that, theory that describes the way things are. The theory of perfect competition in economics simply describes the effects that firms will experience when operating in an intensely competitive environment. At a micro level, a learning organization, for example, aims to develop a better theory of itself. Specifically, learning (accumulated knowledge) is put to use acquiring resources that enable the organization to outperform others.[4] At a macro level, the overall quality of business practices in a nation is often tied directly to the quality of basic research produced there. Indeed, some say the United Kingdom's difficulties in effectively managing its railway and telephone systems are a result of an inability to develop research-based theory.[5] The Business Research Dashboard illustrates how theory is impacting the Internet.

Theory seeks to explain and predict. Researchers' goals are much the same. Theory and practice are inseparable because businesses hope to use theory to do a better job of explaining and predicting. **Rational decision making** is based on explanation and

---

■————Business Research Dashboard————■
Google: Mathematical Theory Can Be Useful

Michel Laroche is a professor at Concordia University in Montreal, Canada. His students have been heard to say, "I don't see the use of these math courses." Even if you see value in math courses, you might question the value of pure mathematical theory. But new search technologies have taken advantage of mathematical theories. Google (www.google.com) is perhaps the most effective commercial search tool available to business. The secret to Google's effectiveness lies in an esoteric branch of mathematics known as graph theory. Graph theory defines the location of points in space mathematically. Graph theory seeks to model edges, which are connections among multiple points. A special class of graphs are directed graphs, in which one end of a connection has more weight than the other. In 1995, the founders of Google, Larry Page and Sergey Brin, were students at Stanford University and realized that the hyperlink structure of the World Wide Web could be represented as an enormous directed graph. The connections among Web pages could be used to calculate "relevance scores" for Web pages in order to identify the best match for particular key words. The relevance of a node or Web page is determined in part by how often other Web pages link to it and how important these linking pages (called backlinks) are. You can see that Page and Brin used theory, in this case graph theory, to develop search software that defines the best search results in terms of mathematical edges. Perhaps you will be thankful for theory the next time Google helps you to find important information.

Sources: Tom Leighton and Ronitt Rubinfeld, "Graph Theory III," lecture notes, October 3, 2006, http://courses.csail.mit.edu/6.042/fall06/lec8.pdf; Jim Hedger, "Unified Theory of Google," *Search Engine Guide*, January 27, 2006, http://www.searchengineguide.com/jim-hedger/unified-theory.php; and Google News Archive, WebmasterWorld.com, October 2002, http://www.webmasterworld.com/forum3/5863.htm, accessed November 12, 2009.

---

prediction. Ultimately, good decisions are based on explanations and predictions that have high truth content; in other words the theory and its explanations and predictions are valid.

Decisions can be made without the benefit of theory and research. But when this happens they are either wild guesses or decisions based on pure intuition. Exhibit 2.2 shows the difference between theory-based and intuition-based decisions. Since businesses normally have a great deal at stake in their decision making, which is the best way to proceed?

Perhaps you've heard people try to explain their reasons for investing in certain stocks or their theory of the stock market. If so, did the theory encourage you to follow their advice? Exhibit 2.2 shows some of the benefits of using research-based theory. Which set of decisions is likely to describe ways of winning more often? The intuition-based rules can be tested just as can the theory-based rules, but the theory-based rules generally offer superior explanations. The explanations are derived from basic probabilities or expected values given that the game is played with a finite number of cards with equal numbers of each particular card value. In contrast, intuition-based decision rules generally do not have a compelling rationale. An exception to this is that some managers develop judgment or intuitions based on their experiences that are sound and relatively sophisticated. Thus, while intuition does play a role in deci-

Exhibit 2.2

Contrasting Theory- and Intuition-Based Decisions: An Illustration Based on a Theory of Playing the Card Game Blackjack

Theory-based decision rules	Intuition-based decision rules
Generally, stand (do not take another card) on more than seventeen.	Always sit on an end seat at the blackjack table.
Draw (ask for another card) when the dealer is showing a face card.	Tuesdays are the best days to play blackjack.
The decision to stand (not take another card) or draw depends on the cards that have been seen so far.	Wear a green shirt whenever playing cards.

sion making, businesspeople prefer to know why a certain course of action should be taken and how likely it is to bring success. Theory helps provide answers to these questions in the form of explanation and prediction.

THE SCIENTIFIC METHOD AND BUSINESS RESEARCH

Most students first study the scientific method in lessons at school. Students are usually able to associate the scientific method with testing a hypothesis through the use of observation and experimentation. The scientific method used by business researchers is really no different from that learned in school.

Science is the body of knowledge about some definable subject. The **scientific method** is the approach researchers use to gain this knowledge. The basic business research process described previously in the book relies on the scientific method. The business research process seeks to accurately describe the realities of business actions and interactions.

Exhibit 2.3 illustrates the scientific method. The top portion contains observation, discovery, and development of hypotheses. These three stages together describe the process of scientific discovery. There is no right way to discover ideas. Ideas can come from intuition, hunches, and deductive or inductive reasoning. Once some order can be imposed on the observations, the ideas can be stated as a discovery. A review of previously conducted research on similar topics is often helpful in moving from pure observation toward some working discovery or idea. The researcher then begins a preliminary investigation to translate the discovery into a testable hypothesis or set of hypotheses.

A **research question** poses an issue of interest to the researcher and is related to the specific decision faced by the company. A **hypothesis** is a formal statement of some unproven supposition that tentatively explains certain facts or phenomena. A hypothesis often describes some systematic (nonrandom) events that can be tested using data. Exhibit 2.4 provides some examples of business hypotheses. Generally, a hypothesis restates a research question in more specific terms. For example, a research question may imply the existence of some relationship, but the hypothesis typically goes further by stating the direction of the relationship.

Exhibit 2.3 **The Scientific Method Contributes to Business Decision Making Through Research**

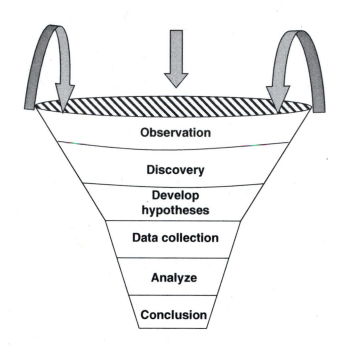

Exhibit 2.4

Research Questions Lead to Hypotheses

Research question	Corresponding hypothesis
Are company share prices affected by unexpected capital investment announcements?	Share price performance is positively and instantaneously impacted by unexpected capital investment announcements.
Does advertising influence sales?	Advertising is positively related to sales.
Is sales territory size related to customer service ratings?	Sales territory size is negatively related to customer service ratings.
Do flexible schedules create increased labor efficiency?	Business units using flextime have lower unit labor costs than do those using standard schedule procedures.
Does package color affect product quality ratings?	Consumers rate products with blue packages as higher in quality than products in orange packages.
Are equity risk premiums related to company size?	Equity investors require larger returns from smaller companies to justify investing funds.
Is beverage consumption related to region?	People living in countries near the equator drink more beer per capita than do people from the countries further from the equator.
Is job satisfaction related to an employee's gender?	Female employees report higher job satisfaction than do male employees with the same job.

Exhibit 2.5 **Flow of Knowledge Between Key Research Tasks**

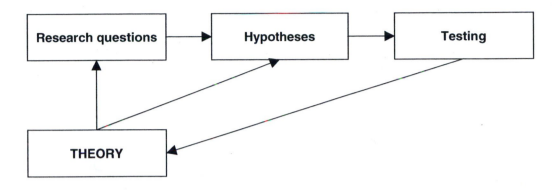

Research questions, hypotheses, and theory are all interrelated, as shown in Exhibit 2.5. Theory provides help in making sense of the decision-making situation. Current events and business problems are compared with existing knowledge. Then research questions are developed with the help of theory, which often identifies things that are related to one another. Further knowledge may result in stating more specific research questions and formal hypotheses. The hypotheses can then be tested by collecting data and analyzing the results. The results are expected to provide answers to the hypothesized relationships and to reinforce or modify existing theory.

The ability to translate research questions and hypotheses into words represents significant progress. This is illustrated in the Business Research Dashboard on so-called casual Fridays.

■————**Business Research Dashboard**————■
Does Wearing Casual Clothing Improve Worker Performance?

In recent years "casual Friday" has become commonplace in business. It refers to company dress codes being relaxed on Fridays. Suits and ties are replaced with jeans and casual shirts. This change was based on the theory that more relaxed workers are better workers. The theory can be expressed as a research question: Is employee dress related to job performance? Still more specificity allows the following hypothesis to be written: Employees in casual clothing will show higher job performance than employees in business clothing. This could be tested by comparing performance between two dress groups. Ten years of studies of this type have not supported this hypothesis. In fact, businesspeople are beginning to believe that for many jobs performance is actually harmed by casual dress. As a result, estimates indicate the number of firms offering casual Fridays has dropped in recent years. The finding that performance is lower when employees dress casually will cause a reexamination of the original theory. Perhaps relaxed workers are not always better!

Source: Lindsey Remington, "Arizona Firms Return to More Conservative Dress," *Tribune,* Mesa, Arizona (February 8, 2002).

RIGOR OF SCIENCE

After hypothesis development, the scientific method moves on to the testing phase (the lower half of Exhibit 2.3), where data is collected. Relevant data represents facts about hypothesized variables. This data is then examined to determine if the findings either support or do not support the hypotheses. If the findings match the pattern described in the hypothesis, then the hypothesis is supported. Thus, a conclusion can be drawn that will allow for more informed decision making.

In the discovery phase of the scientific method there are virtually no guidelines and thus no right or wrong ways to develop ideas or inferences. But testing is quite different. Indeed, it is the rigor of testing that distinguishes the scientific method. Testing is the way to get to the conclusion, and the conclusion contributes to an expansion of knowledge and more informed decision making. Testing is highly critical and analytical.

The scientific method, which is the basis of sound science, can be characterized as follows:

1. It is empirical, meaning that it is compared against reality.
2. It is replicable or objective, meaning that the researcher's opinion is independent of the results; other researchers conducting the study would obtain the same results.
3. It is analytical, in that empirical facts are chosen, specified, and measured in a way that will address research questions.
4. It is theory driven—it relies on an existing body of knowledge.
5. It is logical, meaning conclusions are drawn from the results based on logic.
6. It is rigorous—every effort is made to minimize error.

THE PRAGMATICS OF BUSINESS

The rigor of science is often traded off against the pragmatics of business. Businesspeople usually cannot get an answer too quickly. Thus, there is give-and-take between the businessperson and the researcher in terms of approach. For example, while the researcher may wish to use a sample representative of an entire population, that may take longer and cost more than the decision maker wishes to spend. Researchers almost always sacrifice some rigor for expediency. While this may introduce error, as long as the decision maker is informed of that possibility and the results are qualified based on any shortcuts, the researcher should proceed with the project. Good research also follows the principle of **parsimony**, meaning a simpler solution is better than a complex one. Parsimonious research means applying the simplest approach that will address the research questions satisfactorily.

RESEARCH PROPOSALS

Before conducting a research project, the business researcher must clearly understand the problem to be investigated. Once the problem has been defined, a plan of action is developed to investigate and make recommendations for solving the problem. A **research proposal** is a formal document summarizing what the problem is, how it will be investigated, how much the investigation will cost, and how long the research will take to complete. If accepted, it typically represents a contract between the researcher and the client (the one requesting the research).

The research proposal has a critical role in any research project. It defines the problem, outlines the researcher's approach and methods, specifies the project's deliverables (what the client will get from the project), and includes a budget and time frame for completion. A formal written proposal is the result of interactions between the client and the researcher through which the client's concerns (problems) are translated into research problems and a proposed approach to solving the problem(s) is agreed on.

Researchers benefit from preparing written proposals. The first benefit is that the proposal preparation clarifies whether the problem to be investigated is the one the client has requested. Business research helps managers improve their decisions. If the problem as defined in the research proposal does not facilitate improved decision making, then the problem must be redefined or the research should not be undertaken. Once the proposal is accepted, it provides a direction and plan for the researcher. By following the plan, the researcher can assess progress and make adjustments as needed. Finally, the written proposal documents the agreement between the researcher and the client and minimizes the possibility of later misunderstandings. Clients know what information they will receive and researchers know what information they must provide.

Clients also benefit from a written research proposal. First, when the client reviews the proposal he or she can verify the researcher truly understands the problem to be investigated. If changes are needed, they can be made before the project begins. Once the project is underway, the client can use the proposal as a means of ensuring the project's deliverables are what was expected and that the project has been executed as promised. Finally, a written proposal enables the client to evaluate the quality and value of a proposed project. If several proposals have been solicited, the client can compare the scope, methods, and proposed budget of them. This helps to ensure that high-quality research offering value for its cost will be delivered as expected. Exhibit 2.6 provides an example of a research proposal that was submitted to a health-care organization as part of a strategic planning process.

STRUCTURE OF A RESEARCH PROPOSAL

Research proposals can take a variety of forms. Some proposals are long and detailed. Public domain proposals for governmental projects, for example, typically are the most detailed. Others are of moderate length, such as the one for the Children's Health Foundation shown in Exhibit 2.6. Finally, some are very short, perhaps as short as a page, such as that shown in Exhibit 2.7. No matter their length or level of detail, most proposals should include the following:

- Project title
- Background information, specifying the events leading up to the request for the proposal
- Problem statement and research objectives
- Research strategy and methods—data to be collected, how it will be collected and analyzed, thus summarizing the steps that will be taken to achieve the research objectives
- Nature of the final report to be submitted, specifying the type and nature of the report
- Schedule and budget
- Qualifications of project consultants and the research firm

---

Exhibit 2.6

Research Proposal for Children's Health Foundation

Introduction and Objectives

Children's Health Foundation has progressed significantly since our initial strategic planning project in 2006. At that time management was in transition, Children's had no clear strategy, and Regional Health System, a full-service competitor, was applying steady pressure through the board and medical staff to absorb Children's into its system. Much has occurred since that time. Internally, the organization of Children's has matured significantly, the management team has coalesced, programs have been assessed and improved, costs have been reduced, and facilities developed. Externally, the payor environment has changed radically, with managed care spreading and freedom of choice reduced for patients and physicians. In this new age of health care, Children's must establish a strategic direction.

We believe Children's must rethink all aspects of its strategy. The current plan has been updated periodically over the past five years, but the core directions have remained heavily hospital focused and facility/program oriented. These are no longer sufficient strategic foundations for the future. The new plan must be "next generation," concentrating on a health-care market dominated by managed care, physician-hospital integration, a broader service area, and affiliations with other systems. In short, the strategic plan must be redeveloped from the ground up.

The objectives of the proposed planning process for developing this new strategic plan are as follows:

1. Develop and agree upon a new forecast for the health-care market served by Children's Health Foundation, fully understanding the revised geography, demand, competition, and trends
2. Identify and agree upon Children's positioning in the market
3. Identify the best strategy for Children's to achieve its mission, serve its communities, and prosper in the new environment
4. Achieve a common understanding of these requirements among the board, management, and the physician leadership of the organization

Following is a proposed work plan and schedule for achieving these objectives.

Scope of Work and Processes

We recommend developing the plan in four phases of work, beginning in January 2010, and finishing in May 2011, with an interim leadership retreat in April. Following is an overview of the key tasks and expected time frames.

(continued)

1. Project Initiation

Our major goal early in the project will be to define the type of database, analysis, and findings framework that provides good systemwide evaluations. Major tasks include, but are not limited to: agree upon information needed to support discussion; request and obtain data; develop interview lists, generate meeting dates, and preliminary agendas; and agree upon an initial list of issues to focus on. This should be completed by mid-February.

2. Situation and Objectives

The goal of this group of tasks is to develop a shared understanding of the expected market and of Children's position in that market. This will provide the baseline for identifying the critical objectives for the future. Major activities include: forecast the external market for health care in Children's market area; complete a demographic analysis and forecast; forecast outpatient, inpatient, and physician demand under the expected environment; model Children's expected and needed market share positions and volume implications under a range of scenarios; complete a SWOT (Strength, Weakness, Opportunity, Threat) assessment of Children's position; and identify critical success objectives for the hospital over the next five to ten years. These activities should be completed by mid-April.

3. Strategy and Requirements

Working from the objectives, short- and long-term strategies will be developed. Areas we expect to cover include, but are not limited to: assessment of the number of patients needed to support the system; payor interfaces needed to support alternative patient sources, including managed care, indemnity, Medicaid, etc.; medical staff and physician business development initiatives; internal organization and governance requirements to support strategic initiatives; and mission implications. We expect these areas to be initially addressed during the March–April period. At the retreat in late April the board and management can review preliminary strategic directions and provide input as needed.

4. Action Planning

The intent of this final group of activities is to ensure priorities are set and the basis for implementation is outlined. This will also include submission of the database and project documentation to the Children's management team for subsequent use. Areas we anticipate covering include prioritization and time frames for key initiatives; resource requirements needed to support action steps; implementation process with key groups, including physicians, employees, and board and community leaders; and final report submission. These tasks should be completed by late May.

The process we propose includes regular meetings with a planning steering committee of eight to twelve senior management and medical staff, supported by board presentations and perhaps medical staff briefings at key points. In addition, we expect to conduct approximately thirty-five individual interviews with a cross-section of physicians, board members, payors, potential affiliates, and management. Our proposed scope of process includes the following: five sessions with the steering committee, thirty-five individual interviews, presentation at April retreat, six two-day on-site visits, and discussions with key individuals scheduled into the planned site visits.

Consulting Team and Proposed Budget

Assuming the project can be authorized by late December, we are prepared to commit a very strong consulting team to Children's and are holding open our schedules accordingly. John Frusha, principal investigator, will lead this engagement and participate in all aspects of the work. He directed the original plan in 1998 as well as all interim updates. He has a national experience base and is well versed in the issues confronting Children's Health Foundation. Buddy Chen, a manager in our strategy services group, will coordinate the day-to-day activities. He has broad experience with projects and issues of the type proposed. Jana Reynolds will provide staff consulting support. She has a strong health-care background and will be the point person in developing and analyzing the database, as well as in conducting the interviews. Resumes for all three of these individuals are attached.

Our professional fee for conducting this project as proposed is estimated to be $106,000. This estimate is based on the levels of participation identified below:

> John Frusha—100 hours @ $300/hour = $30,000
> Buddy Chen—150 hours @ $250/hour = $37,500
> Jana Reynolds—220 hours @ $175/hour = $38,500

(continued)

Direct out-of-pocket expenses, including travel and lodging, secretarial support, overnight delivery, long distance telephone, and secretarial support, are charged at cost in addition to the above fees. Based on our past experience with Children's, this is a substantial quote. Two perspectives may be helpful in assessing this proposal. First, the current plan must be updated for the future. Other projects of similar scope typically run $130,000 to $150,000. Our past experience and familiarity with Children's situation has allowed us to complete this project on a budget that is 20 to 30 percent lower. Second, the budget for the previous plan was $70,000. Five years of inflation and the increased complexity of the current health-care environment make the current bid very comparable, in our opinion. Also, our proposed team is more experienced than the previous one.

This team, quote, and timetable are good through the end of December 2010, after which time our changing availability may dictate revisions. Please accept this as a working draft, subject to additional discussion to ensure the scope of the project is in line with your needs.

Exhibit 2.7

Proposal to Initiate a Business-to-Business Survey

AdMark International, LLC
10069 Barrett Parkway
Atlanta, Georgia 30044

Engagement Memo

To: Suzanne Wagner, Senior Manager
        Louisiana Specialty Chemicals
From: Bill Black, Principal Investigator
        AdMark International
Re: Project Contract/Engagement, Business-to-Business Survey
Date: February 26, 2010

Project Deliverables:

- Telephone interviews based on list provided by client ($N = 50$)
- Complete approximately twenty-five to thirty interviews (about 55–60 percent)
- Make ten callbacks to customer list over a three-week period
- Questionnaire same as previous survey
- Begin project first week in March; survey programming and data collection will take about four weeks; report preparation will take approximately two weeks; total project time six to eight weeks
- Open-ended questions to be taped and transcribed; client will be provided copy, but respondent identity will be kept confidential
- PowerPoint presentation report provided to client
- Principal investigator available for consultation regarding project

Budget:

- Cost of Project = $12,000
- $6,000 due to initiate project
- $6,000 due upon submission of report
- One-day site visit to discuss findings (optional)
- $2,000 plus travel expenses

Accepted as proposed above:

_____   _____
Suzanne Wagner   Date

The structure of the proposal is dictated by the nature of the research project being proposed. Fundamentally, the proposal should have enough information to ensure that the proposed project will solve the problem and the results will help the client to improve its decisions.

Most business research proposals are moderate in length and level of detail. Exhibit 2.8 shows the research proposal submitted to Phil Samouel to help him improve his restaurant operations.

CONTINUING CASE: SAMOUEL'S GREEK CUISINE
Is Theory Useful in Business Research?

Phil Samouel has been discussing the restaurant with his brother. Although the restaurant is successful, they have concluded there is room for improvement. By observing the dining area, Phil has noticed that there are often open tables. This led them to consider issues such as the number of tables in the dining area relative to the number of customers, particularly at peak serving hours during lunch and dinner. The brothers also spent some time with the head chef and learned that some entrées are selling well but that the dinner specials are seldom as popular as anticipated. Moreover, though the desserts are specially prepared Greek dishes from the old country, they are not selling well.

Last week Phil was reading the *Financial Times*. It had a story on the large number of new restaurants that had opened in London in recent years. The story said there were so many new restaurants that many potential customers were not aware of a lot of them. Phil did some research on the Internet to learn more about how individuals find out about new restaurants, and he found the Hierarchy of Effects theory, illustrated below:

Hierarchy of Effects Model

Hierarchy stage	Description
Unawareness	Not aware of your company, brand, etc.
Awareness	Aware of your brand
Knowledge	Know something about your brand
Liking	Have a positive feeling about your brand
Intention	Intend to buy your brand next
Purchase	Actually purchase your brand
Repurchase/loyalty	Purchase your brand regularly

---

1. Could this theory be useful to Phil and his family in trying to increase the number of customers?
2. Could it help them to understand why some of the menu items are not selling well?
3. Are there some other theories you can think of that would be useful in improving the restaurant's operations?
4. Should qualitative or quantitative research or both kinds be conducted?

Exhibit 2.8

Research Proposal for Samouel's Greek Cuisine Restaurant

Statement of Problem

Phil Samouel, owner of Samouel's Greek Cuisine restaurant, believes his revenues and profits are not as high as they could be. He wants to find out how to attract more new customers, keep his current customers, and convince customers to spend more when they come and to come back more often. He also wants to ensure he is operating his restaurant as effectively and efficiently as possible.

Phil is a successful manager and businessman, but he is fairly new to the restaurant business. He has decided, therefore, that the best way to improve his business is to hire a restaurant consultant. Through a contact at his advertising agency, Phil identified a business research firm called AdMark International. He contacted the firm and asked that it conduct a preliminary assessment of his restaurant operations and prepare a research proposal for him to review. The proposal is expected to include proposed projects, deliverables from the projects, such as recommended strategies and action plans, as well as a schedule and budget. The outcome of this preliminary assessment is summarized below.

Research Questions

After discussions with Phil Samouel and several of his employees, the account manager from the research firm concluded that the primary questions facing Samouel's restaurant are:

- Are employees being managed to maximize their productivity as well as commitment to the success of the restaurant?
- What are the best approaches to attract new customers and to keep and grow existing customers?

Research Approach

To answer these questions, two separate but related research projects were recommended. The first project will evaluate current employees to determine their productivity, job satisfaction, and commitment. To do so, a survey of employees that has been used by a wide variety of organizations will be administered and tabulated. The second project will involve a survey of customers of Samouel's and his major competitor, Gino's Italian Ristorante.

Employee Assessment Project

The employee assessment project can be broken down into three researchable questions. They are:

1. How do employees feel about the work environment at Samouel's?
2. How committed are the employees to helping make the restaurant a success?
3. Do different groups of employees have different feelings about working at Samouel's?

The first research question concerns the work environment at Samouel's. Specific aspects of the work environment to be examined include compensation, supervision, coworkers, and overall satisfaction with the work at Samouel's. Phil Samouel believes he has good employees but knows there is always room for improvement. Moreover, he has never specifically asked his employees how they feel about working at his restaurant, and he has hired a lot of new, young workers in the past year (twenty-six new workers between the ages of eighteen and thirty-four), many who are part-time.

The second employee research question focuses on how committed the employees are to ensuring the success of Samouel's restaurant. From observing employees and listening to their comments, Phil believes the age and the length of time employees have worked at the restaurant may be related to commitment to the organization. Phil's consultant says that he has read some articles in trade publications suggesting this might be typical.

The third employee research question focuses on whether there are any differences among the employees regarding how they feel about working at Samouel's. Phil's observations of employees suggest this is true, and his consultant says his informal discussions with employees would support this.

(continued)

Customer Assessment Project

The customer assessment project can be broken down into three researchable questions. They are:

1. What is the level of satisfaction of Samouel's customers relative to that of the customers of its primary competitor, Gino's?
2. Do customers of Gino's rate it more favorably than do customers of Samouel's?
3. What factors contribute to restaurant customer satisfaction?

The first research question concerns the competitive positioning of Samouel's relative to Gino's. Phil Samouel's opinion is that Gino's has the advantage of being located in a more established residential area, and that its longer history has resulted in a larger, more loyal customer base. In addition, Phil believes that Gino's is able to charge higher prices without sacrificing business. Since satisfied customers may be willing to reward the restaurant by paying higher prices, it is important to examine these issues.

The second research question addresses whether customers evaluate Samouel's and Gino's differently. Customers will be asked to rate the two restaurants on ten attributes. The question, then, is, Do the ratings of the two restaurants differ significantly in ways that might influence satisfaction and loyalty? If the perceptions differ on critical selection variables, then action plans can be developed to overcome the problems.

The third research question asks which factors determine customer satisfaction. Phil Samouel has expressed belief that satisfaction is determined mostly by food quality and the service of his employees. This belief is supported by a search of existing basic research reported in trade and academic journals. Other researchers have documented that customers evaluate service industries in general based on two classes of attributes. Core attributes represent those that most directly provide the primary benefit sought by most customers. In the case of a restaurant, food-related attributes would qualify as a core attribute. Relational attributes represent those that are less tangible and include human-human and human-environment interactions. Customer perceptions of the environment and employees fall into this category for restaurants.

Several articles in restaurant trade publications report this breakdown between core and relational factors. They discuss the importance of food quality, including the freshness and variety, and restaurant cleanliness as two key factors shaping customers' service quality perceptions. (See, for example, Klara 1999, and Stern and Stern 2000.) Thus, when customer perceptions of food, employees, and atmosphere improve, their satisfaction with the restaurant should also improve. The results of this survey will be important in assessing Samuel's restaurant to identify strategies for improvement.

Methodology

Samples

Data must be collected to examine the issues posed above. Exit interviews as patrons depart Gino's Italian Ristorante and Samouel's Greek Cuisine are proposed because this will be a good way to identify and interview Gino's customers. Interviews will be conducted between 12:00 and 2:00 P.M. and 7:00 and 10:00 P.M., Monday through Saturday, for a period of ten days. Interviews during these hours will enable comparisons between lunch and dinner patrons. Customers will be approached randomly and asked two screening questions. One, did they just dine in the restaurant? Two, have they completed the questionnaire before? A "yes" for the first question and a "no" for the second will prompt a request to participate in the survey. If the customer agrees, they will be provided with a clipboard containing the study questionnaire, a comfortable place to complete it, and $5 for their participation. The goal will be to obtain at least 100 interviews with customers of each restaurant. An employee survey will also be conducted. An attempt will be made to interview as many employees as possible but not fewer than sixty.

Measures

Measures for the study will be developed following interviews with Phillip Samouel and his management team, as well as from consulting previous industry research. The employee survey will have been previously validated and its reliability assessed. The survey will include questions about

(continued)

the working conditions, compensation, coworkers, supervision, commitment to the organization, likelihood to search for another job, and classification variables such as age and gender. The customer survey will include perceptions of the food, atmosphere, prices, employees, and so forth. Classification questions such as age and gender as well as relationship variables like satisfaction and future patronage will also be included.

Data Analysis Approach

After the data is collected, it will be analyzed and summarized in an easy-to-understand format. The statistical software SPSS will be used to ensure relevant issues are examined in a comprehensive and cost effective manner. Both simple as well as advanced statistical techniques will be used where appropriate. Usage of the statistical techniques will be according to commonly accepted research assumptions and practices.

Schedule and Budget

Schedule

The two projects are extensive. The initial operational assessment will take approximately two weeks. But it will not be in final form until information has been collected and analyzed for relevance from the employee and customer surveys. The employee survey will take approximately thirty days to complete. This will entail obtaining interviews from as many employees as possible but no fewer than 50 percent of the workforce at the restaurant, and representation from all management employees. The customer survey will take the longest time. To design the questionnaire, collect data, and analyze and interpret the findings will take approximately eight weeks. Preliminary findings of the other projects and updates will be given every two weeks. The final report, including recommendations, will be available ten weeks after the contract has been signed and the initial payment has been received.

Budget

The total cost for the two projects is shown below:

Employee survey	$15,000
Customer survey	35,000
Total cost	$50,000

Terms: Fifty percent will be due to initiate the project, and the balance is to be paid when the final report is submitted.

Qualifications

Consultants assigned to this project have a combined thirty-five years of experience in the restaurant industry. The principal investigator has completed projects with over 400 clients in the past fourteen years. Biographical sketches of the research team assigned to this project are attached for your review.

References

Robert Klara, "Fast and Fancy," *Restaurant Business*, 98 (6/1/98), 19–21.
Jane Stern and Michael Stern, "Familiarity Usually Breeds Regular Restaurant Customers," *Nation's Restaurant News*, 34 (11/20/2000), 24–26.

SUMMARY

DESCRIBE THE PHASES OF THE BUSINESS RESEARCH PROCESS

This chapter has introduced the basic research process. Three phases are involved. Phase I translates the overall research issues into research questions and hypotheses. Theory plays a key role in translating information about a business situation into a researchable idea. Theory, business practices, and intuition enable translating research questions into hypotheses. A research design is then selected to test the hypotheses. Phase II, the **execution phase**, is concerned with the activities of collecting data, ensuring the data is valid and reliable, and preparing it for analysis. Phase III, the analytical phase, is where the data is analyzed and interpreted relative to the hypotheses. Hypotheses are either supported or not supported based on these results. Finally, a report is written and often presented to communicate the research results.

UNDERSTAND THEORY AND HOW IT IS USED IN BUSINESS RESEARCH

The first half of the basic business research process is oriented toward discovery. There are few if any rules about discovery. The primary objective is to develop some ideas worthy of testing. Testing is the second half of the research process. There is only one way to test ideas; an idea must be compared with reality or expectations. This is known as empirical testing.

A theory is a set of systematically related statements that can be tested empirically. A specific theory is a proposed explanation for some event. Sometimes theories have been confirmed by past research; other times they are proposed theories with either limited or no validation.

Theories provide key inputs into the research process. Business theories explain and predict business phenomena. Decision makers want to know the likelihood these explanations and predictions are accurate. Thus, theory helps shape the research questions and specific predictions as expressed in hypotheses. Research projects then validate or invalidate these predictions.

EXPLAIN HOW THE SCIENTIFIC METHOD IMPROVES BUSINESS RESEARCH

In many ways, the basic business research process follows the same methodology as the scientific method. The process starts by considering all relevant input. This input is combined with current knowledge to produce research questions or hypotheses. They are then tested in an analytical way. It is important to note that no recommendation is provided for the most acceptable way of discovering ideas. However, ideas can be supported or not supported only through testing. The scientific method provides a process for discovering and testing ideas.

CONTRAST THE RIGOR OF SCIENCE WITH THE PRAGMATICS OF BUSINESS

The rigor of testing is what distinguishes the scientific method from business pragmatics. Testing is highly critical and analytical; it is the way to form conclusions, and conclusions enable us to expand knowledge and make more-informed decisions. The rigor of science is often traded off against the pragmatics of business. Businesspeople usually cannot get an answer too quickly. Researchers almost always sacrifice some rigor for expediency. While this may introduce error, as long as the decision maker is informed of that possibility and the results are qualified based on any shortcuts, the researcher should proceed with the project.

UNDERSTAND THE ROLE AND IMPORTANCE OF RESEARCH PROPOSALS

Before conducting a research project, business researchers must understand the problem to be investigated. Once the problem has been defined, a plan of action is developed to investigate and make recommendations for solving the problem. A research proposal is a formal document summarizing what the problem is, how it will be investigated, how much the investigation will cost, and how long the research will take to complete. If accepted, it typically represents a contract between the researcher and the client. The research proposal has a critical role in any research project: it defines the problem, outlines the researcher's approach and methods, specifies the project's deliverables, and includes a budget and time frame for completion. A formal written proposal is the result of interactions between the client and the researcher through which the client's problems are translated into research problems and a proposed approach to solving the problem(s) is agreed on.

ETHICAL DILEMMA

Jean-Charles Chebat is account manager for Burgoyne Research, Ltd. He tells customers his firm recommends that customers begin by conducting a survey to benchmark customer perceptions before undertaking any experiments to determine how customers would react to any new business decisions. Jean-Charles's assistant is aware that Burgoyne already has the information about public perceptions of a client from a recent survey conducted on behalf of this client's major competitor. Therefore, he feels Burgoyne should present the results of the other survey as secondary research to save the client money. When he mentions his concern to Jean-Charles, Jean-Charles says it is not unethical to conduct a new survey even if they know the probable results. Instead, he believes it would be unethical to disclose the results of work conducted on behalf of another client. With whom do you agree?

REVIEW QUESTIONS

1. What are the three phases of the basic business research process? Briefly explain each.
2. What role(s) does theory play in the basic business research process?
3. What is the scientific method and how is it used in business research?
4. What are the characteristics of good science?
5. Why is the preparation of a written research proposal important?

DISCUSSION AND APPLICATION ACTIVITIES

1. Suppose you work for a major consumer goods company. One of the products that you represent is salad dressing. A competitor is beginning a test market involving a new spicy ranch flavor. Its salespeople are going from store to store placing it on the shelves. Your boss asks you to go to these stores and buy all the salad dressing. Why might he or she ask you to do this? What would be your reaction? Consider the ethical implications of this behavior.
2. What are normative decision rules? Are they theory? How can they be used by business researchers?
3. Why is theory important in the design of business research studies?

INTERNET EXERCISES

1. Use a Web-based search engine such as Google or Yahoo! to find the following information:
   a. The number of people employed in automobile manufacturing in the United States, the United Kingdom, Germany, and Japan.
   b. Demographic profiles for the following states: Georgia, California, Vermont, and Nebraska.
2. Visit the Keirsey Web site (http://www.keirsey.com/). Follow the first-time user instructions to take the Keirsey Temperament Sorter II. Which personality type are you? Discuss the different types in class. What types of jobs would you recommend to someone with your personality type? Which would you not recommend to someone with your personality type?

NOTES

1. Shelby Hunt, *Marketing Theory: The Philosophy of Marketing Science* (Homewood, IL: Irwin, 1983).

2. Olin Chamberlin, *The Theory of Monopolistic Competition* (Cambridge, MA: Harvard University Press, 1939).

3. Curt Lewin, *Resolving Conflicts and Field Theory in Social Science* (New York: Harper & Row, 1948).

4. Peter R. Dickson, "Toward a General Theory of Competitive Rationality," *Journal of Marketing*, 56 (January 1992), 69–83; Shelby D. Hunt and Robert M. Morgan, "The Resource-Advantage Theory of Competition: Dynamics, Path Dependencies, and Evolutionary Dimensions," *Journal of Marketing*, 60 (October 1996), 107, 114; Shelby D. Hunt and Robert M. Morgan, "Resource-Advantage Theory: A Snake Swallowing Its Tail or a General Theory of Competition," *Journal of Marketing*, 61 (October 1997), 74–83.

5. Simon Caulkin, "Management: A Mess in Theory, a Mess in Practice," *Observer* (January 13, 2002), 9.

3 Ethics in Business Research

Business ethics is a growing field. Events such as the Enron, Ahold, Parmalat, and WorldCom scandals have attracted attention to abuses of power and authority in the business world and created a demand for more ethical businesspeople. This in turn has created a greater emphasis on the formal study of business ethics. In this chapter we define business ethics and explain its importance to business and society. We then explain ethics from three different perspectives—that of business researchers, business decision makers, and participants in business research. We conclude the chapter with a discussion of gaining access to participants and convincing them to participate in research studies. The ethical issues of gaining cooperation and participation from respondents are discussed as well.

BUSINESS ETHICS DEFINED

Trust is an overriding issue in business ethics. If all parties involved in an exchange truly trusted one another, there would be no need for any oversight of the exchange process. Where trust is lacking, some codified standards need to be enforced. There are professional codes of ethics that govern behavior. For example, two principal aims of the Marketing Research Association (MRA) are to increase professionalism and promote confidence in market research. In part, this is achieved by requiring that all members ensure that execution, data-collection, and data-processing responsibilities are met through following appropriate procedures and methods. Codes alone do not ensure ethical behavior. Top managers and leaders must support and enforce ethics codes for them to be effective.

Stronger replacements for trust include rules, laws, and regulations. Most of us would like to believe that employers can be trusted to take adequate measures to ensure employee safety. However, the number and severity of worker injuries around the world bring into question this trust and results in the imposition of laws through numerous legislative processes. National and supranational bodies such as the Occupational Safety and Health Administration and the European Agency for Safety and Health at Work have been established to determine and monitor standards of occupational safety and health (OSH). Although OSH legislation results in inspections that are sometimes seen as a nuisance, they also help protect workers and reduce costs resulting from industrial injuries, compensation claims, and the like. Estimates within the European Union are that a work-related accident occurs every five seconds and that one worker dies every two hours, so costs can be significant.

As a field of study, **business ethics** addresses the application of moral principles and ethical standards to human actions in the exchange process. Moral principles imply responsibility. Like other businesspeople, business researchers have social, market, legal, and ethical responsibilities.[1] **Social responsibilities** involve a concern for the way actions affect society or groups of people, including employees, customers, and the community. **Market responsibility** means a concern for making sure that products will not harm consumers and that their prices are fair. Business researchers and business decision makers are concerned with all these responsibilities in the performance of their jobs. As individuals, business researchers should exercise integrity, "a voluntary, spontaneous, positive form of honesty, where one takes initiative in being honest and being almost aggressive about it. The person with integrity says or stands up for what he thinks is right without waiting for anyone to ask him how he feels."[2] Consider the relevance of business ethics to university students based on the behavior reported in the Business Research Dashboard.

RELEVANCE OF BUSINESS ETHICS

Business ethics is relevant to business researchers because ethical issues occur in many phases of the research process. Ethical dilemmas are situations when a person is faced with courses of action that have ethical implications. For example, a business researcher may be placed in a situation in which two major competitors have both asked a research firm for similar research projects. Several dilemmas occur. For example, the researcher could take both jobs and use proprietary information to help make recommendations to each company. Alternatively, the researcher could use research paid for by one client as a basis for the recommendations to another.

Ethical dilemmas arise from questions of fairness and justice, potential conflicts of interest, responsibility issues, power discrepancies, and honesty issues. All of these can occur in business research situations. Such dilemmas require sound ethical judg-

---

■————**Business Research Dashboard**————■
Are the Brightest and the Best the Most Ethical?

How ethical are university business students? Several international studies of the ethical ideologies of business students have been conducted. Some have been country specific while others have undertaken cross-cultural comparisons. Numerous studies find that managers place more importance on ethical issues than students do. Experienced businesspeople report lower tolerance of unethical behavior than do business students. Additionally, male students report higher tolerance of unethical behavior than female students do. Evidence has also been presented to show that taking ethics courses does not seem to affect respondents' ethical behavior. Business schools and universities need to find new ways of making students more aware of the consequences of unethical behavior so that they become less relativistic in their perception of right and wrong. More disconcertingly for business schools, a recent cross-cultural study finds that the time spent studying business does not seem to have any positive impact on the ethical awareness of students and, in some samples, studying business appeared to have a negative impact on the ability to identify ethical problems.

How do the ethical standards of university students impact business research? What can be done to improve the ethical awareness of students?

Sources: Catherine N. Axinn, M. Elizabeth Blair, Alla Heorhiadi, and Sharon V. Thach, "Comparing Ethical Ideologies Across Cultures," *Journal of Business Ethics*, 54 (2004), 103–119; Mohamed M. Ahmed, Kung Young Chung, and John W. Eichenseher, "Business Students' Perception of Ethics and Moral Judgment: A Cross-Cultural Study," *Journal of Business Ethics*, 43 (2003), 89–102; Barbara C. Cole and Dennie L. Smith, "Effects of Ethics Instruction on the Ethical Perceptions of College Business Students," *Journal of Education for Business*, 70 (July/August 1995), 351–357; Philip H. Varherr, Joseph A. Petrick, John F. Quinn, and Thomas J. Brady, "The Impact of Gender and Major on Ethical Perceptions of Business Students: Management Implications for the Accounting Profession," *Journal of the Academy of Business Administration*, 1 (Spring 1995), 46–50; A. Singhapakdi and S.J. Vitell, "Ethical Ideologies of Future Marketers: The Relative Influences of Machiavellianism and Gender," *Journal of Marketing Education* (Spring 1994), 34–42.

---

ment. Ethical judgments ultimately involve an assessment of the fairness and justness of some course of action. Note that an ethical judgment is sometimes distinct from a contractual or legal obligation.[3]

Exhibit 3.1 helps demonstrate how various organizational, professional, and individual elements create pressures and conflicts which produce ethical dilemmas. However, organizational, professional, and individual elements also provide checkpoints that counter motivations toward unethical actions. In the end, these three groups of elements help balance business decision making.

This balance can be illustrated with a research example. An organization may be motivated to take advantage of a data collection opportunity. Perhaps this would involve collecting information in a way that violates the rights of research respondents, such as disclosing personal information (discussed later in this chapter). Or perhaps, it might ask a researcher to provide contact information on research respondents for use in sales activities. Neither action would be ethical. Researchers are guided by a professional code of conduct intended to stop them from participating in unethical and misrepresentative data collection. A researcher's own personal value system may

Exhibit 3.1   **Ethical Balance between Individual, Professional, and Organizational Values**

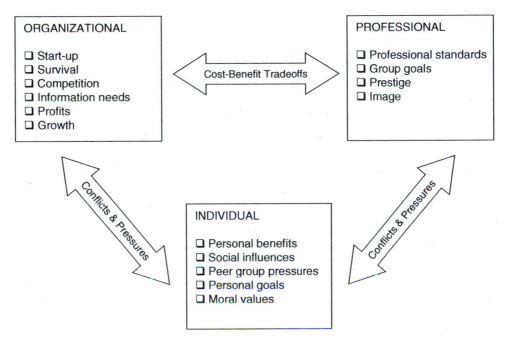

also prevent taking unethical action. The Business Research Dashboard suggests that organizational culture may play a role as well.

ETHICAL OBLIGATIONS OF THE RESEARCHER

Business researchers are faced with ethical considerations and possible ethical dilemmas throughout a research project. They involve the researcher's dealings with management, respondents, and their own professional integrity. Here we focus on the ethical considerations between the client requesting the research and the researchers before, during, and after the project.

BEFORE THE RESEARCH PROJECT

The period just prior to the initiation of a research project is perhaps the most critical point in the entire research process. During this time, the researcher must interview key decision makers to gain a working knowledge of the situation. The researcher acquires an understanding of the project objectives during these interviews. The key here is to translate a decision issue into a researchable proposition. Once a study is envisioned, researchers need to honestly assess their capabilities, and if they lack the skills or resources to carry out the project, they should decline it. Also, if the researcher is unable to reach a consensus with the client on the primary research questions, they should probe more or turn down the job.

■————**Business Research Dashboard**————■
Can Organizational Culture Affect Business Research Ethics?

Researchers have conceptualized organizational cultures as having three dimensions: bureaucratic, supportive, and innovative. Bureaucratic cultures are characterized by rules and systematic procedures, formality and hierarchy. Supportive cultures are friendly, warm, and trusting. Such cultures are more like those of families or clans and are characterized by members sharing the values and beliefs of the organization. Innovative cultures are exciting, creative, and results oriented. Employees are encouraged to try new ideas and use new processes in their work. A cluster analysis of 174 market researchers who responded to the study identified three types of organizational cultures:

Type 1: Innovative-supportive organizations are high in innovativeness and supportiveness and lower in bureaucracy.

Type 2: Bureaucratic-innovative-supportive organizations are high on all cultural dimensions.

Type 3: Bureaucratic-only organizations are high in bureaucracy and low in innovativeness and supportiveness.

Research professionals in all three organizational clusters reported that their organizations are mostly ethical. Nevertheless, research ethics were reported to be highest in the type 2 organizations, bureaucratic-innovative-supportive organizations. Type 1 organizations—innovative-supportive—reported the second-most ethical behavior. Type 3 organizations—bureaucratic-only—reported the lowest research ethics. The author of the study had hypothesized that the bureaucratic organizations would be the most rather than the least ethical because they would be most likely to follow rules. How would you account for the finding that bureaucratic-only organizations reported the lowest research ethics standards?

Sources: Ishmael P. Akaah, "Organizational Culture and Ethical Research Behavior," *Journal of the Academy of Marketing Science*, 21, 1 (1993), 59–63; Ellen J. Wallach, "Individuals and Organizations: The Cultural Match," *Training Journal*, 37 (February 1983), 29–36; Phapruke Ussahawanitchakit; Wichanee Iamchum; Jirapan Choojan; Salakjit Nillaphay; Nantana Ngamtampong; Kornkanok Tiparos; Supapong Pinwaha, "Organizational Culture, Business Ethics, and Earnings Quality: An Empirical Study of SMEs in Thailand," *International Journal of Business Strategy*, January 1, 2009, http://www.highbeam.com/doc/1G1–208534986.html, accessed December 14, 2009.

The researcher must communicate exactly what the research will be able to do. This typically is referred to as project deliverables. Both the researcher and the client must make sure that the project deliverables will address the research questions. The deliverables are listed in the research proposal for the client to review and approve. The research project should begin only when the researcher and the research client are in agreement on the deliverables.

Decision makers and researchers both should realize that sometimes the best decision is not to do any research at all. The following questions can be useful in addressing this key issue. If several of these questions lack answers, perhaps the research should be postponed. Before beginning a research project, the decision maker should ask:

- What information do I need that is now unavailable?
- How could I use that information?
- What will it cost to get this information and how long will it take?
- Does the potential benefit exceed the cost?
- Do my competitors have the information? If so, how is this affecting their performance?
- What aspects of my current business situation do I not understand?

DURING AND AFTER THE RESEARCH

Researcher–Decision Maker Relationship

The researcher has an ethical obligation to have a thorough working knowledge of the analytical and statistical tools necessary to complete the project. Researchers should not apply a technique unless they can do so competently and confidently. Researchers sometimes are tempted to apply a more complex tool than is needed in an effort to seem more sophisticated or perhaps even to increase the perceived worth of the research. But only the right tool should be used. This is usually the simplest tool that will provide the necessary results.

The researcher is responsible for interpreting the results honestly and fully. Researchers may have an opinion about the research questions being examined, or they may know the research outcome that management desires. But if the results disagree with a key decision maker's desires, the researcher faces a dilemma. In the late 1980s, R.J. Reynolds (RJR) invested over $300 million in Premier cigarettes, an innovative smokeless tobacco.[4] At the time, F. Ross Johnson was RJR's chief executive officer (CEO). He was a tough, aggressive, no-nonsense leader who was very enthusiastic about Premier.[5] The initial concept test results were generally positive. Consumers, both smokers and nonsmokers alike, were favorable toward the concept of a smokeless cigarette. RJR researchers were enthusiastic in presenting these results. Further tests, using actual Premier cigarettes produced in small quantities, provided some good and some bad results. Among the discoveries was that a Premier cigarette emitted a very familiar but very undesirable odor when lit with a match. Couple this with the fact that taste is tied closely to smell, and the recipe is disastrous for any product consumed by mouth. Researchers presented these smell and taste results less forthrightly than they had the fact that nonsmokers were favorable toward the idea of Premier cigarettes. In the end, Premier cigarettes were introduced to the market despite the mixed results. The point of this story is that the researcher is obligated to present the results fully and faithfully, even if the decision maker may not want to hear the results.

The researcher generally presents results both through a formal written report and a presentation. The presentation may be formal or informal. Chapter 16 discusses both the report and presentation in more detail. In presenting the findings, the researcher has an obligation to present any limitations of the research. By acknowledging and fully communicating any limitations, the decision maker has a more complete understanding of how much the results should affect the ultimate decision.

Researcher Obligations to Participants

Researchers should serve as advocates for research participants. Without their participation, the researcher might well be without a job. The researcher should show respect to participants at all times. For example, the researcher should accurately describe the nature and extent of the participation required when they are soliciting respondents. It is also essential that the researcher provide a fair estimate of the amount of time required to complete the research task.

Researcher-Participant Relationship: Ethics and Technology

Many technological breakthroughs like those discussed in Chapter 1 benefit researchers tremendously. This benefit does not come without a cost. These new technologies also introduce new ethical dilemmas.

Technology increases the possibility that a research participant's privacy might be violated. Much of the information collected and stored in data warehouses is done so with the promise that it will not be shared with others beyond those individuals directly involved with the research. Researchers have a duty to safeguard the privacy of this information. Personal data should not be shared with outside agencies in any form in which it could be traced back to an individual respondent. Research participant lists should not be sold to other companies to be mined for potential customers. Likewise, employee and corporate financial data is equally sensitive. The appropriate safeguards such as electronic firewalls should be in place to prohibit unauthorized access to this information. Additionally, technology improves the researcher's ability to monitor a research participant's behavior. The researcher must exercise caution with respect to using such monitoring for purposes that would reach beyond the scope of the specific research project. The Business Research Dashboard indicates how difficult it is to protect data and maintain privacy.

Researcher-Participant Relationship: Ethical Dimensions of Experimental Designs

Researchers have an obligation to treat participants in a research project ethically.[6] The following ethical issues are always important, but they become especially relevant during research studies:

- Coercing participation
- Causing potential physical or psychological harm
- Maintaining privacy
- Informing subjects of the nature of the research

Coercion. Subjects should not be forced to participate in a research study. Researchers often provide a modest incentive for participation. Should a potential subject choose not to participate, he or she would forgo the incentive. The incentives are usually small and involve money, merchandise, leave time, or a few points of credit depending on the type of participant required and the extensiveness of the research.

■————**Business Research Dashboard**————■
When Anonymous Data Isn't

In 2006, the online retailer, Netflix, published a database containing the movie rankings of 500,000 of their customers. The idea was to challenge researchers and others to analyze the data and come up with a better movie recommendation system for customers. The data did not include personal details. Names of customers were replaced by random numbers that Netflix believed would protect the privacy of its customers.

However, two researchers at the University of Texas at Austin, Arvind Narayanan and Vitaly Shmatikov, showed that at least some of the data could be "de-anonymized," meaning individual customers could be identified. The researchers compared rankings and timestamps with information in the Internet Movie Data Base (IMDb). Thus, data that customers and Netflix assumed was private could in fact be associated with specific IMDb users.

As Bruce Schneier, author of a book on online security points out, the researchers were not able to reverse the anonymity of the entire Netflix dataset, only those users who also posted to IMDb. In his analysis, Schneier concludes that "The risks of anonymous databases have been written about before . . . [what is troubling is that] the researchers working with the anonymous Netflix data didn't painstakingly figure out people's identities . . . they just compared [the Netflix dataset] with an already identified subset of similar data: a standard data-mining technique . . . as opportunities for this kind of analysis pop up more frequently, lots of anonymous data could end up at risk."

Other research suggests cause for concern as well. A researcher from Carnegie Mellon University, Latanya Sweeney, used public anonymous data from the 1990 census and determined that almost 90 percent of the U.S. population could be uniquely identified by their gender, date of birth and five-digit zip code. Professor Sweeney concludes that "few characteristics are needed to uniquely identify a person." Philipe Golle, a Stanford researcher, suggests that date of birth alone is very useful in "disambiguating" identity.

Business researchers may seek to identify people so that they can match data and improve the quality of decision-making, not because they are intrinsically interested in the identities themselves. But is de-anonymizing data ethical? Business researchers have long combined census data with other available data to better understand and serve customers. While the associated privacy issues have always been challenging for researchers, the depth and breadth of data available in a digital age result in many more opportunities to invade privacy.

Sources: Bruce Schneier, "When 'Anonymous' Data Sometimes Isn't," *Wired*, December 13, 2007, http://www.wired.com/print/politics/security/commentary/securitymatters/2007/12/security-matters_1213, accessed December 2, 2009; Phillipe Golle, "Revisiting the Uniqueness of Simple Demographics in the US Population," Workshop on Privacy in the Electronic Society, Proceedings of the Fifth ACM Workshop on Privacy in Electronic Society (New York: Association for Computing Machinery, 2006); Latanya Sweeney, "Uniqueness of Simple Demographics in the U.S. Population," LIDAP-WP4 Carnegie Mellon University, Laboratory for International Data Privacy (Pittsburgh, PA, 2000).

Volunteer participants in the famous Pepsi Challenge received a free six-pack of the beverage they thought tasted better. Researchers may feel obligated to find an appropriate compensation for the volunteer's time and effort. As in many areas of ethics, the line between incentive and coercion is not always clear. The incentive should never be of the type that a subject's well-being would be damaged by choosing not to participate. For example, docking an employee's pay for not participating in a research experiment compromises the principle of willing participation. Undue social pressure could represent coercion as well. Likewise, if a professor threatened to withhold a student's grade at the end of a semester because of refusal to participate in an experiment, the student would rightly feel coerced into participation. Colleges and universities generally have regulations regarding collecting research from students for preventing coercion.

In some research studies, it is impractical to gain permission from participants. Practically every reader of this book has been a test-market participant in the past few months without even knowing it. For example, consumers who enter a store where a new product test is being conducted are all test-market participants. In visiting a grocery store, you are being subjected to a test market. In most of these cases, the experiment has such a trivial effect on any participant that there is little possibility that someone's well-being has been harmed or that their privacy has been violated. In such cases, the obligation to ask permission is not needed. Marketing research ethics guidelines normally exempt public behavior from the informed consent requirement.

Freedom from Harm. Research study participants have the right to be protected from physical or psychological harm. Subjects stand the potential to be harmed even in business research studies. It is clear that potential harm may occur if a researcher studies job performance using three levels of nicotine or some other drug. Unfortunately, the potential harm isn't always obvious. For example, a researcher may wish to perform an odor study relating scents to employee alertness. Such a study would be useful for understanding whether certain job environments should be impregnated with the scents artificially. A research study could be conducted by changing the scent in a room in which a task will be accomplished. Is there potential for harm? Perhaps! It's possible that a subject may have a severe allergic reaction to one of the scents.

Another example is a study of job stress. Such a study could put a participant under undue stress. To study the effect of stress on job performance, a researcher may allow participants to take different amounts of time to complete a task, and then observe if performance differs based on the amount of time allowed. Another research design may involve telling participants that there will be a punishment for poor performance. Poor performance could be punished by informing subjects that the 15 percent lowest performers in the task would (a) have to work weekends for extra training, (b) have their pay cut, or (c) be fired. Even if the study could significantly benefit the company, is it ethical to place employees under such stress as part of a research project?

Sometimes the harm isn't physical. For example, a researcher may wish to study the effect of confidence on the ability to choose successful stocks. To manipulate confidence levels during the warm-up phase of the study, one group of research participants would be told that their stock-picking strategies are very profitable, whether they are or not. A second group of research participants would be told that their stock-picking strategies are unprofitable. Could subjects be harmed by this research?

While some research behaviors are clearly unethical, sometimes the line between ethical and unethical is unclear. Two questions can serve as a useful guide:

1. Is it impossible to restore the subject to his or her original condition?
2. Has the subject been exposed to unreasonable stress or risk without his or her knowledge?

If the answer to either of these questions is yes, the researcher should not proceed with the design. In the case of the fake stock market exercise, it is likely that debriefing the subject, which involves explaining the deception in the study, will return subjects to their original state. If the participants leave the study with a false impression of their ability to play the stock market (in either direction), however, then they have been harmed.

Privacy. Research participants have a right to privacy. Any research results should be used only for the intended purpose. Data is generally reported in aggregate, and individual responses are held in strict confidence unless some other prior agreement has been reached. Participants typically are promised anonymity when they are solicited for studies, and their data and any research report should maintain that anonymity. Not only is this the more ethical approach but it also protects the research from the bias that results when respondents give socially desirable responses.

Under no circumstances should a research project be used as a cover for some other purpose. On occasion, dishonest salespeople may recruit "research" participants via the telephone, e-mail, or in person. Such participation is only a ploy, however, used to try to sell something at the end of the project or to add the participant to a prospect list. This practice is unethical from both a business and a research viewpoint. Research efforts should be clearly distinguished from direct marketing or selling and vice versa. Researchers should never act as sales agents in any capacity. If the client wishes to add a sales appeal, the researcher should refuse to do the project.

Similarly, "push polls" are sometimes used in political campaigns. **Push polls** are short telephone calls used to spread negative and often false information about a candidate or issue under the guise of a poll. The interview is usually less than one minute and does contain some opinion questions. However, the entire effort is designed to produce a known outcome through the information provided and the manner in which the questions are asked. Selling under the guise of research and push polling clearly represent blatant and avoidable dishonesty.

Disclosure. Researchers conducting most kinds of survey research have no reason to hide the research purpose. Thus, the instructions will generally provide a statement of the research's purpose. This statement should be as specific as necessary to enable the respondent to understand it. Some surveys, however, may present quite a different picture from standard survey research.

Some research studies must utilize mild deception to accomplish the research objective. In this case, the researcher cannot disclose information about the purpose of the study prior to collecting the data from participants. For example, in the hypothetical stock market experiment mentioned previously, if the researcher were to reveal ahead of time that the study would be providing false profits from hypothetical stock purchases, there would be little point in conducting the study. In other words, complete disclosure would influence the results. However, the deception involved must be mild, and research participants must be debriefed after participating in the study.

Many of you have probably heard of a placebo. A **placebo** is an inert substance used in place of another being tested for effectiveness. In a medical experiment testing a drug's effectiveness on weight loss, for example, the drug might be administered intravenously in one of three ways: high dosage, low dosage, and no dosage (i.e., the placebo, which is often saline). All participants, even the placebo group, get an injection. Quite often the placebo group will also show some effect despite not receiving the treatment. Clearly participants cannot be told that they are receiving the placebo, or researchers would not be able to measure and compare the effect of the results from the placebo condition to those from experimental groups who received the medical intervention.

Thus, it may be impossible to fully inform a potential research participant prior to or during an actual research study. In such a case, a potential participant should be provided with a general description of the study's events and enough information to make possible an informed decision about participation. Such participants should be given a full explanation of the research study once their participation is complete. This allows participants to be restored to their original condition. The Business Research Dashboard provides examples of situations in which respondents were not informed but perhaps should have been.

Debriefing. Debriefing takes place after an experimental session is complete and involves revealing the true purpose of the experiment, the sponsor of the experiment, and generally a question-and-answer session. Finally, subjects should be offered a summary of results should they so desire.

Human Resource Review Committee. Research organizations sometimes form a human resource (sometimes known as human subjects) review committee to review all research designs using human participants. The committee should check research procedures to make sure all participants are treated ethically. Research universities routinely perform such reviews prior to providing support for university-sponsored research.

Countries around the world often require that a thorough human resource review be undertaken when seeking government grant money. This applies particularly to government organizations such as the U.S. government and the European Union. As an illustration, the U.S. federal government acted to withhold money from Johns Hopkins University researchers based on what was perceived as a poorly designed human resource review. This action was motivated by the death of a research subject participating voluntarily in university-sponsored research. The death occurred when a subject was given a medication not approved for use in humans. It caused a fatal toxic reaction in the victim's lungs. A government review ruled that even a cursory investigation of the drug would have revealed that it was (a) not approved and (b) potentially dangerous.[7]

Although business research is often much safer than medical research, businesses should nonetheless have a high degree of concern for the welfare of participants.

■————**Business Research Dashboard**————■
Research Ethics Scenarios

The following scenarios have been used in studies of the ethics of marketing researchers. The items were used originally in a 1970 study that has been repeated several times since the original study was performed, including in international settings. Are these practices unethical? Why or why not?

1. Use of Ultraviolet Ink. A project director went to the marketing research director's office and requested permission to use an ultraviolet ink to precode a questionnaire for a mail survey. The project director pointed out that although the cover letter promised confidentiality, respondent identification was needed to permit adequate cross-tabulations of the data. The marketing research director gave approval.

2. Hidden Tape Recorders. In a study intended to probe deeply into the buying motives of a group of wholesale customers, the marketing research director authorized the use of the department's special attaché cases equipped with hidden tape recorders to record the interviews.

3. One-Way Mirrors. One of the products of X Company is brassieres. Recently, the company has been having difficulty making decisions on a new product line. Information was critically needed regarding how women put on their brassieres. The marketing research director therefore designed a study in which two local stores agreed to put one-way mirrors in the dressing rooms of their foundations departments. Observers behind these mirrors successfully gathered the necessary information.

4. Fake Research Company. In a study concerning consumers' magazine-reading habits, the marketing research director decided to survey a sample of consumers using the fictitious company name Media Research Institute. This successfully camouflaged the identity of X Company as the sponsor of the study.

5. Distortions by Marketing Vice President. In the trial run of a major presentation to the board of directors, the marketing vice president deliberately distorted some recent research findings. After some thought, the marketing research director decided to ignore the matter since the vice president obviously knew what he was doing.

6. Advertising and Product Misuse. A recent study showed that several customers of X Company were misusing Product B. Although this posed no danger, customers were wasting their money by using too much of the product at a time. But yesterday, the marketing research director saw final sketches of Product B's new advertising campaign, which actually seemed to encourage misuse. The marketing research director quietly referred the advertising manager to the research results, well-known to all the people involved with product B's advertising, but did nothing beyond that.

Sources: Merle C. Crawford, "Attitudes of Marketing Executives Toward Ethics in Marketing Research," *Journal of Marketing*, 34 (April 1970), 46–52; Ishmael P. Akaah and Edward A. Riordan, "Judgments of Marketing Professionals About Ethical Issues in Marketing Research: A Replication and Extension," *Journal of Marketing Research*, 26 (February 1989), 112–120; Ishmael P. Akaah, "Attitudes of Marketing Professionals Toward Ethics in Marketing Research: A Cross-National Comparison," *Journal of Business Ethics*, 9, 1 (January 1990), 45–53.

Companies in general, and research firms in particular, should consider the benefits of a human resource review committee for favorably balancing ethical dilemmas. Given recent corporate scandals, perhaps the role should be expanded beyond research participants to considering the ethical consequences of business decisions on customers and employees. The Business Research Dashboard poses several ethics scenarios for business researchers.

ETHICAL OBLIGATIONS OF THE CLIENT

Ethics typically is not a one-way street. We have investigated the issues faced by the researcher, but the client has ethical obligations as well. The client faces several important ethical obligations that, if breached, diminish the quality and usefulness of the entire decision-making process.

BEFORE THE RESEARCH

The decision maker should participate fully and openly with the researcher. It is absolutely essential that the decision maker and researcher come to a consensus on the research objectives. Generally, when both parties agree on the research questions involved, consensus is reached. Consensus on research questions becomes a key part of the research proposal, as do the research objectives. If consensus cannot be reached, the research proposal should not be approved. Furthermore, if a researcher is denied access to some piece of information that is crucial in performing the research, the researcher's obligation is reduced.

The client ultimately sets the time frame and budget for the project. But researchers generally make initial requests for time and money, and the two sets of demands meet somewhere in the middle. However, the researcher should communicate and the client should accept the fact that limitations may reduce the quality of the research project correspondingly.

Additionally, the client has an obligation to develop an understanding of the researcher and the research project. This understanding doesn't require that the client become a researcher, but it does mean a client should know enough about research to ask intelligent questions. If not, the client should include someone else in the discussion who understands the nature of research projects.

DURING AND AFTER THE RESEARCH

The client has an obligation to give genuine consideration to the research results. That is, the research should not be commissioned simply to be able to show that it was done. If the client has already made up their mind on the key issue prior to the research project, they should not request that the project be done. The researcher is placed in an awkward position when the results conflict with the client's desires. It is also a waste of the researcher's time and the company's money.

There is an issue that is especially of interest to anyone thinking of becoming a researcher. The client has an obligation to pay the researcher in full and on time. If

Exhibit 3.2 **Ethical Dimensions of the Business Researcher–Decision Maker Relationship**

RESEARCHER	DECISION MAKER
❑ Maintain scientific rigor ❑ Confidentiality (avoid involvement in research with a competitor) ❑ Search for truth (do not try to confirm desires) ❑ Arrive at a consensus "reason" for the research ❑ Admit research limitations including those resulting from budget and time constraints ❑ Present results understandably	❑ Educate oneself (be able to understand researcher) ❑ Establish budget ❑ Give due consideration to the results of the research ❑ Arrive at a consensus "reason" for the research ❑ Have realistic expectations ❑ Pay on time

the researcher successfully completes the project described in the research proposal, they should be paid regardless of the results. For instance, a real estate developer once requested a study of the traffic patterns and market potential for several different possible residential development sites. The developer agreed on a proposal with a researcher, who conducted the study and presented the results. However, the results did not indicate that any of the potential sites had the value the developer had been envisioning. The developer became upset and finally paid the researcher only half the agreed-upon fee and only after some months had passed. Likewise, an in-house researcher should not face negative repercussions if the results of a project are well thought out but undesirable. Exhibit 3.2 summarizes some of the ethical dimensions of business research.

ETHICAL OBLIGATIONS OF RESEARCH PARTICIPANTS

Participants in research also have obligations. Although it is difficult to control participation, the researcher should be aware of issues of voluntary and faithful participation as well as the need for participants to respond honestly and respect research privacy when asked to do so prior to their participation.

VOLUNTARY PARTICIPATION

Researcher participants should decline the opportunity to participate if they have any doubt about whether they possess sufficient motivation to go through with the study. Most studies do not require a great deal of effort. After agreeing to participate, a respondent should cooperate fully. This also means that participants should answer any screening questions honestly. Screening questions are preliminary questions that qualify participants as valid sample members. For example, a researcher studying aspects of retail employment may wish to develop a sample of people with recent retail experience. A participant may be tempted to falsely claim that they qualify for the research if there is a desirable incentive for participating. Such action will lead to inaccurate results since the participant lacks the necessary qualifications.

FAITHFUL PARTICIPATION

Participants should follow the research instructions to the best of their ability. On occasion, a participant may grow weary and begin responding without being fully attentive. The researcher is better off with no response than with an inaccurate response.

The participant should pay attention and follow instructions. These instructions may contain important information pertaining to the appropriate sequence of items or the perspective that the respondent should take. Sometimes the sequence is contingent upon a previous response. Also, the researcher may ask the respondent to respond with something other than his or her own view. For example, in an ethics research project, a researcher may ask a sales manager participating in research how a typical salesperson would respond in a give ethical dilemma. Again, the failure to follow instructions could create error.

HONESTY

It goes without saying that a participant should be honest. On occasion, however, a respondent may have an ulterior motive. A participant may try to respond in a fashion that will benefit him personally. For instance, an employer might commission an opinion survey asking unit managers whether small units should be closed. A manager might be torn between giving an honest response about the viability of such units and a response that will help ensure his or her job is not threatened. Potential participants should refuse to take part in research if they are hesitant to answer questions honestly.

PRIVACY

Researchers may sometimes request that a participant not discuss details of procedures with anyone else for a specified time. There could be many reasons for such a request. The researcher may have legitimate concerns about corporate espionage. If savvy competitors know what a company is studying, they may be able to make an educated guess about its strategy or tactics. In an ongoing study, a researcher may want to avoid an earlier subject's contaminating findings from later subjects. Instructions or debriefing often include a statement requesting those who have completed the task not inform others about the details of the study.

IMPLICATIONS OF UNETHICAL ACTIONS

It is easy for students of business to be lulled into a false sense of security, believing that the ethical implications of business decisions are less serious than those associated with other disciplines, such as medicine or engineering. However, this view is misguided. Businesses provide value. They provide value to customers, shareholders, employees, and to society at large. A breach of responsibility by one party can seriously affect the value equation in a way that harms others.

A breakdown in responsibility during the research process means that business decisions will be based on untrustworthy information. For example, a company CEO who commissions research investigating the advantages and disadvantages of two acquisitions-related strategies, "A" and "B," might request research simply to appease the board of directors. That is, the CEO may already have chosen strategy "A." However, the research may strongly suggest that strategy "B" is the better business decision. Now the CEO must accept the research and abandon his preferred alternative or ignore the research. Worse yet, the CEO could ask the researcher to present results in a way that makes strategy "A," his preferred alternative, seem most attractive. By adopting the strategy "A" nonetheless, the CEO increases the likelihood that critical decisions will not lead to the best outcome.

Such an action could be bad for customers, employees, shareholders, and society more broadly. The implications for customers might mean they buy a less-desirable product. This could have dire consequences in the case of potentially hazardous products. Employees may end up working in conditions that are not as good as they might have been had the research recommendation been followed. For shareholders, a lower long-term return might result. So, customers may suffer health- and safety-related harm; shareholders may have their portfolios become stagnant or decline; and employees may face long periods without pay raises or even lose their jobs.

The impacts on each or all of these stakeholders may also have a negative ripple effect on society. Business decision makers should be ever mindful that the lives of families of employees, customers, shareholders, and communities are affected significantly by the quality of their decisions. Likewise, since researchers provide input into these decisions, they share in this responsibility. Thus, ethics should be taken very seriously. Unethical decisions usually cause harm to at least one of the parties involved in a business exchange. The Business Research Dashboard features the European Society for Opinion and Marketing Research (ESOMAR), a global organization with 5,000 members in over 100 countries. ESOMAR seeks to establish a global standard for ethics in opinion research.

Ethics in decision making does not mean a CEO should always follow the research recommendations. However, it does mean that the researcher should only undertake research that will be considered in the decision-making process. Other issues may enter evaluation of the research results, including, for example, experience and intuition.

Researchers should also be mindful of protecting their own integrity, the reputation of their company, and the image of their profession. Recent public perceptions of questionable behavior committed by auditors overseeing the financial reporting of Enron have seriously damaged the reputation of individual auditors, their employer, Arthur Andersen, and the accounting industry overall.[8] Similarly, accusations were made against Price Waterhouse auditors when the Bank of Credit and Commerce International collapsed, and against Deloitte and Touche following the Barings bankruptcy. Thus, the unethical actions of a small number of researchers can severely damage the overall industry.

■————**Business Research Dashboard**————■
Establishing Global Research Standards

Successful business research depends on public confidence that it is carried out honestly and objectively, and that it respects the impact it may have on respondents. This confidence is best achieved by the adherence of researchers to appropriate professional codes of practice. The European Society for Opinion and Marketing Research (ESOMAR), a global organization with 5,000 members in over 100 countries, has the mission of "enabling better research into markets, consumers, and societies." "ESOMAR developed the first Code of Marketing and Social Research in 1948. In 1976, the International Chamber of Commerce and ESOMAR decided that a single international code should be developed, and they combined forces to publish, for the first time, in 1977, a single international code of practice. Significant revisions have followed in response to the changing nature of business research methods and to the significant increase in the international activities of many practitioners. The code addresses in its fourteen articles research issues that relate to the general public as well as to the business community, and it stresses the need for professionals to follow both the letter and spirit of the document.

Eight key fundamentals are laid out in the document:

1. Researchers shall conform to all relevant national and international laws.
2. Researchers shall behave ethically and shall not do anything which might damage the reputation of the research profession.
3. Researchers shall take special care when carrying out research among children and young people.
4. Respondents' cooperation is voluntary and must be based on adequate, and not misleading, information about the general purpose and nature of the project when their agreement to participate is being obtained, and all such statements shall be honored.
5. The rights of respondents as private individuals shall be respected by researchers and they shall not be harmed or adversely affected as the direct result of cooperating in a research project.
6. Researchers shall never allow personal data collected in a research project to be used for any other purpose.
7. Researchers shall ensure that projects and activities are designed, carried out, reported and documented accurately, transparently, and objectively.
8. Researchers shall conform to the accepted principles of market competition.

Log on to ESOMAR's Web site, at http://www.esomar.org, and read all fourteen articles of the ICC/ESOMAR code. Are the provisions of this document sufficient to meet today's needs for business researchers?

Source: ICC/ESOMAR (2008), "International Code of Marketing and Social Research Practice," http://www.esomar.org, accessed December 16, 2009.

One simple guide for business researchers and researchers generally is to always act as though your actions will be public. This guideline is based on the assumption that your superiors, family, and friends will all know what you have done. This emphasizes the role played by one's conscience in shaping ethical behavior.

An **ethics checklist** can also be useful in guiding decision making. The following questions are useful for ensuring an ethical decision-making climate.

- Will the actions taken harm the institution?
- Will the actions taken harm individuals, including coworkers, clients, research participants, or customers?
- Will the information involved be misused by others?
- Will the actions taken harm my profession, company, or industry?
- Will the actions taken do harm to the personal integrity of researchers and decision makers?
- Will the actions taken harm society at large?

ACCESS TO RESPONDENTS: STRATEGIES AND TACTICS

The purpose of collecting data is to answer research questions. Therefore the key to successful business research is obtaining relevant data to address the questions. Without data business researchers cannot develop solutions.

Access to data sources is critical whether one is conducting secondary or primary research, or both. When the research design is being selected, attention must be given to strategies and tactics for gaining access to respondents so the data can actually be collected from the data sources that have been identified. By following appropriate strategies and tactics, valid, reliable data can be obtained for addressing the research questions. Finally, the issue of research ethics, as discussed earlier, cannot be overlooked.

ISSUES IN OBTAINING ACCESS

Business research is dependent on the cooperation of individuals and the willingness of the organization to participate in providing data pertinent to the research. Thus, it is incumbent on the researcher to ensure that the research design for data collection minimizes obstacles that may hinder access.

A strategy for access should be both pragmatic and systematic. Considerations for achieving this requirement are listed below:

1. The nature of the research question and adopted research paradigm
2. The source(s) from which data is required
3. Gaining access to the source(s)
4. A plan for collecting data

The impact of the research question and research paradigm on obtaining access to respondents is illustrated by the two examples in Exhibit 3.3. The following illustrates how some of the issues can be resolved in developing a strategy for access to respondents in example 1 of Exhibit 3.3.

• If the study requires the views of the CEO or managing director, as in this situation, careful consideration of how to gain access to such individuals is vital. Intermediaries may or may not be able to facilitate an introduction. Therefore, identifying gatekeepers may be a critical component of your access strategy. Developing a relationship with the gatekeeper can be helpful in obtaining that person's support to encourage and

Exhibit 3.3

Issues Associated with Obtaining Access to Respondents

Example 1. The research question was concerned with strategic orientation, executive values, and organizational performance. The objective was to obtain cooperation of knowledgeable individuals who were managers and executives of large organizations.

Issues to be considered:

- Is the research concerned with a single organization or a cross-section of organizations?
- Is the research in a single industrial sector or across sectors?
- What data is already available and what needs to be collected?
- Will the views of the CEO suffice, or is input needed from other executives?
- Will the data be collected through face-to-face interviews, computer-assisted interviews, telephone, mail, or Internet questionnaires?
- Timing of data collection may be very important.
- Number of participants required, length of time to complete the interview, and number of times participants must be interviewed can all impact access.

Example 2. The research question was concerned with business-to-business relationships and the relational norms or supportive norms that help with the trading exchange. Responses were needed from both trading partners, for example, from both the supplier and the buyer.

Issues to be considered:

- Identifying the bilateral relationship—franchisor and franchisee, OEM and manufacturers, banks and corporate client, brewers/distillers/wineries and businesses selling alcoholic beverages, etc.
- Identifying key respondents from both trading partners
- Obtaining views of both sides of a business relationship

remind the respondent to cooperate. But if this is not possible, then consider shipping the questionnaire via overnight delivery. When this is done the gatekeeper will place it on the respondent's desk in a prominent location, and the respondent will believe it is truly important to respond.

• Sometimes researchers find it difficult to contact organizations directly. On such occasions the researchers may use intermediaries such as trade associations, the Institute of Directors, management research companies, management consultants, or university research centers.

The following illustrates how some of the issues can be resolved in developing a strategy for access to respondents in example 2 of Exhibit 3.3.

• Access to both sides of the bilateral exchange may be achieved by first identifying the principal trading partner. This individual can in turn identify and provide an introduction to the main account holders in the bilateral exchange. Ethical consideration becomes paramount here. For example, confidentiality surrounding any information provided rests with the researcher.

• Timing considerations may be important. In the case of the exchange related to the seller of alcoholic beverages, access to the owner/manager is difficult during business hours. Thus, if a face-to-face or telephone survey is used to gather the data, the best time to do a survey is outside those hours. In both cases, however, this could be inconvenient for either the respondent or the researcher.

An effective plan for access to data collection may not materialize because of unforeseen circumstances. Therefore, contingency strategies should be considered in the initial planning stage.

BARRIERS TO ACCESS

There are some obstacles to accessing key sources for data, including:

- Little or no opportunity of direct access to key informants
- Lack of interest in the research questions
- The sensitive nature of the research questions
- Lack of credibility and perceived value of the research
- Minimal confidence in the researcher's ability to articulate the purpose and sponsorship of the research
- The overall impression formed of the researcher, including physical appearance, trustworthiness, and intrusiveness

These obstacles need to be considered in any operational approach for gaining entry to an individual or organization. A key consideration in developing the plan is to factor in ample time. The amount of time required is dependent on the level of access required. It is likely there will be several interactions before the relevant informant has been identified and the individual or organization has agreed to participate by providing data. Gaining access may therefore take two to three months, so start this process early.

The operational plan must incorporate tactics to assist in gaining access. Tactics for gaining access are dependent on the approach taken, which can be direct or indirect. The approach used will have a significant impact on the willingness of individuals or organizations to participate.

A direct approach could be mailing a questionnaire accompanied by a cover letter, or a direct telephone call or e-mail. An indirect approach involves the use of intermediaries to arrange an introduction, or even to help with the data collection.

To encourage access and participation some or all the points set out below can be included in a letter or presentation to potential participants:

- Purpose of the research
- Nature of the desired access
- Usefulness of the findings
- Manner in which sensitivity and confidentiality will be dealt with
- Credentials and affiliation of the researcher
- Benefits to the individual or organization, which could be in the form of a report of the results or even assistance with an in-house project or some other inducement

Throughout the process of attempting to gain access a researcher needs to adhere to the highest ethical standards. This extends to delivering on the promises made, particularly with regard to privacy.

Different methods of data collection involve different approaches to contacting potential respondents. If the method of data collection is a self-completion mail questionnaire, overnight or similar delivery and a clear, detailed cover letter are important. Exhibit 3.4 provides an example of a cover letter. For telephone or Internet studies, and some types of personal interviews, a cover letter can be mailed to potential respondents before the questionnaire is sent.

Exhibit 3.4

Sample Cover Letter to Gain Participant Cooperation

Henley Management College
Henley-on-Thames, Oxfordshire, U.K.

May 1, 2010

Name
Address of Individual
City,Country, etc.

Hello,

You are one of a select group of people who, within the past two years, purchased a Weber outdoor barbecue.

My name is Dr. Arthur Money, and I am a Business Professor at Henley Management College, U.K. I have been retained by Floyds Group, Ltd. to collect information that will help you and other customers be served better.

I am writing to ask for your help with this study. Please know that:

- We are not trying to sell you anything. We just want your opinions.
- Your answers will be reported in combination with others and will not be associated with your name, address, or other personal identifying information.
- We do not sell personal information or opinions to third parties.

The survey is easy to complete and will take about 15 minutes of your time. Please have the person who was most involved with the purchase of your new Weber outdoor barbecue complete the survey and return it in the postage paid envelope.

As a token of our appreciation, when we receive your completed questionnaire we will notify your local dealer to credit your account $50.00 toward your next purchase of barbecue accessory products.

In addition, to solicit early participation, each response postmarked by December 15 will be entered into a drawing whereby two (2) customers will be awarded a $1,000 coupon toward your next purchase of outdoor barbecue and furniture products.

We appreciate the invaluable role you are playing in this study and thank you for your time and input. If you have any questions, please call me at +44 (0) 1491 418989.

Sincerely,

Arthur Money, Ph.D.

It is impossible to develop a standardized cover letter that will be effective in all survey situations. There are, however, guidelines that provide direction for communicating with potential respondents, whether through a cover letter, a telephone contact, a personal interview, or a request for cooperation in an Internet-based survey. Exhibit 3.5 lists the factors and a general description of how to use them to obtain higher respondent cooperation.

Exhibit 3.5

Guidelines for Obtaining Respondent Cooperation

Factors	Description
Personalization	Email or written contacts with respondents should be addressed to the specific respondent and be on either the research firm's stationery or that of a well-known and respected organization. Personally signed communications from the individual conducting the research also are helpful.
Identify the organization doing the study	Identify the name of the research firm or university conducting the study. The actual sponsor of the study may be disguised or revealed, depending on its potential impact on the study's findings.
Establish credibility	Different appeals work with different audiences. If the researcher is a professor with a prestigious university this can be a positive attribute and showing their name and title in the communication can be helpful. A well-known organization affiliated with the study can also help.
Clearly identify study's importance and purpose	Describe the general nature of the research and emphasize its importance to the respondent. Explain how the respondent was chosen and stress the importance of their input in the study's success.
Anonymity and confidentiality	Provide assurance that the respondent's name or identifying information will not be revealed or shared with any other groups.
Time frame for completing the study	Indicate how long the study will last and when the questionnaire is due. Do not say "Can we have a few moments of your time to . . ." as it is easy to say "No" to such a request.
Reinforce importance of respondent's participation	Where appropriate, communicate the importance of the respondent's participation in the study. Clearly explain and emphasize who is to complete the questionnaire and why.
Time requirements and compensation	Tell respondent the approximate time required to complete the questionnaire and point out incentives.
Completion date and where and how to return the questionnaire or get answers to questions	Provide clear and complete instructions for returning the completed questionnaire, and say whom to contact if questions arise.
Advance thank you for willingness to participate	Thank the respondent for his or her cooperation.

Source: Adapted from J.F. Hair Jr., R. Bush, and D. Ortinau, *Marketing Research*, 4th ed. (New York: McGraw-Hill, 2010).

Continuing Case: Samouel's Greek Cuisine

Phil Samouel is a successful manager and businessman, but he is fairly new to the restaurant business. He and his brother have decided the best way to improve their business is to hire a restaurant consultant. Through a business associate, Phil identified a research firm called AdMark International. He contacted it and asked that it conduct a preliminary assessment of his restaurant operations and prepare a research proposal. The proposal is expected to include proposed projects, deliverables such as objectives and action plans, as well as a schedule and budget.

After discussions with Phil, his brother, and several of his employees, the account manager from the research firm recommended two separate but related research projects. The objective of the first project would be to evaluate current employees to determine their productivity, job satisfaction, and commitment to the restaurant. Possible topics of interest include compensation, supervision, coworkers, loyalty, understanding of job responsibilities, and likelihood of searching for another job in the next year. The second project would involve collecting information from customers of Samouel's restaurant and his major competitor, Gino's Italian Ristorante. Possible topics of investigation include prices, food quality, service, and overall satisfaction.

1. Are there any ethical considerations that need to be explored with the employee survey?
2. What about the customer survey?
3. If yes, what are the considerations and how should they be dealt with?
4. Should Phil develop a code of ethics for his restaurant? What about an ethics checklist?

SUMMARY

DEFINE BUSINESS ETHICS AND DISCUSS ITS RELEVANCE TO RESEARCH

Business ethics is defined as the application of ethical standards to human actions in the exchange process. The ethical dimensions of the researcher–decision maker and researcher-participant relationships have been discussed. All actors have important duties before, during, and after the research. Above all, researchers and decision makers should behave as professionals. Being professional means working with the knowledge that your actions affect other people's lives. Therefore, research should be done with great care and with as much precision as the time and budget allow. Above all, effective communication is a key to minimizing conflict between researchers and decision makers.

UNDERSTAND THE ETHICAL OBLIGATIONS OF BUSINESS RESEARCHERS

Business researchers have several important ethical obligations. They should strive to communicate effectively and to develop a consensus regarding the research among all the key actors involved. Researchers should also use the right tool for the job, which means avoiding overly complex research tools. Researchers should decline a job for which they lack expertise. They should also take great care to treat research participants fairly. Human resource committees can provide useful reviews ensuring the research is carried out in an ethical way. Researchers should strive to communicate simply and clearly. Reports and presentations should be prepared with the level of sophistication of the audience in mind. Finally, researchers should clearly communicate all research limitations.

UNDERSTAND THE ETHICAL OBLIGATIONS OF BUSINESS DECISION MAKERS

Decision makers also have important ethical obligations, which involve the treatment of researchers, other employees, consumers, and the public in general. Decision makers should also work to establish a consensus in connection with the proposed research. They should not order research without the intention of seriously considering it when making decisions. Decision makers should not hold the researcher responsible in any way for results that may be considered undesirable.

UNDERSTAND THE ETHICAL OBLIGATIONS OF BUSINESS RESEARCH PARTICIPANTS

Research participants can also negatively influence business decision making. Unethical participant actions can lead to response error, which in turn leads to poor decision making. Research participants should participate willingly or decline participation. This means they should follow the research instructions faithfully and give the task the level of needed involvement. Participants should provide honest responses and not respond in a manner meant to bias the results and thereby affect any eventual decisions. Also, participants should respect the confidentiality of the research project if requested to do so by the researcher.

DESCRIBE THE POTENTIAL CONSEQUENCES OF UNETHICAL ACTIONS

Finally, researchers and decision makers should be mindful of the direct and indirect effects of unethical actions. The quality of decision making is affected by the integrity of the research. If decisions are made that serve to do something other than accomplish socially legitimate business goals, someone is likely to be harmed. Those potentially harmed include employees, consumers, society, the institution, and the discipline or industry.

APPRECIATE THE CHALLENGES OF GAINING ACCESS TO RESPONDENTS

Access to data sources is critical whether one is conducting secondary or primary research. When the research design is selected, attention must be given to strategies and tactics for gaining access to respondents so the data can actually be collected from the identified data sources. Business research is dependent on the cooperation of individuals and the willingness of the organization to participate in providing data pertinent to the research. Thus, it is incumbent on the researcher to ensure that the research design for data collection minimizes obstacles that may hinder access. The strategy for access should be both pragmatic and systematic. Considerations for achieving this include the nature of the research questions and adopted research paradigm, the source(s) from which data is required, gaining access to the source(s), and having a plan for collecting the data.

ETHICAL DILEMMA

Mr. Ralf Sanders owns a data-imaging firm with over 100 employees in the main office. Ralf commissions a study of the organizational culture in his company. The researcher suggests that employees may not respond accurately to a structured questionnaire because of the sensitivity of some of the topics. Instead, he suggests recording the conversations of employees in the company lunchroom using hidden microphones. The resulting conversations could be analyzed using content-analysis software. This would reveal key themes around which organizational culture may be structured. Should Mr. Sanders agree to this approach for collecting information? Why or why not? If not, what changes can be made to the proposed research design to make it more ethically acceptable?

REVIEW QUESTIONS

1. Define business ethics.
2. What takes the place of trust in the exchange process?
3. What is an ethical dilemma? List at least three ways one can occur in the business decision-making process.
4. What are four important considerations that should be given to research participants?
5. What is a human resource review committee? What benefits does it provide?
6. What does it mean for a decision maker to give "due consideration" to business research results?

DISCUSSION AND APPLICATION ACTIVITIES

1. Several recent studies raise questions about student integrity, as described previously in this chapter in the text piece entitled "Are the 'Brightest and the Best' the Most Ethical?" Do you believe there is a relationship between the ethical behavior exhibited by a university student and the ethical behavior he or she will exhibit in the business world? Prepare a one-page position statement that either agrees or disagrees with the statement that "unethical university students will make unethical businesspeople."
2. How might the balancing act depicted in Exhibit 3.1 help ensure that human resources are not treated unfairly even if there are a few employees of questionable moral character involved in decision making?

3. Find information on a current event that questions the ethics of a particular business. Did or could researchers have had a role in preventing this event?

4. What steps do you believe business researchers should take to ensure that research participants fulfill their ethical obligations in the research process?

INTERNET EXERCISES

1. Go to http://ec.europa.eu/eracareers/pdf/am509774CEE_EN_E4.pdf, or Google "European Charter for Researchers." This Web site presents the European Commission perspective on research, including a European Charter for Researchers and perspectives on ethics in research. What elements of the European Commission's perspectives on ethics in research do you consider most relevant to business research?

2. Go to http://www.qrca.org/displaycommon.cfm?an=1&subarticlenbr=26, or search www.qrca.org for their "Code of Ethics." Comment on codes of ethics and practices of the Qualitative Research Consultants Association. How closely do you feel the perspectives presented for this association conform to the ideas presented in this chapter? What other points, if any, does the association emphasize that you believe add value to your understanding of ethics in business research? In which of the aspects it presents do you feel training can be employed to improve the quality of decision making? Which areas do you feel are harder to develop through training interventions and must be controlled by legal means?

NOTES

1. O.C. Ferrell and John Fraedrich, *Business Ethics* (Boston, MA: Houghton Mifflin, 1997).

2. A.B. Blankenship, "Some Aspects of Ethics in Marketing Research," *Journal of Marketing Research*, 1 (May 1964), 26–31.

3. Donald P. Robin, Eric R. Reidenbach, and Barry J. Babin, "Ethical Judgments," *Psychological Review*, 76 (1976).

4. Robert M. McNath, "Smokeless Isn't Smoking," *American Demographics*, 18 (October 2002), 60.

5. B. Saporito, "The Tough Cookie at RJR Nabisco," *Fortune*, 118, 2 (1988), 32–41.

6. Kathinka Evers, *Codes of Conduct: Standards for Ethics in Research* (Luxembourg: Office for Official Publications of the European Communities, 2004).

7. Sharon Begley, Donna Foote, and Adam Rogers, "Dying for Science," *Newsweek*, 138 (July 30, 2001), 36.

8. Ken Brown and Jonathan Weil, "When Enron Auditors Were on a Tear," *Wall Street Journal*, 239 (March 21, 2002), C1.

Part II

Beginning the Research Process

4 Defining the Research Problem and Reviewing the Literature

LEARNING OUTCOMES

1. Identify the characteristics of a quality research topic
2. Describe how to convert research ideas into research questions
3. Understand what a literature review is and how it helps your research
4. Identify the major sources for a literature search
5. Explain how to plan and write a literature review
6. Confirm research questions with the literature review

To a significant extent, success in any research project begins with a clear definition of the research problem. While this may seem self-evident, defining the research problem is often the most difficult part of the research process to execute properly. Researchers should avoid being too rigid at this early stage. A poorly defined problem results in lack of direction and purpose that may become apparent only after considerable time, effort, and money have been spent pursuing nonproductive avenues. For example, a poorly defined research problem is likely to result in an incorrectly structured field study that does not deliver the required data.

Once research problems are initially identified, researchers undertake background research to further refine the definition of the problem and to ensure that past work has been considered in clarifying the scope of the proposed research project. The background research, often referred to as a literature review, provides the basis for converting research problems into research questions and objectives. In this chapter we first discuss selecting good research problems. Then we cover converting research problems into questions and objectives. Next we explain how to plan and conduct background research and synthesize it into a literature review, and we end with an overview of how to write a literature review.

CHARACTERISTICS OF A QUALITY RESEARCH TOPIC

When undertaking commissioned research, the research brief often represents the primary means by which the sponsor communicates an initial perception of the research problems or questions. The **research brief** is an overview of the sponsor's (company or individual) initial perceptions of the problem or opportunity and may be written or presented orally. The proposal prepared in response by the researcher provides a diagnosis and understanding of the problem previously summarized by the sponsor. Dialogue between the two parties (researcher and sponsor) prior to finally signing off on the research is vital in ensuring that a common understanding exists. Focusing this dialogue on the problem definition before selecting the methodology is the best way of achieving the clarity of purpose necessary for a successful outcome.

Whether or not the research is commissioned by a third party, defining the research problem can be quite time-consuming and needs to be specified in both general and specific terms. What is the broad nature of the problem that needs to be addressed by the research activities? What are the specific components of the problem that need to be examined? Experienced researchers iterate through these questions many times to achieve the clarity of purpose considered necessary for success. They recognize that time devoted to problem definition prevents misunderstanding and avoids errors. It also produces better research questions and objectives, an improved research design, and ultimately a better execution.

Research topics are identified and examined by businesses to better understand problems or opportunities and to develop the best solutions. Research topics are also identified and pursued in upper-level academic programs. Whether developed for academic or business purposes, good research topics exhibit numerous common characteristics. They are presented in Exhibit 4.1 and discussed in depth below.

First among these guidelines is that the topic should be developed from and supported by a sound theoretical base. Topics that are informed by theory have a clearer overall purpose, method, and expected outcome. This ensures that well-informed and rigorous decisions flow from the research. Theory places the research topic in the context of a broader field of business and enables both the sponsor and the researcher to leverage prior work in the field, enhance the quality of the research project, and limit the resources needed to achieve the research objectives.

Theoretical underpinnings of research projects are particularly important when the research is undertaken as part of an academic thesis or dissertation. Not only is examining the literature a necessary step in ensuring that the topic meets the requirements of the examiners, but it also helps confirm your interest in the broader field of study. Although a lot has been written about the importance of selecting a research topic that can sustain your interest for the entire duration of the project, an underlying objective of your thesis (or dissertation) must be to help confirm your career choice and improve your employability in the field you have selected. Your thesis is an important part of this process.

The second characteristic relates to the importance of the topic to the research sponsor. Greater commitment by the sponsor increases his or her engagement and reduces the potential for conflict as the process continues. This is obviously important when

Exhibit 4.1

Characteristics of a Quality Research Topic

- The research is developed from and supported by a sound theoretical base.
- The research is of interest to both the sponsor and the researcher.
- The research problem is well defined and the research questions and objectives that flow from it are specific and possible to address through a rigorous research design.
- Resource requirements in terms of time, money, and data access are well understood early in the research process.
- The research is expected to make a contribution to knowledge independently of the orientation of the findings. This characteristic is particularly important for academic theses and dissertations.

---

carrying out research for commercial purposes. The sponsor plays a role not only in specifying the objectives of the research and approving its scope but also in ensuring the inevitable unknowns that arise during the research process will be discussed in an honest and open fashion. This increases the likelihood the researcher will be able to make decisions deemed necessary in a mutually supportive environment.

While academic research topics may not have an obvious external sponsor, the research supervisor can be viewed in this role. The supervisor guides the research and provides support when problems arise. This person also understands the requirements for success with regard to the theoretical background, the primary data-collection requirements, and the depth of analysis required. For instance, some degrees may require that the thesis investigate an actual business problem and gather new primary data, while others find a less-applied approach acceptable with little or no primary data collection required. The greater the supervisor's interest in the topic, the more likely will be a commitment to the process and a generous allotment of time and energy. No matter how passionate you may feel about a thesis topic, success is significantly enhanced if your supervisor shares this passion.

The third element of the research topic relates to how the problem is defined, the quality of the research questions, and the way the objectives of the research have been articulated. Defining the problem requires the sponsor to focus on the business decisions that will be based on the research once it is completed. This ensures the research design addresses gaps in the knowledge necessary to make these decisions and, as such, helps in developing questions and setting objectives. **Quality research topics** are those that address gaps in existing knowledge and are likely to result in more informed management decision making. Consequently, well-stated research questions focus on the organization or personal objectives of the research sponsor.

Once questions have been established and full agreement exists between the sponsor and the researcher, the questions need to be converted into explicit research objectives. Ultimately, the research design flows from the specific research objectives, and, not surprisingly, quality research projects that deliver on their promise have explicit, focused, and well-articulated objectives.

Establishing objectives represents a significant challenge for researchers undertaking research on behalf of others. It is not unusual for research sponsors to find it difficult to set clear objectives for the research. Sponsors with limited research experience tend to state their desires in general terms, and so it is up to the researchers to convert those desires into objectives that are of operational importance and that make the scope of the research more explicit.

The fourth characteristic of research topics concerns the resource requirements for achieving the desired outcome. These resources include knowledge, time, money, and access to needed data. No matter how worthy of research the initial problem is, little will be achieved if the researcher lacks the ability to investigate the topic properly. Researchers who are skilled in quantitative research using closed-ended and well-structured questionnaires often do not have the skills or temperament to undertake qualitative research based on **focus groups** and in-depth interviews. Before accepting a research assignment, researchers need to honestly examine their skill sets and their capacity to develop the knowledge and approaches necessary for it.

While the importance of assessing skill sets may be apparent for commercial research, it is no less important that students undertaking research projects reflect carefully on their own capacities when selecting their topics. The time and financial resources necessary to complete research projects vary widely. Some topics may lend themselves to a much higher proportion of desk research, while others might require extensive travel to interview key stakeholders. A rigorous assessment of the time and finances required to complete a research project should be made as early as possible in the research process. For commissioned research this is necessitated by the need to quote a research budget. But students also must reflect on these points to reduce the possibility they cannot meet deadlines set by the university or college. It may be necessary to adjust the scope of a project in order to meet financial and time constraints.

Data accessibility also should never be taken for granted. Early in the research process researchers need to confirm they can gain access to the required data, since promises and assumptions made about secondary data availability may not be justified. As an example, accounting data for microbusinesses generally is far more difficult to access than may seem apparent from the taxation obligations these organizations have in common with their larger counterparts. If researchers are collecting primary data from respondents, they should have reason to believe that they can gain access to and cooperation from the targeted population.

Finally, an important characteristic of a research topic particularly relevant for academic purposes is that it should produce a valuable outcome independent of the orientation of the findings. In other words, research projects undertaken as part of the requirements for a degree or qualification should be worthwhile, whether or not the research hypotheses are confirmed. This requirement greatly reduces the probability that months of effort will be discarded because the outcome of the research does not make the necessary scholarly contribution to knowledge. It is important that students anticipate possible outcomes and the research value under various scenarios before spending too much effort pursuing the research topic. The Business Research Dashboard poses the question of whether a problem is a quality research topic and can provide useful findings.

■————Business Research Dashboard————■
What Kind of Research Is Necessary?

One Stop is a convenience store business that employs over 6,000 staff in over 500 neighborhood shops throughout England and Wales. Until recently, the retailer outsourced its financial management system for the management of general operations and financial accounting, backups, recoveries, disaster recovery, hardware maintenance of the computer operating system and its Oracle database. With the contract up for renewal, One Stop decided to look at alternative solutions for its financial management system and the possibility of bringing its financial business processes in-house.

Do you consider this a quality research topic? Could research be useful in making a decision between outsourcing financial management functions and bringing them in-house?

Sources: http://www.hoovers.com/t&s-stores/—ID_90419—/free-co-factsheet.xhtml?cm_ven=PAID&cm_cat=INK&cm_pla=CO1&cm_ite=t&s-stores; http://www.manta.com/comsite5/bin/pddnb_company.pl?pdlanding=1&referid=3810&id=1y2myk&pub_code=0194IBIR&item_id=0194-IBIR; Yahoo! Finance, "One Stop Stores Limited Company Profile," http://biz.yahoo.com/ic/90/90419.html; One Stop, "Who Are We?" http://www.onestop.co.uk/about/aboutus.asp; Wikipedia, "Tesco," http://en.wikipedia.org/wiki/Tesco, accessed November 2009.

CONVERTING RESEARCH IDEAS INTO RESEARCH QUESTIONS AND OBJECTIVES

Research ideas may be generated by the researcher or provided by the sponsor in the form of a business problem around which an informed decision needs to be made. When the researcher rather than the sponsor is expected to come up with the idea, a variety of approaches can be adopted to generate the initial idea and refine it into a research problem worthy of investigation. When the idea is provided by somebody else, such as the sponsor in commissioned research projects, the researcher still must refine the idea by transforming it into explicit questions and objectives.

Research ideas that do not flow immediately from a business problem often may be clarified by questioning senior researchers, executives, and decision makers about problems they face, by examining published research in fields of interest, or by examining past research projects that may suggest areas worthy of subsequent investigation.

Discussions with individuals who are experienced researchers or those who frequently use research to inform their own decision making can produce quality ideas and a path for further research. Experienced researchers are well aware of the fact that most research projects can be an interesting source of new questions. Research conducted to test one or more specific hypotheses can lead researchers to reflect on new hypotheses and questions. Similarly, commissioned research designed to support a specific management decision results in action by the decision maker that can lead to further decision requirements and other research opportunities. Dialogue with experienced researchers and decision makers offers a good opportunity to develop research ideas grounded in prior empirical work.

Published literature is an additional source of research ideas. Textbooks and academic and professional articles are fruitful sources of research ideas. Academic articles are probably the best source of new thinking, and research ideas generated from them are likely to be topical and of value because they will naturally reflect current research interest. Professional articles and research reports may offer less-explicit insight into potential research ideas, but they definitely increase the probability that they will be of practical significance and are considered important by the business community.

Although textbooks may seem an obvious source of ideas for individuals new to research, they should be used with some caution if their publication date is long past. Most textbooks contain research ideas that have already been published elsewhere and are somewhat outdated and thus less-promising as sources of new ideas. Business reports occupy a position between articles and textbooks. Their content is usually considerably fresher than that contained in textbooks, but they generally occupy a position closer to that of applied or professional articles than to academic articles, which are typically more rigorous and theoretical than applied research.

The capacity to extract a vast number of articles at the click of a mouse means the need for focus prior to beginning a literature scan has become increasingly important. Personal motivation and excitement about a particular field of study should inform the initial focus when scanning the literature.

A final external source of research ideas is past empirical research of both a professional and academic nature. The nature of research is that it raises new questions as it answers others. Areas for further research are often explicitly mentioned in the conclusions of academic research papers and, if not explicitly, often implicitly in research commissioned for professional or business purposes.

Once a suitable research idea has been identified, the researcher needs to narrow the topic to produce research questions that can be answered through the application of appropriate research techniques as well as produce clear, succinct objectives. Initial discussions, literature searches, and reviews of past research can help develop great research ideas, but research success requires that these broad ideas be further refined and developed.

Before attempting to refine the idea, the researcher should convince himself or herself that the topic is of personal interest. This is particularly important when the objective of the research is satisfying an academic degree requirement. Feeling passionate about an initial research idea is important but insufficient until the researcher has a better grasp of the likely avenue the research will take as the idea is transformed into a set of specific research questions. Initial research ideas are often far broader than desirable for a research topic. This can be fortunate, because it provides the opportunity to scale back an idea provided by someone else into a topic of specific interest. For example, a prospective employer might suggest that you investigate how to increase organizational commitment and thereby enhance service quality among the organization's frontline staff. Such a topic is unlikely to be feasible for a single piece of research but does contain elements that might have considerable appeal to you and are of sufficient scope to constitute worthwhile research ideas. Some of these elements include (a) the degree of organizational commitment among employees,[1,2] (b) the antecedents of service quality proposed by prior researchers and how they manifest themselves in the company,[3,4] and (c) the levels of service quality and service-quality gaps.[5,6] Each of these elements could form the basis of research ideas for an in-company project and could be considered a necessary first step in addressing the overall topic for the prospective employer.

Exploratory work undertaken while developing the idea should be extended through robust questioning and an examination of the literature. A preliminary study might even be helpful. The study may be restricted to further desk research or it may involve some initial fieldwork. Whatever the approach, the work must be done comprehensively enough to address the areas mentioned in Exhibit 4.1 as important for a quality research topic.

While it can be debated whether research questions precede or follow from research objectives, both are crucial components that help focus the research idea and produce the specificity necessary for the project plan. The dictionary reveals that the word "objective" means both "goal or aim" and, more narrowly, "the lens in a telescope or microscope nearest to the object observed." Both meanings are useful when seeking to convert initial ideas into research questions and objectives. Each objective needs to explicitly state the goal or aim of the research or a particular element of it. Consequently, the researcher needs to reflect closely on the desired outcome when stating these objectives. That is, he or she needs to project forward to the desired endpoint of the research. Stated objectives can also be viewed as the starting point of rigorous research in that they demonstrate the potential legitimacy of the research project in far stronger terms than a statement of the research idea can. Experienced researchers can assess the feasibility of a stated research objective precisely because of its specificity. This is far more difficult to do when presented with a more general statement of an idea.

Research questions can range from the broad (How do corporate incentive systems work?) to the narrow (What is the relationship between executive stock options and corporate performance?) Clearly, the first question does not meet the requirement of specificity. It provides no focus for a research topic examining incentive systems, and it is of no help in developing research objectives or a research agenda to explore the relationship between incentive systems and corporate performance. The second question does meet these demands and is therefore appropriate as a research question.

Developing appropriate research questions is not easy because they need to occupy the space between what is considered too easy and probably not worthy of research in the first place and what is considered too complex for guiding the research design and execution plan. Easy questions are those that require mere descriptive answers; for example, What is the average term of employment of staff? or What are the sick leave statistics for the company? While both questions may be relevant to an investigation of organizational commitment, they are insufficient for the task because their answers provide no insight into how to go about pursuing the investigation nor ultimately into a possible solution to the business problem under investigation. A more appropriate set of research questions would be: To what extent does organizational commitment correlate with incidents of sick leave? and Does length of service influence this relationship in any way?

Developing research questions and objectives can be made easier by continually

---

■————**Business Research Dashboard**————■
Cash, Credit Card, or Debit Card?

Developed countries have used some form of money for more than 3,000 years. But with new technology customers are increasingly migrating to digital money payment systems. Check usage has fallen to its lowest level ever in many countries, and even credit cards are being used less by some individuals. Moreover, online billing, Internet banking, and other forms of digital transactions are replacing traditional payment methods. In Japan, such "proximity payment" methods as waving personal digital assistants and mobile phones in front of a reader are being used to pay at, for example, fast food restaurants, vending machines, gas stations, cinemas, shops, and similar purchasing situations. Indeed, trading shares and betting at the horse races are becoming a commonplace digital transaction.

Customers, particularly younger people, are quickly and easily embracing digital payment systems. But the spread of digital transactions has been slow because merchants and retailers must adopt the payment system, which requires the purchase of expensive new technology.

What is the research problem? How would you conduct a literature review to learn more about obstacles slowing the adoption of digital payment systems? What key words would you try in your search?

Sources: "Time Runs Short for Cash as Electronic Money Grows," *The Business*, http://www.thebusinessonline.com, April 30, 2006, 8; http://www.virtualschool.edu/mon/ElectronicProperty/ElectronicMoney.html; http://www.digitalmoneyforum.com/, accessed October 2009; Ross Clark, "Don't Let Them Kill Off the Cheque," *Spectator*, February 23, 2008, http://www.thebusinessonline.com; "What Is Virtual Cash?" http://www.virtualschool.edu, accessed November 6, 2009; and "Conferences on Virtual Money," http://www.digitalmoneyforum.com, accessed November 6, 2009.

---

referring to your background research. Keep in mind that research questions ultimately inform the exact plan of execution. The questions you ask when undertaking fieldwork, the data you compile from secondary sources, and the method of analysis you apply are all greatly informed by the questions you have set. The Business Research Dashboard provides an example of the challenges of formulating research questions and objectives.

The Role of Theory in Research

The importance of theory in research cannot be overstated, because it provides the foundation on which quality research is built. This applies whether the research is for an academic thesis or a commercial client. It is likely that most readers of this book have heard someone comment, "Oh, that's too theoretical and has no relevance to the real world!" This is usually the statement of an individual who does not fully understand theory or who is trying to justify a weak argument or personal bias with anecdotal observation.

Theory can be viewed as a conceptual model based on foundational statements that are presumed true. A theory postulates a relationship between two or more variables under certain environmental conditions. In other words, theory provides the informed framework for analysis by suggesting relationships or causalities that may be worthy of investigation and that have the potential for generalization to a larger population. Researchers must avoid the trap of considering theory as being the opposite of practice and recognize that "there is nothing as practical as a good theory." Equally, practitioners need to realize that their decisions are often based on some internalized theory that they are perhaps unable to make explicit. As Keynes stated as long ago as 1953, "Practical men, who believe themselves to be quite exempt from any intellectual influences, are usually the slaves of some defunct economist."

Developing a research project with a sound theoretical footing offers numerous benefits. First, reviewing theory helps you refine your measurement constructs, and is particularly useful when you need to measure complex variables like commitment, loyalty, and quality. Second, theory provides justification for relationships you wish to investigate and suggests causality that helps guide a research project. For instance, an experimental design seeking to examine the strength of the relationship between two variables of interest may be far more robustly constructed if theory suggests which variable is causal. Equally, theory may suggest that there is a third variable in the relationship. Leaving the third variable unmeasured might greatly reduce the potential of the research to confirm the relationship between the two variables initially of interest.

As long as the purpose of the research extends beyond mere intelligence gathering, as is usually the case, it involves some form of theoretical reflection. Research seeking to demonstrate cause and effect relationships presumes some underlying theoretical relationship between the cause, or independent variable, and the effect, or dependent variable. Providing conceptual definitions of the variables of interest is part of the theoretical construction and a vital first step in developing operational definitions of the variables that are amenable to measurement and observation in practice. Variables may be measured directly or through the use of appropriate indicators. For example, while an operational definition of performance can be established when investigating the causal relationship between incentive systems (independent variables) and performance (dependent variable), performance needs to be measured using indicators such as revenues, profits, and share price appreciation.

Just as theory is necessary to inform the overall research topic, it also provides structure and the rationale when converting research questions into hypotheses or statements that can be tested with empirical data and found to be probably true or probably false. In this sense, theory can be viewed as explaining the why of a research plan, while hypotheses provide the means for answering the questions arising from the why. The Business Research Dashboard asks about the role of theory in formulating research questions.

PREPARING A LITERATURE REVIEW

Business students may wonder why it is necessary to undertake a literature review. But understanding fully what a literature review is and how it can help them in their research can answer the question. For one thing, a literature review prevents researchers from duplicating previous research. It also may answer research questions and

---

■————**Business Research Dashboard**————■

Craigslist: Competition for Newspaper Classifieds?

Craig Newmark set up a Web site with local classified listings in his garage in San Francisco in 1995. Craigslist has more than 20 billion page views per month and is visited by more than 50 million people each month. Almost 14 million new classified ads are published on Craigslist each month. The Web site is the seventh most visited English language site on the Web, and there are more than 450 Craigslist sites in the fifty U.S. states and in over fifty countries. The site offers consumers free classified listings and makes money by charging for postings only in a few categories, such as job listings.

Revenues from classified ads in newspapers represent about half the total revenue of U.S. newspapers. The growth of Craigslist has newspaper executives reeling; they lament, "The List is not bad news; it's terrible news." The central problem: Craigslist ads are free and newspaper ads are expensive. Ads posted to Craigslist are available 24-7 and can be updated and enhanced with all the beauty of digital publishing, while print newspapers offer consumers relatively unattractive formats. Online classified ads reach folks around the corner and around the world; print is still anchored in one place. And the digital medium is home to a whole new generation. Newspapers that react by simply putting their current print ads online are not using the full capability of the online environment. In a nutshell, Craigslist is the collision of the digital economy with traditional business models.

If you were a newspaper executive, what kind of research would you undertake to prepare yourself for this kind of competition? How would you define the business problem? How might theory be useful in researching this topic?

Sources: Craig's blog at www.cnewmark.com; Craigslist fact sheet, http://www.craigslist.org/about/factsheet.html; Craigslist UK, http://london.craigslist.org/; and Reynolds_Writing, "How to Use Craigslist to Generate Free Traffic to Your Website, Blog or Hub Pages," HubPages, http://hubpages.com/hub/UseCraigsList-GenerateFreeTraffictoYourWebsite, accessed July 2010.

---

therefore eliminate the need for a particular research project. Whatever the situation, the literature review typically has two broad objectives. First, it helps to develop and expand research ideas. Second, although a researcher may have some knowledge of the research topic, the literature review ensures a familiarity with recent developments and a complete understanding of the relevant topics.

The literature review follows the clarification of the problem in the formal research process. Likely you have previously researched the topic. But that research typically would have involved searching briefly for publications or reports that help in better understanding the research problem. It may also have consisted of informal interviews with colleagues or coworkers with similar research interests. No matter which approach you took, previous efforts to gather information were probably less formal and not as organized.

Literature reviews are often divided into two stages. The first stage is a review of the literature to identify existing themes, trends, and relationships between variables. The end result of this initial effort is to generate ideas related to your topic that have not been researched in the past or have not been examined using the same methods you propose to use. For example, there may be previous research examining your ideas or theory using qualitative approaches but none based on a quantitative, empirical approach.

The second stage of your literature review is much more extensive. It focuses on identifying and describing past theoretical research related to your topic. Theories are then included in your work if they are directly relevant. If they are not closely related and therefore not included, likely you will need to explain how and why. But ultimately a literature review must examine and comment on what has already been researched.

The literature review provides an understanding of the relevant previous research. If your research interest is examining why employees are quitting your organization, you would first look at research findings addressing employee loss. In this case, there will be a lot of previous work related to your area of interest. If findings are few, you are likely researching a topic that has emerged from recent changes in the business environment. For example, research on how the Internet is affecting organizational policies and plans is limited. If relevant research is limited, you must attempt to adapt previous research approaches to your new and likely innovative topic. For example, if you chose to study factors influencing the adoption of information technologies that facilitate electronic records capture and storage in the medical field, research would be limited. On the other hand, there is a great deal of previous research on the adoption of innovations in general. Consequently, you could examine this general area to determine what is applicable to your research.

Some of the previous research may be directly related to your research. If you are examining how employees accept and adopt change in the workplace, or the concepts of trust and loyalty, there will be many directly related previous studies. But there will be other work that is less directly related. For example, there are fewer studies of shared values in an organization or the climate for acceptance, yet these factors may influence whether change in an organization is readily accepted. Therefore, these areas must be examined to determine how they might relate to your research.

Reviewing previous research related to your topic should identify variables that are used to measure concepts such as job satisfaction, corporate reputation, organizational performance, motivation, and so forth. Such a review should also suggest how these variables are related to one another. As you conduct your literature review, however, you will often find that the same variables are defined differently by different researchers. Moreover, the literature may reveal different views on how the variables are related. Thus, a necessary outcome of the literature review is resolving the dilemmas when research variables are defined differently and findings about relationships between variables are inconsistent.

If there is little research related to your topic, you may be concerned that there is nothing of value to build upon. But this also can be encouraging because you can easily answer another frequent question related to research topics: What can I do that is unique and will make a contribution? If you are finding it difficult to obtain related research, another possibility is you're looking at it from too narrow a perspective. For example, if you are looking for information on adoption of new software to increase productivity in not-for-profit organizations, you likely will find literature on the adoption process and productivity but may find none on the adoption process for new software or the adoption process in a not-for-profit setting. When confronted with a situation like this, you must look for ways to adapt previous research to your context. For example, find previous research on the adoption process for software or similar new processes in a for-profit setting and adapt it to fit your context.

The literature review has purposes other than understanding previous work in the area. It may help to refine existing research questions and objectives or to develop new ones. In other instances you may identify problems or issues that have been overlooked in previous research. Previous researchers may have suggested areas for future research, to which you can refer in identifying your own area to investigate. Of course at a minimum you should examine current trends and opinions contained in scholarly and trade journals as well as in newspapers and industry reports that will likely provide insights into the research questions and objectives you may not have otherwise considered.

The literature review is one of the first steps in your research project. But even though it begins early in the process, it often continues to the end. For example, assume you are researching the relationships between job satisfaction, organizational commitment, and employee turnover. Early in the process, you may be searching for information on how supervision and compensation influence job satisfaction. Later, you may read an article or, in discussion with someone, decide that attitudes toward coworkers should also be examined. You will then have to expand the scope of your research to include coworkers and their possible influence on job satisfaction.

An important question that will eventually have to be answered is, When do I have enough literature and so can stop searching? The answer to that question is not obvious. At the least you must include all the most recent studies (those published in the last ten years) as well as the most important literature on the topic historically. There may also be less important work that nonetheless needs to be included because it is topical or was conducted by the person supervising your research. One strategy is to look at the references cited in recent and important research and include those most often cited. The answer given most often is you need to make sure you include the literature on all relevant issues. But since the definition of "relevant" often changes in the course of your research, you need to be prepared to reopen your literature search if necessary.

Another important consideration is the balance between applied or business sources and scholarly sources. To distinguish between the two types, consider the following. Scholarly sources are written in a more formal and rigorous style and have many citations from the most prestigious journals. In contrast, applied or business sources are written in a much less formal style and typically have only a few references. Moreover, scholarly sources are always subject to peer review by two to four researchers knowledgeable about the topic, while business publications are generally reviewed only by the publication's editor. Business sources include *BusinessWeek*, *Forbes*, the *Financial Times*, and the *Wall Street Journal*. On the other hand, the *Journal of Management*, *Economic Business Review*, *Corporate Reputation Review*, the *Journal of Marketing*, *MIS Quarterly*, and the *European Journal of Operational Research* are

Exhibit 4.2

Steps in Conducting a Literature Review

1. Clarify research questions and objectives
2. Locate and evaluate sources of information
3. Start collecting the literature
4. Review and make a record of the information
5. Start writing the initial literature review
6. Identify gaps in the literature
7. Reexamine research questions and objectives
8. Collect additional literature to fill gaps
9. Prepare final literature review

considered scholarly sources, and their content generally emphasizes theory as much as or more than practice. Consulting business publications is useful because their stories tend to cover the most recent developments. In contrast, scholarly journals typically take several years for studies to be published so they do not report the most recent developments. Ultimately, the balance depends on the audience for your research. For a predominantly academic audience the emphasis is on scholarly publications; for a business audience applied sources are more often cited.

An important point to remember when conducting your literature review is you will need to examine publications across a wide range of fields. Depending on your specific topic, you should first consider looking at the literature in all major business disciplines, including management, marketing, information technology, finance, accounting, and economics. Unlike some other fields of study, however, in business you also need to examine the literature from the social science disciplines in general, such as psychology, sociology, agriculture, geography, and others. These disciplines often feature similar research or have previously developed theories or concepts that can be adapted to business situations.

How do you actually conduct a literature review? Exhibit 4.2 lists the typical steps to follow in doing a literature review.

CONTRIBUTIONS OF THE LITERATURE REVIEW

Most research reports include an overview of the literature related to the research topic. Only applied reports limited in scope will not include a literature review. The reason for including a literature review is that it helps your research in many ways. Specifically, the literature review helps define the research problem and clarify your research questions, provides the background of the major issues, suggests potential hypotheses, and identifies research methods and data analysis and interpretation approaches used by other researchers on similar projects.

DEFINING THE RESEARCH PROBLEM

Recall that defining the research problem is an important first step in the research project. If you focus on the symptoms and not the problem, your project will be a waste of time. One way to ensure you focus on the problem and not the symptoms is to conduct preliminary interviews with knowledgeable people. Another way is to examine the scholarly literature and business publications to identify similar situations. The literature published in academic journals will be heavily focused on defining and testing business theories. In contrast, popular business publications typically are much more applied and more recent. For example, wireless technology, whether cell phones, Internet access, or tracking inventory and employees through radio frequency identification devices (RFID) is creating new workplace issues. The field is so new, however, that it is being reported in business publications but has little or no coverage in scholarly publications. Thus, scholarly publications can suggest appropriate research methods, but business publications are likely better sources for identifying issues and problems to study.

BACKGROUND INFORMATION

There are several ways in which background information can be important to your research project. Among the most important is that previously published literature can be used to justify your particular research problem as deserving further study. If it is a cutting-edge topic under consideration, the business literature may be the best source of information. If the problem is an extension or new application of an established problem, then academic as well as business literature should be helpful.

A background study also helps you to summarize all the major aspects of a problem. The relevant literature is identified and described to demonstrate you have a full understanding of past research and how it relates to your project. Background information can be extensive, depending on what is considered relevant. An early strategy is to examine and collect information on almost any topic that may be related. But as the process continues you must decide what the most important issues are and what can be left out. In using this approach the end result is a summary of the theories, arguments, and findings from both the business and scholarly literature. It is often helpful to identify the gaps in previous research that may suggest directions for your own work. The end result is a document that identifies what has and has not been done on the subject and where your research fits into this body of knowledge.

Students considering a graduate-level thesis or doctoral dissertation frequently want to know what they can do that is unique. Experienced researchers knowledgeable about a particular field can help. Exhibit 4.3 can serve as a place to begin when considering different approaches.

For graduate students it is important to follow well-established procedures and thus be able to claim the research has been rigorous and made an intellectual contribution to the literature. If research approaches are taken that are not well recognized, the risk of an examiner's rejecting the research is considerable. It is useful to think of the risk profile of a proposed research project as having two dimensions. The first dimension is the novelty of the research method and the second is the degree to which the field of study is established. As can be seen from Exhibit 4.3, if a new methodology is used in a new field of study, the risk of the research's rejection is high. But if an old methodology is applied to a well-researched field of study, there is the possibility the

Exhibit 4.3 **Risk Profile of a Research Topic**

	New method	Old method
New field	High risk of criticism and possibly failure	Should produce a satisfactory result
Old field of study	Should produce a satisfactory result	May be of little value and not worthy of a degree

researcher will not be able to argue convincingly that something new has been added to the body of theoretical knowledge. The safer areas are applying a new methodology in an established filed of study or using an established methodology in a new field of study.

Settling on a research approach is an important part of the research process. Thus, the supervisor needs to take a lot of time to explain the decision criteria for selecting a topic. Indeed, the process of selecting a topic may have to be explained several times. The issues often are so complex that it takes time for the full implications of different strategic choices to be fully absorbed. Students that ignore the advice of their supervisors in selecting a topic do so at a high risk.

RESEARCH QUESTIONS AND HYPOTHESES

The literature review also helps to refine your research questions and develop hypotheses. Possible relationships are identified and those that are unlikely are rejected. Factors influencing relationships should also be identified. For example, you may find that younger workers change jobs more often, or that older workers adapt to innovations in the workplace more slowly. You may also find that gender is associated with the frequency of changing jobs or the willingness to accept change. By using the literature to identify and suggest relationships, you can create hypotheses for testing in your study. We discuss developing research hypotheses in Chapter 6.

METHODOLOGY

The literature can be very helpful in identifying the methods used by previous researchers to study a problem. There is no need to reinvent what has proven useful in the past, unless you can identify a clear and important shortcoming of current methods. Questionnaires, measurement scales, statistical techniques, and research designs from other studies should be examined to see if they might be useful. If they produced valid findings before, they will likely bear fruit in another study. Statistical methods and research designs often require few changes, but questionnaires and scales often must be updated and revised to meet the needs of a new study. For example, a study that used a perceived self-efficacy scale as part of a study of decision making in an industrial plant would have to be adapted for use in a health-care setting. In other situations, there may not be a previously published scale, and the researcher will have to develop a new one.

Scales that require only small revisions can often be adapted based on the input of knowledgeable experts. Scales that must be extensively revised should always be pretested. Where there is no existing scale, an entirely new scale must be developed. New scale development is described in Chapter 9.

Whether using a qualitative or quantitative approach, researchers can almost always learn from the data analysis approaches used in previous research. In a qualitative approach, the literature review may help you decide when and how to use software in analysis and which packages are best. If you are doing quantitative research, other studies can suggest the appropriate statistical technique, or whether to use summated scales or factor scores to represent constructs. Using the literature to learn about possible methodologies and to support a particular research method is therefore an important step in designing your research.

INTERPRETATION

When reviewing the literature you should also look at how other researchers are interpreting their findings. What levels of statistical significance are acceptable? Which relationships are positive and which are negative? How are decisions made regarding acceptance or rejection of hypotheses? What sources are other researchers citing to support their interpretations? When the findings of your research are consistent with those of other studies you can use those studies to support your interpretation. If your findings oppose previous studies, then you must explain why. Previous research may identify reasons for your findings being different, such as using a different sample or difficulty with a particular published scale. Your task as a researcher, therefore, is to use the literature to design and execute research in a way that increases the likelihood you will obtain accurate results.

LITERATURE SOURCES

There are many sources of literature. Until recently much of the literature was difficult to locate. But developments in information technology have made locating sources much easier. Most college libraries have Web sites from which you can locate published work on almost any topic of interest. Some information is more limited, confined to bibliographic citations or abstracts only. But increasingly there are databases that provide the complete text of an article. In some cases, journal articles are accessible on campus without having to go through the library's gateway. You can conduct searches for scholarly articles and related information through Google

Scholar (http://scholar.google.com). Some of these articles will be instantly available to you as long as you are logged in through your campus, but some will require that you go through your college library's online gateway. Articles in JSTOR, a database that houses many major marketing and management scholarly publications, are often directly accessible via Google Scholar.

Newspaper articles, conference proceedings, textbooks, syndicated studies, and government documents, as well as many other sources, are all available online in databases. Information technology has facilitated the copying, storage, updating, and display of many documents. Most scholarly journals in management, marketing, accounting, and other functional areas of business are available online from their date of origin. Many newspaper articles and other publications dating from the early 1900s are also available. For most researchers, locating relevant work begins with turning on the computer and going online.

BOOKS

New researchers usually begin their literature search by reviewing books. For most topics, there are many books from which to choose. Textbooks in particular provide an overview of most recent and relevant research and cite the most important journal articles. The material is organized by topic and generally easy to read, so books are a good source for developing an overview of your research. But researchers never rely entirely on books because the information is typically at least several years old.

JOURNALS AND CONFERENCE PROCEEDINGS

Until recently, most scholarly journals were available only in hard copy. Today, most universities have electronic catalogs that enable users to find relevant research using the appropriate search terms and key words. For example, ABI/Inform enables users to search using key words or author names. The result is abstracts, PDF files, and sometimes the full text of an article. Unfortunately, some journals are not available through a user's library. Also, even if journals are available, generally the most recent articles (six to twelve months) are not included. Thus, while journals are an important source, it is often a challenge to access the material.

Professional and trade journals, as well as practitioner publications, should also be examined for relevant articles. These journals and online resources are published by professional associations, such as the Knowledge Management Professional Society, the European Society for Opinion and Marketing Research (ESOMAR), the Direct Marketing Association, the Association for Information Management, the Risk Management Association, the Internet Advertising Bureau, and the American Institute for Certified Public Accountants (AICPA). They generally contain more applied articles on topics of interest to their members as well as news items, notices of new products and services, and, on occasion, summaries of research published in other sources. These articles can seldom be used by themselves but often point researchers in new directions because of the "thought" pieces they include by prominent individuals in the field.

Professional associations typically sponsor annual meetings. These meetings often publish proceedings of the papers presented. Examples of associations that publish proceedings include the Academy of Management, the Association for Consumer Research, the Association for Information Systems, the American Marketing Association, the Academy of Marketing Science, the Decision Sciences Institute, the American Accounting Association, and the Financial Management Association International. The quality of research published in proceedings is generally not as good as that in journals, but it is more recent and often indicates new research directions.

Government and Industry

Government and industry reports can be helpful for some research topics. This is particularly true in accounting, finance, economics, sociology, and demography. More developed countries publish much statistical information and often have catalogs of their materials. The U.S. Department of Commerce is an example of a government agency that publishes many research reports (http://www.stat-usa.gov). The U.S. Census Bureau also publishes information of interest to businesses (http://www.census.gov). For Europe and some other areas, finding and using government and industry reports can be challenging because the studies are usually published in the country's native language. In addition to national government and industry reports, there are those from international organizations. These include, but are not limited to, the United Nations, the International Monetary Fund, the European Central Bank, the European Commission, the Council of Europe, the Association of African Universities, the Association of Southeast Asian Nations, and the World Bank. Access to these reports generally requires some payment, but in some cases summaries are available. Reports from such agencies are increasingly available from Internet databases.

Theses and Dissertations

Universities keep copies of theses and dissertations in their libraries. Master's theses are generally not indexed and therefore difficult to locate. Doctoral dissertations can often be found by Internet searches. If dissertation research is not readily available, which it generally is not, we recommend sending an e-mail directly to the author. We have found that researchers generally respond favorably to such inquiries, often sending electronic copies of summaries of their research.

Electronic Databases

Another source of information for financial, economic, marketing, and other statistics is online directories and databases. These databases cover a wide range of topics across many disciplines. Examples include the Wall Street Journal Index, the Business Periodicals Index, Datastream, Fame, Bloomberg, Reuters, ABI/Inform Global, InfoTrac, and others. These and other databases can be accessed anywhere you can connect to the Internet. Google, Yahoo! and other search engines can help locate additional sources. Electronic databases are discussed further in Chapter 5.

INTERNET SEARCHES

The Internet, and particularly search engines like Google, have had a significant impact on literature searches. Search engines look in Web sites for key words and phrases matching user requests. Thus, the key to success in finding relevant material is using the correct words and phrases. Indeed, more often than not a user is faced with information overload because of the difficulty of determining the best key words for obtaining the desired results. If you are searching for scholarly articles, one way to limit the search is to use Google Scholar. Google Scholar gives the number of times an article has been cited by others, which helps you determine its relative importance. Additional guidelines on conducting Internet searches are provided in Chapter 5.

PLANNING THE LITERATURE SEARCH

The literature search process can be tedious and time-consuming, often taking much longer than originally planned. Careful planning of the literature search is therefore important. Exhibit 4.4 offers guidelines for planning your literature search.

The objective of a literature review is to summarize the major issues related to your research. In most cases you will discuss what different authors have reported, the methodology used, and how their findings are similar or different. For research findings that are similar, you likely will point out why. Where the findings differ, you should suggest reasons for this as well. In all cases you should indicate how their findings influenced your own research.

The literature review constitutes a critical analysis of the research that has been conducted on your topic. The topics included in the literature review are based on your research questions and objectives. For example, if your research is looking at factors that cause employees to search for a new job, then your literature review would examine work environment factors such as compensation, supervision, teamwork, communications, and so forth. Your literature review will summarize what you found out about the questions posed by your research. The issues not addressed, often called gaps, will be identified, and your research will focus on one such research gap.

The format and length of the literature review varies depending on the type of research project. Commercial and consulting projects have a limited literature review, covering only the essential information. Projects seeking funding support, such as government grants, usually include a more extensive literature review. Graduate-level theses have the most extensive literature reviews. Shorter reviews are generally limited to a few pages, while longer ones are at least a chapter and sometimes more.

You start your literature review by reflecting on your research objectives. Review each objective and identify the topics that are the same and those that differ across objectives. For example, if your research objectives involve examining factors related to job satisfaction and loyalty, then there are at least four topics to be included in your literature review: (1) What is job satisfaction and how is it defined? (2) What is loyalty and how is it defined? (3) What factors are related to job satisfaction and how are they defined? and (4) What factors are related to loyalty and how are they

Exhibit 4.4

Guidelines for Planning a Literature Search

- Define the scope of your subject area, for example, leadership, conflict management, customer satisfaction.
- Determine which disciplines must be examined, for example, marketing, psychology, or management, among others.
- Identify the context of your research, whether business to business or consumer.
- Decide on the geographic area to be studied—North America, Europe, Asia.
- Decide the time period to be examined, generally a minimum of the most recent ten years, but likely a quick review of at least twenty years.
- Identify the languages in which relevant research is likely to be published and sources of translation for any materials in a language you cannot read.
- Identify, beyond books and scholarly journals, other sources to be examined, such as conference proceedings and industry publications.

defined? Of course, there will likely be some overlap in topics, particularly with the factors related to job satisfaction and loyalty.

Once you have identified the topics to be covered, you should start generating search terms or key words. This is particularly true today since most literature reviews rely on a computer search engine to locate relevant research. If you have the correct search terms, you will find the appropriate literature. If your search terms do not include all your topics, then you will not find the literature you need to fully understand the background of your topic.

Identification of search terms and key words often begins with the most recent articles published in the literature. Review articles and meta-analyses of a particular topic are generally the most helpful. They will not only identify key words but also reference other, similar articles worthy of review. Another excellent source is theses and dissertations in the libraries of research universities. Handbooks, encyclopedias, dictionaries, and thesauruses are also useful. Fortunately, most of these are now available electronically. Brainstorming with fellow students or colleagues as well as with scholars in your field of study once you have a good idea of your topic can generate many productive search terms. Finally, do not overlook the power of e-mail. In the past, researchers were limited to contacting individuals close by or over the telephone, but today one should never hesitate to contact scholars publishing in your area for ideas. The main stipulation is to be well prepared and able to ask intelligent questions. Do not just send a general inquiry such as, What key words would you use to find out about job satisfaction?

WRITING A LITERATURE REVIEW

Writing the literature review can be a challenging task, particularly for inexperienced researchers. Conflicting findings should be reported, but you must comment on and explain the differences. For example, if the research focuses on the concept of motivation among employees, then it would be important to discuss how motivation is defined in each study and whether the same or a similar scale was used to measure

Exhibit 4.5

Guidelines for Preparing a Literature Review

- Start from a broad perspective and move to a narrow one that focuses on your specific topic, a method often referred to as a funnel approach.
- Ensure your review relates closely to your research objectives and questions.
- Cite the major experts in the field in which you are working.
- Cite the most recent of any publications considered important to your research.
- Identify gaps in existing research, how your research is related, and what its contribution will be.
- Include publications that suggest a different viewpoint from your own, indicating how and why your research is different.
- Be objective in evaluating the contributions of other researchers. If in doubt, ask knowledgeable individuals less involved in your work to evaluate your comments.
- Include a comprehensive conceptual model showing all relevant constructs and variables and their proposed relationships.

motivation. Motivation could easily be defined differently for employees in different job settings, and if so this must be explained. A good literature review demonstrates the researcher has an excellent understanding of previous research and how it is related. Citing an extensive list of references is not sufficient and could be risky. An examiner might question you about a particular one and be unimpressed if you are unable to comment on it.

Researchers must be able to clearly interpret previous research and show the links among studies. Exhibit 4.5 provides guidelines for preparing your literature review.

The library is a critical resource for the researcher because it provides access to the literature. It contains not only the books relevant to your topic but also, and often more important, it allows through its annual subscription fees access to applied and scholarly publications, government documents, and some industry reports.

Start your literature review by looking at your library's catalog to determine which publications it has and what it may be able to obtain over the Internet. Another source is interlibrary loan, but in most cases this service must be paid for, so users should make sure items ordered this way are relevant. A good rule of thumb is that books, well-known journals, and government publications not otherwise available are generally worth the expense associated with interlibrary loan.

As you collect your literature, you should begin evaluating it. Indeed, during the process of locating information you will be examining what you have collected to determine if it justifies further effort. Some articles will be discarded immediately while others will be set aside. We have found that dividing the literature into three categories is useful: (1) definitely useful, (2) likely useful, at least in a limited way, and (3) possibly useful but set aside until later. Suggestions for what to include in a literature review are given in Exhibit 4.6.

During the literature review you will download articles from the Internet and photocopy material from books, reports, and journal articles. While you are collecting information, it is important to prepare notes. Your notes will summarize the contribution of each publication to your research as well as the complete bibliographic

Exhibit 4.6

Deciding What to Include in a Literature Review

- Is the reference more than ten years old? If yes, make sure a more recent publication has not replaced the earlier reference.
- Is the source reliable, or potentially biased? If the source is potentially biased, be careful about relying on it in your work and indicate potential biases.
- Has the reference been cited in reliable sources?
- Beyond the theory, is the methodology useful as a guide to your approach?
- Can the topics reported in the research be used to organize your report?
- Which conclusions can be built upon and need to be cited?
- If the findings are different from your research, how do you explain the discrepancy? It is not a good idea to simply ignore contradictory studies, because others, such as research supervisors, will often be familiar with these studies.

information. This will make it easier to properly cite sources used in your research. Database software is available to help you do this, so be sure to check it out. The process of preparing notes will help you organize your thinking and make you more efficient when you are actually writing down your ideas.

When is your literature search completed? In reality, it is not complete until you stop researching a particular field. You should continue to search and review until you finish your research. Doing so will help you avoid overlooking a recently published or significant study. At a minimum, you must review all the major literature closely related to your topic. For topics that have been extensively researched for many years, it is generally easier to focus on the most relevant research. But for new and emerging topics, you will necessarily have to extend your review to related fields. An indication of when this process is nearing completion is that you will begin seeing citations already in your list of references. The Business Research Dashboard gives an example of an emerging issue for which locating sources of information may require a researcher to extend the review to other applicable fields.

CONFIRMING RESEARCH QUESTIONS WITH THE LITERATURE REVIEW

The literature review should lead to a redefinition of the research problem or opportunity in scientific terms. That is, the literature review enables you to develop research questions that focus on the underlying issues and not the symptoms. Issues are not the same as symptoms. **Issues** are points or matters in question that, if altered, will close the gap between the actual and desired states. Like a medical doctor, the business professional will create a much better long-term outcome if the real issues are treated, not just the symptoms. **Symptoms** are signals that a change may be needed to avoid further problems or take advantage of an important opportunity. A runny nose and a sore throat are symptoms that could indicate some type of viral or bacterial infection. Likewise, decreased employee productivity could be symptomatic of some organizational management problem or of one within the workplace environment. These two issues would produce research questions involving entirely different variables. In either case, simply treating the symptom itself may make the problem worse.

■————**Business Research Dashboard**————■
The Post-Geographic Office

Technology companies have been at the forefront of restructuring offices and work hours. Forty percent of IBM's workforce and one third of AT&T's employees do not have an official office. Sun Microsystems believes that it has saved $400 million in real estate costs because half of all employees work wherever they want, as long as they get their work done. In a recent study, Boston Consulting Group found that fully 85 percent of executives expect the number of employees who work away from the office to rise considerably over the next five years.

Perhaps the most innovative restructuring of time in the workplace is happening outside the technology industry, at Best Buy corporate headquarters. The program is not a flextime program: the time employees put in at the office is not tracked at all. Instead, the results of their work are measured. According to *BusinessWeek*, the "nation's leading electronics retailer has embarked on a radical—if risky—experiment to transform a culture once known for killer hours and herd-riding bosses. The endeavor, called ROWE, for 'results-only work environment,' seeks to demolish decades-old business dogma that equates physical presence with productivity." Best Buy is "smashing the clock."

At Best Buy, people are free to work whenever or wherever they want. There are no mandatory meetings. And there's more to come: the company plans to implement ROWE in its retail stores. The upside of this approach for companies like Best Buy is that programs like ROWE may let employees make better work/life balance decisions, which in turn could boost morale, employee loyalty, job satisfaction, and productivity.

Best Buy's idea of measuring productivity rather than time spent at work is a relatively new idea. If you wrote a thesis on the effects of "smashing the clock," what topics would you include in your literature review? How would you go about conducting your literature review? What general types of sources would you consult?

Source: "Smashing the Clock," *BusinessWeek,* December 11, 2006, http://www.businessweek.com/magazine/content/06_50/b4013001.htm?chan=search, and www.bestbuy.com, accessed July 2010.

Research questions are often phrased in a what, when, where, who, and why form. Such questions can be specific or broad. Specific research questions are more useful, however, in developing actionable research ideas related to managerial issues. Research questions rephrase research issues into a researchable form. In other words, the variables are described in a way that provides helpful information to business decision makers. Examples of symptoms, issues, and research questions are given in Exhibit 4.7. Clarifying research issues and questions is important because they occupy a prominent role not only in the research design but also in the research outcome.

A group effort generally results in the most effective research questions. The researcher is responsible for posing the initial questions based on the literature review; but after that, involving experts or other knowledgeable people can often be helpful in revising or expanding the questions. Such brainstorming is increasingly accomplished via e-mail.

After the research questions have been developed, research objectives must be formulated. Examples of research questions converted into objectives are provided in Exhibit 4.8.

Exhibit 4.7

Examples of Symptoms, Issues, and Research Questions

Symptoms	Issues	Research questions
Low customer service ratings	Sales territories too large, inadequate training	What factors influence customer service ratings?
Stock-outs higher than previous year	Shelf space increases have lowered retail inventories	What is the relationship between shelf space and retail sales?
Sales lower than expected	Inadequate forecasting techniques	What variables are the best predictors of sales?
Churn rate highest in the market	Poor product quality, prices too high, service employees unfriendly	What factors are related to churn rate?
Labor costs higher than those of competition	Too many employee sick days, low productivity	Do flexible schedules create increased labor efficiency (lower labor costs)?

Exhibit 4.8

Converting Research Questions into Objectives

Research Questions	Research Objectives
What can be done to improve employee morale?	Identify factors influencing employee morale.
When has employee training been effective?	Describe the situations and criteria when employee training has been effective.
Where should we sell our products?	Determine in which geographic areas (countries or regions) our products are most likely to sell.
Who should we consider outsourcing our manufacturing to, and for which products?	Determine the criteria for selecting countries and companies for possible outsourcing.
Why is employee productivity low?	Identify which conditions are related to productivity and how those conditions are influencing our firm's productivity.

As defined in Chapter 2, a theory is a set of systematically related statements or a proposed explanation for some event that can be tested empirically. We noted that some theories have been confirmed by past research while others have either limited or no validation. Whether your theory has been confirmed or is a new proposition, it should be used to develop research questions and objectives. As an example, Exhibit 4.9 illustrates a marketing theory called the hierarchy of effects. The theory proposes to explain how individuals become customers in a series of stages, from lack of awareness to awareness, knowledge, and so on. We could use this theory to develop research questions, objectives, and ultimately hypotheses. For example, a potential question is, In which stage of the hierarchy is the 50+ market segment? This question could then lead to the research objective to describe what the 50+ market segment knows about our company and products and services. Finally, a hypothesis to test

Exhibit 4.9

Theory of Hierarchy of Effects

	Hierarchy stages	Description
1.	Unawareness	Unaware of brand
2.	Awareness	Aware of brand
3.	Knowledge	Some knowledge of brand
4.	Liking	Positive feeling about brand
5.	Intention	Intention to buy brand next time
6.	Purchase	Purchase of brand.
7.	Repurchase/loyalty	Regular purchase of brand

might be that the 50+ market segment is not buying our products because they are not familiar with their features and benefits.

From the research questions and objectives a preliminary idea of the types of data necessary to complete the research project is also formulated. This process involves answering a series of questions, such as: Is data available in the firm's data warehouse that can solve the problem or clarify the opportunity? Can secondary data be obtained from trade associations, government documents, or similar sources? and What are the budget and time constraints for the project? At this point, it is common to make adjustments in the initial research objectives because of time and budget constraints. Ultimately, the researcher and the manager must decide if the value of the information is greater than the cost of obtaining it and whether the data can be obtained quickly enough to be useful. If the answer is yes on both counts, the research questions are translated into research objectives, and the research design is selected.

CONTINUING CASE: SAMOUEL'S GREEK CUISINE
Developing Research Questions and Objectives

Phil Samouel has concluded that the problems needing to be investigated for his restaurant should involve research on both customers and employees. To obtain a better understanding of these issues he logged on to the Yahoo! and Google search engines. He also spent some time at the local library. From his review of the literature, he identified some best practices guidelines on how restaurants should be run. Below is a summary of what he found.

- If you do not have enough customers, first examine the quality of your food, the items on your menu, and the service.
- Your wait staff must fit the image and character of your restaurant. How your employees behave is extremely important. They must be well groomed, knowledgeable, and polite and must speak clearly and confidently.
- Your menu items must represent a good value for the money.
- Service must be efficient, timely, polished, and cordial.
- Cleanliness in and around your restaurant has a strong effect on the success of your business.

(continued)

- Follow the marketing premise of "underpromise and overdeliver," always finding ways to please your customers.
- Empower your employees to make decisions to keep your customers happy. For almost all customer complaints, and it is hoped there will be few, train your employees on ways of resolving the situation instead of coming to the manager.
- Create a pleasant dining atmosphere, including furniture and fixtures, decorations, lighting, music, and temperature.
- Find out if your restaurant appeals to women. For family outings or special occasions, women make the decision on where to dine about 75 percent of the time.

With this information, Phil and his brother need to specify the research questions to be examined.

1. What research questions should be examined in the employee research?
2. What research questions should be examined in the customer research?
3. Should Phil continue his literature search? If yes, for what additional topics should he seek information?

SUMMARY

IDENTIFY THE CHARACTERISTICS OF A QUALITY RESEARCH TOPIC

The characteristics of a quality research topic include: the research is developed on a sound theoretical base; the research is of interest to both the sponsor and the researcher; the research problem is well defined and the research questions and objectives that flow from it are specific and possible to address through a rigorous research design; resource requirements in terms of time, finances, and data access are well understood early in the research process; and the research is expected to make a contribution to knowledge independently of the orientation of the findings.

DESCRIBE HOW TO CONVERT RESEARCH IDEAS INTO RESEARCH QUESTIONS

Research ideas may be generated by the researcher or provided by the sponsor in the form of a business problem around which an informed decision needs to be made. Research ideas that do not flow immediately from a business problem may often be clarified by questioning senior researchers, executives, and decision makers about problems they face; by examining published research in fields of interest; or by examining past research projects that may suggest areas worthy of subsequent investigation. Once a suitable research idea has been identified, the researcher needs to narrow the topic to produce research questions that can be answered through the application of appropriate research techniques, as well as clear, succinct objectives. Initial discussions, literature searches, and reviews of past research can help develop great research ideas, but research success requires that these broad ideas be further refined and developed into good research questions and specific objectives.

UNDERSTAND WHAT A LITERATURE REVIEW IS AND HOW IT HELPS YOUR RESEARCH

The literature review follows the clarification of the problem or opportunity in the formal research process. Likely you have previously researched the topic. But that research typically would have involved searching briefly for publications that help you to better understand the research problem. It may also have consisted of informal interviews with colleagues or coworkers with similar research interests. No matter which approach you used, previous efforts to gather information were probably less formal and less organized than you need to be in your literature review. The literature review helps you to develop an understanding of the relevant previous research. Some previous research may be directly related to your research. But other work will be less directly related. You use a literature review to demonstrate your knowledge of the relevant research and how your research makes a unique contribution to the field.

IDENTIFY THE MAJOR SOURCES FOR A LITERATURE SEARCH

There are many sources of literature. Until recently much of the literature was difficult to locate. But developments in information technology have made locating sources much easier. Most libraries have online resources to help you locate published work on almost any topic of interest. Some of the information is limited to bibliographic citations or abstracts only. But increasingly there are databases that provide the complete text of an article. Newspapers, journal articles, conference proceedings, textbooks, syndicated studies, and government documents, as well as many other sources, are all available now in online databases.

EXPLAIN HOW TO PLAN AND WRITE A LITERATURE REVIEW

The literature search process can be tedious and time-consuming, often taking much longer than originally planned. Careful planning is therefore important for efficiently locating the literature most relevant to your research topic. The objective of a literature review is to summarize the major issues related to your research. In most cases you will discuss what different authors have reported, what methodology they used, and how their findings are similar or different. Both similar and differing findings should be explained. In all cases you should indicate how their findings influenced your own research.

Writing the literature review can be a challenging task, particularly for inexperienced researchers. Conflicting findings should be reported, but you must comment on and explain the differences. For example, if the research focuses on the concept of employee motivation, then it would be important to discuss how motivation is defined in each study and whether the same or a similar scale was used to measure motivation. Motivation could easily be defined differently for employees in different job settings, and, if so, this must be pointed out. A good literature review demonstrates the researcher has an excellent understanding of previous work and how it is related. Citing an extensive list of references is not sufficient. Researchers must be able to clearly interpret previous research and show the links among studies.

CONFIRM RESEARCH QUESTIONS WITH THE LITERATURE REVIEW

The literature review should lead to a redefinition of the research problem or opportunity in scientific terms. That is, the research questions must focus on underlying issues and not the symptoms. Research questions are often phrased in a what, when, where, who, and why form. Such questions can be specific or broad. Specific research questions are more useful for providing helpful information to business decision makers. By clarifying the issues, your research questions will lead to more accurate objectives.

ETHICAL DILEMMA

The CEO for a chain of retail clothing stores has observed that the number of employees choosing to quit is very high, particularly in certain stores. She wants to identify ways of reducing employee loss. One possibility involves improving the compensation plan. The CEO does not believe she has enough information on what compensation options are possible and what might be more desirable to employees. Carmen Roberts, head of personnel, is asked to research compensation options and recommend the best alternative at the next management meeting. Carmen is asked to survey other retailers about the compensation packages they offer their employees and to interview employees about what they want. Because of pressure to fill several unexpected employee openings that same month, Carmen has time only to check with the chain's major competitor and contact three small retailers about their benefits packages. In addition, the only employee input she has gathered has come from the group of employees who eat lunch with her regularly. When the time for the meeting arrives, Carmen claims she has done the requested research herself. Based on the results, she recommends that the firm adopt a plan similar to the one used by the major competitor. She presents only this idea and recommends approval. The next day an employee who has been offered a job in another industry shows Carmen the compensation package she has been offered. It seems much more desirable and perhaps more economical than the package Carmen has recommended. What should Carmen do now? Where did Carmen go wrong?

REVIEW QUESTIONS

1. What are the characteristics of a quality research topic?
2. What is a literature review and why is it important to the research process?
3. What are the major sources of business literature?
4. What are the steps in planning a literature review?
5. Describe the differences between research questions and research objectives.

DISCUSSION AND APPLICATION ACTIVITIES

1. You are having difficulty deciding whether your research topic will make a unique intellectual contribution. Suggest an approach that could help you determine if your topic is unique.

2. You are trying to begin your literature search on the adoption of new technology in business organizations. What are some issues you need to resolve before actually starting to collect and review the literature?

INTERNET EXERCISE

Go to http://www.testq.com/career/quizzes/show/121. You can take this online test for free, and you will get a preliminary summary of the results.

a. What is the research problem and objectives that the Classic IQ test addresses?
b. What about this online survey methodology is unique? Do you think these unique aspects help to more effectively address the research problem and objectives that you identified? Why or why not?

NOTES

1. B.B. Brown, "Employees' Organizational Commitment and Their Perception of Supervisors' Relations-Oriented and Task-Oriented Leadership Behaviors" (PhD diss., Virginia Polytechnic Institute and State University, 2003).

2. P. Lok and J. Crawford, "The Relationship Between Commitment and Organizational Culture, Subculture, Leadership Style and Job Satisfaction in Organizational Change and Development," *Leadership and Organization Development Journal*, 20, 7 (1999), 365–374.

3. N.J. Allen and J.P. Meyer, "The Measurement and Antecedents of Affective, Continuance and Normative Commitment to the Organization," *Journal of Occupational Psychology*, 63 (1990), 1–18.

4. L.F. Pitt, S.K. Foreman, and D. Bromfield, "Organizational Commitment and Service Delivery: Evidence from an Industrial Setting in the UK," *International Journal of Human Resource Management*, 6, 1 (1995), 369–389.

5. G. Philip and S.A. Hazlett, "The Measurement of Service Quality: A New P-C-P Attributes Model," *International Journal of Quality & Reliability Management*, 14, 3 (1995), 260–286.

6. V. Zeithaml, L. Berry, and A. Parasuraman, "The Behavioral Consequences of Service Quality," *Journal of Marketing*, 60, 2 (1996), 31.

5 The Nature and Sources of Secondary Business Data

LEARNING OUTCOMES

1. Define the nature and scope of secondary business data
2. Discuss the advantages and disadvantages of using secondary business data
3. Describe the various sources of secondary business data
4. Evaluate the validity, reliability, and potential bias of different types of secondary data
5. Appreciate ethical issues that may be associated with secondary data

We are living in an information age. A quick perusal of the information available to the general public as well as to students and faculty is mind-boggling. We see that not only do we need to figure out what kind of information we are looking for but also we have to decide which of the many available sources we want to utilize to get this information. In addition, we are forced to consider how we want the information delivered. The Internet has brought an unwieldy amount of information to us through the computers we have in our classrooms, computer laboratories, homes, and libraries. And that information can be delivered to us online, in paper form, or in multiple other formats.

To prepare and educate ourselves for our information needs we need to examine the types of information we can access and determine what information can help us answer our research questions. Although the natural inclination of researchers seeking answers to business questions is to gather new data on the topic or objective, this approach is not always optimal. Researchers should give serious thought to whether data may already exist that could answer the research question. Searching for existing data can save time, effort, and expense and be of value also in spite of the fact that the data may not have been collected originally with the current research question in mind. In other words, such data may still represent a practical, valid, and useful source of both quantitative and qualitative information.

The high cost of collecting data makes it important that researchers check to see if data already collected by others is available. This should be done whether the project concerns itself with quantitative or qualitative approaches. This chapter begins by defining secondary business data. Next we outline sources and types of secondary data as well as its advantages and disadvantages. We end with comments on the quality of secondary business data.

SECONDARY BUSINESS DATA DEFINED

Data used for research that was not gathered directly and purposefully for the project under consideration is termed **secondary data**. As this chapter shows, such data can, and does, play an important role in answering many research questions. However, because the original purpose for collecting data does not relate to the study under consideration the researcher needs to devote considerably more thought to questions of validity, reliability, and potential bias.

Sources of secondary data include the researcher's company as well as various external agencies such as data collection companies, municipal or other governmental agencies, nongovernment organizations (NGOs), and trade or consumer associations. Whatever the source, the data may be provided in either raw or summarized form, be free of charge or available only for a one-off or some form of license fee, and available in either printed or digital form.

At some point many of us have been called upon by one or more of the above groups to provide data on ourselves. Sometimes the purpose for the data collection is narrow and explained to us at the time it is collected. An example of this would be when you are stopped in a supermarket and asked to sample and comment on a particular product. Other times the purpose of data collection is broader, and it is less clear how the data will be used. The data provided by households during national census studies are a good illustration of the type of collection where people generally do not know how or where the data will be used.

The difference between primary and secondary data is not always clear. For example, a researcher may decide to add more data to that initially collected for a report or research paper that has already been published. Whether the new data, which extends the original study, is considered secondary is open to debate. The answer is based on the extent to which the scope of the revised report expands the original study.

SOURCES AND TYPES OF SECONDARY BUSINESS DATA

Business research uses various forms of secondary data for both descriptive and explanatory purposes. This type of data is used to support studies designed for extrapolation to general populations and for specific case study analyses where the ability to generalize plays a lesser role in the research design.

Traditionally, economists have been the leading users of secondary data in the broad field of business research. Statistics gathered from stock markets, bond markets, national governments and agencies such as the U.S. Federal Reserve Bank (http://www.federalreserve.gov), and international agencies such as the International Monetary

Fund (IMF) (http://www.imf.org) and the World Bank (http://econ.worldbank.org) are extensively used by econometricians to investigate relationships between policy choices and economic performance. In recent years, however, secondary data has become important also in research studies ranging from education and health care to corporate governance, ethics, and social responsibility. From a demand side, this growth has also been driven by an expanded interest in large comparative studies undertaken nationally and internationally. From a supply side, technology has greatly enhanced the capacity of data providers to leverage their databases for commercial purposes, and this has increased the nature and extent of the data they provide.

Data obtained from secondary sources can be either qualitative or quantitative. For instance, secondary data consisting of summary comments or graphical presentation of the underlying raw data permit only qualitative interpretation. Although the original data may have met all the requirements for quantitative analysis, it may have been compiled by the researcher in a manner that makes it amenable only to qualitative analysis as a secondary source. Conversely, a research organization providing the raw data used in the original study or providing compiled tabular summaries of that data is offering secondary data that may lend itself to further quantitative analyses. For example, data on population and income statistics by country might be used to develop a trend analysis.

A useful way to categorize secondary data is by source, format, and type, as shown in Exhibit 5.1. While secondary data is generally considered to be data that is obtained from third-party or external sources, it can also come from within a company. When it comes from within the company, it is considered an **internal source**. When it is obtained outside the company, it is considered an **external source**. External sources include organizations or individuals that are the primary gatherers of the data and syndicated service organizations that act as brokers and consolidators of data initially gathered by others. Sometimes you can obtain data from a single external source. Other times you will need to use multiple external sources to compile the data needed for your research. This occurs when there is no single provider of all the needed data or when a provider is unwilling to allow access to third parties.

External providers of secondary data also include local, regional, and national governments, industry and professional associations, supranational organizations, such as the European Union, NGOs, and commercial enterprises that are either direct distributors of data or gather data and sell it to others. Investment firms are a good example of commercial organizations that generate data for their own purposes but also sell or distribute it to their clients.

Secondary data provided by nonbusiness entities includes census and other macroeconomic and social statistics published by various governmental agencies as well as reports developed by NGOs as part of their service mission and to substantiate lobbying activities they may be engaged in. Increasingly, such data is stored electronically and can be obtained via the Internet.

Whatever its source, secondary business data may not be available in a format that is immediately useful. For example, written reports, recorded discussions, and meeting notes are illustrations of secondary sources that require considerable analysis to convert them to a convenient format for further processing. Sometimes even

Exhibit 5.1 **Secondary Data and Its Sources**

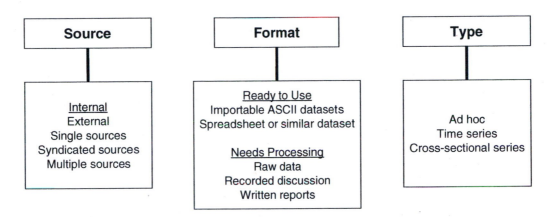

raw data may be stored in a way that requires reentry into an electronic database for analysis. This possibility is not restricted to external sources. Even internal secondary data may be stored in a format requiring work to get it into an appropriate form for analysis. Examples include certain customer characteristics gathered from customers at the start of the business relationship and kept on file, such as brands previously purchased or lifestyle information, but that have not been fully integrated into a company's customer relationship management (CRM) system. Generally, however, internally sourced secondary data is part of a company's standard management information structure and services. As such, the data can be extracted in a format that is relatively easy to integrate with newly acquired primary data gathered specifically for the research project being undertaken.

Increasingly, individual and syndicated sources are also making their data available electronically via the Internet and through proprietary online services. This data is usually in a convenient format that includes text, spreadsheet, and database files.

Finally, secondary data can be classified by type. It can be sourced from single, ad-hoc investigations undertaken for a specific purpose with no initial intention to expand the research over time, or across market segments. Alternatively, it may come from a source, or sources, that repeatedly collect data as part of longitudinal studies or to compare findings across different markets. For example, the European Union and its constituent governments produce large quantities of secondary data that is relevant for business researchers. This data is readily accessible from the central statistical offices of the national governments and the Statistical Office of the European Commission. Some of the data is gathered according to a regular schedule and presented as time series in raw or indexed form. Other data is collected to compare market, social, or environmental conditions across member countries. Finally, data is also collected for specialized, one-off reports.

Examples of longitudinal data include gross domestic product, interest rates, inflation statistics, and employment data. Given that these types of data are also collected for individual countries, they also represent cross-sectional secondary data. An example of a one-off report is the Board of Governors of the Federal Reserve System's

"Proposed Guidance on Sound Incentive Compensation Policies," which proposes compensation adjustments designed to help ensure that bank incentive policies do not encourage the kind of excessive risk taking believed to be responsible for the 2008 global financial crisis. The importance of this report and the responses it received from the public to the banking sector and the wider community cannot be overstated.[1] The Business Research Dashboard offers an example of secondary data gathered for trend assessment purposes.

LOCATING SECONDARY BUSINESS DATA

The list of potential sources of secondary data is nearly endless. Generally, the researcher begins by examining internal sources. Data previously collected by the organization itself includes primary data from prior studies and routine record inventories. Useful data from the sales domain includes sales staff itineraries, sales invoices, customer complaint records, product returns, and prior customer surveys. In the financial realm, company financial reports and records provide information on assets acquisition, cash flows, research and development, marketing expenditures, and financial performance. Minutes of meetings as well as strategic planning documents and the like are also key internal sources of secondary data. Finally, research into motivation and commitment of staff members may be developed from secondary data on pay, employee coaching and evaluation reports, and training investment.

Once internal sources have been exhausted, researchers can turn to external secondary data sources. The amount of secondary data available from both profit and nonprofit organizations is almost unlimited, but the quality and appropriateness of the data must be critically appraised relative to your study. Fortunately, this data is increasingly accessible through electronic means. Many of us know from our daily Web browsing that the key to a successful electronic search is isolating key words. A poor choice of key words leads to either too restrictive a list of identified items or, worse, one that is so long as to be useless.

Most libraries have access to several specialized search engines that can identify relevant research articles and data. Individuals and private companies also can subscribe to an online database for a fee. These specialist search engines typically provide access to abstracts or full-text articles in trade periodicals, academic journals, and general business magazines. Some also provide access to specialized statistical data.

Although electronic searches now dominate the landscape, some historical material of interest may still be available only in library archives. You should not assume that all interesting and valid sources of external secondary data will be accessible via an electronic search. In addition, be aware that electronic sources and their data are subject to change. Companies, government agencies, and nonprofit organizations may change their Internet addresses (URLs) and Web page content. Downloadable files may also be updated periodically as statistics are revised by the initial provider. For example, the Japanese Camera and Imaging Products Association, which produces statistics on digital cameras, revised its estimate of the production of digital still cameras for January 2006 upward by 8.4 percent, from 3,712,406 units to 4,024,586 units, on April 3, 2006.[2] This is a significant adjustment for someone tracking market

■————**Business Research Dashboard**————■
Employment Trends in the United States

As part of the services it provides to U.S. workers, the U.S. Department of Labor produces a biannual publication entitled the *Occupational Outlook Handbook*. In addition to providing comprehensive information about the nature of innumerable job categories ranging from apparel-pattern makers to information systems managers and zookeepers, the handbook provides insight into the training and qualifications requirements, development possibilities, and earnings potential. Also of note, the handbook provides projections of the expected growth or decline of an employment category over the next five to ten years. This searchable electronic publication can be found at http://www.bls.gov/oco/.

Although presented in a far more aggregated form, the Department of Labor also provides downloadable (HTML) historical data of employment in various sectors of the U.S. economy. This data can also be obtained on a more regional basis and is useful for assessing the longer-term trends in employment across the United States. The graph presented below provides a powerful illustration of the shifting employment patterns in the nonfarming sector between 1960 and 2008 (http://www.bls.gov/cps/cps_over.htm#available).

In 1960, the three production sectors of mining and logging, construction, and manufacturing employed a total of 19.18 million people, as opposed to the four service sectors of financial activities, professional and business, leisure and hospitality, and government, which employed 18.15 million. By 2008 the three production sectors were employing 21.42 million, versus 61.88 million for the four service sectors, an undeniable shift in the American economy from production to services, with relative growth represented by these three and four sectors, respectively, aggregating to a 12 percent growth in production-sector employment over half a century versus 241 percent growth for the service sector.

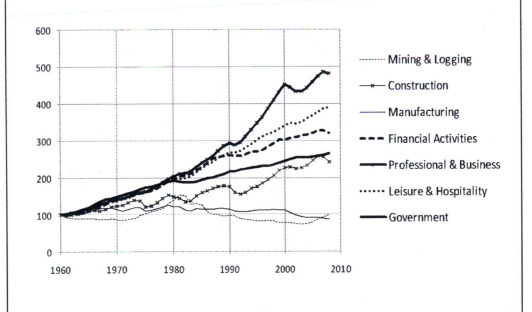

■————Business Research Dashboard————■
Data Can Be Fishy!

Secondary data is abundant online. All one needs is a good search engine and a little imagination. Suppose you are interested in a statistical overview of aquaculture (fish farming) as part of an environmental analysis for a prospective entrepreneurial business venture in British Columbia, Canada.

Google can supply the bait! Go to http://www.google.com/, enter "Canadian aquaculture statistics" in the search window, and search. Google will recommend several sites. One is the Statistics Canada site, at http://www.statcan.gc.ca/start-debut-eng.html, which will direct you to the aquaculture statistics section (http://www.statcan.gc.ca/bsolc/olc-cel/olc-cel?lang=eng&catno=23-222-X), which provides the latest aquaculture statistics report as either an HTML or PDF viewable file. Toward the bottom of the page, a hyperlink takes you to a chronological index of the reports dating back to 2001. Additionally, a further hyperlink to "Livestock and Aquaculture" enables you, for a modest fee, to access summary and comprehensive downloadable Excel files of data. Searching through the site reveals numerous interesting articles and statistics on the fishing industry, including the commercial production (aquaculture) of shellfish, salmon, and trout production across Canada and elsewhere internationally. Since the data is charted over a number of years, it could be useful in plotting and analyzing trends in the marketplace.

From this example you can likely see how easy it is to find volumes of information from reputable sources on even the seemingly most obscure topics if you are prepared to spend a little time and think in a logical and structured way.

---

size and growth in this sector. The Business Research Dashboard gives an example of what you might find using an electronic search engine.

Exhibit 5.2 provides a list of some external secondary data sources clustered into various groupings. The list includes important and reliable sources, but the almost limitless supply of secondary data sources means the search has only begun. Efforts must now focus on identifying the best sources. For example, a Google search of unemployment statistics for the United States of America results in 25,400,000 hits. Narrowing this search by requesting that all hits include the exact word combination "official statistics" still produces 65,100 hits. Clearly, other criteria must be applied to select the most useful sources for the research at hand.

The potential for large and indiscriminate search results means that experienced researchers often use other platforms and networks to provide focus. A literature review may suggest the sort of data that is available and provide some indication of its quality. Articles and books you read while doing the literature research should have given you references to the sources of secondary data that prior researchers have tapped. You should also speak to people knowledgeable about the area, since they can usually help with achieving focus. Published guides like indexes and catalogs can also be helpful in finding useful secondary data. They are often available online in a downloadable format.

Data held by companies and other private organizations is sometimes difficult to obtain because it is not commonly made public. In such a case, you need to locate a key person in the organization with access to the data and the authority to release it to you. This may require you to pay for and sign a statement of confidentiality.

Exhibit 5.2

Secondary Data Sources Available on the Internet

Source	Description from Web site
Governmental and Nongovernmental Agencies	
http://www.un.org	This official site of the United Nations includes an extensive database of information on international treaties and humanitarian and nongovernmental directories. Video clips of General Assembly meetings can also be accessed via the site.
http://www.federalreserve.gov	The Federal Reserve System, often referred to as the Federal Reserve, or simply the Fed, is the central bank of the United States. It was created by Congress on December 23, 1913, with the signing of the Federal Reserve Act by President Woodrow Wilson to provide the nation with a safer, more flexible, and more stable monetary and financial system. The site provides a comprehensive database of economic and financial indicators, much of which is downloadable.
http://www.census.gov	The U.S. Census Bureau has the stated mission of serving as the leading source of quality data about the nation's people and economy. Its goal is to provide the best mix of timeliness, relevancy, quality, and cost for the data it collects and services it provides. This site also provides the U.S. census data in downloadable formats.
http://www.fda.gov	The U.S. Food and Drug Administration (FDA) is responsible for protecting the public health by ensuring the safety, efficacy, and security of human and veterinary drugs, biological products, medical devices, the nation's food supply, cosmetics, and products that emit radiation.
http://www.ngo.org	The site serves as the home page for global nongovernmental organizations (NGOs) associated with the United Nations. Its alphabetic listing of NGOs includes organizations concerned with refugees, drug abuse, peace and security, sustainable development, human rights, and ethics and values, among others.
http://www.aspeninstitute.org	The Aspen Institute fosters values-based leadership and encourages individuals to reflect on the ideals and ideas that define a good society. It also provides a venue for discussing and acting on critical issues and produces numerous publications in this domain.
Industry bodies	
http://www.itaa.org	The Information Technology Association of America is a leading industry trade group for information technology companies whose membership accounts for in excess of 90 percent of ICT goods and services sold in North America.

(continued)

Exhibit 5.2 *(continued)*

http://www.nada.org	The National Automobile Dealers Association represents more than 19,700 new car and truck dealers, both domestic and international, with more than 43,000 separate franchises.
http://www.nrf.com	The National Retail Federation is the world's largest retail trade association, with membership that comprises all retail formats and channels of distribution. The federation is a nonprofit 501(c)3 foundation that conducts industry research, develops education and workforce development programs, and promotes retailing as a career destination.

Commercial Providers and Library Search Engines

http://money.cnn.com/	The CNN investor research center of CNN. This site provides information on the U.S. and world financial markets.
http://www.bloomberg.com	Bloomberg provides current and historical market information that is particularly well used by the financial sector. While considerable data is available on the public site, full access requires that one sign up for the professional service.
http://www.standardandpoors.com	Standard & Poor's (S&P) is known as a leader in financial-market intelligence. In addition to being an independent provider of credit ratings, the organization maintains a number of widely followed stock indices and undertakes independent equity and mutual fund research.
http://www.reuters.com	Reuters is a worldwide provider of news and information that is sourced by many professional reporters and used extensively by the global financial markets. Although considerable data is available on the public site, full access requires that one log in to the site.
http://www.hoovers.com	Hoovers has a database of over 32 million international public and private companies and provides enhanced company and industry information and access to financial statement data for many of them.
http://www.emeraldinsight.com	Emerald is one of the world's largest providers of management journals and online support for libraries. Articles are provided in either abstract or as full-text documents. The database includes over 100 full-text journals and reviews from approximately 300 management journals.
http://www.lexisnexis.com	LexisNexis is a pioneer in online information and an excellent source for identifying current events as reported in newspapers and business periodicals. Access to government statistics is also provided, as well as some private statistical tables.

ADVANTAGES AND DISADVANTAGES OF SECONDARY DATA

As with all data collected for research purposes, there are a number of advantages and disadvantages that need to be kept in mind when using secondary data sources. They are summarized in Exhibit 5.3 and discussed in some depth below.

Exhibit 5.3

Advantages and Disadvantages of Secondary Data

Advantages	Disadvantages
• Resource efficiency	• Misalignment of purpose
• Capacity for evaluation	• Access complications
• Potential for comparative analysis	–Cost
–Longitudinal	–Familiarity
–Cross-sectional	–Impact of reporting methods
–Contextual	• Quality concerns
• Avoids respondent fatigue	–Source
• Potential for triangulation	–Data collection methods
• Potential for new insights	–Definitions
	• Age of data

ADVANTAGES OF SECONDARY DATA

Considerable cost, time, and human capital savings can be realized when secondary data is used. **Cost savings** arise because data that have already been collected and compiled into a suitable format present the initial owner with the opportunity to provide it to third parties for considerably less than the original cost. For example, Bloomberg Professional[3] provides robustly compiled risk measures for thousands of U.S. and internationally listed companies. The service is used extensively by a wide range of investment professionals to assess risk and estimate company cost of capital. The large quantities of data and the sophisticated statistical techniques used make it far more cost effective for users to buy the data than to undertake the necessary research themselves. Even when the purchase price of data equals or slightly exceeds the cost of gathering equivalent primary data, time and personnel savings occur when secondary data sources are utilized.

The time and personnel requirements necessary to design and execute a field study can be considerable. Using existing data sources to replace or supplement primary data collection can significantly reduce the length of a research project. Additionally, resource constraints can result in compromises when only primary data is considered. Such compromises can be avoided by using secondary sources, thus leading to an improved research outcome. The Business Research Dashboard gives an example of the type of secondary data available from a typical provider.

■————**Business Research Dashboard**————■
Do Major Life Events Impact Media Consumption Patterns
and Buying Behavior?

The Interactive Advertising Bureau (IAB) is made up of more than 375 leading media and technology companies that are responsible for selling 86 percent of online advertising in the United States. The bureau cooperates with over twenty IAB affiliates worldwide that are independently organized and operated but that are collectively dedicated to the growth of the interactive advertising marketplace and of its share of total marketing spend.

In early 2007, the IAB commissioned Simmons Market Research Bureau to conduct a segmentation study designed to offer new insights regarding the impact of major life events such as marriage, buying a first home, and having a first child on consumers' media consumption patterns and buying behavior. The study found that individuals experiencing major life events at a younger age are greater users of interactive media for research and purchasing and that they display a greater propensity to take risks and enjoy life. They are also heavier consumers of financial and electronic products and relatively more health conscious.

As a business researcher, how could you use this information for a consulting assignment with a financial services company? What other types of secondary information would be helpful in getting a consulting job with a financial services company?

For more information on IAB, go to http://www.iab.net.

Source: IAB, "Lifestages: Understanding Early Life Changers," http://www.iab.net/insights_research/1672/223276, accessed July 2010.

EVALUATING SECONDARY SOURCES

Secondary data sources should be evaluated before they are integrated into a research project. Sometimes the methods used by the original researcher are provided with the secondary data and they can be studied to determine if the collection process is appropriate for the anticipated use of the data. Alternatively, the reputation of the research entity or organization itself can often be relied on as an indication of data quality. For instance, researchers using raw data, indexes, or summary statistics provided by national and international statistical services or by organizations such as the U.S. Federal Reserve and the World Bank generally accept that rigorous collection and verification techniques have been applied throughout. The reputation of these organizations is taken as a signal of data quality.

Several forms of **comparative analysis** may be considered crucial for a particular research project. Comparative analysis involves evaluating the accuracy of secondary data by looking at the same data from multiple sources or by evaluating trends to see if there is any questionable data at a particular time. Secondary data sources offer the possibility of undertaking analyses that would otherwise be impossible or prohibitively expensive. **Longitudinal analysis** pertains to comparing findings across time to identify trends or seasonal patterns. For example, a fashion company wishing to enhance its understanding of consumer purchasing behavior under various psychographic, demographic, and economic conditions would need to supplement its internal sales and CRM data with longitudinal data and time-series indexes generally available from secondary data sources. **Cross-sectional analysis** is used when a researcher wants to compare findings across various clusters or market segments at a particular time to identify points of difference or similarity in performance or response patterns. Secondary data sources in this type of research may be vital for obtaining comparable data for selected competitors. For example, a researcher employed by Tesco PLC, a leading U.K. retailer that recently entered the United States, might use Hoover's™ (www.hoovers.com), a subsidiary of the D&B Group, to source much of the standardized competitor information necessary to undertake a comparative study identifying the sources of value creation for U.S. retail companies.

Researchers need to ensure they are fully aware of the context in which their research is being done. Secondary data sources play an important role in identifying contextual issues relevant to a particular research agenda. Consider a business that is looking to increase its access to capital for investment and growth purposes. Although management may believe listing on a stock exchange is an obvious solution, contextual issues need to be considered. For example, the historical performance of the firm, its market profile, strategy, and short-, medium-, and longer-term financial needs all have a role in determining what exchange it should consider. Secondary data sources can be used to investigate the listing requirements of local and international stock exchanges. But what criteria determine whether a privatized Russian enterprise should select France, the United Kingdom, or the United States for its initial listing? If it selects the United States, should it list on the New York Stock Exchange, the National Association of Security Dealers Automated Quotations (NASDAQ) exchange, the Over-the-Counter Bulletin Board, or should it use Pink Sheets? These are all contextual issues that must be addressed in making the proper decision.

Unlike behavioral tracking or observation techniques, survey research generally requires considerable time and effort from respondents. Researchers need to create an appropriate response environment (structure, length, location, and timing) when conducting survey research as a means of avoiding respondent fatigue and ensuring questionnaires are completed diligently. This concern has historically been addressed in the context of single study research design rather than in terms of the fatigue that occurs when individuals find themselves repeatedly surveyed for similar but varied reasons. The growth of the Internet and the potential it offers for conducting large and sometimes indiscriminate survey research has significantly increased how frequently many of us are approached and asked for our opinions. For example, consider the growth in the number of business school ranking surveys that are conducted by the international press and business magazines like *BusinessWeek* (http://www.businessweek.com/), the *Financial Times* (http://rankings.ft.com/), *U.S. News & World Report* (http://colleges.usnews.rankingsandreviews.com/), and *Forbes* (http://www.forbes.com/), to name a few. Many of these surveys require that questionnaires be completed by the same generation of alumni and corporate sponsors or employers. Researchers should consider using secondary data sources whenever they can reduce the scale and frequency of questionnaire usage without reducing the research value.

Secondary data can be used as an unobtrusive supplement to direct survey research and to corroborate its findings. In other words, the researcher should consider whether archived data can be used to confirm that conclusions drawn from the primary collection method are appropriate. Such an approach triangulates findings established from the primary collection method and confirms the validity of the research. The approach offers particular advantages when primary data collection methods limit the researcher to small samples where extrapolation to a broader population group might be problematic. Secondary sources can also provide qualitative analyses to supplement quantitative techniques used in primary research, or they may present quantitative census or large sample results confirming a smaller but more in-depth qualitative research design.

Reexamination of secondary data and the conclusions extracted from the data presents the researcher with the opportunity to develop **new insights**. Although the initial data collection method undoubtedly focused on gathering data relevant to the initial research objectives and hypotheses, a reexamination and analysis may provide additional insight. Using alternative or more recently established frameworks to examine previously collected data can offer additional perspectives of value for hypothesis generation or confirmation purposes. Excellent examples of new interpretations of historically compiled data can be found in the fields of economics, finance, and medicine. Policy makers regularly review previously collected national statistics on consumption, investment, productivity, trade, and inflation and combine them with interest rates and market price indexes to develop new insights for purposes of setting monetary and fiscal policy. In the medical field, complex data collected to investigate the carcinogenic properties of certain chemical compounds may subsequently be used in research investigating their psychological impact.

DISADVANTAGES OF SECONDARY DATA

Data collected with a particular research agenda in mind is gathered using techniques and approaches specifically designed for that purpose. Consequently, it should meet the requirements for drawing valid and reliable conclusions. Unfortunately, the same cannot always be said of secondary data, and it may therefore be inappropriate for your purposes.

Whenever possible, you should carefully examine the data collection methods when using secondary data sources to ensure that there is not a misalignment of purpose making the data unacceptable. This examination will confirm whether the sampling technique used and questions asked can answer your research questions fully, partially, or not at all. If the secondary source offers only a partial solution, then combining it with primary data may be the preferred solution rather than discarding it entirely.

Sometimes you may find it difficult to use secondary data because of lack of familiarity with the data sources, or because of the way the data is summarized and the conclusions drawn from it are reported. These **access complications** have been significantly reduced with the growth of the Internet and the tendency for greater transparency in primary data collection organizations. But they have not been eliminated. Some providers offer a restricted subset of their data at no cost but require subscription or purchase for their more comprehensive and better validated data sets. The cost of this higher quality data can be high. Bloomberg (http://www.bloomberg.

com/) and Professional and Emerald (www.emeraldinsight.com), an international electronic management research library database, are two examples of secondary data providers that offer some data services free of charge but require subscription payments for full access.

Lack of familiarity with the initial motivation and processes followed when gathering the data also represents a potential weakness in using secondary data. Although many government and private sector collection agencies that provide significant volumes of important secondary data use transparent and well-understood techniques and approaches when reporting their data, this is by no means always the case. The growth of the Internet and the ability to search internationally for multiple sources of data have significantly increased the likelihood of not being familiar with key aspects of the secondary data being reviewed. For example, the format used to present historical data on restaurant habits that you may have extracted from an Internet search may not clearly state who the initial provider was, and it may disguise the fact that a convenience sample was used. If the purpose of your study is to investigate the pattern of usage of suburban restaurants, a convenience sample developed by interviewing young professionals in the central shopping district at lunchtime will underrepresent, if not totally ignore, the influence of parents who work in the home.

Most secondary data you will access comes in the form of published reports. These reports present the research data in a summarized or aggregated form that may not meet the requirements of your research. Definitions of terms and the methods used for aggregation and drawing inferences are well described in most quality reports. But the possibility exists that the included tables and interpretations reflect the biases of the initial researcher rather than an objective interpretation of the gathered evidence. Clearly, the impact of reporting methods on your capacity to interpret and use secondary source reports needs to be considered.

Potential quality concerns with secondary data relate to source, definition of terms and constructs, and the nature of the collection methods. All of these can have a significant impact on the overall reliability and validity of your research.

Data sourced from supranational agencies such as the United Nations (http://www.un.org/); national agencies such as the U.S. Census Bureau (http://www.census.gov/) and the U.K. Office for National Statistics (http://www.statistics.gov.uk/); leading NGOs such as Médecins Sans Frontières (http://www.msf.org/); and major private sector originators and redistributors of data such as Reuters (http://www.reuters.com/) are generally considered reliable and of high quality. Other producers of secondary data, however, may have lesser resources or an institutional agenda that calls into question the quality and completeness of the data they provide. The quality of your secondary data sources should be carefully assessed and not accepted at face value. This assessment can include an additional search to see how often and by whom the data and the data provider are cited. Broad usage of a particular data set or provider by other reputable researchers is an important signal of quality.

Attention needs to be paid to the definitions used for various variables and constructs in the initial research. Even reliable sources of secondary data can produce research of little value if the original definitions and constructs are inappropriate for the current study. For instance, is the service quality construct summarized in a published report defined and measured using the original SERVQUAL construct of Parasuraman, Zeithaml, and Berry (1988),[4] or the SERVPERF construct of Cronin and Taylor (1992)?[5] Whichever approach was used, could it have an impact on your study? These types of questions need to be asked whenever secondary data are being considered as a key component of a particular study.

Finally, the age of the secondary data needs to be considered. No matter how legitimate the original study, the passage of time may have changed how data needs to be gathered to measure constructs or how relationships are defined. The age of the secondary data is also influenced by the time between collection and publication of the summarized results. For example, national census studies are sometimes considered problematic because of the significant lag between successive studies and because of delays in publishing the comprehensive results. Economic trends, demographic and lifestyle changes, and technology evolution must also be considered when thinking about using older secondary data. For example, research undertaken to study patterns associated with university students conducted twenty years ago may be of questionable value because of the development of distance-learning technologies over the past decade and their pervasive use today.

EVALUATING THE QUALITY OF SECONDARY BUSINESS DATA

Secondary business data needs to be rigorously evaluated so that its advantages can be captured and its disadvantages controlled. The process begins with an investigation of the original provider of the data. But whenever possible the evaluation should also include a review of the research design and of the data collection methods that were used. These steps are presented in Exhibit 5.4.

EVALUATING THE SOURCE

A general reputation for ethical and trustworthy behavior increases the likelihood that the secondary data will have been collected using credible methodologies and appropriate expertise. This expertise may be in-house or obtained through contracting with third parties. Whenever it is clear that third parties have been used, they should also be investigated. If the source of the secondary data is considered suspicious, then alternative methods for obtaining the required information should be used in spite of a loss of anticipated cost savings and efficiencies. This critical approach should be taken throughout your appraisal of the secondary data.

EVALUATING THE RESEARCH DESIGN

Once the qualifications of the secondary data provider have been established, particulars of the research design need to be examined. Data is always collected with one or more objective in mind. Appreciating this is important in establishing whether the data are appropriate for an alternative application. The sampling design and measures used in the original research may not be fully applicable to a new study. The value of secondary data is reduced when the definition of the measures used is not consistent

Exhibit 5.4

Evaluating the Quality of Secondary Data

Source of data	Research design	Data collection methods
Reputation	Objective	Sampling
Expertise	Definition of constructs	Respondent intention and response rate
	Examined relationships	Measurement techniques
	Report structure	

with the requirements of the new study. Hypothesized and confirmed relationships presented in published reports also need to be interpreted with the original objective in mind before assuming that these insights are relevant. Relationships examined in the original study need to be considered carefully because a slight change of emphasis can affect the validity of secondary data. For example, a study examining actual buyer behavior in response to certain marketing strategies would find prior research that inferred patterns of behavior from attitudinal responses of limited use.

How the report is written can give additional insight into the appropriateness of the source. Summary tables, frequency diagrams, or report conclusions that use unusual clustering approaches may indicate the initial research was undertaken with a particular political agenda in mind rather than as an unbiased investigation. This can also occur when a study is commissioned inside a commercial organization with the intent of substantiating firmly held management beliefs and justifying a previously decided course of action.

EVALUATING DATA COLLECTION METHODS

Assuming you are satisfied with the quality of the secondary data provider and that the objectives of the initial study make it suitable for your purposes, the final step you need to take to confirm that the data is suitable is to review the data collection methods that were employed. Whenever possible, the sampling frame, response rate, and measurement techniques should all be examined when evaluating secondary data.

Although the sample frame may have been ideally suited for the original study, it may not fully suit new research objectives. To the extent that this is the case, raw data and summary statistics should be translated with caution. For example, an earlier study of private vehicle purchasing behavior undertaken for the sport utility vehicle (SUV) market may have restricted itself to sampling higher-income households. This may make it inappropriate as a secondary source for a subsequent study of five-door hatchbacks that are more targeted toward less-wealthy individuals and families with small children.

The purpose of a particular research project can influence the state of mind of those surveyed. This can have an impact on the response pattern and the response rate. Two studies with different objectives may ask a similar series of questions, but the responses may differ because of the subjects' understanding of the purpose of the study. For example, many readers of this book may have been approached by a student surveyor while traveling on their national railway system. Consider how you might respond to a question concerning the visibility of railway staff on trains if the survey is introduced as a means of investigating convenience and cleanliness versus the response you might give if the survey is introduced as a means of investigating railway security!

Low response rates may result in biased conclusions because nonrespondents may have a different perspective on the topic under investigation. Research into issues considered sensitive, such as abortion, legalization of certain drugs, and immigration are particularly susceptible to this type of bias because those who feel most strongly one way or the other about the issue are more inclined to take the time and effort to complete the research questionnaire or make themselves available for interviews. A good example of this response bias is television and radio studies where the presenter raises a topic and asks people to telephone or e-mail their yes or no response to a particular question.

Correctly measuring topics of interest is extremely important, and the difficulty of doing this when gathering primary data is often compounded if secondary data is also being gathered. For example, research investigating stakeholder awareness among company executives might ideally require a large sample design and the use of questionnaires and interviews. However, doing so might be prohibitively expensive. Consequently, the researcher may consider undertaking a content analysis of secondary data sources, such as company financial statements and published minutes of company meetings, to construct proxies for executive awareness of stakeholders. To the extent that they do not actually measure company executive stakeholder awareness, conclusions drawn from the research may suffer from questionable measurement validity.

Measurement validity is difficult to establish with any degree of certainty, and judgment is often necessary when considering secondary data.[6] Because of this you should investigate the extent to which the approach you intend to take has been used by prior researchers who have experienced similar difficulties.

The potential for measurement bias when using secondary data exists for a number of reasons. They include changing methods of collecting data over time and deliberate distortion as a result of political agendas. Technological development has also significantly changed the methods commonly used to collect household and other data over the past two decades. For example, Internet shopping and the shift away from cash usage have transformed how companies are able to monitor customer spending behavior. This means that longitudinal studies by these organizations need to adjust for the changing way the data is gathered over time. Real-time data collection using electronic capture techniques clearly eliminates the recall bias that existed when purchasing behavior was captured by respondents in diary form at periodic intervals.

Measurement bias can also arise when a technique does not truly measure the topic of interest. For example, inflation data that is computed using a stable basket of goods suffers from this deficiency. Cost-of-living increases for the typical household in a country will be correctly measured only if the basket of goods used to determine the consumer price index represents the actual purchasing preferences of an average household. Considerable effort is required to optimally determine when to change the basket of goods and how to link the prior basket to a new one so as to retain the longitudinal character of the index.

■————**Business Research Dashboard**————■
Online Resource for Business Insights

Looking for an online resource for business insights? Try http://www.allbusiness.com. AllBusiness.com is an online media and e-commerce company designed to serve business professionals. A subsidiary of Dun & Bradstreet, the company is based in San Francisco and has been recognized by publications such as the *Wall Street Journal* and *U.S. News & World Report*. AllBusiness.com offers resources that include how-to articles; business forms, contracts, and agreements; expert advice; blogs; business news; business directory listings; product comparisons; business guides; a business association; and more (http://www.allbusiness.com/2984614-1.html), and its content and services can be accessed through numerous electronic media channels.

Would this be a good source of secondary data for business research? Explain your answer.

Distortion can also happen when data is gathered to substantiate a particular perspective or because respondents find themselves wanting to please the researcher or interviewer. The extent to which measurement bias exists because of a deliberate desire to confirm a particular perspective is often difficult to discover when considering secondary data precisely because the initial intention is to deceive. Consequently, researchers may need to rely on the reputation of the initial researcher or on collaborative evidence obtained through some form of triangulation. Equally deliberate, although less malicious, distortion also occurs when respondents to questionnaires wish to expedite the process or please the researcher. Individual responses to telephone surveys may be biased by the desire of the respondent to terminate the discussion speedily and by the belief that a particular response will achieve that goal. Similarly, surveys conducted about animal welfare, the environment, nuclear power, or the willingness to support marginalized segments of society may result in biased response patterns if not handled with a great deal of care and diligence.

ETHICAL ISSUES RELATED TO THE USE OF SECONDARY DATA

Numerous ethical dilemmas need to be considered when deciding whether to use secondary data. These include attempting to use the data when the specificity of the research question requires that primary data be obtained, insisting on collecting primary data when appropriate secondary data is inexpensive or even free, using secondary data gathered under guarantees of anonymity in a manner that may undermine that initial promise, and using secondary data that has been collected using questionable methods.

Researchers may be considered morally obliged to use secondary data that is appropriate for the research at hand if it can reduce the time and cost of a research project. Equally, they should ensure that data used from other sources is relevant and that it was collected in an appropriate way when drawing inferences or conclusions from it in their own studies.

Commissioned research that does not include a fully specified research design provides an opportunity for increased profitability if compromises are made on the data collection side through an overreliance on secondary data when primary data is really required. Clearly, following this type of strategy is ethically questionable. It is an unwarranted financial expense to the customer if the budget was based on collecting primary data. Moreover, it may represent an unwarranted performance expense for the customer if the conclusions are compromised as a result of the inappropriate use of previously published secondary data.

CONTINUING CASE:
USING SECONDARY DATA WITH SAMOUEL'S RESTAURANT

Phil Samouel's business consultant suggests that secondary data may be useful in better understanding how to run a restaurant. Based on what you have learned about secondary data, that should be true. What kinds of secondary data are likely to be useful? Conduct a search of secondary data sources for material that could be used in the Samouel's restaurant project. Use Google, Yahoo! or other search engines to do so. What key words would you use in the employee research? What key words would you use in the customer research?

Summarize what you found in your search.

SUMMARY

DEFINE THE NATURE AND SCOPE OF SECONDARY BUSINESS DATA

Secondary business data is data originally collected for some other purpose but that has relevance for a subsequent research project. This data, collected from various sources, may appear in summarized form as tables or graphs, or in raw form. Whatever the format, this data may offer significant insight and advantages to the researcher and it should therefore be given serious consideration before deciding to collect primary data.

In addition to a fundamental classification based on its quantitative or qualitative nature, secondary data can be classified by source, format, and type. It may be obtained inside an organization through its standard information gathering processes or as the result of a prior specific piece of research. Alternatively, it can be sourced from external providers, including the originators of the research as well as organizations that consolidate and distribute data collected by others. These syndicated sources can also play a role in categorizing and assuring the quality of the original source.

Increasingly, secondary data is being made available in electronic form. This applies to both written reports and data sets. However, even when provided electronically, data sometimes requires further processing before it can be properly analyzed. Content-analysis techniques that enable researchers to cluster and categorize text have greatly increased the use of written documents as important secondary sources of data.

Finally, secondary data can be classified according to its usefulness for longitudinal and cross-sectional studies. Although data can relate to one-off studies, in other cases, it is longitudinal or cross-sectional in nature. The latter types are important for comparative purposes in many fields of business research.

DISCUSS THE ADVANTAGES AND DISADVANTAGES OF SECONDARY BUSINESS DATA

The advantages to using secondary business data include potential savings in cost, time, and human capital investment. These savings are not limited to the researcher; they also apply to respondents when their use means less respondent fatigue, which can significantly increase response quality. The attractiveness of secondary data as a comparative source of longitudinal, cross-sectional, and contextual analyses, as well as its potential for triangulation, should not lead to uncritical application. Secondary sources should always be evaluated before being used because they can present numerous disadvantages.

Lack of familiarity with the secondary source, including some doubt as to original method and purpose, can result in drawing invalid conclusions. This misalignment can occur even when the original research is of a high caliber. Public reporting methods may, deceitfully or merely for brevity's sake, hide key elements of the original sampling and data collection methods or the research design.

DESCRIBE THE VARIOUS SOURCES OF SECONDARY BUSINESS DATA

The Internet has become increasingly important in helping researchers find suitable business data from secondary sources. The Web and today's culture of transparency and disclosure have greatly increased the volume of data that is provided in conveniently searchable form. Supranational agencies, governments, nonprofit organizations, and companies increasingly provide information and reports via their Web sites. This does not mean that researchers can limit themselves to investigating sources that are just a click away. Sometimes key internal and external data may be held in more traditional archive formats.

Secondary sources include commercial providers that may be considered as primary gatherers or collators of relevant information, such as Reuters, as well as resellers or syndicated providers, such as Emerald, that offer convenient search engines for reports and data sets originally written and compiled by others. Industry bodies that exist primarily to serve their members are also important and interesting sources of secondary data. But researchers must be aware of their potential biases when considering them as sources of secondary data. Triangulation may be important in such cases. Government agencies such as the U.S. Federal Reserve and supranational agencies such as the World Bank and the International Monetary Fund freely offer significant quantities of statistics across a wide range of topics. These agencies tend to provide a lot of detail as to their collection and processing methodologies. This means that researchers can consider more than reputation when assessing the appropriateness of such secondary data for a particular study.

EVALUATE THE VALIDITY, RELIABILITY, AND POTENTIAL BIAS OF DIFFERENT TYPES OF SECONDARY DATA

Evaluating the quality of secondary data involves investigating the credibility of the data source, the robustness of the research design, and the data-collection methods that were employed. In many respects, validating and checking the reliability of secondary sources of data mirror the requirements for a diligent review of a piece of academic research—an assessment needs to be made of its purpose, method, collection, and analysis.

APPRECIATE THE ETHICAL ISSUES THAT MAY BE ASSOCIATED WITH SECONDARY DATA

The ethical issues underlying the use of secondary data may be summarized as inappropriately using these sources when you should not and inappropriately not using them when you should!

Secondary sources should not be used surreptitiously as a way of avoiding research effort. This is particularly important when there is a misalignment of purpose and the sourced data cannot be expected to address the research problem in an unbiased fashion. Data collected in an inappropriate manner which involves misleading respondents about the purpose or compensation or designing sample frames with the intention of influencing the outcome are unethical. Confidentiality and exclusivity should be respected at all times, and researchers should confirm that data gathered and analyzed for a particular client may be used as a secondary source for another one. Secondary data should be employed when it can robustly answer research questions in a more efficient manner and when confidentiality and conflict of interest concerns are not an issue.

ETHICAL DILEMMA

Joshua is part of the research team that is working on the project for Samouel's Greek Cuisine. The deadline for completing his part of the project, which involves collecting secondary data, is tomorrow morning. He has spent several hours searching for information and has found some conflicting information about demographic and economic trends in the neighborhood where Samouel's restaurant is located. Two of the studies are from what appears to be reputable firms that process and sell studies based on government data. The third study, which has findings conflicting with the two nongovernmental studies, is from a government-sponsored Web site. It is late in the afternoon and he wants to finish so he can meet his friends later that evening. What should he do—ignore the information from the government Web site, or stay late and miss going out with his friends?

REVIEW QUESTIONS

1. Discuss the pros and cons of using internal versus external sources of secondary data.

2. Data provided by national statistical offices are often classified as being both time series and cross-sectional in nature. Provide some specific illustrations of your country's central statistical data that meet this definition.
3. Provide two specific ways in which using secondary data can reduce instances of respondent fatigue.
4. Discuss any potential disadvantages of using Web sites of organizations such as the Independent Petroleum Association of America (http://www.ipaa.org/) or Greenpeace (http://www.greenpeace.org/) as secondary data sources for an investigation into sustainable energy.
5. How might the disadvantages discussed in question 4 above be controlled?
6. A suggested advantage of secondary data is that it provides access to insights of experienced researchers. Discuss.
7. A California client of an international market research agency has asked it to conduct primary research into consumer perceptions of the Internet purchase of home improvement products. The U.K. office of the agency has recently completed a similar study for B&Q (a British DIY home improvement company) that confirmed earlier published research undertaken for the Home Depot. Should the market research company do the primary research as requested? If so, should it discuss the findings of the Home Depot study and that its own research has already confirmed its validity?

DISCUSSION AND APPLICATION EXERCISES

1. Discuss three disadvantages of using secondary data when assessing the impact of compensation on employee commitment in a firm.
2. The capacity to quickly and cheaply search for possible sources of secondary data using the Internet means that you often find a huge number of possible sources in mere seconds. What methods would you consider using to confirm the quality of secondary data sources that you finally focus on?
3. What secondary data sources would you consider appropriate for use in an investigation into trends in the consumption of wine and beer in California?
4. A private executive education provider is considering opening a campus in Shanghai.
   a. How would you determine the size of the market and its responsiveness to foreign providers?
   b. In what way do you think secondary data sources can be used to investigate the nature of the competition you are likely to be exposed to (benchmarking)?
   c. Can secondary data be used to determine your pricing strategy, and, if so, how?
5. A researcher who has collected primary data from a sample of eastern European economic refugees in London wishes to confirm the validity of her conclusions concerning the pay discrimination these people experience. What kind of secondary data might she use to triangulate her findings?
6. As part of your investigation into commuter perceptions of the service quality provided by the New York City subway you have found a secondary source

giving satisfaction ratings of the subway. A review of the methodology employed by this prior study reveals that it was carried out by university students at midday. In what way might this secondary data be inappropriate given the purposes of your study?

INTERNET EXERCISES

1. Visit the Bureau of Labor Statistics of the U.S. Department of Labor, at http://www.bls.gov/data. See if you can find monthly time series of private-sector weekly earnings between January 1999 and 2010 and the consumer price index over the same period. Use the data to plot the nominal and real increases in weekly earnings over the eleven-year period. (Nominal increases are based on the actual quoted hourly rates, while real increases are obtained by first adjusting the actual quoted rates by dividing them by the inflation or consumer price index). How might these graphs and data prove useful for a company?

2. Go to the Web site of the European Travel Commission, at http://www.etc-corporate.org/. Extract information that you believe would be useful to an individual running a restaurant like Phil Samouel's Greek Cuisine but one that is located in England. How might tourism seasonality and trends impact on the management of the restaurant?

3. Search the U.S. Food and Drug Administration Web site, at http://www.fda.gov/, for information on genetically modified food and food safety. How might this information prove useful to international pharmaceutical and agri-food industries?

NOTES

1. "Notices," *Federal Register*, 74, 206 (Tuesday, October 27, 2009).

2. Camera & Imaging Products Association (CIPA), "Corrections in Statistical Data of Digital Still Camera (Actual Results for January 2006)" (April 3, 2006), http://www.cipa.jp/english/pdf/revise060403.pdf.

3. Bloomberg Professional, https://software.bloomberg.com/bb/service.

4. A. Parasuraman, V.A. Zeithaml, and L.L. Berry, "SERVQUAL: A Multiple-Item Scale for Measuring Consumer Perceptions of Service Quality," *Journal of Retailing*, 64, 1 (1988), 12–40.

5. J. Cronin and S. Taylor, "Measuring Service Quality: A Re-examination and Extension," *Journal of Marketing*, 56 (July 1992), 5–68.

6. M. Denscombe, *The Good Research Guide for Small-Scale Social Research Projects* (Maidenhead, Berkshire, UK: Open University Press, 1998).

6 | Conceptualization and Research Design

Researchers must make sure managers understand how research leads to improved decision making. One way to do this is to communicate the relationships that will be tested with the research. For many people, a visual representation of the relationships will simplify their understanding and more effectively communicate what is being done in the research. This process is called conceptualization. Once the conceptualization process has been completed, the researcher can more accurately select the appropriate research design. In this chapter we first explain how to develop a conceptual model for hypothesized relationships. Then we clarify the difference between qualitative and quantitative research. Finally, we describe the basic types of research designs and when they are best used.

DEVELOPING A CONCEPTUAL MODEL

An important outcome of your literature review is the development of a conceptual model of the relationships you will be studying. The process of developing a model is called **conceptualization**. Conceptualization involves three tasks: (1) identifying the variables and constructs for your research, (2) specifying hypotheses and relationships, and (3) preparing a diagram (conceptual model) that visually represents the theoretical basis of the relationships you will examine.

IDENTIFYING VARIABLES AND CONSTRUCTS

The process of conceptualization begins with the identification of variables and constructs. **Variables** are the observable and measurable characteristics in a conceptual model. Researchers assign values to variables that enable their measurement. Examples of variables include sales, brand awareness, production level, purchases, search behavior, demographic characteristics, and so on. When characteristics are measured with a single question or statement, we generally refer to them as variables. Variables are linked directly to observable, verifiable facts, such as watching a checkout counter in a store and observing customers' purchasing behavior or an individual's age.

When several questions or statements are used in combination to represent a characteristic or concept, we call this combination a **construct**. A big difference between a variable and a construct is that variables are measured directly. In contrast, constructs can be measured only indirectly by the several indicator variables, often using survey questionnaires. Thus, constructs are concepts that represent a higher level of abstraction than variables and are defined on the basis of theory. Examples of constructs used in business are service quality, brand attitude, organizational commitment, likelihood of searching for a new job, trust, satisfaction, leadership, and so forth. Each of these constructs would be measured indirectly.

As another example of a construct, the following questions all asked together on a questionnaire would be considered a service-quality construct.

> How strongly do you agree or disagree that firms should
> . . . have their customers' best interests at heart?
> . . . be dependable?
> . . . be expected to give customers personal attention?
> . . . keep a promise to do something by a certain time?
> . . . keep accurate records?

In sum, the primary difference between variables and constructs is that variables directly measure a single characteristic or attribute at a lower level of abstraction, whereas constructs consist of several related characteristics and are measured indirectly and characterized by a higher level of abstraction than variables. We discuss constructs in greater detail in Chapter 9.

Types of Variables

When developing a conceptual model, we must think about two types of variables and constructs—independent and dependent. An **independent variable** is a measurable characteristic that influences or explains the dependent variable. A **dependent variable** is the variable you are trying to understand, explain, or predict. For example, employee job satisfaction would be a dependent variable that is explained by two independent variables, compensation level and quality of supervision. The appropriate hypothesis would then be that higher compensation and better supervision (independent variables) explain or predict higher job satisfaction (dependent variable). Constructs, like variables, are also classified as either independent or dependent.

Specifying Hypotheses and Relationships

Researchers often have some preliminary ideas regarding data relationships based on the research objectives. These ideas are derived from previous research, theory, or the current business situation and typically are called hypotheses. In statistics a **hypothesis** is an unproven supposition or proposition that tentatively explains certain facts or phenomena. A hypothesis may also be thought of as an assumption about the nature of a particular situation. Business researchers test hypotheses to verify that any relationships thought to exist among the variables being studied are because of true relationships and not chance. Some examples of hypotheses business researchers might test include:

- Organizational commitment is related to supervision, coworkers, and satisfaction with the work environment.
- Teenage customers will use more wireless minutes per month if we offer package plans with free downloading of music.
- Share prices are positively impacted by favorable performance announcements.
- Customer loyalty is positively related to product quality, pricing, customer service, purchasing convenience, business hours, and so forth.
- Sales are positively related to the amount spent on advertising, the price of the product or service, and the number of sales representatives.
- The announcement of share splits has a positive impact on share price.
- Fund managers are unable to time the market and thereby earn superior portfolio returns.
- Emerging stock markets exhibit long-term overreaction patterns.

How to Develop Hypotheses. Hypotheses are developed prior to data collection and generally emerge from the literature review, research questions, and theory. Researchers use hypotheses to explain and test propositions. For example, Phil Samouel may want to test the proposition that 70 percent of his employees are proud to be working at his restaurant. Similarly, he may wish to compare two or more groups of employees, for example female workers and male workers, and determine if there are important differences between the two groups. He might also want to use the results of his employee survey to test the proposition that part-time employees are more likely to search for another job than are full-time employees.

Two Important Questions in Hypothesis Development. In developing hypotheses, the researcher must always be concerned about whether the hypotheses can actually be tested. To test a hypothesis, you must be able to identify the group you are focusing on and measure the appropriate variables. Thus, in developing hypotheses researchers must constantly ask, What group will be examined with the hypothesis? and, What variables are being tested? For example, if you want to determine whether older workers (defined as fifty years or older) who have younger supervisors (thirty-nine or younger) are more likely to search for another job than are older workers with older supervisors, then you must ask specific questions about these variables on your questionnaire. Moreover, in stating your hypotheses you must be specific about which group you are talking about and which variables. Consider the following hypotheses recently posed by one of the authors' students in a thesis proposal:

1. Older workers who expect more from their younger supervisors will elicit more effective leadership from their younger supervisors.
2. There is a relationship between the younger supervisor's leadership behavior and the expectations of the older worker.

To test these hypotheses, what groups and what variables are involved? Clearly you must have collected data on older workers with a younger supervisor. But do you also have to have data on older workers with older supervisors? In hypothesis 1, to measure the effectiveness of the younger supervisors' leadership do you need data on the leadership behavior of older supervisors as a benchmark to measure younger supervisors' effectiveness? Moreover, what is meant by "will elicit more effective leadership"? How will this variable be measured? Finally, in the second hypothesis what is meant by "the expectations of the older worker" and how will that be measured? Other questions are possible to ensure these hypotheses can be tested, but those here give you an idea of how precise you must be in developing hypotheses.

Correctly stating hypotheses can be difficult. The researcher must be specific about the variables being measured and the groups being questioned. Consider, for example, the following hypothesis.

H: Older workers' (50+) expectations of their immediate supervisor's leadership behavior are positively associated with their immediate supervisor's actual leadership behavior.

With this hypothesis, data must be collected from only one group, older workers (fifty and older). Second, the variables being measured are (1) what older workers expect from their immediate supervisor in terms of leadership and (2) how their immediate supervisor actually behaves as a leader. To test this hypothesis, you must have data that measures leadership expectations and the behavior of immediate supervisors as perceived by older workers. If you devote time to developing good hypotheses, it will ensure that data is collected from the correct group of individuals and that the appropriate questions are asked on the survey.

Null and Alternative Hypotheses. Hypotheses sometimes are stated in the null form. The **null hypothesis** states there is no difference in the group statistics, for example in means, medians, and so forth. A null hypothesis is based on the notion that any change or difference is entirely the result of random error. In our older worker example, the null hypothesis would be:

H_0: There is no difference in the leadership behavior of immediate supervisors of older workers with high leadership expectations versus those with lower leadership expectations.

Statisticians almost always test the null hypothesis. But business researchers often test hypotheses stated in other ways.

Another hypothesis, called the alternative hypothesis, states the opposite of the null hypothesis. The **alternative hypothesis** says that there is a difference between the groups being compared. If the null hypothesis is accepted there is no difference between the groups. But if the null hypothesis is rejected and the alternative hypothesis is accepted, the conclusion is there is a change or difference in behavior, attitudes, or a similar measure of the groups.

Directional and Nondirectional Hypotheses. Hypotheses can be stated as directional or nondirectional. If you use terms like "more than," "less than," "positive" or "negative" in stating the relationship between two groups or two variables, then these hypotheses are directional. An example of a **directional hypothesis** would be:

H: The greater the stress experienced on the job the more likely an employee is to search for another job.

Another way of stating a directional hypothesis is by means of the if-then approach:

H: If employees are given more safety training, then they will have fewer accidents.

Nondirectional hypotheses postulate a difference or relationship but do not indicate a direction for the differences or relationship. That is, we may postulate a significant relationship between two groups or two variables, but we are not able to say whether the relationship is positive or negative. An example of a nondirectional hypothesis would be:

H: There is a relationship between stress experienced on the job and the likelihood an employee will search for another job.

Another example of a nondirectional hypothesis is:

H: There is a relationship between organizational commitment and the likelihood of searching for another job.

Directional and nondirectional hypotheses are both acceptable in business research. The advantage of a directional hypothesis, however, is that you can use a one-tailed statistical test for hypothesis testing instead of a two-tailed test. Indeed, if a two-tailed statistical test is used to test a directional hypothesis, it is quite possible the researcher will conclude a relationship does not exist when in fact one does. This is an important concept to understand since most commercially available statistical software, like SPSS, reports only the results of two-tailed tests.

Hypothesis Testing. **Hypothesis tests** are systematic procedures followed to accept or reject hypotheses about certain patterns or relationships. The proposed connections or relationships need to be tested to conclude whether they are true relationships. Researchers can test hypotheses whether they are doing qualitative or quantitative research. When testing qualitative hypotheses researchers look for alternative explanations or negative (opposing) examples that are not consistent with the patterns being tested. If information is gathered that differs from the proposed relationship, the hypothesis is rejected. When testing quantitative hypotheses researchers collect quantitative data and apply statistical tests.

The variables and constructs measured in business research have relationships that connect them. A **relationship** is a meaningful link believed to exist between two variables or two constructs. For example, lower prices are related to higher sales, bad working conditions are associated with a higher likelihood of searching for a new job, and so on. Typically, relationships are identified as meaningful and deserving of attention based on theory, business experience, or expert judgment. Other examples of relationships we study in business research include:

- Employees are absent from work less often when they have good working conditions.
- Accounts that frequently do not balance should be audited.
- Healthy people exercise more often and eat more nutritious foods.
- Conglomerate firms underperform relative to focused firms with respect to the returns they achieve for shareholders.
- Individuals from diverse backgrounds have greater natural networking ability.
- Dominant firms in mature markets generate greater proportions of free cash flow.

When describing the relationships we typically label some of the variables as independent and others as dependent. The independent variables have arrows coming from them; the dependent variables have arrows pointing to them. If arrows are going to and coming from a variable, then those variables are used as both independent and dependent variables in the same conceptual model.

The logic we use in deciding how to describe the relationships is based on the research hypotheses. Recall that hypotheses are preconceptions regarding the relationships represented in data. Two more examples of hypotheses are:

H: Teenage customers will use more wireless minutes per month if we offer package plans with free downloading of music.
H: Loyalty is positively related to product quality, pricing, customer service, purchasing convenience, business hours, and so forth.

We test hypotheses such as these to enable us first to confirm that a relationship does or does not exist and, second, to help us better understand relationships.

PREPARING A CONCEPTUAL MODEL

In the initial stages of a research project, an important first step is to prepare a diagram that illustrates the research hypotheses and displays the variable relationships that will be examined. Specifically, a **conceptual model** is a diagram connecting variables and constructs based on theory and logic that displays the hypotheses to be tested. Preparing a conceptual model early in the research process enables researchers to organize their thoughts and visually consider the relationships between the variables of interest. Conceptual models are also an efficient means of sharing ideas among researchers working on or reviewing a research project.

There are five basic elements of conceptual models: (1) theoretical constructs, (2) measured variables, (3) unidirectional relationships, (4) bidirectional relationships, and (5) error terms. The **theoretical constructs** are latent, nonmeasured composite or component variables. In the diagram they are typically represented as ovals (ellipses) or circles. The **measured variables** represent the actual observations (raw data) and are referred to as indicator variables. In the diagram measured variables are typically represented as rectangles. The error terms are represented by circles.

The theoretical constructs are connected by either single-headed or double-headed arrows. **Single-headed arrows** indicate unidirectional relationships between two theoretical constructs or between a theoretical construct and its measured variables. In addition, single-headed arrows represent predictive relationships that, with theoretical support, can be interpreted as causal relationships. Double-headed arrows indicate bidirectional relationships and represent correlations or covariances between constructs that are neither predictive nor causal.

There are two other terms associated with conceptual models that will help you to better understand conceptual modeling. First, there is an **inner model** that represents the latent theoretical constructs. The inner model displays the relationships (paths) between the ovals and is referred to as the structural model. These relationships between ovals can be either unidirectional or bidirectional. Second, there is an **outer model** that displays the relationships between the theoretical latent constructs and the indicator variables (rectangles). These relationships between ovals and rectangles are unidirectional and represent predictive relationships. The outer model is typically referred to as the measurement model because it displays the relationships between the indicator variables (actual, observed measurements) and the theoretical constructs.

Two examples of conceptual models are shown in Exhibit 6.1. The top model has two measured variables (ad budget and sales) connected by a single-headed arrow and is an example of a model of a bivariate regression. The measured variables are represented as rectangles, and the arrow indicates that advertising budget is related to or predicts sales. The model at the bottom of the exhibit is more complex and represents a multiple regression model. There are four measured variables, all represented as rectangles. The three measured variables on the left are independent variables, and the single measured variable on the right is a dependent variable. Each independent variable has an arrow that indicates that it is related to or predicts the dependent variable, sales. Thus, the model indicates that sales are predicted by the advertising budget,

Exhibit 6.1   **Conceptual Model of Demographics and Wireless Minutes Usage**

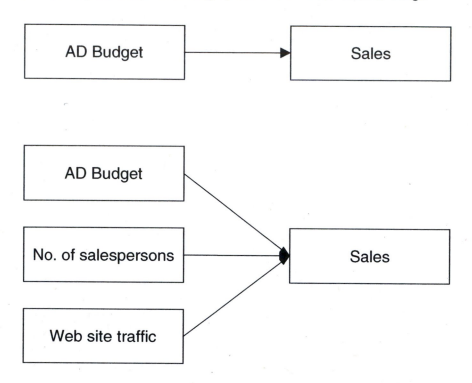

the number of salespeople, and the amount of Web site traffic. All these variables are measured with a single question, and we think of them as individual variables. Also, no signs (+ or –) are shown on the arrows to represent the orientation of relationships between the independent and dependent variables. Therefore, our hypotheses show only that there is a relationship between the variables but not whether the relationship is positive or negative (directional).

The conceptual model in Exhibit 6.2 illustrates a more sophisticated analysis of relationships. There are four variables, shown as ovals. In this situation, we refer to them as constructs because each variable is considered latent and not directly measured. Instead, there are several questions that measure the construct indirectly. The measured variables are not shown in Exhibit 6.2 but are illustrated in Exhibit 6.3. Note that researchers sometimes use the terms "variable" and "construct" interchangeably, but constructs are always measured indirectly by indicator variables.

To understand the model in Exhibit 6.2, the constructs must be defined. First, the construct "technology acceptance climate" means the extent to which employees' ongoing use of information technology is rewarded, supported, and expected in the organization. Although not shown in the model, it is measured indirectly by several questions (measured indicator variables). Second, the construct "shared values" represents the feelings and beliefs that form an organization's culture and provide a basis for individuals to understand the organization's functioning and norms of behavior. Examples of shared values include customer orientation, entrepreneurial values,

Exhibit 6.2 **Technology Implementation Model**

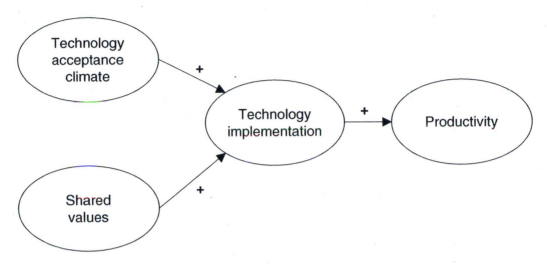

adaptive cultural expectations, and information sharing norms. The shared values construct is also measured by several questions. Third, "technology implementation" refers to how quickly and completely new information technology is integrated into ongoing operations, and "productivity" means higher output per day. The "technology implementation" and "productivity" constructs are both measured by means of several questions as well.

The constructs "technology acceptance climate" and "shared values" are independent constructs in the conceptual model. In contrast, the construct "productivity" is a dependent variable. The construct "technology implementation" is more complicated in the model because it is both a dependent and an independent variable. In other words, it is a dependent variable because it is predicted by two independent variables ("technology acceptance climate" and "shared values"), but it is also an independent variable because it is shown as predicting the construct "productivity."

Three hypotheses are illustrated by the arrows in this conceptual model: (1) technology implementation is positively related to the technology acceptance climate, (2) technology implementation is positively related to the organization's shared values, and (3) productivity is positively related to technology implementation. There is a plus sign by all three arrows, indicating all three relationships are represented as directional and positive.

Note that constructs in all conceptual models are represented in a sequence based on theory, logic, or the researcher's knowledge and experience. The sequence of the constructs is illustrated from left to right, with independent (predictor) constructs on the left and dependent (outcome) variables to the right. That is, constructs to the left are assumed to precede and predict constructs to the right. When there are more than two sets of constructs represented in a conceptual model, constructs on the right are always assumed to be predicted by constructs on the left. Moreover, constructs considered as dependent in a conceptual model are often referred to as **endogenous variables**. Any construct that has an arrow pointing to it is an endogenous variable. Constructs that operate as both independent and dependent variables in a model are also considered endogenous. Finally, constructs that are always only independent variables are generally referred to as **exogenous variables**. Exogenous variables (constructs) only have arrows pointing from them and no arrows pointing to them. In Exhibit 6.2 "technology acceptance climate" and "shared values" are exogenous constructs. In contrast, "technology implementation" and "productivity" are endogenous constructs.

Determining the sequence can be difficult. Sometimes the underlying theory has not been confirmed and scholars disagree on the sequence. For example, some scholars believe job satisfaction precedes and predicts organizational commitment. But other scholars believe organizational commitment precedes and predicts job satisfaction. Theory and logic should always determine the sequence of constructs in a conceptual model, but when the literature is inconsistent or unclear, researchers must use their best judgment to determine the sequence. It is also possible to have alternative, competing models that test a different sequence. But selecting the best sequence among several competing alternatives can be challenging.

The order of the constructs in the conceptual model shown in Exhibit 6.2 is based on the following assumptions. In an organization the climate of acceptance of new technology and the shared values both influence the extent to which new technology is implemented. Thus, implementation of new technology is dependent on and predicted by the climate of acceptance and shared values. The "technology acceptance climate" and "shared values" constructs are referred to as antecedents of technology implementation. In addition, implementation of new technology is expected to lead to higher productivity, so the "technology implementation" construct is an independent variable that predicts productivity, a dependent, or outcome, construct.

When the sequence of the constructs has been decided, then the connecting arrows representing the hypothesized relationships must be drawn. The arrows are inserted pointing to the right, indicating the sequence and that the constructs on the left predict the constructs to the right. The predictive relationships are sometimes referred to as causal links if the theory supports a causal relationship. If it does not support a causal relationship, the link between constructs is considered a correlation. In connecting the constructs with arrows, all the possible connections may not be included. For example, the model in Exhibit 6.2 does not have an arrow between "technology acceptance climate" and "productivity," even though one could be drawn between the two constructs. An arrow is not drawn there because theory does not support such a relationship. Thus, arrows are drawn in conceptual models only where theory or logic supports a hypothesized relationship.

The conceptual model shown in Exhibit 6.3 extends the model in Exhibit 6.2 by adding the measured indicator variables for three of the latent constructs and the error terms. To simplify the example we have included only three of the four constructs and their respective measured variables. The two independent variable constructs each have three measured indicator variables, X_1 to X_3 for "technology acceptance climate" and X_4 to X_6 for "shared values." The dependent variable construct "technology implementation" has two measured indicator variables, Y_1 and Y_2. Most theoretical constructs will be measured by six or seven indicator variables, but our example includes fewer measured variables to make it easier to understand.

Exhibit 6.3   **Conceptual Model with Three Constructs and Eight Measured Variables**

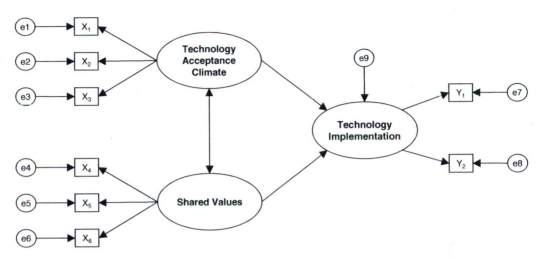

To further explain the concept of measured indicator variables and constructs, consider the conceptual model in Exhibit 6.3. There are three measured variables for the construct "technology acceptance climate," X_1, X_2, and X_3. Using a scale of 1 to 10, with 10 indicating "strongly agree" and 1 indicating "strongly disagree," indicate the extent to which you agree or disagree with the following statements: (a) My organization rewards employees willing to embrace new technology, (b) My organization supports acceptance of new technology by providing the training to learn how to use it, and (c) Employees in my organization are expected to quickly apply new technology. The answers to these three questions represent the measures for this construct. The construct itself is measured indirectly by these three indicator variables and for that reason is referred to as a latent construct. The other constructs in the model could be described in a similar manner. That is, each of the other constructs is measured by two or more indicator variables that are directly measured by responses to specific questions.

There are two other new concepts shown in Exhibit 6.3. First, there is a double-headed arrow between the "technology acceptance climate" and "shared values" constructs. This double-headed arrow indicates the two latent constructs are correlated. The second new concept is the error term. **Error terms** are represented by the circles that are connected to the rectangles (indicator variables). There is an error term for each indicator variable, and in the exhibit they are labeled e1 to e8. Note that there is also an error term (e9) for the latent construct "technology implementation." The e9 error term is included because the two independent variable constructs ("technology acceptance climate" and "shared values") would never be expected to predict 100 percent of the variance in the dependent variable construct "Technology Implementation." Thus, the error terms are included in the conceptual model to represent the amount of variance not explained by the hypothesized relationships between the variables (or constructs). In regression and some other statistical techniques the unexplained variance is referred to as residual variance.

Exhibit 6.4

Guidelines for Preparing a Conceptual Framework

- Clearly identify and define the variables and constructs considered relevant to the study.
- Clearly identify the sources of constructs. If new constructs are developed for the study, explain the process for developing the constructs and report on their validity and reliability.
- If published constructs are used, report on their validity and reliability for both the published study and for your own research.
- Discuss how the variables and constructs are related to one another. That is, which variables are dependent (endogenous) and which are independent (exogenous).
- If possible, hypothesize the nature (positive or negative) of the relationships as well as their direction on the basis of theory, logic, previous research, or researcher judgment.
- Clearly explain why you expect these relationships to exist. Cite theory, business practice, or some other credible source.
- Prepare a conceptual model or framework to clearly illustrate the hypothetical relationships.

When you prepare your literature review you should include a written description of your conceptual model as well as an actual drawing of the model. The section of your literature review that describes your model typically is called a **conceptual framework**. The written description integrates all the information about the problem or opportunity in a logical manner, describes the relationships among the variables, explains the theory underlying these relationships, indicates the nature and direction of the relationships, and includes a conceptual model. Exhibit 6.4 provides guidelines for preparing a good conceptual framework.

Business researchers could collect empirical data using a questionnaire from a cross-section of firms and test the hypotheses described in the technology implementation model. Indeed, in many instances business research involves collecting information to test hypotheses. Sometimes the research design is qualitative and uses, for example, case studies to test hypotheses. Other times it is quantitative and uses surveys to test hypotheses. In the rest of this chapter we describe how to select the appropriate research design to either identify relationships, or, if relationships are already known, such as those depicted in the conceptual models, how they can be examined.

BASIC RESEARCH DESIGNS

A **research design** provides the basic directions or "recipe" for carrying out the project. Following the principle of parsimony, the researcher should choose a design that will (1) provide relevant information on the research questions and hypotheses and (2) complete the job in the most efficient manner. Once the researcher has decided on a study design, the formulation phase of the basic research process is complete.

Recall that the literature review identifies existing themes, trends, and relationships among variables. Relevant theories are described, and a reexamination or restatement of the preliminary research questions may be necessary. Sometimes the theory is well developed and leads to a formal conceptual framework, including hypotheses to be tested. Other times, the theory is limited or perhaps nonexistent. When hypotheses can be developed, the researcher typically relies on a combination of both qualitative and quantitative approaches to conduct the research. If the topic of interest is a new area and the theory is not well established, then the researcher will most likely rely on a qualitative approach.

QUALITATIVE VERSUS QUANTITATIVE APPROACHES

Many students fear business research courses because they are associated in their minds with math and statistics. But business research is a discipline that uses statistics. The statistics are used with quantitative data collected from company financial records, sales reports, questionnaires, and similar sources. **Quantitative data** refers to measurements in which numbers are used directly to represent the characteristics of something. Since they are recorded directly with numbers, they are in a form that lends itself to statistical analysis. Chapter 8 describes data collection methods.

Qualitative data represents descriptions of things made without assigning numbers directly. Qualitative data is generally collected using some type of unstructured interviews or observation. Focus groups and in-depth interviews are frequently applied qualitative research approaches. Rather than being collected by assigning numbers, the data is gathered by recording words, phrases, and sometimes pictures. For example, a researcher asks respondents to describe how they feel about a particular issue, such as globalization, or to narrate a particular event that is important to them. The researcher then analyzes the comments on globalization or the event for potential meaning. Exhibit 6.5 compares qualitative and quantitative approaches.

An important point to remember with qualitative research is that hypotheses are less frequently developed. In qualitative research the concern is that if hypotheses are

Exhibit 6.5

Comparison of Qualitative and Quantitative Approaches

Description	Quantitative approach	Qualitative approach
Purpose	Collect quantitative data More useful for testing Provides summary information on many characteristics Useful in tracking trends	Collect qualitative data More useful for discovering Provides in-depth (deeper understanding) information on a few characteristics Discovers hidden motivations and values
Properties	More structured data collection techniques and objective ratings Higher concern for representativeness Emphasis on achieving reliability and validity of measures used Relatively short interviews (one to twenty minutes) Interviewer questions directly but does not probe deeply Large samples (over fifty) Results relatively objective	More unstructured data collection techniques requiring subjective interpretation Less concern for representativeness Emphasis on the trustworthiness of respondents Relatively long interviews (thirty minutes to many hours) Interviewer actively probes and must be highly skilled Small samples (one to fifty) Results relatively subjective

developed they will influence the direction and outcome of the findings. Consequently, the literature review in qualitative research leads to a conceptual framework that is to be examined. But rather than proposing hypotheses, the researcher is guided by the conceptual framework in collecting data to identify concepts and ideas. Thus, the data collection interacts with the conceptual framework to move the research toward its conclusion. At some point in the data collection the researcher begins identifying the common themes and organizing them into patterns. The patterns are then summarized into a set of findings and ultimately conclusions.

The research components that are strengths of a quantitative study, such as structure and representativeness, are not typical in qualitative research. Qualitative researchers use unstructured interviews as a way of probing deeply into an issue. Since respondents are free to choose their own words, the researcher cannot predict the specific direction of the interview. The lack of structure allows identification of issues that would not be revealed by a structured questionnaire. Respondents who are atypical in some way may be preferred, and individuals highly involved in a situation are especially desirable because new discoveries are often somewhat extreme.

Objectivity is an important component of science. Quantitative approaches provide objectivity in that hypotheses are tested by applying statistical criteria to the measures. Since the respondents provide the numbers, the researcher's opinion does not affect the testing of the hypotheses, although it clearly does influence the design of the study questions. In contrast, qualitative approaches require interpretation. For example, it should be obvious that "cool" clothing usually means the respondent likes it. If clothing is referred to as "funky" or "comfortable," however, does that indicate desirability? These terms represent ambiguity for the researcher when reading an interview transcript. "Comfortable" could mean loose fitting and allowing freedom of movement, or it could mean the clothing makes consumers feel comfortable about their bodies.[1] Thus, the researcher's judgment is used to resolve the ambiguous meaning. Experienced qualitative researchers are good at resolving ambiguities and use approaches minimizing problems with interpretation. Finally, since judgment is involved, the findings of qualitative approaches can be more difficult to replicate, particularly if the methods followed have not been fully documented.

Does subjectivity make qualitative research unscientific and less useful? Absolutely not! Qualitative researchers usually assess inter-rater reliability. **Inter-rater reliability** means that multiple raters will evaluate the same qualitative data point. Reliable data exists when the raters agree on its meaning, and this provides an indication that the results can be replicated. This is not often required, however, because most qualitative research is conducted for purposes other than testing hypotheses. It stops short of the testing phase of the scientific method. Since it is discovery oriented, the criticism of subjectivity isn't relevant. Subjectivity becomes a weakness only when researchers try to generalize based on a single researcher's opinion.

Some researchers assert the superiority of qualitative research over quantitative research or vice versa. However, this view is shortsighted. A comparison of the two approaches suggests that they complement each other quite well. Qualitative techniques are more often part of an exploratory design. Thus, an important alliance between the two occurs when qualitative studies can develop ideas that can be tested with some type of quantitative approach. Effective decision making often requires input from both quantitative and qualitative research approaches.

THREE TYPES OF RESEARCH DESIGNS

Many research designs could be used to study business problems. To simplify your understanding of the different designs, we have grouped them into three types. Researchers generally choose from among an (1) exploratory, (2) descriptive, or (3) causal design. An exploratory research project is useful when the research questions are vague or when there is little theory available to guide the development of hypotheses. At times, decision makers and researchers may find it impossible to formulate a basic statement of the research problem. **Exploratory research** is used to develop a better understanding of a business problem or opportunity. **Descriptive research** describes a situation. Generally, the situation is described by providing measures of an event or activity. Descriptive research often accomplishes this by using descriptive statistics. Typical descriptive statistics include frequency counts (how many), measures of central tendency like the mean, median, or mode, or a measure of dispersion (variation) such as the standard deviation. Statistical tests are used to assess the relationships using descriptive statistics. **Causal research designs** are the most complex. They are designed to test whether one event causes another. For example, does one event x (smoking) cause y (cancer)? The three basic research designs are explained in greater detail below.

1. Exploratory Research

Exploratory research is performed when the researcher has little information. In other words, an exploratory design is appropriate when the researcher knows little about the problem or opportunity. It is meant to discover new relationships, patterns, themes, ideas, and so on. Thus, it is not intended to test specific research hypotheses.

Exploratory research is particularly useful in highly innovative industries. Vodafone, Microsoft, Siemens, Cisco, and Apple, for instance, are companies that place a high priority on discovering new ideas from exploratory research. The research not only identifies new technologies but also aims to discover technologies that address practical business or consumer needs. Siemens, the German-based telecommunications firm, employs over 40,000 people in research-related positions.[2] Their programmatic exploratory research program is aimed at discovering potential matches between needs and technologies one, two, or three decades in advance.

The importance of exploratory research in product innovation has been described by Swaddling and Zobel as follows:[3]

> When conducted well, exploratory research provides a window into consumer perceptions, behaviors, and needs. It enables companies to develop successful new products more consistently. This superior understanding of the consumer leads to effective decision making and recognition of market opportunities, a distinct definition of the business in which your company competes, and a high probability of producing innovative new products that drive extraordinary profits (p. 21).

Exploratory research was instrumental in helping Apple develop the iPod. From exploratory research, Apple learned that consumers wanted a portable device that could play their favorite songs, with high quality, and provide ample storage (over 1,000 songs). Exploratory research later helped Apple develop follow-up products such as the iPod Nano and Shuffle, and later the iPhone. Exploratory research is useful in other situations as well, such as identifying innovative production and management practices, auditing approaches, strategies for diagnosing medical problems, developing messages for political candidates, and incentive compensation systems for managers to increase unit innovativeness.[4]

Exploratory research can take many forms. A literature review can be a useful first step in providing a better understanding of an issue. Literature reviews are conducted by searching through company records, trade and academic journals, as well as other sources where research is reported. But a literature review can also be an early part of a descriptive or causal design. Electronic search engines like Google or Yahoo! have made the search process simpler. Researchers can enter key terms related to the research question and locate dozens, perhaps hundreds of potential sources containing related research.

Exploratory research relies more heavily on qualitative techniques, although it is possible to use quantitative approaches. The following situations are typical of exploratory designs using qualitative approaches:

- Use of focus groups to identify the factors important in purchasing a new wireless telephone
- Use of in-depth interviews to identify what issues are causing employees to be less productive
- Case studies to determine what conditions or events are causing companies in a particular industry to have financial problems
- Digital video recorders or photographs to record the experiences or events impacting the group of individuals being examined
- Experience surveys to collect information from individuals considered to be knowledgeable on the research topic
- Document observation and analysis to examine recorded opinions, reports, news stories, and similar secondary data
- Projective techniques to explore difficult-to-obtain information, such as motivation or justification for supporting a less-popular or extreme viewpoint

2. Descriptive Research

Descriptive research is designed to obtain data that describes the characteristics of the topic of interest in the research. As examples, questions like, Who is likely to be most satisfied? When should we maximize production? How much investment is required? Which brands are most preferred? What advertisements are most effective? How are experience and performance related? and, Why do skiers prefer the Colorado Rockies? can be answered by descriptive research. Hypotheses, derived from theory, usually serve to guide the process and provide a list of what needs to be measured.

Descriptive research designs are usually structured and specifically designed to measure the characteristics described in the research questions.

Studies tracking seasonal trends are good examples of descriptive studies. A company that brews beer and ale can benefit from seasonality information for numerous reasons. For example, beer and ale sales differ during the year, so seasonality information would improve decisions regarding flexible production capacity. Exploratory research might reveal that consumers feel more like drinking beer for certain types of occasions and that they prefer beer with certain foods, such as pizza or spicy food dishes. A research question might ask whether beer and ale consumption is seasonal. Further consideration may suggest hypotheses that lager beer sales are highest in the summer while ale and dark beer sales are highest in the winter. A descriptive study could track monthly sales of each product over a five-year period. The results would describe the seasonality of beer and ale consumption and directly address the hypotheses and research question.

In descriptive studies, data collection usually involves some type of structured process, either observation of data or interviews with structured questions. For example, the research may rely on a questionnaire containing specific items that ask respondents to select from a fixed number of choices, or it may involve an individual's observing (collecting) financial or economic data from government or industry documents. Data may be collected on production processes, stores visited, products or services used, political candidates or issues, employee attitudes, and so on. Bar codes can be scanned to obtain information on the movement of goods, and Web sites can be monitored to determine the number of visits, type of information requested, purchasing data, and so forth. A descriptive study using scanner data from supermarkets would be able to compare weekly sales of Tabasco hot sauce with and without a price promotion. Unlike exploratory studies, descriptive studies are often confirmatory. In other words, they are used to test hypotheses.

Descriptive studies are generally classified as either cross-sectional or longitudinal. We discuss both in the following paragraphs. Descriptive studies provide a snapshot or description of business elements at a given time and are considered **cross-sectional**. Data is collected at a given time and summarized statistically. As an example of a cross-sectional study, data could be collected in North America to examine different attitudes of individuals from various regions about the value of obtaining a university degree. Findings of this study could be examined by cross-sections of the respondents, such as residence location, age, gender, rural versus suburban versus city, and so forth. This is a one-shot or cross-sectional study examining attitudes about the idea of having a university degree. Most surveys fall into this category.

Sample surveys are good examples of cross-sectional studies. Perhaps you have seen a civil engineer or surveyor examining a piece of land where a new freeway will be built. They are surveying the land to describe its characteristics. What are its boundaries and elevation and what are its distinguishing characteristics? Likewise, business researchers survey a sample of business elements in an effort to describe a population's characteristics. When surveying land, the surveyor looks through a transit to take measurements. Generally, business research takes measurements using a questionnaire or some other structured response form. The business elements could be business units, retail stores, hospitals, salespeople, production workers, brands, products, or customers, among others. A distinguishing feature of cross-sectional studies is that the elements are measured only once during the survey process.

Descriptive statistics based on sample measurements describe the population. Typical statistics include rankings (best to worst), frequency counts (how many), cross-classifications (comparisons of frequencies), group means, correlations, and predictions using regression. Each of these is discussed in Chapters 13 and 14.

Since population characteristics are being inferred from a sample, or subset, of the population, cross-sectional descriptive studies must carefully consider how well the selected subset represents the larger population. Researchers assume that the sample characteristics are comparable to those of the population. Error is introduced into the process to the extent that the sample and population are actually different. Thus, for convenience a researcher may use MBA students as a sample in a study of how managers evaluate subordinates. The MBA students would play the role of managers in the study. Error is introduced to the extent that MBA students are indeed different from practicing managers. Sampling approaches and ways to minimize error are discussed in Chapter 7.

Suppose a researcher wanted to study the effect of background music on service quality perceptions. A specific research question deals with whether men and women rate background music and service quality similarly. Questionnaires could be used to measure customers' perceptions of background music and service quality using a seven-point scale. A sample of 800 department store customers could be surveyed over a one-week period. Answers to the questions could then be used to describe the population's beliefs. After data has been collected results would be tabulated and summarized statistically, and conclusions drawn.

Exhibit 6.6 shows the descriptive, cross-sectional results of a study on the use of music in department stores. Several conclusions are possible from these results. For instance, men rate the store's service quality higher, but women like the background music more. Further analysis might show whether or not reactions to the music are related to service quality and perhaps even to buying behavior. Conclusions derived from these results are valid to the extent that the 800 department store shoppers are representative of all department store shoppers. Studies of this type are fairly common and a good example of cross-sectional data.[5]

Longitudinal studies also use a sample to describe business activities. Rather than describing business activities at a single time, however, longitudinal data describes events over time. Longitudinal studies are appropriate when research questions and hypotheses are affected by how things vary over time. Unlike cross-sectional studies, longitudinal studies require data collection from the same sample units at multiple times. The data represents a time series of observations. Longitudinal data enables tracking of business elements so that trends can be observed.

Time is critical to business. Organizations often track employee performance over time. This data enables managers to know how performance varies with time. Similarly, many financial statistics are tracked, including all well-known stock exchange indexes. In most industrialized nations consumer confidence is also tracked. By ana-

Exhibit 6.6

Department Store Shopper Ratings of Background Music and Service Quality

	n	Background music (mean)	Service quality (mean)
Women	500	5.07	6.04
Men	300	4.61	6.22
Overall	800	4.89	6.11

Note: A seven-point scale was used by shoppers to rate the music and service quality, with 1 = "unfavorable" and 7 = "very favorable."

■————**Business Research Dashboard**————■
Is There a Bad Time for a Beer?

Is beer seasonal? Time and beer are related. First, beer shows a fairly strong seasonal trend. Research shows that beer sales are about 15 percent higher during the summer months than they are during the rest of the year. But, it isn't quite that simple. There are spikes in beer sales around the winter holidays. Wintertime beer sales are concentrated around those times. However, time and beer go together in other ways too. Cyclical patterns in demand over long periods of time can be observed. Theoretically, these patterns are due to cyclical patterns in consumer choices of alcoholic beverages. If wine is in, beer is out. And there is even more. Forty percent of all weekly beer sales are sold in the twelve-hour period from 4 P.M. to 10 P.M. Friday and Saturday.

Both beer companies and retailers tie their promotional efforts to these trends. During these times, co-promotions may be used. Research is conducted in a certain area to determine which foods are most often consumed with beer. Promotions might be run on these foods and beer simultaneously to try to make up for the usual drop in sales.

Sources: Becky Kelly, "Beer for All Seasons," *National Petroleum News*, 91 (August 1999), 34–36; Wikipedia, "List of Countries by Beer Consumption per Capita," http://en.wikipedia.org/wiki/List_of_countries_by_beer_consumption_per_capita; Brewers of Europe, *The Benefits of Moderate Beer Consumption*, 3rd ed. (2004), http://www.brewersofeurope.org/docs/publications/pdf-Mei04.pdf, accessed December 2009.

---

lyzing these two trends together, we can see how closely the two indexes correspond. Is this information useful for making investment decisions? Product sales are usually tracked since many products experience seasonal demand, meaning consumption is not constant through time. The Business Research Dashboard illustrates seasonality in beer, wine, and alcohol consumption.

Longitudinal studies sometimes use a panel for collecting data. A **panel** is a fixed sample established for the purpose of collecting data over time. Although panels can include any business element as a unit, they are generally made up of human elements. People in such a panel agree to have repeated measurements taken over an extended period of time. For example, television ratings are derived from a panel of viewers who agree to have their program selection automatically monitored. Monitoring companies provide each panel member a meter that is connected to their television. The

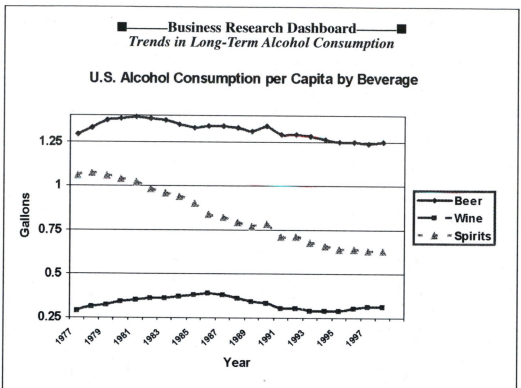

■————Business Research Dashboard————■
Trends in Long-Term Alcohol Consumption

U.S. Alcohol Consumption per Capita by Beverage

This chart tracks how much alcohol the average American consumes each year. To read this chart, keep in mind that each beverage is only partially alcoholic. A typical wine, for example, is 10 to 13 percent alcohol, spirits (whiskey) are 40 to 50 percent alcohol, and beer is 4 to 6 percent alcohol. The chart shows a downturn in spirits consumption over the time period beginning in 1977. Beer consumption also shows a slight decrease, although the average American still consumed 1.25 gallons of alcohol by beer in 1998, which equates to 25 gallons per year. Alcohol consumption via wine displays a peak during the mid-1980s and perhaps the start of an upward trend toward the end of the 1990s. This data might be useful to beverage companies in identifying competitive and market pressures that affect sales and operations.

meter electronically records which channels are being watched at what times of the day and on what days of the week. Some electronic meters include a heat sensor to determine whether the room the television is located in has humans or the family pet! Each panel member also records their television watching habits in a diary. The diary is used to record demographics and other personal details about the household.

Panel surveys collect data from the same group of respondents over a period of time. A large pool of panel members is recruited, and when they are involved in a survey they record their responses in a diary. Information on panel members, such as demographic and household characteristics, is collected and used to determine which individuals will be used for a particular survey. Panels can represent any type of group, from consumer groups to business groups to those including doctors, lawyers, CEOs, and so forth. One online example is a panel of children ages six to fourteen that can be viewed at http://www.kidzeyes.com. Typically, the research company maintaining the panel will randomly select individuals as a representative sample to participate in a particular survey. Sometimes panel members are asked the same questions repeatedly over time, which is called a longitudinal panel study. Other times, the questions are asked only once. Traditional methods of data collection have been by mail, telephone, personal interviews, and fax. But electronic data collection is rapidly increasing for panel surveys. Also, panel surveys can be either self-completion or interviewer assisted. An advantage of panel data is response rates are fast and substantially higher than with other methods of data collection. The Business Research Dashboard tells more about the emergence of electronic panel surveys.

■————Business Research Dashboard————■
Decision Analyst, Inc. Enters Internet Panel Sector in a Big Way!

Decision Analyst, Inc. is a leader in using technology to collect data. President Jerry Thomas believes the future of marketing research belongs to the Internet. In the United States almost 80 percent of adults currently have access to the Internet at home or at work. Moreover, Internet users represent over 75 percent of total U.S. purchasing power and are becoming representative of the U.S. population. Other countries or regions, such as the United Kingdom, Germany, France, the Netherlands, Australia, and Scandinavia, exhibit similar trends of Internet access and usage.

  As a global leader in Internet-based research, Decision Analyst has conducted hundreds of online surveys via their worldwide online consumer opinion panels of more than 3.5 million consumers in the United States, Canada, Europe, Latin America, and Asia, as well as via their specialty panels of technology professionals, physicians, executives, and contractors. Based on its own experiences as well as observations from other professionals, Decision Analyst believes Internet-based surveys provide higher-quality data and are faster and less costly than telephone surveys. For more information on this innovative company, visit its Website, at http://www.decisionanalyst.com/Index.dai.

---

3. Causal Research

Causal research tests whether one event causes another. Does x cause y? More precisely, a causal relationship means that a change in one event brings about a corresponding change in another event. **Causality** means a change in x (the cause) makes a change in y (the effect) occur. There are four conditions researchers look for in testing cause-and-effect relationships:[6]

1. Time sequence—the cause must occur before the effect.
2. Covariance—a change in the cause is associated with a change in the effect. In other words, the two variables are related to each other.
3. Nonspurious association—the relationship is true and not due to something else that just happens to affect both the cause and effect. This requires that other potential causes be controlled or eliminated.
4. Theoretical support—a logical explanation exists for why the cause and effect relationship exists.

■————**Business Research Dashboard**————■
Do Mobile Phone Users Want Advertisements?

The mobile phone video download market is expected to increase by 1000 percent by 2012. Some consumers prefer free downloads supported by advertisements, while others prefer to pay a small monthly fee for commercial-free programs. The big appeal of mobile phone advertising is being able to communicate with the youth market. Most of this segment spends little time reading or viewing traditional mediums like television, newspapers, and magazines. The medium appears particularly good for products like music and movies, which the youth market consumes a lot of. For example, Maiden Group, PLC, an advertising company based in the United Kingdom, promoted a new album by rock band Coldplay using thirty-second spots featuring interviews with musicians and clips from their music videos. To ensure a higher quality sound, the clips were adjusted to better match mobile phone technology. The clips were used in six London train stations, and large video advertising screens told mobile phone users to switch on their Bluetooth phones to receive a message. The album became a number one hit in the United Kingdom, and the agency plans to use the approach with other promotions for this segment. Similarly, in Plaça Catalunya, in Barcelona, Spain, Nike installed a huge outdoor advertisement featuring tennis player Rafael Nadal and powered with Bluetooth technology. By using their Bluetooth mobile phone connection, users could download the new Nike Pro television spot and an exclusive Nadal screensaver.

How do you feel about mobile phone advertising? What research design would you use to determine consumers' reactions to mobile phone advertising?

Sources: Enid Burns, "Users Prefer Ad-Supported Video," *ClickZ*, January 11, 2006, http://www. clickz.com/3576816; Enid Burns, "Mobile Video Market Set for Growth," *ClickZ*, March 28, 2006, http://www.clickz.com/3579236; "Wireless Phone Advertising Has Promise," In-Stat press release, September 14, 2005, http://www.instat.com/press.asp?ID=1441&sku=IN0502096MCM; Paul Korzeniowski, "Cell Phones Emerge as New Advertising Medium," *TechNewsWorld*, November 16, 2005, http://www.technewsworld.com/story/46630.html?wlc=1268166256; http://www.marketingdirecto. com/noticias/noticia.php?idnoticia=16532 (accessed November 2009).

The following example illustrates these four conditions. Suppose a researcher is testing whether a change in compensation systems causes a change in employee turnover. First, the time sequence condition means the researcher must study changes in turnover occurring after the compensation system has been altered. Since a change cannot affect what has happened in the past, it is illogical to suspect that a change in the compensation plan announced and implemented in July 2010 caused employees to quit their jobs in December 2009.

Second, the researcher examines whether a change in compensation is systematically related to employee turnover rates. This is done by comparing turnover rates before and after a change.

Third, even if a relationship is observed, is there something else going on at the same time that could explain any observed changes? For example, what if a competing firm had opened a new facility at the same time the data was collected? Would any changes in turnover have been caused only by the compensation system changes, or could they have been caused by the increased demand for labor brought about by the competition?

Fourth, a theoretical explanation is needed. A change in compensation may affect how workers feel about their jobs, which will affect whether they continue working for the company. Causality can be established to the extent that these conditions are met.

Decision makers are helped by known cause-and-effect relationships. Knowledge enables them to predict what will happen if they effect a change. Causality is a powerful concept, and causal designs thus require precise execution. Moreover, they can be complex and expensive, and often take a long time from planning to execution.

USING SEVERAL RESEARCH DESIGNS

Researchers often use more than one research design in a single project. It is common to collect secondary data to help decide if primary data needs to be gathered. Similarly, we often conduct exploratory research using qualitative approaches before moving on to quantitative research using descriptive designs. For example, Kaiser Permanente (www.kaiserpermanente.org) may want to relocate its health clinics to better serve users. But it may not know how patients decide to use a particular clinic or what factors to consider. To learn of these factors it may first make use of focus groups and follow this exploratory research with descriptive research to determine which findings are valid for the overall population of clinic users.

Selecting the right research design depends on the research questions and objectives. If a research question involves primarily discovery or clarification of an issue, an exploratory design is best. Research questions emphasizing the description of a quantity, the relative amounts of a variable, or the extent to which some variables are related probably call for a descriptive design. On the other hand, exploratory research may be used to help design a questionnaire for a descriptive research project. Finally, if a research question focuses on cause and effect, then a causal design with an experiment is appropriate. The Business Research Dashboard addresses selecting the best research design.

■————Business Research Dashboard————■
How Can Europe Keep Older Workers Employed Longer?

The European Commission has gone on record urging the European Union to make better use of the potential of its older workers. Increased life expectancy means that people have more opportunities to fulfill their potentials over a longer life span, and their employment will be a key factor in maintaining living standards. The European Commission says that the number of workers between the ages of twenty and twenty-nine will fall by 11 million, or 20 percent, during the period 1995 to 2015, while the number of people between fifty and sixty-four will increase by 16.5 million, or more than 25 percent. Over the next twenty years the population above the standard retirement age, sixty-five years, will increase by 17 million. Companies are going to have to learn how to manage older workers, because there are going to be a lot more of them.

(continued)

Summits in Stockholm and Barcelona in 2001 and 2002 adopted a target of 50 percent for the employment rate of individuals in the fifty-five to sixty-four age group. But progress toward achieving that target has been disappointing, and employment for this age group remains at about 40 percent. A commission report has suggested the following conditions will reinforce the employment of older workers:

- Appropriate financial incentives
- Continuing access to training
- Good health and safety conditions at work
- Flexible forms of work organization
- Effective labor market policies
- Improved quality of work

What kind of research design should be utilized to determine how Europe can make better use of it older workers?

Sources: http://europa.eu.int/comm/employment_social/news/2004/mar/ip_04_295_en.html; Steve Zwick, "Not Over the Hill Yet!" *Time Europe*, 156, 7 (August 14, 2000), http://www.time.com/time/europe/magazine/2000/0814/wrinklies.html; Sara E. Rix, "Rethinking the Role of Older Workers: Promoting Older Worker Employment in Europe and Japan," AARP Issue Brief No. 77, http://assets.aarp.org/rgcenter/econ/ib77_workers.pdf; "Europe Needs to Make Better Use of Its Older Workers," press release, Sheila Pantry Associates, Ltd., March 2004, http://www.sheilapantry.com/oshworld/news/2004/200403.html, accessed November 2009.

CONTINUING CASE: SAMOUEL'S GREEK CUISINE

A business consultant with experience in the restaurant industry was hired to assist Phil and his brother. After an initial consultation, the business consultant recommended a comprehensive assessment of the restaurant. The assessment would focus on three areas. The first area was the actual operations of the restaurant, and the proposed variables to be investigated in this first project included:

- prices
- menu items
- interior decorations and atmosphere
- customer counts at lunch and dinner
- average amount spent per customer

The second area of study involved better understanding Phil's employees. To do so, the consultant recommended a research project to obtain information regarding the work environment at the restaurant and how employees felt about working there. Variables to be examined on the employee project included:

- relationship with supervisor
- relationship with coworkers
- compensation

- training
- job satisfaction
- classification characteristics for employees

The third area focused on learning more about Samouel's and Gino's customers. Variables to be examined on the customer project included:

- food quality
- customer contact employees
- pricing
- atmosphere
- dining out habits
- customer characteristics

Results from examining these three areas are to be used to prepare a business plan to compete with Gino's Italian Ristorante.

1. Do the three research projects proposed by the consultant include all the areas that need to be researched? If not, which others need to be studied?
2. Is there other information that needs to be collected in the project on restaurant operations?
3. Should other variables be examined in the employee and customer projects? If yes, what specifically are these variables?
4. What kind of research design would be most appropriate for the three projects, exploratory, descriptive, causal, or more than one type of research design? Justify your choice.

SUMMARY

UNDERSTAND THE ROLE OF CONCEPTUALIZATION IN RESEARCH

An important outcome of your literature review is the development of a conceptual model of the relationships you will be studying. The process of developing a model is called conceptualization. Conceptualization involves three tasks: (1) identifying the variables and constructs for your research, (2) specifying the hypotheses and relationships, and (3) preparing a diagram (conceptual model) that visually represents the theoretical basis of the relationships you will examine.

Researchers often have some preliminary ideas regarding data relationships based on the research objectives. These ideas are derived from previous research, theory, or the current business situation and are typically called hypotheses. In statistics a hypothesis is an unproven supposition or proposition that tentatively explains certain facts or phenomena. A hypothesis may also be thought of as an assumption about the nature of a particular situation. Business researchers test hypotheses to verify that any relationships found in the variables being studied are true relationships and not the result of chance.

CLARIFY HOW TO DEVELOP AND TEST HYPOTHESES

Researchers can test hypotheses whether they are doing qualitative or quantitative research. When testing qualitative hypotheses researchers look for alternative explanations or negative (opposing) examples that are not consistent with the patterns being tested. If information is gathered that differs from the proposed relationship, the hypothesis is rejected. When testing quantitative hypotheses researchers collect quantitative data and apply statistical tests. Researchers often develop conceptual models to visually communicate their hypotheses and the relationships between variables. The models visually represent a conceptual framework for the research. Research reports include a written description of the conceptual framework that integrates information about the problem or opportunity in a logical manner, describes the relationships among the variables, explains the theory underlying these relationships, and indicates the nature and direction of the relationships.

DESCRIBE THE THREE BASIC BUSINESS RESEARCH DESIGNS

A research design is selected based on the scientific method. If the researcher knows little about the topic of interest, then an exploratory design is the best approach. Exploratory designs are discovery oriented. Descriptive research is designed to obtain data that describes the characteristics of the topic of interest. If a researcher wants to develop frequencies of certain variables or describe basic relationships, a descriptive design is probably appropriate. If the researcher is interested in testing whether one variable causes another, then a causal design should be used.

EXPLAIN THE DIFFERENCE BETWEEN CROSS-SECTIONAL AND LONGITUDINAL STUDIES

Descriptive studies are generally classified as either cross-sectional or longitudinal. Descriptive studies providing a snapshot or description of business elements at a given time are cross-sectional. Cross-sectional and longitudinal studies both use a sample to describe business activities. Whereas cross-sectional studies describe business activities at a single time, longitudinal studies describe events over time. Longitudinal studies are therefore appropriate when research questions and hypotheses are concerned with how things vary over time.

REVIEW QUESTIONS

1. What is a conceptual framework?
2. What is the difference between a null and an alternative hypothesis?
3. What are the major differences between the three types of research designs?
4. How does a researcher select the best design?
5. Under what circumstances can more than one design be used in the same research project?

DISCUSSION AND APPLICATION ACTIVITIES

1. Write two hypotheses for a research project on how to motivate employees in an organization. Be sure the hypotheses can actually be tested by making sure you clarify the group that will be interviewed and the variables to be measured.
2. You are a regional manager for twenty retail stores. Your monthly reports indicate a large number of employees are quitting in five of your stores but very few in the other fifteen stores. What kind of research design would be best to identify the problem and potential solutions to reduce the loss of employees in the five stores?

INTERNET EXERCISES

1. Go to http://www.socialresearchmethods.net/kb/desdes.htm and scroll down to the section on "Minimizing Threats to Validity." Prepare a summary report on how to improve validity of research designs.
2. Go to http://www.greenfield-ciaosurveys.com/html/home.htm. What can you learn from this Web site? How can this Web site help business researchers?
3. Go to http://us.lightspeedpanel.com/US/public/index.us. What does this company do with its Web site? Take the poll on the Web site and prepare a report explaining what you learned about business research.

NOTES

1. John Teresko, "Research Renaissance," *Industry Week*, 246 (June 9, 1997), 139–150.
2. Ibid.
3. Jeffrey D. Swaddling and Mark W. Zobel, "Beating the Odds," *Marketing Management*, 4 (Spring/Winter 1996), 20–34.
4. Robert Holthausen and David F. Larcker, "Business Unit Innovation and the Structure of Executive Compensation," *Journal of Accounting and Economics*, 19 (May 1995), 279–304.
5. For a review of similar studies, see Jean-Charles Chebat, Claire Gélinas-Chebat, and Dominique Vaillant, "Environmental Background Music and In-Store Selling," *Journal of Business Research,* 54 (November 2001): 115–124.
6. Shelby D. Hunt, *Marketing Theory: The Philosophy of Marketing Science* (Homewood, IL: Irwin, 1983); Shelby Hunt, *Modern Marketing Theory* (Cincinnati, OH: South-Western, 1991).

Part III

Sampling and Data Collection

7 | Sampling Approaches and Considerations

LEARNING OUTCOMES

1. Understand the key principles of sampling in business research
2. Appreciate the difference between the target population and the sampling frame
3. Recognize the difference between probability and nonprobability sampling procedures
4. Describe different sampling methods commonly used by business researchers
5. Determine the appropriate sample size for various situations encountered in practice

Data is essential for business research irrespective of whether an investigation is quantitative or qualitative in nature. The data can be obtained in a number of ways. Ideally the researcher would like to collect data from all members of a population under investigation. This is known as a **census**. But in most situations this is not feasible. Therefore a sample of the population is drawn.

A **sample** is a relatively small subset of the population. It is drawn using either probability or nonprobability procedures. Whether a probability or nonprobability approach is used, careful consideration of sampling design issues is necessary in selecting the sample.

Probability sampling is typically used in quantitative research. This involves a selection of a representative sample from the population using a random procedure to ensure objectivity in selecting the sample. The findings from the sample data can then be generalized to the population with a specified degree of accuracy.

Nonprobability sampling is typically used in qualitative research. Judgment is used to select the sample in qualitative research. Findings from the sample can be used to describe, discover, and develop theory. While the findings can be used to generalize to the population, it cannot be done with a specified degree of accuracy.

Sample size is an important consideration in both quantitative and qualitative research. For example, to generalize to the population a sufficiently large sample is required. In contrast, when using a qualitative approach to develop theory on organizational behavior a small number of cases may be sufficient.

In this chapter we discuss the basics of sampling. This includes what sampling is, the different probability and nonprobability sample designs, and the determination of sample size. Examples are given to illustrate the use of sampling designs in practice.

SAMPLING

Sampling design is part of the basic business research process. The sampling design process involves answering the following questions: (1) Should a sample or a census be used? (2) If a sample, then which sampling approach is best? and (3) How large a sample is necessary? In answering these questions, the researcher must always consider ways to minimize error that might occur in the sampling process.

Business research involves collecting information to improve decision making. Collecting information involves contacting people who are knowledgeable about a particular topic. We refer to the group of knowledgeable people as a **population** or **universe**. A population is thus the total of all the **elements** that share a common set of characteristics. The elements in a population can be people, supermarkets, churches, hospitals, and so on. But all the elements must share a set of common characteristics. A census investigates all the elements in the population. In contrast, a sample investigates a small subset of the population to derive conclusions about the characteristics of the population.

While it may be possible to conduct a complete census of the population, business researchers seldom do. Contacting the entire population would generally be costly and time-consuming. It is often difficult if not impossible to locate all the elements (people, objects, businesses, etc.). Also, use of the elements may destroy them. For example, quality control tests of products such as drugs, chemicals, light bulbs, and others always use sampling because the testing destroys the product.

Properly selected samples provide information that is sufficiently accurate to be used in business decision making. In probability sampling, business researchers are able at a minimum to calculate the error associated with a particular sampling design and can make decisions with this knowledge in hand. In nonprobability sampling, researchers are not able to calculate the error but have made informed judgments in an effort to obtain usable sample information.

In the case study in this book, Phil Samouel had to make sampling decisions for his survey of customers. Before conducting the survey, Phil had to define his research problem. His Greek restaurant is reasonably successful but not as successful as he initially expected. Gino's Italian Ristorante, his major competitor, is doing much better in attracting and retaining customers. Phil would like to know why. To fully understand this situation, he must know both customer and employee perceptions. He decided to conduct a survey of customers of both restaurants, as well as a survey of his employees. The customer survey consisted of exit interviews, and the employee survey involved completing interviews with as many employees as possible within a specified period.

Phil Samouel concluded that taking a census by collecting information from every element (individual) in the target population would be impossible. In the case of the customer survey, it would have required getting information from all potential restaurant customers in New York City. But since New York City has a population of over 8 million people, a census was not realistic. A census is feasible if the population is small and relatively easy to contact in a short time. For example, many business-to-business populations are small (e.g., CEOs of motor companies or agents for financial services companies). But in consumer studies, in most instances the population is large and some form of sampling is necessary.

A sample must be **representative** of the population from which it is drawn. In other words, the sample should mirror characteristics of the population, thereby minimizing the error associated with sampling. Use of an appropriate sampling design can achieve this objective.

THE SAMPLING PROCESS

Representative samples are generally obtained by following a set of well-defined procedures:

1. Defining the target population
2. Choosing the sampling frame
3. Selecting the sampling method
4. Determining the sample size
5. Implementing the sampling plan

We discuss each of these steps in the following paragraphs.

Business researchers must assist their clients in making decisions at each of these steps. But a lot of help is available from companies that specialize in working with researchers to obtain a representative sample. One of the most well known sampling vendors is described in the Business Research Dashboard.

DEFINING THE TARGET POPULATION

The research objectives and scope of the study are critical in defining the target population. The **target population** is the complete group of objects or elements relevant to the research project. They are relevant because they possess the information the research project is designed to collect. Other practical factors may influence the definition of the target population. They include knowledge of the topic of interest, access to elements (individuals, companies, etc.), availability of elements, and time frame. Elements or objects available for selection during the sampling process are known as the **sampling unit**. Sampling units can be people, households, businesses, or any logical unit relevant to the study's objective. When the sampling plan is executed, sampling units are drawn from the target population to use in making estimates of

---

■————**Business Research Dashboard**————■
Survey Sampling Goes Online

For over thirty years, Survey Sampling International (SSI) has provided business researchers, marketers, pollsters, and survey organizations with samples. Realizing the research possibilities available through the Internet, SSI now utilizes Web surveys as well as the more traditional methods of contacting respondents, such as telephone, mail, or personal interviews. To successfully conduct Web surveys, SSI has learned that many factors, including hardware, software, questionnaire design, and appropriate sampling have to be taken into consideration. With this in mind, SSI has filled the need for e-mail samples (eSamples) with two types of eSampling services, SurveySpot and SSI LITe eSamples (low incidence targeted samples).

SSI's SurveySpot panel provides researchers with access to a multisourced Internet panel of people interested in participating in online research. Because SurveySpot records come from many sources, including banner ads, online recruitment methods, and RDD (random digit dialing) telephone recruitment, this service can deliver higher response rates than can be obtained using most other sources. SurveySpot panelists can be targeted by education, ethnic group, gender, income, occupation, and race, and family members living in the same household can be targeted by age and gender.

SSI LITe eSamples are designed to allow researchers to conduct directional research, particularly when low-incidence segments of the population are being targeted. Panelists can be targeted by hundreds of lifestyle categories, including advertising, education, family, health, hobbies, the Internet, and travel.

Both SurveySpot and SSI LITe records come from many sources, and panelists are recruited through a variety of permission-based techniques. Files are created from self-reported, respondent-specific information, which gives researchers the advantage of reaching the exact targets they are after. Further, since the panelists have agreed to being contacted by e-mail concerning specific areas of interest, they are never spammed when receiving an eSample survey invitation.

The process of SSI's eSampling is simple. When a researcher secures SSI services, SSI invites panelists, selected according to prequalifying requirements, via e-mail to participate in a survey located on the researcher's Web site. SSI does not collect the data since the company works in a noncompete position in the marketing research process. All data is collected at the researcher's own Web site. SSI can handle the infrastructure, servers, hardware, software, and timing of the study. SSI is also equipped to handle random selection of prizewinners and administration of monetary rewards.

With the addition of Web surveys, SSI is continuing its mission of providing quality samples for research projects. Through eSamples, SSI offers researchers a low cost per completed interview with national and international samples targeted by demographics, lifestyles, and topics of interest.

---

population characteristics. Exhibit 7.1 defines a target population for a survey of employees of a bank who participate in an incentive plan.

CHOOSING THE SAMPLING FRAME

The sampling frame provides a working definition of the target population. A **sampling frame** is a comprehensive list of the elements from which the sample is drawn. Examples of sampling frames are a Yellow Pages listing of restaurants, a telephone

Exhibit 7.1

Target Population for Employees with Incentive Pay

Element	Employees with incentive pay
Sampling unit	Customer service representatives and branch managers
Extent	All branch locations in the Los Angeles, California, market
Time	March 2011

directory listing of individuals, a company's internal database listing its employees or customers, electronic directories available on a hard drive or the Internet, and even university registration lists. A sampling frame is thus as complete a list as possible of all the elements in the population from which the sample is drawn.

Ideally, a sampling frame is an accurate, complete listing of all the elements in the population targeted by the research. In reality, a sampling frame is often flawed in a number of ways:

- It may not be up-to-date.
- It may include elements that do not belong to the target population.
- It may not include elements that do belong to the target population.
- It may have been compiled from multiple lists and contain duplicate elements as a result of the manner in which the list was constructed.

Before drawing a sample from the sampling frame list, the researcher must therefore confirm the list's accuracy irrespective of its origin. This will be discussed further in a later section dealing with sampling design issues.

SELECTING THE SAMPLING METHOD

Selection of the sampling method to use in a study depends on a number of related theoretical and practical issues. They include considering the nature of the study, the objectives of the study, and the time and budget available. The Business Research Dashboard illustrates how the Internet is impacting sampling.

Traditional sampling methods can be divided into two broad categories: probability and nonprobability. Probability methods are based on the premise that each element of the target population has a known, but not necessarily equal, probability of being selected in a sample. In **probability sampling**, sampling elements are selected randomly and the probability of being selected is determined ahead of time by the researcher. If done properly, probability sampling ensures that the sample is representative.

In **nonprobability sampling**, the inclusion or exclusion of elements in a sample is left to the discretion of the researcher. In other words, not every element of the target population has a chance of being selected into the sample. Despite this, a skillful selection process should result in a reasonably "representative" sample. By "representative" we mean it represents the researcher's judgment of what she or he wants but is not based on chance. The most common types of sampling methods are shown in Exhibit 7.2.

Exhibit 7.2

Types of Sampling Methods

Probability	Nonprobability
Simple random	Convenience
Systematic	Judgment
Stratified	Snowball/Referral
Cluster	Quota
Multistage	

■————**Business Research Dashboard**————■
Online Sampling Methods

The big switch to online advertising as part of the media mix continues across the United States. Research from the Interactive Advertising Bureau (IAB) indicates that U.S. online advertising spending will exceed $35 billion in 2012. IAB members are responsible for selling 86 percent of online advertising in the United States. Online advertising spending will continue to grow as more and more firms discover the power of Internet advertising as both a branding and direct marketing medium. It is not surprising that businesses are examining online advertising with audiences across the United States spending 25 percent or more of their media time online. But online marketing involves more than advertising; it supports every aspect of a customer's journey, from raising awareness of a brand through the sale itself and even service after the sale.

Search engine ads have become a popular approach to acquiring new customers. But other formats are also driving the growth of online advertising. A new generation of Web banners is using sophisticated behavioral targeting techniques to understand viewers' interests and to provide tailored messaging. For example, television-style commercials can now be easily rebroadcast online; the creative power of the rich media formats can display commercial messages across an entire Web page; and affiliate marketing is extending the reach of online retailers, thus giving customers more choice.

As you read the rest of this chapter, reflect on what kind of sampling method you would recommend for businesses wishing to learn more about the potential for their business using online marketing. Explain your decision.

Sources: IAB Europe, http://www.iabeurope.eu/; Interactive Advertising Bureau, http://www.iab.net/; Tech Crunchies—Internet Statistics and Numbers, http://techcrunchies.com/, accessed July 2010.

PROBABILITY SAMPLING

In drawing a probability sample the selection of elements is based on a random procedure that gives elements a known and nonzero chance of being selected, thereby minimizing selection bias. Probability sampling usually involves taking large samples considered to be representative of the target population from which they are drawn. Findings based on a probability sample can be generalized to the target population with a specified level of confidence. The most commonly employed probability sampling techniques are described in the following paragraphs.

Simple Random Sampling

Simple random sampling is a straightforward method of sampling that assigns each element of the target population an equal probability of being selected. Drawing names from a hat or selecting the winning ticket from a container in a raffle are examples of simple random sampling. It is easy to draw names or numbers from a hat when working with a small population. But when the target population is large, other approaches are necessary.

One method of simple random sampling is random digit dialing in a telephone survey. This technique is used because it overcomes the bias introduced when telephone directories do not include recent listings or unpublished numbers. Unfortunately, it has the disadvantage of creating nonworking numbers as well as the problem of refusals to answer a telephone. Indeed, telemarketing has created a huge refusal rate problem in the United States. Ten years ago, business researchers were able to complete telephone interviews using a sample-to-completion ratio of 4 to 1 (completion ratio = start with a total sample of 2,000 listings to complete a sample of 500; i.e., 1,500 refused, would not answer telephone, etc.). Today, this ratio is often 10 to 1 (start with 5,000 listings to complete 500 interviews). Part of the problem is certainly that potential respondents are not at home, or there may be a lack of time or interest in the topic. But technology such as caller ID and other issues, such as simply not wanting to be bothered, are having a substantial impact on telephone refusal rates.

The procedure for drawing large samples involves the following steps:

1. Sequentially assign a unique identification number to each element in the sampling frame.
2. Use a random number generator to identify the appropriate elements to be selected into the sample.
3. Ensure that no element is selected more than once.

Software packages like SPSS will execute the above steps for you. If the determined sample size is sufficiently large, the resulting sample will be representative of the target population. In the Data Analysis box we illustrate the SPSS click-through sequence to draw a random sample of fifty cases from the one hundred Samouel's customers in our restaurant database. If you are not familiar with SPSS, go to the book's Web site (www.mesharpe-student.com) for more detailed information. The Data Analysis box describes how to use SPSS to select a random sample.

Systematic Sampling

Systematic sampling is a process that involves randomly selecting an initial starting point on a list, and thereafter every nth element in the sampling frame is selected. For example, suppose you have a list of 10,000 students attending a particular university and you want a sample of 500 students. Your sampling objective is a representative cross-section of the student body. To draw the sample you must determine the sample size and then calculate the sampling interval. The **sampling**

■————DATA ANALYSIS————■
Using SPSS to Select a Random Sample
for Samouel's Greek Cuisine Restaurant

Our sampling objective is to draw a random sample of 50 customers of Samouel's Greek Cuisine restaurant who were interviewed in the survey. Each of the 100 Samouel's customer interviews represents a sampling unit. The sampling frame is the list of 100 customers of Samouel's included in the restaurant database. To access this list, you must first arrange the sample so Samouel's customers are first. To do so, follow this sequence: DATA → SPLIT FILE → Compare Groups, highlight X_{28}, and move it to the Groups based on box, and click OK. The first 100 respondents in the database are now Samouel's customers. If you want to check this out, go to variable X_{28} and you will notice that the first 100 interviews are coded 0. These are the Samouel's customers.

The SPSS click-through sequence to select the random sample of Samouel's customers is DATA → SELECT CASES → RANDOM SAMPLE OF CASES → SAMPLE → EXACTLY → 50 CASES → FROM THE FIRST 100 CASES → CONTINUE → OK. In the preceding sequence you must click on each of the options and place "50" in the cases box and "100" in the from the first __ cases box. The customers (cases) not included in the random sample are indicated by the slash (/) through the case ID number on the left side of your computer screen.

Any subsequent data analysis will be based on only the random sample of 50 customers of Samouel's restaurant. For example, the table below shows the number and percentage of occasional, somewhat frequent, and very frequent diners (X_{20}) at Samouel's restaurant who were included in the sample. Data in the "Frequency" column indicates we selected 27 occasional diners, 10 somewhat frequent diners, and 13 very frequent diners, for a total of 50 diners. This table is an example of what you get when you use the SPSS software. Another random sample of 50 customers will likely result in slightly different frequencies.

	X_{20}, "frequency of dining"		
	Frequency	Percent	Cumulative percent
Occasional diner	27	54.0	54.0
Somewhat frequent diner	10	20.0	74.0
Very frequent diner	13	26.0	100.0
Total	50	100.0	

interval is the number of population elements between each unit selected for your sample. In this case, the sampling interval is 20 (10,000 students/sample of 500 = 20). To draw the sample, you randomly select a number between 1 and 20 as a starting point. For example, say you randomly choose 7, then the sample would be the sampling elements numbered 7, 27, 47, 67, and so on. Similarly, in the Data Analysis box we tell you how to develop a systematic sampling procedure to survey Samouel's restaurant customers.

Systematic sampling produces representative data if executed properly. To work properly, the sampling interval must divide the sampling frame into relatively homogeneous groups. If there is a cyclical sequence to the sampling frame instead of a random sequence, systematic sampling will not work. For example, alphabetical listings are considered random and not cyclical. In contrast, if we wanted to do weekly

---

■————DATA ANALYSIS————■
Selecting a Systematic Random Sample
for Samouel's Greek Cuisine Restaurant

Over the past four years, Phil Samouel has compiled a listing of 1,030 customers arranged in alphabetical order. A systematic sample of 100 customers' opinions is his research objective. Having decided on a sample size of 100 to be selected from the sampling frame of 1,030 customers, Phil calculates the size of the interval between successive elements of the sample dividing the sampling frame size by the desired sample size (1,030/100 = 10.3). In situations like this, where we end up with a decimal instead of a round number, you ignore the decimal to be sure of a minimum sample of 100. Thus, we have effectively partitioned the sampling frame into 100 intervals of size 10. From the numbers in the interval of 1 to 10, we then must randomly select a number to identify the first element for the systematic sample. If, for example, that number is 4, then we begin with the 4th element in the sampling frame and every 10th element thereafter is chosen. The initial starting point is the 4th element and the remaining elements selected for the sample are the 14th, 24th, 34th, and so on, until the final element chosen is the 1,024th. This will result in a sample of 103 customers to be interviewed in the survey.

---

interviews with Samouel's customers and our interval was 7, the sample would produce biased information because we would always interview on the same day of the week. To be truly random, we must conduct interviews across at least several different days of the week. Similarly, if our list of 1,030 Samouel's customers is arranged according to frequency of dining, and the first 100 names on the list eat at Samouel's at least once a week and the remaining 930 eat at Samouel's an average of four times a year, we would have a problem using systematic sampling. If the sampling interval is 10 and our sample size is 103, then our sample would underrepresent the frequent customers (only 10 frequent customers) and overrepresent the less frequent customers (93 nonfrequent customers). Thus, we must know ahead of time if there are underlying systematic patterns in the data so we can account for them in our sampling plan.

Stratified Sampling

Stratified sampling requires the researcher to partition the sampling frame into relatively homogeneous subgroups that are distinct and nonoverlapping, called strata. The researcher usually does the stratification on the basis of some predetermined criteria that may be the result of his or her past experience, or stratification could even be specified by the client. For example, in his survey Phil Samouel may wish to stratify his customers on the basis of a characteristic such as age, marital status, family size, income level, frequency of eating out, level of satisfaction, who selected the restaurant, or a combination of these.

The researcher determines the total sample size as well as the required sample sizes for each of the individual strata. For example, the total sample size might be 400 and the four individual strata might each have a sample size of 100. The stratified sample is the composite of the samples taken from the strata. Elements for the stratified sample are usually selected either by drawing simple random or systematic samples of the specified size from the strata of the target population. With stratified sampling, elements must be selected from all the strata of the total sample. When done properly, stratified sampling increases the accuracy of the sample information but does not necessarily increase the cost. In practice a stratified sample is selected in one of two ways, proportionately or disproportionately. Descriptions of these two approaches follow:

In **proportionately stratified sampling**, the overall sample size will be the total of all the elements from each of the strata. The number of elements chosen from each stratum is proportionate to the size of a particular stratum relative to the overall sample size. So if we have a stratum that is 25 percent of the target population, then the size of the sample for that stratum will be 25 percent of the total sample. For example, if we use proportionately stratified sampling to select a sample of males and females at a university with 10,000 students, and 6,000 students are females and 4,000 students are males, then the overall sample would include 60 percent females and 40 percent males.

In **disproportionately stratified sampling** the sample elements are chosen in one of two ways. One approach involves choosing the elements from each stratum according to its relative importance. Relative importance is usually based on practical considerations such as the economic importance of the various strata. For example, if Samouel's restaurant is located in an area dominated by older individuals who dine out less frequently, then sampling a higher proportion of younger customers that dine out more often would be viewed as more important to him. This is illustrated in the far-right column of the table in the Continuing Case box.

With disproportionately stratified sampling based on economic or other reasons, the sample size from each stratum is determined independently without considering the size of the stratum relative to the overall sample size. The more important a particular stratum is considered, the higher will be the proportion of the sample elements from the stratum.

CONTINUING CASE: SAMOUEL'S GREEK CUISINE
Which Is Better, Proportionately
or Disproportionately Stratified Samples?

Phil Samouel, owner of Samouel's Greek Cuisine, has a list of 3,000 potential customers broken down by age. His business consultant has determined through the use of a statistical formula that a proportionately stratified sample of 200 will produce information that is sufficiently accurate for decision making. The number of elements to be chosen from each stratum using a proportionate sample based on age is shown in the fourth column of the table that follows. But, if the consultant believes it is necessary that the sample size in each stratum be relative to its economic importance, and those in the 18 to 49 age group are the most frequent diners and spend the most when dining out, then the number of selected elements would be disproportionate to stratum size, as illustrated in the fifth column. The numbers in the disproportionate column would be determined based on the researcher's judgment of each stratum's economic importance.

Age group	Number of elements selected for the sample	Percentage of elements in stratum	Number of elements in stratum	
			Proportionate sample size	Disproportionate sample size
(1)	(2)	(3)	(4)	(5)
18–25	600	20	40 = 20%	50 = 25%
26–34	900	30	60 = 30%	50 = 25%
35–49	270	9	18 = 9%	50 = 25%
50–59	1,020	34	68 = 34%	30 = 15%
60 and older	210	7	14 = 7%	20 = 10%
Total	3,000	100	200	200

Should the consultant recommend proportionate or disproportionate sampling? Should the decision be based on economic importance or some other criteria?

Another approach to selecting a disproportionately stratified sample considers the variability of the data within each stratum. Elements from each stratum are selected based on the relative variability of the elements. Strata with high relative variability will contribute a higher proportion of elements to the total sample. Similarly, the lower the variability of a stratum the lower will be its proportional representation in the total sample. For example, assume a university with 10,000 students has 50 percent male students and 50 percent female students. We know that almost all the males drink beer, and there is wide variation in beer drinking habits, with some drinking beer every day and a very small number not drinking beer at all. On the other hand, only a small proportion of the female students drink beer and not very often (the female students prefer wine), so there is not much variation in their beer consumption patterns. In this example, we would sample a larger number of male students in our survey so we could more accurately represent male beer consumption patterns. Since female students do not vary much in their beer consumption habits, the smaller sample of females should still accurately represent their behavior.

Cluster Sampling

In **cluster sampling** the target population is viewed as being made up of heterogeneous groups, called clusters. Examples of clusters are ethnic groups, companies, households, business units, and geographic areas. We illustrate the use of cluster sampling with an example.

The most frequently used type of cluster sampling is geographic area sampling. For example, assume you want to interview managers of banks in San Diego, California. The researcher could obtain a list of zip codes in which banks are located: each area is then a cluster. The clusters to be sampled would be randomly selected, and then all bank managers or a random sample of managers of banks would be interviewed in each of the selected clusters. This process generally works well and produces representative data. The procedure for taking a cluster sample is as follows:

1. Define the cluster characteristics in a way that ensures the clusters are unambiguously identified in the target population. In this manner, the total number of clusters in the population will be known ahead of time.
2. Decide on how many clusters to sample.
3. Choose the cluster(s) in a random manner.
4. Obtain a sampling frame for the chosen clusters.
5. Decide whether to conduct a census on the chosen cluster(s) or whether to take a probability sample from the cluster(s).
6. If a probability sample is desired, determine the total sample size. If more than one cluster will be used, then the sample size should be allocated appropriately. This is generally done on a proportionate sampling basis.

The Continuing Case example explains how Phil Samouel might use a cluster sampling process to identify the relevant customers to interview.

CONTINUING CASE: SAMOUEL'S GREEK CUISINE
Cluster Sampling of Restaurant Customers

Phil Samouel would like to know the perceptions of his weekend customers, because the average bill size is $110. In contrast, the average bill of weekday customers is only $65. For this research project a cluster is defined as customers who dine at the restaurant on weekends. This results in fifty-two clusters (one for each week) from which a random sample of clusters (weekends) can be drawn. One of two possible options may be followed. The first option is that all customers from the selected clusters can be interviewed. In this case a census is conducted. The second option is that elements (customers) can be drawn from the selected clusters by one of the above probability sampling methods, or by one of the nonprobability approaches discussed in the following paragraphs.

Which approach is most realistic and why? What problems are associated with each approach?

Multistage Sampling

Multistage cluster sampling involves a sequence of stages. These stages are illustrated by the following example. The problem is to investigate the views of medical practitioners in the United States concerning the use of medical software to assist in patient diagnosis. The first stage is to select a random sample of regions in the United States. The regions are the clusters. The second stage is to select a random sample of hospitals from the selected regions, and then either collect information from all medical practitioners from the chosen hospitals or a random sample from within each of the chosen hospitals. Even more complex multistage sampling is possible.

NONPROBABILITY SAMPLING

In nonprobability sampling the selection of sample elements is not necessarily made with the aim of being statistically representative of the population. Rather, the researcher uses subjective methods such as personal experience, convenience, expert judgment, and so on to select the elements in the sample. As a result, the probability of any element of the population being chosen is not known. Moreover, there are no statistical methods for measuring the sampling error for a nonprobability sample. Thus, the researcher cannot generalize the findings to the target population with any measured degree of confidence, which is possible with probability samples. This does not mean nonprobability samples should not be used. Indeed, in some situations they may be the preferred alternative. The most frequently used nonprobability sampling methods are described in the following sections.

Convenience Sampling

A **convenience sample** involves selecting sample elements that are most readily available to participate in the study and can provide the information required. For example, exit interviews used with restaurant customers who have just finished a meal at the restaurant represent a convenience sample. Similarly, when a college professor interviews students at his university, he/she is making use of a convenience sample. Convenience samples are used because they enable the researcher to complete a large number of interviews quickly and cost effectively. But they suffer from selection bias, because the individuals interviewed are often different from the target population. It is therefore difficult and risky to generalize to the target population when a convenience sample is used.

Judgment Sampling

A **judgment sample**, sometimes referred to as a **purposive sample**, involves selecting elements in the sample for a specific purpose. It is a form of convenience sampling in which the researcher's judgment is used to select the sample elements. Sample elements are chosen because the researcher believes they represent the target population, but they are not necessarily representative. An example of a judgment sample might be a group of experts with knowledge about a particular problem or issue; for example, physicians who specialize in treating diabetes might be interviewed in a survey to learn about the most effective ways to convince diabetics to adopt good diets and exercise properly. The advantages of judgment samples are their convenience, speed, and low cost.

Quota Sampling

Quota sampling is similar to stratified random sampling. The objective is for the total sample to have proportional representation of the strata of the target population. It differs from stratified sampling in that the selection of elements is done on a convenience basis.

In quota sampling the researcher defines the strata of the target population, determines the total sample size, and sets a quota for the sample elements from each stratum. In addition, the researcher specifies the characteristics of the elements to be selected but leaves the actual choice of elements to the discretion of the person collecting the information. Thus, while quota sampling ensures proportionate representation of each stratum in the total sample, the findings from the sample cannot be generalized because the choice of elements is not done using a probability sampling method. As with judgment sampling, the advantages of quota samples are their convenience, speed, and low cost.

Snowball Sampling

A **snowball sample**, also called a **referral sample**, is one where the initial respondents are typically chosen using probability methods. The researcher then uses the initial respondents to help identify the other respondents in the target population. This process is continued until the required sample size is reached. Snowball sampling uses referrals to facilitate the location of rare populations or those where a list does not exist. For example, the 2010 FIFA World Cup football games were held in South Africa. There is a list of individuals who purchased tickets, but not a list of who actually attended the games. The situation is complicated further by the fact that many companies purchased multiple tickets either for their own employees or for resale. If the organizing committee wanted to conduct a survey of individuals who attended the 2010 games in order to better plan for the 2014 games, the available list likely would not be very accurate. An effective approach might be to use the available names, contact those individuals, and ask them for referrals to other individuals or groups that attended the games. This is a particularly good approach when the target population is narrow, such as when identifying individuals who frequently attend the World Cup versus those who go less frequently.

DETERMINING SAMPLE SIZE

Efficient sample sizes can be drawn from either large (infinite) populations or small (finite) populations. Below we discuss the determination of the sample size for both cases.

SAMPLING FROM A LARGE POPULATION

Researchers often need to estimate characteristics of large populations. To achieve this in an efficient manner, it is necessary to determine the appropriate sample size prior to data collection.

Determination of the sample size is complex because of the many factors that need to be taken into account simultaneously. The challenge is to obtain an acceptable balance among several of these factors. These factors include the variability of elements in the target population, the type of sample required, time available, budget, required estimation precision, and whether the findings are to be generalized and, if so, with what degree of confidence.

Formulas based on statistical theory can be used to compute the sample size. For pragmatic reasons, such as budget and time constraints, alternative ad-hoc methods are often used. Examples are sample sizes based on rules of thumb, previous similar studies, one's own experience, or simply what is affordable. Irrespective of how the sample size is determined, it is essential that it be of a sufficient size and quality to yield results that are seen to be credible in terms of their accuracy and consistency.

When statistical formulas are used to determine the sample size, three decisions must be made: (1) the degree of confidence (often 95 percent), (2) the specified level of precision (amount of acceptable error), and (3) the amount of variability (population homogeneity). The degree of confidence (confidence level) is typically based on management or researcher judgment. Historically, a 95 percent confidence level has been used, but a lower confidence level is acceptable where less risk is involved. Managerial or researcher judgment is also involved in determining the level of precision. The level of precision is the maximum acceptable difference between the estimated sample value and the true population value.

The third decision relates to the variability, or homogeneity, of the population. The variability of the population is measured by its standard deviation. If the population is homogeneous, it has a small standard deviation. For example, the standard deviation in the age of college students is small and therefore requires a relatively smaller sample size. But if the population is heterogeneous, such as people attending a football game, then a relatively large sample is necessary because the standard deviation in the age of this population is larger. In practice, it is unlikely the true standard deviation is known. Consequently, the researcher typically uses an estimate of the standard deviation based on previous, similar studies or a pilot study.

If you have information on these three factors, the sample size can be calculated as follows:

$$Sample\ Size\ (SS) = \left[\frac{DC \times TV}{DP} \right]^2$$

where

DC (Degree of Confidence) = the number of standard errors for the degree of confidence specified for the research results.

TV (True Variability) = the standard deviation of the population.

DP (Desired Precision) = the acceptable difference between the sample estimate and the population value.

Note that the above formula does not include the population size. This is because, except with finite populations, the size of the population has no impact on the determination of sample size. Specifically, a sample size of 500 is equally useful in understanding the opinions of a target population of 15 million as it is for one of 100,000. This is always true for large populations. The Business Research Dashboard on page 179 describes an emerging problem in selecting the best sampling method.

The calculated sample size does not necessarily ensure the sample is representative of the target population. The extent to which a sample is representative is dependent on the process used in the selection of the elements. A representative sample is more likely to be achieved through probability rather than nonprobability sampling. Two examples of how to determine sample size are provided in Exhibit 7.3.

Exhibit 7.3

Estimating the Sample Size for a Mean

Case 1: Using a Rating Scale

Phil Samouel asked his research consultant to estimate the appropriate sample size considering the rating scale questions that will be asked on his survey of restaurant customers. The researcher must determine the sample size that will estimate the true perceived mean score for the characteristics of the restaurants (i.e., food quality, reasonable prices, etc.) to a desired level of precision and to a specified level of confidence. To do so, the researcher must consider all three elements in the sample size formula, the degree of variability in the population as measured by the standard deviation, the acceptable level of precision, and the specified level of confidence. The researcher is likely to proceed as follows:

The first component of the sample size formula that must be decided on is the true variability. Generally speaking, the true variability as measured by the standard deviation is not known. In most cases, therefore, it will have to be estimated either through the use of a pilot test sample or by some subjective method, such as the researcher's experience with similar types of questions.

It is also necessary to make some assumptions about the properties of the distribution of responses to the questions. In general, it is assumed that the measure for the characteristics to be estimated follows a normal distribution. In Phil Samouel's study the characteristics are measured with a one to seven rating scale. This gives a range of six units (7 − 1 = 6). Once we know the range, we estimate the standard deviation of the rating scale by dividing the range by four (6/4 = 1.5). The division by four is based on the assumption that the distribution of the responses to the restaurant characteristic questions is normal. When we have a normal distribution business researchers typically use a confidence interval of plus or minus two standard errors (95 percent). When plus or minus two standard errors is used, the range of standard errors is four. Hence, we divide the range of responses by four to get the estimated standard deviation.

In consultation with the client the researcher generally determines the acceptable level of precision and the desired level of confidence. Suppose that the precision is specified as one third of a unit on the rating scale. This means the sample estimate should be accurate within one third of a unit. A confidence level of 95 percent is desired.

We now have sufficient information to calculate our sample size using the formula:

$$Sample\ Size = \left[\frac{(degree\ of\ confidence\ required \times variability)}{desired\ precision} \right]^2$$

$$Sample\ Size = \left[\frac{(2 \times 1.5)}{.33} \right]^2 = 82.6$$

Thus, eighty-three is the minimum sample size the researcher should aim for in order to meet the specified precision and confidence goals.

Case 2: Using a Ratio Scale

Consider the case where we wish to estimate the average monthly expenditure on eating out. Although the true standard deviation (variability) is unknown, a pilot test study of thirty customers provides an estimate of the unknown standard deviation of $14. We want to be 95 percent confident that our estimate of the mean monthly expenditure on eating out is within $2 of the true population mean. Assuming the distribution of expenditures follows a normal distribution, then the sample size is determined as follows:

$$Sample\ Size = \left[\frac{(degree\ of\ confidence\ required \times variability)}{desired\ precision} \right]^2$$

$$Sample\ Size = \left[\frac{(2 \times 14)}{2} \right]^2 = 196$$

We should aim for a sample of at least 196 to meet our preset criteria of an efficient sample size.

■————**Business Research Dashboard**————■
Will Biometric IDs Be Accepted by Customers?

Cashpoint fraud and theft cost banks in excess of $900 million in losses every year. In an effort to reduce this, banks have considered fingerprints and eye scanning for identification. Customers in some countries, such as the United States and the United Kingdom, have resisted fingerprint identification because it is associated with criminals. Similarly, many people believe the eye is too vulnerable to permit a regular and invasive search approach like iris scanning. As a result, banks and other businesses have been searching for an authentication method acceptable to customers.

For several years, Japanese manufacturer Hitachi has been selling biometric scanners that check customers' finger and palm veins at banks for identification purposes. Now it is hoping to enter both the U.S. and European markets. The system can not only use biometric identification with false acceptance at less than .0001 percent but also designate a particular finger as a duress signal. Thus, if a customer is being forced to withdraw cash, they simply place the previously identified duress finger on the scanner and it alerts authorities in less than half a second that a problem exists.

How do you feel about submitting your finger and palm vein pattern to banks or other businesses for identification purposes? What kind of research design and sampling method are best to ensure valid results for a study to determine customer acceptance of the use of this technology?

Sources: Tony Glover, "Hitachi Launches Biometric ID to Stop Cashpoint Fraud," *The Business Online*, April 30, 2006, http://www.orisys.com/infocenter/article_173.shtml; Tom Geoghegan, "I've Got a Biometric ID Card," *BBC News Online*, August 12, 2004, http://news.bbc.co.uk/2/hi/uk_news/3556720.stm; Jennifer Maselli, "Speeding Up the Checkout Line with Biometrics," *InformationWeek*, March 13, 2002, http://www.informationweek.com/news/software/showArticle.jhtml?articleID=6501491, accessed July 2010.

SAMPLING FROM A SMALL POPULATION

The size of the population in the preceding formula has no impact on the determination of the sample size. This is always true for large populations. When working with small populations, however, use of the above formula may lead to an unnecessarily large sample size. If, for example, the sample size is larger than 5 percent of the population, then the calculated sample size should be multiplied by the following correction factor:

$$\frac{N}{[N+(n-1)]}$$

where

N = population size.
n = the calculated sample size determined by the original formula.

Thus, the adjusted sample size is:

$$\text{Sample Size (SS)} = \left[\frac{DC \times TV}{DP}\right]^2$$

$$\text{Sample Size} = \left[\frac{2 \times 1.5}{.33}\right]^2 = 82.6$$

Use of this formula is illustrated in Exhibit 7.4.

Exhibit 7.4

Estimating Sample Size Adjusted by the Correction Factor

Suppose a bank has 5,000 ATMs installed in the United States. The bank wishes to establish its users' views of this service. A researcher commissioned by the bank estimates the required sample size given their agreed criteria is 750. This sample size is 13 percent of the population and is larger than is necessary for an efficient sample size. In this case the sample size correction factor needs to be applied, as illustrated below:

$$\text{Adjusted Sample Size} = 750 \times \left[\frac{5000}{(5000 + 750 - 1)}\right] = 653$$

The reduction in the sample size could lead to significant savings in time and money.

Business researchers working with clients who serve the business-to-business market are also sampling from a small population. That is, the number of customers for a company selling to the business sector may be several hundred or fewer. This contrasts with the several thousand customers for a company selling to consumers. In this situation the question arises, What is an adequate sample size? This is because using a sample size formula can result in a sample size that cannot be achieved. In such a situation it is typical to interview 10 to 20 percent of the total number of individuals in the population. Also, a minimum sample size of thirty is recommended, and larger if possible. In all situations dealing with sample sizes this small it is necessary to examine the characteristics of the sample respondents to ensure they are reasonably representative. That is, do the respondents represent all types of customers, such as larger and smaller businesses, or only one type? If all types of customers are not represented in sufficient numbers, then the findings must be interpreted accordingly.

Many issues must be considered in selecting the best sampling method and the proper sample size. Consider the issues posed in the Business Research Dashboard on women's usage of the Internet.

IMPLEMENTING THE SAMPLING PLAN

The researcher implements the sampling plan after all the details of the sampling design have been agreed upon. The target population has been defined, the sampling

---

■————Business Research Dashboard————■
Are Online Usage Patterns Changing?

Recent research shows women throughout the U.S. and Europe are using the Internet almost as much as men. Men spend an average of twelve hours a week online, while women spend eleven hours a week on the Web. But women are increasing their Web usage at a faster rate than men. Where are women spending less time—reading magazines? The increase in Internet usage among women is mostly in the sixteen to thirty-four age group, which includes young professional women and those with young children. The Web sites visited most often by women include those related to travel, banking, shopping, medical, and auctions. Based on this research, the implication is that advertisers must consider how women's shopping habits and use of different mediums are changing if they are to be successful in communicating with this segment. The research was based on random telephone interviews with respondents from the United Kingdom, Germany, France, Spain, Belgium, the Netherlands and the Scandinavian countries, as well as interviews in the United States.

Similar studies in the United States have shown younger women are more likely than younger men to be online. In fact, 86 percent of women ages eighteen to twenty-nine are online compared with 80 percent of men in that age range. Further, women are more likely to use the Internet to send and receive e-mail, get maps and directions, look for health and medical information, get support for health or personal problems, and obtain religious information. Men, on the other hand, are more likely to use the Internet to check the weather, get news, find do-it-yourself and sports information, obtain political and financial information, do job-related research, download software, listen to music, rate a product, person, or service, download music files, use a webcam, play games, and take a class. This research has implications for determining appropriate samples and sample representativeness so advertisers can identify and target potential customers.

What kind of research design would answer the question as to why women are increasing their Web usage faster than men?

Sources: Enid Burns, "Euro Women to Outpace Men Online in Near Future," *ClickZ*, March 29, 2006, http://www.clickz.com/3595241; Deborah Fallows, "How Women and Men Use the Internet," Pew Internet & American Life Project Report, December 28, 2005, http://www.pewinternet.org/Reports/2005/How-Women-and-Men-Use-the-Internet.aspx; European Interactive Advertising Association, "EIAA Digital Women Report 2006," http://www.eiaa.net/Ftp/casestudiesppt/Digital%20Women%20-%20Exec%20Summary%20-%20FINAL%2016.3.pdf, and http://www.encyclopedia.com/doc, accessed July 2010.

---

frame has been chosen, the sampling method has been selected, and the appropriate sample size determined. If the sampling unit is companies, then the types of companies must be specified as well as the titles and perhaps names of the individuals who will be interviewed. Many details must be decided on before a final sampling plan is accepted and implemented, because once the data is collected, it is too late to change the sampling design.

> ### CONTINUING CASE: SAMOUEL'S GREEK CUISINE
> #### Which Sampling Method Is Best?
>
> The business consultant hired by Phil Samouel has recommended a survey of his customers and his employees. The consultant has also recommended a survey of Gino's customers. Samouel has a total of seventy-seven employees. Some work full-time and others part-time.
>
> Samouel's is open seven days a week for lunch and dinner and so is Gino's. The consultant is considering both probability and nonprobability sampling methods as ways to collect customer data.
>
> 1. Is a sampling method needed for the employee survey? Why?
> 2. Which of the sampling options is best for the survey of Samouel's customers? Why?
> 3. What are some possible ways to collect data from Gino's customers? Recommend a sampling method you believe will work best.

SUMMARY

UNDERSTAND THE KEY PRINCIPLES OF SAMPLING IN BUSINESS RESEARCH

The key issues in sampling are to identify the target population, the sampling frame, and the method of sampling. Generally, a researcher seeks to draw a representative sample from the target population using either probability or nonprobability procedures. Access to and participation of respondents, whether they are companies or individuals, is therefore an important consideration to ensure that the sample size is credible, efficient, and representative.

APPRECIATE THE DIFFERENCE BETWEEN THE TARGET POPULATION AND THE SAMPLING FRAME

Before beginning sampling it is necessary for us to identify all the elements of interest to our study. These elements could be individuals or objects such as companies, or even events. These elements are the target population. In practice there may not be an exhaustive list of these elements, so we make use of one or more lists that provide a good proxy for the population. It is this proxy that forms the sampling frame from which we draw the sample.

RECOGNIZE THE DIFFERENCE BETWEEN PROBABILITY AND NONPROBABILITY SAMPLING PROCEDURES

The difference between the two sampling approaches is simple. For probability sampling methods the chances of selection of elements into a sample are known. In contrast, for nonprobability sampling methods the chances of selection are not known. Also, for inferring from a sample to a population, probability sampling must be used.

DESCRIBE DIFFERENT SAMPLING METHODS COMMONLY USED BY BUSINESS RESEARCHERS

Probability sampling, generally used in large-scale surveys, is based on a random procedure for selecting elements from the target population. If the sample size is sufficiently large, the sample selected should be representative. Probability sampling approaches include simple random sampling, systematic sampling, stratified sampling, cluster sampling, and multistage sampling. Each one of these sampling designs has advantages and disadvantages that must be considered before selecting a particular approach. If executed properly probability sampling enables you to make generalizations about the population with a specified degree of confidence.

Nonprobability sampling, generally used in exploratory research, involves selecting elements into the sample based on convenience, judgment, referral, or quotas, without attaching probabilities to the elements in the target population. For such samples it is difficult to ensure they are representative, and thus the findings cannot be generalized to the population with a specified degree of confidence.

DETERMINE THE APPROPRIATE SAMPLE SIZE FOR VARIOUS SITUATIONS ENCOUNTERED IN PRACTICE

To determine the sample size, three pieces of information are needed: (1) the degree of confidence necessary to estimate the true value, (2) the precision of the estimate, and (3) the amount of true variability present in the data. In practice the researcher and client discuss and agree upon the desired level confidence and the precision of the estimate. Further, since the true variability is unlikely to be known, it is typically estimated based on judgment or through a pilot study.

ETHICAL DILEMMA

Mark Stephenson is an account manager for a business research firm. At the request of a local hospital's marketing director, he submits a proposal to conduct a patient satisfaction survey. His opinion is the sample should be random and collected by telephone or the Internet. After his presentation to the marketing director and the hospital chief executive, the marketing director asks Mark to use exit interviews to collect the data instead. She explains that her boss feels exit interviews are just as valid and will save the hospital money.

What should Mark do?

REVIEW QUESTIONS

1. What is the difference between a sample and a population?
2. Why interview a sample instead of the population?

3. What are the steps in the sampling process?
4. What is the difference between probability and nonprobability sampling?

DISCUSSION AND THINKING ACTIVITIES

1. Discuss the difficulties researchers face in defining the target population and its associated sampling frame. Comment with examples of how you would overcome them.
2. In which situations is nonprobability sampling preferred to probability sampling? Comment with examples.
3. For each of the probability sampling designs, illustrate its use with examples.
4. What considerations need to be taken into account when determining the appropriate sample size?
5. Would you prefer to use a sample of 20,000 voters or 2,000 voters to describe voting behavior in national elections? Explain your choice.

INTERNET EXERCISES

1. Go to the Google or Yahoo! search engines and type in the words "population" and "sampling." Prepare a brief summary of what you find.
2. Go to the following Web sites: www.surveysystem.com/sscalc.htm and www.svys.com/. Use the functions on the Web sites. Prepare a brief report of what the Web sites do and how they work. Comment on how useful these Web sites would be to the business researcher.
3. Go to http://random.mat.sbg.ac.at/links/. Use the functions on the Web site to prepare a brief report of what the Web site does and how it works. Include comments about how useful this Web site would be to business researchers.

8 Methods of Collecting Primary Data

LEARNING OUTCOMES

1. Provide an overview of the different data collection methods
2. Describe differences between qualitative and quantitative data collection
3. Understand the differences between observation and interview methods
4. Explain the role of the various interview methods in obtaining data
5. Assess the use of self-completed versus interviewer-completed surveys

Researchers describe and explain phenomena that exist in the business world. To do so they examine, for example, demographics, behavior, attitudes, beliefs, lifestyles, and expectations of consumers or organizations. To complete this task, researchers must have data. Data is collected by means of one or more of the following: interviews, observation, and questionnaires. Once data is obtained, it is analyzed and becomes the basis for informed decision making, which in turn helps to reduce the risk of making costly errors.

Data collection requires considerable knowledge and skills. We provide an overview of qualitative and quantitative data collection methods in this chapter. This stage of the research process is important because once the data is collected, you cannot return to an earlier step to correct decisions that led to limitations in the study. At that point, the only choice is to collect the data again after correcting the problem, and this can be expensive and sometimes impossible.

DATA COLLECTION METHODS

The type and amount of data to be collected depend on the nature of the study and its research objectives. If the study is exploratory the researcher collects narrative data through the use of focus groups, personal interviews, or by observing behavior or events. This type of data is referred to as qualitative. Such studies typically involve the use of smaller samples or case studies. But if the study is descriptive or causal, the researcher is likely to require a relatively large amount of quantitative data obtained through large-scale surveys or by accessing electronic databases.

Until recently, face-to-face interviews, telephone surveys, mall intercepts, and mail surveys were the primary methods of data collection. Information technology is revolutionizing data collection, however, and large amounts of data, both qualitative and quantitative, can be obtained and integrated into databases relatively fast and at a very low cost compared to more traditional methods. These new methods include computerized questionnaires administered over the Internet, electronic capture of data at the point of sale, and electronic "conversations" or "discussions," both internally over an intranet and externally over the Internet. Indeed, globally electronic methods of collecting data now account for almost 30 percent of all data collection.

The various data collection approaches are depicted in Exhibit 8.1. The process of data collection begins by examining secondary data. A limited amount of data may already have been collected through informal observation and interviews, or by scanning easily accessible information. But now the process becomes much more formal. The initial objective is to determine whether the research objectives can be achieved using secondary data. If they can, there is no need to collect primary data. The secondary data collection process involves examining internal data sources as well as external data. We discussed secondary data in Chapter 5. The focus in this chapter is on the collection of primary data.

When the research objectives cannot be achieved using secondary data, primary data must be collected. Primary data collection methods can be divided into two types—qualitative and quantitative. An overview of both types is provided in the rest of this chapter. Exhibit 8.2 shows the frequency of usage of selected qualitative methods.

QUALITATIVE DATA COLLECTION

There are two broad approaches to qualitative data collection—observation and interviews. If the objective of your research is to examine the behavior of people or events, then observation is the appropriate method. On the other hand, if your objective is to understand why something happens, then you will need to interview people. We discuss observation and interviews as methods of qualitative data collection in this section.

OBSERVATION

Observational data is collected by systematically recording observations of people, events, or objects. Observational data can be obtained by use of human, electronic, or mechanical observation. An observational approach results in either narrative or numerical data. If narrative data is collected, it typically involves researchers preparing written descriptions of behavior, behavior recorded on an electronic medium such as an audio- or video digital recorder, or information obtained from an electronic

Exhibit 8.1   **Primary Data Collection Methods**

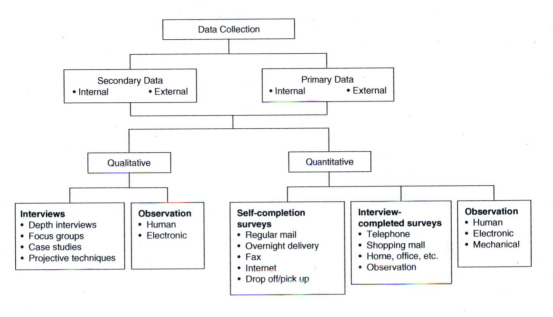

Exhibit 8.2

Frequency of Usage of Selected Qualitative Methods

Traditional focus groups	59%
In-depth interviews (in person)	11%
In-depth interviews (telephone without Internet)	9%
Chat (text)-based online focus groups	3%
Video-based online focus groups	2%
Interviews/groups using online communities	2%
Monitoring blogs	2%
Ethnography	1%
Other	3%

Source: Research Industry Trends, 2008 Report, Pioneer Marketing Research, GreenBook, Rockhopper Research, GMI, Peanut Labs, and MRG.

database (e.g., a blog). If numerical data is gathered, it involves either a trained observer recording events using a structured questionnaire or a device that counts or tracks specific actions. For example, a researcher may study fruit, vegetable, or meat selection behavior in a supermarket by having an observer record the amount of time between the approach of the individual and the decision to purchase a particular item, whether the item is picked up or turned over, and so forth. This information could be recorded on a questionnaire along with purchasing information. Similarly, Phil Samouel might evaluate the competence of the waiters in his restaurant on a number of predetermined criteria.

Today, however, probably the most widespread means of observational data collection is either through the scanning of purchases in supermarkets, drugstores, or other retail outlets, or over the Internet when companies observe an individual's click-through behavior. But what you may not realize is that when you telephone a business and are informed the call may be recorded for quality control monitoring and training, what often happens is the recording is being used to collect observational data. Recording such calls provides a rich source of qualitative data for assessing company procedures, employee performance, and customer comments.

A disadvantage of observation is there is no opportunity to observe any unseen thoughts or attitudes. For example, if behavior is being observed in a supermarket, we do not know the vegetable or fruit customer's attitude, hunger level, or whether the purchase is for her or his own consumption. In contrast, a primary advantage of observational data is its unobtrusive approach. "**Unobtrusive**" means the respondent is unaware of his or her participation in a research project. Because individuals being observed have had no interaction with a researcher, such as being given instructions or a questionnaire, they cannot be influenced by any activities associated with collecting data. Thus, observational data collection avoids interview bias since no instructions are given or questions asked.

Does this unobtrusive approach violate the research participant's right to privacy? Or is it possible the participant can be harmed in any way? If the behavior being observed is typically performed in public with the likelihood that others may notice it, it is unlikely the person's privacy has been violated or that they will be harmed. But, observations of human behavior for research purposes should avoid recording the person's name. This is another way in which privacy is protected. On the other hand, private acts should not be observed. For example, retail store dressing rooms should not be used for collecting observational data even though the data might be very useful in understanding how and why people buy clothes.

As a general rule, individuals do not know their behavior is being observed. But occasionally researchers may choose to request the participation of potential respondents in an observational study. As an example, mall shoppers may be given a Global Positioning System (GPS) transmitter that allows their behavior to be tracked throughout the mall. This provides researchers with useful information on shopping patterns. Researchers hope shoppers will forget they have the device so it will not influence their behavior. Similarly, GPS technology is being used to observe the location and driving patterns of commercial trucks and buses, railroads, and school buses. GPS technology is expected to be standard equipment on most new vehicles within five years.

Ethnographic research and content analysis are two special forms of the observational approach. We discuss both in the following paragraphs.

ETHNOGRAPHIC RESEARCH

Ethnographic researchers prefer to interpret behavior through observation of actual life experiences. Researchers typically will spend long periods of time with a respondent, and then write narratives that describe the respondent's behavior. For example, a researcher studying heavy beer consumption may actually spend days or weeks with a "heavy" beer consumer to try to discover all the needs addressed by beer consumption.[1] Similarly, a researcher may spend weeks or months as an "employee" in a workplace in an effort to understand the organization and the behavior of its employees. Ethnographic approaches to observation are often referred to as participant-observer research.

Ethnographic observational studies sometimes pay participants to place small video cameras in their homes or cars.[2] For example, 3M paid consumers to track their in-home movements via video in an effort to better understand how its Ergo handheld electronic Internet appliance would be used. This eventually led to the belief that people would use it differently than they do the Internet via a computer. Similarly, Moen, one of the largest plumbing fixture manufacturers in the world, got permission to video record people in their showers! This enabled them to discover several aspects of shower behavior that people couldn't or wouldn't voice. For example, they noticed that many women used a faucet handle for balance while shaving their legs. Findings like these enabled Moen to design shower fixtures that improve your shower experience! We discuss ethnographic methods more thoroughly in Chapter 11.

CONTENT ANALYSIS

Content analysis obtains data by observing and analyzing the content or message of written text. Examples of text where content analysis is typically used include reports, contracts, advertisements, letters, blogs, open-ended questions on surveys, in-depth interviews, and similar content. Through systematic analysis as well as observation, the researcher examines the frequency that words and main themes occur and identifies information content and characteristics embedded in the text. The end result is often a quantification of qualitative data.

The initial content analysis may count word or phrase frequency. For example, a researcher could analyze transcripts from employment interviews. Typically the transcripts are analyzed by software that counts the frequency of occurrence of words and expressions. One successful application of content analysis has been the discovery of expressions that indicate a dishonest response. A job candidate with a high count of short, negative expressions such as "never" and "nothing," or a high number of qualifiers such as "kind of" or "I don't think" may be classified as dishonest.[3] Moreover, "kind of" and "sort of" may both be interpreted as "hedging." An initial content analysis may reveal many words that have essentially the same meaning. If this occurs, categories of "common meaning" are developed.

Researchers have used content analysis to discover the primary theme and purpose of business codes of ethics. Codes of ethics are available as secondary data for many large public firms. Content analysis of codes found in the Fortune 500 database and *Business Review Weekly* database provides an interesting comparison among British, Australian, and American codes of ethics. For example, the themes that were identified suggested that codes are directed toward owners, management, or all employees of an organization. Themes most often involve employee conduct, community involvement, and customer treatment. Identified activities most often include gift giving and receiving, conflicts of interest, and accurate record keeping. Relatively few passages describe specific guidance on what is acceptable. The themes were similar across the United Kingdom, Australia, and the United States. But U.K. codes contained more community welfare references, and Australian and U.S. codes contained more references to customer treatment and equal opportunity.[4]

Content analysis is frequently used to interpret text interviews. It is also commonly used to discover themes and orientations of media programs and advertising. Given the visual nature of advertising, content analysis often involves identifying the frequency of themes expressed both in words and in pictures.[5] For example, a content analysis of television commercials directed at teenagers in the United States revealed that U.S. teens are exposed to over 14,000 ads a year containing sexual references. Similarly, news and other types of television programs are analyzed to determine the amount and type of violence included. Indeed, even video and computer games are examined to determine and classify their content.

INTERVIEWS

An **interview** is where the researcher speaks to the respondent directly. Interviews are particularly helpful in gathering data when dealing with complex or sensitive issues, and when open-ended questions are used to collect data. Interviews also enable the researcher to obtain feedback and to use visual aids if the interviews are face-to-face. For example, respondents might be shown a new corporate logo, a new corporate mission statement, building designs, automobile styles and colors, and so on and asked to comment. Finally, interviews are flexible with regard to where they can be conducted (e.g., at work, home, or in malls), and researchers can increase participation rates by explaining the project and its value.

To get the cooperation of the interviewee in a face-to-face interview and thereby obtain quality information, the interviewer must create a relaxed atmosphere in which to conduct the interview. Once this has been achieved, interviewers will ask the respondents to describe the situation or phenomenon of interest, followed by why, how, when, where, and who questions. For example, if Phil Samouel wanted information about the food being served in his Greek restaurant, he might ask customers, What do you think about the quality of my food? If their response is, We think it is very good, then he would follow up by asking, Why do you say that? as well as ask them to give examples, such as: I really like the special of the day, or a particular dessert is very good. In this way, Phil can really begin to understand what customers think about the food in his restaurant. In short, Phil can get actionable information for his business plan, not just general information that is of little value in taking corrective action. In formulating questions for interviews, therefore, always ask yourself, Will the answers I get to this question help me make a better decision about a particular business approach? If not, don't ask the question.

Interviews can vary from being highly unstructured to highly structured. Unstructured interviews are generally conducted using a flexible approach. In contrast, the interviewer controls structured interviews in a consistent and orderly manner. Whether structured or unstructured, interviewing can take a variety of forms, such as face-to-face or via telephone.

Structured Interviews

In **structured interviews** the interviewer uses an interview sequence with predetermined questions for each interview and is required to use the same interview sequence and to conduct the interview in exactly the same way to avoid biases that may result from inconsistent interviewing practices. Additionally, a standardized approach will ensure responses are comparable among interviews.

Each respondent is provided with an identical opportunity to respond to the questions. The interviewer may collect the responses in the form of notes or may record the interview. Recording should be done only with the permission of the interviewee. If the interview is not recorded, it is good practice to provide the interviewee with a copy of the interviewer's notes after they are completed, since this will help ensure the interview has been captured accurately.

Semistructured Interviews

Sometimes **semistructured interviews** are used. Here researchers are free to exercise their own initiative in following up an interviewee's answer to a question. For example, the interviewer may want to ask related, unanticipated questions that were not originally included. This approach may result in unexpected and insightful information coming to light, thus enhancing the findings.

Semistructured interviews have an overall structure and direction but allow a lot of flexibility to include unstructured questioning. Perhaps the best-known semistructured interview approach is the **focus group**. Focus groups involve semistructured interviews that use an exploratory research approach and are considered a type of qualitative research. Focus groups are unstructured in that the moderator allows participants to answer questions in their own words and encourages them to elaborate on their responses. But focus groups are also structured in that the moderator has a list of topics or questions to guide the discussion.

Focus groups consist of relatively informal discussions among eight to twelve respondents. Respondents usually share something in common. They may all have the same job, work for the same company, be a customer of the same bank, or do the same household chores. This common ground is usually very much involved in the discussion. Unlike other survey approaches, a random sample is neither required nor desired.

Focus groups are guided by a **moderator**, who encourages discussion and keeps the group on track, meaning they don't stray too far from the primary topic. A good moderator is key to a successful focus group. Good moderators possess some or all of the following characteristics:[6]

1. Personable—the moderator should have good conversation and people skills. Focus group participants need to feel comfortable discussing the subject matter with this person. The moderator must be able to encourage comments from quiet respondents and suppress those from any dominant participants.
2. Attentive—focus group sessions usually last one to two hours. The moderator

has to pay close attention the entire time and allocate time so that all topics are covered.

3. Professional training—focus group moderators usually need a background in communications, psychology, advertising, or marketing research.

4. Well organized—the moderator should be prepared to lead the discussion in a logical sequence. A focus group outline is an essential part of this process. The outline is a discussion guide that lists all key discussion points that should be covered by the group. It's a good idea to get input from key decision makers in constructing this outline.

5. Objective—the moderator should not let his or her opinion interfere with the interview in any way. A moderator who has a strong opinion on the subject matter may very well lead the discussion toward a personally desirable outcome. Sometimes this effect is unintentional. That is why it is often advisable to have an outsider conduct the focus group interview. A good moderator may not even require a great deal of knowledge about the situation to be effective.

6. Good listener—generally, the less a moderator says the better the focus group session. The key is getting the respondents to discuss the issues without having to individually ask each to answer every question. A quiet moderator is less likely to adversely influence the responses and their direction.

The Business Research Dashboard tells you what focus groups revealed as important reasons for selecting a family-style restaurant.

Focus groups are used across all business disciplines. For example, focus groups can be instrumental in developing ideas related to supervisory issues, including compensation systems and flexible work scheduling.[7] Focus groups have also played a role in developing professional certification programs in finance and accounting.[8]

Politicians frequently use focus groups. Focus groups are useful in discovering issues that can reinforce or build a candidate's image. In the United States, focus groups are used in presidential campaigns, in most campaigns for the U.S. Senate, and in many statewide elections. They are particularly useful when the public's opinion is diverse. President Obama relied on focus groups throughout his election campaign, and President Clinton used them his entire term.[9] Taglines and phrases were developed from focus group sessions that effectively communicated the intended messages. American politicians aren't the only ones using focus group research. Australian politicians successfully used input from focus groups to position candidates and policies based on tax issues.[10]

Making decisions based solely on focus group research is risky. Focus groups are discovery oriented. The group size is small. Thus, the results are much less likely to represent the population as a whole. Sometimes opinions are dependent on a particular group's chemistry. Researchers usually recommend two or three focus groups at a minimum to find consistent opinions. Therefore, conclusions drawn from focus groups are best tested using another, more confirmatory approach.

There are hundreds of research firms worldwide specializing in focus group research.[11] Focus group interviews generally require human and physical resources in addition to a moderator. A support staff is needed to recruit participants, who

---

■————Business Research Dashboard————■
It's All About the Quality of the Food!

One of the authors of this book was asked to conduct a series of focus groups in seven different geographic areas. The client was a large chain of family-style restaurants that wanted to know what motivated customers to go to a particular restaurant. The information would help management better understand dining behavior and be used in developing an advertising and promotion campaign. Eleven unique reasons were identified in the focus groups. They are listed below:

Reason	Percent of time mentioned
Quality of food	88
Variety of menu items	51
Expected cost of meal	39
Convenient locations	34
Friendly service	31
Nutritious food	19
Speed of service	17
Competent, knowledgeable employees	17
Atmosphere	15
Portion size	14
Special promotions, coupons, and discounts	9

Two focus groups were held in each geographic area and a total of 137 individuals participated. How valid are these findings? How can they be used? Can they be generalized to the overall market for family-style restaurants?

---

are usually paid ($100–$150) for their time and participation. People are needed to coordinate the group and provide basic hospitality. Focus group interviews are usually recorded. A typical focus group room includes a two-way mirror and recording equipment. Focus group sponsors generally observe the interview through the mirror, and the entire session is recorded. Respondents should be informed of the recording and given an option not to participate should they object. By now it should be no surprise that focus groups are expensive. A typical focus group session costs about $5,000 to $10,000 to conduct, including a fee for analysis and report preparation.

Technological developments are providing additional focus group opportunities. Electronic focus groups are conducted using password-protected Web site bulletin boards. A moderator posts a question and waits for participants to respond. If the group gets off course, or when enough discussion on a topic has been obtained, the moderator will post a new comment. Generally, this process will go on for a week to a month. Electronic focus groups are not seen as a replacement for traditional focus groups. While they are useful in obtaining large quantities of highly elaborate responses, they are even more expensive than a traditional focus group (about $12,000), and they are unable to capture the real-time, face-to-face interactions of participants.[12]

Unstructured Interviews

An **unstructured interview** is conducted without the use of an interview sequence. This allows the researcher to elicit information by engaging the interviewee in free and open discussion on the topic of interest. A particular advantage of this approach is the researcher has the opportunity to explore in depth issues raised during the interview.

Unstructured interviews are a type of qualitative research. They are used when research is directed toward an area that is relatively unexplored. By obtaining a deeper understanding of the critical issues involved, the researcher is in a better position not only to more clearly define the research problem but also develop a conceptual framework for the research. This will then form the basis for subsequent empirical research to test the ideas, concepts, and hypotheses that emerge.

The Business Research Dashboard provides an example of how a corporate policy on document shredding might be developed. An in-depth semistructured interviewing approach was used instead of focus groups because it was believed employees would not be as open in their comments in a focus group setting.

■————**Business Research Dashboard**————■
Developing Company Policies Requires Effort!

All large accounting firms have a policy on the shredding of documents. One would think such policies would be specific and well thought out. The Arthur Andersen/Enron situation indicates this is not necessarily true. A smaller accounting firm retained one of the authors of this book to conduct unstructured interviews with employees. The purpose of the interviews was to obtain information to assist in updating and improving its document shredding policy. The interviews were conducted individually and anonymity was guaranteed. In-depth interviews were used instead of focus groups because it was anticipated employees would be more open and honest in their comments if interviewed separately instead of in a focus group setting. Questions were asked about how the policy had been applied in the past, if it had worked well, if there were situations in which they had doubts about whether the policy was appropriately applied, how it could be improved, and so forth. Since more than forty individuals had to be interviewed and their responses tabulated, the process took a substantial amount of time. But several gaps in the policy were identified and management felt the outcome, a substantially improved policy, had been worth the effort.

Depth Interviews

A **depth**, or **in-depth interview**, is an unstructured one-to-one discussion session between a trained interviewer and a respondent. Respondents are usually chosen because they have some specialized insight. For example, a researcher exploring employee turnover might conduct a depth interview with someone who has worked for five different restaurants in a period of two years. As in a focus group, the interviewer first prepares an outline that guides the interview (this is the structured part of an in-depth interview). Also like a focus group, the responses are unstructured. Indeed, a depth interview allows much deeper probing than does a focus group. **Probing** means that a researcher delves deeply into a response to identify possibly hidden reasons for a particular behavior. The why, why, why technique (asking why several times) is a popular probing technique.

Depth interview participants are usually more comfortable discussing potentially sensitive topics. For example, employees are far more likely to be candid in discussing their superiors' behavior in a one-to-one setting than among a dozen coworkers. Some consumer issues also fall into the sensitive category. Consumers may discuss hygiene, financial, or sexual-preference issues more readily in a depth interview than in a focus group setting. Likewise, executives and top managers are more comfortable in a one-to-one setting. You can imagine that a focus group of product design engineers from Honda, Toyota, Mercedes, and Ford might be a very quiet session.

Like focus groups, depth interviews can be useful in clarifying concepts. Researchers need an operational definition for something before they can measure it. For example, what does a work climate of trust and responsibility mean? Depth interviews have proven useful in identifying observable workplace events that employees identified with coworker responsibility. Depth interview participants have indicated that the "CYA principle" (cover your ass) is associated with low trust in the workplace. Depth interviews have also been used with restaurant employees to examine issues such as hiding tips to prevent their being shared with coworkers and the effects of stress on workplace behavior, including food preparation and wholesomeness.

Depth interviews are generally more expensive than focus groups. Since the interviews are one-on-one as opposed to one on twelve, fees charged by the interviewer are multiplied. The interviewer may spend twelve or more hours with only six respondents. Further, since more text is generated, more analysis time is generally required. This adds up to a higher bill. Exhibit 8.3 compares depth interviews and focus groups.

Projective Techniques

Focus groups, depth interviews, and many surveys involve some type of interview process. Both the researcher and the respondent are actively engaged. When we conduct interviews there is always a risk the interview process itself will influence respondents. Perhaps respondent comments are not entirely accurate. The inaccuracy may be because of incomplete recall, a suppression of information because of social concerns, or an unwillingness to provide an accurate response to the question. There are some things people simply will not tell an interviewer.

Projective data can be collected in an interview as well. In **projective interviewing**, the researcher presents the respondent with an ambiguous stimulus. For example, the interviewer may provide the respondent with a stick-figure cartoon showing a grocery store employee eating an apple in the store. The respondent, a grocery store employee, is then asked to complete the picture in words and/or images. Since the respondent is describing another person and not him- or herself, the researcher is more confident the response will be reliable. For example, a respondent is more likely to mention whether the apple was purchased or pilfered. This picture completion exercise is known as **thematic apperception**. As with all projective approaches, the researcher will infer that the characteristics applied to the ambiguous figure actually reside in

Exhibit 8.3

Comparison of Focus Groups and Depth Interviews

Benefits of exploratory research	Focus groups	Depth interviews
Clarifying thinking, identifying researchable propositions, help in forming hypotheses	* * * * *	* * * * *
Identifying salient attributes such as product or job characteristics	* * * * *	* * * * *
Aiding measurement in future studies by providing operational definition of concepts	* * * * *	* * * * *
Identifying usage patterns	* * * *	* * *
Identifying key sources of difficulties for respondents	* * * *	* * * * *
Identifying novel ideas	* * * * *	* * *
Concept testing of new ideas	* * * * *	* *
Discussing sensitive issues	0	* * * * *
Identifying personal problems of respondents	0	* * *
Effective hypothesis testing	0	0
Economical	0	0

Note: The number of stars indicates how effective a technique is in producing the listed benefit. Five stars = highly effective, fewer stars = less effective, 0 = ineffective.

the respondent. Projective approaches are thus a good way to discover hidden motivations. Other projective approaches include sentence completion, word association, balloon test, and role-playing. The Business Research Dashboard describes a classic study that used the projective technique approach.

Case Studies

Case studies focus on collecting information about a specific event or activity, often about a particular firm or industry. The logic of conducting a case study is that obtaining a complete picture of the entire situation requires examining a real-life example. Doing so enables the researcher to identify interactions among all the variables in a real-life setting.

Several decisions are necessary in case studies. The first is the unit of analysis. That is, what will be the focus of the study? Will it be a division of the company, a particular department, or perhaps even a project that is being implemented by the company as a whole. A second decision relates to the time frame. When does the study period begin and when does it end? Incorrect decisions on either of these issues could invalidate the study's findings. Case studies involving comparisons of two or more companies, events, or activities are even more complex. For example, it would not be appropriate to compare a family business to a publicly traded one, just as it would not be appropriate to compare a situation in the year 2012 with one that occurred in 2001. Comparisons are necessary, but the situations must be comparable.

■———Business Research Dashboard———■
Are Instant Coffee Drinkers Really That Bad?

Suppose you found a grocery list containing the following items: a loaf of bread, five pounds of flour, an eight-ounce jar of Maxwell House Instant Coffee, two pounds of ground beef, a fifteen-ounce can of cling peaches. How would you describe the owner of this grocery list? This projective approach was applied by a researcher studying the reasons people select instant versus ground coffee. A group of respondents were asked to respond to a list of this type. Another group responded to a list identical in all respects with the exception that instant coffee was replaced by ground coffee. The respondents were asked to describe the woman purchasing these groceries in as much detail as possible based on nothing but the list. While the ground coffee purchaser received generally positive responses, the instant coffee buyer was often described as "lazy," "living alone," "a poor homemaker," "careless with her money," and even as "an old maid!" This led to the theory that the process of purchasing and making instant coffee was not as fulfilling as making coffee in a more traditional way. Keep in mind that this data was collected nearly sixty years ago. Do you think things have changed?

Sources: Mason Haire, "Projective Techniques in Marketing Research," *Journal of Marketing*, 14 (April 1950), 649–656; George S. Lane and Gayne L. Watson, "A Canadian Replication of Mason Haire's 'Shopping List' Study," *Journal of the Academy of Marketing Science*, 3, 1 (Winter 1975), 48–59; Mason Haire, Edwin E. Ghiselli, and Lyman W. Porter, *Managerial Thinking: An International Study* (New York: Wiley, 1966).

QUANTITATIVE DATA COLLECTION

Quantitative data collection involves gathering numerical data using structured questionnaires or observation guides to collect primary data from individuals. The data ranges from beliefs, opinions, attitudes, behavior, and lifestyles to general background information on individuals such as gender, age, education, and income, as well as company characteristics like revenue and number of employees. Business researchers often refer to quantitative data collection as survey research. When the research project involves collecting information from a large sample of individuals, survey research is the best approach. An important consideration with surveys is that respondents are aware information about their behavior or attitudes is being collected. It is thus always possible this awareness may influence their responses and create response bias.

Methods of collecting quantitative survey data fall into three broad categories—self-completion, interviewer completed, and observation. **Self-completion methods** include mail surveys, Internet or other electronic surveys, and drop-off and pickup surveys and similar approaches. **Interviewer-completed methods** involve direct contact with the respondents through personal interviews, either face-to-face or via telephone. Quantitative observation studies involve collecting a large amount of numerical data, such as that from individuals' click-through behavior on the Internet or purchasing behavior monitored via scanner methods. The primary difference in observation techniques between qualitative research and quantitative research is that qualitative observation involves mostly human observation and the recording of

Exhibit 8.4

Frequency of Usage of Selected Survey Methods

Method	Percent
Online	59
CATI (computer-assisted telephone interviewing)	22
Face-to-face/intercepts	11
Mail	3
Mobile phone	1
Other	4
Total	100

Source: Research Industry Trends 2008 Report, Pioneer Marketing Research, GreenBook, Rockhopper Research, GMI, Peanut Labs and MRG

narrative information, whereas quantitative observation approaches involve counting and numerical information on behavior, actions, or events instead of narrative. Exhibit 8.4 shows the frequency of usage of selected survey methods.

As noted, personal interviews, whether structured or unstructured, are often used to obtain detailed qualitative information from a relatively small number of individuals. This approach is sometimes referred to as an in-depth survey. On the other hand, structured questionnaires are used to collect quantitative data from large numbers of individuals in a relatively quick and convenient manner. Finding a company to assist in conducting a survey is a lot easier with the Internet, as the Business Research Dashboard on Quirks.com shows.

SELF-COMPLETION SURVEYS

Self-completion approaches to collecting data use structured questionnaires. A structured questionnaire is a predetermined set of questions designed to capture data from respondents. It is a scientifically developed instrument for measurement of key characteristics of individuals, companies, events, and other phenomena. Good survey research requires good questionnaires to ensure accuracy of the data.

In conducting a questionnaire-based study there are a number of interrelated activities that must be considered: the general design of the questionnaire, validation of the questionnaire by pretesting, and the method by which the questionnaire is administered.

Questionnaire surveys are generally designed to obtain large quantities of data, usually in numerical form. A questionnaire consists of a standard set of questions with answers to the questions often limited to a few predetermined, mutually exclusive and exhaustive outcomes. "Mutually exclusive" means each answer has a separate response category, while "exhaustive" means a response category has been included for every possible answer. Questionnaire wording is important for accuracy of the information collected, and in Chapter 10 we give you guidelines on how to deal with this topic as well as other questionnaire design considerations.

Questionnaires are frequently completed without a researcher being present. The

---

■————**Business Research Dashboard**————■
Quirk's, Your Online Source for Research Services

For over fifteen years Quirk's Marketing Research Review has been producing a monthly print magazine that reports on research trends and techniques in a simple and straightforward manner to promote the value of research. The company's Web site (http://www.quirks.com) is designed to encourage the use, understanding, and value of research while providing free access to as many research resources as possible. On the Web site business researchers can search for and purchase over 40,000 research reports from more than 350 publishers.

The site also allows researchers access to archived articles from the magazine, including case histories on successful research projects, discussion of research techniques, the statistical use of data in marketing research, and other topics relevant to the research industry. Some of the directories available online include the Researcher SourceBook, which contains listings of more than 7,300 firms providing marketing research products and services, of worldwide focus group facilities, and of more than 300 data processing and statistical analysis firms. For example, if you log on to the Web site and select focus group facilities, you will get a listing of five recent articles involving focus group research. After using the online directories to locate a firm, business researchers can then use the online Request For Proposal Form to send project parameters directly to a particular firm.

Another unique feature of the site is the Job Postings page that enables researchers to view or post research related employment opportunities and view or post online resumes. From job postings and case studies to directories and a glossary of research terms, Quirk's offers marketing and business research professionals the tools, information, and solutions to almost any research question they might face.

---

assumption is respondents have the knowledge and motivation to complete them on their own. It does mean, however, the topic, design, and format must be sufficiently appealing that respondents actually complete and return the questionnaire. Examples of self-completion questionnaires include surveys given to theater patrons either before or after a show, or perhaps at intermission; "tabletop" surveys at restaurants or in doctors' offices, and questionnaires sent by auto dealerships following service visits.

Self-completion questionnaires are delivered to respondents in several ways. Traditional approaches include mail and fax surveys. More recently, electronic delivery approaches are being utilized. A major problem with any kind of self-completion questionnaire is the loss of researcher control. You typically do not know whether the intended person has completed the questionnaire, if respondents have answered the questions in their formatted sequence, or whether they have asked for input from others. Any of these deviations can introduce response bias. But perhaps the biggest problem with this type of questionnaire is the low response rate, raising the question of whether those who responded are representative of the target population for the research project.

Mail Surveys

Surveys delivered to respondents via regular mail, fax, and overnight delivery are typically thought of as **mail surveys**. Some mail surveys are short, others are quite long, as many as five or six pages, and in some instances booklets requesting extensive information are used. With fax surveys the researcher has few options. The major limiting factor is that only individuals with fax machines can be surveyed. For business surveys this is not much of a problem, but few individuals have a fax machine at home.

With traditional mail and overnight delivery, however, decisions must be made regarding the envelope, cover letter, length, and incentive. All these factors impact the response rate in some way. Attractive envelopes and stationery, well-written cover letters, and reasonable length questionnaires will all increase response rates. With longer surveys, an incentive will increase responsiveness. While overnight delivery is a costly alternative, it is often used in business-to-business surveys if the budget permits. Prior agreement to participate is generally obtained over the telephone. But actual delivery is by overnight courier, because experience has shown that overnight packages are delivered to the respondent's desk and bypass traditional gatekeepers such as secretaries. If time is a factor, then traditional mail is not a good alternative. Generally speaking, researchers must allow at least three weeks for individuals to respond. But even then, in most instances it will be necessary to send follow-up reminders to achieve a sufficient sample size, and this will take another two or three weeks. Some suggested approaches to increase mail survey response rates are summarized in the Business Research Dashboard.

To conduct mail surveys you must have a list. If you are surveying your own customers or other individuals with whom you already have a relationship, a list will be available. If you are soliciting information from other individuals or organizations, however, it will be necessary to purchase a list from a direct marketing company. Several large companies sell lists. The Business Research Dashboard tells you about the services of one of the larger direct marketing companies.

Electronic

Several approaches are taken with electronic self-completion questionnaires. The traditional approach is to deliver a computer diskette to the respondents. The questionnaire is programmed on the diskette, and respondents simply place the diskette in their computers, follow the instructions, and, when completed, return the diskette to the research company. But e-mail and Web-hosted Internet have replaced this approach in recent years.

E-mail surveys are popular, inexpensive, can be completed in a short period of time, and generally produce high quality data. But Web-hosted Internet surveys have more flexibility. To maintain the anonymity of respondents and increase response rates, **Web-hosted Internet surveys** are typically created and hosted by an independent research company on their own server (computer). But companies sometimes host them on an in-house server. The greater flexibility of Internet surveys is due to the questionnaires' being located on the in-house server, which can include manipulations not possible in e-mail surveys, in which the questionnaire is located on the respondent's side (i.e., it is sent to the respondent and completed on his or her own computer). Access to Web-hosted surveys can be controlled by a password to ensure

■————**Business Research Dashboard**————■
How to Increase Mail Survey Response Rates

Below are some suggested ways to increase response rates in mail surveys.

Approach	Examples
Preliminary contact	Letter, email, or telephone call ahead of time.
Personalization	Individually typed, addressed letter, personal signature, etc.
Response deadline	Provide a due date in the letter.
Appeal	Convince respondent survey is important and has some social or other important value.
Sponsorship	Survey is sponsored by an important organization, such as a national trade organization or prestigious university.
Incentives	Nonmonetary gifts like summary of findings or a ballpoint pen. Monetary incentive like $2.00 to buy a cup of coffee.
Questionnaire length	Print on both sides of the paper and make no longer than four pages.
Type of postage	Special commemorative stamp. If the budget permits; sending by overnight delivery such as FedEx will bypass "gatekeepers" to directly reach the intended recipient. Always include a postage-paid envelope for returning the questionnaire.
Follow-up	Send follow-up reminders such as a postcard. Sometimes respondents lose the questionnaire, so sending a letter with a second copy can help.

Source: Adapted from J. Conant, D. Smart, and B. Walker, "Mail Survey Facilitation Techniques: An Assessment and Proposal Regarding Reporting Practices," *Journal of the Market Research Society*, 32, 4 (1990), 569–580.

■————**Business Research Dashboard**————■
Direct Marketing Campaigns for Individuals and Organizations

USADATA is one of the leading U.S. direct marketing companies. It uses a variety of methods to develop lists of business-to-business and business-to-consumer mailing lists covering the United States. It notes that it has provided successful sales leads for more than 100,000 businesses. Direct marketing represents an excellent method of efficiently contacting potential customers. Its proprietary modeling approaches help to identify highly targeted segments and lists with the greatest potential to produce high response rates. It also offers e-mail and mobile marketing capabilities that have the added benefits of interactivity and lower costs. USADATA is privacy compliant, with 38 million opt-in e-mail addresses of customers and 15 million opt-in e-mail addresses of businesses, a significant resource!

Sources: USADATA, http://www.usadata.com/; US Data Corporation, http://usdatacorporation.com/; "USDATA Corporation Acquired by Tecnomatix," press release, July 30, 2003, http://www.automation.com/content/usdata-corporation-acquired-by-tecnomatix, accessed November 2009.

only qualified respondents complete the survey according to specified instructions. Respondents are contacted and asked to participate and then given a unique password. In general, Internet surveys provide quick responses and high quality data. But they can be expensive because of the Web-site programming costs. When evaluating the option of an Internet data collection approach, researchers must ensure that the profile of Internet users includes their targeted respondents. For example, consumers that are sixty or older are less likely to respond to Internet surveys.

Another type of self-completion interview is the **kiosk survey**. A self-contained kiosk is located in a high-traffic area, and individuals sign on to obtain information and submit survey information. Drug stores use them to dispense medical information. Supermarkets use them to provide recipes and related information for food purchases. Conferences and trade shows use them at hotels to collect and disperse information, and fuel stops on highways use them to collect and disperse travel information. The main problem is the lack of control over who uses a kiosk to fill out a questionnaire. But they do provide 24-7 access to information and data collection ability.

Data is also collected electronically via scanner equipment when customers pay for merchandise. The Business Research Dashboard illustrates how scanning devices provide a means for businesses to collect data electronically.

■————**Business Research Dashboard**————■
Scanner Data Improves Understanding of Purchasing Behavior

When you purchase something in a drugstore, supermarket, or almost any retail store, the item you purchase is scanned into a computer. The bar code enables each store to know exactly what products are selling, when, and at what price. In addition, store managers can keep accurate control of inventory, making it easy to order more products when they run low. Walmart is among the leaders in the use of scanner data. Walmart does not own most of the products on its shelves. Instead, the product manufacturers arrange to put them on Walmart shelves but still own the products. With its scanning system, Walmart always knows what is on its shelves, where in the store it is placed, what products are selling, and which ones need to be reordered. Scanner data has enabled Walmart and other retailers to build and manage larger inventories than would have been possible a few years ago.

Scanner equipment can also be used with bar-coded customer cards, so customers can be associated with their purchases and the data stored in a central database. The process takes a second or two per transaction and requires only that the customer produce the card at purchase time. Scanner technology is widely used in the marketing research industry. Questionnaires can be prepared using word-processing software and printed with a laser printer. Respondents can complete the questionnaire with any type of writing instrument. With the appropriate software and scanning device, the researcher can scan the completed questionnaires, after which the data is checked for errors, categorized, and stored—all in a matter of seconds. Retailers often collect 400 to 500 completed surveys in a week or so. Thus, scanner technology offers many benefits for data collection at a reasonable cost.

Sources: Barry Deville, "The Data Assembly Challenge," *Marketing Research Magazine* (Fall/ Winter 1995), 4; "Experience with an IT Asset Management System," BNET white paper 2003-03-24, http://resources.bnet.com/topic/scanner+data.html; "IRI Launches InfoScan Advantage to Track Wal-Mart Sales," *Appliance Design*, August 21, 2001, http://www.appliancedesign.com/Articles/Breaking_News/f94150f96b938010VgnVCM100000f932a8c0, accessed December 2009.

INTERVIEWER-COMPLETED SURVEYS

Interviewer administered questionnaires are completed either face-to-face or over the telephone. Face-to-face and telephone interviews are the most prevalent methods of collecting interviewer-completed survey data.

Personal interviews involve face-to-face contact with respondents. Telephone interviews, though not face-to-face, can still be effective. Telephone interviewing is generally faster and less expensive than personal interviews, but it precludes the possibility of using visuals, and generally respondents will not tolerate as long an interview as in a face-to-face situation. Telephone surveys do enable greater control, however, particularly when conducted from a central facility under a supervisor's monitoring.

The objectives of the research can impact the decision on which method of administering questionnaires is best. Exhibit 8.5 summarizes the advantages and disadvantages of the major methods of administering survey questionnaires.

Exhibit 8.5

Advantages and Disadvantages of Methods of Administering Survey Questionnaires

Method	Advantages	Disadvantages
Ordinary mail, fax, or drop off: Involves sending the questionnaire to predetermined respondents with a cover letter. Generally used when there is a large number of geographically dispersed respondents.	Wider access and better coverage Provides anonymity Relatively low cost Large sample size Respondents complete questionnaire at own pace	Questionnaire must be simple Low response rate Points of clarification are not possible Follow-up of nonresponses is difficult
In person: Requires face-to-face contact with respondents. Generally used with smaller samples to gather opinions and when dealing with sensitive issues.	Establishes empathy and interest in the study Can probe complex issues Clarifies respondents queries High response rate	Expensive in time and money May lead to interviewer bias Difficult to obtain wide access Relatively small sample size
Over the telephone: A form of personal interviewing used to obtain information quickly. Generally used to gain access to respondents who are geographically dispersed.	Provides personal contact Wide geographic coverage Easy and quick access Can be done with the aid of a computer	Short interview time Limited to listed telephone owners Can be expensive
Electronic: Administered via intranet and Internet through the use of e-mail. An increasingly popular method for collecting data.	Easy to administer Low cost Global reach Fast data collection and analysis No interviewer bias	Loss of anonymity Can be complex to design and program Limited to computer users

OBSERVATION

Observation is increasingly being used for quantitative research. Scanner and Internet-tracking technologies enable researchers to count sales of products and services, observe behavior on Web sites, and assess advertising response and e-commerce behavior. Thus, while observation has traditionally been mostly a qualitative data collection tool, it is now being used for many more quantitative studies.

CONTINUING CASE: SAMOUEL'S GREEK CUISINE
Choosing the Best Data Collection Method

The business consultant hired by Phil Samouel has recommended a survey of his customers and his employees. The consultant has also recommended a survey of Gino's customers. For the survey of Samouel's employees, the consultant has said there are several options. One is to give all employees a copy of the questionnaire and ask them to return it to Phil. A second option is to give employees a copy of the questionnaire and ask them to return it to the consultant. The third option is to require all employees to come to a meeting and complete the questionnaire. He says there are other alternatives, but they are likely too expensive.

For the survey of Samouel's customers, the consultant has suggested a couple of approaches for collecting the data. One approach involves asking customers to complete the questionnaires at their tables either before or after they get their food. Another is to stop them on the way out of the restaurant and ask them to complete a questionnaire. A third option is to give it to them and ask that they complete it at home and mail it back. A fourth option is to load software on the computer, write a program to randomly select customers, and, when paying their bills, give them instructions on how to go to a Web site and complete the survey. The last option is the most expensive one, however, because the programming and computer setup are costly.

The consultant has been brainstorming with other restaurant industry experts on how best to collect data from Gino's customers. He does not yet have any options he feels comfortable suggesting to Phil.

Which of the data collection options is best for the employee survey? Why? Which of the data collection options is best for the customer survey? Why? What are some possible ways to collect data from Gino's customers? Recommend a method you believe will work best.

SUMMARY

PROVIDE AN OVERVIEW OF THE DIFFERENT DATA COLLECTION METHODS

There are many different data collection methods. The selection of a particular data collection method can influence the accuracy and reliability of the data. It is thus important to select the correct method. Data collection can be divided into two types—qualitative and quantitative. Both methods can be used to capture narrative or numeric data using observation, trained interviewers, and technology. Electronic data collection approaches are emerging as one of the most efficient and cost-effective means of collecting data. But traditional methods will continue to have their roles long into the future.

Describe Differences Between Qualitative and Quantitative Data Collection

Qualitative data is usually captured in narrative form and is used to describe human behavior or business phenomena. Quantitative data, on the other hand, is captured through the use of various numeric means, such as scales. Qualitative approaches to data collection are frequently used at the exploratory stage of the research process. Their role is to identify or refine research problems, which may help to formulate and test conceptual frameworks. In contrast, quantitative approaches to data collection are often used when we have well-defined research problems or theoretical models. Validation of these concepts and models usually involves the use of data obtained from large-scale questionnaire surveys.

Understand the Differences Between Observation and Interview Methods

Data is obtained through observation, self-completion, or interviews. Observation data is collected through a systematic approach to recognizing and recording occurrences associated with people, events, behavior, and objects. Collection of such data can be achieved through trained observers or through mechanical or electronic means like videos, scanning at checkout counters, or other electronic methods. Observation data can be narrative, graphic, or numeric.

A survey usually involves the collection of large amounts of quantitative data through the use of self-completion or interviewer-completed questionnaires, or through observation using structured guides. Questionnaires can include both closed-ended and open-ended questions, which yield numeric and narrative data, respectively. In cases where narrative data is obtained, it can be converted to numbers through coding techniques. An example of this is content analysis.

Explain the Role of the Various Interview Methods in Obtaining Data

An interview is the interaction between interviewer and interviewee through face-to-face, telephone, or computer dialogue. Interviews are an appropriate means for gathering complex and sensitive information, or where a lot of elaboration is necessary to understand concepts. It is important that an interview be conducted in a relaxed and friendly atmosphere.

The nature of the interview can range from being highly unstructured to highly structured. Highly unstructured interviews do not require an interview schedule, and this makes free and open dialogue between interviewer and interviewee possible. On the other hand, a highly structured interview requires an interview schedule of prepared questions to be followed when conducting the interview. In both types of interviews care must be taken to avoid biases and inconsistencies in the data collected.

Focus group interviews and depth interviews are both important discovery-oriented exploratory research tools. Depth interviews are preferable when a respondent may be more open in a private setting as opposed to a group setting. Focus groups are preferable when the group dynamics will not hinder comment. In fact, the group dynamics often encourage discussion.

ASSESS THE USE OF SELF-COMPLETION VERSUS INTERVIEWER-COMPLETED SURVEYS

Surveys collect data using questionnaires. When the questionnaires are completed by the individual taking the survey, it is referred to as a self-completion survey. When the questionnaires are completed by having an interviewer ask the individual the questions, it is referred to as an interviewer-completed survey.

A questionnaire is a means of obtaining data not already available in written or electronic form as secondary data, or that cannot be easily obtained by observation. An example of data that cannot be readily obtained by observation is feelings or beliefs. Data generated by a questionnaire is generally referred to as primary data.

A questionnaire can be unstructured, semistructured, or highly structured. Irrespective of its structure, a questionnaire must produce accurate and reliable data amenable to statistical analysis using software packages such as SPSS. Key to achieving this objective is the design and development of the questionnaire.

ETHICAL DILEMMA

Midway through a series of focus groups about the new mobile data package a regional telecommunications company is planning to offer, the research firm tells the product manager, Salvador Andretti, that customer response has been overwhelmingly positive. Salvador reported the early feedback to his boss, who was excited because the company needs a new product that will boost company sales before the end of the year if bonuses are to be paid. In anticipation, Salvador decides to observe the final focus group himself. While observing, he begins to sense that the focus group facilitator is leading the subjects toward favorable responses. He fears the research is flawed but still believes the product will be popular with consumers. He is also aware that if he reschedules the focus groups with a new facilitator, he will not have the data his boss needs to make the final decision about releasing the product until the first quarter of next year. If you were Salvador, what would you do? Should you present the focus group findings to your boss without voicing your concerns? Did the researcher act unethically in disclosing the early but incomplete results?

REVIEW QUESTIONS

1. Why would a business researcher want to collect data?
2. What are the main data gathering methods? Comment on their strengths and weaknesses and illustrate their use with examples.

3. What are the advantages and disadvantages of conducting surveys on the Internet?
4. What is the difference between structured and unstructured interviews?
5. What are focus groups and when would the business researcher use them?

DISCUSSION AND THINKING ACTIVITIES

1. An organization is experiencing low morale among its employees. Why and how might survey research be used in this situation?
2. What are the main issues that need to be considered in selecting a method of data collection for a survey of opinions about diversity in the workplace?
3. What type of questions would one expect to find on a survey of opinions about business ethics? Illustrate, with examples, their purpose, wording, and coding. Would the topics in a business ethics survey differ from those in a survey of political ethics?
4. How would you go about creating a relaxed and friendly atmosphere during an interview? Give examples.
5. Go to the Web site for this book, at www.mesharpe-student.com. Click on the link to "Bar Soap Focus Groups" and review the list of bar soap purchase criteria that were identified in the focus groups. Rank the criteria from most important to least important in deciding which brand of soap to purchase. Now click on "Ranking Answer" to see if your answers are the same as those in the original sample. Can you think of any criteria that were not identified? If so, send and e-mail them to one of the authors of this book to see if they agree. Their e-mail addresses are provided on the home page of this Web site.
6. How have recent technology developments facilitated data collection?
7. "Bias in data collection cannot be avoided." Give your view on this statement and suggest ways to minimize bias.
8. Critique the following methods of data collection.
    a. A shopping mall places interviewers in the parking lot every Saturday to ask respondents where they live and the two to three stores they came to visit on this shopping trip.
    b. To evaluate the popularity of a new television series, the Fox channel invited people to call a number and vote yes, they would watch it again, or no, they would not watch it again. Each caller was charged $2.00.
    c. A supermarket recently completed a major renovation. To obtain customer reactions, the checkout personnel placed a short questionnaire into each customer's grocery bag while putting the groceries in.

INTERNET EXERCISES

1. Go to http://www.nielsen.com and http://www.symphonyiri.com. Prepare a report on what these two companies are saying about their latest scanner-based technology.

2. Use an Internet Web browser such as Yahoo! or Google. Conduct a search using the words "data collection." Prepare a report summarizing what you found.

3. The Web site www.stat-usa.gov offers a single point of access to authoritative business, trade, and economic information from across the federal government. Go to http://www.stat-usa.gov/ and prepare a report summarizing the information available on this Web site and the methods used to collect the data.

4. The Web site for the Princeton University Survey Research Center is located at http://www.princeton.edu/~psrc/. Go to this Web site and prepare a report summarizing the types of information located there and why it might be of interest to business researchers.

NOTES

1. Arch G. Woodside and Elizabeth J. Wilson, "Applying the Long Interview in Direct Marketing Research," *Journal of Direct Marketing Research*, 9, 1 (1995), 37–65.

2. Gary Khermouch, "Consumers in the Mist," *BusinessWeek* (February 26, 2001), 92–93.

3. William Hunt, "Getting the Word on Deception," *Security Management*, 39 (June 1995), 26–27.

4. Donald P. Robin, M.F. Giallourakis, F. David, and T.E. Moritz, "A Different Look at Codes of Ethics," *Business Horizons*, 32, 1 (1989), 66–73; Brian J. Farrell and Deirdre M. Cobin, "A Content Analysis of Codes of Ethics in Australian Enterprises," *Journal of Managerial Psychology*, 11, 1 (1996), 37–56.

5. Michael L. Maynard and Charles R. Taylor, "Girlish Images Across Cultures: Analyzing Japanese versus U.S. *Seventeen* Magazine Ads," *Journal of Advertising*, 28 (Spring 1999), 39–49.

6. Jennifer Lawrence and Paul Berger, "Let's Hold a Focus Group," *Direct Marketing*, 61 (December 1999), 40–44; Thomas L. Greenbaum, *Handbook of Focus Group Research* (New York: Lexington, 1993).

7. Robert N. Lussier, "Flexible Work Arrangements from Policy to Implementation," *Supervision*, 56 (September 1995), 10.

8. "EAR Focus Groups Target ISO 14000," *Internal Auditor*, 54 (June 1997), 8.

9. Pamela Hunter, "Using Focus Groups in Campaigns: A Caution," *Campaigns and Elections*, 21 (August 2000), 38–41.

10. Max Walsh, "Focus Groups Set a New Agenda," *Newsweek*, 117 (February 9, 1999), 7.

11. See *Marketing News*, 36 (March 4), for a directory of focus group firms and facilities. See also Quirk's Marketing Research Review, at http://www.quirks.com.

12. Dana James, "This Bulletin Just In: Online Research Technique Proving Invaluable," *Marketing News*, 36 (March 4, 2002), 45–46.

9 Measurement and Scaling

LEARNING OUTCOMES

1. Understand the role of concepts in business research
2. Explain the notion of measurement
3. Provide an overview of the types of measurement scales
4. Distinguish between reliability and validity

Measurement is an important issue in business research. We must correctly measure the concepts we are examining, otherwise our interpretations and conclusions will not be accurate. To ensure the accuracy of our findings, we must consider how we measure as well as whether our measures are valid and reliable.

Measurement is a common occurrence for most people. College entrance examinations are measuring devices. So are employment tests. Exams in university classes measure achievement. Similarly, quarterly and annual reviews at work measure our progress. In a group setting, measurement is involved if we count the number of individuals, classify them as either male or female, or judge them as introverted or extroverted. Likewise, when we purchase automobile insurance or take an exam to get a driver's license, measurement is involved. These are only a few examples of measurement in our everyday lives. In most instances we take the measurement process for granted. We seldom think about how we measure and the accuracy of the measurement. This chapter examines some of the more important issues we need to be aware of in measurement.

WHAT IS A CONCEPT?

A **concept** is an abstraction or idea formed by the perception of phenomena. The idea is a combination of a number of similar characteristics of the concept. The characteristics are the variables that, collectively, define the concept and make its measurement possible. Indeed, together they indirectly measure the concept, which is also referred to as a construct. For example, the variables listed below were used to measure the concept "customer interaction."[1]

- This customer was easy to talk with.
- This customer genuinely enjoyed my helping her or him.
- This customer likes to talk to people.
- This customer was interested in socializing.
- This customer was friendly.
- This customer tried to establish a personal relationship.
- This customer seemed interested in me, not only as a salesperson but also as a person.

By obtaining scores on each of the individual variables, you can indirectly measure the overall concept of customer interaction. The individual scores are then combined into a single summary score, according to a predefined set of rules. The resulting score is often referred to as a scale, an index, or a summated rating scale. In the example of customer interaction, the individual variables were scored using a five-point scale, with 1 = "strongly disagree" and 5 = "strongly agree."

Suppose the research objective is to identify the characteristics (variables) associated with a theory of restaurant satisfaction. The researcher is likely to review the literature on satisfaction, conduct both formal and informal interviews, and then draw on his or her own experiences to identify characteristics such as quality of food, quality of service, and value for money as important components of a conceptual model of restaurant satisfaction. Logical integration of these characteristics then provides a theoretical framework and a conceptual model, which can facilitate empirical investigation of the concept of restaurant satisfaction.

MEASUREMENT IN BUSINESS RESEARCH

Measurement is a fundamental concept of business research. To understand business research, or really any concept, we must be able to measure it. Without measurement, it is difficult if not impossible to comment on business behavior or phenomena. This is because we subconsciously measure something when we say something about it. For example, if we buy an ice cream cone and say it tastes good, we are measuring. We are saying it tastes good compared to other flavors we have tasted previously. Similarly, if we say an employee is lazy or irresponsible or uncooperative, we are measuring.

Managers are interested in measuring many aspects of business. Supervisors measure employee performance, motivation, turnover rates, and other performance indicators. Accountants measure profits and losses, assets and liabilities, depreciation, and so forth. Marketing managers measure awareness of a particular store or restaurant; favorable or unfavorable perceptions of various characteristics, such as service quality, portion size, or taste; brand preference, volume of traditional "brick-

and-mortar" versus online sales, and so on. The more effectively managers measure these business aspects, the better their decisions.

Measurement Difficulties

When we think of measurement, most of us think in terms of our own experiences. How fast am I driving, or how high is that airplane flying? How much do I weigh, or how tall am I? Measurement of such things is easy because their measurement is not complex. It is easy to use a ruler or set of scales to measure height or weight. In contrast, when we attempt to measure attitudes, opinions, or perceptions, it is more difficult. Often we do not have precise definitions of concepts such as satisfaction. Consequently, we have to develop new scales (questions) to measure a concept; we do not have tools like rulers or speedometers to measure concepts precisely.

In business research we work with concepts that can range from being simple and concrete to those that are complex and abstract. Therefore, one of the first things we have to do is develop precise definitions of the concepts we are examining in our research, thereby ensuring there is no ambiguity in their interpretation. In this book we use the terms "concept" and "construct" interchangeably. Recall that a concept is an abstraction or idea formed in your mind based on perceptions of phenomena. Examples of concepts in business include job satisfaction, job commitment, brand awareness, brand loyalty, service quality, image, risk, channel conflict, empathy, strategic orientation, executive values, motivation to search online, and so on.

Consider concepts such as "age" and "income" as opposed to "satisfaction" and "competence of employees." For "age" and "income" there will, generally speaking, be agreement about their definitions because they are directly observable and represent facts. But for "satisfaction" and "competence of employees" there is unlikely to be a common interpretation of their meanings, and these concepts can be measured only indirectly. The more complex and abstract the concept is—for example, "executive values"—the more we need to provide an explicit definition.

Once we have defined the concepts, we still must be sure we measure them properly. The measurement process involves specifying the variables that serve as proxies for the concepts (constructs). A **proxy** is a variable that represents a single component of a larger concept, and, taken together, several proxies are said to measure a concept. Proxies are also referred to in business research as indicator or manifest variables because they indirectly measure constructs. Identification of proxy variables (indicators) is important because the variables provide the numerical scores used to measure concepts in quantitative terms. The Business Research Dashboard gives examples of the proxy variables for several concepts—source credibility, financial and performance risks, and pricing perceptions.

Variables that are relatively concrete in nature, such as gender, age, height, household income, food prices, and even social class, are relatively easy to define and thus can be measured in an objective and fairly precise manner through observation, questioning, or the use of a calibrated instrument, such as a ruler. The following examples illustrate how we might measure the demographic variables mentioned above.

■———**Business Research Dashboard**———■
Examples of Proxy Variables for Concepts

Business researchers use proxy (indicator) variables to help them measure concepts or constructs for their research. The examples here are typical of a wide variety of business research studies. Excerpts from the study are reported, but the entire scale can be viewed in the original article.

Source Credibility Check

A six-item, seven-point scale was used. Respondents were asked to rate the spokesperson on each of the following:

Trustworthy—Not trustworthy
Open-minded—Not open-minded
Good—Bad
Expert—Not expert
Experienced—Not experienced
Trained—Untrained

Perceived Financial Risk

A three-item, seven-point scale was used. Respondents were asked:

Considering the potential investment involved, for you to purchase the Hito VCR would be:
Not risky at all—Very risky

I think the purchase of the Hito brand VCR would lead to financial risk for me because of the possibility of such things as higher maintenance and/or repair costs.
Improbable—Very probable

Given the potential financial expenses associated with purchasing the Hito brand VCR, how much overall financial risk is associated with purchasing the Hito brand VCR?
Very little risk—Substantial risk

Perceived Performance Risk

A three-item, seven-point scale was used. Respondents were asked:

How confident are you that the Hito brand VCR will perform as described?
Very confident—Not confident at all

How certain are you that the Hito brand VCR will work satisfactorily?
Certain—Uncertain

Do you feel that the Hito brand VCR will perform the functions that were described in the advertisement?
Do feel sure—Do not feel sure

(continued)

Message Framing Check

Respondents were provided an aided-recall question:

How did the spokesperson in the advertisement rate most of the features of the Hito VCR?
Hito rated superior to Toshiba   _____
Toshiba rated superior to Hito   _____

Price Check

Respondents were asked the following using a seven-point scale:

The price of the Hito VCR is:
Very high—Very low

Source: D. Grewal, J. Gotlieb, and H. Marmorstein, "The Moderating Effects of Message Framing and Source Credibility on the Price-Perceived Risk Relationship," *Journal of Consumer Research,* 21 (June 1994), 145–153.

Gender

Suppose we need to know the gender of a customer. There is no need for a definition of gender since people have a clear understanding of the concept. We determine the gender of a person either by observation or, in a survey, by including a question asking the respondent to state their gender. Thus, a simple concept like gender can be measured without error, assuming it is recorded correctly. The measurement involves assigning numerical scores to the outcome of the gender variable, such as 1 for male and 0 for female. Note the assignment of numbers is arbitrary and could just as easily be 1 for female and 0 for male.

Dining Out Expenditures

Now consider having to measure the average weekly eating out expenditures of a family. Again, the concept is easily understood and not in need of an explicit definition. To measure this concept all we need do is to include a question in our survey that asks the respondent to state his or her family's average weekly expenditure on eating out. In this case, while the respondent will be clear as to what is being asked, he or she is likely to find it difficult to give a precise answer. In such a situation measurement of the variable can be achieved by assigning a number on a continuum, with a lower limit of 0. There will still be some error, because the individual will be responding based on an ability to recall a previous period (assuming no record of expenditures was kept). But ideally, the error will be minimal because the concept is easily understood.

Total Family Wealth

Contrast the examples above on gender and dining out expenditures with the concept of "total family wealth." It is highly unlikely there is a common understanding of the concept "total family wealth." The understanding will depend on how well we define the concept. The definition can include tangible variables like cash, property, stocks and bonds, and even cars, as well as intangible variables such as education, health, and so on. In this case, a definition of the concept "total family wealth" will be complex, incorporating a combination of some or all of the variables considered as being manifestations or indicators of total family wealth. Further, measurement of the concept will involve the use of a series of questions to represent the variables that make up the concept. Then, from each participant in a survey a numerical response to each of the questions will be obtained. An overall measure of the concept is usually determined by combining the individual scores, by calculating either their sum or their average. The amount of error associated with this question will depend on how precise the researcher was in defining the concept and its individual variables.

The preceding examples demonstrate the definitional and measurement problems confronting business researchers. Concepts such as gender and expenditure, for example, are easily defined and objectively measured in absolute terms. In contrast, concepts that are complex and abstract in nature, for example, wealth, satisfaction, organizational commitment, and image are relatively difficult to define and measure objectively. To measure such concepts researchers are likely to use subjective measures that include perceptions, attitudes, beliefs, opinions, and values. In the next section we describe how complex concepts can be measured.

How to Measure Concepts

Measurement involves assigning numbers to a variable according to certain rules. The assigned numbers must reflect the characteristics of the phenomenon being measured. For example, if we are measuring how important food quality is in the selection of a restaurant, we might say the number 5 represents "very important" and the number 0 represents "not important at all." In this case, the rule is a higher number means something is relatively more important, and a lower number means it is relatively unimportant.

There are four levels of measurement available to the researcher. The levels determine the sophistication of the measurement employed. The researcher must decide on the level of measurement to be used before the research is conducted. Such a decision is also influenced by the nature of the concept. For example, a respondent must be willing and able to provide information at the level sought. This may not be true if the researcher is asking questions about sensitive issues like sexual orientation, birth control use, medical condition, or even income. Similarly, if data is obtained by observation, the variable's measurement will depend on the situational context and the ability of the observer to accurately record the observed behavior. For example, if we are measuring online purchases, measurement is easy because all the information is collected from the online transactions. Similarly, measurement of scanner data at a store checkout counter is easy because the information is automatically collected and stored in a computer database. On the other hand, if we are watching people walk out of a movie theater in an attempt to determine whether they enjoyed the movie, we are faced with a more difficult task. It is more difficult to accurately measure a quality such as enjoyment via observation.

As you may recall, the business consultant hired by Phil Samouel recommended an employee survey as well as a customer survey. It would be difficult if not impossible to interview Gino's employees, because he would likely not permit it. Therefore, the employee survey is based on a sample of Samouel's employees. The employee survey questionnaire is shown in Exhibit 9.1. We use it to illustrate several points on questionnaire design in this chapter and in Chapter 10.

Measurement is achieved through the use of scales. A **scale** is a measurement tool that can be used to measure a question with a predetermined number of outcomes. These outcomes can be directional or categorical (labels). For example, a yes/no scale measures a directional outcome, either yes or no. Other examples of such a scale might measure whether an employee agrees or disagrees with a supervisor or company policy, or likes or dislikes a particular product or service. For some scales the number of distinct outcomes can be more than two. For example, a question on industry type would represent more than two outcomes and might include categories for financial, manufacturing, retailing, and so on. In this case the outcome is strictly a label.

In contrast, when scales are continuous they measure not only direction or classification but intensity as well. Examples of such scales are time to complete task, age of an investment project, preference or importance, and so on. Thus, in addition to measuring agree/disagree, a continuous scale can measure the intensity of agreement, such as "strongly agree" or "somewhat agree." Furthermore, the intensity of the scale can vary, with a three-point scale measuring little intensity and a ten-point scale providing the opportunity for measuring a great deal of respondent variation in intensity of feeling.

TYPES OF SCALES

The four levels of measurement are represented by different types of scales: nominal, ordinal, interval, and ratio. Variables measured at the nominal or ordinal levels are discrete and are referred to as either categorical or nonmetric. Variables measured at the interval or ratio levels are continuous and referred to as either quantitative or metric. In the following paragraphs we discuss the different measurement scales in more detail.

NOMINAL SCALE

A **nominal scale** uses numbers as labels to identify and classify objects, individuals, or events. For example, when an athlete is assigned a number, this is an example of the use of a nominal scale. In using a nominal scale each number is given to only one object (individual). Numbers used in this manner serve as a label identifying, for example, basketball players. In business research, nominal scales are used to identify individuals, job titles or positions, brands, stores, and other objects. Consider the following example:

A survey of diners poses the following question:

Are you happy with the service at Samouel's Greek Cuisine? _____ Yes _____ No

In this case the restaurant is the object and the measured characteristic is happiness with the service. The predetermined categories are "happy" or "not happy," as reflected by the nominal scale, with two discrete scale points, yes or no. Each respondent can be placed in one of the two categories—yes I am happy, or no I am not happy. The Samouel's employee survey shown in Exhibit 9.1 has two nominal questions, X_{18}, "work type," and X_{19}, "gender."

Nominal scales are not limited to just two categories. For example, we may characterize a restaurant according to ownership type, sole ownership, partnership, or corporation. Similarly, we might measure occupation with a nominal scale using the categories "teacher," "banker," "doctor," "lawyer," and so forth. A requirement for a nominal scale is that its categories are mutually exclusive and exhaustive. This means each category must be different (no overlap), and all possible categories must be included.

To ensure all possible categories are considered, researchers typically use an "other" category. But care must be taken to ensure that not too many respondents choose this category. More than 15 percent response to an "other" category is usually considered too high. In such cases we must learn more about why individuals are choosing the "other" category. For example, it is typical to indicate "Please specify _____" beside the "other" category. We can then determine how individuals are responding and create another category to represent the responses that make up a large portion of the "other" responses.

Nominal scales are the lowest level of measurement. Data analysis is restricted mostly to counts of the number of responses in each category, calculation of the mode or percentage for a particular question, and use of the chi-square statistic.

ORDINAL SCALE

An **ordinal scale** is a ranking scale. It places objects in a predetermined category that is ordered according to a criterion such as preference, age, income group, importance, and so forth. This scale enables the researcher to determine if an object has more or less of a characteristic than some other object. But it does not enable the researcher to determine how much more or less of the characteristic an object has. The following example illustrates this point:

A survey of diners poses the following question:

Regarding your visits to restaurants in the last month, please rank the following attributes from 1 to 4, with 4 being the most important reason for selecting the restaurant and 1 being the least important. Please ensure no ties.

Food quality _____

Atmosphere _____

Prices _____

Employees _____

Exhibit 9.1

The Samouel's Employee Questionnaire

Screening and Rapport Questions

Hello. My name is _____ and I work for DSS Research. As you know, Phil Samouel has hired my company to conduct a survey of its employees to better understand the work environment and suggest improvements as needed. The survey will take only a few minutes and will be very helpful to management in ensuring the work environment meets both employee and company needs. All your answers will be kept strictly confidential. In fact, once the questionnaires have been completed, they will be taken to my office and kept there.

1. Are you currently an employee of Samouel's Greek Cuisine restaurant? ____ Yes ____ No
2. Do you have any questions before you take the survey?   ____ Yes ____ No

If they are currently employed by Samouel's restaurant and do not have any questions, hand them the survey and ask them to complete it. Tell them to ask you if there is anything they do not understand.

WORK ENVIRONMENT SURVEY

Please read all questions carefully. If you do not understand a question, ask the interviewer to help you.

Section 1. Perception Measures

Listed below is a series of statements that could be used to describe <u>Samouel's Greek Cuisine</u> restaurant. Using a scale from 1 to 7, with 7 being "Strongly Agree" and 1 being "Strongly Disagree," to what extent do you agree or disagree that each statement describes your work environment at Samouel's?

		Strongly agree						Strongly disagree
1.	I am paid fairly for the work I do.	1	2	3	4	5	6	7
2.	I am doing the kind of work I want.	1	2	3	4	5	6	7
3.	My supervisor gives credit and praise for work well done.	1	2	3	4	5	6	7
4.	There is a lot of cooperation among the members of my work group.	1	2	3	4	5	6	7
5.	My job allows me to learn new skills.	1	2	3	4	5	6	7
6.	My supervisor recognizes my potential.	1	2	3	4	5	6	7
7.	My work gives me a sense of accomplishment.	1	2	3	4	5	6	7
8.	My immediate work group functions as a team.	1	2	3	4	5	6	7
9.	My pay reflects the effort I put into doing my work.	1	2	3	4	5	6	7
10.	My supervisor is friendly and helpful.	1	2	3	4	5	6	7
11.	The members of my work group have the skills and/or training to do their job well.	1	2	3	4	5	6	7
12.	The benefits I receive are reasonable.	1	2	3	4	5	6	7

(continued)

Section 2. Relationship Measures

Please indicate your view on each of the following questions:

		Strongly agree						Strongly disagree
13.	I have a sense of loyalty to Samouel's Greek Cuisine restaurant.	1	2	3	4	5	6	7
14.	I am willing to put in a great deal of effort beyond that normally expected to help Samouel's Greek Cuisine restaurant to be successful.	1	2	3	4	5	6	7
15.	I am proud to tell others that I work for Samouel's Greek Cuisine restaurant.	1	2	3	4	5	6	7

16. How likely are you to search for another job in the next six months?

7 = Extremely likely
6 = Very likely
5 = Somewhat likely
4 = Neither—about 50-50
3 = Somewhat unlikely
2 = Very unlikely
1 = Extremely unlikely

17. How long have you been an employee of Samouel's Greek Cuisine restaurant?

1 = Less than one year
2 = One year to three years
3 = More than three years

Section 3. Classification Questions

Please indicate the number that classifies you best.

18. Your work type   0   Full-time
                         1   Part-time

19. Your gender   0   Male
                         1   Female

20. Your age in years   _____

Thank you very much for your help. Please give your questionnaire to the interviewer.

Note: The following question was input by the researcher based on performance information provided by management.

21. Performance – employees were rated on a seven-point scale, with 1 = very low performance and 7 = very high performance.

If we tabulated the results of the survey of restaurant selection factors and found that 40 percent of the respondents assigned a 4 to food quality, 30 percent a 4 to atmosphere, 20 percent a 4 to prices, and 10 percent a 4 to employees, then we would know that, relatively speaking, food quality is the most important reason, followed by atmosphere, prices, and employees. Thus, employees would be the least important reason for selecting a restaurant. This same question is used in the Samouel's and Gino's customer surveys shown in Chapter 10.

The points on an ordinal scale do not indicate equal distance between the rankings. For example, the difference between a ranking of 3 and 4 is not necessarily the same as the difference between a ranking of 1 and 2. But we do know that a ranking of 4 is different from 3, just not how much different. When designing ordinal scales the researcher decides whether larger numbers are better, as in our example, where 4 is more important than 3, or smaller numbers are more favorable, such as 1 being more important than 4. In summary, ordinal scales allow entities to be placed into ordered groups.

A higher level of analysis is possible with ordinal data than with nominal data. We can now calculate the median as well as percentages. We can also use Spearman rank-order correlation statistics.

INTERVAL SCALE

An **interval scale** uses numbers to rate objects or events so that the distances between the numbers are equal. Thus, with an interval scale differences between points on the scale can be interpreted and compared meaningfully. The difference between a rating of 3 and 4 is the same as the difference between a rating of 1 and 2. An interval scale has all the qualities of nominal and ordinal scales, but also, because the differences between the scale points are considered to be equal, it is possible to compare the differences between objects.

With an interval scale the location of the zero point is not fixed. Both the zero point and the units of measurement are arbitrary. The temperature scale is frequently mentioned as an example of an interval scale. For the Fahrenheit scale, a 1°F increase in temperature has the same meaning anywhere on the scale, but it is not true that 64°F is twice as hot as 32°F. The explanation for not being able to state 64°F is twice as hot as 32°F is that the origin, or freezing point, for the Fahrenheit scale is arbitrarily set at 32°F.

When researchers use interval scales in business, they attempt to measure concepts such as attitudes, perceptions, feelings, opinions, and values through the use of rating scales. **Rating scales** typically involve the use of statements on a questionnaire accompanied by precoded categories, one of which is selected by the respondent to indicate the extent of agreement or disagreement with a given statement. To illustrate the use of rating scales, consider the following, typical statement on a questionnaire:

Please indicate the extent of your agreement or disagreement with the following statement by circling the appropriate number.

	Strongly disagree	Disagree	Neither agree nor disagree	Agree	Strongly agree
Samouel's restaurant is a fun place to go	1	2	3	4	5

Strictly speaking, the above rating scale is an ordinal scale. It has become customary in business research, however, to treat the scale as if it were an interval. Empirical evidence that people treat the intervals between points on such scales as being equal in magnitude provides justification for treating them as measures on an interval scale. To further illustrate this point, let us consider the following responses:

	Strongly disagree	Disagree	Neither agree nor disagree	Agree	Strongly agree
Response 1 Samouel's restaurant is a fun place to go	①	2	3	4	5
Response 2 Samouel's restaurant is a fun place to go	1	②	3	4	5
Response 3 Samouel's restaurant is a fun place to go	1	2	③	4	5

First, the responses can be ordered in terms of strength of agreement. Response 1 strongly disagrees, response 2 disagrees, and response 3 neither agrees nor disagrees. Second, we observe that respondent 1 is one unit away from respondent 2, who in turn is one unit away from respondent 3. Also, respondent 3 is two units away from respondent 1. Third, we cannot conclude the rating point 2 is twice the intensity of rating point 1 in terms of strength of agreement. Similarly, we cannot conclude that the strength of agreement of respondent 3 is three times that of respondent 1. All we can conclude is that respondent 1 disagrees with the statement by two units more than respondent 3.

In summary, the numbers on an interval scale possess all the properties of nominal and ordinal scales and also allow for objects (respondents) to be compared in terms of their differences on the scale. When constructing rating scales the researcher arbitrarily chooses the origin, or anchor, point of the scale. In the preceding example the scale ranged from 1 to 5. But it could just as easily have ranged from 0 to 4. Moreover, it was a five-point scale, but it could also have been a seven-point or ten-point scale.

The Samouel's employee survey questionnaire has several interval scales. First, all twelve statements representing the work environment perceptions are measured using a seven-point Likert-type interval scale. Similarly, the questions measuring organizational commitment to Samouel's restaurant (X_{13}–X_{15}) are considered interval scales.

Interval scales include the properties of both nominal and ordinal scales. Therefore, data obtained using an interval scale is amenable to the same calculations as the other two scales but can also handle more sophisticated calculations, such as the mean, standard deviation, and Pearson's product-moment correlation coefficient.

RATIO SCALE

A **ratio scale** provides the highest level of measurement. A distinguishing characteristic of a ratio scale is that it possesses a unique origin, or zero point, which makes it possible to compute ratios of points on the scale. A bathroom scale or other common weighing machines are examples of ratio scales because they have absolute zero points. When comparing one point to another, for example, you can say that a 200-pound person is twice as heavy as a 100-pound person. The following example illustrates how a ratio scale might be used in business research. Consider the question:

How many children are there in your household? _____

A response of "0" to the question can be interpreted in only one way. Namely, that there are no children in the household. On the other hand, if we compare two responses, a response of "2" with a response of "4," we can conclude that the number of children in the households are "2" and "4," respectively. Further, we can state that the first household has fewer children than the second household by two children. Finally, we can compute the ratio (4/2) = 2 and conclude that the second household has twice as many children as the first. Ratio scales possess all the properties of the other scales plus an absolute zero point. In terms of statistics, we can compute the coefficient of variation as well as the standard deviation and product-moment correlation.

FREQUENTLY USED MEASUREMENT SCALES

Broadly speaking, there are two types of scales—metric and nonmetric. Metric scales are often referred to as quantitative, and nonmetric as qualitative. Nominal and ordinal scales are nonmetric, and interval and ratio scales are metric. Business researchers use several types of metric and nonmetric scales. Exhibit 9.2 lists the various types of metric and nonmetric scales that are most frequently used in business research.

Exhibit 9.2

Types of Measurement Scales

Metric	Nonmetric
• Likert (summated ratings)	• Categorical
• Numerical	• Rank order
• Semantic differential	• Sorting
• Graphic ratings	• Constant sum

METRIC SCALES

We describe each of the types of metric scales and give examples in the following paragraphs.

Likert Scale

A **Likert scale** attempts to measure attitudes or opinions. Likert scales often use a five-point scale to assess the strength of agreement or disagreement about a statement. For each point on the scale you can develop a label to express the intensity of the respondent's feelings. If you have several statements that all relate to a single concept, such as opinions about a company or product, and you combine the individual statement ratings, the result is referred to as a **summated ratings scale**. Thus, when you sum the scales for all the statements, it is referred to as a summated ratings scale. When you use the scale individually, it is referred to as a **Likert scale**. An example of a Likert scale is:

	Strongly Disagree	Disagree Somewhat	Neither Agree nor Disagree	Somewhat Agree	Strongly Agree
When I hear about a new restaurant I eat there to see what it is like.	1	2	3	4	5

A seven-point Likert scale is also frequently used. The more points you use, the more precision you get with regard to the extent of the agreement or disagreement with a statement. But it is difficult to develop labels for individual numbers when the number of scale points is larger than seven. An example of a seven-point Likert scale is:

	Strongly Disagree	Disagree Somewhat	Disgree Slightly	Neither Agree nor Disagree	Agree Slightly	Agree Somewhat	Agree Strongly
Gino's Italian Ristorante has a wide variety of menu choices.	1	2	3	4	5	6	7

Likert-type scales are also used to measure other concepts in business research, such as importance. An example of an importance measure using a Likert-type scale is shown below:

	Very Unimportant	Somewhat Unimportant	Neither Important nor Unimportant	Somewhat Important	Very Important
How important are credit terms in selecting a vendor to do business with?	1	2	3	4	5

Question X_{16} on the Samouel's employee questionnaire is an example of this type of scale, but it uses a seven-point scale instead of a five-point scale.

A frequent adaptation of Likert-type scales is the **behavioral intention scale**. Business researchers use this type of scale to assess how likely customers are to demonstrate some type of behavior. Examples include likelihood of visiting a particular Web site, of shopping at a particular store, and of purchasing a product or service. In designing behavioral intention scales researchers should include a specific time frame (e.g., likely to purchase within the next three months) in the question, typically based on purchasing frequency for a particular product or the frequency of visiting a Web site or store. An example of a behavioral intention scale follows:

	Not Likely At All					Highly Likely	
How likely are you to purchase a new laptop in the next 12 months?	1	2	3	4	5	6	7

Numerical Scales

Numerical scales have numbers as response options rather than verbal descriptions. The numbers correspond with categories (response options). For example, if there are seven response positions, the scale is called a seven-point numerical scale. This type of scale can be used to assess the level of agreement or disagreement. But it is often used to measure other concepts, such as important/unimportant, essential/not essential, likely/unlikely, satisfied/dissatisfied, and so on. An example follows using the phrasing "important/not at all important" in the question:

> Using a 10-point scale, where 1 is not at all important and 10 is very important, how important is [blank] in your decision to do business with a particular vendor? _____

You fill in the blank with an attribute, such as reliable delivery, product quality, complaint resolution, competitive pricing, credit terms, and so forth. This type of scale can also be designed with a 100-point scale. For example:

> Please indicate your satisfaction with your current job by placing a percentage in the blank, with 0% = Not Satisfied At All and 100% = Highly Satisfied. _____

Numerical scales are frequently used to measure behavioral intentions. Typical concepts examined with this type of scale include intention to buy, likelihood of seeking additional information, likelihood of seeking another job (turnover), likelihood of visiting a particular Web site, probability of investing in a particular stock, and so forth. Scales that measure behavioral components of an individual's attitudes ask about a respondent's likelihood or intention to perform some future action.

We noted earlier that Likert-type scales can be used to measure intentions or likelihood. A method other than Likert-type or numerical scores for measuring likelihood uses descriptive phrases such as in the following examples:

Example 1:
How likely is it that you will pursue your MBA in the next three years?
_____   I definitely will pursue my MBA in the next three years.
_____   I probably will pursue my MBA in the next three years.
_____   I might pursue my MBA in the next three years.
_____   I probably will not pursue my MBA in the next three years.
_____   I definitely will not pursue my MBA in the next three years.

Example 2:
How likely is it that you will look for another job in the next six months?
_____   Extremely Likely
_____   Very Likely
_____   Somewhat Likely
_____   Neither—about a 50-50 chance
_____   Somewhat Unlikely
_____   Very Unlikely
_____   Extremely Unlikely

The choice of a particular method of measuring behavioral concepts depends on the nature of the group being measured and the researcher's preference. All the approaches are considered acceptable. An example of how a numerical scale has been used in business research is reported in the Business Research Dashboard.

■———Business Research Dashboard———■
Measuring Service Quality Expectations in Business Research

Service quality has been studied extensively in many industries. Initial applications were in consumer studies, but more recently the concept is being used in business-to-business studies. Examples of the approach suggested could be used to measure customer expectations via a telephone interviewing approach, as follows:

Instructions: Please think of the kind of company that would deliver excellent service quality, the kind of company with which customers would be pleased to do business. Please indicate the extent to which you think such a company would possess the characteristic described by each statement. If you feel a characteristic is not at all essential for an excellent company, then say the number "one" for the statement. If you feel a characteristic is absolutely essential for excellent companies, say "seven." If your feelings are less strong, give me one of the numbers between one and seven. There are no right or wrong answers—all we are interested in is a number that truly reflects your feelings regarding companies that deliver excellent quality service to their customers.

1. When customers have a problem, an excellent company will show a sincere interest in solving it.   ____
2. Employees of excellent companies will give prompt service to customers.   ____
3. Excellent companies will have the customers' best interests at heart.   ____
4. Employees of excellent companies will have the knowledge to answer customer questions.   ____
5. Excellent companies will perform services right the first time.   ____
6. Excellent companies will give customers individual attention.   ____
7. Materials associated with products and services (such as pamphlets or statements) will be visually appealing in excellent companies.   ____
8. Employees of excellent companies will never be too busy to respond to customer requests.   ____

Source: A. Parasuraman, V.A. Zeithaml, and L.L. Berry, "A Conceptual Model of Service Quality and Its Implications for Future Research," *Journal of Marketing*, 49 (Fall 1985), 41–50.

Semantic Differential Scale

A **semantic differential scale** is another approach to measuring attitudes. Both five-point and seven-point scales are used, depending on the level of precision desired and the education level of the targeted population. The distinguishing feature of semantic differential scales is the use of bipolar end points (or anchors), with the intermediate points typically numbered. The end points are chosen to describe individuals, objects, or events with opposite adjectives or adverbs. Respondents are asked to check which space between a set of bipolar adjectives or phrases best describes their feelings toward the stimulus object. An example of how you might use the semantic differential to rate a supervisor follows.

My supervisor is . . .

Courteous	___	___	___	___	___	Discourteous
Friendly	___	___	___	___	___	Unfriendly
Helpful	___	___	___	___	___	Unhelpful
Supportive	___	___	___	___	___	Hostile
Competent	___	___	___	___	___	Incompetent
Honest	___	___	___	___	___	Dishonest
Enthusiastic	___	___	___	___	___	Unenthusiastic

As another example, let's consider Phil Samouel's Greek Cuisine restaurant. After having observed his customers, Phil Samouel believes a particular personality type patronizes his restaurant. To confirm this he identifies a number of personality characteristics that could describe restaurant customers. A semantic differential format is then used to collect data from his customers. For example:

Instructions: A number of personality characteristics that can be used to describe people are shown below. Notice that each feature has an opposite. Please look at each characteristic and then rate yourself according to whichever end of the scale you feel best applies. For example, if you think you are more modern, you would place a mark on the modern end of the scale that most closely fits you. On the other hand, if you think you are more traditional, then you would place a mark on this end of the scale. Please rate yourself on every feature, and try to be as honest about yourself as possible.

Traditional	___	___	___	___	___	Modern
Self-confident	___	___	___	___	___	Not Confident
Reserved	___	___	___	___	___	Sociable
Outgoing	___	___	___	___	___	Introverted
Liberal	___	___	___	___	___	Conservative
Sophisticated	___	___	___	___	___	Down-to-earth

Semantic differential scales are easy to understand and are considered a metric measure. The difficulty in using this type scale is being able to come up with adjectives that are opposite. The Business Research Dashboard (page 226) provides an example of how the semantic differential scale was used to measure "product complexity."

Graphic Ratings Scale

A **graphic ratings scale** is one that provides measurement on a continuum in the form of a line with anchors that are numbered and named. The respondent gives an opinion about a question by placing a mark on the line. Sometimes the midpoint is labeled and other times it is not. An example of how this scale might be used to assess restaurant perceptions follows:

On a scale from 0 to 10 how would you rate the atmosphere of Samouel's Greek Cuisine restaurant?

```
Poor                              OK                            Excellent
|------------------------------------|------------------------------------|
0                                    5                                   10
```

Graphic rating scales are used in other types of business research as well. An example of how this type of scale could be used to examine the concept "organizational commitment" follows. Notice that the midpoint is not labeled and that numbers are not placed beside the scales. Respondents simply mark an X on the line at the appropriate place.

I talk about this company to my friends as a great place to work.
```
Strongly Disagree                                          Strongly Agree
|------------------------------------------------------------------------|
```

I really care about the future of this company.
```
Strongly Disagree                                          Strongly Agree
|------------------------------------------------------------------------|
```

For me this is the best of all companies to work for.
```
Strongly Disagree                                          Strongly Agree
|------------------------------------------------------------------------|
```

■————**Business Research Dashboard**————■
Measuring Perceived Product Complexity

An example of product complexity, a concept that has been measured in business research using a five-point semantic differential, is shown below (product name goes in blank space).

Instructions: Using the rating scale shown below, please circle one number for each set of factors listed. The numbers have no specific values and are designed only to represent a continuous scale between the high and low definitions provided for each factor. Circle the number that reflects your opinion of where [*blank*] falls on such a continuum. (Product name goes in [*blank*].)

Standardized product	1 2 3 4 5				Differentiated product
Technically simple	1 2 3 4 5				Technically complex
Easy to install/use	1 2 3 4 5				Specialized installation/use
No after sales service	1 2 3 4 5				Technical after sales service
No consequential adjustment	1 2 3 4 5				Large consequential adjustment

Source: D. McCabe, "Group Structure: Constriction at the Top," *Journal of Marketing*, 51 (October 1987), 88–89.

NONMETRIC SCALES

Nonmetric scales provide data that describes differences in the type or kind of response by indicating the absence or presence of a particular characteristic or property. Nonmetric scales can also be comparative in design so that two or more objects are evaluated relative to each other rather than independently. The following examples illustrate the variety of nonmetric scales.

Categorical Scale

Categorical scales are nominally measured opinion scales that have two or more response categories. When there are more categories, the researcher can be more precise in measuring a particular concept. Categorical scales are often used to measure respondent characteristics such as gender, age, education level, product type, industry sector, and so on. But they can also be used to measure other concepts, as follows:

What is your job title?
_____ Attorney
_____ Professor
_____ Physician
_____ Manager
_____ CEO (Chief Executive Officer)
_____ Other (please specify) _____

How interested are you in learning more about what is expected of you in your new job assignment?
_____ Very interested
_____ Somewhat interested
_____ Not very interested
_____ Never thought about it

Which of the following is your favorite soft drink?
_____ Coca Cola
_____ Pepsi
_____ Mountain Dew
_____ None of the above

A **paired-comparison scale** is a type of categorical scale that includes a set of traits, product characteristics, or features that are paired against one another. Respondents are asked to make a series of paired judgments and select the feature that most closely represents their feelings. Below is an example of a paired-comparison scale.

Several pairs of characteristics associated with a salesperson's job activities are listed below. For each pair of characteristics, please check only one trait you believe is more important in the sales success of a salesperson.

1. ____	Competence	____	Trust
2. ____	Competence	____	Communication Skills
3. ____	Trust	____	Communication Skills
4. ____	Social Skills	____	Competence

The benefit of this scale is that it requires the respondent to choose between the two items being compared. A problem, however, is respondents can find it difficult to choose one over the other and may either skip the question or stop answering the questionnaire.

Rank Order Scale

Individuals often place items or alternatives in a rank order. A **rank order scale** is an ordinal scale that asks respondents to rank a set of objects or characteristics in terms of preference, similarity, importance, or similar adjectives. An example of a rank order scale using "importance" follows:

Please rank the following five attributes on a scale from 1 (most important) to 5 (least important) in searching for a job. No ties please.

Job Attributes	Ranking
Pay	_____
Benefits	_____
Coworkers	_____
Flexible scheduling of work hours	_____
Working conditions	_____

This scale measures only relative importance. That is, the importance of each job attribute relative to the others. If pay is ranked highest in a sample survey, we know only that, relatively speaking, it is higher, but we do not know how much higher.

Sorting

Sorting scales ask respondents to indicate their beliefs or opinions by arranging objects (items) on the basis of perceived similarity or some other attribute. Sorting can also be used to rank order objects. It is particularly useful when there are a large number of objects. To use this scale, you prepare a card for each object and write the object on the card. Then the cards are given to the respondent and they're asked to arrange them in the order of their preference or importance. For example, let's say you wanted to rank order students' preferences for taking courses from different areas of study. There are many fields of study, including accounting, finance, management, information systems, psychology, marketing, education, law, and so on. You would give respondents a stack of cards with the names of the fields of study you want them to compare and ask them to stack them in the order of their preference for each of the fields of study. The technique is particularly useful in ranking the importance of objects, because it prevents respondents from giving all objects a high rating, as often happens when rating scales are used.

Constant Sum Scale

With a **constant sum scale** respondents are asked to divide a constant sum over several categories to indicate, for example, the relative importance of the attributes. For example, suppose FedEx wants to determine the importance of several attributes in the selection of an overnight delivery service. Respondents might be asked to allocate 100 points across the following attributes to indicate their relative importance.

Attribute	Score
On-time delivery	_____
Price	_____
Tracking capability	_____
Invoice accuracy	_____
Sum	100

Generally speaking, the constant sum scale can be used only with respondents who are well educated. When respondents follow instructions, the results approximate an interval scale. But the technique becomes increasingly difficult as the number of attributes increases. Unfortunately, the likelihood of the scores not adding up to 100 can be a problem.

Another example of a constant sum scale follows. It demonstrates how data could be collected to determine the relative importance of components of a compensation package.

Suppose your monthly salary is $5,000. Think of an ideal compensation plan to meet your needs. How much would you like to allocate to each type of benefit? Please be sure that the points allocated among the benefits sum to 100.

Benefits	Score
Life insurance	_____
Disability insurance	_____
Health insurance	_____
Savings	_____
Salary	_____
Retirement	_____
Sum	100

The constant sum scale provides both a ranking and the magnitude of relative importance of each attribute. In this example, if salary is given a score of 40 and life insurance is given a 20, then we know salary is much more important than life insurance. It should be noted that some analysts consider this scale to be metric, while others consider it nonmetric.

Practical Decisions When Developing Scales

Several practical decisions are necessary when developing scales. They include number of scale categories, odd or even number of categories, balanced or unbalanced scales, forced or nonforced choice, and nature and degree of verbal description.

Number of Scale Categories

Should your scale have three, five, seven, ten, or more categories? From a research design perspective, the larger the number of categories the greater the precision of the measurement scale. But, with more categories it is more difficult to discriminate between the levels, and some respondents face greater difficulty in processing the information. Thus, the desire for a higher level of precision must be balanced with the demands placed on the respondent and the respondent's experience in answering questions using scales.

Respondents must be reasonably well educated to process the information associated with larger numbers of categories. For example, children may have difficulty using a three-point scale, but with a high school or comparable education, a seven-point scale is acceptable. College-educated individuals can typically respond to an eleven-point scale, and a zero to one hundred scale can be useful if this level of variability is relevant. Likewise, individuals with experience in responding to scaling questions can respond to more categories of discrimination. But individuals less exposed to scaling questions, from countries where interviewing is not commonplace, for example, can more easily respond to scales with fewer categories. From the researcher's perspective, you would almost always prefer to use no fewer than five categories. This is because respondents frequently avoid the extremes, and a five-point scale, for example, may effectively become a three-point scale. In fact, seven-point scales are the norm today, and increasingly scales with a larger number of categories are being used to increase variability and precision in measurement. In fact, the authors recommend eleven-point scales (with a neutral middle point) should be used where appropriate.

Number of Items in Measuring a Concept

Concepts should be measured using scales with multiple items. In such cases, the scales are referred to as multi-item scales. A **multi-item scale** consists of a number of closely related individual statements (items or indicators) whose responses are combined into a composite score or summated rating used to measure a concept. But are two items enough, or should the researcher use ten or even twenty items to measure a concept? The general guideline is the statements need to be closely related, represent only a single construct, and must completely represent the construct to be measured with the multi-item scale. Moreover, a minimum of three items is necessary to achieve acceptable reliability, but it is common to see at least five to seven items, and sometimes more.

ODD OR EVEN NUMBER OF CATEGORIES

The midpoint typically represents a neutral position when an odd number of categories is used in a scale. This type of scale is used when, based on the experience or judgment of the researcher, it is believed that some portion of the sample is likely to feel neutral about the issue being examined. On the other hand, if the researcher believes it is unlikely there will be many neutral respondents or wants to force a choice on a particular issue, then an even number of categories is used.

BALANCED OR UNBALANCED SCALES

Scales can be either balanced or unbalanced. In a **balanced scale** the number of favorable and unfavorable categories is equal. In an **unbalanced scale** the number of favorable and unfavorable categories is unequal. Examples of balanced and unbalanced scales follow:

To what extent do you consider TV shows with sex and violence to be acceptable for teenagers to view?

Balanced:
_____ Very acceptable
_____ Somewhat acceptable
_____ Neither acceptable or unacceptable
_____ Somewhat unacceptable
_____ Very unacceptable

Unbalanced:
_____ Very acceptable
_____ Somewhat acceptable
_____ Unacceptable

Unbalanced scales are used when the researcher expects responses to be skewed toward one end of the scale. For example, in satisfaction studies it is common for respondents to give very favorable responses. Therefore, researchers may choose to use an unbalanced scale to the positive end to provide an opportunity for more variation in the responses. This is an example of the importance of considering the research problem when deciding whether to use a balanced or unbalanced number of scale categories.

It should be noted, however, that unbalanced scales can create bias in the responses by giving more options toward one end of the scale. For example, in the unbalanced acceptable/unacceptable scale above, the two options for acceptable and one for unacceptable would result in a higher proportion of acceptable responses than with a balanced scale.

FORCED OR NONFORCED CHOICE

In a **forced choice scale** respondents are forced to make a choice. There is no midpoint that can be considered a neutral or no opinion category. If many respondents are likely to have not formed an opinion about a particular issue then a forced-choice scale will make them respond in one direction or another. It will, for example, make them respond either favorably or unfavorably, likely or unlikely, agree or disagree, aware or unaware, and so on. If a respondent selects the middle category when they have no opinion or are neutral it will cause an error in the responses. In such cases it is better to use a forced-choice scale and provide a "no opinion" option. "No opinion" response categories are typically placed at the far right of the scale, as follows:

Very unlikely					Very likely	No Opinion
1	2	3	4	5	6	____

CATEGORY LABELS FOR SCALES

The scales we have discussed included three types of choices – verbal labels, numerical labels, and unlabeled choices. Some researchers prefer scales with only verbal labels, typically because they believe it helps respondents give more precise answers. Using numerical labels gives some guidance to respondents on label interpretation but less than verbal labels. Numerical labels are helpful because they tend to make responses more closely resemble interval data.

Numerical labels and unlabeled scales are used when researchers have difficulty developing appropriate verbal descriptions for the middle categories. This typically occurs when the number of scale points exceeds seven. A compromise is to label the end points and the middle category if one uses an odd number of scale points. Examples of the three types of scale labeling follow:

Verbal Label. How important is the size of the hard drive in selecting a laptop PC to purchase?

Very Unimportant	Somewhat Unimportant	Neither Important or Unimportant	Somewhat Important	Very Important
1	2	3	4	5

Numerical Label. How likely are you to purchase a laptop PC in the next six months?

Very Unlikely						Very Likely
1	2	3	4	5	6	7

Unlabeled. How important is the weight of the laptop PC in deciding which brand to purchase?

Very Important					Very Unimportant
____	____	____	____	____

CRITERIA FOR ASSESSING MEASUREMENT SCALES

Before using the scores from any concept (construct) for analysis, the researcher must ensure the variables (indicators) selected to represent and measure the concept do so in an accurate and consistent manner. Accuracy is associated with the term **validity,** while consistency is associated with the term **reliability**. The most com-

Exhibit 9.3

Criteria for Assessing Measurement Scales

Reliability
- Test-retest reliability
- Alternative-forms reliability
- Internal consistency reliability

Validity
- Content validity
- Construct validity
  - Convergent validity
  - Discriminant validity
- Criterion validity
  - Concurrent validity
  - Predictive validity

mon criteria for assessing the accuracy and consistency of scales are displayed in Exhibit 9.3.

Our concern in selecting scales for questionnaires is with the quality of the measurement obtained. A scientific study must always address these two issues, reliability and validity. When these issues are properly addressed, measurement error is reduced. Measurement error occurs when the values obtained in a survey (observed values) are not the same as the true value. For example, if you ask a respondent to answer the following question:

> Using a 10-point scale, where 1 is poor and 10 is excellent, how does Samouel's Greek Cuisine restaurant rate on competitive prices?

You have measurement error if the response is 8 when in fact the true answer is 6. Measurement error is the result of interviewer bias or errors, data input errors, respondent's misunderstanding or misrepresentation, and so forth. In conducting business research we always strive to reduce measurement error as much as possible. Measurement error is minimized when the observed numbers accurately represent the characteristics being measured and nothing else.

RELIABILITY

A survey instrument (questionnaire) is considered reliable if its repeated application results in consistent scores. This is contingent on the definition of the concept (construct) being unchanged from application to application. Reliability is concerned with the consistency of the research findings. Reliability is important no matter what form the question takes, but it is most frequently associated with multi-item scales. Multi-item scales consist of multiple items (variables, indicators) representing a concept. A single item is one statement or question that respondents evaluate as part of the entire concept.

If the instrument is a multi-item scale, then for it to be reliable the scores (ratings) for the individual questions (items) making up the scale should be correlated. The stronger the correlations, the higher the reliability of the scale. Similarly, the weaker the correlations, the more unreliable the scale will be. Exhibit 9.4 is an example of

Exhibit 9.4

Confirmation of Expectations of a Distributor

Purpose: Measures the extent to which a distributor rates the performance of a manufacturer as meeting expectations.

Instructions: Following is a list of supplier (manufacturer) characteristics that might be important to your operations. Please indicate how well [*blank*] has performed relative to the original level at which you expected them to perform for each item listed. Circle the number that most accurately reflects your belief. (Supplier name goes in [*blank*].)

1 = Much worse than expected
2 = Somewhat worse than expected
3 = About as expected
4 = Somewhat better than expected
5 = Much better than expected

1.	Product quality	1	2	3	4	5
2.	Reliable delivery	1	2	3	4	5
3.	Quality of advertising	1	2	3	4	5
4.	Pricing	1	2	3	4	5
5.	Technical support	1	2	3	4	5
6.	Order processing speed	1	2	3	4	5
7.	Credit terms	1	2	3	4	5
8.	Problem resolution	1	2	3	4	5
9.	Salesforce call frequency	1	2	3	4	5
10.	Responsiveness of salesforce	1	2	3	4	5

Source: Excerpt from J.J. Cronin Jr. and M.H. Morris, "Satisfying Customer Expectations: The Effect of Conflict and Repurchase Intentions in Industrial Marketing Channels," *Journal of the Academy of Marketing Science*, 17, 1 (Winter 1989), 41–49.

a multi-item scale that was used to measure the construct "confirmation of expectations." To be reliable as a scale, the questions must be answered by respondents consistently and in a manner that is highly correlated. If they do not, the scale will not be reliable.

Test-Retest Reliability

Test-retest reliability is obtained through repeated measurement of the same respondent or group of respondents using the same measurement device and under similar conditions. Results are compared to determine how similar they are. If they are similar, typically measured by a correlation coefficient, we say they have high test-retest reliability.

Several factors cause problems when using test-retest reliability. Respondents' first taking of a test (survey) may influence their response the second time they take it. In addition, situational factors such as how respondents feel on a particular day may influence how respondents answer the questions, and something may change in the time between repeated sessions of the test. Finally, it is often difficult and sometimes impossible to have the same respondents take a survey twice.

Alternative Forms Reliability

Alternative-forms reliability can be used to reduce some of these problems. To assess this type of reliability the researcher develops two equivalent forms of the construct. The same respondents are measured at two different times using equivalent alternative constructs. The measure of reliability is the correlation between the responses to the two versions of the construct.

Internal Consistency Reliability

Internal consistency reliability is used to assess a summated scale where several statements (items) are summed to form a total score for a construct. For example, one could assess the internal consistency reliability of a satisfaction/loyalty construct with the following three items:

1. How satisfied are you with Samouel's Greek Cuisine restaurant?
2. How likely are you to return to Samouel's Greek Cuisine in the future?
3. How likely are you to recommend Samouel's Greek Cuisine to a friend?

Each of the above three questions measures some aspect of the satisfaction construct. Responses to the questions should be consistent in what they indicate about Samouel's restaurant. That is, a respondent who is very satisfied should be very likely to return in the future and very likely to recommend the restaurant to a friend. The Business Research Dashboard shows how businesses are using multi-item scales to measure the satisfaction construct.

There are two types of internal consistency reliability. The simplest is **split-half reliability**. To determine split-half reliability, the researcher randomly divides the group of scale items in half and correlates the two sets of items. A high correlation between the two halves indicates high reliability. The second type of internal consistency reliability is **coefficient alpha**, also referred to as Cronbach's alpha. To obtain coefficient alpha you calculate the average of the coefficients from all possible combinations of split halves. Coefficient alpha ranges from zero to one. Your can use the guidelines in Exhibit 9.5 as rules of thumb for interpreting alpha values. Researchers generally consider an alpha of .7 as a minimum, although lower coefficients may be acceptable, depending on the research objectives.

Exhibit 9.5

Rules of Thumb About Cronbach's Alpha Coefficient Size

Alpha coefficient range	Strength of association
< .6	Poor
.6 to < .7	Moderate
.7 to < .8	Good
.8 to < .9	Very Good
≥ .9	Excellent

Note: If alpha > .95, items should be inspected to ensure they measure different aspects of the concept.

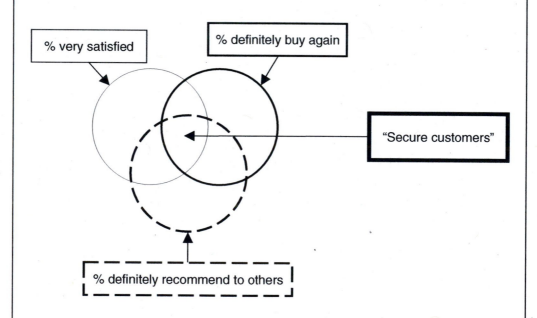

Business Research Dashboard
*Multi-Item Concepts Are Widely
Used in Business Research*

If you think only academic researchers use multi-item concepts, think again. Burke, Inc., one of the largest business research firms in the world, developed the Secure Customer Index to use in customer satisfaction and retention projects

The index is a three-item scale that asks respondents about satisfaction, likelihood to purchase or return in the future, and likelihood of recommending a particular business to others. The three items (indicators) are measured using a five-point Likert-type scale. Secure customers are those respondents who choose a five on all three items. It is typically measured in terms of the percentage of customers who check the top box (5) of a particular item. Burke has had good success using this approach in satisfaction studies with its clients.

The Secure Customer Index™ (Burke, Inc.)

% very satisfied

% definitely buy again

"Secure customers"

% definitely recommend to others

For more information on Burke and its services, go to http://www.burke.com.

The following case of Samouel's restaurant tells you how to use SPSS to calculate Cronbach's alpha for three of the perceptions variables on the Samouel's and Gino's questionnaire.

CONTINUING CASE: SAMOUEL'S GREEK CUISINE
Using SPSS to Calculate Cronbach's Alpha

We can use SPSS to calculate Cronbach's alpha for the variables in the customer database. Questions X_6, on employee friendliness, X_{11}, on employee courteousness, and X_{12}, on employee competence, relate to characteristics reflecting different aspects of employee quality. Cronbach's alpha can be used to determine whether the three items, combined into a single index, capture in a consistent manner the quality of employees. To perform a Cronbach's-alpha analysis using SPSS, the click-through sequence is as follows: ANALYZE → SCALE → RELIABILTY ANALYSIS. Scroll down and highlight X_6, Friendly Employees, click on the arrow box to move it into the Items box. Repeat this procedure for X_{11}, Courteous Employees, and X_{12}, Competent Employees. Next click on OK to run the program. The resulting output is as follows:

R E L I A B I L I T Y A N A L Y S I S — S C A L E (A L P H A)

Reliability Coefficients

N of Cases = 200.0   N of Items = 3

Alpha = .8176

The alpha value of 0.82 is "very good." Thus, we conclude that the three items can be combined to measure the quality of restaurant employees in a consistent manner.
Where else might you calculate reliability in either the employee or customer surveys? A copy of the customer survey is included in Chapter 10.

Words of Caution on Reliability

An acceptable level of reliability indicates respondents are answering the questions in a consistent manner. Good research requires acceptable reliability. The following guidelines can be used to ensure reliability in your scales:

1. The minimum number of items in a scale to measure a particular concept should be at least three.
2. The items included in the scale must be positively correlated. Where negative correlations arise between items:
   - Check the wording of the questions, and if a question is negatively worded, then the scores for that question must be "reverse-coded." By "reverse-coded," we mean that on a five-point scale a 1 is recoded 5, a 2 is recoded as a 4, and so on. You can use the RECODE function in SPSS to do this.

- Should the "negative wording" check fail, then remove the offending item from the scale.

3. Items in a scale that are correlated with other items in the scale at a level lower than 0.30 should be evaluated for removal from the scale.

VALIDITY

Validity is the extent to which a construct measures what it is supposed to measure. For example, if you want to know a family's disposable income, it must be kept in mind that it is different from total household income. You may start with questions about total family income to arrive at disposable income, but total family income by itself is not a valid indicator of disposable income. A construct with perfect validity contains no measurement error. An easy measure of validity is comparing observed measurements with the true measurement. The problem is we seldom know the true measure. To assess measurement validity we use one or more of the following approaches:

- Content validity
- Construct validity
- Criterion validity

Content Validity

Establishing the **content validity** (or **face validity**) of a scale involves a systematic but subjective assessment of a scale's ability to measure what it is supposed to measure. Validation, in general, involves consulting a small sample of typical respondents or experts to pass judgment on the suitability of the items (indicators) chosen to represent the construct. This is a commonly used validation method in business research. Generally speaking, content validity is not considered an adequate measure of validity, and business researchers typically go on to assess either construct or criterion validity.

To illustrate content validity, let's consider the construct "job satisfaction." A scale designed to measure job satisfaction should include items on compensation, working conditions, communication, relationship with coworkers, supervisory style, empowerment, opportunities for advancement, and so on. If any one of these major areas does not have items to measure it, then the scale would not have content validity.

Construct Validity

Construct validity assesses what the construct (concept) or scale is in fact measuring. To assess construct validity you must understand the theoretical rationale underlying the measurements you obtain. The theory is used to explain why the scale works and how the results of its application can be interpreted.

To assess construct validity two checks have to be performed. The checks are convergent and discriminant validity. **Convergent validity** is the extent to which the construct is positively correlated with other measures of the same construct. **Discriminant validity** is the extent to which the construct does not correlate with other measures that are different from it. These are objective tests, based on numerical scores, of how well the construct conforms to theoretical expectations.

Convergent Validity

Establishing convergent validity of a scale requires that the following be done:

Step 1: Based on theory and experience, identify another established construct that is claimed to measure the same concept as the one being validated.

Step 2: Obtain scores on both constructs and compute the correlation between the scores.

If the scores are highly correlated, then it is concluded that convergent validity is evident.

Discriminant Validity

Establishing the discriminant validity of a construct requires a similar set of steps:

Step 1. Based on theory and experience, identify a construct that is claimed to be different from the concept being validated.

Step 2. Specify the manner in which the two scales representing the constructs are expected to differ. It is expected that the scores resulting from administering the scales on the same respondents will be uncorrelated.

Step 3. Obtain scores on both scales and compute the correlation between the scores.

If the correlation is low, we conclude the construct exhibits discriminant validity.

Criterion Validity

Criterion validity assesses whether a construct performs as expected relative to other variables identified as meaningful criteria. For example, theory suggests employees who are highly committed to a company would exhibit high job satisfaction. Thus, correlations between measures of employee commitment and job satisfaction should be positive and significant. If this is so, then we have established criterion validity for our construct. Similarly, when we measure the construct of customer loyalty, a criterion for validating it would be the construct "satisfaction." Very loyal customers should be highly satisfied with the business.

To establish criterion validity we need to show that the scores obtained from the application of the scale being validated are able to predict scores obtained on a theoretically identified dependent variable, referred to as the criterion variable. One or both of two types of criterion validity checks can be performed. These checks are referred to as concurrent and predictive validity.

Concurrent Validity

To demonstrate **concurrent validity** of a construct some prespecified association must be established between the scores on the construct being validated and the scores on a dependent variable as determined by theory. The scores of both variables are obtained at approximately the same time and should be highly correlated. For example, Samouel's highly satisfied customers should also be frequent patrons of his restaurant.

Predictive Validity

Predictive validity assesses the ability of a construct measured at a specific time to predict another criterion at a future time. The other criterion can be either another individual variable or a multi-item scale. Thus, for a construct to have predictive validity it must be possible to predict future values of a dependent variable from scores obtained on the construct being tested. So predictive validity differs from concurrent validity in that the scores on the dependent variable are obtained sometime after the scores for the construct that is being validated. Validity is established if the scores are highly correlated. An example of predictive validity would be assessing whether the Graduate Management Admission Test (GMAT) is a valid predictor of performance in a business graduate school.

HOW TO DEVELOP A SCALE

In developing a scaling approach, we must consider the underlying theory as well as the reliability and validity of the scale. We must also consider the level of measurement (nominal, ordinal, interval, and ratio), any problems that might arise administering the scale, and respondents' knowledge of the research issues. Our research objective is that the scale will be theoretically valid, reliable, and include the highest possible level of measurement. Moreover, respondents must be able and willing to respond to questions accurately and must not have negative attitudes regarding a particular issue being examined.

Consider the following problem that may concern our restaurant owner. Phil Samouel is interested in determining the image of his restaurant. A prerequisite for this is the development of a scale to measure the concept "image." The process of developing a scale involves a number of steps:

1. Definition of the concept or concepts to be measured
2. Identification of the components of the concept
3. Specification of a sample of observable and measurable items (indicators or proxy variables) that represent the components of the concept
4. Selection of the appropriate scales to measure the items
5. Combination of the items into a composite scale, sometimes referred to as an

instrument, which in turn serves as a means of measuring the concept
6. Administering the scale to a sample and assessing respondent understanding
7. Confirming scale reliability and validity
8. Revising the scale as needed

The scale obtains perceptions of different components of the concept being measured. For example, components of the concept "restaurant image" might include assessments of the employees, food, atmosphere, and so on. Each of these components should have several indicators to measure them. A rule of thumb is each component should have a minimum of three items to be adequately measured. For example, measuring the image of a restaurant involves acquiring perceptions on such characteristics as the friendliness of the staff, parking facilities, the physical layout of the restaurant, the prices, and so on. Similarly, measuring the concept "satisfaction" involves several components. Possible components of the "satisfaction" concept are illustrated in Exhibit 9.6.

In developing an instrument to measure a concept, we generally look for previously developed scales. This is because scale development is difficult and time consuming. Fortunately, in the past twenty-five or thirty years many excellent scales have been developed and published. Several sources of scales are described in the Business Research Dashboard.

Exhibit 9.6

Potential Components of the Concept "Restaurant Satisfaction"

Concept:	Satisfaction		
Components:	Quality of food	Quality of service	Price of meals
Items/Questions:	1. The food served must be of the highest quality.	1. When I visit a restaurant I expect its employees to be courteous.	1. When I visit a restaurant for a special occasion, price is not important to me.
	2. The food served must be fresh.	2. I expect prompt service from a restaurant.	2. I am prepared to pay more for specialty dishes.
	3. The menu should offer a wide range of choices.	3. I expect the restaurant staff to be knowledgeable about the menu offerings.	3. When taking the family out to a restaurant, price is important to me.

SUMMARY

UNDERSTAND THE ROLE OF CONCEPTS IN BUSINESS RESEARCH

In business research we examine concepts of varying degrees of complexity. These concepts describe business phenomena that we must understand and explain to make

■———Business Research Dashboard———■
Where to Find Scales to Measure Research Concepts

Researchers like to use previously published scales in their research. This saves them a lot of time and effort in their own research. Sometimes these scales are used exactly as they were developed. Other times small modifications are made to the original instrument to more closely fit the needs of the specific research objectives. Several valuable sources of previously used scales are listed below. References are organized by the relevant discipline.

Organizational Behavior and Management

James L. Price, "Handbook of Organizational Measurement," *International Journal of Manpower*, 18, 4/5/6 (1997), 305–558.

This is a reference handbook and research tool that focuses on constructs to measure organizational behavior. It includes twenty-eight chapters reporting on constructs that measure a wide variety of type of work behavior. Examples of constructs include absenteeism, commitment, communication, innovation, involvement, compensation, power, productivity, technology, turnover, and others.

Management Information Systems (MIS)

Two Web sites provide measures of constructs associated with user reactions to computer systems.

Peter Newsted, Sid Huff, Malcolm Munro, and Andrew Schwartz, "Survey Instruments in IS," http://www.misq.org/discovery/surveys98/surveys.html. This Web site provides listings of constructs and attributes relevant to information systems research. All measures in the database were published in research journals.

MISQ Archivist, http://www.misq.org/archivist/home.html. This Web site is affiliated with *MIS Quarterly* and includes data and measures from articles published in the journal.

Marketing

William O. Bearden and Richard Netemeyer, *Handbook of Marketing Scales*, 3rd ed. (Thousand Oaks, CA: Sage, 2005).

This book has information on over 130 scales, including a definition of the scale, type of scale and number of scale points, how the scale was developed, including the sample, and evidence of validity and reliability. It includes the following types of scales: individual traits such as opinion leadership and innovativeness; values such as social responsibility and materialism; involvement and information processing; reactions to advertising stimuli; performance of business firms; social agencies; and the marketplace, including ethical issues, sales, sales management, and inter- and intrafirm issues.

Gordon C. Bruner II and Paul J. Hensel, *Marketing Scales Handbook* (Cincinnati, OH: Thompson Learning, 2005).

(continued)

This handbook includes scales in three primary areas: consumer behavior, advertising and sales force, and general. Specific examples include assertiveness, aggressiveness, arousal, brand switching, brand loyalty, complaining behavior, convenience, curiosity, information seeker, innovativeness, opinion leadership, risk, satisfaction, store image, novelty, source credibility, acceptance of coworkers, alienation from work, channel conflict, customer orientation, and so on. It reports scale name, origin, reliability and validity, and so on, for almost 600 scales.

General

John P. Robinson, Phillip R. Shaver, and Lawrence S. Wrightsman, *Measures of Personality and Social Psychological Attitudes* (San Diego, CA: Academic Press, 1991).

This book contains published scales in eleven different areas: response bias, subjective well-being, self-esteem, social anxiety and shyness, depression and loneliness, alienation and anomie, trust and human nature, authoritarianism, sex roles, and values. Over 150 scales are reviewed and summarized.

Buros Institute, "Buros Institute of Mental Measurements," http://www.unl.edu/buros/. This Web site allows the user to search, locate, and obtain reviews of published tests and measurements.

effective decisions. Successful research requires clearly delineated definitions of concepts to avoid ambiguity in measuring them. In defining concepts, the researcher will draw on established theory, literature, and business experience.

EXPLAIN THE NOTION OF MEASUREMENT

Measurement involves quantifying the outcomes of variables by assigning numbers to the outcomes according to preset rules. Managers measure many aspects of business, including employee performance and satisfaction, motivation, turnover, and profits. The measurement process involves specifying the variables (indicators) serving as proxies for the concepts. Variables that are relatively concrete in nature, such as gender and age, are easy to define and measure. But many concepts are much less precise and more difficult to accurately measure.

PROVIDE AN OVERVIEW OF THE DIFFERENT TYPES OF MEASUREMENT SCALES

To measure business phenomena we use four types of scales: nominal, ordinal, interval, and ratio. Nominal and ordinal scales are nonmetric variables. Interval and ratio scales are metric measurement tools.

Data analysis for nonmetric variables is limited. For nominal data, only counts, percentages, and the mode can be computed. For ordinal data, we can compute the percentiles, median, and range. Data analysis is much more extensive for metric variables. In addition to the above, it is possible to compute means, standard deviations, and other statistics.

When measuring a complex concept, we typically use multi-item scales, where the individual items of the scale collectively capture different aspects of the concept. The multi-item scale index is a composite derived from the scores on its individual questions or statements.

DISTINGUISH BETWEEN RELIABILITY AND VALIDITY

Before using a multi-item scale, the researcher must perform certain essential checks to ensure that the items selected to represent and measure a concept do so in an accurate and consistent manner. Accuracy is associated with the term "validity," while consistency is associated with the term "reliability."

ETHICAL DILEMMAS

CENTROID SYSTEMS, LTD.

Five years ago, when a new CEO was hired, a business research firm conducted an organizational climate survey for Centroid Systems, Ltd. Since that time the new CEO has reorganized departments and tightened budgets. As a result company performance has improved and shareholders are happy. Richard Johnson, Centroid's human resources director, believes employees are also feeling better about their work environment. To measure the changes, Richard decides to conduct another organizational climate survey. However, in order to save money, Richard decides to conduct the survey himself using the questionnaire and scales that were used in the previous survey without consulting the original research firm. Is this unethical?

NUTRIX, LTD.

Nutrix, Ltd., the maker of dietary supplements, has recently launched a new marketing campaign for Slender, an herbal supplement to increase weight loss. According to the product marketing materials, in an experiment conducted by Nutrix, people using Slender lost 5 percent more weight than those using a placebo. In addition, the people using Slender reported none of the side effects, such as increased heart rate, commonly reported to be caused by other weight loss products. As the product has gained popularity, critics have begun to attack the company's claims, arguing that Nutrix's research is not comprehensive enough, because it fails to measure the long-term effects of Slender. In fact, according to critics, most people who use the product report that they are unable to maintain the weight loss after they quit taking Slender. Many also report experiencing withdrawal symptoms, such as migraine headaches. Nutrix stands by its research, which shows the product is a safe weight loss alternative, arguing that, since patents are not available on herbal supplements, the company cannot afford expensive, long-term studies. What do you think? Is the short-term measurement of effects adequate? Or should Nutrix be required to conduct long-term experiments before making these claims for current or new products?

Review Questions

1. What is a concept in business research?
2. How do we measure concepts?
3. What is the difference between metric and nonmetric scales? Give an example of each.
4. What is reliability? How does it differ from validity?
5. What are the steps to follow in developing a scale?

Discussion and Thinking Activities

1. Why would a business researcher want to measure concepts?
2. What key issues need to be considered by the business researcher in defining a concept? Illustrate with a concept that you are familiar with.
3. What considerations need to be taken into account in determining the level of measurement of variables?
4. Make a list of concepts that college students might want to learn more about. Prepare a list of indicators (statements) for each concept. Decide on the type of measurement scale you will use and justify your selection.
5. *SPSS Application:* We are interested in measuring a concept labeled "work environment." From the list of variables in the Samouel's employee database, select those you believe will collectively capture restaurant "work environment." Assess the reliability of your chosen items in measuring this concept.
6. *SPSS Application:* Identify the "work environment" variables from the Samouel's employee survey. Select the six statements covering coworkers and supervision and calculate their reliability using SPSS. What did you find?
7. The Samouel's employee questionnaire has three indicators of "organizational commitment" (variables 13, 14, and 15). Develop a more comprehensive measure of "organizational commitment" covering areas not included in that questionnaire.

Internet Exercises

1. Complete a survey at the following Web site and prepare a report on your experience: http://www.strategicbusiness insights.com/vals/presurvey.shtml.
2. Go to http://www.icpsr.umich.edu/icpsrweb/ICPSR. Find the General Social Survey and prepare a report telling what it is. How does it compare to the Yankelovich MONITOR, found at http://www.yankelovich.com?

3. VALS is a Values, Attitudes, and Lifestyles survey that has been conducted for many years by SRI International. The VALS approach is well-known and respected as a profiling approach that groups Americans based on questions about their values and lifestyles. Go to http://www.strategicbusiness insights. com/vals/presurvey.shtml, click on VALS, and complete the survey. Prepare a brief report on what you found.

NOTE

1. K.C. Williams and R.L. Spiro, "Communication Style in the Salesperson-Customer Dyad," *Journal of Marketing Research*, 22 (November 1985), 434–442.

10 Questionnaire Design

LEARNING OUTCOMES

1. Understand that questionnaire design is difficult and why
2. Explain the steps involved in designing an effective questionnaire
3. Recognize how the method of data collection influences questionnaire design
4. Understand the types of questions and how they are used
5. Describe the major sections of the questionnaire and how they relate to one another

Few managers dispute the value of accurate information in improving decision making. The purpose of business research is to provide managers with accurate information, often from surveys. But information from surveys is accurate only if the questionnaire is properly designed. Many individuals believe questionnaires are easy to design. But those with experience in designing questionnaires know this is not true. Indeed, experienced researchers can easily make mistakes in questionnaire design if they overlook essential steps, such as pretesting.

This chapter describes the importance of careful questionnaire design and suggests an approach for developing good questionnaires. Specific guidelines to be followed at each stage in the design process are provided. But, unfortunately, few of the guidelines hold in all situations. Indeed, many individuals believe questionnaire design is more art than science.

QUESTIONNAIRES

Questionnaire design is only one phase of several interrelated business research steps. But it is a very important phase because data collected with questionnaires is used to improve decision making. A **questionnaire** is a prepared set of questions (or measures) used by respondents or interviewers to record answers (data). Moreover, it is a structured framework consisting of a set of questions and scales designed to generate primary data. When designing a questionnaire, researchers must realize that there will be only one opportunity to interact with respondents, since a reasonable interval of time is necessary before the same respondent can be contacted again, and then it should generally involve either another topic or a different approach to the same topic. We review the essentials of questionnaire design in this chapter, but entire books have been written on the topic. We refer those who wish to review more extensive coverage of questionnaire design to the Business Research Dashboard below.

There are two methods other than questionnaires to record data. One is an interview guide and the other is an observation guide. Both are much less structured than questionnaires. An **interview guide** specifies the topics to cover, the questions to be asked, the sequence of questions or topics, and the wording of the questions (which is fixed), but there are no scales for measuring concepts. The role of the interviewer is to explain the survey, motivate the respondent to answer, make sure the respondent understands the questions, and probe for clarification or elaboration of open-ended questions. **Observation guides** are used to record observed data. They indicate what the observer is to look for and provide a place to record the information. The initial structure of the guide is based on the conceptual framework for the research, but during the data collection process it may expand to include new information that emerges.

■————**Business Research Dashboard**————■
The Art and Science of Questionnaire Design

Is questionnaire design an art or a science? We say it is both. We refer you to the following sources for more detailed treatments of this important topic. The sources are organized into practical and theoretical categories.

Practically Oriented Books

Douglas Berdie and John Anderson, *Questionnaires: Design and Use* (Metuchen, NJ: Scarecrow Press, 1974).
Arlene Fink, *How to Ask Survey Questions* (Thousand Oaks, CA: Sage,1995).
Mildred Patten, *Questionnaire Research* (Los Angeles, CA: Pyrczak, 1998).
Stanley Payne, *The Art of Asking Questions* (Princeton, NJ: Princeton University Press, 1951).
Robert Peterson, *Constructing Effective Questionnaires* (Thousand Oaks, CA: Sage, 2000).

Theoretically Oriented Books

William Belson, *The Design and Understanding of Survey Questions* (London: Gower, 1981).
Howard Schuman and Stanley Presser, *Questions and Answers in Attitude Surveys* (New York: Academic Press, 1981).
Seymour Sudman and Norman Bradburn, *Asking Questions* (San Francisco, CA: Jossey-Bass, 1982).

STEPS IN THE QUESTIONNAIRE DESIGN PROCESS

The final outcome of a well-constructed questionnaire is reliable and valid data if the related phases of the research have also been well executed. To develop questionnaires that produce reliable and valid data, you must follow a systematic process, such as that shown in Exhibit 10.1. We discuss each of the steps in this chapter. Guidelines are given on the best approach for designing questionnaires. Similarly, examples of specific types of questions are provided. Finally, the questionnaire used for the customer survey in the Samouel's and Gino's case study is shown in Exhibit 10.2. It is used to illustrate many of the above issues.

Exhibit 10.1

Steps to Be Followed in the Design of a Questionnaire

1. Initial Considerations

- Clarify the nature of the research problem and objectives.
- Develop research questions to meet research objectives.
- Define target population and sampling frame (identify potential respondents).
- Determine sampling approach, sample size, and expected response rate.
- Make a preliminary decision about the method of data collection.

2. Clarifying Concepts

- Ensure the concept(s) can be clearly defined.
- Select the variables/indicators to represent the concepts.
- Determine the level of measurement.

3. Determining Question Types, Format, and Sequence

- Determine the types of questions to include and their order.
- Check the wording and coding of questions.
- Decide on the grouping of the questions and the overall length of the questionnaire.
- Determine the structure and layout of the questionnaire.

4. Pretesting the Questionnaire

- Determine the nature of the pretest for the preliminary questionnaire.
- Analyze initial data to identify limitations of the preliminary questionnaire.
- Refine the questionnaire as needed.
- Revisit some or all of the above steps, if necessary.

5. Administering the Questionnaire

- Identify the best practice for administering the type of questionnaire utilized.
- Train and audit field workers, if required.
- Ensure a process is in place to handle completed questionnaires.
- Determine the deadline and follow-up methods.

Exhibit 10.2

The Samouel's and Gino's Customer Questionnaire

Screening and Rapport Questions

Hello. My name is _____ and I work for Whitehall Research. We are talking to individuals today/tonight about dining out habits.

1. Do you occasionally dine out in restaurants?
   ____ Yes
   ____ No
2. Did you just eat at Samouel's/Gino's?
   ____ Yes
   ____ No
3. Is your annual household income $20,000 or more?
   ____ Yes
   ____ No
4. Have you completed a restaurant questionnaire for our company before?
   ____ Yes
   ____ No

If person answers yes to the first three questions and no to the fourth question, then say:

> We would like you to answer a few questions about your experience today/tonight at Samouel's/Gino's restaurant, and we hope you will be willing to give us your opinions. The survey will take only a few minutes and will be very helpful to management in better serving its customers. We will pay you $5.00 for completing the questionnaire.

If person agrees, give them a clipboard with the questionnaire on it, briefly explain the questionnaire, and show them where to complete the survey.

DINING OUT SURVEY

Please read all questions carefully. If you do not understand a question, ask the interviewer to help you.

Section 1. Perception Measures

Listed below is a set of characteristics that could be used to describe Samouel's Greek Cuisine/ Gino's Italian Ristorante. Using a scale from 1 to 7, with 7 being "strongly agree" and 1 being "strongly disagree," to what extent do you agree or disagree that Samouel's/Gino's has:

		Strongly Disagree						Strongly Agree
1.	Excellent food quality	1	2	3	4	5	6	7
2.	Attractive interior	1	2	3	4	5	6	7
3.	Generous portions	1	2	3	4	5	6	7
4.	Excellent food taste	1	2	3	4	5	6	7
5.	Good value for the money	1	2	3	4	5	6	7
6.	Friendly employees	1	2	3	4	5	6	7
7.	Appears clean and neat	1	2	3	4	5	6	7
8.	Fun place to go	1	2	3	4	5	6	7
9.	Wide variety of menu items	1	2	3	4	5	6	7
10.	Reasonable prices	1	2	3	4	5	6	7
11.	Courteous employees	1	2	3	4	5	6	7
12.	Competent employees	1	2	3	4	5	6	7

Section 2: Selection Factors

Listed below are some factors (reasons) many people use in selecting a restaurant where they want to dine. Think about your visits to fine dining restaurants in the last thirty days and rank each attribute from 1 to 4, with 4 being the most important reason for selecting the restaurant and 1 being the least important reason. There can be no ties, so make sure you rank each attribute with a different number.

	Attribute	Ranking
13.	Food quality	_____
14.	Atmosphere	_____
15.	Prices	_____
16.	Employees	_____

Section 3: Relationship Measures

Please indicate your view on each of the following questions:

		Not satisfied at all						Very satisfied
17.	How satisfied are you with Samouel's/Gino's restaurant?	1	2	3	4	5	6	7

		Definitely will not return						Definitely will return
18.	How likely are you to return to Samouel's/Gino's restaurant in the future?	1	2	3	4	5	6	7

		Definitely will not recommend						Definitely will recommend
19.	How likely are you to recommend Samouel's/Gino's restaurant to a friend?	1	2	3	4	5	6	7

20. How often do you eat at Samouel's/Gino's restaurant? (circle one)
    1 = Occasionally (less than once a month)
    2 = Frequently (1–3 times a month)
    3 = Very frequently (4 or more times a month)

21. Have you seen any advertisements for Samouel's/Gino's restaurant in the last three months?
    _____ Yes
    _____ No (skip to Q. 24)

22. Which advertisement did you see? (Interviewer: show respondent the three ads)
    _____ Ad 1
    _____ Ad 2
    _____ Ad 3

23. Please rate each of the advertisements, using a seven-point scale, with 1 = "poor" and 7 = "excellent."
    Ad Ratings:
    _____ Ad 1
    _____ Ad 2
    _____ Ad 3

24. How long have you been a customer of Samouel's/Gino's?
    _____ months

(continued)

Section 4: Classification Questions

Please indicate the answer that classifies you best.

25.	Your gender	0	Male
		1	Female
26.	What is your age in years?		_____
27.	What is your total annual household income?		$_____

Interviewer Record

28.   Samouel's customer = 0; Gino's customer = 1

Thank you very much for your help. Please give your questionnaire to the interviewer and you will be given $5.00.

Note: There were two forms of the questionnaire. One had questions that referred to Samouel's, and the other referred to Gino's.

INITIAL CONSIDERATIONS

Before developing a questionnaire the researcher must be clear as to exactly what is being studied and what is expected from the study. This means the research problem must be clearly defined, project objectives must be clarified, and research questions agreed upon. If these tasks are completed properly, it is much more likely the research questions will be accurately answered. Once they are in place, the questionnaire can be designed.

Developing questions is one of the critical early tasks in questionnaire design. When an initial list of questions is developed, they must be evaluated to determine if answers to the questions will provide the information needed to make a decision, understand a problem, or test a theory. The more specific the questions, the easier they are to evaluate. The following possible research questions are examples:

- Is sexual harassment a problem in this organization?
- Do employees in this organization support diversity in the workplace?
- Does religious affiliation influence support for human cloning?
- What are the most important factors influencing the purchase of a laptop computer?
- How can you determine if an individual's actions are ethical?

These questions provide an initial start for the researcher, but a final evaluation requires them to be stated even more specifically. As an example, with the sexual harassment question the researcher would want to clarify what kinds of sexual harassment problems exist, how often they occur, if employees understand what harassment means, and so forth. This level of specificity is necessary if training is to be implemented to resolve any potential problems.

When the preliminary list of questions to be included in the questionnaire has been agreed upon, the researcher must evaluate them from the respondent's perspective. First, can respondents understand the questions? This is particularly important when respondents are children, are less familiar with a particular research topic, or if the study examines technical issues. Along with understanding the questions, one must consider whether the potential respondents have the knowledge to answer the questions. If the research is designed to understand the purchasing decision process for software in an organization, then those who will be asked to respond to the questions must be knowledgeable about this process. Finally, respondents must be willing to answer the questions. If the questions focus on sensitive topics, or if answering the questions might reveal an organization's competitive advantage, it is likely to be difficult if not impossible to obtain answers. Evaluation of questions in terms of respondents' ability and willingness to answer them is an important early step in questionnaire design.

To enable the researcher to evaluate questions from the respondent's perspective, the target population for the study must be specified. If the target population is not precisely defined, the researcher cannot evaluate the questions. It is at this point that the researcher considers to what extent respondents can be contacted and convinced to respond. If the survey must obtain information from a group of CEOs of large companies, physicians, or even schoolchildren, it may be difficult to accomplish. Understanding the target population can also influence the method of data collection and questionnaire administration. For example, to determine children's preferences for various shapes and tastes of cookies shaped like animals, one company chose to observe which cookies children ate and in which order rather than asking them questions. Similarly, because different methods of questionnaire administration (e.g., telephone versus face-to-face) can influence the nature of the responses, the method used must be carefully considered, particularly when questionnaires include attitude and behavior questions.

In addition to respondent capabilities, the researcher needs to consider whether the questions can be answered using a self-completion approach or if an interviewer-assisted approach will be necessary. To some extent it depends on the potential respondents, because some may be able to successfully answer self-completion questionnaires while others may not. For example, educational background, language capabilities such as vocabulary level, prior experience completing questionnaires, age, and cultural issues related to responding can be important, particularly when these factors are different from the researcher's.

Researchers must be concerned not only with whether respondents will answer a particular question but also with whether they will respond accurately. Potential respondents may refuse to answer questions on sensitive issues, or those they consider an invasion of their privacy. But what is sensitive or an invasion of privacy to one group may not be so with another group. For example, in a recent survey of U.S. teenagers they willingly answered questions regarding personal experiences with various types of sexual practices, whereas older individuals are reluctant to answer such questions. When answering questions of such a sensitive nature, however, all groups of respondents are likely to underreport their personal experiences.

In addition, respondents may not answer a question because it is perceived as being too long or too difficult to answer. On the other hand, respondents may willingly respond but do so in a manner they perceive to be socially responsible. For example, if asked about alcohol consumption, individuals who drink daily will almost always identify themselves as occasional drinkers, if they answer the question at all. Similarly, if asked about a belief in God, few individuals will deny such a belief. Finally, respondents may answer by guessing at a response simply because they want to be helpful. Close consideration of all these issues is important in minimizing error in data collected with questionnaires.

CLARIFICATION OF CONCEPTS

In designing the content, structure, and appearance of a questionnaire a number of aspects need to be taken into account. First, the concepts (constructs) to be measured must be identified and clearly defined, and then a method of measurement must be found. Second, decisions about other questions to include, such as classification and outcome information (e.g., intention to search for a job or likelihood to visit a particular Web site), types and wording of questions, questionnaire sequence, and general layout must be made by the researcher. As a general rule, only questions relevant to the research objectives should be included. When done properly, these decisions will result in a questionnaire with a high response rate and minimal error. Good questions will also ensure that the necessary kind of data analysis can be used.

If the questionnaire requires attitudinal or opinion questions about a particular concept, the indicators and the level of measurement must be determined. For example, if management wants to better understand employee turnover, it would include questions related to the work environment, pay, benefits, coworkers, job expectations, role clarity, supervisory style, and so forth. Information on each of these topics could help clarify issues impacting employee turnover. Moreover, the target population must be considered in determining how to measure the indicators. When Step 2 (clarification of concepts) has been completed, the researcher should have a list of potential questions to address the research objectives.

The Samouel's employee survey addressed some of these issues associated with job satisfaction and employee turnover. Recall from Chapter 9 that the first section of the employee questionnaire asked questions about the work environment. Four topics were included: supervision, compensation, coworkers, and overall satisfaction. Three indicators (statements) were included for each of these topics. Indicators on organizational commitment and likelihood to search for another job were also included. Thus, several concepts were measured in the Samouel's employee questionnaire.

DETERMINING QUESTION TYPES, FORMAT, AND SEQUENCE

To achieve a high response rate and a high quality of responses, the researcher must pay particular attention to the length of the questionnaire as well as the manner in which the questions are structured, sequenced, and coded. This will also facilitate the data collection and statistical analysis.

Typically, in gathering information through questionnaires we make use of different types of questions. The form of these questions and the order in which they appear in the questionnaire are important. The types of questions and their order in the questionnaire depend on the nature of the topic, how the questionnaire is administered, the target population's ability and willingness to respond, the type of statistical analysis, and similar factors. We describe in the following what we believe to be the most important considerations.

Closed-Ended Versus Open-Ended Questions

In broad terms, two forms of questions are used in questionnaires. The two types are **closed-ended** and **open-ended** questions. With closed-ended questions the respondent is given the option of choosing from a number of predetermined answers. An open-ended question places no constraints on respondents, who are free to answer in their own words. Examples of open-ended and closed-ended questions follow.

Open-Ended Questions:

- What do you think about the Internal Revenue Service?
- Which mutual funds have you been investing in for the past year?
- How are the funds you have invested in performing?
- What do you think of airport security?

Closed-Ended Questions:

- Did you check your e-mail this morning?
  - _____ Yes
  - _____ No
- Should the United Kingdom adopt the euro, or keep the pound?
  - _____ Adopt the euro
  - _____ Keep the pound
- Which countries in Europe have you traveled to in the past six months?
  - _____ Belgium
  - _____ Germany
  - _____ France
  - _____ Holland
  - _____ Italy
  - _____ Switzerland
  - _____ Spain
  - _____ Other (Please specify): _____
- How often do you eat at Samouel's Greek Cuisine restaurant?
  - _____ Never
  - _____ 1–4 times per year
  - _____ 5–8 times per year
  - _____ 9–12 times per year
  - _____ More than 12 times per year

Open-ended questions are relatively easy to develop because the researcher does not have to specify the answer alternatives ahead of time. Indeed, in instances where the researcher does not know the answer alternatives (e.g., exploratory research), open-ended questions are the only possibility. Open-ended questions are also useful when the researcher believes the alternatives may influence the answer, or for unaided recall and "top-of-mind" awareness questions. For example, to determine unaided recall or awareness the researcher might ask, When you think of banks in your area, which one comes to mind first? Open-ended questions often follow an initial question, whether that question is open-ended or closed-ended. In response to the question about banks, when a bank is mentioned, the researcher might follow up with the question, And is there a second bank that comes to mind? Similarly, an open-ended question might follow a closed-ended question like the following:

> On a scale of 1 to 10, where 1 is "not at all customer oriented" and 10 is "very customer oriented," how customer oriented do you consider Barclays Bank to be?

Following the response to this question, the interviewer could then ask:

> Why do you say that?

Open-ended questions elicit rich information and often insight from responses. But respondents need to be articulate and willing to spend time giving a full answer. The main drawback to open-ended questions is that it takes a great deal more time and effort to understand the responses. In self-completion questionnaires, open-ended questions should be used sparingly.

The design of closed-ended questions is more difficult and time consuming than that of open-ended questions. This means closed-ended questions are typically more expensive to design. But closed-ended questions can be precoded, making data collection, data input, and computer analysis relatively easy and less expensive. Closed-ended questions are generally used in quantitative studies employing large-scale surveys. All the questions in the Samouel's and Gino's customer and employee surveys are closed-ended. Note also that the process of creating a data file is greatly simplified with closed-ended questions because all the answers have been precoded.

Questionnaire Sections

After the researcher has decided the types of questions to be asked, the preliminary questionnaire structure must be determined. The structure follows a three-part sequence of **questionnaire sections**. The questions in the initial section are referred to as opening questions. The middle section has questions directed specifically at the topics addressed by the research objectives. The final section includes the classification questions that help the researcher to better understand the results. The Business Research Dashboard shows a typical example of the three questionnaire sections from the hospitality industry.

■————Business Research Dashboard————■
Service Quality Drives Competitive Strategies
in the Hospitality Industry

Almost all types of businesses in the hospitality industry, from hotels to restaurants and entertainment facilities, are realizing the importance of service quality as part of a competitive strategy. To improve service quality, businesses must have data for decision making. To obtain that data, they rely on customer surveys. The following is an example of a typical questionnaire a hotel might use to collect this type of data.

GUEST SATISFACTION SURVEY

Thank you for your recent stay at [*name of hotel*]! Because we value your business, we would like your opinion as to how well we meet our goal of delivering excellent service to you every time you visit. A postage-paid envelope has been included for you to return your completed questionnaire.

Sincerely,
Jens E. Jorgensen
Senior Vice President, Customer Relations

Please check the boxes as requested.

1. Were you a recent guest at [*name of hotel*] in [*name of city*]?
   _____ Yes
   _____ No

2. Was this your first visit to this particular hotel?
   _____ Yes
   _____ No

3. Was this your first visit to any of our hotels?
   _____ Yes
   _____ No

4. What was the primary reason for your stay?
   _____ Business
   _____ Pleasure
   _____ Both business and pleasure

Please think of your stay at this hotel when completing the following questions.

5. How did you make your reservation?
   _____ 800 number (Continue with Q. 6)
   _____ Called hotel directly (Continue with Q. 6)
   _____ Travel agent (Skip to Q. 7)
   _____ Web site (Skip to Q. 7)
   _____ Someone else made my reservation (Skip to Q. 7)
   _____ Did not have a reservation (Skip to Q. 7)

(continued)

6. If you made an advanced reservation, please rate the person you spoke with using a report card grade, where "A" is "Excellent" and "F" is "Poor." Circle the correct response.

	Excellent				Poor
How quickly was the call answered?	A	B	C	D	F
How courteous was the person you talked to?	A	B	C	D	F
How knowledgeable was the person you talked to?	A	B	C	D	F

7. Was the type of room you requested available?

_____ Yes

_____ No

8. For the following question, please rate your satisfaction with the hotel you stayed at using a report card grade, where "A" is "Excellent" and "F" is "Poor." Circle the correct response. If a question is not applicable to your stay, please circle the NA response.

Check-In	Excellent				Poor	
Exterior appearance of hotel	A	B	C	D	F	NA
Appearance of lobby	A	B	C	D	F	NA
Speed of check-in	A	B	C	D	F	NA
Courtesy of front desk staff	A	B	C	D	F	NA
Knowledge of front desk staff	A	B	C	D	F	NA

Hotel Staff						
Knowledgeable hotel staff	A	B	C	D	F	NA
Helpful housekeeping staff	A	B	C	D	F	NA
On-time wake up call	A	B	C	D	F	NA
Courtesy of hotel staff	A	B	C	D	F	NA

Guest Room						
Cleanliness of room	A	B	C	D	F	NA
Cleanliness of bathroom	A	B	C	D	F	NA
Cleanliness of carpet	A	B	C	D	F	NA
Cleanliness of bed linens	A	B	C	D	F	NA
Comfort of the bed	A	B	C	D	F	NA
Quietness of room	A	B	C	D	F	NA
Bathroom supplies sufficient	A	B	C	D	F	NA
Adequacy of phone equipment	A	B	C	D	F	NA
Working order of TV, radio, etc.	A	B	C	D	F	NA
Working order of heating and AC	A	B	C	D	F	NA

Other Facilities						
Condition of pool/spa	A	B	C	D	F	NA
Cleanliness of pool/spa	A	B	C	D	F	NA
Cleanliness of exercise facility	A	B	C	D	F	NA
Variety of exercise machines	A	B	C	D	F	NA
Convenience of business center	A	B	C	D	F	NA
Usefulness of business center	A	B	C	D	F	NA

9. What one thing could we have done to make your stay more satisfactory?

_____

_____

_____

10. Thinking of your overall experience at this hotel, how would you rate each of the following using a report card grade, where "A" is "Excellent" and "F" is "Poor." Circle the correct response.

	Excellent				Poor
Overall condition/appearance of hotel	A	B	C	D	F
Overall staff service	A	B	C	D	F
Overall stay	A	B	C	D	F

	Very likely				Very unlikely
11. If you were to return to this area, how likely would you be to stay at this hotel? Respond using a report card grade, where "A" is "Very likely" and "F" is "Very unlikely." Circle the correct response.	A	B	C	D	F
12. If a friend were planning a trip to this area, how likely would you be to recommend this hotel? Respond using a report card grade, where "A" is "Very likely" and "F" is "Very unlikely." Circle the correct response.	A	B	C	D	F

Classification Information

13. How many nights during the last year did you stay at a hotel?
    _____ nights

14. What is your gender?
    _____ Male
    _____ Female

15. What is your age?
    _____ Under 25
    _____ 25–34
    _____ 35–49
    _____ 50–64
    _____ 65 and over

16. Which category best describes your total annual household income before taxes?
    _____ Under $30,000
    _____ $30,000–$45,000
    _____ $45,001–$60,000
    _____ $60,001–$90,000
    _____ $90,001–$150,000
    _____ $150,001 and over

If you have additional comments, please use a separate sheet of paper and mail it with your survey. Your comments are important to us.

Opening Questions

The first questions on a questionnaire are referred to as **opening questions**. Usually the first couple of opening questions are designed to establish rapport with the respondent by gaining his or her attention and stimulating interest in the topic. It is typical to ask the respondent to express an opinion on an issue that is likely to be considered important but still relevant to the study. Opening questions should be simple and nonthreatening, such as the following:

- Tell me about a movie (or television show) you have recently seen?
- What is your favorite restaurant? Why is this your favorite restaurant?

While rapport questions must be simple and easy to answer, they must nonetheless be relevant to the topic being researched.

Screening questions, sometimes referred to as filtering questions, are another type of opening question. They are used to ensure that respondents included in the study are those that meet the predetermined criteria of the target population. They may also be in the form of **skipping questions** that direct respondents to the appropriate section of the questionnaire. This ensures the respondent will not be required to answer irrelevant questions. An example of a screening question for a financial services telephone survey follows. It was used to ensure that the most knowledgeable individual in the household responded to the survey.

Tonight we are talking with individuals who are eighteen years of age or older and have 50 percent or more of the responsibility for banking decisions in your household. Are you that person?

    _____ Yes
    _____ No

If the person says yes, that person continues with the survey. If the response is no, then the interviewer asks for the person who meets those criteria.

To summarize, the main objective of the opening questions is to include relevant participants and to create an atmosphere that encourages participation. Under no circumstances should the opening questions be of a sensitive nature. Note that the Samouel's and Gino's customer survey opening questions were easy to answer, relevant, and made sure the respondents had eaten at the restaurant and had not previously completed a questionnaire. The question about income may, however, be threatening to some individuals.

Research Topic Questions

The second group, referred to as **research topic questions**, includes those designed to provide information on the topic being researched. This series of questions typically asks about things such as attitudes, beliefs, opinions, behavior, and so on. These questions are usually grouped into sections by topic, because respondents then find it is easier to respond. This format also helps to maintain interest and avoid confusion. Moreover, since early questions can influence responses to later questions, the nature of question sequencing is to ask general questions early and more specific ones later. Moving from general to specific questions is referred to as a **funnel approach**. Note that the questions on Samouel's and Gino's customer questionnaires were organized by logical sections, starting with opinions about the restaurant. People like to give their opinions, so it is easy to get them to answer these questions. The ranking of selection factors requires more thought, so these questions were placed second. The ranking questions were also placed there because it minimizes the likelihood of the earlier perception questions influencing answers to the relationship measures. Finally, the classification questions were at the end of the questionnaire, with the income question being the very last one.

Branching Questions

Branching questions are used to direct respondents to answer the right questions as well as doing so in the proper sequence. Branching questions enable respondents to skip irrelevant questions or to more specifically explain a particular response. An example of a branching question follows:

Q: Have you heard or seen any advertisements for wireless telephone service in the past thirty days?

No →	If no, go to question 10.
Yes →	If yes, were the advertisements on TV or radio or both?
TV/both →	If the advertisements were on TV or both, go to question 6.
Radio →	If the advertisements were on radio, go to question 8.

For both question 6 and question 8, the next question would be:

Q:	Were any of the advertisements for Verizon?
Yes →	If yes (meaning Verizon), then ask, What did the advertisement say?
No →	If no, go to question 10.

The main disadvantage of funnel questions is the possibility that respondents will become confused if the questionnaire is a self-completion one. For this reason, funnel questions work best with interviewer-administered questionnaires. This is particularly true with computer-assisted interviewing, where funnel questions can easily be used with both open-ended and closed-ended questions.

Classification Questions

With the exception of screening questions, demographic and socioeconomic questions used for classification of respondents should be placed at the end of the questionnaire. The reason for this is that **classification questions** often seek information of a more personal nature, for example, age and income, and if asked early on may affect the nature of responses to subsequent questions or even result in nonparticipation. Being at the end does not mean classification questions are less important. Putting them there is simply an effort to increase responsiveness and reduce error.

Because many classification questions are considered sensitive or an invasion of privacy, researchers have found that a funnel approach can be used to increase the response rate. Below is an example of how funneling might be used with the income question.

- Is your total annual household income above or below $30,000?
- If the answer is below $30,000, then the next question might be, Is your total annual household income above or below $20,000?

This process can continue until the answer is as precise as the researcher would like it to be. In the above example, however, the funnel would probably stop at this point if the response were "above," because knowing the annual household income is between $20,000 and $30,000 is generally as precise as the researcher needs.

PREPARING AND PRESENTING GOOD QUESTIONS

Converting research objectives into questions that will be understood and correctly answered by respondents is not an easy task. As noted earlier, entire books have been written on this topic. To assist you in preparing good questions, we suggest you observe the following guidelines.

Use Simple Words

Questions must be in a language familiar to the respondent. Avoid using jargon or technical terms unless absolutely necessary. In situations where technical terms must be used, it is good practice to provide definitions for all words where misunderstandings could occur.

Be Brief

Questions should be short and to the point, and if possible not exceed one line. The longer a question is, the more likely it will be misunderstood by respondents. Long questions have higher nonresponse rates and produce more error in responses. The higher error rate is a result of respondents' tending to answer long questions before fully reading them because they are in a hurry to complete the questionnaire.

Avoid Ambiguity

Wording should be clear and concise. Questions are ambiguous when they contain words possibly unfamiliar to respondents or of more than one meaning. Such terms include "often," "frequently," "sometimes," "occasionally," "generally," "normally," "good," "bad," "fair," "poor," and so forth. An example of a poorly worded, ambiguous question follows:

How often do you consider your supervisor to be fair with all her/his subordinates?

_____   Never
_____   Occasionally
_____   Quite often
_____   All the time

The words "consider" and "fair" can both be interpreted differently. Moreover, the response alternatives can mean different things to different respondents. Finally, to eliminate ambiguity, researchers often quantify vague alternatives. For example, if a researcher is investigating church attendance, the question could be worded:

How often do you attend church?

_____   Regularly
_____   Often
_____   Occasionally
_____   Never

But this wording is clearly ambiguous. Three of the four frequency of attendance alternatives could mean different things to different respondents ("never" is the only clear one). A much better way to word this question is:

How often do you attend church?

_____   Every week
_____   1–3 times a month
_____   Once a month
_____   Between 2 and 12 times a year
_____   Never

Open-ended questions are typically more ambiguous than closed-ended questions. For example, consider the following question:

Do you like orange juice?

If a parent answered this question with a simple yes, and the interviewer did not follow with a probing question like, Why? there would be at least two possible interpretations of the answer. One is the parent personally likes orange juice. But the other possibility is the parent likes orange juice because he or she believes it is healthy for his or her children to drink.

When using open-ended questions, it can sometimes be useful to provide respondents with some help in answering questions. An **aided question** is one that provides the respondent with a stimulus that jogs the memory, whereas **unaided questions** do not have a stimulus. Stimulus information in aided questions should be neutral in nature to avoid biasing the response. For example, a researcher may aid the respondent by asking for a recall on the most recent visit to a restaurant. Instead of just saying, Where did you last eat out? which is an unaided question, the researcher might ask: When you ate out the last time, did you go to Samouel's Greek Cuisine, Gino's Ristorante, Juban's Creole Restaurant, the Swan Pub, or somewhere else? The latter phrasing is called an aided-response question.

Avoid Leading Questions

Leading questions imply that a particular answer is correct, or they lead a respondent to a socially desirable answer. This is sometimes referred to as framing the question to encourage a particular response. The Business Research Dashboard provides an example of how framing can bias responses.

Avoid Double-Barreled Questions

Double-barreled questions include two or more issues and make interpretation difficult, and often impossible. For example, it is not uncommon to see questions like the following on a survey:

To what extent do you agree or disagree with the following statements:
• Macy's employees are friendly and helpful.
• Macy's employees are courteous and knowledgeable.

When such questions are used, it is impossible to know which of the two adjectives a respondent is reacting to. Moreover, respondents do not know how to answer if they have a different opinion about the two descriptors.

■————**Business Research Dashboard**————■
Framing Your Questions Can Introduce Bias!

On a Saturday morning one spring day one of the authors of this book was out working in the yard. A group of young folks got out of a van and began knocking on doors to solicit participation in a survey of exercise-related topics. They were students from a small university doing a class project for a local health club. The students were pleasant and polite in soliciting participation, and upon receiving agreement to participate they began asking the questions on the survey. About halfway through the survey they said the following:

When people were asked this question in the past, 90 percent said "Yes." "Do you think belonging to a health club motivates people to exercise?" Yes or No?

The author refused to answer the question and proceeded to inform the student interviewers that they were not in fact asking if he believed belonging to a health club motivates people to exercise. They, in essence, asked: How willing are you to give a response that differs from 90 percent of the others who have responded to this question in the past? The young folks were shocked but courteous. The author then informed them if they would like to learn how to design valid questionnaires they should take his research methods course at the university where he worked.

Be Careful About Question Order and Context Effects

Questions should be asked in a logical order that is organized by topics. Early questions should be general in nature and later ones more specific to minimize **position bias** introduced by the order of the questions. Examples of position bias and how to eliminate it are shown below.

Position Bias:
  Q_1:   How important are flexible hours in evaluating job alternatives?
  Q_2:   What factors are important in evaluating job alternatives?

No Position Bias:
  Q_1:   What factors are important in evaluating job alternatives?
  Q_2:   How important are flexible hours in evaluating job alternatives?

Position bias occurs in the first example because asking the specific question about flexible hours before the more general question may make the respondent more likely to include a reference to flexible hours in responding to the general question.

An **order bias** is also possible with questions like the perceptions measures on the Samouel's and Gino's customer surveys. Answers to questions posed early in a survey can influence how respondents answer the later questions. For example, the first question in both surveys is on the food quality. If a respondent "strongly agrees" in response to the first (or early) question, then all later responses in that section are likely to be nearer the "strongly agree" end of the scale. Similarly, if early opinions toward questions are "strongly disagree," then opinions in response to later questions are more likely to be toward the "strongly disagree" end of the scale. To avoid this type of order bias, researchers generally rotate the sequence in which respondents are asked a particular question. This is easy to do in telephone or Internet surveys. But in self-completed surveys, like mail surveys or the self-complete ones used with the Samouel's and Gino's case study, the only way to overcome this is to have two or more versions of the questionnaire with a different sequence of the questions in a particular section.

A **context effect** occurs when the position of a question relative to other questions influences the response. Marsh and Yeung[1] reported context effects when they studied global self-esteem as measured by items like, I feel good about myself," or, "Overall, I have a lot to be proud of." They noted that if the statement, I feel good about myself, is positioned on the questionnaire where the statements refer to academic situations, then respondents will respond in terms of how they feel about themselves academically. But if the same question is positioned near statements that refer to an individual's physical condition, they are more likely to rate the statement relative to how they feel about themselves physically.

Check Questionnaire Layout

Presentation, spacing, and layout of the questions can influence responses. This is particularly true with mail, Internet, or other self-completion questionnaires. Note that the questions on the Samouel's and Gino's questionnaire (Exhibit 10.2) have been grouped into sections. Each section has a clearly marked heading and, where required, specific instructions on how to answer the questions. Finally, care was taken to avoid splitting a question over two pages.

Preparing Clear Instructions

Almost all questionnaires have instructions of some sort. Self-completion and interviewer-assisted questionnaires are likely to include instructions in the following areas:

Self-Completion Instructions

- Introducing and explaining how to answer a series of questions on a particular topic
- Transition statements from one section (topic) of the questionnaire to another
- Which question to go to next
- How many answers are acceptable; for example, "Check only one response," or, "Check as many as apply"
- Whether respondents are supposed to answer the question by themselves or can consult another person or reference materials
- What to do when the questionnaire is completed; that is, how to return it

Interviewer-Assisted Instructions

- How to increase respondent participation
- How to screen out respondents who are not wanted and still keep them happy
- What to say when respondents ask how to answer a particular question
- When concepts may not be easily understood, how to define them
- When answer alternatives are to be read to respondents (aided response) or not to be read (unaided response)
- How to follow branching or skip patterns
- When and how to probe
- How to end the interview

Whether the instructions are for self-completion or interviewer-assisted questionnaires, they must be clear, concise, and consistent throughout the questionnaire. Researchers often make instructions bold, italic, or full capitals to distinguish them from the questions and to increase the likelihood they will be noticed and understood.

With the growth of the Internet, several online support facilities have emerged to assist researchers in designing questionnaires. The Web site addresses of several vendors are provided in the Business Research Dashboard. Many of these sites are helpful, particularly in the mechanical aspects of questionnaire design. But none of them can replace the knowledge and judgment of a researcher experienced in questionnaire design.

■————Business Research Dashboard————■
Online Software Revolutionizes Questionnaire Development

Need some help developing a questionnaire? Researchers are increasingly turning to resources on the Internet. Below are some of the better Web sites that provide help in the design of questionnaires and the collection of data online.

Qualtrics (http://www.qualtrics.com)	Qualtrics is the leading portal in the United States for questionnaire development. Many universities teach methods of business and market research, political polling, and statistical modeling with the Qualtrics Research Suite, which is fully equipped and versatile enough to handle almost any project. It can assist in survey design, questionnaire development, data collection, panels, data analysis, and many other research challenges.
Socratic Technologies (http://www.sotech.com)	The Socratic Web Survey system operates on a CATI-like platform. It allows for quota controls and skip patterns as well as randomization of lists and attributes. Other features make it flexible and comprehensive, including a system for handling multiple languages in international surveys.
SurveyPro.com (http://www.surveypro.com)	This site claims their breakthrough technology creates "on the fly" e-mail surveys and forms in less than five minutes. Its format includes radio buttons, check boxes, and data-entry fields. Students and faculty are offered free access to this site for surveys.
The Survey System (http://www.surveysystem.com)	This is a comprehensive software package that is simple enough for occasional users but powerful and flexible enough for business research professionals. The system is written in a modular format, so the researcher can purchase only the modules needed.
SurveyMonkey (http://www.surveymonkey.com)	This company says it has a single purpose: to enable anyone to create professional online surveys quickly and easily. It is easy, but the claim of anyone is a stretch.

PRETESTING THE QUESTIONNAIRE

No questionnaire should be administered before the researcher has evaluated the likely accuracy and consistency of the responses. This is achieved by **pretesting** the questionnaire using a small sample of respondents with characteristics similar to those of the target population. Respondents should complete the questionnaire in a setting similar to that of the actual research project. Moreover, they should be asked probing questions about each part of the questionnaire, from instructions to scaling to format to wording, to ensure each question is relevant, clearly worded, and unambiguous. Pretesting is relatively easy with consumer surveys because generally there is a large number of available participants. But with employee surveys there is often only a small number of individuals available for pretesting and you do not want to include too many in the pretest. In such cases, researchers may choose to have the questionnaire evaluated by other experts or by individuals as similar to the employees as possible.

The pretesting approach depends on several factors. When a research topic is new to a researcher the questionnaire should always be pretested. But even if the researcher has extensive experience with a topic, the questionnaire must be pretested if it will be used with a different group of respondents. Clearly, if a researcher has used a questionnaire in the United States and is asked to use it in England, it must be pretested. And of course if the questionnaire were translated into French for use in France, it must be extensively pretested. But even a questionnaire used in one geographic location of the United States, such as Georgia or Louisiana, would need to be pretested if it were to be used in California or New England. Finally, longer questionnaires are more likely to need more extensive pretesting, and pretesting is always required if the mode of administration has changed, such as using an Internet approach instead of the telephone.

How large should the sample size be in a pretest? The smallest number would likely be four or five individuals, and the largest no more than about twenty. In the authors' experiences pretest sample sizes larger than twenty typically do not provide substantial incremental information for use in revising the questionnaire. Sample size is covered in more detail in Chapter 7.

Based on feedback from the pretest, including the coding and analysis of the responses to individual questions, the questionnaire may require some refinement. The pretest may have to be undertaken several times, using a different set of respondents, depending on the nature and extent of the revisions, before the researcher feels confident to proceed with the survey. In situations where multi-item scales are used to measure concepts, this process provides at a minimum a check of face validity.

ADMINISTERING THE QUESTIONNAIRE

There are five major ways of administering a questionnaire in order to collect data:

1. By mail, including overnight delivery
2. Via fax
3. In person
4. Over the telephone
5. Electronically via email or hosted Web site

For each of these approaches, there is an accepted best practice for increasing the likelihood of higher response rates and quality responses to the questions. Each of these ways of administering a questionnaire is discussed in Chapter 8. But the final decision on how to administer the questionnaire cannot be made until the questionnaire has been pretested and agreed upon.

CONTINUING CASE: EVALUATING THE SAMOUEL'S AND GINO'S CUSTOMER SURVEY QUESTIONNAIRES

The questionnaire used in the customer surveys was introduced in Exhibit 10.2. Review the questionnaire and consider the ease of completion, sequence of questions, topics covered, scaling, and so on. Does the questionnaire flow well? Is the sequence of questions correct? Are any topics missing that should have been included? List any questions that need to be rewritten. Give suggestions on how to rewrite them to overcome any weaknesses.

SUMMARY

UNDERSTAND THAT QUESTIONNAIRE DESIGN IS DIFFICULT AND WHY

Few managers dispute the value of accurate information in improving decision making. The purpose of business research is to provide managers with accurate information, often from surveys. But information from surveys is accurate only if the questionnaire is properly designed. Many individuals believe questionnaires are easy to design. But those with experience in designing questionnaires know this is not true. Indeed, experienced researchers can easily make mistakes in questionnaire design if they overlook essential steps, such as pretesting. In designing a questionnaire researchers must realize there will be only one opportunity to interact with respondents, since a reasonable interval of time is necessary before the same respondent can be contacted again, and then it should generally involve either another topic or a different approach to the same topic. For this reason, great care must be taken to ensure the questionnaire will produce reliable and valid data.

EXPLAIN THE STEPS INVOLVED IN DESIGNING AN EFFECTIVE QUESTIONNAIRE

In developing a questionnaire careful planning and a systematic approach are necessary to ensure the collected data is accurate. Clear definitions of concepts and how they might be communicated and measured are prerequisites for the design of a good questionnaire. Consideration must be given to the readability, presentation, structure, and length of a questionnaire, because previous research has shown that these affect response quality and rate. Finally, researchers must also be cautious about the type of questions used, their wording, and the coding of the responses.

RECOGNIZE HOW THE METHOD OF DATA COLLECTION INFLUENCES QUESTIONNAIRE DESIGN

There are five major ways of administering the questionnaire: mail, including overnight delivery; fax; face-to-face; by telephone; and electronic (Internet or kiosk). Each of the approaches has an accepted best practice. The method chosen must be appropriate for the study and yield an acceptable response quality and rate.

UNDERSTAND THE TYPES OF QUESTIONS AND HOW THEY ARE USED

Typically, in gathering information through questionnaires we make use of different types of questions. The form of these questions and the order in which they appear in the questionnaire are important. The types of questions and their order in the questionnaire depend on the nature of the topic, how the questionnaire is administered, the target population's ability and willingness to respond, the type of statistical analysis, and similar factors. Sometimes open-ended questions are best, while other times closed-ended questions best achieve the research objectives. Similarly, rating scales are used sometimes, while other times dichotomous questions are better.

DESCRIBE THE MAJOR SECTIONS OF THE QUESTIONNAIRE AND HOW THEY RELATE TO ONE ANOTHER

After the researcher has decided the type of questions to be asked, the preliminary questionnaire structure must be determined. The structure follows a three-part sequence. The initial questions are referred to as opening questions. The middle section has questions directed specifically at the topics addressed by the research objectives. The final section includes the classification questions that help the researcher better understand the results.

ETHICAL DILEMMA

Shelly Appleby graduated from college in May and has just started working for a marketing research firm. She has been doing a great job, and as a reward her supervisor asks her to write the survey questions for a telephone survey of customer perceptions about local grocery store chains. She turns in her questions and is told by her supervisor that they look good and require only minor editing. A month later, Shelly is included in the meeting to present the results to the grocery store that had commissioned the survey. During the meeting, Shelly notices that the survey questions have been altered and, in her opinion, slanted to produce positive results about the client's stores. When she mentions her thoughts to her supervisor, her supervisor explains that while objectivity is fine in the academic world, in the real world, the most important thing is to make the client happy. Shelly disagrees with her supervisor. What should she do?

REVIEW QUESTIONS

1. What are the steps to follow in questionnaire design?
2. What is the difference between closed-ended and open-ended questions? Give an example of each.

3. What is an opening question and why would a business researcher use one?
4. What is a classification question?
5. What are the guidelines for preparing good questions?
6. Why pretest a questionnaire?

DISCUSSION AND THINKING ACTIVITIES

1. How does the researcher know which questions should be included in a questionnaire?
2. Design an open-ended questionnaire to obtain college students' opinions about diversity on campus.
3. Design a closed-ended questionnaire to obtain college students' opinions about binge drinking on campus. Include questions to determine whether respondents themselves are binge drinkers.
4. Pretest the binge-drinking questionnaire prepared in question 3 on eight to ten students. Prepare a report on your findings.
5. How can questionnaire design help to minimize error in research data?
6. Go to the Web site for this book (www.mesharpe-student.com). Click on the link for the survey of Public Houses and Brewers in London. Could this questionnaire be used in the United States? If yes, how would it have to be changed, if at all? What is your opinion of the structure, layout, and wording of the questionnaire?
7. Go to the Web site for this book (www.mesharpe-student.com). Click on the link to the restaurant Neighborhood Survey. Would you complete and return this survey? Why or why not? Are there questions that should have been asked that were not included on the survey? Identify any questions you feel were unnecessary and could be deleted. Prepare a report on your conclusions about this survey.
8. Go to the Web site for this book (www.mesharpe-student.com). Click on the link to the Binge Drinking survey questionnaire. Evaluate the questionnaire in terms of wording, question sequence, layout, and scales. Pay particular attention to the definition of binge drinking, and comment on its validity and possible influence on answers to the questions.
9. *SPSS Application:* We are interested in measuring a concept labeled "work environment." From the list of variables in the Samouel's employee survey database, select those you believe will collectively capture "work environment." Assess the reliability of your chosen items in measuring this concept. Are there any weak or confusing items that relate to this concept?
10. *SPSS Application:* We are interested in measuring a concept labeled "restaurant atmosphere." From the list of variables in the Samouel's and Gino's customer survey database, select those you believe will collectively capture "restaurant atmosphere." Assess the reliability of your chosen items in measuring this concept.

INTERNET EXERCISES

1. Go to http://www.qualtrics.com. Use the software to design a questionnaire to obtain student evaluations of college professors.
2. Go to http://www.google.com. Type in the phrase "questionnaire design" and conduct a search. What did you find? Try this at http://www.yahoo.com. How do the results differ?
3. Complete a survey on one of the following Web sites and prepare a report that evaluates the questionnaire.
   a. http://www.survey.net
   b. http://www.cc.gatech.edu/gvu/user_surveys/
4. Go to http://www.markettools.com/products/customersat. Prepare a report on what you learned about customer satisfaction surveys.

NOTE

1. Herbert W. Marsh and Alexander S. Yeung, "The Liability of Psychological Ratings: The Chameleon Effect in Global Self-Esteem," *Personality and Social Psychology Bulletin*, 25, 1 (1999), 49–64.

Part IV

Analysis and Interpretation of Data

11 Basic Data Analysis for Qualitative Research

Business research involves a lot more than numbers and statistics. Some researchers have criticized qualitative research as being "soft" and lacking rigor. However, quantifying findings does not ensure that business research is useful or even accurate. Good research is the result of a careful, thoughtful, knowledgeable approach, whether qualitative or quantitative research methods are used. Indeed, we advocate using both qualitative and quantitative approaches in the same research in many instances because each has its role, and sometimes both are used in the same research project.

In this chapter, we first review the differences between qualitative and quantitative research. Then we explain various research approaches to the analysis of qualitative data. Next we describe the process of analyzing qualitative data. This process includes data collection, data reduction, data display, and movement back and forth between these steps. We end the chapter with an overview of how to draw conclusions and bolster the credibility of qualitative findings.

UNDERSTANDING QUALITATIVE RESEARCH

To understand qualitative data analysis it's necessary to first understand qualitative research. Qualitative research is discovery oriented, with analysts using the data collected to generate ideas and theories, and it is therefore based on inductive reasoning.

Inductive reasoning is a type of thinking that involves identifying patterns in a data set to reach conclusions and build theories.[1] When researchers use an inductive approach they are attempting to build their theory or conceptual framework from the data they collect. Theory built through inductive reasoning is called **grounded theory**. The opposite, analytical approach, referred to as **deductive reasoning**, starts with theory and hypotheses before collection or analysis of data. Thus, qualitative research emphasizes the development of hypotheses, while quantitative research focuses on testing hypotheses. Many qualitative projects are not followed up with quantitative research, however. This happens either when precise results are not necessary and when the topic under study does not lend itself to precise quantification. For example, intensive studies of cultures, subcultures, symbolism, and subconscious motivations may not lend themselves to parallel quantitative studies.

A qualitative research approach is the most appropriate and indeed the only way to achieve some research objectives. Situations in which qualitative research is likely to be the preferred method include (1) when little is known about a research problem or opportunity, (2) where previous research only partially or incompletely explains the research question, (3) when current knowledge involves subconscious, psychological, or cultural material that is not accessible using surveys and experiments, and (4) if the primary purpose of the research is to propose new ideas and hypotheses that can eventually be tested with quantitative research. For example, if the research goal is to identify all the kinds of issues older workers might have with a younger supervisor, then a qualitative approach is preferred, unless previous research has already identified these issues. But, if the goal is to test a specific hypothesis, that, for example, older workers are less satisfied with their younger supervisors, then a survey or experiment using a quantitative approach is best.

QUALITATIVE RESEARCH APPROACHES

All qualitative research is grounded in the sense that it is based on the evidence gathered about the context or topic being studied. The data collected for grounded research provides the basis for inductive reasoning and theory development. The general goal of grounded theory research is to construct theories to understand specific contexts and phenomena. Grounded theory may create, elaborate on, and even validate theory, but the emphasis is generally on theory creation and elaboration. Examples of questions used in a grounded theory approach include, Tell me about the process of (shopping online, buying a house, playing video games)? and, How is it different from (shopping in a store or catalog, renting a house, playing a board game)? Grounded theory procedures are neither statistical nor quantitative and begin by focusing on an area of study. Data may be gathered from a variety of sources, such as participant interviews, observation, field notes, photographs, video recordings, or diaries.

Once gathered, the textual data and any images are coded using categories or themes that researchers find in the data. For example, a study of online shopping investigating motives for online shopping may code the motives as goal oriented (better price, selection, information, and convenience) or hedonic (fun, surprise, and deals). In the grounded theory approach, theories are generated based on interpretive procedures. The interpretive procedures involve reviewing the codes (themes and categories) appearing in the data, recoding and aggregating themes, and collecting more data to fill in categories and themes that, during the analysis process, appear undeveloped. Finally, the findings are summarized in a report. Often a diagram or table is used to provide a model of the context or to summarize or provide sample verbatims from the theoretical categories. Verbatims are exact copies of the words or phrases obtained in the interviews. Although grounded theory emanates from the field of sociology, it has been used successfully by researchers in a variety of disciplines, including business, education, medicine, political science, and psychology.

While all qualitative research is essentially grounded, there are several different ways to collect and analyze the data and four possible "stances" regarding the analytical approach. Also, several data-collection techniques can be used. Chapter 8 covers focus groups, in-depth interviews, projective techniques, ethnography, and case studies, which all result in qualitative data. The researcher's approach to collecting and analyzing qualitative data is generally informed by a particular interpretive stance. The four interpretive stances are positivistic, postpositivistic, interpretive, and critical.[2] **Positivism** is a research philosophy that views reality as something that can be objectively ascertained and described through research. **Postpositivism** is a modern revision of positivism. Postpositivists believe that there is an objective reality but acknowledge that it is difficult to describe or analyze that reality without sociocultural and psychological lenses filtering interpretation. However, postpositivists continue to try to interpret research findings in a bias-free fashion under the assumption that there is an objective reality to describe. Quantitative researchers fall in the positivist or postpositivist category, but qualitative researchers may be positivists or postpositivists as well.

Interpretivism asserts that all access to reality is socially constructed. Interpretive researchers attempt to understand phenomena through meanings assigned to them by individuals rather than seeking an objective, bias-free reality. Thus, interpretivists embrace relativism and believe that neither truth nor reality is independent of social construction. Interpretivists may utilize a research approach called **phenomenology** to study human experiences and consciousness. Phenomenological studies examine conscious experiences from the first-person (interviewer or observer) point of view and range from experiences involving perceptions, thoughts, desires, memories, emotions, and imagination to bodily awareness and social interactions. The focus of phenomenological studies is "lived experience," or the conscious emotions and thoughts associated with life events these studies analyze.

A specialized analytical approach in phenomenology is **hermeneutics**, which explains human behavior based on an analysis of the stories people tell about themselves. In business research, these stories may be about buying and consumption or organizations and work, for instance. Researchers interpret such narratives with special attention to personal identity and to the social and cultural contexts in which the narratives are embedded. Thus, hermeneutic analysis requires immersion in background research about the historical and cultural conditions relevant to the topic being researched. To conduct the analysis, the analyst reads the text from all the interviews to understand each participant's narrative. Then the researcher reads back and forth across the interviews to understand patterns and themes.[3] An example of a phenomenological, hermeneutic analysis appears in the Business Research Dashboard.

Critical approaches actively seek to change social and economic circumstances. Researchers in the critical paradigm seek to undertake research that is "emancipatory." Critical knowledge is sought to enable people to free themselves, through self-reflection, from all forms of domination. Examples of critical approaches to research include feminist theory and psychoanalysis. Critical theory is not common in business research applications, but it does appear in scholarly business research. For example, critical theorists may study the excesses of marketing, consumption, and corporations with the explicit research goal of freeing consumers, workers, and societies from those excesses.

Managing Qualitative Data

Qualitative data generally originates from two sources, field-generated data and "found" data. **Field-generated data** comes from interviews or focus groups in the field and may include transcriptions, photographs, and video recordings. In contrast, **found data** comes from existing sources like online social networks, newspaper articles, speeches, diaries, advertisements, and audio and video records. Qualitative data management presents different challenges depending on the source of the qualitative data.

Unless collected in an online focus group or interview, field-generated data must be transcribed to enable qualitative analysis. Researchers differ in their resources, assumptions, and objectives, and what is actually transcribed into text will differ depending on each of these. For example, it is expensive to transcribe all data collected in the field, so researchers with a limited budget may choose to transcribe only portions of their video or audio files based on their relevance to their research objectives. Typically, however, video and audio files are transcribed. A great deal of information can be lost if researchers rely only on their memories and notes, and worse, memory may be incorrect.

The issue of choosing material to collect can be difficult for found data. The reason is that both the Internet and business are producing large amounts of digital records, and search techniques must be used to harvest relevant information from the data. Qualitative researchers may have access to millions of sources of information on a particular topic and must use certain criteria for deciding what to examine in their research. For example, if you conduct a Google search under "case study," the result is 611 million entries. Clearly it is impossible to examine that much information. Researchers must therefore identify relevant search terms and choose the information sources that will yield the greatest depth for their research topic, or they can sample the sources. An example of the latter approach involves the open-ended responses provided at the end of the "Did You Feel It?" survey designed by geologist David Wald. Most of the survey is quantitative, but a box for comments appears at the end of the survey. The site has collected tens of thousands of responses from respondents who have logged on to report their earthquake experiences. Researchers interested

■————Business Research Dashboard————■
A Hermeneutic Analysis of the "Juggling" Lifestyle

Hermeneutic analysis requires knowledge of the social and cultural history of the subject being studied by the researcher. For instance, a study of professional working mothers engaged in the "juggling" lifestyle uncovered two themes, which were expressed as binary contrasts: (1) envisioned ideals versus practical considerations and (2) holding it together versus falling apart. Expressing themes as binary contrasts is common in narrative analysis. The researcher contextualizes his or her findings in cultural and historical ideas about femininity and motherhood. Each of the themes has subthemes. For example, taking care of self versus taking care of others is a subcategory of the envisioned ideals/practical considerations theme, because taking care of others is an envisioned ideal in the juggling lifestyle.

In the following we present verbatims from a study of professional women and the juggling lifestyle, followed by the researcher's hermeneutic analysis. This table presents only a small part of the researcher's analysis, but you can see clearly how the analysis is situated in the historical and cultural context of women's roles.

Verbatim from in-depth interview	Researcher's interpretation
Susan: "My mom was home all the time, which was the norm when I was growing up. Looking back I realize that we were really lucky to have that. I don't know how Daddy, how they made ends meet with all of us, without her working, but they did. A lot of things that I do for my children they couldn't do for me with only Daddy working. Like gymnastics lessons and Cub Scouts and stuff like that, those were like luxuries that we didn't have that I am happy I can give to my kids."	Few concepts are more culturally sanctified than motherhood. As such, it would be a social taboo for a woman with children to not place motherhood at the center of her identity . . . Throughout the twentieth century, however, the social influences of mass marketing and advertising have drawn a close association between motherhood and consumption choices, such that being a good mother is equated with choosing the "correct" brands . . . By justifying career pursuits in terms of consumer benefits to one's children, primacy is granted to the role of motherhood and the pursuit of a career outside the home is reconfigured . . . Public work becomes a means to provide children with a more enriching consumer lifestyle.
Elsa: "I mean this kinda sounds cliché, but somebody's got to hold it all together. He's [her husband] got more responsibilities at work. But somebody's gotta tie it all together and I guess I feel like, OK, you're the woman, children are your charge. You know, Dad has the number one job. And it boils down to what you've been ingrained for years and years and years. That your place is with the children is your castle, and you take care of it."	The "holding it together" aspect of this theme captures a series of higher-level meanings that are manifested in the participant experience—near concern with staying on schedule. In one sense, this theme stands as a major motivation, and in some cases justification, for tolerating the juggling lifestyle . . . [Elsa's] qualifier of "I know this sounds cliché" and the reference to cultural norms of traditional motherhood suggest an awareness that her orientation is very much a product of cultural and situational factors that cannot be readily ignored.

(continued)

Verbatim from in-depth interview	Researcher's interpretation
Betty: "I usually do it [eat out for dinner] on days when I've just been working so hard and the thought of having to come home and to just work harder still is just more than I can take. I perceive fixing dinner as falling in the category of the straw that breaks the camel's back. I've worked real hard and all I want to do is go out and have someone else do the work. So, I don't want to have to worry about the cooking and the fixing and the thinking about what to make. I want to go and see a menu and just on the spur of the moment say, '"Yeah, that's what I want."'"	Betty interprets her unusually hard workdays as those where she has been heavily immersed in the interpersonal dimensions of her job and has spent the day "responding to other people's needs and problems" rather than "getting her own work done" ... In addressing this aspect of her narrative, I became sensitized to a distinction between doing for self and doing for others that emerged in her interviews and framed her interpretation of cooking ... "Cooking at home" is interpreted as the normal routine ... which then allows "eating out" to be interpreted as a much-coveted experience of being cared for.

These three verbatims are only a small part of the researcher's analysis, but they do show how narratives intersect with personal identity and cultural context. Why might business researchers (both managers and marketers) be interested in a hermeneutic analysis of professional women and the juggling lifestyle?

Sources: Craig J. Thompson "Caring Consumers: Gendered Consumption Meanings and the Juggling Lifestyle," *Journal of Consumer Research*, 22 (March 1996), 388–407; Craig J. Thompson, "Interpreting Consumers: A Hermeneutical Framework for Deriving Marketing Insights from the Texts of Consumers' Consumption Stories," *Journal of Marketing Research*, 34, 4 (November 1997), 438–455.

in understanding how citizens experience earthquakes have sampled responses from various types, locations, and sizes of earthquake events rather than trying to review all the responses.[4]

Many organizations are starting their own community sites to collect data from consumers. These sites are referred to as Market Research Online Communities (MROCs). The Business Research Dashboard addresses efforts by General Mills to move its qualitative research online.

Computers are increasingly providing a great deal of help to qualitative researchers with managing data collection, storage, and analysis. Software facilitates a wide range of approaches for managing data using document names, themes, definitions, memos, codes, shapes, colors, and so on. Even if computer software is used to manage qualitative data, researchers will always need quick and easy access to the original data to verify patterns, themes, and conclusions. Software is also increasingly used in a technique called **Web scraping**. Web-scraping tools locate and transform Internet content into structured data that can be stored and analyzed in a central, local database or spreadsheet.

■———**Business Research Dashboard**———■
General Mills Moves Qualitative Research Effort
to Market Research Online Communities (MROCs)

Over the past sixty years, quantitative methods have evolved from door-to-door techniques to direct mail, telephone, and finally to online research. On the other hand, qualitative research has relied heavily on focus groups during the same period and experienced little change. However, Market Research Online Communities are starting to transform qualitative research. Jane Mount, executive vice president of Digital Research Inc., explains the current change in qualitative research as being "a shift from asking questions to get reactive consumer feedback to listening to dialogue to get proactive consumer insight."

One company that has experimented heavily with MROCs is General Mills (GM), which had already engaged in twenty-two online community projects by fall 2009. GM's research efforts are moving online because, "Online consumer communities meet the needs of consumers, brand teams and agencies with busy lives. They allow you to innovate with consumers better, faster and cheaper . . . We listen, we build; we listen, we tweak. This can be done very quickly, with a lot of flexibility." The speed of qualitative research projects has now increased substantially. For instance, one project that would have taken six months only took six weeks.

What the company has learned about online qualitative research so far has resulted in changes to its research approach. GM has learned that online communities are better in discovering new ideas for products but not as good at choosing the best ideas once GM has started to build the product. GM's researchers have also learned that smaller communities, of thirty to fifty people, are generally better than larger communities, unless it wants to investigate several distinct market segments. Fewer members make it easier for researchers to get greater depth from those members.

Another finding has been that shorter duration communities, focused on specific projects, are more useful than an ongoing community. Compensation for participation has also been adjusted over time. Fifty dollars for six weeks of participation was not successful at garnering the feedback it desired. GM now offers $40 to $50 for each week of participation.

The manager of consumer networks at GM, Ned Winsborough, has heard everything from "Traditional research is dead" to "Online research is useless." Winsborough says "the truth is somewhere in the middle . . . It has a place, and we need to approach it like any other new technology. What questions can it answer? What objectives can it meet? What objectives can't it meet? . . . It certainly doesn't obsolete core quantitative methods, but it has powerful potential to transform qualitative research as we know it."

Sources: Jim Bryson, "General Mills Has 'Mandate' to Do Qualitative Research Online," QualBlog, November 9, 2009, http://www.qualblog.com/2009/11/general-mills-has-mandate-to-do-qualitative-research-online.php#more, accessed December 5, 2009; Jeffrey Henning, "From Bedrock to MROC: Member Activities beyond Discussions," Vovici, November 5, 2009, http://blog.vovici.com/blog/bid/23263/From-Bedrock-to-MROC-Member-Activities-beyond-Discussions, accessed December 5, 2009.

ANALYZING QUALITATIVE DATA

The objective of qualitative data analysis is to identify, examine, compare, and interpret patterns and themes. Recall that in quantitative data analysis, the process of data collection and analysis follows a set of steps that are usually followed in order.

In contrast, qualitative analysis is an iterative process in which the data is revisited as new questions and connections surface, or as the overall understanding of the research situation emerges. Indeed, in qualitative research, data collection and analysis are often concurrent, with analysis initiating additional data collection, which in turn stimulates more analysis. Thus, with qualitative research data collection, analysis, and theory development are intertwined. Qualitative researchers develop categories and themes as they work through transcripts or other artifacts and allow the theory and ideas to emerge from the data. When analyzing data in qualitative research, the following questions should be continually asked:

- What themes and common patterns are emerging that relate to the research objectives?
- How are these themes and patterns related to the focus of the research?
- Are there examples of responses that are inconsistent with the typical patterns and themes?
- Can these inconsistencies be explained or perhaps be used to expand or redirect the research?
- Do the patterns or themes indicate additional data, perhaps in a new area, needs to be collected? (If yes, then proceed to collect that data.)

To help them conduct qualitative analyses, researchers often use coding. **Coding** is the process of assigning meaningful numerical values or names that reduce data from a large amount of undifferentiated text to a much smaller number of relevant and representative chunks. The purpose of coding is to enable the researcher to simplify and focus on meaningful characteristics of the data.

Coding data begins with selecting coding units. Examples of **coding units** include words, phrases, sentences, paragraphs, images, graphics, and photographs. Some material that is collected may not be coded at all if there is nothing in the material that is relevant to the research. Researchers may sometimes count the number of times a word or theme appears, the proportion of time or space representing a particular topic or theme. However, care must be taken when anything in the data is counted. The sample is generally not representative, and in most qualitative research the interviews are not conducted in a standard fashion. However, counting can occasionally be of use. The end result of coding is data linked to or tagged with topics, themes, and concepts, allowing it to be manipulated, organized, and eventually categorized.

To clarify the process of qualitative data analysis, it is helpful to review the framework developed by Miles and Huberman.[5] Their steps in qualitative analysis are shown in Exhibit 11.1. They include data collection, data reduction, data display, drawing conclusions, and verification of findings.

DATA REDUCTION

When qualitative data is collected, it needs to be organized and reduced. **Data reduction** involves selecting, simplifying, and transforming the data to make it more

Exhibit 11.1 **Steps in Qualitative Data Analysis**

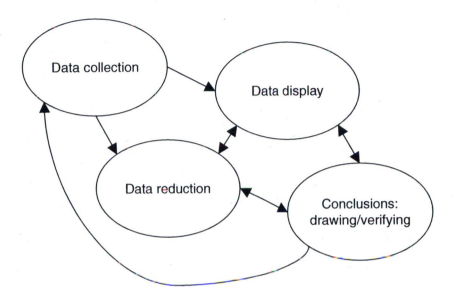

manageable and understandable. The process requires choices about what should be emphasized, minimized, and eliminated from further study. Initial decisions are guided by the predetermined research purpose and questions, but the analyst continually looks for new meanings and relationships. The objective is to reduce the data without eliminating anything that is relevant to the research.

DATA DISPLAY

A second step in the process of qualitative data analysis is data display. **Data display** goes beyond data reduction by organizing the information in a way that facilitates drawing conclusions. The process of data display helps qualitative researchers to organize information and view it in a way that enables them to identify links and develop explanations that relate their findings to existing theory. During the data display process, higher-order themes or patterns are likely to be extracted from the data. Examples of displays are charts or diagrams listing, defining, or linking themes that are central to the research. A table may show sample verbatims exemplifying the major themes and links in the study. A diagram may sometimes look like a conceptual model in quantitative research, with boxes and arrows between concepts. However, the qualitative version of these models may use double-sided arrows, meaning a theme or variable can both affect and be affected by another theme or variable.

The data reduction and data display processes described in the Business Research Dashboard come from a research project on Amway. The research describes how Amway uses "dream building" (a concept that emerged from the data collection effort) to recruit and motivate Amway distributors.

■————**Business Research Dashboard**————■
Data Reduction and Display: "Dream Building" and Identification in Amway

A researcher at the University of Illinois at Urbana-Champaign, Michael G. Pratt, performed an ethnographic study of distributors for Amway, a network marketing organization. The researcher engaged in participant observation, performed in-depth interviews, and collected archival data. Pratt joined the organization but let them know that he was collecting information for a study. In his research report, Pratt describes his participant observation as follows: "I listened to Amway tapes, read their books, sold their products, and did product ordering and bookkeeping tasks. I also attended various formal functions, such as weekend seminars and daylong workshops, and informal functions, such as casual meetings with upline members."

Pratt ultimately reduced the data he collected to data displays, two of which are presented below. The first display explains one of his themes, "dream building," by showing the various categories of dreams that Amway used in its appeals to distributors. (See Data Display 1 below.) For each category of dream building, Pratt lists an illustrative verbatim quote from his data. Tables of verbatims exemplifying themes and subcategories of themes are common ways of displaying data in qualitative analysis.

A second prominent data display device in qualitative research is a flow chart or conceptual model. (See Data Display 2 below.) Pratt used a flow chart to model the way that Amway distributors work to make sense of the organization and either identify, disidentify, or ambivalently identify with Amway. The flow chart suggests that if dream building is successful at motivating a distributor, that person will establish a relationship with a mentor. Also, through attempts to sell the product to family and friends, the distributor finds that his or her preexisting social network may not want to buy the products, and relationships suffer. When Amway's positive programming is successful, distributors validate their identities through Amway rather than through their social network; they engage in something Pratt calls encapsulated sense making, wherein meaning is sought almost exclusively through Amway relationships.

Data Display 1
Table of Sample Verbatims Explaining "Dream-Building Categories"

Dream categories and types	Illustrations from data
Lifestyle:	
Material wealth/possessions	"I would like to own my own home. [It should have] about 55 rooms and 100 acres and you know, some kind of stables." (Excerpt from dream-building session)
Freedom (no J.O.B.)	"The best part, really, absolutely, without hesitation is doing what you want to do every day. How many of you can get excited about that concept? [*Crowd claps and cheers.*] Eat breakfast with your children. Have lunch when you're hungry. Take a nap in the middle of the day. Do whatever you want to do. I go out on the swing set with my little girl and we sing our favorite song, 'I Love You.'" (Excerpt from tape *This Is Where You Don't Need an Ad Pack*.)

(continued)

Family:

"Traditional" American family

"My wife is pretty burned out in her job and yet she does not want to retire from her job until I am able to . . . My daughter wants to have swimming lessons. She's two and a half years old and our life does not really afford the time to have swimming lessons with both of us working. That's something we'll be much better able to do when we have more time to share with our children and our children aren't in day care five days a week." (Excerpt from an interview with a distributor.)

Helping:

Business opportunity

"Michael, do you really want to help people? If so, you can help more people by showing them this business that you can from teaching. God meant more for you than academia." (Excerpt from my field journal: my upline distributor is instructing me on why I should be a distributor.)

Altruism

"I want to own my own foster home for women who have Alzheimer's disease and do my research about the environment in that foster home so that this, our Amway business, would support that and if it [the home] didn't make money, it doesn't matter because it will just be an altruistic service to society." (Excerpt from an interview with a distributor.)

Data Display 2
Flow Chart of Dream Building and Identification with Amway

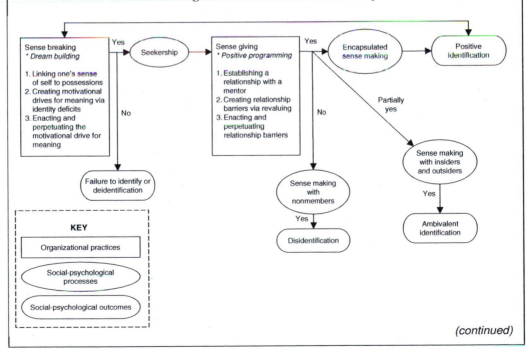

(continued)

Pratt spent two years studying Amway. He collected an extensive amount of primary and archival data. Through data display, he effectively reduced this data and helped to communicate what he learned. Looking at the diagrams, do you think the processes uncovered might apply to other organizations?

Sources: Michael G. Pratt, "The Good, the Bad, and the Ambivalent: Managing Identification among Amway Distributors," *Administrative Science Quarterly*, 45, 3 (September 2000), 456–493; Amway Global, http://www.amway.com/en/about-amway/our-story?aid=About+Amway-Our+Story/, accessed June 2010.

DRAWING AND VERIFYING CONCLUSIONS

The third step in qualitative data analysis is drawing conclusions and verifying their accuracy through cross-checking. **Drawing conclusions** involves deciding what the identified themes and patterns mean and how they help to answer the research questions. Qualitative researchers begin drawing conclusions during the process of data collection. In a process called **memoing**, qualitative researchers write their initial conclusions and observations, sometimes after every focus group, interview, or observational event. These conclusions are initially preliminary, subject to revision as the project proceeds. Interim analyses may suggest new questions for future interviews and different types of participants to sample.

Verification involves checking and rechecking the data to ensure the initial conclusions are credible. Recall that validity in quantitative research is the extent to which a construct measures what it is supposed to measure. **Credibility** is the qualitative analogue to the quantitative researcher's concept of validity: both credibility and validity involve assessing the extent to which the conclusions that have been drawn are logical, believable, and justified by the data. Any identified patterns should be supportable even when there are alternative explanations.

The process of drawing and verifying conclusions is driven by the objective of identifying the best of several alternative conclusions or explanations, not by looking for a single explanation. To enhance the likelihood the best conclusion has been drawn, it is advisable to collect data from multiple sources using different approaches. Thus, when possible, using information collected in focus groups as well as from in-depth interviews and perhaps even through observation could produce more valid conclusions. For example, information obtained in focus groups with managing directors of European software companies about how decisions are made to develop software for the Asian market might suggest that group consensus is important. But individual in-depth interviews could reveal that senior management support and knowledge are really more important. Thus, analyzing data from multiple sources involves more than deciding who may be right or wrong, or relying on who talks most often or speaks the loudest. It is a much more subtle process of hearing different viewpoints, assessing their plausibility and significance, and ultimately drawing the conclusion that is most consistent with the data.

In analyzing qualitative data the researcher can be unduly influenced by extreme, deviant, or outlier cases, because they suggest a new direction for data collection or analysis, or an alternative explanation or approach to solving a problem. This contrasts with quantitative research, where outliers or extreme cases are typically removed. However, the qualitative researcher has to use judgment about these outlier cases—is the participant merely an outlier, or is the individual a lone wolf who has articulated an insightful idea that other participants were unable or unwilling to provide?

Finally, some analysts use computer software to help with the process of analyzing qualitative data. Indeed, there are many packages that have become available in recent years, all of which have strengths and weaknesses. Before selecting a particular software package the researcher should consider the amount and type of data to be collected, the sources of data, and the anticipated types of analysis. While they can help manage the data, software packages are simply a method of more efficiently completing tasks that involve counting or organizing data. They do not develop codes for the data or define themes or phrases to be examined. In sum, even when software is used, the researcher cannot skip the intensive intellectual examination and assessment that is required to properly complete qualitative research.

Qualitative analysis software was initially used mostly in academic or scholarly research. But applied business researchers and industry in general are now finding applications. An example of the use of computer-aided software to examine qualitative interviews asking questions on organizational behavior and worker productivity is described in the Business Research Dashboard (see page 288). The example also shows that when a research topic is very focused, qualitative research can be analyzed quantitatively.

ASSESSING CREDIBILITY

An important requirement in qualitative research, just as in quantitative approaches, is that the methods used produce reliable findings. In **qualitative research, reliability** is the degree of consistency in the assignment of similar words, phrases, or other kinds of data to the same pattern or theme by different researchers. This is referred to as **inter-rater reliability**. Reliability can also mean the degree of consistency with which the same researcher assigns similar observations and interpretations at different times. Qualitative research often employs multiple member teams to code data into themes. The members of the team must work together to agree on categories for themes. Then they must define those categories so that the data can be consistently coded. Members of the team may all assess some of the same transcripts to ensure coding consistency.

Questions also arise as to the validity of qualitative findings. Qualitative researchers often use the terms "credibility" or "trustworthiness," rather than validity, but the concepts are similar. In quantitative research, methods for assessing validity involve inserting numbers into formulas and calculating a numerical index. But because qualitative research involves working with text and images, researchers cannot simply calculate a validity index for a particular study. This does not mean, however, that the validity or credibility of qualitative research cannot be assessed. In fact, there are several ways for qualitative researchers to establish credibility. To achieve credibility,

■————Business Research Dashboard————■
*An Application of Computer-Assisted Qualitative
Data-Analysis Software*

Researchers interviewed sixteen sales managers to identify organizational variables considered important in the effective implementation of sales force automation systems. Responses were transcribed and submitted to computer-aided content analysis. The relative occurrence of key concepts and value-laden terms was tabulated, and categories of themes were developed for each question. A panel of experts then defined the categories by developing a list of key words that described each category. The software searched the entire text of the interviews and placed information into the categories. Then the panel of experts again examined the results to eliminate any information miscategorized because of contextual issues. The four questions asked, the categories developed, and the relative percentage of hits for each category in each question are reported below:

1. What employee behaviors should firms reward, support, and expect if they are interested in effectively implementing an SFA system?

Teamwork	28%
Computer skills	35%
SFA competence	37%

2. What kinds of information can SFA provide that would be valuable in terms of helping increase a firm's productivity?

Prospecting	34%
Account development	32%
Buyer profile	34%

3. Please describe the kind of organizational culture or shared values necessary to effectively implement an SFA system

Information sharing	41%
Teamwork	33%
SFA commitment/ownership	26%

4. Please describe issues that might limit or enhance the effectiveness of an SFA system.

Resistance to change	61%
Insufficient support for SFA	39%

As an example, for question 1, three categories were identified. Their relative importance was 28 percent for teamwork, 35 percent for computer skills, and 37 percent for SFA competence. The other questions are interpreted in a similar manner. Computer-aided content-analysis software enables the business researcher to quickly and confidently analyze open-ended responses and report the findings in an effective manner.

Source: Chris Pullig, Trey Maxham, and Joe Hair, "Salesforce Automation Systems: An Exploratory Examination of Organizational Factors Associated with Effective Implementation and Salesforce Productivity," *Journal of Business Research*, 55, 5 (May 2002), 401–416.

qualitative researchers adopt a systematic and consistent process in data collection and analysis. They also document their fieldwork and analysis procedures in a manner that enables others to examine and confirm the soundness of their procedures and conclusions.

Perhaps the most important concept in establishing credibility in qualitative research is triangulation. There are four types of triangulation in qualitative research: researcher, data, method, and theory. **Researcher triangulation** involves the analysis and interpretation of multiple researchers on the same team, particularly if they come from different backgrounds. **Data triangulation** requires collecting data from several different sources or at different times. **Method triangulation** involves conducting the research project using several different methods and comparing the findings, including sometimes findings from both qualitative and quantitative approaches. Finally, **theory triangulation** is using multiple theories and perspectives to interpret and explain the data. Qualitative researchers cannot use all types of triangulation in a single research project but should be aware of them and think about the opportunities for building safeguards wherever a project would otherwise be weak.

In addition to triangulation, there are other approaches to enhancing the credibility of qualitative research. **Extended fieldwork** is collection of data over an extended period, which is likely to improve both discovery and interpretation. Extended contact with the field, as in ethnographic research, enhances the knowledge and theoretical sensitivity of researchers. **External peer review** by other research experts, including those both familiar with the research as well as disinterested parties, can verify or alter interpretations and conclusions. In **member checking**, researchers ask key informants in their study to read their results and verify or offer alternative interpretations of their data.

Qualitative researchers must constantly think critically about their results as they perform the analysis of the data. The Business Research Dashboard (see page 290) covers several questions that qualitative researchers should keep in mind as they analyze their findings.

CONTINUING CASE: SAMOUEL'S GREEK CUISINE
The Role of Qualitative Research

The business consultant hired by Phil Samouel has recommended two quantitative surveys, one of Samouel's employees and customer surveys for both Samouel's and Gino's. He did not recommend any qualitative research. Phil Samouel is not an expert in research methods, but he does know the difference between qualitative and quantitative research. He is wondering if some kind of qualitative research method should be used to better understand the challenges facing him in improving his restaurant.

Could observation be used to collect qualitative information? If yes, what kind of information could be collected using observation? What about focus groups? What topics could be explored using focus groups? What about the possibility of collecting qualitative data online from customers? How could the data be collected and what kinds of information could be collected in the online setting?

■————**Business Research Dashboard**————■
Interrogating Qualitative Research Results

All research has the potential to reflect researcher biases, but qualitative research may be particularly susceptible. Both the strength and the weakness of qualitative research is its reliance on human beings as research instruments. To build trustworthy analyses, qualitative researchers need to subject their conclusions to a great deal of critical thinking. Here are some questions to consider in establishing credibility for your analysis.

1. Does the analysis generalize too much from one or a very few cases? In particular, did a case that is vivid or interesting unduly affect my analysis?
2. Did I look for "boundary conditions" that limit the generalizability of my findings?
3. Did I explicitly search for negative cases, or cases that would disprove my assertions?
4. On my research team or among colleagues that I asked to review the work, were there individuals who have different points of view?
5. Did I explicitly consider alternative theories that explain my results and then select the most plausible concepts rather than prematurely settling on my ideas?
6. Did I continue to collect data until my understanding of the research topic was complete, and subsequent data collection provided no new insights?
7. Did I submit my final report to key research informants and ask for their feedback?

SUMMARY

CLARIFY WHEN QUALITATIVE RESEARCH IS BEST AT ACHIEVING YOUR RESEARCH OBJECTIVES

A qualitative research approach is the most appropriate and indeed the only way of achieving some research objectives. Situations in which qualitative research is likely to be the preferred method include (1) when little is known about a research problem or opportunity, (2) where previous research only partially or incompletely explains the research question, (3) when current knowledge involves subconscious, psychological, or cultural material that is not accessible using surveys and experiments, and (4) if the primary purpose of the research is to propose new ideas and hypotheses that can eventually be tested with quantitative research.

UNDERSTAND THE DIFFERENT PHILOSOPHICAL APPROACHES TO CONDUCTING QUALITATIVE RESEARCH

Many approaches are available for conducting qualitative research. Almost all qualitative research is "grounded," in the sense that the conclusions emerge from the data collected, rather than being based on preexisting hypotheses. The data collected for grounded research provides the basis for inductive reasoning and theory development. The general goal of **grounded theory** research is to construct theories to understand specific contexts and phenomena. Data may be gathered from a variety of sources, such as participant interviews, observation, field notes, photographs, video recordings, or diaries.

There are several different ways to collect and analyze the data and four possible "stances" regarding the analytical approach. The four interpretive stances are positivism, postpositivistic, interpretive, and critical. Positivism is a research philosophy that views reality as something that can be objectively ascertained and described through research. Postpositivists believe that there is an objective reality but acknowledge that it is difficult to describe or analyze that reality without sociocultural and psychological lenses filtering interpretation. Interpretivism asserts that all access to reality is socially constructed. Interpretive researchers attempt to understand phenomena through meanings assigned to them by individuals rather than seeking an objective, bias-free reality. Critical approaches actively seek to change social and economic circumstances. Researchers in the critical paradigm seek to undertake research that is "emancipatory." Critical knowledge is sought to enable people to free themselves, through self-reflection, from all forms of domination.

EXPLAIN THE IMPORTANCE OF MANAGING QUALITATIVE DATA

Qualitative data generally originates from two sources—field-generated data and "found" data. Field-generated data typically comes from interviews or focus groups in the field and consists of words and phrases in textual format. In contrast, found data is from existing sources like online social networks, newspaper articles, speeches, diaries, advertisements, and audio and video records. Qualitative data management presents different challenges depending on the source of the qualitative data. Field-generated data must be transcribed into a textual format to enable qualitative analysis. Found data must be selected, categorized, tagged, and stored.

The issue of what is actually analyzed in qualitative research can be difficult for found data because society is producing so much data, and the search techniques have improved so much that it is impossible to include even a small portion of what is being generated about a particular topic. Search techniques and terms must be used to choose the most relevant data, and if there is still too much information, sampling must be used. Managing data in qualitative research is important because decisions made early in the process of conducting qualitative research about how to manage the data can have consequences later in the study.

DESCRIBE THE PROCESS FOR ANALYZING QUALITATIVE DATA

The process of qualitative data analysis is to identify, examine, compare, and interpret patterns and themes. Qualitative analysis is an iterative process in which the data is revisited regularly as new questions and connections emerge, or as the overall understanding of the research situation emerges. Indeed, in qualitative research, data collection and analysis are often concurrent, with new analysis initiating additional data collection, which in turn stimulates subsequent analysis. The specific steps in qualitative research include data collection, data reduction, data display, drawing conclusions, and verification of findings.

ETHICAL DILEMMA

Stavros Kalafatis is an experienced qualitative researcher with Mayfair Research, Ltd. His company contracted to conduct a series of twenty employee focus groups in five countries to use in completing a training needs assessment for a large industrial manufacturing firm. The budget submitted in the initial proposal, prepared by a former employee of Mayfair, covered only the cost of collecting the data, not transcribing participant comments and preparing a report. When Stavros presented the budget for transcribing the twenty focus-group sessions, the client said it was too much and suggested that Stavros transcribe either half the focus-group sessions or only selected portions of all the focus groups. What should he do? How could Stavros develop criteria to select which focus groups to transcribe, or which portions?

REVIEW QUESTIONS

1. What are the situations in which qualitative research is the preferred approach?
2. What is the difference between the postpositivist and interpretive approaches to analyzing qualitative data?
3. What are the steps in the analysis of qualitative data? How are they related?
4. Can the reliability and validity of qualitative research be determined? If yes, what are some methods to do so?

DISCUSSION AND APPLICATION ACTIVITIES

1. How are data collection, data reduction, and data display interrelated in qualitative research?
2. How can qualitative researchers verify the conclusions they develop from their data?
3. Discuss the role of coding in qualitative data analysis.
4. How does triangulation help qualitative researchers achieve credibility for their research?

INTERNET ACTIVITIES

1. Suppose you decide to study consumers' feelings about coffee by using found data on the Internet. Come up with a list of sites and places that are publicly available where you could find postings about coffee. Now, design a study based on data collection from some or all of these sites. Which sites would you use and how much information would you collect at these sites (i.e., would you collect all consumer postings, or just a sample, and, if so, how would you sample?)? How would the study you design based on found data be better, the same as, or inferior to a series of focus groups with coffee consumers?

2. Run an online search for two to three research firms that specialize in ethnography. Find sample ethnographic reports at the sites. Do you have confidence that these businesses produce credible research? What factors influence your level of confidence?

3. Visit QualVu, at http://www.qualvu.com. How does QualVu collect qualitative data? What are the advantages and disadvantages compared to traditional online focus groups and in-depth interviews?

NOTES

1. M.B. Miles and A.M. Huberman, *Qualitative Data Analysis* (Newbury Park, CA: Sage, 1994).

2. Y.S. Lincoln and E.G. Guba, "Competing Paradigms in Qualitative Research," in *Handbook of Qualitative Research*, ed. N.K. Denzin and Y.S. Lincoln (Thousand Oaks, CA: Sage, 1994), 105–117.

3. C.J. Thompson, "Interpreting Consumers: A Hermeneutical Framework for Deriving Marketing Insights from the Texts of Consumers' Consumption Stories," *Journal of Marketing Research*, 34, 4 (November 1997), 438–455.

4. R. Celsi, M. Wolfinbarger, and D. Wald, "The Effects of Earthquake Measurement Concepts and Magnitude Anchoring on Individuals' Perceptions of Earthquake Risk," *Earthquake Spectra*, 21, 4 (November 2005), 987–1008.

5. Ibid.; Miles and Huberman, *Qualitative Data Analysis*.

SUGGESTED READINGS

Bryman, A., and R.G. Burgess. *Analyzing Qualitative Data.* London: Routledge, 1994.

Dey, I. *Qualitative Data Analysis: A User-Friendly Guide for Social Scientists.* London: Routledge, 1993.

Fielding, N.G., and R.M. Lee. *Computer Analysis and Qualitative Research.* London: Sage, 1998.

Hardy, M.A., and A.E. Bryman. *Handbook of Data Analysis.* Newbury Park, CA: Sage, 2004.

Lofland, J., and L.H. Lofland. *Analyzing Social Settings: A Guide to Qualitative Observation and Analysis.* 3rd ed. Belmont, CA: Wadsworth, 1995.

Miles, M.B., and A.M. Huberman. *Qualitative Data Analysis.* Newbury Park, CA: Sage, 1994.

Morse, J.M., and L. Richards. *Read Me First for a User's Guide to Qualitative Methods.* Newbury Park, CA: Sage, 2002.

Strauss, A.L. *Qualitative Analysis for Social Scientists.* Cambridge: Cambridge University Press, 1987.

Strauss, A.L., and J. Corbin. *Basics of Qualitative Research: Grounded Theory Procedures and Techniques.* Newbury Park, CA: Sage, 1990.

12 Basic Data Analysis for Quantitative Research

LEARNING OUTCOMES

1. Describe the process of conducting quantitative data analysis
2. Understand the importance of data preparation
3. Explain how descriptive statistics enable you to better understand your data
4. Clarify how to identify and deal with outliers

Business researchers typically have lots of data to help managers improve their decision making. One of their primary tasks is to convert the data into knowledge. With quantitative research, this means examining the data to identify and confirm relationships. Before quantitative data can be analyzed, it must be edited, coded, and in some instances, transformed to ensure that it can be properly used in statistical analysis. In discussing quantitative analysis, we begin with the process of data preparation. We then show you how to graphically display data so decision makers can better understand it. For example, if you conducted a survey of Safeway customers, you would be able to determine how frequently they shopped in that store, identify which respondents are the most frequent customers compared with the least frequent customers, and perhaps why, and make comparisons with shoppers at competitive food stores.

In many situations today there are "too many numbers" to look at and identify relationships that might be useful. Information must be developed, therefore, to summarize and describe the numbers. The basic statistics and descriptive analysis covered in this chapter were developed for this purpose. In later chapters we show you more sophisticated methods to use when the simple approaches cannot adequately explain the data relationships.

ANALYZING QUANTITATIVE DATA

Many research projects have numerical data or information that can be quantified to enable research questions to be answered. Recall that quantitative data is measurements in which numbers are used to directly represent the properties of phenomena. To be useful the data needs to be analyzed and interpreted. Data analysis in quantitative research involves a series of steps, as shown below:

1. Review conceptual framework and relationships to be studied
2. Prepare data for analysis
3. Determine if research involves descriptive analysis or hypothesis testing
4. Conduct analysis
5. Evaluate findings to assess whether they are meaningful

An overview of basic approaches to data examination is provided in this section. The discussion begins with data preparation, which is the initial step in data examination following review of the conceptual framework.

DATA PREPARATION

After data has been collected and before it is analyzed, the researcher must examine it to ensure its completeness and validity. If the questions were precoded, then they can be input into a database. If they were not precoded, then a system must be developed so they can be coded for input into the database. Blank responses, referred to as **missing data**, must be dealt with in some way. The typical tasks are editing, dealing with missing data, coding, transformation, and entering data. We discuss each below.

Editing

Before survey data can be used it must be **edited**. This means the data must be inspected for completeness and consistency. Some inconsistencies can be corrected at this point. For example, a respondent may not have answered a question on marriage. But their answers to other questions indicated they had been married ten years and had three children, all under the age of eighteen. In such cases the researcher may choose to fill in the response to the unanswered marriage question. Of course, this has some risk because the individual may have recently divorced, or in some instances individuals choose to have children but not be married. If either is true, the researcher would be introducing bias in the data if the married category were indicated. Thus, it is always best to contact individuals, if possible, to complete missing responses.

Editing also involves checking to see if respondents understood the question or followed a particular sequence they were supposed to in a branching question. For example, assume the researcher is conducting a study about two types of work situations. One situation describes a supportive work environment and the other a work environment with little or no support from management. To verify that a respondent interpreted the description of the work environment properly, the researcher may do what is called a **manipulation check**. That is, after a respondent has answered the questions they are asked to comment on the level of management support in the two work environments. If the respondent indicates both work environments are equally supportive, it means he or she did not understand the differences in the two work situations. In such situations, the researcher may choose to remove that particular respondent from the data analysis.

When collecting primary data, editing may result in the elimination of questionnaires. For example, if there is a large proportion of missing data, then the entire questionnaire may have to be removed from the database. The general rule of thumb for eliminating an entire questionnaire is when the proportion of missing data exceeds 15 percent of the total responses. Similarly, a screening question may indicate you want to interview only persons who own their own home. But the response on a completed questionnaire may say a particular respondent is a renter. In such cases, the questionnaire must not be included in the data analysis. We talk about how to deal with missing data in the next section.

Missing Data

Business researchers often have missing data, whether from surveys or internal sources such as data warehouses. Missing data can impact the validity of a researcher's findings and therefore must be identified and the problems resolved. Missing data typically arises because of data collection or data entry problems. The business researcher must assess how widespread the missing data problem is and whether it is systematic or random. If the problem is of limited scope, the typical solution is to simply eliminate respondents or questions with missing data. When missing data is more widespread the researcher must deal with that because by removing respondents with missing data, the sample size may become too small to provide meaningful results. In the Samouel's restaurant survey, a total of seventy-one employee surveys were completed. But eight employee surveys had missing data on one or more of the questions, and the proportion of missing data exceeded 15 percent. In this case, we chose to simply remove the eight surveys with missing data and work with the remaining sixty-three interviews.

We will cover two approaches to dealing with missing data, although other alternatives are possible.[1] The first approach is to identify the respondents and variables that have a large proportion (15 percent or more) of missing data points. These respondents or variables are then eliminated from the analysis. The second approach is to estimate the missing values by substituting the mean, or some other appropriate number. Unfortunately, this is appropriate only for metrically measured variables. When nonmetric variables have missing data the respondent or question must be eliminated from the analysis in most situations.

One approach to replacing missing values is to calculate the mean and input it into your data file. Another approach is to use SPSS software, which has a procedure for substituting the mean before any data analysis. To do so, go to the Transform pulldown menu, scroll down, and click on Replace Missing Values. Highlight and move variables with missing data into the box. Several methods of replacement are possible, but we recommend you use the default, that is, Series mean, and then click OK.

Recall that we stated previously that almost 60 percent of primary data collection is via Internet surveys. When surveys are completed on the Internet, controls are included that prevent respondents from going to the next question if they have not answered a particular question. These controls eliminate missing data in surveys conducted online but may cause other problems. First, respondents may simply provide a random response in order to move to the next question. They may also guess at a response. Either of these types of responses results in invalid data. Another problem is respondents may simply stop completing the survey and log off, resulting in an incomplete questionnaire. To reduce these problems and increase the likelihood of accurate completion of surveys, business researchers need to design questionnaires in a way that eliminates difficult or confusing questions.

Coding and Data Entry

Responses must be coded either before or after the data is collected. If at all possible, it is best to code it ahead of time. Coding means a number is assigned to a particular response so the answer can be entered into a database. For example, if we are using a five-point agree-disagree scale, then we must decide if "strongly agree" will be coded with a 5 or a 1. Most researchers will assign the largest number (5) to "strongly agree" and the smallest (1) to "strongly disagree," with the points in between being assigned 2, 3, or 4. A special situation arises when the researcher has a two-category variable like gender. Some researchers use a coding approach that assigns a 1 to male and a 2 to female. But we recommend that in such instances a coding approach be used that assigns a 1 to one of the categories and a 0 to the other category. This approach, referred to as dummy variable coding, enables greater flexibility in data analysis. We discuss this approach in Chapter 14.

When interviews are completed using a computer-assisted approach, the responses are entered directly into the database. But when self-completed questionnaires are used, business researchers should use a scanner sheet, because then responses can be directly scanned into the database. In other instances, however, the raw data must be manually keyed into the database. It is best to avoid manual keying of data, because doing so eliminates a step that could introduce error.

Open-ended questions are occasionally used with quantitative surveys. Such questions must be coded after the survey has been completed. Coding of open-ended questions is necessary whether the data is collected online or in some type of interviewer-assisted approach. To accomplish the coding, responses are reviewed to identify common words, phrases, themes, and other types of patterns in the responses. Codes are then assigned to facilitate quantitative data analysis. Chapter 11 further discusses coding qualitative data.

Most popular software includes a data editor, similar to a spreadsheet, that can be used to enter, edit, and view the contents of the database. Missing values are typically represented by a dot (.) in a cell, so they must be coded in a way that will be recognized by the software. For example, if a seven-point Likert-scaled question is missing a response, we could code a missing value as 9. Similarly, a question may include a "don't know" option, and we may choose to code that as an 8, for "don't know," and a 9 for any other response that represents an actual missing value. Researchers need to anticipate these situations and plan for them ahead of time.

Human errors can occur when completing the questionnaire, when coding it, or during data entry. Therefore, at least 10 percent of the coded questionnaires as well as the actual database are typically checked for possible coding or data entry errors. Selecting questionnaires for checking usually involves a systematic, random sampling process.

Data Transformation

Data transformation is the process of changing the original form of the data to a new format. This is done typically to more easily understand the data or achieve some other research objective. For example, with measurement scales we often have both negatively and positively worded statements. In such cases, the researcher will typically reverse code the questions that are negatively worded so a summated scale can be calculated to interpret the results. That is, if a five-point scale is used a 5 will be transformed to a 1, a 4 to a 2, and so on (a 3 does not have to be changed). Another situation that might require transformation is when data is collected on the respondent's age. Generally less response bias is associated when respondents are asked what year they were born in rather than how old they are. In such cases, the researcher would simply transform the birth year into the age of the respondent.

Researchers may also choose to collapse or combine adjacent categories of a variable in a way that reduces the number of categories. For example, the number of categories for the age variable can be reduced to two: respondents aged thirty years and younger versus those older than thirty. Similarly, a seven-point agree-disagree scale may be reduced to a three-point scale by combining the 5, 6, and 7 responses and the 1, 2, and 3 responses. The number 4 responses would remain the middle, or neutral, category.

Another important data transformation involves creating new variables by respecifying the data with logical transformations. For example, we may choose to combine Likert scales into a summated rating. This would involve combining the scores (raw data) for several attitudinal statements into a single summated score. The **summated score** for a three-statement attitude scale is calculated as shown below:

Summated score = variable 1 + variable 2 + variable 3

Another approach the researcher could use is to calculate the **average summated score**. This involves calculating the summated score and then dividing it by the number of variables. When this approach is used the new transformed, composite variable is comparable in scaling to the original scale. For example, if we had three five-point statements, the summated score might be 4 + 4 + 5 = 13. But if we used the average summated score, the result would be 4 + 4 + 5 = 13/3 = 4.3. SPSS software calculates summated scores, as shown in the Data Analysis box.

Many businesses today are assembling their data in data warehouses. A **data warehouse** is a computerized electronic storage device that holds all the information the business has collected. The information may be secondary data, such as accounting

---

■————DATA ANALYSIS————■
Using SPSS to Calculate Summated and Average Summated Scores

The work environment statements on the Samouel's employee survey include three measures related to the supervisor. They are variables X_3, X_6, and X_{10}. To calculate the summated score, load the employee survey data (Employee Survey $N = 63$.sav). The click-through sequence is: TRANSFORM → COMPUTE. First type a variable name in the Target Variable box. In this case we are calculating a summated score for the supervisory statements, so let's use the abbreviation SUMSUP for Summated Supervisor. Next click on the Numeric Expression box to move the cursor there. Look below at the buttons and click on the parenthesis to place it in the Numeric Expression box. Now highlight variable X_3 and click on the arrow box to move it into the parenthesis. Go to the buttons below and click on the plus (+) sign. Go back and highlight variable X_6 and click on the arrow box to move it into the parenthesis. Again click on the plus (+) sign. Finally, go back and highlight variable X_{10} and click on the arrow box to move it into the parenthesis. Next click on OK and you will get the summated score for the three variables. You can find it as a new variable at the far right side of your data editor screen.

To calculate the average summated score, you follow the same procedure as before. This time you must type a different Target Variable name than what was used before. Let's use the abbreviation ASUMSUP to indicate average summated supervisor rating. After you have moved all three variables into the parentheses and before you click on OK, you click the cursor to place it after the parentheses. Next go to the buttons below the Numeric Expression box and click on the slash sign ($/$ = the division sign) to place it after the parenthesis. Now again go to the buttons below the Numeric Expression box and click on 3. You click on 3 because you are calculating the average of the three variables. Next click on OK, and you will get the average summated score for the three variables. You can find it as a new variable at the far right side of your data editor screen.

---

records or customer lists. Primary data from observation (e.g., Web site traffic) or surveys is also stored in the data warehouse. Managers and business researchers can access and analyze this information to answer questions, solve business problems, or make decisions. The Business Research Dashboard summarizes the challenges involved in using information from data warehouses.

DATA ANALYSIS USING DESCRIPTIVE STATISTICS

Quantitative data analysis involves one of two approaches: (1) using descriptive statistics to obtain an understanding of the data, or (2) testing hypotheses using statistical tests. In the rest of this chapter we provide an overview of descriptive data analysis. Chapters 13, 14, and 15 describe the major statistical methods that can be used to test hypotheses.

Graphics and charts help you to more easily understand and describe your data. They also more effectively communicate complex issues and make your business research reports more visually appealing. We show you how to use frequency distributions, histograms, bar charts, pie charts, and line charts, as well as measures of central tendency and dispersion.

■————**Business Research Dashboard**————■
Dealing with Data from Data Warehouses

Increasingly researchers must analyze and make recommendations on data from data warehouses. This trend has both advantages and disadvantages. The advantages are related mostly to the fact that data from data warehouses is secondary data and therefore quicker and easier to obtain, as well as less expensive. But there are numerous disadvantages that must be dealt with before the data can be analyzed and used. Below is a list of typical problems business researchers and managers face in using data from data warehouses.

- Outdated data, that is, too old to be relevant.
- Incomplete data, that is, data available from one period but not another.
- Data that is supposedly available but cannot be found—in large companies often because of there being several data warehouses in different locations maintained by different divisions of the company.
- Data that is supposedly the same from various internal sources actually being different—for example, information on sales by territory is different from two different sources, internal sales records versus scanner data, which generally does not represent all distribution outlets. Researchers must decide which source to rely on in a particular situation, or how to combine the data from two sources.
- Data that is in an unusable or incompatible format, or cannot be understood.
- Disorganized data, not in a central location.
- Software to access data is not working, or not working as it should.
- Too much data.

How are the above problems resolved? Sometimes they cannot be resolved, at least in a timely manner—that is, in time for decision making. The best approach to avoid or minimize such problems is to establish a good working relationship among management, information technology personnel, and business researchers. This means the individuals involved in using data must start early to communicate their expectations of what data is needed, how often, in what format, and so on, than on an ongoing basis continue to work closely to anticipate and deal with data management and utilization issues as they arise.

Source: J. Hair, M. Wolfinbarger, D. Ortinau, and R. Bush, *Essentials of Marketing Research*, 2nd ed. (New York: McGraw-Hill/Irwin, 2010), 245. Reprinted with permission.

THE FREQUENCY DISTRIBUTION

Business researchers often answer research questions based on a single variable. For example, the researcher may need to answer questions such as the following:

1. How likely is it that the employees of a particular business will search for another job? For example, are they very likely, somewhat likely, or not likely at all to search for a new job in the next six months?
2. What percentage of the patrons of a restaurant should be classified as very frequent, somewhat frequent, or infrequent users? For example, if you interview a sample of individuals as they leave McDonald's, what percentage of them come to the restaurant frequently versus infrequently?

3. What is the geographic location of customers? For example, are there more owners of Mercedes in Germany than in the United States?

Questions like these can be answered by examining a table that describes the data. The table is called a frequency distribution. **Frequency distributions** examine the data one variable at a time and provide counts of the different responses for the various values of the variable. The objective of a frequency distribution is to display the number of responses associated with each value of a variable. Typically, a frequency distribution shows the variable name and description, the frequency counts for each value of the variable, and the cumulative percentages for each value associated with a variable.

Let' use our Samouel's and Gino's employee survey database to illustrate a frequency distribution. Exhibit 12.1 shows three questions from the employee survey used in many of the examples in this chapter. Note that employees were asked to indicate their feelings about working at Samouel's restaurant by responding to a seven-point agree-disagree scale. In the examples question 13 is labeled "loyalty," question 14 is labeled "effort," and 15 is labeled "proud."

Exhibit 12.1

Employee Survey Questions Used as Examples

Please indicate your view on each of the following questions:

	Strongly disagree						Strongly agree
13. I have a sense of loyalty to Samouel's Greek Cuisine restaurant.	1	2	3	4	5	6	7
14. I am willing to put in a great deal of effort beyond that normally expected to help Samouel's Greek Cuisine restaurant to be successful.	1	2	3	4	5	6	7
15. I am proud to tell others that I work for Samouel's Greek Cuisine restaurant.	1	2	3	4	5	6	7

The frequency distribution for variable X_{15} "proud," is shown in Exhibit 12.2. In the frequency distribution table, the first column with numbers in it shows the various responses (ratings) to the question. For example, responses to this question were on a seven-point scale, but the lowest rating was a 4 and the highest a 7. The second column, labeled "Frequency," is the count of the number of times a particular rating was given by respondents. In this example, a rating of 5 was given by twenty-eight respondents. The third column, "Percent," shows the percentage of all respondents ($N = 71$) selecting the value for this variable. For example, 39.4 percent of the respondents gave a rating of 5 on this question ($28/71 = 39.4$ percent). The fourth column, "Valid Percent," displays the percentage of valid responses ($N = 69$). In other words, this column represents the percentage of responses, not the percent of respondents. For the survey there were eight respondents that had missing data on one or more of the questions. But, for this question (X_{15}), there were only two respondents (2.8 percent)

Exhibit 12.2

Frequency Distribution for Variable X_{15} "Proud" on Employee Survey with Missing Data

Valid Responses	Frequency	Percent	Valid Percent	Cumulative Percent
4	10	14.1	14.5	14.5
5	28	39.4	40.6	55.1
6	21	29.6	30.4	85.5
Definitely agree = 7	10	14.1	14.5	100.0
Total	69	97.2	100.0	
Missing	2	2.8		
Total	71	100.0		

with missing data. If there is no missing data, the percentages in the "Percent" and "Valid Percent" columns will be the same. "Cumulative Percent," the last column, is the cumulative percentage from the top to the bottom based on the "Valid Response" column. The cumulative percentage is simply the sum of the "Valid Percents." In this survey, 55.1 percent of the respondents gave a rating of 5 or below.

Frequency distributions have many uses in business research. They are used to describe the responses to a particular variable by displaying the counts and percentages both before and after adjustment for nonresponses (missing data). A frequency distribution can be used to perform an "eyeball" check of the data and to easily determine the number of nonresponses, if any. If a rating appears in the frequency distribution that is not a valid response, the researcher can also determine when there are data inaccuracies. For example, seeing a 0 on the frequency distribution in Exhibit 12.2 (where a 1 to 7 scale was used) would indicate a problem with the data, since that rating was not possible given the coding of this variable. Cases in which ratings are out of range would be investigated and corrective actions taken. The researcher can also examine the data for each variable to see if there are any outliers—cases with extreme values that may distort the total picture. For example, an individual who eats at a fast food hamburger restaurant more than ten times each week would be likely to be so unusual the person may be considered an outlier.

HISTOGRAMS

A frequency distribution also provides evidence of the shape of the distribution for the variable. Are most of the responses on the high or low end of the response values? A vertical bar chart, or **histogram**, can be constructed from the information in the frequency distribution, and the shape of the actual data as presented in the histogram can be compared with the expected shape. Exhibit 12.3 is a histogram for the "proud" variable (X_{15}). It shows that most employees of Samouel's restaurant are moderately proud to be working there. That is, most of the employees gave a "proud" rating of 5, 6, or 7. A normal (bell-shaped) curve is superimposed over the histogram to facilitate comparison of the actual distribution with the normal curve. The distribution in this example conforms reasonably well to a normal curve. At the lower right-hand corner of

Exhibit 12.3

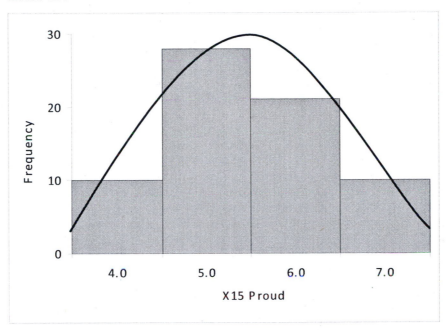

DATA ANALYSIS
Using SPSS to Prepare a Frequency Distribution Table and Histogram

It is easy to use SPSS to calculate the frequency distribution table in Exhibit 12.2. Set up your SPSS software and load the employee survey database with missing data (Employee Survey_N = 71 with Missing Data.sav). The click-through sequence is: ANALYZE → DESCRIPTIVE STATISTICS → FREQUENCIES. Scroll down and highlight X_{15}, "proud," and click on the arrow box to move it into the Variables box. Click on Charts and then under Chart Type, click on Histograms and right below it "With Normal Curve," and finally on Continue. Next click on OK to execute the program. The result will be the frequency chart and histogram shown in Exhibits 12.2 and 12.3.

the graph the mean, standard deviation, and sample size are indicated. Note the sample size is sixty-nine. This indicates there is missing data on this variable for two respondents. (Note that for this analysis the employee database with missing data was used.)

The results shown above would be of interest to Phil Samouel, owner of Samouel's Greek Cuisine. But a comparison of the satisfaction of his customers with that of Gino's would also be of interest to him. By making this comparison he could determine if there are differences in the satisfaction levels of the customers of the two restaurants. The question used to measure satisfaction on the Samouel's and Gino's customer surveys is shown in Exhibit 12.4.

The frequency tables in Exhibit 12.5 show the customer satisfaction ratings for the two restaurants. Note that you can now compare the satisfaction ratings for the two res-

Exhibit 12.4

Customer Survey Question Measuring Satisfaction

Please indicate your view on the following question:

	Not satisfied at all						Very satisfied
17. How satisfied are you with Samouel's/Gino's restaurant?	1	2	3	4	5	6	7

Exhibit 12.5

Frequency Table Comparing Samouel's and Gino's

X_{17}, "satisfaction" X_{28}, "competitor"	Frequency		Percent	Valid Percent	Cumulative Percent
Samouel's	3	10	10.0	10.0	10.0
	4	42	42.0	42.0	52.0
	5	16	16.0	16.0	68.0
	6	24	24.0	24.0	92.0
	Highly satisfied = 7	8	8.0	8.0	100.0
	Total	100	100.0	100.0	
Gino's	4	7	7.0	7.0	7.0
	5	28	28.0	28.0	35.0
	6	27	27.0	27.0	62.0
	Highly satisfied = 7	38	38.0	38.0	100.0
	Total	100	100.0	100.0	

taurants. First, go to the "Frequency" column and look at the total for both Samouel's and Gino's. You will see that each total is 100, the number of customers interviewed at each restaurant that had no missing data on their questionnaires. Now let's look at how the two customer groups responded to this question. To the far right is a column labeled "Cumulative Percent." If you look at the third from the top number in this column you will see the number 68.0 percent for Samouel's. This is the percentage of satisfaction ratings of 5 or lower. But when you look at Gino's, you see that only 35.0 percent of his customers gave a satisfaction rating of 5 or below. These numbers tell us that Gino's customers are more satisfied than are Samouel's customers. How do we know this? It is based on the fact that Gino's customers give higher ratings on the "satisfaction" variable (X_{17}) than do Samouel's customers. For example, as noted earlier, 68 percent of Samouel's customers rate his restaurant 5 or below, while only 35 percent of Gino's customers rate his restaurant 5 or below. Information such as this can be useful to business researchers, owners, and managers.

Visual comparisons using a histogram of the satisfaction ratings of the two restaurants make it even easier to compare the ratings. A histogram simply takes the information in a frequency table and displays it in a chart. We quickly see from Exhibit 12.6 that Samouel's has very few ratings of 7 ("highly satisfied"), whereas Gino's has many. Moreover, Samouel's has many ratings of 4, while Gino's has very few ratings of 4. Thus, it is easy to see that Gino's customers are more highly satisfied than are Samouel's.

Exhibit 12.6

X25: Samouel's

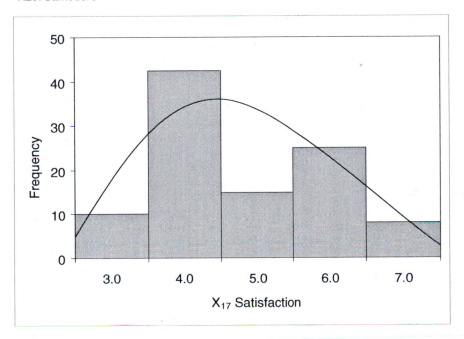

X25: Gino's

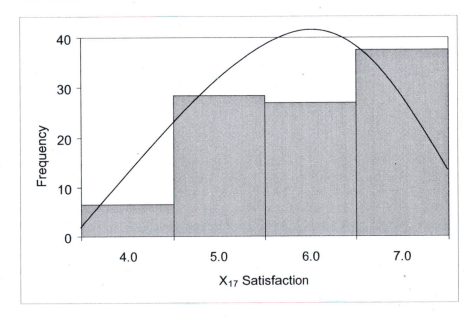

■————DATA ANALYSIS————■
Using SPSS to Compare Samouel's and Gino's on Customer Satisfaction

To make this comparison first load the customer database into your SPSS software—Customer Database_2e.sav. Recall that we want to compare the two restaurants on customer satisfaction. To do so, you must first go to your SPSS software and click on the pull-down menu labeled "Data." Scroll down and click on Split File, then on Compare Groups. Now scroll down and highlight variable $X_{28,}$ "competitor," and move it into the window labeled "Groups based on:" and click OK.

Now you can compare the two restaurants. The click-through sequence is: ANALYZE → DESCRIPTIVE STATISTICS → FREQUENCIES. Highlight $X_{17,}$ "satisfaction," and click on the arrow tab to move it into the Variables window. Click on Charts and then under Chart Type click on Histograms, and right below it "With Normal Curve" and finally Continue. Next click on OK to run the program. The results will be the same as shown in Exhibits 12.5 and 12.6.

BAR CHARTS

Bar charts show the data in the form of bars that can be displayed either horizontally or vertically. Note that the only difference between a bar chart and a histogram is that there is no space between the bars in a histogram. Bar charts and histograms are useful for showing both absolute and relative magnitudes, and for comparing differences. Exhibit 12.7 is an example of a vertical bar chart of the distribution of responses to a question in the Samouel's employee survey ($X_{15,}$ "proud"). The question asked how proud an employee is that she or he works at Samouel's restaurant. Respondents rated the question using a seven-point scale, where 7 = "definitely agree" and 1 = "definitely disagree." For example, the frequency (10) for the value of "definitely agree" = 7 is the vertical bar on the right side of the chart. This chart shows that a moderately high proportion of Samouel's employees are proud to work there (a high proportion of employees responded with a 5, 6, or 7 on the seven-point scale). Note that none of the responses was lower than a 4 on the seven-point scale.

PIE CHARTS

Pie charts display relative proportions of responses. Each section of the pie is the relative proportion. That is, the pie sections are shown as a percentage of the total area of the pie. In Exhibit 12.8 there is a pie chart for variable $X_{15,}$ "proud," in the Samouel's employee survey. Generally, six or seven sections in a pie chart are considered the maximum possible, and three to four is ideal.

The pie chart is another way to present data visually. The proportion of Samouel's employees who indicated they were very proud to work there (responded with a 5, 6, or 7) was very high—over 80 percent. Check out the Business Research Dashboard on page 308 for an interesting historical perspective on the pie chart.

Exhibit 12.7

Bar Chart and Frequency Table for Variable X_{15}, "Proud to Work at Samouel's"

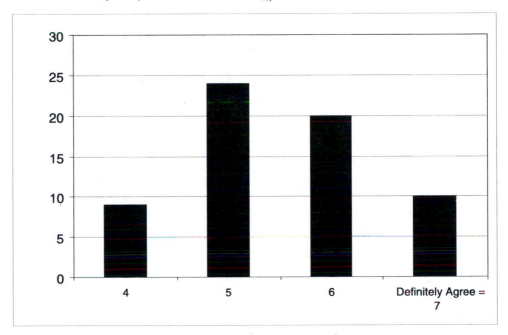

Response	Frequency	Percent	Valid percent	Cumulative percent
4	9	14.3	14.3	14.3
5	24	38.1	38.1	52.4
6	20	31.7	31.7	84.1
Definitely agree = 7	10	15.9	15.9	100.0
Total	63	100.0	100.0	

Exhibit 12.8

Pie Chart of Variable X_{15}, "Proud"

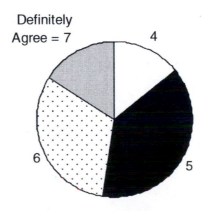

■————**Business Research Dashboard**————■
Florence Nightingale and the Pie Chart

Florence Nightingale is best remembered as the mother of modern nursing. Few realize, however, that she occupies a place in history also for her use of graphical methods to convey complex statistical information.

After witnessing deplorable sanitary conditions in the Crimea, she wrote *Notes on Matters Affecting the Health, Efficiency and Hospital Administration of the British Army* (1858), which included colorful polar-area diagrams where statistics being represented were proportional to the area of a wedge in a circular diagram. These charts illustrated that far more deaths were attributable to nonbattle causes, such as unsanitary conditions, rather than to battle-related causes.

With this information, Nightingale helped to promote the idea that social phenomena could be objectively measured and subjected to mathematical analysis. And through this statistical approach, Nightingale convinced military authorities, Parliament, and Queen Victoria to carry out her proposed hospital reforms, which resulted in a decline in the mortality rate for soldiers.

As Nightingale demonstrated, statistics provided an organized way of learning and led to improvements in medical and surgical practices. She also developed a Model Hospital Statistical Form that could be used to collect and generate consistent data and statistics. She became a fellow of the Royal Statistical Society in 1858, an honorary member of the American Statistical Association in 1874, and has been acknowledged as a "prophetess" in the development of applied statistics.

Sources: "Florence Nightingale—Statistical Links," www.math.yorku.ca/SCS/Gallery/flo.html; Wikipedia, "Pie Chart," http://en.wikipedia.org/wiki/Pie_chart; Wolfram Math World, "Pie Chart," http://mathworld.wolfram.com/PieChart.html, accessed December 2009.

The numbers and percentages in our restaurant examples show how customers and employees rate various aspects of the restaurant operations. Because numbers were involved, frequency distributions, bar charts, and pie charts could all be used to display descriptive statistics. We next discuss the normal curve and then measures of central tendency and dispersion.

THE NORMAL DISTRIBUTION

One of the most useful distributions for business researchers is the normal distribution, also called the normal curve. It describes many chance occurrences encountered in business research. The **normal distribution** is a continuous curve that describes all possible values of a variable. The normal curve is symmetrical, bell shaped, and almost all (99.7 percent) of its values are within plus or minus three standard deviations from its mean.

An example of a normal curve is shown in Exhibit 12.9. Note that 68 percent of the values are within plus or minus one standard deviation, and 95 percent are within plus or minus two standard deviations. The normal distribution is particularly important

Exhibit 12.9 **The Normal Curve**

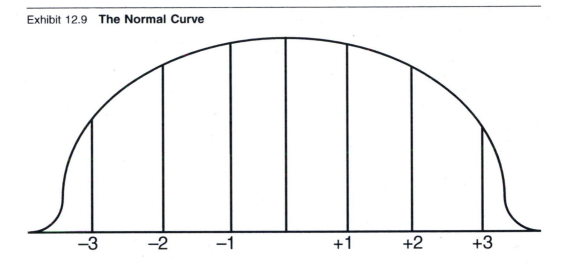

because it provides the underlying basis for many of the inferences made by business researchers who collect data using sampling. For example, recall that the mean satisfaction rating for Samouel's customers was 4.8 and the standard deviation was 1.16. Using this information we can be 95 percent confident that the ratings for all of Samouel's customers is between a low of 2.53 and a high of 7.00 (two standard deviations around the mean).

A particularly important theoretical result is that for sufficiently large samples (typically of thirty or more) the normal distribution describes the expected distribution of sample means. The standard deviation of the distribution of sample means is a measure of the dispersion in sample means about the population mean, which is given a special name, the standard error. The **standard error** is the standard deviation of the individual values of the sample divided by the square root of the sample size.

A special type of normal curve is the standard normal distribution. The **standard normal distribution** has a mean of 0 and a standard deviation of 1. It is also referred to as the Z distribution. The standard normal distribution is used when we wish to illustrate variables with different means or standard deviations on a single scale. For example, assume that several different instructors at a university teach the basic statistics course. It is logical that the different instructors would use different teaching methods and grading approaches, and as a result, the distribution of grades for the instructors would be different. To overcome this problem and enable the distributions to be compared, the different instructors could first calculate the means and standard deviations for the courses they teach, and then calculate a Z value for each student. This would make it possible to compare the Z distributions for each class and interpret them.

A common use for Z values and the standard normal distribution is in calculating probabilities for making inferences from sample findings to the population. Indeed, this is what enables business researchers to apply the empirical rules that approximately 68 percent of the data fall within one standard deviation of the mean, about 95 percent fall within two standard deviations of the mean, and almost all fall within three standard deviations of the mean. When business researchers use these empirical rules with real data they collect, the distribution of the data must be approximately symmetrical and bell shaped, and the sample size relatively large (at least thirty). When the data is skewed left or right researchers must be careful in applying these empirical rules.

MEASURES OF CENTRAL TENDENCY

Frequency distribution tables are easy to read and provide a great deal of basic information about the data. Many times, however, researchers need to summarize and condense information to better understand it. Measures of central tendency can be used for this. The mean, median, and mode are measures of central tendency. **Measures of central tendency** locate the center of the distribution as well as other useful information.

Mean

The **mean** is the arithmetic average and is one of the most commonly used measures of central tendency. For example, if you are interested in knowing the daily consumption of soft drinks, you can calculate the mean (average) number of soft drinks an individual drinks each day. The mean can be used when your data is measured with either an interval or a ratio scale (also called metric). The data typically shows some degree of central tendency, with most of the responses distributed close to the average, or mean, value.

If extreme values (referred to as outliers) occur in the distribution, the mean can misrepresent the true characteristics of the data. For example, suppose you ask four individuals how many colas they drink in a single day. Respondent answers are as follows: respondent A = 1 cola, respondent B = 10, respondent C = 5, and Respondent D = 6. In addition, you have observed that respondents A and B are females and respondents C and D are males. With this knowledge, you can now compare consumption of colas between males and females. Looking at the females first (respondents A and B), we calculate the mean number of colas to be 5.5 (1 + 10 = 11/2 = 5.5). Similarly, looking at the males next (respondents C and D), we calculate the mean number of colas to be 5.5 (5 + 6 = 11/2 = 5.5). We could conclude there are no differences in the consumption patterns of males and females if we consider only the mean number of colas consumed per day. But if we consider the underlying distribution, it is obvious there are some differences. The two females are at the extremes, while both males are in the middle of the distribution. Drawing conclusions based on only the mean can distort our understanding of the cola-consumption patterns of males and females in situations like the above. Of course, we must also consider that in the example we were referring to a small sample and that, as the sample size increases, the ability to accurately infer to the larger population improves. So sample size must be considered also in drawing conclusions about distributions, such as means, and their characteristics.

The mean is most often used with interval or ratio data (metric). But, as noted above, when extreme values occur in the data, the mean can distort the results. In such a situation, the median and the mode should be considered to represent your research findings.

Median

The next measure of central tendency, the **median**, is the value in the middle of the distribution. In other words, the median is the value below (and above) which half the values in the sample distribution fall. For this reason, it is sometimes referred to as the fiftieth percentile. For example, let's assume you interviewed a sample of individuals about the number of soft drinks they drink in a typical week. You might find the median number of soft drinks consumed is ten, with the number of soft drinks consumed above and below that number being the same (the median number is the exact middle of the distribution). If you have an even number of data observations, the median is, by definition, the average of the two middle values. If you have an odd number of observations, the median is the middle value. The median is the appropriate measure of central tendency for ordinal data.

Mode

The **mode** is the measure of central tendency that identifies the value that occurs most often in the sample distribution. For example, the typical individual may drink an average of three colas a day, but the number of colas that most people drink is only two (the mode). The mode is the value that represents the highest peak in the distribution's graph. The mode is the appropriate measure of central tendency for data that is nominal (categorical).

EXAMPLES OF MEASURES OF CENTRAL TENDENCY

The table in Exhibit 12.10 contains the measures of central tendency for the sixty-three employee surveys with no missing data. Note that the mean is 5.49, the median is 5.0, the mode is 5, and there is no missing data. Since this variable is measured on a seven-point scale, with 1 = "definitely disagree" and 7 = "definitely agree," this shows that employees feel very proud to work at Samouel's (the middle of the seven-point scale = 4).

Next look at the histogram in Exhibit 12.11. We have imposed a normal curve on the chart to enable you to compare it with the responses. The chart shows you the lowest point on the seven-point scale for X_{15}, "proud," is 4 and the highest is 7. It also shows the distribution is fairly normal and does not represent a problem.

Exhibit 12.10

Measures of Central Tendency for X_{15} "Proud" Statistics

X_{15} Proud

N	Valid	63
	Missing	0
Mean		5.49
Median		5.00
Mode		5

Exhibit 12.11

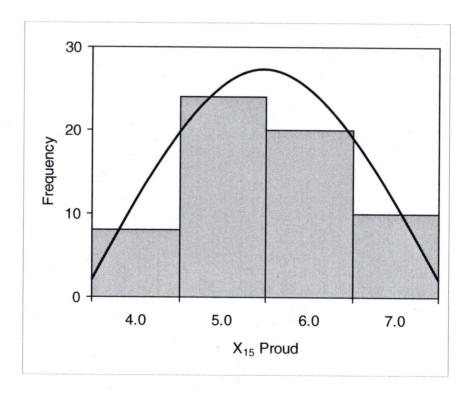

MEASURES OF DISPERSION

Measures of central tendency seldom give a complete picture of a sample distribution. For example, if the Gaucho Grill in New York collects data about customers' attitudes toward a new steak sandwich, you could calculate the mean, median, and mode of the distribution of answers. But you also might want to know if there is much variability in the respondents' opinions about the steak sandwich. For example, recall our discussion of the mean and cola consumption, where males and females averaged the same consumption but females were very high and very low in the distribution and males were in the middle. If the Gaucho Grill's survey of attitudes toward the new steak sandwich is very consistent (little variation) and on the positive end of the scale, the restaurant would likely be pleased. On the other hand, if the responses varied from the very low extreme (negative) to the very high extreme (positive), the restaurant would want to investigate the new sandwich more before adding it to the menu. Specifically, the owner or management would want to know why there are negative responses (very low extreme) and what could be done to eliminate or minimize them. Management could learn more about this problem by examining the measures of dispersion associated with the distribution of sample responses on the customer survey.

Measures of dispersion describe the tendency for sample responses to depart from the central tendency. Calculating the dispersion of the data, or how the responses vary from the mean, is another approach for summarizing data. Typical measures of dispersion used to describe the variability in a distribution of numbers include the range, variance, standard deviation, skewness, and kurtosis.

Range

The **range** is the simplest measure of dispersion. It defines the spread of the data and is the distance between the largest and the smallest values of a sample frequency distribution. We can also define the range by saying it identifies the end points of the sample distribution. For example, if the Gaucho Grill's survey of opinions about a new steak sandwich asked the likelihood of purchasing the sandwich using a ten-point scale and the highest likelihood rating is 8 and the lowest rating is 1, the range is seven (8 − 1 = 7).

Variance

To determine how far away a respondent is from the mean we can calculate individual deviation scores for each respondent. If the deviation scores are large, we will find that the distribution has a wide spread or variability. The problem with deviation scores is that when we try to calculate an average deviation for all respondents, the positive deviation scores always cancel out the negative ones, thus leaving an average deviation value of 0. To eliminate this problem we can square the deviation scores and then calculate the average. The result is a measure called the **variance**. It is useful for describing the variability of the distribution and is a good index of the degree of dispersion. The variance is equal to 0 if each and every respondent in the distribution is the same as the mean. The variance becomes larger as the observations tend to differ increasingly from one another and from the mean.

Standard Deviation

The variance is used often in statistics. But it does have a major drawback. The variance is a unit of measurement that has been squared. For example, if we measure the number of colas consumed in a day and wish to calculate an average for the sample of respondents, the mean will be the average number of colas and the variance will be in squared numbers. To overcome the problem of having the measure of dispersion in squared units instead of the original measurement units, we use the square root of the variance, which is called the standard deviation. The **standard deviation** describes the spread or variability of the sample distribution values from the mean and is perhaps the most valuable index of dispersion.

To obtain the squared deviation we square the individual deviation scores before adding them (squaring a negative number produces a positive result). Once the sum of the squared deviations is determined, it is divided by the number of respondents minus 1. The number 1 is subtracted from the number of respondents to help produce an unbiased estimate of the standard deviation. If the estimated standard deviation is large, the responses in a sample distribution of numbers do not fall very close to the mean of the distribution. If the estimated standard deviation is small, you know that the distribution values are close to the mean.

Another way to think about the estimated standard deviation is that its size tells us something about the level of agreement among the respondents when they answered a particular question. For example, in Samouel's employee survey, respondents were asked to indicate their loyalty and pride about working at Samouel's Greek Cuisine (X_{13} and X_{15}) using a seven-point scale. If the estimated standard deviation of these two variables is small (< 1.0), it means the respondents were very consistent in their opinions about working at Samouel's. In contrast, if the estimated standard deviation of these two variables is large (> 3.0), then there is a lot of variability in their opinions.

One final concept to be clarified is the standard error of the mean. The standard deviation of the sampling distribution of the mean is referred to as the **standard error of the mean**. When we have information on the population we can determine the standard deviation. Since we seldom have population information we typically draw a sample and estimate the standard deviation. When we draw only one sample, we refer to this as the estimated standard deviation. When we draw many samples from the same population, we have a sampling distribution of all the possible values of the sample means. The standard deviation of this distribution of means is the standard error of the mean.

Skewness and Kurtosis

We are often interested in the shape of our distribution. Two measures we typically look at are skewness and kurtosis. **Skewness** measures the departure from a symmetrical (or balanced) distribution. In a symmetrical distribution the mean, median, and mode are in the same location. A distribution that has respondents stretching toward one tail or the other is called skewed. When the tail stretches to the left (smaller values), it is negatively skewed. When the tail stretches to the right (larger values), it is skewed positively. When a distribution is symmetrical the skewness is 0, and the larger the number the larger the skewness. With a positive skew we get a positive number, and with a negative skew we get a negative number. When skewness values are larger than +1 or smaller than −1 this indicates a substantially skewed distribution.

Kurtosis is a measure of a distribution's peakedness (or flatness). Distributions where responses cluster heavily in the center are peaked. Distributions with scores more widely distributed and tails farther apart are considered flat. For a normal curve the value of kurtosis is $0.^2$ A large positive value means the distribution is too peaked, while a large negative value means the distribution is too flat. A curve is too peaked when the kurtosis exceeds +1 and is too flat when it is below −1.

Measures of central tendency and dispersion can reveal a lot about the distribution of a set of numbers from a survey. Business researchers are often interested in solving research problems involving more than one variable at a time. We will explain how to do this in later chapters.

EXAMPLES OF MEASURES OF DISPERSION

The measures of dispersion for X_{15}, "proud," on Samouel's employee survey are shown in Exhibit 12.12. The highest response on the seven-point scale is a 7 (maximum), and the lowest response is a 4 (minimum). None of the respondents gave a 1, 2, or 3 on this question. The range is calculated as the distance between the smallest and the largest values in the set of responses and is 3 (7 − 4 = 3). The standard deviation is .931 and the variance is .867. A standard deviation of .931 on a seven-point scale is relatively small and indicates the responses are reasonably close to the sample mean of 5.49.

Exhibit 12.12

Measures of Dispersion for X_{15} "Proud" Statistics

X_{15} Proud

Valid N	63
Missing	0
Mean	5.49
Median	5.00
Mode	5
Std. Deviation	.931
Variance	.867
Skewness	.086
Std. Error of Skewness	.302
Kurtosis	−.809
Std. Error of Kurtosis	.595
Range	3
Minimum	4
Maximum	7

OUTLIERS

An outlier is a respondent (observation) that has one or more values that are distinctly different from the values of other respondents. Like missing data, outliers can impact the validity of the researcher's findings and therefore must be identified and dealt with as well. Outliers may result from data collection or data entry errors. Data collection or data entry outliers are typically identified and corrected in the data cleaning phase of the research project. Another type of outlier is an accurate observation that represents the true characteristics of the population but still distorts the findings. For example, if we calculated the average net worth of the households located in the neighborhood where Bill Gates of Microsoft lives, the resulting average would be much higher with Gates included as opposed to being eliminated, because his extremely high net worth makes him an outlier. Certainly Gates's neighbors are wealthy, but they have a far smaller net worth than he does. In this situation, the question would be, Is the average net worth of households in Bill Gates's neighborhood more representative with him included, or excluded? The answer here is that it depends on the research objectives. The true average would include Bill Gates. But removing him would be much more representative of the typical net worth in the neighborhood. See the Business Research Dashboard for more on this point.

A final type of outlier is a respondent(s) who has one or more values that are unique, and there is no apparent reason for it (in the Bill Gates example we know the reason; here we do not). In a case like this, if the researcher cannot determine that the outlier represents a valid segment of the population, it must be removed. For more information on the nature of outliers and how to deal with them, we suggest you refer to more advanced texts.[3]

■———Business Research Dashboard———■
Is Bill Gates an Outlier?

Bill Gates lives in Medina, Washington, near Seattle. The number of households in the town of Medina is 1,206. His net worth and that of the next two most wealthy individuals in his town are shown below. The net worth for his town changes dramatically when he is removed from the calculation of average net worth of the town of Medina. It changes even more when the other two individuals are removed from the calculation.

Is Bill Gates an Outlier?

Individual	Net worth in $	Source
Bill Gates	46.0 billion	Microsoft
Jeff Bezos	5.1 billion	Amazon.com
Craig McCaw	2.0 billion	Telecommunications

Number of households, Medina, Washington =	1,206
Average net worth (1,206 households) =	$44,253,482
Average net worth (remove Bill Gates) =	$6,115,934
Average net worth (remove top three) =	$224,189

Source: Calculated from Forbes 2007 and U.S. Census Bureau data

CONTINUING CASE: SAMOUEL'S GREEK CUISINE
Using Descriptive Statistics with the Restaurant
Employee Survey

As you learned in Chapter 9, the employees of Samouel's Greek Cuisine were interviewed as part of the research studies conducted by the consultant. On the Web site for this text (www. mesharpe-student.com) there is a data set with the responses of the employee survey. It is named Employee Database_2e. Start your computer, load the SPSS statistical software, and download the database from the Web site. While you are getting the employee survey database, download and save the customer survey titled Customer Database_2e.

When the employee database is loaded, run bar charts for the following variables: X_4, X_6, X_{13}, X_{16}, and X_{21}. What did you learn about Samouel's employees? Are there some indications that Phil Samouel should be concerned about? If yes, explain why.

SUMMARY

DESCRIBE THE PROCESS FOR CONDUCTING QUANTITATIVE-DATA ANALYSIS

Many research projects have data that can be quantified to enable research questions to be answered. Quantitative data is measurements in which numbers are used to directly represent the properties of phenomena. To be useful the data need to be analyzed and interpreted. Data analysis in quantitative research involves the following steps: (1) review conceptual framework and proposed relationships, (2) prepare data for analysis, (3) determine if research involves descriptive analysis or hypothesis testing, (4) conduct analysis, and (5) evaluate findings to assess whether they are meaningful.

UNDERSTAND THE IMPORTANCE OF DATA PREPARATION

After data has been collected and before it is analyzed, the researcher must examine it to ensure its validity. Blank responses, referred to as missing data, must be dealt with in some way. If the questions were precoded, then they can simply be input into a database. If they were not precoded, then a system must be developed so they can be input into the database. The typical tasks involved are editing, dealing with missing data, coding, transformation, and entering data.

EXPLAIN HOW DESCRIPTIVE STATISTICS ENABLE YOU TO BETTER UNDERSTAND YOUR DATA

Descriptive statistics such as graphics and charts help you to more easily understand your data. They not only add clarity but also impact research reports. The most often used charts and graphs include frequency distributions, bar charts, pie charts, and line charts.

Measures of central tendency enable researchers to summarize and condense information to better understand it. The mean, median, and mode are measures of central tendency. Measures of central tendency locate the center of the distribution as well as other useful information.

Measures of dispersion describe the tendency for responses to depart from the central tendency (mean, median, and mode). Calculating the dispersion of the data, or how the responses vary from the mean, is another means of summarizing the data. Typical measures of dispersion used to describe the variability in a distribution of numbers include the range, variance, standard deviation, skewness, and kurtosis.

Clarify How to Identify and Deal with Outliers

When you have outliers, as well as observations with missing data, you must decide whether to retain or eliminate them. The most conservative approach is to eliminate them to avoid distorting or misrepresenting your findings. If you retain them, you must have a valid reason for doing so. This is also true if you decide to replace the missing data with an estimate of the value and then retain it in your analysis. Retaining observations with missing or replaced data is risky and must be done cautiously.

Ethical Dilemma

Ann Webster is a sales analyst for a large retailer. The company is planning its annual meeting, and Ann's boss has asked her to prepare visuals for the company's performance presentation. The company president is planning to downplay the fact that the company's overall sales are slipping by focusing on the performance of the company's top five stores. Ann is therefore asked to prepare separate bar charts for each of the top stores listing the sales periods in ascending order and to prepare a bar chart of the overall sales figures with sales periods in descending order. Although the data will be factual, Ann realizes that the graphics could mislead board members. What should she do?

Review Questions

1. What are the steps in analyzing quantitative data?
2. Why is it necessary to prepare data before analyzing it?
3. How can frequency distributions help us to better understand our data?
4. How do measures of central tendency differ from measures of dispersion?
5. What is an outlier?

Discussion and Application Activities

1. Why would the business researcher want to use charts and graphs?
2. What is the value of measures of central tendency and dispersion?
3. Why are missing data and outliers a problem?

4. *SPSS Application:* Examine all the variables in the employee database using histograms, skewness, and range to determine if you have any problems with the data.

INTERNET ACTIVITIES

1. The SPSS statistical software package has a home page at http://www.spss .com. Go to the Web site and identify and summarize the statistical techniques that can be used with the activities in this chapter.
2. The home page for the American Statistical Association is at http://www .amstat.org. Go to its Web site and identify and summarize the career options that one might have if interested in statistics.
3. Go to http://www.yankelovich.com. Prepare a report summarizing the MONI-TOR. How can business researchers use the data from this research?
4. Go to http://www.acop.com. Prepare a report summarizing the Web site and the types of surveys featured.
5. Go to http://www.shodor.org/interactivate/activities/piechart/. Prepare a report explaining how the information helps you to better understand pie charts.

NOTES

1. J.F. Hair, B. Black, B. Babin, and R. Anderson, *Multivariate Data Analysis*, 7th ed. (Upper Saddle River, NJ: Prentice Hall, 2010).

2. There are two alternative ways that kurtosis is calculated. For a normal distribution, the kurtosis is determined directly from the moments of the normal distribution and is equal to 3. Another more practical definition expresses the kurtosis as the amount it differs from 3, sometimes referred to as excess of kurtosis. It is this latter estimate of kurtosis that is reported by SPSS.

3. Hair et al., *Multivariate Data Analysis*.

13 | Testing Hypotheses in Quantitative Research

Data becomes knowledge only after analysis has confirmed that a set of proposed relationships can be used to improve business decision making. In quantitative research we examine hypothesized relationships to see what kinds of conclusions are appropriate. Examples of relationships that would be of interest to business researchers include:

- Ford Motor Company wants to confirm what types of individuals will respond favorably to the new 2010 fuel-efficient Ford Escape Hybrid.
- The *New York Times* wants information about who reads its newspaper and who does not so it can either add or delete sections to increase circulation.
- Apple, Inc. wants to know which factors are likely to increase productivity on its iPad production lines.
- Companies want to know if there is a difference in preference for flextime in the workplace between female and male workers.
- Organizations would like to know whether offering employee profit sharing plans will result in higher worker productivity.

In this chapter we first show you several conceptual models of relationships that can be tested using the Samouel's databases. These conceptual models will help you to better understand how relationships in any type of business research can be tested using statistics. Next we review and explain the relationship between sample statistics and population parameters as well as how to select the appropriate statistical test. We then cover several univariate and bivariate statistics used to test hypotheses. The software package SPSS® is used to illustrate hypothesis testing.

UNDERSTANDING HYPOTHESIZED RELATIONSHIPS

Although measures of central tendency and dispersion provide an overview of research results, researchers often want to test one or more hypotheses. Statistical techniques enable us to determine whether the empirical evidence can confirm the proposed hypotheses. Consider the two conceptual models for the Samouel's employee database shown in Exhibit 13.1. The models are based on organizational behavior theory and display relationships between a single dependent variable and two independent variables. The dependent variable for model A is "loyalty," and it is measured by a single variable (X_{13} in the data set). The dependent variable for model B is "intention to search," and it, too, is measured by a single variable (X_{16} in the data set). Both models have the same independent variables: supervision and work groups. Recall from our earlier discussion that constructs are typically made up of several variables. Constructs are preferable in testing hypotheses because using multiple variables usually creates more valid and reliable measures of a concept. When you examine the Samouel's employee database, you will see that the "supervision" construct is measured by three variables: X_3, X_6, and X_{10}, and the "work group" construct is measured by three other variables: X_4, X_8, and X_{11}. These six variables are not shown in the exhibit but can be found in the listing of variables for the survey in Chapter 9.

The conceptual models display several testable hypotheses. The hypothesis for model A is: More favorable perceptions of supervision and work groups are associated with higher loyalty. The hypothesis for model B is: More favorable perceptions of supervision and work groups are associated with lower intention to search for another job. These are directional hypotheses—for model A the dependent variable is positively related to the two independent variables, and for model B the dependent variable is negatively related to the two independent variables.

In this chapter we show you how to use statistical tools to empirically test whether hypothesized relationships can be confirmed as being true. We also explain how to determine if these relationships differ between groups, such as male employees versus female employees. Exhibit 13.2 lists the steps in developing and testing quantitative hypotheses.

SAMPLE STATISTICS VERSUS POPULATION PARAMETERS

Inferential statistics help us to make judgments about the population from a sample. A sample is a small subset of the total number of respondents in a population. For example, in the Samouel's employee survey the sample of sixty-three respondents

Exhibit 13.1 **Conceptual Models: Samouel's Employee Survey**

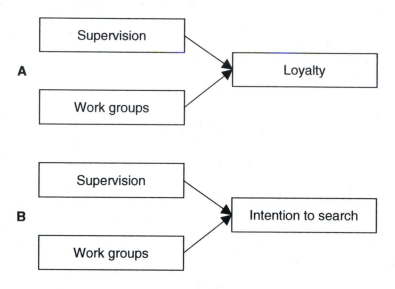

Hypotheses:
- More favorable perceptions of Supervision and Work groups are associated with higher Loyalty.
- More favorable perceptions of Supervision and Work groups are associated with higher Intention to search.

Exhibit 13.2

Steps in Hypothesis Development and Testing in Quantitative Research

1. State the null and alternative hypotheses.
2. Make a judgment about the sampling distribution of the population, and then select the appropriate statistical test based on whether you believe the data is parametric or nonparametric.
3. Decide on the desired level of significance ($p = < 0.05$, < 0.01, or other).
4. Collect the sample data and compute the appropriate test statistic to see if the level of significance is met.
5. Reject or do not reject the null hypothesis. That is, determine whether the deviation of the sample value from the expected value would have occurred by chance alone, for example, five times out of a hundred.
6. Evaluate your findings to determine if they are meaningful.

---

is used to project to all his employees. Similarly, for the customer survey the sample of 100 Samouel's respondents is used to project to all customers of Samouel's Greek Cuisine, and the sample of 100 Gino's respondents is used to project to all customers of Gino's Italian Ristorante.

We use different terminology to refer to characteristics of the sample from what we use to refer to characteristics of the population. **Sample statistics** are the characteristics computed from the sample. **Population parameters** are the characteristics of the population. We use sample statistics to estimate population parameters because we have data only from the sample. An example of a sample statistic would be the number of glasses of wine the sample of 100 Samouel's customers said they consumed at their last meal eaten at the restaurant. Similarly, it might be the number of cups of Starbucks coffee consumed by a sample of students in a survey at the London School of Economics, or the percentage of individuals in a sample from Ireland who say they prefer Guinness stout over lager, compared to a sample of Germans who likely would say they prefer lager over ale. The sample statistic is based on the sample data but is used to estimate the population parameter. The actual population parameters are seldom known, since the cost to conduct a census of the population is very high.

A **null hypothesis** concerns a population parameter, not a sample statistic. Based on the sample data, the business researcher can reject the null hypothesis or accept the alternative hypothesis. In other words, the researcher can conclude there is either a meaningful difference between the two population groups being compared (for example, males and females) or no meaningful difference. If there is no meaningful difference, the researcher would not detect any significant differences between the two groups.

In business research the null hypothesis is developed so that by rejecting it we accept what we think is correct—the **alternative hypothesis**. Using our Samouel's employee survey data, an example of a null hypothesis is: No relationship exists between supervision and loyalty. The alternative hypothesis is: A relationship exists between supervision and loyalty. In statistical terminology, the null hypothesis is notated as H_0 and the alternative hypothesis is notated as H_1. If the null hypothesis H_0 is rejected, then the alternative hypothesis H_1 is accepted. The Business Research Dashboard describes a situation where several hypotheses might be tested.

TYPE I AND TYPE II ERRORS

There is always the risk the inference a researcher draws about a population from the sample may be incorrect. In business research error can never be completely avoided. Therefore, statistical tests the researcher performs to accept or reject the null hypothesis may still lead to an incorrect conclusion. Two types of errors are associated with hypothesis testing. The first type of error is termed Type I. A **Type I error**, referred to as an alpha (α) error, occurs when the sample results lead to the rejection of the null hypothesis when it is true. In the Samouel's customer survey, a Type I error would occur if we concluded, based on the sample data, that satisfaction with Samouel's and Gino's is different when in fact it is the same. The probability of this type of error (α), also referred to as the level of significance, is the amount of risk the researcher is willing to accept. Thus, the level of significance is the probability of making an error by rejecting the null hypothesis when it is in fact true.

Depending on the situation, business researchers typically consider < 0.05 an acceptable level of significance. The proper interpretation of < 0.05 is that a researcher is willing to accept the risk of making five errors out of every 100 decisions made as to whether a hypothesis can be accepted or should be rejected. The researcher is thus

---

■————Business Research Dashboard————■
Harrison Global Transportation: Making Better Use of Drivers

Harrison Global is a limo and transportation company founded in 1986 to meet the limo service needs in the Boston area. Since its founding, the company has expanded to serve numerous U.S. and international cities. The Boston area office is located in Waltham, Massachusetts, and provides limousine, sedan, and other chauffeured driving services, mainly to the corporate market. A considerable number of the company's customers travel to and from towns west of Boston and Logan International Airport. Traffic problems in recent years on the Massachusetts Turnpike (I-90), I-93, and I-95, as well as on feeder roads, have created significant problems in estimating journey time for customers. For the past two years the company has been collecting information on origin of pickups, destination, travel time in towns, travel time outside towns, travel time on highways, and total journey time. All the time data is in minutes. It has also added limited comments about weather and time of day for the journey. The company hopes to use the information to better predict journey time.

What hypotheses could be tested using this data? What statistical technique would be most helpful, and how might the technique be applied? What other data might be collected to improve the company's estimates?

Sources: "Harrison Global Transportation," CitySquares Online, http://ma.citysquares.com/waltham/moody-street/travel-transportation/transportation-services/harrison-global-transportation; Harrison Global, http://www.smartertransportation.com; "Harrison Global," Local Database, http://www.localdatabase.com/business/28129849/Harrison_Global.html, accessed December 2009.

---

willing to accept some risk (5 percent) that the null hypothesis will be inappropriately rejected. But the level of risk is specified before the research project is carried out. If the research situation involves testing relationships where the risk of making the mistake of falsely rejecting the null hypothesis is very costly, the researcher would specify a higher level of significance, for example < 0.01. For instance, in examining the relationship between two chemicals that might explode, or the failure rate of an expensive piece of equipment, such as an aircraft engine, the researcher would not be willing to take very much risk. Conversely, when examining behavioral or attitudinal relationships where the risk of a Type I error is generally less costly, then the researcher is willing to take more risk. In some situations, the researcher may even accept a 0.10 level of significance.

The second type of error is referred to as a Type II error. A **Type II error** occurs when, based on the sample results, the null hypothesis is not rejected when it is in fact false. A Type II error is generally referred to as a beta (β) error. The researcher specifies the alpha error ahead of time, but the beta error is based on the population parameter (that is, mean or proportion). This concept is summarized in the table below:

	H_0 is true	H_0 is false
Accept H_0	X	Type II
Reject H_0	Type I	X

A third important concept in testing hypotheses for statistical significance is the **statistical power** of the test. The power of a test is the ability to reject the null hypothesis when in fact the null hypothesis is false. The statistical power of a test can be described as $1-\beta$, the probability of correctly rejecting the null hypothesis. The probability of a Type II error is unknown, but it is related to the probability of a Type I error. Extremely low levels of α will result in a high level of β error. Therefore, it is necessary to reach an acceptable compromise between the two types of error. Sample size can help control both Type I and Type II errors. Generally, the researcher will select the α and the sample size in order to increase the power of the test and to minimize α and β errors.

HYPOTHESIS TESTING

After the researcher has developed the hypotheses and selected an acceptable level of risk (statistical significance), the next step is to test the hypotheses. In this section we discuss the statistics used to actually test hypotheses. First we tell you how to select the appropriate statistical technique. Then we discuss the use of the *t* test, chi square, and ANOVA to test hypotheses.

CHOOSING THE APPROPRIATE STATISTICAL TECHNIQUE

When we test hypotheses we are converting data to knowledge. A number of statistical techniques can be used to test hypotheses. The choice of a particular technique depends, first, on the number of variables and, second, on the scale of measurement.

Number of Variables

The number of variables examined together is a major consideration in the selection of the appropriate statistical technique. A univariate statistical technique involves only one variable at a time to generalize about a population from a sample. For example, if the researcher wants to examine the average number of cups of Dunkin' Donuts coffee college students drink during finals, only a single variable is used, and a univariate statistic is appropriate. If the business researcher is interested in the relationship between the average number of cups of Dunkin' Donuts coffee college students drink during finals and the number of hours spent studying for finals, two variables are involved and a bivariate statistical technique is required. Often business researchers need to examine many variables at the same time to represent the real world and fully explain relationships in the data. In such cases, multivariate statistical techniques are required. We examine univariate and bivariate statistical techniques in this chapter and multivariate statistical techniques in Chapters 14 and 15.

Scale of Measurement

We discussed measurement and scaling in Chapter 9. We use that information here to show which statistical techniques are used with a particular type of scale. Exhibit 13.3

Exhibit 13.3

Scale Type and Appropriate Statistical Test

Scale Type	Measure of Central Tendency	Measure of Dispersion	Statistical Test
Nominal	Mode	None	Chi square
Ordinal	Median	Percentiles or quartiles	Chi square
Interval or ratio	Mean	Standard deviation	t test, ANOVA

provides an overview of the types of scales used in different situations. Suppose a researcher wants to compare two groups: Dunkin' Donuts coffee drinkers and Starbucks coffee drinkers. In such a comparison, the groups are identified with a nominal scale, and the mode would be the only appropriate measure of central tendency. That is, we could compare only the number of individuals who say they prefer Dunkin' Donuts versus those who prefer Starbucks.

Nominal data is a name or label that is used to enable the researcher to place respondents into categories, but it does not allow for comparisons like bigger/smaller or faster/slower. A chi-square test could be used to test whether the observed number of Starbucks coffee drinkers is what one would expect it to be. For example, if a sample survey showed that 24 percent of college students at a particular university drink Starbucks coffee and you expected it to be 30 percent based on a survey of all the college students in the United States, you could use the chi square test to determine if the difference is statistically significant.

Ordinal data is the next higher level of data, and it makes possible responses' being ordered in a hierarchical pattern such as higher/lower or greater than/less than. With ordinal data you can use the median, percentile, and chi square, plus anything you can use with nominal data. For example, if we have ranking data for two factors that are thought to be important in the selection of a coffee shop, we would use the median, percentile, and chi square. If the two ranking factors are coffee taste and atmosphere, we could use the chi square statistic to determine whether customers of Dunkin' Donuts and those of Starbucks ranked these factors differently.

Interval data and **ratio data** are the highest level of measurement. The units of measurement are constant so differences in any two adjacent points on a scale are equal, and almost any mathematical procedure, such as a mean or standard deviation, can be calculated with them. Thus, if we have the actual count of the number of cups of coffee the typical customer of Dunkin' Donuts and that of Starbucks drank each time they were in the store, we have ratio data and could calculate means and standard deviations. This would enable us to determine, using the t test or ANOVA, if there are differences in the average number of cups consumed.

OTHER CONSIDERATIONS IN HYPOTHESIS TESTING

There are two major types of statistical procedures. They are referred to as parametric and nonparametric. The major difference between them lies in the underlying assumptions about the data. When the data is measured using an interval or ratio scale and the sample size is large, **parametric statistical procedures** are appropriate. It is also assumed the sample data is collected from populations with normal (bell-shaped) distributions. When the assumption of a normal distribution is not possible, the researcher should use **nonparametric statistical procedures**. When data is measured using an ordinal or nominal scale, it is generally not appropriate to make the assumption the distribution is normal. Therefore, nonparametric, or distribution-free, statistical procedures should be used. In this chapter we discuss a nonparametric statistical procedure, the chi square, and two parametric statistical procedures, the *t* test and ANOVA.

While parametric statistical tests assume the data has a normal distribution, most tests are quite robust, and this assumption seldom causes problems when the data is only approximately normal. The same is true for the assumption that two or more groups will have the same variance. That is, problems seldom arise when parametric tests are used to compare two groups with different variances (or standard deviations) when the groups are comparable in size.

We previously defined a population as the total of all the elements that share a common set of characteristics. For example, a population could be all the students at a given university or all the employees at a particular company; it could be all the persons living in a particular city or country, or all the customers of Samouel's and Gino's restaurants. In contrast, a sample is a small subset or some part of all the individuals in the population. For example, if we wanted to determine the average number of glasses of wine consumed with dinner at Samouel's restaurant, we would not interview all the customers. That would be expensive, take a long time, and likely be impossible because of the difficulty of finding all the customers. Instead, a sample of 100 customers (out of a total of over 1,000 customers) might be considered large enough by Phil to provide accurate information about the average number of glasses of wine consumed.

SINGLE GROUP HYPOTHESIS TESTING

Testing hypotheses using statistical tests involves much more than the tabulations included in a frequency distribution or the calculation of measures of central tendency or dispersion. Researchers describe data using not only means or percentages. They also apply statistical tests that determine the likelihood the sample numbers correctly or incorrectly estimate the population characteristics. The simplest types of statistical tests are univariate tests of significance. **Univariate tests** of significance are used to test hypotheses when the researcher wishes to test a proposition about a sample characteristic against a known or given standard. The following are examples of such propositions:

- The new product will be preferred by 90 percent of our current customers.
- The average monthly electric bill in Seattle, Washington, exceeds $200.
- The market share for Tetley teas in Houston is at least 30 percent.
- The average cost of living in the United States is higher than that in Japan.

• More than 50 percent of current Diet Coke customers will prefer the new Diet Coke, which includes a taste of lime.

We can translate these propositions into null hypotheses and test them. In the following paragraphs we provide an example from our restaurant database of a univariate hypothesis test.

Phil Samouel would like to know if his customers think his prices are reasonable. He would also like to know how Gino's customers perceive that restaurant's prices. Survey respondents indicated their perceptions of prices using a seven-point scale, on which 1 = "strongly disagree" the restaurant has reasonable prices and 7 = "strongly agree." Phil's business consultant has told him the question is typically measured with an interval scale and previous research has shown the responses are approximately normally distributed.

To examine Phil's question about pricing we must first develop the hypothesis and agree on the level of significance for rejecting or accepting the hypothesis. Phil thinks customers consider the menu prices to be somewhat reasonable. After talking with his consultant, they have agreed that a rating of 5 on a seven-point scale would represent somewhat reasonable prices. They would therefore expect the responses to the question on prices to have a mean of 5.0. The null hypothesis is that the sample mean will not be different from 5.0 (the standard for reasonable prices established by Phil and his consultant). The alternative hypothesis is that the sample mean of the answers to X_7, "reasonable prices," will be different from 5.0.

Recall that researchers often consider <0.05 (5 percent) as the most risk they want to take in rejecting the null hypothesis. In this case, however, Phil has decided he needs to be only 90 percent certain the mean is different from 5.0. That is, he is willing to assume a 10 percent risk in examining the pricing issue. Using this significance level means that if the survey of customers were conducted many times, the probability of incorrectly rejecting the null hypothesis when it is actually true would occur 10 or fewer times out of 100 (< 0.10).

The null hypothesis that the mean of the perceptions of pricing is not different from 5.0 can be tested using the **one-sample t test.** The results of using this test are shown in Exhibit 13.4. The top half, "One-Sample Statistics," displays the mean and standard deviation for X_{10}, "reasonable prices." Phil Samouel's customers give him a mean of 4.14, and Gino's customers give Gino a 3.97. The respective standard deviations are 0.932 and 0.937. The lower portion of the table shows the results of the t test for the null hypothesis that the mean response to X_{10}, "reasonable prices," is 5.0. The t-test statistic for Samouel's is –9.225, and the significance level is 0.000. Similarly, the t-test statistic for Gino's is –10.993, and the significance level is 0.000. This means that the null hypothesis for both restaurants can be rejected and the alternative hypothesis accepted with a high level of confidence. The level of significance of 0.000 means there are no chances in 10,000 that rejecting the null hypothesis would be incorrect. The use of the software SPSS to execute this test is explained in the Data Analysis box.

From a practical standpoint, the results of the univariate hypothesis test indicate that customers from both restaurants felt the prices of the menu items were not very reasonable. This is because in both instances the mean response is significantly below

Exhibit 13.4

One-Sample *t* Test of Samouel's and Gino's Prices

One-sample statistics

X_{28} – competitor		N	Mean	Standard deviation
Samouel's	X_{10} – reasonable prices	100	4.14	0.932
Gino's	X_{10} – reasonable prices	100	3.97	0.937

One-sample test

Test value = 5.0

X_{28} – competitor		t	df	Significance (2-tailed)	Mean difference
Samouel's	X_{10} – reasonable prices	−9.225	99	0.000	−0.86
Gino's	X_{10} – reasonable prices	−10.993	99	0.000	−1.03

■————DATA ANALYSIS————■
Using SPSS to Calculate a One-Sample *t* Test

Since Phil would like to know the answer for both his restaurant and for Gino's before testing the hypotheses, we must split the sample into Samouel's customers and Gino's customers. Recall that this involves going to the Data pull-down menu and doing the following: Data → Split File and then click on Compare groups. Next highlight X_{28}, "competitor," and click on the arrow button to move it in the Groups Based on: box. Now click OK and you will be back to the SPSS Data Editor screen. All data analysis will now be comparing customers from the two restaurants.

The click-through sequence to run the one-sample *t* test is: ANALYZE → COMPARE MEANS → ONE-SAMPLE T-TEST. Click on X_{10}, "reasonable prices," to highlight it and then click on the arrow box to move X_{10} into the Test Variables window. In the box labeled "Test Value," enter the number 5.0. This is the number you want to compare the respondents' answers against. When you click on the Options tab, note that 95 is the default in the Confidence Interval box. This is the same as setting the significance level at 0.05. Since Phil has decided to accept more risk, we must change this number. The level of risk Phil will accept is 10 percent (0.10), so change the 95 in the Confidence Interval box to 90. Then, click on the Continue button and OK to execute the program. The results are shown in Exhibit 13.4.

---

the standard of 5.0 that Phil set as being reasonable. From Phil's point of view, this means his customers believe his prices are not as reasonable as he had thought. Of course, Gino's customers think his prices are not very reasonable either, so neither restaurant has a competitive advantage, although perceptions for Phil's restaurant are slightly more favorable than those for Gino's.

Phil needs to determine if the problem is real. That is, are his prices really considered not very reasonable? Or is the problem one of customer misperception. That is, are his prices perceived as being too high when in fact they are not? Once this is determined, he must develop a plan to improve customer perceptions of the pricing of his menu items. It may involve actually changing prices, or it may require changing portion sizes or some other approach. An improvement in pricing perceptions from a mean of 4.14 could become a significant competitive advantage for Samouel's restaurant.

MULTIPLE GROUP HYPOTHESIS TESTING

Business researchers often test hypotheses that one group differs from another group in terms of attitudes, behavior, or some other characteristic. For example, Phil Samouel might like to know if there are any differences in the perceptions of older and younger patrons of his restaurant. If there are differences, he could develop separate marketing strategies to appeal to each segment. Where more than one group is involved, **bivariate statistical tests** must be used. In statistical terminology, the null hypothesis is that there are no significant differences between the two groups.

In the following section, we describe three multiple group hypothesis tests. We first show you how to use chi square to test for differences between groups measured with nominal data. Then we explain how to use the *t* test and ANOVA to test for differences in group means measured with metric (interval) data.

Cross-Tabulation Using Chi Square (χ^2) Analysis

One of the simplest methods for describing sets of relationships is cross-tabulation. A **cross tabulation** is a frequency distribution of responses on two or more sets of variables. For example, a cross tabulation might compare the number of individuals at the Ryder Cup golf tournament who say they are U.S. supporters versus the number who say they support the Europeans. To do a cross tabulation, we count the responses for each of the groups and compare them. Chi square (χ^2) analysis enables us to test whether there are statistical differences between the numbers of individuals at the golf tournament who support the United States versus those supporting the Europeans. Below are examples of questions that could be answered using cross tabulations and testing with chi square analysis:

- Is brand awareness of Samuel Adams beer (aware, not aware) related to the geographic area in which individuals live (central United States, East Coast, West Coast, etc.)?
- Do males and females differ in their recall of an advertisement?
- Is there a relationship between gender and work type (full-time versus part-time) for Samouel's restaurant employees?
- Does frequency of patronage (very frequent, somewhat frequent and occasional) differ between Samouel's and Gino's restaurants?
- Is usage (heavy, moderate, and low) of the Internet related to educational level?
- Does job satisfaction differ between blue-collar and white-collar workers?

Business researchers use the chi square test to determine whether responses observed in a survey follow the expected pattern. For example, Phil Samouel might believe there is no difference in the frequency of patronage between male and female customers. Similarly, he may think there is no difference in the number of male and female customers who saw an advertisement he ran in the *New York Times*. Thus, the null hypotheses would be, first, there is no difference in frequency of patronage between male and female customers, and, second, there is no difference in advertisement recall between male and female customers. Hypotheses such as these can be tested using the chi square statistical test. Phil would want to know the validity of his claims because if there are differences he could use that knowledge in developing his business plan.

The **chi square (χ^2) statistical test** can be used to test whether the frequencies of two nominally scaled variables are related. Nominal data from questions about job type (professor, physician, manager, etc.), gender, advertisement recall, or other categorical variables can be examined. The chi-square statistic compares the observed frequencies (sometimes referred to as actual) of the responses with the expected frequencies. The observed frequencies are the actual cell counts of data from our survey. The expected frequencies are the theoretical frequencies derived from your null hypothesis of no relationship between the two variables. The statistic tests whether or not the observed frequencies "fit" the expected frequencies. In other words, it tests the goodness of fit for the observed frequency distribution with the expected distribution. The Business Research Dashboard illustrates an example of the appropriate application of chi square.

When we conduct a chi square analysis, we set up a contingency table with a number of cells. A cell refers to the intersection of a row and a column and represents a specific combination of two variables. For example, in Exhibit 13.5 the number of Japanese who prefer Macallan single malt Scotch ($N = 145$) over Laphroaig is a cell. The number of British respondents who prefer Laphroaig ($N = 270$) is another cell.

■————Business Research Dashboard————■
Can People Tell the Differences in the Taste of Beer?

We have conducted many blind taste tests with our students. Taste tests provide a good example of how to use chi square to determine if people are able to identify the taste of brand name beers in a blind taste test. Suppose you have twenty students in your class. You pour Samuel Adams beer in twenty paper cups that have no identification on them. Next you ask your students to taste the beer and tell you whether it is Samuel Adams or Budweiser. Since there are an even number of students in the test, if they all guess randomly you would expect the results to be 50 percent Samuel Adams and 50 percent Budweiser. The null hypothesis is then that there is no relationship between the Samuel Adams beer being tested and the brand the students select based on the taste test. Following the taste test you count the number of times each brand is selected and find that fourteen of the students said the beer was Budweiser and six said it was Samuel Adams. Your expected frequencies were ten and ten, but your observed frequencies are fourteen and six. There seems to be a relationship that indicates students definitely cannot identify the brand of beer based on a taste test. But to be certain we must use a statistical test like chi square to determine if the difference between expected and observed frequencies is statistically significant.

Exhibit 13.5

**Cross Tabulation Table for Macallan versus Laphroaig Brand
Single Malt Scotch Drinkers**

Frequencies Table

Ethnic heritage	Prefer Macallan	Prefer Laphroaig	Totals
Japanese count	145	305	450
Expected count	203.57	246.43	
British count	330	270	600
Expected count	271.43	328.57	
Totals	475	575	1,050

A 2 × 2 contingency table has four cells, as does our example. A 3 × 3 contingency table has nine cells. Proper use of chi square requires that each expected cell frequency have a sample size of at least five. If this sample size minimum cannot be met, the researcher can either take a larger sample or combine individual response categories so the minimum cell size can be met. The observed counts are the actual number of responses from the sample in each cell. The expected counts are the number of responses we expect to get in each cell.

How do we determine the expected counts? To get the expected count (number), multiply the column and row totals together and divide by the total sample size. For example, looking in the far-right column, you see that there were 450 Japanese respondents in the sample. Looking at the sample sizes (bottom of table), you see that there were 475 respondents who prefer Macallan and 575 who prefer Laphroaig. Multiplying 575 (cell column total) times 450 (cell row total) gives 258,750. Divide this number by 1,050 (total sample), and you get 246.43 (the number of Japanese one would expect to prefer Laphroaig if choice of Scotch was independent of ethnic heritage). All the expected counts are calculated in a similar manner. The chi square test has not been calculated, but it appears there is a significant difference in the actual versus expected preference for the two brands of Scotch. In short, British respondents prefer Macallan more than expected and Laphroaig less than expected, while Japanese prefer Laphroaig more than expected and Macallan less than expected.

When testing hypotheses, we begin by formulating the null hypothesis and selecting the appropriate level of statistical significance for our research problem. Phil ran an advertisement for his restaurant about two weeks before the survey. He wants to see if there is a difference in recall of the advertisement between males and females. He does not think advertisement recall will differ between males and females, but he would like to know. The null hypothesis is that males and females do not differ in their recall of the advertisement. We will assume the acceptable level of statistical significance is 0.05.

Exhibit 13.6

**Observed and Expected Counts for Gender Cross Tabulated
with Advertisement Recall**

$X_{21,}$ "saw advertisement"		$X_{25,}$ "gender" Male	Female	Total
Did not see advertisement	Count	13	10	23
	Expected count	12.2	10.8	23.0
Saw advertisement	Count	93	84	177
	Expected count	93.8	83.2	177.0
Total	Count	106	94	200

Chi-square test	Value	df	Asymp. sig. (2-sided)
Pearson chi square	0.129*	1	0.719
N of valid cases	200		

*0 cells (0.0 percent) have an expected count less than 5.
The minimum expected count is 10.81.

The observed and expected counts for males and females interviewed in his survey cross-tabulated with advertisement recall are shown in Exhibit 13.6. Looking at the observed count in the column of males we see that the survey found there were 13 males who did not see the advertisement. If we compare this to the expected count of 12.2, we see there is little difference between observed and expected. Recall that the expected counts (number) in a cell are calculated by multiplying the cell column total times the cell row total and dividing it by the total sample size. For example, looking in the far-right column, you see that 177 individuals in the sample saw the advertisement. Looking at the sample sizes (bottom of table), you see there were 106 males and 94 females. Multiplying 94 females (cell column total) times 177 (cell row total) gives 16,638. Dividing this number by 200 gives 83.2 (the number of expected females who saw the advertisement). All the expected counts are calculated in a similar manner.

Looking at the results, we see there is little difference in the actual and expected counts for both males and females. Moreover, the Pearson chi square test results in the lower portion of the exhibit show that indeed there are no statistically significant differences (sig. = 0.719) in the expected versus actual number of males and females who saw the advertisement. In fact, a very high percentage of both males and females recall having seen the advertisement. We therefore accept the null hypothesis that there is no difference in advertisement recall between females and males.

The chi square statistical test should be estimated only on counts of data. When the data is in percentage form, we must first convert it to absolute counts or numbers. Additionally, we assume the observations are drawn independently. This means one group of respondents does not in any way influence the other group's responses. That is, women's responses to the question in the advertisement recall example, Do you recall an ad by Samouel's Greek Cuisine? in no way influence men's responses to the same question.

Testing Differences in Group Means

One of the most frequently examined questions in business research is whether the means of two groups of respondents on some attitude or behavior are significantly different. For example, in a sample survey we might examine any of the following questions:

- Do the coffee consumption patterns (measured using the mean number of cups consumed daily) differ between males and females?
- Does the number of hours an individual spends on the Internet each week differ by income level, gender, or level of education?
- Do younger workers exhibit higher job satisfaction than older workers?
- Do multinational firms have a more favorable image than local, family-owned businesses?

When we examine questions like the above, we first develop the null and alternative hypotheses. Then we select the significance level for testing the null hypothesis. Finally, we select the appropriate statistical test and apply it to our sample data. In this section we cover two statistical tests that can be used to examine questions that compare the means of two groups.

Independent and Related Samples. Business researchers often find it useful to compare the means of two groups. When comparing group means, two situations are possible. The first situation is when the means are from independent samples. The second situation is when the samples are related. An example of the first situation, independent samples, might be when the researcher interviews a sample of females and males. If the researcher is comparing the average number of colas consumed per day by females with the average number of colas consumed by males, this is considered an independent sample situation. An example of the second situation, related samples, is when the researcher collects data from a sample of females only and compares the average number of times a week they drink bottled water with the average number of times a week they drink a glass of fruit juice. The following paragraph presents a brief overview of related sample testing. But the remainder of our discussion of hypothesis testing assumes independent samples.

The researcher must examine the information cautiously when confronted with a related sample problem. In this situation, the researcher wants to test for differences between the means for two variables in the same sample. While the two questions (variables) are independent, the respondents are the same, so the researcher does not have independent samples. Instead the researcher is dealing with what is referred to as paired samples, which require the use of a paired samples t test. SPSS software has options for both the related samples and independent samples t tests, and it is important that the appropriate test be chosen for each situation.

Comparing Two Means with the t *Test.* The t test can be used to test a hypothesis stating that the means for the variables associated with two independent samples or groups will be the same. The use of a t test requires interval or ratio data, and we assume the sample populations have normal distributions and the variances are equal. The t test assesses whether the observed differences between two sample means occurred by chance, or if there is a true difference. Although a normal distribution is assumed with the t test, it is quite robust relevant to departures from normality.

The t test is appropriate in situations where the sample size is small ($n = 30$ or less) and the population standard deviation is unknown. The t test uses the t distribution, also called the student's t distribution, to test hypotheses. The standard t distribution is a symmetrical, bell-shaped distribution with a mean of 0 and a standard deviation of 1. Other statistical distributions may be used in situations where the sample size (n) is larger than 30. But the t distribution is often used for sample sizes larger than 30 because the distributions are almost identical with larger sample sizes.

To demonstrate the use of a t test to compare two means, we examine the level of satisfaction for Phil Samouel's customers and Gino's customers. The null hypothesis is there are no differences in the level of satisfaction of the customers of the two restaurants. This hypothesis is tested using a t test, and the results are shown in Exhibit 13.7. The independent samples test was used because we are comparing Samouel's customers to Gino's customers. The SPSS instructions for calculating this test are shown in the Data Analysis box.

The top half of Exhibit 13.7 contains the group statistics. The mean satisfaction level for Samouel's customers was considerably lower at 4.78, compared with 5.96 for Gino's customers. The standard deviation for Samouel's was somewhat larger (1.16), however, than that for Gino's (0.974). To determine if the mean satisfaction levels are significantly different, we look at the information on the independent samples test in the lower portion of the table. Information in the column labeled "Sig. (2 tailed)" shows the means are significantly different (< 0.05) for assumptions of either equal or unequal variances. Thus, Samouel's customers are significantly less satisfied than Gino's customers, so Phil Samouel definitely needs to develop strategies to improve the satisfaction level of his customers.

Exhibit 13.7

Testing Differences in Two Means Using the t Test

Group Statistics

X_{17} "Satisfaction"	X_{28} "Competitor"	N	Mean	Standard deviation
	Samouel's	100	4.78	1.16
	Gino's	100	5.96	0.974

Independent Samples Test

		t-test for equality of means			
		t	df	Sig. (2-tailed)	Mean difference
X_{17} "Satisfaction"	Equal variances assumed	−7.793	198	0.000	−1.18
	Equal variances not assumed	−7.793	192.232	0.000	−1.18

■————DATA ANALYSIS————■
Using SPSS to Test the Differences in Two Means:
Comparison of Samouel's and Gino's Customers

To make the comparison, we can use the SPSS Compare Means program. First make sure you are analyzing all 200 cases. To do so, go to the Data pull-down menu and click on Split File. If the Analyze all cases is checked, click OK and go back to the Data Editor. If Compare Groups is checked, then click on Analyze all cases and then on OK to go back to the Data Editor.

The SPSS click-through sequence is: ANALYZE → COMPARE MEANS → INDEPENDENT-SAMPLES T TEST. When you get to the dialogue box click variable X_{17}, "satisfaction," into the Test Variables window and variable X_{28}, "competitor," into the Grouping Variable window. Now click on Define Groups and put a 0 for group 1 (Samouel's) and a 1 for group 2 (Gino's) and then click on Continue. For the Options we will use the defaults, so just click on OK to execute the program. The results will be the same as in Exhibit 13.7.

ANOVA (ANALYSIS OF VARIANCE)

ANOVA is used to assess the statistical differences between the means of two or more groups. For example, the circulation manager of the *New York Times* conducted a readership survey and found that individuals thirty-nine and younger read the paper an average of 2.5 times a week, individuals forty to forty-nine read the paper an average of 3.1 times a week, and individuals fifty and older read the paper an average of 4.7 times a week. The circulation manager wants to know whether these observed differences are statistically significant. Such information would be useful to managers and business researchers generally and to the circulation manager in particular. ANOVA can test for statistical differences among the average number of times the *New York Times* is read by several age groups, whereas the *t* test can compare at most two means. In our example, the null hypothesis is that the average frequency of readership of the three age groups is the same.

We discuss **one-way ANOVA** in this section. "One way" is used since there is only one independent variable. ANOVA can also examine research problems that involve several independent variables. When several independent variables are included, it is called **N-way ANOVA**. The independent variable (or variables) in an ANOVA must be categorical (nonmetric). In ANOVA, we refer to the categorical independent variables as **factors**. Each factor has two or more levels or groups. Each level is referred to as a treatment. For example, if we are examining the preference of a sample of individuals for Coca Cola Light, the dependent variable might be a preference measure using a seven-point scale, with 7 = "very strong preference" and 1 = "no preference at all." Likewise, the independent variable (factor) might be consumption measured using a scale of heavy, medium, and light. Since we have only one independent variable, this is a one-way ANOVA. If we added a second independent variable, such as brand loyalty (measured using highly loyal versus not loyal at all), this would be a two-way ANOVA.

■————**Business Research Dashboard**————■
Which Statistic Is Appropriate?

Richard and his fellow students are planning which classes they will take next fall and want to know which professors are rated most favorably by their students. They obtain information in student evaluations over the past year for several professors from a Web site that collects the data. The evaluations were obtained using a ten-point scale of "strongly agree" to "strongly disagree" relevant to eight statements about teaching methods. Information was also collected on which classes a particular professor taught and which time of the day.

   Which statistic could be used to answer the question of which professors have significantly more favorable ratings?

Differences between the group means are examined with the *F* test instead of the *t* test when we use ANOVA. To conduct the test, the total variance is partitioned into two forms of variation and then compared. The first is the variation within the groups and the second is the variation between the groups. The *F* distribution is the ratio of these two forms of variance and can be calculated as follows:

$$F = \text{Variance between groups (VB)} / \text{Variance within groups (VW)}$$

When the variance between the groups relative to that within the groups is larger, then the *F* ratio is larger. Larger *F* ratios indicate significant differences between the groups and a high likelihood the null hypothesis will be rejected. The Business Research Dashboard poses a question about the appropriate application of statistics.

   In our example we want to compare the satisfaction of three groups of restaurant customers, so a *t* test cannot be used. ANOVA that uses the *F* test, however, can be used with three or more groups, as long as the dependent variable is measured either as an interval or ratio. Also, the independent variable(s) must be categorical. All these conditions are met, so ANOVA can be used. As with other bivariate tests, the null hypothesis is that all three groups of restaurant customers (groups based on frequency of eating at $-X_{20}$) will express the same level of satisfaction with the restaurants.

   Our research question has two parts. First, we must determine if significant differences in satisfaction exist among any of the three customer groups defined by frequency of eating at $-X_{20}$. Second, if differences are identified, we must determine between which groups the differences are statistically significant. We will do this using ANOVA and the Scheffé follow-up test. The results of testing this hypothesis are shown in Exhibit 13.8.

   The upper table in Exhibit 13.8 shows the number of diners in each of the frequency groups and the mean level of satisfaction by frequency of dining. Note that in all cases higher frequency of dining is associated with higher satisfaction. In the *N* column at the right we see that Gino's has many more very frequent and somewhat frequent diners than Samouel's. Moreover, customer satisfaction for Samouel's restaurant is not as high (4.78) as it is for Gino's (5.96). The task for Phil Samouel, therefore, is to

Exhibit 13.8

Analysis of Variance Testing Mean Differences in Satisfaction Levels of Samouel's and Gino's Customers Based on Frequency of Dining

Descriptive Statistics

Dependent Variable: X_{17}, "Satisfaction"

X_{28}, "competitor"	X_{20}, "Frequency of eating at"	Mean	N
Samouel's	Occasional diner	4.04	47
	Somewhat frequent diner	4.62	21
	Very frequent diner	5.97	32
	Total	4.78	100
Gino's	Occasional diner	4.78	9
	Somewhat frequent diner	5.69	29
	Very frequent diner	6.26	62
	Total	5.96	100

Tests of between-subject effects

Dependent Variable: X_{17}

X_{28}	Source	Type III sum of squares	df	Mean square	F	Sig.
Samouel's	Corrected model	71.324[a]	2	35.662	55.942	0.000
	Intercept	2,137.359	1	2,137.359	3,352.800	0.000
	X_{20}	71.324	2	35.662	55.942	0.000
	Error	61.836	97	0.637		
	Total	2,418.000	100			
	Corrected total	133.160	99			
Gino's	Corrected model	20.207[b]	2	10.103	13.309	0.000
	Intercept	1,729.763	1	1,729.763	2,278.680	0.000
	X_{20}	20.207	2	10.103	13.309	0.000
	Error	73.633	97	0.759		
	Total	3,646.000	100			
	Corrected total	93.840	99			

[a]R squared = 0.536 (Samouel's); [b]R squared = 0.215 (Gino's)

analyze the survey data and develop a strategy to improve customer satisfaction levels, attract new customers, and increase the frequency of dining at his restaurant.

Information in the lower table reveals that satisfaction levels differ significantly among the groups identified by their frequency of dining. You determine this by looking under the "Sig." column for variable X_{20} (located in the "Source" column). Note the level of significance is 0.000 for Samouel's and 0.000 for Gino's, so satisfaction levels for customers of both restaurants vary significantly based on frequency of dining. The null hypothesis of no differences is therefore rejected.

Unfortunately, ANOVA enables the researcher to conclude only that statistical differences are present somewhere among the group means. It does not identify where the differences are. In our example of satisfaction levels of customers, we could conclude that differences in satisfaction levels based on frequency of dining are statistically significant, but we would not know if the differences are between very frequent and somewhat frequent diners, somewhat frequent and occasional, or occasional and very frequent. We would be able to say only that there are significant differences somewhere among the groups. For this reason, business researchers must use follow-up tests to determine where the differences lie.

ANOVA Using Follow-Up Tests

Several follow-up tests have been developed to identify the location of significant differences. Many are available in statistical software packages such as SPSS or SAS. All the follow-up tests involve simultaneous assessment of differences among several means. Discussion of these techniques is well beyond the scope of this book, but the techniques differ in the extent to which they are able to control for the error rate. SPSS software has fourteen tests that assume equal variances and four where equal variance is not assumed. In our example we use the Scheffé procedure because it is the most conservative method of assessing significant differences among group means. But the Tukey and Duncan tests are widely utilized in the literature.

The information in Exhibit 13.9 shows which group means are significantly different. The far-right column, labeled "Sig.," shows the level of significance. For both Samouel's and Gino's there are statistically significant differences among all the groups. This means the "very frequent," "somewhat frequent," and "occasional" diners differ significantly in their satisfaction levels. If there were any comparisons in which the group means were not significantly different, they would have been shown in the "Sig." column of numbers.

Exhibit 13.9

Comparisons of Individual Group Means for Significant Differences

Multiple Comparisons
Dependent Variable: X_{17} "satisfaction"

Scheffé test

X_{28} "competitor"	(I) X_{20} "frequency of dining"	(J) X_{20}	(I − J) Mean diff.	Sig.
Samouel's	Occasional diner	Somewhat frequent diner	−0.58*	0.026
		Very frequent diner	−1.93*	0.000
	Somewhat frequent diner	Occasional diner	0.58*	0.026
		Very frequent diner	−1.35*	0.000
	Very frequent diner	Occasional diner	1.93*	0.000
		Somewhat frequent diner	1.35*	0.000
Gino's	Occasional diner	Somewhat frequent diner	−0.91*	0.027
		Very frequent diner	−1.48*	0.000
	Somewhat frequent diner	Occasional diner	0.91*	0.027
		Very frequent diner	−0.57*	0.018
	Very frequent diner	Occasional diner	1.48*	0.000
		Somewhat frequent diner	0.57*	0.018

*The mean difference is significant at the 0.05 level.

To determine the nature of the differences we look back at the means shown in Exhibit 13.8. For Samouel's the mean satisfaction level of the "very frequent" diners is 5.97, for the "somewhat frequent" diners the mean is 4.62, and for the "occasional" diners it is 4.04. Thus, as would be expected, the more frequent diners are significantly more satisfied. A similar finding is true for Gino's. The mean satisfaction level of the "very frequent" diners is 6.26, for the "somewhat frequent" diners the mean is 5.69, and for the "occasional" diners the mean is 4.78. Phil would be concerned that Gino's has more frequent customers than he does. A business plan must be devised to increase frequency of dining as well as other performance indicators.

FACTORIAL DESIGN: TWO-WAY ANOVA

One-way ANOVA designs involve a single nonmetric independent variable and a single metric dependent variable. A **factorial design** examines the effect (if any) of two or more nonmetric independent variables on a single metric dependent variable. With one-way ANOVA the total variance is partitioned into the between-group variance and the within-group variance. But in factorial designs (**two-way ANOVA**), the between-group variance itself is partitioned into (1) variation due to each of the independent variables (factors) and (2) variation due to the interaction of the two variables. That is, their combined effects on the dependent variable beyond the separate influences of each. Therefore, three null hypotheses are tested simultaneously by a two-way factorial design: (1) the effect of variable one on the dependent variable; (2) the effect of variable two on the dependent variable; and (3) the combined (joint) effect of variables one and two on the dependent variable. The effects of the two independent variables are referred to as **main effects**, and their combined effect is referred to as the **interaction effect**.

Example of Two-Way ANOVA

Phil Samouel has observed that the frequency of dining of his male and female customers appears to be different. If in fact the dining frequencies are statistically different, he would like to better understand why and determine how he could use that information to grow his business. He would also like to know how customer gender and frequency of dining are related to satisfaction. The null hypotheses are: (1) there are no differences in mean satisfaction levels based on frequency of dining; (2) there are no differences in mean satisfaction levels based on gender; and (3) there are no differences in mean satisfaction levels based on the combined effects of frequency of dining and gender. The metric dependent variable for these hypotheses is X_{17}, "satisfaction," and the nonmetric independent variables are X_{20}, "frequency of dining," and X_{25}, "gender." The results of the tests of the hypotheses are reported in Exhibits 13.10 to 13.12. Instructions on how to use SPSS to execute these tests are shown in the Data Analysis box.

Exhibit 13.10 shows the results of the two-way ANOVA program. The null hypotheses were that there would be no difference between the mean scores for X_{17},

Exhibit 13.10

Two-Way ANOVA for Frequency of Dining and Gender

Tests of between-subject effects—Samouel's Greek Cuisine restaurant
Dependent variable: X_{17} "satisfaction"

Source	Type III sum of squares	df	Mean square	F	Sig.
Corrected model	86.828[a]	5	17.366	35.232	.000
Intercept	1,848.007	1	1,848.007	3,749.330	.000
X_{20}	39.076	2	19.538	39.639	.000
X_{25}	12.620	1	12.620	25.604	.000
$X_{20} \times X_{25}$	2.377	2	1.189	2.412	.095
Error	46.332	94	.493		
Total	2,418.000	100			
Corrected total	133.160	99			

[a]R squared = 0.652 (adjusted R squared = 0.634)

■————DATA ANALYSIS————■
Using SPSS to Execute a Two-Way ANOVA

We must separate Samouel's customers from Gino's for this analysis. To do so we go to the Data pull-down menu and then scroll down and click on Select Cases. Next click on If condition satisfied, and then on If . . . Now highlight variable X_{28} and click the arrow box to move it into the box on the top right side. Next click below on the equal sign (=) and then click on 0. This tells the program to select for analysis only cases coded 0 for variable X_{28} (i.e., Samouel's customers). Finally click on Continue and then on OK. We use this process to select only Samouel's customers for this analysis.

The click-through sequence is: ANALYZE → GENERAL LINEAR MODEL → UNIVARIATE. Highlight the dependent variable X_{17} "satisfaction," by clicking on it and move it to the Dependent variable window. Next, highlight X_{20} "frequency of dining," and move it into the window labeled "Fixed Factors." Now do the same for variable X_{25} "gender." Click on the Post Hoc tab to the right and highlight X_{20} in the Factor(s) window and then click on the arrow box to move this variable to the window for Post Hoc Tests. We do not move X_{25} because it has only two groups and not three. Look to the lower left side of the screen and click on Scheffé's test and then on Continue (we are assuming the variances are equal, or approximately equal). Now go to the Options tab and click on Descriptive statistics and then on Continue. Finally, click on OK, since we do not need to specify anything else for this test. The results are shown in Exhibit 13.10.

"satisfaction," for customers with different dining rates (X_{20}), no difference in mean scores on X_{17} "satisfaction," between females and males (X_{25}), and no interaction effect. The purpose of the N-Way ANOVA analysis is first to see if statistically significant differences exist and, if they do, among which groups.

To assess the mean differences for each independent variable comparison, an *F* ratio is used. As discussed earlier, the approach used in a two-way ANOVA compares the variance from the between groups grand mean to the variance within the groups. In this case, the groups are the three groups of customers exhibiting different dining

Exhibit 13.11

Means and Standard Deviations for Customer Satisfaction by Gender and Frequency of Dining

Descriptive statistics—Samouel's Greek Cuisine restaurant
Dependent variable: X_{17}, "satisfaction"

X_{20}, "frequency of dining"	X_{25}, "gender"	Mean	Standard deviation	N
Occasional diner	Male	4.38	0.805	21
	Female	3.77	0.430	26
	Total	4.04	0.690	47
Somewhat frequent diner	Male	4.89	0.782	9
	Female	4.42	0.793	12
	Total	4.62	0.805	21
Very frequent diner	Male	6.29	0.464	24
	Female	5.00	1.309	8
	Total	5.97	0.933	32
Total	Male	5.31	1.113	54
	Female	4.15	0.868	46
	Total	4.78	1.160	100

rates and the two gender groups. When the *F* ratio is large, we are more likely to have larger differences among the means of the various groups examined.

The first main effect we examine is the impact of variable X_{20}, "frequency of dining," on variable X_{17}, "satisfaction." The *F* ratio for X_{20}, "frequency of dining," for Samouel's customers is 39.639, which is statistically significant at the 0.000 level. From Exhibit 13.11 we can see that for Samouel's restaurant satisfaction is higher for "somewhat frequent" (mean = 4.62) and "very frequent" customers (5.97) than it is for the "occasional" diner (4.04). Thus, we reject the null hypothesis and conclude satisfaction does vary by frequency of dining at Samouel's restaurant. Moreover, as would be expected the more-frequent customers are significantly more satisfied than the less-frequent diners.

The second main comparison was whether there is a difference in satisfaction based on X_{25}, "gender." The *F* ratio for gender is 25.604 and statistically significant (0.000). (See Exhibit 13.10.) We therefore reject the null hypothesis of no difference and conclude that satisfaction of Samouel's customers differs based on gender. Specifically, for Samouel's Greek Cuisine females are significantly less satisfied than males (female mean satisfaction levels are consistently lower than those for males).

The third hypothesis was there are no differences based on the combined effect of frequency of dining and gender. The interaction between dining frequency and gender is nonsignificant (0.095), meaning that the difference in satisfaction when both independent variables are considered together is very small. The null hypothesis of no difference is therefore not rejected for the interaction effect.

Exhibit 13.12

Multiple Groups Tests of Significance

Multiple comparisons—Samouel's Greek Cuisine restaurant
Dependent variable: $X_{17,}$ "satisfaction"

Scheffé test

(I)	(J)	(I – J)	
$X_{20,}$ "frequency of dining"	X_{20}	Mean diff.	Sig.
Occasional diner	Somewhat frequent diner	−0.58*	0.010
	Very frequent diner	−1.93*	0.000
Somewhat frequent diner	Occasional diner	0.58*	0.010
	Very frequent diner	−1.35*	0.000
Very frequent diner	Occasional diner	1.93*	0.000
	Somewhat frequent diner	1.35*	0.000

*The mean difference is significant at the 0.05 level.

To better understand the results let's look first at the information in Exhibit 13.12. There are significant differences among all the groups of diners—"occasional," "somewhat frequent," and "very frequent." Thus, higher frequency of dining does indicate a higher level of satisfaction, and significant differences exist for all the group comparisons.

Now that you have learned about ANOVA, try answering the questions in the Business Research Dashboard (see next page).

MULTIVARIATE ANALYSIS OF VARIANCE (MANOVA)

MANOVA (multivariate analysis of variance) is similar to ANOVA. The difference is that instead of one metric dependent variable, the technique can examine two or more. The objective is the same since both techniques assess differences in groups (categorical variables) as they impact metric dependent variables. While ANOVA examines differences in a single metric dependent variable, MANOVA examines group differences across multiple metric dependent variables at the same time. With ANOVA the null hypothesis is that the means of the single dependent variable are the same across the groups. In MANOVA the null hypothesis is that the means of the multiple dependent variables are the same across the groups.

As an example, our customer survey has three relationship outcome variables: satisfaction, recommend to a friend, and likelihood of returning in the future. All of these variables are measured metrically. An appropriate MANOVA would be to examine the relationship between gender (nonmetric) and the three outcome variables (metric). Similarly, another appropriate MANOVA application to our customer survey would be to examine the relationship between frequency of dining (nonmetric) and the three outcome variables. MANOVA will not be covered in this text.

■————**Business Research Dashboard**————■
Application of ANOVA to Resolve a Quality Control Issue

Lynne Larson is chief work-study analyst for a large international chemical company. Duncan Jones, production manager of the agricultural division, approached her for help because far too many production runs in the fertilizer plant were failing quality checks performed by analysts in the company's chemical laboratory. Jones wondered how this situation could have arisen when there had been no recent changes in procedure at the plant. In fifteen years as division production manager he had never experienced this level of rejection.

Jones was adamant that the fertilizer met the required standards and that the fault lay with the laboratory analysts. But the chief chemist, Fred Lions, insisted that the fertilizer runs were being correctly rejected. His analysts were highly qualified and experienced and there was no possibility that they could be at fault.

Larson recognized there were only two key sources of variation that could be at the root of the problem. The source had to be either the production runs or the analysts. To assist her in finding the problem, she called in her chief statistician, Johan Avery, to design a study to examine the situation.

Avery recognized this as an analysis of variance (ANOVA) problem. He asked that five samples be taken at random from a production run and that four randomly chosen analysts analyze each sample. The samples were to be analyzed for nitrogen and iron content. Thus, two separate ANOVAs were to be performed: one comparing the five samples and another comparing the analysts.

The results of the ANOVA revealed that the variation between the five samples (rows) was not significant at the 5 percent level for both nitrogen and iron content. This revealed that the sample results did not differ significantly. In other words, the analysts did not find real differences between the samples. Further, it was established that the variation between the analysts (columns) was significant at the 1 percent level, indicating that the analysts did differ significantly among themselves with respect to their evaluations of the samples. This was the case for both nitrogen and iron content. Thus it was concluded that the analysts were unreliable in their evaluation of the samples.

What are the independent and dependent variables in this ANOVA? What should Lynne Larson report to Duncan Jones? The above formulation is for a simple two-way ANOVA since there is only one observation recorded for each combination of sample and analyst. What is the limitation of such a formulation?

CONTINUING CASE: SAMOUEL'S GREEK CUISINE
Developing Relationships and Testing Hypotheses

With the surveys completed, edited, and entered into a computer file, a decision has to be made regarding the best way to analyze the data to understand the individuals interviewed and how the information could be used to help Phil and his brother improve the restaurant's operations. The data analysis should be led by the theory used to guide the design of the studies as well as by the business experience of Phil and his brother. Phil, his brother, and the consultant have been brainstorming on how to best analyze the data to understand both the customer and employee surveys.

1. Draw several conceptual models to represent relationships that could be tested with the Samouel's restaurant surveys.
2. Which statistical techniques would be appropriate for testing the proposed relationships?
3. Give examples of relationships that could be tested with chi square and ANOVA.

SUMMARY

UNDERSTAND HOW TO REPRESENT HYPOTHESIZED RELATIONSHIPS FOR TESTING

Conceptual models are an excellent way to visually display hypothesized relationships among independent and dependent variables. The relationships can indicate whether they are positive or negative in direction. Statistical techniques enable us to determine whether the empirical evidence confirms the proposed hypotheses.

CLARIFY THE DIFFERENCE BETWEEN SAMPLE STATISTICS AND POPULATION PARAMETERS

The purpose of inferential statistics is to develop estimates about a population using a sample from that population. A sample is a small subset of all the elements in the population. Sample statistics refers to measures obtained directly from the sample or calculated from the data in the sample. A population parameter is a variable or some sort of measured characteristic of the entire population. Sample statistics are useful in making inferences regarding the population's parameters. Generally, the actual population parameters are unknown, since the cost to perform a census of the population often is prohibitively high.

DESCRIBE HOW TO CHOOSE THE APPROPRIATE STATISTICAL TECHNIQUE TO TEST HYPOTHESES

The choice of a particular technique depends on (1) the number of variables and (2) the scale of measurement. Univariate statistical techniques can assess only a single variable. Bivariate statistical techniques can assess two variables. Multivariate statistical techniques can examine many variables simultaneously and can handle both multiple dependent and independent variables. The appropriate statistical technique also varies depending on whether your data is nominal, ordinal, interval, or ratio.

EXPLAIN WHEN AND HOW TO USE THE T TEST, ANOVA, AND CHI SQUARE TO EXAMINE HYPOTHESES

Business researchers frequently want to test the hypothesis that one group differs from another group in terms of attitudes, behavior, or some other characteristic. Where more than one group is involved, bivariate or multivariate tests must be used. In statistical terminology, the null hypothesis is that there are no significant differences among the two (or more) groups. Three bivariate hypothesis tests were discussed in this chapter. The first, chi square, tests differences between groups using data that is measured on either a nominal or ordinal scale. The t test and ANOVA are used to test group mean differences when data is measured with either an interval or ratio scale. Moreover, the t test is appropriate for testing differences in only two groups, while ANOVA can test differences in three or more groups.

ETHICAL DILEMMA

Dan Henderson, president of a family owned business with a total of seven stores, believes the company needs to create a customer loyalty program designed to reward customers who spend more than $200 per shopping trip. Therefore, he asks his younger sister to create a program that can help the company identify and profile its most profitable customers. When the report is completed, the data indicates that the more affluent shoppers who spend more than $200 per shopping trip represent only a small part of the company's overall sales because they shop only three to four times a year and tend to buy only lower margin designer clothing. But the report notes that the most profitable store customers tend to be over forty years old, from average income households. They shop at least twice a month, spending an average of $100 per trip on everything from cosmetics to housewares to high margin private label clothing. After reviewing the report, Dan nonetheless decides he wants the customer loyalty program to reward the high-dollar purchase customers, justifying the decision by claiming that they are responsible for the store's upscale image that appeals to the regular store customer.

What do you think about Dan's decision?

REVIEW QUESTIONS

1. What is the difference between sample statistics and population parameters?
2. How does the researcher choose the correct statistical test?
3. What is the difference between the t test, ANOVA, and chi square?
4. Why do we use follow-up tests in ANOVA?
5. What is the difference between one-way and two-way ANOVA?

DISCUSSION AND APPLICATION QUESTIONS

1. Draw a conceptual model of hypothesized relationships for the Samouel's customer database. Identify the hypotheses and indicate whether they are directional or nondirectional.
2. How do you select the appropriate statistical method to test a hypothesis?
3. A business researcher uses two-way ANOVA in a report for a client. The researcher does not check the assumptions for using the technique. Is this a problem?

4. *SPSS Application:* Use the customer survey database and compare the "satisfaction," "likely to recommend," and "likely to return" variables for Samouel's Greek Cuisine and Gino's Italian Ristorante using the *t* test. Are they statistically different and, if so, how would you interpret the findings?

INTERNET EXERCISES

1. Participate in a survey at http://www.survey.net and prepare a report on what you learn.
2. The Federal Reserve Bank of St. Louis has a database called FRED (Federal Reserve Economic Data). Go to its Web site, http://research.stlouisfed.org/fred/abotfred.html, and report what you find. Identify some research questions that can be examined with the statistical techniques covered in this chapter.
3. Want more information on the fundamentals of statistical analysis and definitions of concepts and terms? Go to the Platonic Realms Interactive Mathematics Encyclopedia, at http://www.mathacademy.com/pr/index.asp. Click on Encyclopedia. Prepare a report summarizing the value of this Web site.

14 Examining Relationships Using Correlation and Regression

LEARNING OUTCOMES

1. Describe the nature of relationships between variables
2. Explain the concepts of correlation and regression analysis
3. Clarify the difference between bivariate and multiple regression analysis
4. Understand how multicollinearity can influence regression models
5. Describe how to use dummy variables in regression

Many business questions are concerned with the relationship between two or more variables. Questions such as, Are sales related to advertising? Is product quality related to customer loyalty? Is educational level associated with the purchase of a particular stock? and How much safety training is required to reduce accidents? can be answered by using statistical techniques to examine relationships between variables. This chapter explains how you can use statistical techniques to examine questions like these. To better illustrate the statistical analyses, we use SPSS software. Specific instructions on how to use this software to calculate the results presented in this chapter can be found on this book's Web site at www.mesharpe-student.com.

TYPES OF RELATIONSHIPS BETWEEN VARIABLES

When variables have a consistent and systematic link between them, a relationship is present. Statistical techniques are used to determine whether there is a statistically significant association or link between the variables. If there is a statistically significant association, it is important to understand the relationship is not necessarily causal. That is, statistical association cannot be used to infer that one variable causes another. Correlation and regression are associative techniques that help us to determine if there is a consistent and systematic relationship between two or more variables. There are four basic concepts we need to understand about relationships between variables: presence, nature of the relationship, direction, and strength of association. We describe each of these concepts in the following sections.

PRESENCE

Presence relates to whether a systematic relationship exists between two or more variables. We rely on the concept of statistical significance to measure whether a relationship is present. If statistical significance is found between the variables we say that a relationship is present. That is, we say knowledge about the behavior of one or more variables enables us to predict the behavior of another variable. For example, if we found a statistically significant relationship between customers' perceptions of the employees of Gino's Ristorante and their satisfaction with the restaurant, we would say a relationship is present and that perceptions of the employees will tell us what the level of satisfaction is likely to be. We previously introduced the concept of a null hypothesis. With associative analysis, the null hypothesis is that no association is present between the variables. If we find statistical significance then we reject the null hypothesis and accept the alternative hypothesis that a relationship exists between perceptions of employees and customer satisfaction.

NATURE OF THE RELATIONSHIP

A second important concept is how variables are related to one another. We typically say the relationship between variables is either linear or nonlinear. A **linear relationship** is a straight-line association between two or more variables. A **nonlinear relationship**, often referred to as **curvilinear**, is one in which the relationship is best described by a curve instead of a straight line. In a linear relationship the strength and nature of the relationship between the variables remain the same over the range of the variables. But in a nonlinear relationship the strength and nature change over the range of both variables (i.e., Y's relationship with X first gets weaker as X increases, but then gets stronger as the value of X continues to increase).

Linear relationships between variables are much easier to work with than curvilinear relationships. If we know the value of variable X, we can use the formula for a straight line ($Y = a + bX$) to estimate the value of Y. But when variables have a curvilinear relationship, the formula that best describes that link will be much more complex. Curvilinear relationships are beyond the scope of this book, and most business researchers work with relationships they believe are linear. In fact, most of the statistics covered in this book are based on the assumption that a linear relationship is an efficient way to describe the association between the variables being examined.

DIRECTION

If a relationship is present between the variables we also need to know its direction. The direction of a relationship can be either positive or negative. In our restaurant example, a positive relationship exists if customers who rate employees favorably are also highly satisfied. Similarly, a negative relationship exists if customers who rate the portions as small (low rating) express higher levels of satisfaction with the dining experience (high rating). A negative relationship between two variables is denoted by a minus (–) sign, and a positive relationship has a plus (+) sign.

STRENGTH OF ASSOCIATION

Depending on the type of relationship being examined we generally categorize the strength of association as slight, small but definite, moderate, high, or very strong. The strength of association measures the association between two variables. A slight, almost negligible situation is one in which a consistent and systematic relationship is not present between the variables. When a relationship is present, the business researcher must determine the strength of the association. A very strong association means there is a very high probability the variables have a relationship. A moderate association means there is likely to be a consistent and systematic relationship.

VARIABLE RELATIONSHIPS AND COVARIATION

Business researchers often want to know whether two or more variables are linked. Variables are linked if they exhibit covariation. **Covariation** is when one variable consistently and systematically changes relative to another variable. The correlation coefficient is used to assess this link. Large coefficients indicate high covariation and a strong relationship. Small coefficients indicate little covariation and a weak relationship. The correlation coefficient is a standardized measure of covariation that is used to assess the degree of covariation between two variables. For example, if we know that purchases over the Internet are related to age, then we may want to know the extent to which younger persons make more purchases on the Internet and ultimately what kinds of products they purchase most often and why. Thus, when two variables change together on a reliable or consistent basis (i.e., covary), that information helps us to make predictions for use in developing sound business strategies.

One of the first issues we need to determine is whether the correlation coefficient is statistically significant. Regardless of its absolute size, a correlation coefficient has no meaning unless it is statistically significant. Most popular software programs tell you if a correlation is statistically significant. Statistical significance means you are confident the results of your statistical analysis are reliable. It doesn't mean the findings are important or that they are useful for decision making. Researcher judgment in light of the research objectives determines whether the findings are important and useful. The SPSS program reports significance as the probability the null hypothesis is supported (Excel uses the label p-value for statistical significance). Typical guidelines say that to be considered statistically significant the probability must be at least < 0.05, and in some instances < 0.01. A probability of < 0.05 means there must be fewer than five chances in one hundred you will be wrong if you reject the null hypothesis when it is in fact true. In some business situations, a level of < 0.10 is considered acceptable. But by accepting this probability level the researcher assumes more risk and must decide if the situation warrants the higher level of risk.

Exhibit 14.1

Rules of Thumb About Correlation Coefficient Size

Coefficient Range:	Strength of Association:
± (0.91–1.00)	Very strong
± (0.71–0.90)	High
± (0.41–0.70)	Moderate
± (0.21–0.40)	Small but definite relationship
± (0.00–0.20)	Slight, almost negligible

Note: Assumes correlation coefficient is statistically significant.

Once we have determined the relationship is statistically significant, we must then decide what strength of association is acceptable. The size of the correlation coefficient is used to quantitatively describe the strength of the association between two or more variables. Rules of thumb have been proposed to characterize the strength of the association between variables, based on the absolute size of the correlation coefficient. As Exhibit 14.1 suggests, correlation coefficients between ±0.91 and 1.00 are considered very strong. That is, covariance is definitely shared between the two variables being examined. In contrast, if the correlation coefficient is between 0.00 and ±0.20, even though the coefficient is different from 0 in the sample, there is a good chance that the null hypothesis won't be rejected (unless you are using a large sample). These levels are only suggestions, and other guidelines regarding the strength of the relationship are possible.

Scatter diagrams are an easy way to visually display the covariation between two variables. A **scatter diagram**, sometimes referred to as a **scattergram**, is a plot of the values of two variables for all the observations in the sample. If one variable is considered the dependent variable, it is customary to plot it on the vertical axis, with the independent variable on the horizontal axis. Exhibits 14.2a to 14.2c are examples of possible relationships between two variables plotted on a scatter diagram. In 14.2a, there is no apparent relationship or association between the variables. That is, there is no predictable or identifiable pattern to the points. Knowing the values of Y or X would not tell you very much (probably nothing at all) about the possible values of the other variable. 2a suggests there is no consistent and systematic relationship between Y and X and thus very little or no covariation shared by the two variables. If the amount of covariation shared by these two variables were measured, it would be very close to 0.

In Exhibit 14.2b, the pattern of the two variables shows a very different picture. There is a distinct pattern to the points on the scatter diagram that is easily described as a straight line. We refer to this relationship as positive because increases in the value of Y are associated with increases in the value of X. Similarly, if the values of Y decrease, the values of X will also decrease. If we measured the covariation between the values of Y and X, it would be relatively high. Thus, changes in the value of Y are consistently and systematically related to changes in the value of X.

Exhibit 14.2   **Scatter Diagrams Illustrating Various Relationships**

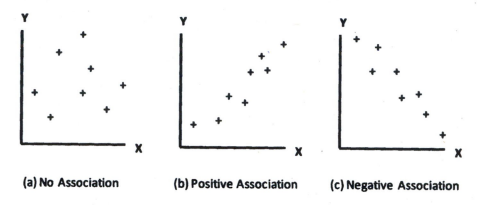

(a) No Association   **(b) Positive Association**   **(c) Negative Association**

Exhibit 14.2c shows a similar pattern between the values of *Y* and *X*, but the direction of the relationship is opposite that in Exhibit 14.2b. There is a linear pattern, but now when the values of *Y* increase the values of *X* decrease. That is, the values of *Y* and *X* change in the opposite direction. This type of relationship is described as a negative relationship. There is a large amount of covariation between the two variables, because *Y* and *X* consistently change together. The difference is they move in the opposite direction from that in 14.2b. Covariation refers to the amount of shared movement between two variables. The direction of the relationship is indicated by the sign of the covariation.

CORRELATION ANALYSIS

Scatter diagrams enable us to visually demonstrate the relationship between two variables and the extent to which they covary. For example, a scatter diagram can tell us that as age increases the average consumption of aspirin increases, too, or that on a hot day we consume more water. But even though a visual display of data is useful, some situations may need a quantitative measure of the covariation between two variables to obtain a complete understanding of the relationship.

The **Pearson correlation** measures the linear association between two metric variables. The number representing the Pearson correlation is referred to as a correlation coefficient. It ranges from -1.00 to $+1.00$, with 0 representing absolutely no association between the two metric variables. While -1.00 or $+1.00$ is possible and either represents a perfect association between two variables, such perfect associations seldom occur. Stronger links or levels of association result in larger absolute-magnitude correlation coefficients. Correlation coefficients can be either positive or negative, depending on the direction of the relationship between the variables. If there is a positive correlation coefficient between *X* and *Y*, then increases in the value of *X* are associated with increases in the value of *Y*, and vice versa.

The correlation coefficient describes the extent of the association between two variables. The null hypothesis states there is no association between two variables and that the correlation coefficient is 0 (or very small). For example, we may hypothesize that there is no relationship between preference for Dunkin' Donuts coffee and income level. If you take measures of the two variables (consumption of Dunkin' Donuts coffee and income) from a sample of the population and calculate the correlation coefficient for that sample to be 0.36, the question is, What is the probability that you would get a correlation coefficient of 0.36 in your sample if the correlation coefficient in the population is actually 0? That is, if you calculate a large correlation coefficient between two variables in your sample—consumption of Dunkin' Donuts coffee and income (and your sample was properly selected from the population of interest)—then the chances the population correlation coefficient is really 0 are small. If the correlation coefficient is statistically significant, you can reject the null hypothesis and conclude with some degree of confidence the two variables share some association in the population. In other words, consumption of Dunkin' Donuts coffee is related to income.

In addition to examining the correlation coefficient, we often square the correlation coefficient to get the **coefficient of determination**, or r^2. The coefficient of determination ranges from 0.00 to 1.00 and represents the amount of variation explained or accounted for in one variable by the other.[1] If a correlation coefficient is 0.54, then the r^2 would be 0.2916, meaning that approximately 29.16 percent of the variation in one variable is associated with the other variable. As is the case with the correlation coefficient, a stronger relationship between the variables results in a larger coefficient of determination.

When we use the Pearson correlation coefficient we must make several assumptions about the nature of the data. First, the two variables are assumed to have been measured using interval or ratio-scaled measures (i.e., metric). Other types of correlation coefficients can be used if the variables are nominal or ordinal measures. Later in the chapter we discuss the Spearman correlation coefficient for use with ordinal data. Another assumption of the Pearson correlation coefficient is that the relationship we are examining is linear. That is, a straight line is an accurate description of the relationship between the two metric variables.

A third assumption of the Pearson correlation coefficient is that the variables you are examining are from normally distributed populations. A normal distribution, also referred to as a bell shaped curve, is a common assumption for many statistical techniques used by business researchers. But it is often difficult to determine whether sample data is normally distributed. Since correlation is considered a reasonably robust statistic when the distribution varies from normal, this assumption is frequently taken for granted.

AN EXAMPLE OF PEARSON BIVARIATE CORRELATION

Phil Samouel collected information in his employee survey on employee cooperation and teamwork as well as likelihood to search for a job. Since a stable workforce is good for his restaurant, he wants to use his survey findings to better understand what can be done to retain good employees. One of the options he is considering implementing is a new training program for employees. He would therefore like to know if the relationship between the perceived cooperation among his employees and likelihood to search for a new job is significant and negative. In other words, greater perceived cooperation is associated with higher loyalty and reduced likelihood to search for another job. If there is a relationship, he can use this information in developing a training program to ensure that his employees cooperate more in preparing meals and serving customers.

The null hypothesis is that no relationship exists between perceived cooperation among Samouel's employees and likelihood to search for a new job. Recall from the employee questionnaire described in Chapter 9 that information was collected on "intention to search for another job" (X_{16}) and perceived cooperation among members of a work group (X_4). To test this hypothesis, we must calculate the correlation between these two variables. This has been done and is reported in Exhibit 14.3. The Data Analysis box explains how to execute this correlation.

Exhibit 14.3 shows us, in the lower half, how the two variables are related. Stated another way, it tells us if the two variables covary. To interpret the table, look at the columns and rows where the variables intersect. For example, the far-right column is variable X_{16}, "intention to search," and the number at the top of the column is –0.416**. This indicates the correlation between variable X_4, "work group cooperation," and X_{16} is –0.416, and the significance level is 0.001 (this number is right below –0.416** and in the row labeled "Sig. (2-tailed)," which is the t test that shows the correlation is significant). The numbers in the row labeled N represent the number of respondents used to compute the correlation. In other words, the sample size of sixty-three Samouel's employees.

The results reported in Exhibit 14.3 confirm that perceived work group cooperation is significantly correlated with intention to search for another job. This means we can reject the null hypothesis of no relationship between these two variables. Moreover, the correlation is negative and moderately strong, so we can conclude that employees who believe there is less work group cooperation exhibit a higher

---

Exhibit 14.3

Bivariate Correlation Between Work Group Cooperation and Intention to Search for Another Job

Descriptive Statistics	Mean	Standard deviation	N
X_4, "work group cooperation"	3.51	1.11	63
X_{16}, "intention to search"	4.32	1.87	63

Correlations		X_4 "work group cooperation"	X_{16}, "intention to search"
X_4, "work group cooperation"	Pearson correlation	1.000	–0.416**
	Sig. (2 tailed)	—	0.001
	N	63	63
X_{16}, "intention to search"	Pearson correlation	–0.416*	1.0
	Sig. (2 tailed)	0.001	—
	N	63	63

**Correlation is significant at the 0.01 level (2 tailed).

■———DATA ANALYSIS———■
Using SPSS to Calculate a Pearson Bivariate Correlation

Load up the Samouel's employee database. The SPSS click-through sequence to execute the Pearson bivariate correlation is: ANALYZE → CORRELATE → BIVARIATE, which leads to a dialogue box where you select the variables. Highlight X_4 and X_{16} and move them into the Variables box. We will use the three default options: Pearson correlation, Two-tailed test of significance, and Flag significant variables. Next go to the Options box and click on Means and Standard Deviations and then on Continue. Finally, click OK at the lower left corner of the dialogue box to run the program. The results will be the same as those in Exhibit 14.3.

intention to search for another job. To ensure a more stable workforce, Phil needs to implement the employee training he is considering so that he can improve cooperation in employee work groups.

Practical Significance of the Correlation Coefficient

If the correlation coefficient is strong and statistically significant, you can conclude there is a relationship between the variables. In our example, Phil Samouel can be reasonably confident the variables "work group cooperation" and "intention to search" are related because the correlation is -0.416 and highly significant (0.001). But if the correlation coefficient is small, there are two possibilities. First, a consistent, systematic relationship does not exist between the variables, or, second, the association exists but it is not linear, and other types of relationships must be considered.

Even if the correlation coefficient is statistically significant, it does not mean it is practically significant. To determine practical significance, we must also ask whether the numbers we calculated are meaningful. In calculating the statistical significance of a correlation coefficient, the sample size is a major influence. With large sample sizes it is possible to have a statistically significant correlation coefficient that is really too small to be of any practical use. For example, if the correlation coefficient between "work group cooperation" and "intention to search" is 0.20 and significant at the 0.05 level, the coefficient of determination would be 0.04. Is this coefficient of determination of practical significance? Does the value of knowing that you have explained 4 percent of the variation justify the cost of developing and implementing a program to improve cooperation in employee work groups? You must always look at both types of significance (statistical and practical) before drawing conclusions, particularly when examining more complex issues.

Measurement Scales and Correlation

Business researchers often find the answers to their questions can be measured with only ordinal or nominal scales. For example, if we wanted to see if gender is related to soft drink consumption, we have a problem because gender is a nominal variable.

If we used the Pearson correlation coefficient to examine fruit juice consumption by males and females and assumed the measure has interval or ratio-scale properties, our results would be misleading. For example, using a two-point scale (nonmetric) instead of a five-point scale (metric) substantially reduces the amount of information available and may result in an understatement of the true correlation coefficient in the population.

When scales used to collect data are ordinal (nonmetric), an analyst can use the Spearman rank order (rho) correlation coefficient rather than the Pearson product-moment correlation. The Spearman correlation coefficient typically results in a lower coefficient but is considered a more conservative statistic.

AN EXAMPLE OF THE SPEARMAN RANK ORDER CORRELATION

The survey of restaurant customers collected data on four restaurant selection factors. Customers were asked to rank the following four factors in terms of their importance in selecting a restaurant: food quality, atmosphere, prices, and employees. The survey variables were X_{13} to X_{16} and were measured using ordinal scales (ranking data). Phil Samouel would like to know whether "food quality" rankings are related to "atmosphere" rankings. An answer to this question will help Phil to know whether to emphasize food quality in his advertising or atmosphere, or both variables. This is ordinal data (ranking), so the Pearson correlation cannot be used. Instead, the Spearman rho is the appropriate correlation to use. The null hypothesis is there is no difference in the rankings of the two restaurant selection factors. Instructions on how to use SPSS to calculate the Spearman rho are provided in the Data Analysis box.

■————DATA ANALYSIS————■
Using SPSS to Calculate the Spearman rho Correlation

Using the Samouel's customer database, the SPSS click-through sequence is: ANALYZE → CORRELATE → BIVARIATE. Highlight variables X_{13} and X_{14} and move them to the Variables box. The Pearson correlation is the default along with the Two-tailed test of significance and Flag significant correlations. Unclick the Pearson Correlation and click on Spearman. Then click on OK at the lower left corner of the dialogue box to run the program. The results will be the same as those shown in Exhibit 14.4.

Exhibit 14.4 shows that the correlation between variables X_{13} "food quality," and X_{14} "atmosphere," is –0.801, and the significance level is 0.000. This demonstrates there is a significant, negative relationship between the two restaurant selection factors. The negative correlation means that customers who rank food quality high in importance as a selection factor will rank atmosphere as significantly less important. The restaurant customers rank food quality as very important much more often than atmosphere, as shown in the bar charts in Exhibit 14.5.

Phil now knows that customers rank food quality as relatively more important than atmosphere. But he does not know the rankings of the selection factors in

Exhibit 14.4

Correlation of Food Quality and Atmosphere Using the Spearman rho Nonparametric

Spearman rho		X_{13}, "food quality" ranking	X_{14}, "atmosphere" ranking
X_{13} ranking	Correlation coefficient	1.000	−0.801*
	Sig. (2 tailed)	—	0.000
	N	200	200
X_{14} ranking	Correlation coefficient	−0.801**	1.000
	Sig. (2 tailed)	0.000	—
	N	200	200

*Correlation is significant at the .01 level (2 tailed).

Exhibit 14.5

Bar Charts of Rankings for Food Quality and Atmosphere

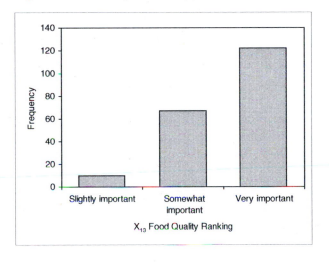

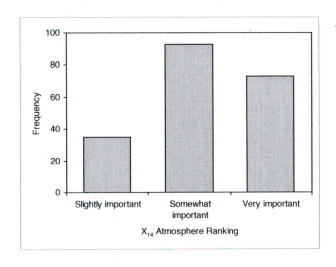

general. Variables X_{13} to X_{16} are ordinal data. Therefore, we cannot compare them by calculating the means. Instead, we must use the median to compare the rankings of the four restaurant selection factors. This will enable us to better understand the relationships.

The rankings are shown in Exhibit 14.6. Recall the four selection factors were ranked from 1 to 4, with 4 = "most important." Thus, the variable with the largest median is ranked the highest and is the most important, and the variable with the lowest median is the least important. "Food quality" (X_{13}) is ranked as the most important (median = 4), while X_{15}, "prices," is the least important (median = 1). Moreover, note that the minimum for variables X_{13} and X_{14} is 2 and for X_{15} and X_{16} it is 1. Thus, based on the median rankings, customers of these two restaurants are interested in food quality first and atmosphere second. Moreover, by comparing the medians we can see that employees and prices are the least important selection factors. This does not mean they are unimportant and can be ignored by Phil, but that relatively speaking food quality and atmosphere are more important. In developing an action plan to compete with Gino's, Phil needs to focus initially on his food, then on atmosphere, and to some extent on his employees (some customers ranked employees most important, as shown by the maximum value of 4).

Exhibit 14.6

Customer Rankings of Restaurant Selection Factors

Statistics		X_{13} "food quality"	X_{14} "atmosphere"	X_{15} "prices"	X_{16} employees
N	Valid	200	200	200	200
	Missing	0	0	0	0
Median		4.00	3.00	1.00	2.00
Minimum		2	2	1	1
Maximum		4	4	3	4

STATISTICAL TECHNIQUES AND DATA ANALYSIS

Most business problems involve many variables. Managers look at multiple performance dimensions when they evaluate their employees. Consumers evaluate many characteristics of products in deciding whether to purchase. Multiple factors influence a broker's recommendation of particular stocks. Restaurant patrons consider many factors in deciding where to dine. As the world becomes more complex, more factors influence the decisions managers make. Thus, increasingly business researchers must rely on more sophisticated methods of data analysis.

Our discussion to this point in the chapter has dealt with **bivariate analysis**, which, unlike **univariate analysis**, involves statistically testing two variables rather than a single variable. When business problems involve three or more variables, they are inherently multidimensional and require the use of multivariate analysis. **Multivariate analysis** involves using statistical methods to analyze multiple variables at the same time. For example, managers trying to better understand their

Exhibit 14.7 **Classification of Statistical Techniques**

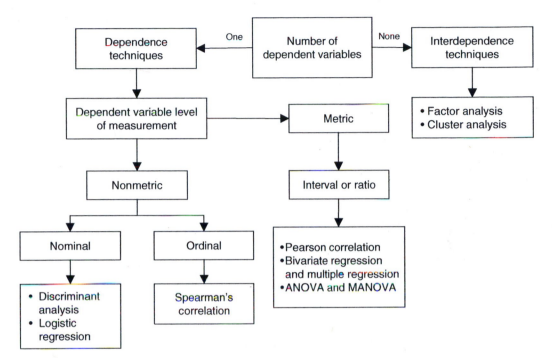

employees might examine job satisfaction, job commitment, work type (part-time versus full-time), shift type (day or night), age, and so on. Similarly, consumers comparing supermarkets might look at the freshness and variety of produce, store location, hours of operation, cleanliness, courtesy and helpfulness of employees, and so forth. Business researchers need multivariate statistical techniques to fully understand such complex problems.

Exhibit 14.7 displays a useful classification of statistical techniques. As you can see looking at the top, we divide the techniques into dependence and interdependence statistical approaches, depending on the number of dependent variables. If there is a single dependent variable, a technique is referred to as a dependence method. That is, we have both dependent and independent variables in our analysis. In contrast, when we do not have a clearly identified dependent variable, we refer to the technique as an interdependence method. That is, when we use interdependence techniques, all variables are analyzed together, and our goal is to form groups or give meaning to a set of variables or respondents. Note also that when we have multiple dependent variables (more than one), the interdependence techniques can also be applied.

Using the classification we can select the appropriate statistical technique. If we have a research problem that involves association or prediction using both dependent and independent variables, we should look at the dependence techniques on the left side of the diagram. The choice of a particular statistical technique also depends on whether we have a metric or nonmetric dependent variable. With nonmetric, ordinal

Exhibit 14.8

Definitions of Statistical Techniques

ANOVA	ANOVA stands for analysis of variance. It is used to examine statistical differences between the means of two or more groups. The dependent variable is metric and the independent variable(s) is nonmetric. One-way ANOVA has a single nonmetric independent variable, and two-way ANOVA can have two or more nonmetric independent variables.
Cluster analysis	Cluster analysis enables researchers to place objects (e.g., customers, brands, products) into groups so that objects in the groups are similar to one another. At the same time, objects in any particular group are different from objects in all other groups.
Correlation	Correlation examines the association between two variables. The strength of the association is measured by the correlation coefficient. a. The *Pearson correlation* is used when the data is interval or ratio in nature. b. The *Spearman rank order correlation* is used for ordinal data.
Discriminant analysis	Discriminant analysis enables the researcher to predict group membership using two or more metric independent variables. The group membership variable is a nonmetric dependent variable.
Factor analysis	Factor analysis is used to summarize the information from a large number of variables into a much smaller number of variables or factors. It is used to combine variables, whereas cluster analysis is used to identify groups with similar characteristics.
MANOVA	MANOVA is the same technique as ANOVA, but it can examine group differences across two or more metric dependent variables at the same time.
Regression	Regression is a technique for measuring linear relationships between two or more variables. Three popular forms of regression are bivariate, multiple, and logistic regression. a. *Bivariate regression* has a single metric dependent variable and a single metric independent variable. b. *Multiple regression* has a single metric dependent variable and several metric independent variables. c. *Logistic regression* is a special type of regression that can have a nonmetric dependent variable.

dependent variables we would use the Spearman correlation, discussed previously. With a nonmetric, nominal dependent we use discriminant analysis or logistic regression. On the other hand, if our dependent variable is metric, we can use correlation, regression, ANOVA, or MANOVA. The various statistical techniques are defined in Exhibit 14.8. In Chapter 13 we discussed ANOVA and MANOVA. In this chapter we discuss correlation and regression. In Chapter 15 we discuss factor analysis, cluster analysis, and discriminant analysis.

REGRESSION ANALYSIS

Regression analysis is perhaps the most widely applied data analysis technique for measuring linear relationships between two or more variables. Correlation tells us if a relationship exists between two variables, as well as the overall strength of the relationship. Sometimes, however, these answers do not provide enough information for management to make the proper decision. For example, Phil Samouel may want to examine the relationship between several work environment measures and the commitment of his employees. Exhibit 14.9 shows the three supervision variables (X_3, X_6, and X_{10}) from the employee survey and one of the commitment variables (X_{14}, "effort"). If Phil Samouel used bivariate regression analysis, he would have to run three regression models, one for each of the three supervision variables. But using multiple regression analysis, Phil could run just one regression model. That is, the metric dependent variable would be X_{14} and the three metric independent variables would be X_3, X_6, and X_{10} (all of these variables measure employee perceptions of supervision at Samouel's Greek Cuisine restaurant).

Exhibit 14.9

Selected Variables from the Samouel's Employee Questionnaire

		Strongly Disagree						Strongly Agree
X_3	My supervisor gives credit and praise for work well done.	1	2	3	4	5	6	7
X_6	My supervisor recognizes my potential.	1	2	3	4	5	6	7
X_{10}	My supervisor is friendly and helpful.	1	2	3	4	5	6	7
X_{14}	I am willing to put in a great deal of effort beyond that normally expected to help Samouel's Greek Cuisine restaurant to be successful.	1	2	3	4	5	6	7

Managers would often like to be able to predict, for example, how much impact an advertising campaign will have on sales. The three typical methods to make these predictions are (1) informed judgment, (2) extrapolation from past behavior, and (3) regression. Informed judgment and extrapolation both assume that past events and behavior will continue into the future. When such past circumstances change, extrapolation and judgment do not help the business researcher predict the future with an acceptable level of accuracy. In such a case, the business researcher needs a technique like regression analysis, which enables the business researcher to predict the future with an assessed level of accuracy.

Our initial discussion will focus on bivariate linear regression. **Bivariate regression** analysis is a statistical technique that makes predictions by examining information about the relationship between one independent (predictor) variable and one dependent (criterion) variable. Values of the independent variable are examined and the behavior of the dependent variable is observed and compared using the formula for a straight line. The formula for linear regression is:

$$Y = a + bX$$

where

Y = the predicted variable

X = the variable used to predict Y

a = the intercept, or point where the line cuts the y axis when $X = 0$

b = the slope or the change in Y for any corresponding change in one unit of X

This is similar to the straight-line relationship we described underlying the correlation coefficient. When the scatter diagram is a straight line, there is a high correlation between the two variables. Regression is directly related to correlation and indeed bivariate regression and correlation analysis may be viewed as being the same.

The task of the business researcher is to find the best method of fitting a straight line to the data. The **least squares method** is a relatively simple mathematical method of ensuring the straight line that runs through the points on the scatter diagram is positioned so as to be the "best" possible. To do this, it minimizes the distances from the straight line to all the points on the scatter diagram. It measures these distances by looking at the errors in predicting Y from X. The least squares criterion minimizes the sum of the squared deviations between the actual values and the straight line predicted by the regression.

We must evaluate certain assumptions when we use regression analysis, just as with correlation. First, regression analysis assumes the relationship between two variables is linear. If the scatter diagram of the values of both variables looks like the plot in Exhibit 14.2b or 14.2c, this assumption would seem to be a good one. If the plot looks like 14.2a, regression analysis is not the appropriate choice.

Second, although we refer to the two variables as independent and dependent, respectively, this does do not mean we can say that one variable causes the behavior of the other. Regression analysis assesses the magnitude and type of association between two variables and makes predictions from this, but it is nothing more than a statistical tool. Although one might be tempted to infer causation from the results of a regression analysis, that would be wrong. Causation must be determined using theory or experimental research, which is beyond the field of pure statistical calculation. Consequently, even though two variables such as sales and advertising are logically related, regression analysis does not permit the business researcher to make cause-and-effect conclusions about them.

The remaining assumptions of simple regression are that the variables are measured using interval or ratio scales and come from normal populations, and, finally, the error terms resulting from the regression are independent and distributed normally. We will cover these assumptions in more detail when we discuss multiple regression. However, an important point is that nominal and ordinal scales can be included in a regression if they are converted to a dummy variable coding. That is discussed later in this chapter.

With bivariate regression analysis, we have one independent variable and one dependent variable. But business researchers are often interested in examining the combined influence of several independent variables on one dependent variable. For example, are purchasing patterns on the Internet related not only to age but also to income, ethnicity, gender, geographic location, education level, and so forth? Similarly, Phil Samouel might want to know whether customer satisfaction at his restaurant is related only to perceptions of the restaurant's food quality (X_1), or is satisfaction also related to perceptions of menu variety (X_9), fun place to go (X_8), reasonable prices (X_{10}), or any of the other perception variables? Multiple regression enables us to measure these relationships without running several separate bivariate regressions. We look first at an example of bivariate, or simple regression analysis, and then move on to multiple regression.

AN EXAMPLE OF BIVARIATE REGRESSION

Phil Samouel regularly reads the American Restaurant Association trade publications to better understand restaurant operations and trends. He consistently sees studies that report food quality as the most important variable used by customers in selecting and deciding to return to a particular restaurant. He wants to know if having high quality food will help him to retain customers and grow his business. Bivariate regression analysis can provide information to help answer this question.

Phil's customer survey collected information on "satisfaction" (X_{17}). This variable was measured as 1 = "not very satisfied" and 7 = "highly satisfied." Variable X_1 was a measure of respondents' perceptions of the quality of food (1 = "strongly disagree" and 7 = "strongly agree"). The null hypothesis in this case is that there is no relationship between X_{17} "satisfaction" and X_1, "excellent food quality." The alternative hypothesis is that X_{17} and X_1 are significantly related. This hypothesis can be tested using bivariate regression because we have a single metric dependent variable and a single metric independent variable. Instructions on how to run bivariate regression are given in the Data Analysis box.

The test results are shown in Exhibit 14.10. Note that we have separated the customer surveys into two groups—customers from Samouel's and customers from Gino's. This enables us to make comparisons between the results for the two restaurants. The upper part of the table displays the mean of Samouel's and Gino's for both the dependent variable, X_{17} (Samouel's = 4.78, Gino's = 5.96) and the independent variable, X_1 (Samouel's = 5.24, Gino's = 5.81). In the lower portion of the table we see that r^2 for Samouel's regression model is .263 and for Gino's is .110. As you may recall from our earlier discussion, r^2 shows the amount of variation in one variable that is accounted for by another variable. In this case, customer perceptions of Samouel's food quality account for 26.3 percent of the total variation in customer satisfaction with the restaurant, while for Gino's it is only 11.0 percent.

There are several other aspects of bivariate regression you need to know about. These include an understanding of the F ratio, the regression and residual sums of squares, and the regression coefficient. Exhibit 14.11 contains this information for the bivariate regression of customer satisfaction and food quality. The table shows the F

Exhibit 14.10

Bivariate Regression of Satisfaction and Food Quality

Descriptive Statistics

$X_{28,}$ "Competitor"		Mean
Samouel's	$X_{17,}$ "Satisfaction"	4.78
	$X_{1,}$ "Excellent Food Quality"	5.24
Gino's	X_{17}	5.96
	X_1	5.81

Model Summary

X_{28}	Model	R	R^2
Samouel's	1	.513	.263
Gino's	1	.331	.110
Predictors	X_1, "Excellent Food Quality"		

■———DATA ANALYSIS———■
Using SPSS to Calculate a Bivariate Regression

Note: Samouel's and Gino's customers are considered separately.

The SPSS software can help us to test the null hypothesis of no relationship between customer satisfaction and food quality. Since we want to look at the customers from the two restaurants separately, we must first use the Data pull-down menu to split the sample into Samouel's and Gino's customers. To do so, go to the Data pull-down menu, click on Compare groups, and then highlight variable $X_{28,}$ "competitor," and move it into the box labeled "Groups based on:" and then click OK. As noted earlier, we do this because Phil wants to compare his restaurant with Gino's.

To run the bivariate regression, the SPSS click-through sequence is: ANALYZE → REGRESSION → LINEAR: Click on $X_{17,}$ "satisfaction," and move it to the Dependent Variable box. Click on $X_{1,}$ "excellent food quality," and move it to the Independent Variables box. Use the default Enter in the box labeled "Method." Click on the Statistics button and use the defaults for Estimates and Model fit, then click on Descriptives. Finally, click Continue and OK to execute the program. The results will be the same as in Exhibit 14.10.

---

ratio for the regression models. This statistic assesses the statistical significance of the overall regression model. Under the "Sum of Squares" column, the variance in $X_{17,}$ "satisfaction" that is associated with X_1 "food quality" is referred to as explained variance (as "regression sum of squares" in the table). The remainder of the total variance in X_{17} that is not associated with X_1 is referred to as unexplained variance (as "residual sum of squares" in the table). The *F* ratio is the result of comparing the amount of explained variance to the unexplained variance. Specifically, if you divide the mean square for the regression (35.001) by the mean square for the residual (1.002), you will get the *F* ratio for Samouel's of 34.945. The larger the *F* ratio, the more variance in the dependent variable is explained by the independent variable.

Exhibit 14.11

Other Aspects of Bivariate Regression

ANOVA

$X_{28,}$ "Competitor"		Sum of Squares	Mean Squares	F	Sig.
Samouel's	Regression	35.001	35.001	34.945	0.000
	Residual	98.159	1.002		
	Total	133.160			
Gino's	Regression	10.310	10.310	12.095	0.001
	Residual	83.530	0.852		
	Total	93.840			
Predictor Variable	$X_{1,}$ "excellent food quality"				
Dependent Variable	$X_{17,}$ "satisfaction"				

Coefficients		Unstandardized Coefficients		Standardized Coefficients			
$X_{28,}$ "Competitor"		B	Std. Error	Beta	t	Sig.	
Samouel's	$X_{1,}$ "food quality"	0.459	0.078	0.513	5.911	0.000	
Gino's	$X_{1,}$ "food quality"	0.284	0.082	0.331	3.478	0.001	
Dependent Variable	$X_{17,}$ "Satisfaction"						

In our bivariate regression example, the F ratio for Samouel's (34.945) indicates the model is highly significant at the 0.000 level. The relationship for Gino's is relatively less significant (F ratio = 12.095) but still very strong (0.001).

The sums of squares also provides useful information for understanding regression. For Samouel's the regression sum of squares is 35.001, and the residual sum of squares is 98.159. For Gino's the regression sum of squares is 10.310, and the residual sum of squares is 83.530. Examination of the regression, residual, and total sums of squares tells us that for both regression models there is a lot of unexplained (residual) variance in the dependent variable. Specifically, to determine the percentage of unexplained variance for a regression model you simply divide the residual variance by the total variance. For Samouel's, you divide 98.159 (residual sum of squares) by 133.160 (total sum of squares) and you find out that 73.7 percent of the total variance is not explained by this bivariate regression model (98.159/133.160 = 0.737). Moreover, if you divide 35.001 (regression sum of squares) by 133.160 (total sum of squares), you find out that 26.3 percent of the total variance is explained by this bivariate regression model (35.001/133.160 = 0.263). Note that dividing the regression sum of squares by the total sum of squares gives you r^2 for this regression model (26.3 percent).

Regression coefficients tell us how much of the variance in the dependent variable is explained by the independent variable. Let's look at the regression coefficient for X_1 for Samouel's restaurant, shown in the lower part of Exhibit 14.11. The column labeled "Unstandardized Coefficients" reveals the unstandardized regression coefficient for X_1 is 0.459. The column labeled "Sig." indicates the statistical significance of the regression coefficient for X_1. The t test tells us whether the regression coefficient is different enough from 0 to be statistically significant. The t statistic is calculated by dividing the regression coefficient by its standard error (labeled "Std. error" in the table). If you divide 0.459 by 0.078, you get a *t* value of 5.911, which is significant at the 0.000 level. (Note that any differences in calculating the numbers are due to rounding errors.)

The relationship between customer satisfaction and food quality for Samouel's is positive but only somewhat strong. The regression coefficient (B) for X_1 is interpreted as, "For every unit that X_1 increases X_{17} will increase by 0.459 units." Recall Phil Samouel wanted to know if excellent quality food would improve customer satisfaction and therefore the ability to attract and retain customers. The answer is "somewhat." The model was significant at the 0.000 level and r^2 was .263, but is this practically significant? An r^2 of .263 suggests Phil should focus on improving his food quality but continue looking for other areas to improve that are also related to customer satisfaction. He must also be concerned because Gino's food is rated as higher in quality (5.81 versus 5.24), and while not as closely related to satisfaction there is still a significant relationship.

The table contains both **"Unstandardized Coefficients"** (B) and **"Standardized Coefficients"** (Beta). We need not be concerned with standardized coefficients in bivariate regression. But in multiple regression, when several independent variables are used, the scales measuring the several independent variables may not always be the same (e.g., using number of salespeople and advertising expenditures to predict sales). **Standardization** is a method of adjusting for different units of measure across variables. In the context, "Beta" refers to regression coefficients that have been standardized.

MULTIPLE REGRESSION ANALYSIS

Recall that in bivariate regression we use a single independent variable to predict a single dependent variable. In multiple regression analysis we enter several independent variables into the same type of regression equation to predict a single dependent variable. A separate regression coefficient is then calculated for each independent variable describing its individual relationship with the dependent variable. These coefficients enable the researcher to evaluate the relative influence of several independent variables on the dependent variable. Multiple regression is a more realistic model because, in the world we live in, prediction depends on multiple factors, not just one.

The relationship between each independent variable and the dependent measure is assumed to be linear, as it was with bivariate regression. The task of the researcher is to find the best means of fitting a straight line to the data. Again, the least squares method is a relatively simple mathematical technique that makes sure the straight line will best represent the relationship between the multiple independent variables and the single dependent variable. The logic of least squares is that no straight line can completely represent every dot in a regression scatter diagram. Even if there were an almost perfect correlation between the variables, there would always be some differences between the actual scores (each dot) and the predicted scores using the regression line. In short, any regression line will produce some errors. The least squares method minimizes the errors in predicting the dependent variable from the independent variables. An *F* test is then used to compare the variance explained by the regression to the unexplained variance (residual), and the result tells us if the overall relationship is statistically significant.

To understand the relationship between the multiple independent variables and the single dependent variable, we examine the regression coefficients for each independent variable. These coefficients describe the average amount of change in *Y* (dependent variable), given a unit change in the independent variable (X_i) being examined. Additionally, a regression coefficient describes the relationship of each independent variable with the dependent variable. For example, assume the dependent variable is the number of bottles of water consumed in an afternoon. The two independent variables are temperature and distance walked. The regression coefficients for both of these independent variables are likely to be rather large because both are logically related to the number of bottles of water consumed.

Because multiple regression is concerned with more than one independent variable, a couple of new issues must be considered. One is whether the independent variables are measured using the same or a different scale. If a different scale is used, we cannot make direct comparisons between the regression coefficients to determine the relative importance of each independent variable in predicting the dependent variable. For example, assume we want to predict annual sales revenue of a Mercedes dealership using number of salespeople and advertising expenditures. These two variables are measured using different scale units. Salespeople are measured using the actual number, and advertising expenditures are measured in dollars. When several independent variables are measured using different scales, it is not proper to directly compare the regression coefficients to see which independent variable most influences the dependent variable.

Since independent variables are often measured using different scale units and business researchers typically want to identify which variables are relatively more important, we must have a way to overcome this problem. To do so, we use the standardized regression coefficient, referred to as a beta coefficient. This standardization process adjusts the regression coefficients to account for the different scales of measurement. Beta coefficients range between −1.00 and +1.00. Using beta coefficients in multiple regression permits making direct comparisons between the independent variables to determine which have the most influence on the dependent variable. The larger the absolute value of a standardized beta coefficient the more relative importance it assumes in predicting the dependent variable.

Another issue we must be concerned about is whether the several independent variables are statistically independent and uncorrelated with one another. If high correlations exist among the independent variables, a multicollinearity problem is considered to exist, particularly in the case of stepwise multiple regression. As a researcher you must test for and remove multicollinearity if it is present. One way is to examine the correlation matrix for the independent variables and use only those that have low correlations. Another approach is to use internal checks included in most software programs that will signal that multicollinearity is a problem and identify where problems exist.

STATISTICAL VERSUS PRACTICAL SIGNIFICANCE

When we discussed bivariate regression, we used the coefficient of determination (denoted as r^2) to see if the variance in the dependent variable was consistently and systematically related to the independent variable. The same concept applies to multiple regression. The term "multiple coefficient of determination" indicates we are measuring the ability of the multiple independent variables to predict the single dependent variable. But when we refer to the **multiple coefficient of determination** (with multiple independent variables) we denote it as R^2. Just as in bivariate regression, the multiple coefficient of determination can be interpreted as the proportion of the variability in the dependent variable that can be explained by the several independent variables in the model.

The first step in examining the overall regression model is to see if it is statistically significant. We do this using the F statistic. If the F statistic is significant, it means it is unlikely your sample will produce a large R^2 when the population R^2 is actually 0. To be considered statistically significant, a rule of thumb is there must be < 0.05 probability the results are due to chance. Some business situations will accept a lower probability level of perhaps < 0.10, but most require a < 0.05 level, and some expect < 0.01.

If R^2 is statistically significant, we then evaluate the strength of the linear association between the dependent variable and the several independent variables. Multiple R^2, also called the multiple coefficient of determination, is a handy measure of the strength of the overall relationship. As you may recall from our discussion of r^2 in the section on correlation analysis, the coefficient of determination is a measure of the amount of variation in the dependent variable associated with the variation in the independent variable. In the case of multiple regression analysis, R^2 shows the amount of variation in the dependent variable associated with all the independent variables considered together (it is also referred to as a measure of the goodness of fit). Multiple R^2 ranges from 0.0 to +1.0 and represents the amount of the dependent variable explained by the independent variables combined. A large multiple R^2 indicates the straight line works well, while a small R^2 indicates the line does not work well.

The larger R^2 the more the dependent variable is associated with the independent variables we are using to predict it. For example, if the multiple R^2 between the numbers of bottles of water consumed in an afternoon (dependent variable) and the independent variables temperature and distance walked is 0.69, that would mean that we can account for, or explain, 69 percent of the variation in bottled water consumption by using the variation in temperature and distance walked. A larger R^2 indicates a stronger relationship between the independent variables and the dependent measure. As before, the measure of the strength of the relationship between an individual independent variable and the dependent measure of interest is shown by the standardized regression coefficient (beta) for that variable. Thus, we would use the beta coefficients to tell us whether temperature or distance walked is a better predictor of bottled water consumption.

Just as we did with bivariate regression, it is necessary in multiple regression to test for the statistical significance of the regression coefficients (betas) for each of the independent variables. Again, we must determine whether sampling error is influencing the regression results. The basic question is still the same: What is the likelihood we would get a coefficient of this size for our sample if the true regression coefficient in the population were 0? SPSS and most other statistical software calculate the t-test statistics for each regression coefficient, so we can easily answer this question. If any of the regression coefficients is not statistically significant, that particular independent variable is not a good predictor of the dependent variable. In other words, an insignificant beta means the relationship is due to sampling error and not a true relationship in the population. In short, the use of an independent variable that has an insignificant beta is meaningless and should be removed from the regression model. Removing insignificant independent variables and rerunning the regression results is the simplest model possible.

In sum, to evaluate the results of a multiple regression analysis do the following: (1) assess the statistical significance of the overall regression model using the F statistic; (2) if the F is significant, then evaluate R^2 to see if it is large enough (see Exhibit 14.11); (3) examine each of the regression coefficients and their t statistics to identify which independent variables have statistically significant coefficients; and (4) rerun the regression using only the significant independent variables and look at the beta coefficients to determine the relative influence of each of the independent variables. If you follow these steps you will have answers to the four basic questions about the relationships between your single dependent variable and your multiple independent variables: Does a relationship exist? If there is a relationship, how strong is it? Is the relationship positive or negative? and If there is a relationship, what is the best way to describe it?

AN EXAMPLE OF MULTIPLE REGRESSION

Phil Samouel would like to predict how satisfied his customers will be while dining in his restaurant based on their experiences. As part of his customer survey, Phil collected information on customer perceptions regarding various characteristics of his restaurant. The first twelve variables in the database are the perception characteristics. They are metric variables and can be used as independent variables in a regression model. The perceptions are measured using a seven-point Likert-type rating scale, with $7 = $ "strongly agree" (favorable) and $1 = $ "strongly disagree" (unfavorable). Variables X_{13} to X_{16} are nonmetric variables because they are ranking data, and it is not appropriate to use them in a regression equation. Variables X_{17}, X_{18}, and X_{19} are metric dependent variables measured on a seven-point Likert-type rating scale. These variables measure customers' reactions to their dining experience, such as satisfaction and likelihood to return in the future. Variable X_{20}, "frequency of eating at," is nonmetric, as are X_{25}, "gender," and X_{28}, "competitor." Thus, Phil's survey has collected information that could be used to develop a multiple regression predictive model that, it is hoped, would be a much better predictor than his judgment or heuristic extrapolation from existing information.

Several empirical studies have shown that food quality is the most important factor in selecting a restaurant. These same studies have shown that when restaurant customers mention food quality they are thinking of taste, proper temperature, good seasoning, variety, and so on. Thus, it is clear Phil Samouel will want to know whether perceptions of his food are related to satisfaction as well as to other outcome vari-

Exhibit 14.12

Selected Variables from Samouel's Customer Questionnaire

		Strongly Disagree						Strongly Agree
X_1	Excellent food quality	1	2	3	4	5	6	7
X_4	Excellent food taste	1	2	3	4	5	6	7
X_9	Wide variety of menu items	1	2	3	4	5	6	7
		Definitely will not return						Definitely will return
X_{18}	How likely are you to return to Samouel's restaurant in the future?	1	2	3	4	5	6	7

ables like recommending the restaurant and returning to it in the future. A multiple regression model can answer these questions. For the initial regression model, we will examine the single dependent metric variable $X_{18,}$ "return in future," and the food independent variables $X_{1,}$ "excellent food quality," $X_{4,}$ "excellent food taste," and $X_{9,}$ "wide variety of menu items." These variables are shown in Exhibit 14.12 as they were used in the survey. The null hypothesis would be that there is no relationship between X_{18} and X_1, X_4, and X_9. The alternative hypothesis would be that X_1, X_4, and X_9 are significantly related to X_{18}.

The results of the initial multiple regression models are shown in Exhibit 14.13. (See the Data Analysis box for instructions on how to run SPSS for this example.) For the example we have divided the sample into two groups, Samouel's customers and Gino's customers, so we can compare them. We show information for each of the multiple regression models. The upper part of the table labeled Descriptive Statistics shows the means of the variables in the regression analysis. Note the means for Samouel's on the independent variables X_1 (5.24), X_4 (5.16), and X_9, (5.45) are above the midpoint of the seven-point scale (4.0) and therefore represent relatively positive perceptions of these attributes. The dependent variable X_{18} (Samouel's = 4.37) is lower but still slightly above the midpoint. What is of concern to Phil, however, is that Gino's customers are more likely to return to his restaurant in the future (mean = 5.55) and on all three food variables Gino's has relatively more positive perceptions. This is information Phil can use to develop an action plan to improve his restaurant.

Information in the lower part of the table labeled Model Summary indicates the R^2 for the regression of Samouel's restaurant is 0.262. This means that 26.2 percent of the variation in "return in future" (dependent variable) can be explained by the three independent variables. In general, R^2 always increases as independent variables are added to a multiple regression model. To avoid overestimating the impact of adding an independent variable to the model, some analysts prefer to use the adjusted R^2 (it recalculates the R^2 based on the number of predictor variables in the model). This makes it easy to compare the explanatory power of regression models with different numbers of independent variables. The adjusted R^2 for the model is 0.239, which indicates only a slight overestimation with this model.

Exhibit 14.13

Multiple Regression of "Return in Future" and Food Independent Variables

Descriptive Statistics

X_{28}, "Competitor"	Variable	Mean
Samouel's	X_{18}, Return in future	4.37
	X_1, Excellent food quality	5.24
	X_4, Excellent food taste	5.16
	X_9, Wide variety of menu items	5.45
Gino's	X_{18}, "Return in future"	5.55
	X_1, "Excellent food quality"	5.81
	X_4, "Excellent food taste"	5.73
	X_9, "Wide variety of menu items"	5.56

Model Summary[a]

X_{28}, "Competitor"	R	R^2	Adjusted R^2
Samouel's	0.512[b]	0.262	0.239
Gino's	0.482[b]	0.232	0.208

[a]Dependent variable: X_{18}, "Return in future"
[b]Predictors: (constant), X_9, X_1, X_4.

■————DATA ANALYSIS————■
Using SPSS to Compute a Multiple Regression Model

Since we will be comparing Samouel's customers' perceptions with those of Gino's, go to the Data pull-down menu to split the sample. Scroll down and click on Split File, then on Compare Groups. Highlight variable X_{28} and move it into the box labeled "Groups based on:" and then click OK. Now you can run the regression.

The SPSS click-through sequence is: ANALYZE → REGRESSION → LINEAR. Highlight X_{18} and move it to the Dependent Variables box. Highlight X_1, X_4, and X_9 and move them to the Independent Variables box. Use the default Enter in the Methods box. Click on the Statistics button and use the defaults for Estimates and Model Fit. Next click on Descriptives and then on Continue. There are several other options you could select at the bottom of this dialogue box, but for now we will use the program defaults. Click on OK at the lower left corner of the dialogue box to run the regression. The results are the same as in Exhibits 14.13 and 14.14.

The remaining diagnostic information for the multiple regression models are shown in Exhibit 14.14. The regression model for Samouel's is statistically significant (F ratio = 11.382; probability level = 0.000). The probability level of 0.000 means that the chances are 0.000 that the regression model results are due to random events instead of a true relationship. The Gino's multiple regression model is also significant at a very high level (0.000). Thus, the food independent variables do predict whether a customer is likely to return in the future for both restaurants. We can therefore reject the null hypothesis of no relationship between the variables.

Information provided in the "Coefficients" section of the table tells us which independent variables are significant predictors of the likelihood of customers' returning

Exhibit 14.14

Other Information for Multiple Regression Models

ANOVA[a]

X_{28}, "Competitor"		Sum of Squares	df	Mean Square	F	Sig.
Samouel's	Regression	28.155	3	9.385	11.382	0.000[b]
	Residual	79.155	96	.825		
	Total	107.310	99			
Gino's	Regression	22.019	3	7.340	9.688	0.000[b]
	Residual	72.731	96	.758		
	Total	94.750	99			

Coefficients[a]		Unstandardized Coefficients		Standardized Coefficients		
X_{28}	"Competitor"	B	Std. Error	Beta	t	Sig.
Samouel's	X_1, "excellent food quality"	0.260	.116	0.324	2.236	0.028
	X_4, "excellent food taste"	0.242	.137	0.291	1.770	0.080
	X_9, "wide variety of menu items"	−0.082	.123	−0.094	−0.668	0.506
Gino's	X_1	0.272	.119	0.316	2.295	0.024
	X_4	0.241	.132	0.264	1.823	0.071
	X_9	−0.053	.125	−0.065	−0.421	0.675

[a]Dependent variable: X_{18}, "return in future"
[b]Predictor variables: X_1, X_4, X_9

in the future. In the "Sig." column, we note that the beta coefficient for Samouel's food quality is significant (0.028). Similarly, with Gino's food quality is the only significant predictor (0.024). Examining the "Standardized coefficients beta" column for Samouel's, we note X_1 is most closely associated with X_{18} (beta = 0.324), and the same situation is true for Gino's (beta = 0.316). For both regression models "excellent food taste" approaches significance but does not meet our criteria of < 0.05. This is based on the use of a two-tailed test, which is discussed later.

A note of caution is in order regarding the beta coefficients and their significance. We have concluded that only one independent variable in each regression model is statistically significant based on the reported significance levels. But levels of significance can vary if there is multicollinearity among the independent variables. Equally, the signs indicating a negative or positive relationship between the independent and dependent variables can be reversed if there is multicollinearity among the independent variables. For this reason, when developing a multiple regression model we always recommend that the simple correlations among the independent and dependent variables be examined closely to ensure the proper interpretation of the findings.

Another concept of importance in interpreting the significance of the regression coefficients is whether a one-tailed or a two-tailed test is used. A **one-tailed test** is used when you can predict the direction of your hypothesized relationship (positive or negative). A **two-tailed test** must be used if you cannot predict the direction of your hypothesized relationship. For example, a one-tailed test would be used to test the hypotheses that "excellent food taste" is positively related to "return in the future," or "excellent food quality" is positively related to "satisfaction." In each case, the hypothesis predicts the direction of the relationship. A two-tailed test would be used to test the hypotheses that there is no relationship between "excellent food taste" and "return in the future" or "excellent food quality" is not related to "satisfaction."

The one-tailed probability is exactly half the value of the two-tailed probability. There is some controversy about whether it is appropriate to use a one-tailed test. It is safer to use two-tailed tests, but there are situations where one-tailed tests seem more appropriate. For example, we recommend a one-tailed test in examining the relationship between "excellent food taste" and "return in the future" for the two restaurants. Since SPSS reports the two-tailed test results, and if we divide the level of significance in half (Samouel's food taste significance = 0.080/2 = 0.040), we can then conclude that indeed perceptions of "excellent food taste" are significantly related to likelihood of returning in the future. Thus, the researcher can choose whether to use one-tailed or two-tailed tests depending on the research situation.

We interpret regression coefficients somewhat differently in multiple regression than we did in bivariate regression. In bivariate regression we interpret the unstandardized regression coefficient as the amount of change in the dependent variable for every one unit of change in the independent variable. But in multiple regression this interpretation must be modified somewhat. In our example above, if we use the beta coefficient for Samouel's X_1, we would say the dependent variable would change 0.324 for every one unit of change in food quality when all other independent variables are constant. Thus, 0.324 is the estimated increase in likelihood to return to the restaurant in the future associated with a one-unit increase in food quality when food taste and variety of menu items are constant. Note the signs of the coefficients are interpreted the same as in a correlation coefficient. Thus, with more positive perceptions of food quality there is an increased likelihood to return in the future. This is consistent with the mean value of 5.24 for food quality, indicating Samouel's customers are relatively happy with his food. Similar findings were found for Gino's, but it should be noted that Gino's food quality is perceived to be somewhat higher (5.81) than Samouel's.

This means we can reject both null hypotheses that the three food independent variables are not associated with X_{18} for Samouel's and Gino's restaurants. For example, using the beta coefficient for food quality, we can conclude that every time X_1 increases by one unit, X_{18} will increase on average by 0.324 units for Samouel's and 0.316 units for Gino's, assuming the other variables are constant. If we apply the one-tailed test for food taste, it is significant, too, but "wide variety of menu items" is not. Thus, since two of the three variables are significant, we can conclude that perceptions of food are definitely a predictor of likelihood to return in the future.

Two other problems remain. The first problem is the initial regression model for Samouel's explains only about 26.2 percent of the variation in X_{18} (23.2 percent in the case of Gino's), so we need to consider other independent variables that might help us increase the predictive capability of our regression model, such as the other perceptions variables. Increasing the predictive capability of our regression by adding other independent variables will help Phil Samouel to develop a more effective business plan to compete with Gino's. The second problem is Gino's customers are more likely to return to his restaurant (5.55 versus 4.37), so Phil's business plan must address this issue as well.

MULTICOLLINEARITY AND MULTIPLE REGRESSION

In our discussion of multiple regression we have used the term "independent variable" to refer to any variable being used to predict or explain the value of the dependent variable. This does not mean the independent variables are independent in a statistical sense. Indeed, most independent variables in multiple regression are correlated. **Multicollinearity** in multiple regression analysis refers, therefore, to the correlation among the independent variables.

Multicollinearity can cause a number of problems in regression. For example, the F test of the overall multiple regression model may indicate a statistically significant relationship. But when we examine the t tests for the individual coefficients, we may find none of them is significant. If this happens it is not possible to determine the individual effect of any particular independent variable on the dependent variable. In addition, in some cases multicollinearity will cause the regression coefficients to have a sign opposite that of the actual relationship (i.e., a negative relationship when in reality the relationship is positive). Thus, with a high degree of multicollinearity we cannot rely on the individual coefficients to interpret the results. Multicollinearity problems do not have an impact on the size of R^2 or on your ability to predict values of the dependent variable. But they certainly can affect the statistical significance of the individual regression coefficients and your ability to use them to explain the relationships.

So how do we know when multicollinearity is too high? A general rule of thumb adopted by statisticians is a correlation coefficient between two independent variables greater than ± 0.60 is evidence of potential problems with multicollinearity. Indeed, when there are several independent variables, all of which are intercorrelated, multicollinearity can be a problem at levels lower than ± 0.60. When this situation exists you should remove one or more of the independent variables from the regression model and rerun it, or combine the highly correlated variables into a single summated variable.

Statisticians have developed more precise tests than the above rule of thumb to determine whether multicollinearity is high enough to cause problems, but these tests are beyond the scope of this book. They are the tolerance and VIF tests. For more information on these tests, see the book's Web site, at www.mesharpe-student.com.

AN EXAMPLE OF MULTICOLLINEARITY

Phil Samouel certainly needs to know whether multicollinearity is a problem in his regression models. An assessment of multicollinearity is necessary to ensure that he can interpret the relative importance of the individual independent variables in the regression models. Based on conversations with his consultant he wants to examine whether compensation issues are related to the loyalty of his employees. He collected information related to this on his employee survey, and we will use that to answer this question. To do so, we will use the single dependent metric variable X_{13}, "loyalty," and the three metric independent variables X_1, "paid fairly," X_9, "pay reflects effort," and X_{12}, "benefits are reasonable." These variables are shown in Exhibit 14.15 as they appear on the employee questionnaire. The null hypothesis is that there is no relationship between X_{13} and the three independent variables. We will test this hypothesis using multiple regression analysis. The instructions on how to use SPSS to examine this relationship are provided in the Data Analysis box.

Exhibit 14.15

Compensation and Loyalty Variables from the Samouel's Employee Questionnaire

		Strongly Disagree						Strongly Agree
X_1	I am paid fairly for the work I do.	1	2	3	4	5	6	7
X_9	My pay reflects the effort I put into doing my work.	1	2	3	4	5	6	7
X_{12}	The benefits I receive are reasonable.	1	2	3	4	5	6	7
X_{13}	I have a sense of loyalty to Samouel's Greek Cuisine restaurant.	1	2	3	4	5	6	7

■———DATA ANALYSIS———■
Multiple Regression and Multicollinearity

The SPSS click-through sequence is: ANALYZE → REGRESSION → LINEAR. Highlight X_{13} and move it to the Dependent Variables box. Highlight X_1, X_9, and X_{12} and move them to the Independent Variables box. Use the default Enter in the Methods box. Click on the Statistics button, and use the defaults for Estimates and Model Fit. Next click on Descriptives and then on Continue. There are several other options you could select at the bottom of this dialogue box, but for now we will use the program defaults. Click on OK on the lower left corner of the dialogue box to run the regression. The results are shown in Exhibits 14.16 and 14.17.

The results from running the multiple regression model are shown in Exhibits 14.16 and 14.17. Information from the Model Summary section of the table in Exhibit 14.16 indicates the R^2 for the model is 0.249. Looking at the ANOVA section of the table we see that the model is highly significant (0.001). The next question is: Which of the three independent variables are contributing to the predictive ability of this regression model and how? To determine this we look at the "Coefficients" section of the table in Exhibit 14.16. Recall the beta coefficients tell us which independent variables contribute the most to explaining the relationship between the dependent and independent variables. Variables X_1 and X_9 are statistically significant (< 0.05). The third independent variable, X_{12}, is not significant in this regression model. The coefficients information thus suggests that only two of the independent variables are statistically significant in this model. But does that mean the other variable is not

Exhibit 14.16

Summary Statistics for Employee Regression Compensation Model

Model Summary

Model	R	R^2	Adjusted R^2	Std. Error of the Estimate
1	0.499[b]	.249	.211	.859

ANOVA[a]

Model		Sum of Squares	df	Mean Square	F	Sig.
1	Regression	14.468	3	4.823	6.536	0.001[b]
	Residual	43.532	59	0.738		
	Total	58.000	62			

Coefficients[b]	Unstandardized coefficients		Standardized coefficients		
Variables	B	Std. Error	Beta	t	Sig.
X_1, "paid fairly"	0.739	0.251	0.699	2.945	0.005
X_9, "pay reflects effort"	−0.625	0.299	−0.491	−2.090	0.041
X_{12}, "benefits reasonable"	0.110	0.377	0.093	0.292	0.771

[a]Dependent variable: X_{13}, "loyalty"
[b]Predictor variables: X_{12}, X_9, X_1

Exhibit 14.17

Bivariate Correlations

	X_{13}, "loyalty"	X_1, "paid fairly"	X_9, "pay reflects effort"	X_{12}, "benefits reasonable"
Pearson correlation				
X_{13}	1.000	0.407	0.124	0.278
X_1	0.407	1.000	0.763	0.880
X_9	0.124	0.763	1.000	0.877
X_{12}	0.278	0.880	0.877	1.000
Sig. (1 tailed)				
X_{13}	—	0.000	0.166	0.014
X_1	0.000	—	0.000	0.000
X_9	0.166	0.000	—	0.000
X_{12}	0.014	0.000	0.000	—

related to the dependent variable? Not necessarily. Another problem is the sign of the beta for X_9. This is not logical because it suggests that employees who are less favorable about their pay are more loyal. We need to look further to explain these results and understand the regression model.

To understand the multicollinearity issue, let's look at the bivariate correlations between the variables shown in Exhibit 14.17. The top of the table shows the correlations and the bottom half the level of significance. Two of the three compensation variables are significantly correlated with the dependent variable "loyalty." With regard to multicollinearity between the independent variables, there are definitely some problems. The correlation between variables X_1 and X_{12} is 0.88, between X_1 and X_9 it is 0.763, and between X_9 and X_{12} the correlation is 0.877. In other words, all three of the bivariate correlations are above the recommended 0.60. Thus, multicollinearity has influenced this regression model. The information provided on the significance of the betas (Exhibit 14.16) indicates that variable X_{12} is not related to the dependent variable when in fact it may be related, and variable X_9 has a negative sign for the beta when in fact the sign is positive based on the bivariate correlations. These findings need to be explored further.

The problems of multicollinearity in regression can be assessed by examining the correlations between the independent variables. If any are too high (> 0.60), you could remove one or more of the highly correlated variables from the regression model. But how do you decide which independent variable to remove? One possibility is to first identify the independent variables that are most closely related to one another (highest correlation). Then keep the independent variable in your regression model that is most highly correlated with the dependent variable. Another approach is to run regression models with all combinations of variables and see which model has the largest R^2. A third possibility is to create new summated variables from the independent variables that are highly correlated. Each regression model involves different issues, so each situation must be considered in light of the research objectives and constraints.

ADVANCED TOPICS IN MULTIPLE REGRESSION

Multiple regression is a very useful statistical technique in business research. Entire books have been written about the topic, so many issues are too advanced for this book. If you wish to learn more, take a look at some of the sources cited at the end of this chapter. You could also go to the Web site for this book, www.mesharpe-student .com, where we provide additional material on topics like advanced diagnostics to examine multicollinearity, stepwise regression, dealing with residuals, and so on.

THE ROLE OF DUMMY VARIABLES IN REGRESSION

A dummy independent variable is a variable that has two (or more) distinct levels, which are coded 0 and 1. Dummy coded variables enable us to use independent variables not measured using interval or ratio scales to predict the dependent variable. For example, if you wanted to include the gender of customers of the two restaurants to understand satisfaction with the restaurant, it is obvious your measure for gender includes only two possible categories, male and female. In this case, we could use gender in a regression model by coding males as 0 and females as 1. Similarly, we might have purchasers versus nonpurchasers and include them as an independent variable using the same 0 and 1 coding method. This represents a slight but acceptable violation of the assumption of metric scaling for the independent variables.

To use dummy variables we must choose one category of the variable to serve as a reference category and then add as many dummy variables as there are possible values of the variable, minus the reference category. Each category is coded as either 0 or 1.

In the example above, if you choose the male category as the reference category, you will have one dummy variable for the female category. That dummy variable would be assigned the value of 1 for females and 0 for males. In the restaurant employee database, X_{19}, "gender," is already coded as a dummy variable for gender using males as the reference category (males are coded 0).

We can also use dummy coding with categorical independent variables that have more than two categories. Let's say you wanted to use an independent variable like "occupation," and you have physicians, attorneys, and professors in your sample. To use dummy variables in your regression, you choose one category as a reference group (physicians) and add two dummy variables for the remaining categories. The variables would be coded as follows, using 0 and 1:

Category	X_1	X_2
Physician	0	0
Attorney	1	0
Professor	0	1

As is shown in the table, when the respondent is a physician, X_1 and X_2 will be 0 (the reference category is always coded 0). For attorneys, the regression coefficient for X_1 represents the difference in the dependent variable compared with physicians. The regression coefficient associated with X_2 represents the difference in the dependent variable for professors compared with physicians.

AN EXAMPLE OF DUMMY VARIABLES

To enable him to prepare a better business plan, Phil wants to know more about his employees and what he can do to increase their productivity and commitment to working at his restaurant. In the employee survey Phil gathered data on the employee work environment, commitment to the restaurant, likelihood of searching for another job, and selected demographic information, such as gender. As stated above, gender is coded as a dummy variable, with 0 = male and 1 = female.

To investigate the relationship between work environment and job commitment, we will use X_{13}, "loyalty," as the dependent variable in a regression model and two of the metric work environment variables used in the preceding multicollinearity example. The two variables we use are X_1, "paid fairly," and X_9, "pay reflects effort." We delete X_{12}, "benefits are reasonable," from this regression model because of the previously identified multicollinearity problems. In addition to the work environment variables, however, Phil wants to determine if the gender of his employees influences their loyalty to the restaurant. Therefore, we also include X_{19}, "gender" (coded male = 0 and female = 1), in our regression model.

Results of the multiple regression analysis are shown in the Exhibits 14.18 and 14.19. R^2 for the model is .597, as shown in the top of the table in Exhibit 14.18. Thus, approximately .597 percent of the total variation in X_{13} can be predicted by X_1, X_9, and X_{19}. The regression model is highly significant, with a probability level of 0.000, as revealed in the ANOVA section of the table.

Exhibit 14.18

Regression Model of Samouel's Employees Using Work Environment and Gender as Independent Variables and Loyalty as a Dependent Variable

Model Summary[a]

R	R^2	Adjusted R^2
0.773	0.597	0.577

ANOVA[b]

	Sum of Squares	df	Mean Square	F	Sig.
Regression	34.638	3	11.546	29.159	0.000
Residual	23.362	59	0.396		
Total	58.000	62			

Coefficients[b]	Unstandardized Coefficients		Standardized Coefficients		
	B	Std. Error	Beta	t	Sig.
X_1, "paid fairly"	0.579	0.138	0.548	4.186	0.000
X_9, "pay reflects effort"	−0.351	0.166	−0.275	−2.117	0.038
X_{19}, "gender"	1.205	0.169	0.605	7.148	0.000

[a]Predictor variables: X_{19}, X_1, X_9
[b]Dependent variable: X_{13}, "loyalty"

■———DATA ANALYSIS———■
Using SPSS to Examine Dummy Variables

The SPSS click-through sequence is: ANALYZE → REGRESSION → LINEAR. Click on X_{13}, "loyalty," and move it to the Dependent Variables box. Click on X_1, X_9, and X_{19} and move them to the Independent Variables box. The box labeled "Method" has ENTER as the default, and we will use it. Click on the Statistics button and use the Estimates and Model fit defaults. Click on Descriptives, then on Continue and OK to run the regression. The results will be the same as shown in Exhibit 14.18.

The lower half of Exhibit 14.18 reveals that X_{19} is a significant and strong predictor of X_{13}, with a beta coefficient of 0.605 (probability of 0.000). X_1 is also significant (0.000) and strong, with a beta coefficient of 0.548, as is X_9, which has only a moderately strong beta coefficient of −0.275 but is still significant (0.038). Thus, gender is the best predictor of loyalty, but the work environment variables are also important in predicting loyalty.

Note that the sign (+/−) for the gender beta is positive, meaning that higher values of the gender variable are associated with higher loyalty. Since females are coded 1 and males 0, this means that females are more loyal than males. The means shown in Exhibit 14.19 confirm this.

To explain the results for gender, let's compare male and female employees' re-

Exhibit 14.19

Comparison of Male and Female Employees

Descriptives	X_{19}, "Gender"	N	Mean	Std. deviation
X_1, "paid fairly"	Males	40	4.18	.903
	Females	23	4.39	.941
	Total	63	4.25	.915
X_9, "pay reflects effort"	Males	40	4.53	.716
	Females	23	4.48	.846
	Total	63	4.51	.759
X_{13}, "loyalty"	Males	40	5.18	.747
	Females	23	6.52	.665
	Total	63	5.67	.967

ANOVA	Sum of Squares	df	Mean Square	F	Sig.
$X_1 * X_{19}$					
Between Groups	0.683	1	0.683	0.813	0.371
Within Groups	51.253	61	0.840		
Total	51.937	62			
$X_9 * X_{19}$					
Between Groups	0.032	1	0.032	0.054	0.816
Within Groups	35.714	61	0.585		
Total	35.746	62			
$X_{13} * X_{19}$					
Between Groups	26.486	1	26.486	51.267	0.000
Within Groups	31.514	61	0.517		
Total	58.000	62			

■————DATA ANALYSIS————■
Using SPSS to Compare Group Means

Using SPSS, it is simple to compare the responses of male and female employees. The SPSS click-through sequence is: ANALYZE → COMPARE MEANS → MEANS. Click on X_{13}, "loyalty," and X_1 and X_9 and move them to the Dependent List box. Now click on X_{19}, "gender," and move it to the Independent List box. Click on the box labeled "Options" and then at the bottom left-hand corner of the screen click on ANOVA and eta, then click Continue and OK to run the program. The results are the same as in Exhibit 14.19.

---

sponses. The results of this comparison are in Exhibit 14.19. As you can see, females are relatively more favorable (higher mean) concerning X_1 and less favorable about X_9, but the differences are not statistically significant. Differences are significant only for X_{13} "loyalty" (as apparent in the ANOVA part of the table). Thus, females are significantly more loyal to Samouel's restaurant than males. This finding suggests that Phil needs to learn more about male and female employees and why they differ in their feelings about working at Samouel's restaurant. Indeed, he needs to go beyond these variables and look at all aspects of working at the restaurant.

Summary

Describe the Nature of Relationships Between Variables

There are four basic concepts we need to understand about relationships between variables: presence, type of relationship, direction, and strength of association. Presence concerns whether a systematic relationship exists between two or more variables. We rely on the concept of statistical significance to measure whether a relationship is present. The second important concept is type of relationship. We typically say there are two types of relationships, linear and nonlinear. A linear relationship is a straight line association between two or more variables. A nonlinear relationship, often referred to as curvilinear, is one in which the relationship is best described by a curve instead of a straight line. If a relationship is present between the variables, we also need to know its direction. The direction of a relationship can be either positive or negative. Finally, when a relationship is present, the business researcher must determine the strength of the association. Depending on the type of relationship being examined, we generally categorize the strength of association as slight, small but definite, moderate, high, or very strong.

Explain the Concepts of Correlation and Regression Analysis

Correlation analysis calculates the association between two variables. The Pearson correlation measures the linear association between two metric variables. The number representing the Pearson correlation is referred to as a correlation coefficient. It ranges from −1.00 to +1.00, with 0 representing absolutely no association between the two metric variables. While −1.00 or +1.00 is possible and either represents a perfect association between two variables, it seldom occurs. A stronger link or level of association is reflected in a larger absolute magnitude correlation coefficient. Correlation coefficients can be either positive or negative, depending on the direction of the relationship between the variables. If there is a positive correlation coefficient between X and Y, then increases in the value of X are associated with increases in the value of Y, and vice versa.

Managers would often like to be able to predict, for example, how much impact an advertising campaign will have on sales. The three typical methods to make such a prediction are (1) informed judgment, (2) heuristic extrapolation from past behavior, and (3) regression. Although all three techniques use historical data and therefore assume that past events and behavior will continue into the future, regression analysis allows the business researcher to predict the future with an assessed level of accuracy.

Regression analysis is perhaps the most widely applied data analysis technique for measuring linear relationships between two or more variables. Correlation tells us if a relationship exists between two variables, as well as the overall strength of the relationship. Sometimes, however, these answers do not provide enough information for management to make the proper decision. For example, Phil Samouel may want to examine how both the atmosphere and food variables are related to satisfaction, instead of examining the variables one at a time. In such a case we use regression analysis because it enables us to use several independent variables to predict a single dependent variable.

CLARIFY THE DIFFERENCE BETWEEN BIVARIATE AND MULTIPLE REGRESSION ANALYSES

Bivariate regression has only two variables: a single metric dependent variable and a single metric independent variable. Multiple regression has a single metric dependent variable and several metric independent variables. In bivariate regression the coefficient of determination is r^2. In multiple regression the multiple coefficient of determination is R^2.

UNDERSTAND HOW MULTICOLLINEARITY CAN INFLUENCE REGRESSION MODELS

Multicollinearity can cause a number of problems with regression. For example, the F test of the overall multiple regression model may indicate a statistically significant relationship. But when we examine the t tests for the individual coefficients, we may find none of them is significant. If this happens it is not possible to determine the individual effect of any particular independent variable on the dependent variable. Multicollinearity problems do not have an impact on the size of R^2 or on your ability to predict values of the dependent variable. But they can certainly affect the statistical significance of the individual regression coefficients.

So how do we know when multicollinearity is too high? A general rule of thumb adopted by statisticians is that a sample correlation coefficient between two independent variables with an absolute value greater than 0.60 is evidence of potential problems with multicollinearity. But statisticians have developed more precise tests than this rule of thumb to determine whether multicollinearity is high enough to cause problems. The tests are referred to as the tolerance and VIF tests. The results of the tests can be examined using SPSS and other statistical software packages.

DESCRIBE HOW TO USE DUMMY VARIABLES IN REGRESSION

A dummy independent variable is a variable that has two (or more) distinct levels, which are coded 0 and 1. Coded dummy variables enable us to use qualitative independent variables not measured using interval or ratio scales to predict the dependent variable. For example, if you wanted to include the gender of customers of the two restaurants to understand satisfaction with the restaurant, it is obvious your measure for gender includes only two possible categories, male and female. In this case, we could use gender in a regression model by coding males as 0 and females as 1. Similarly, we might have purchasers versus nonpurchasers and include them as an independent variable using the same 0 and 1 coding approach. This represents a slight but acceptable violation of the assumption of metric scaling for the independent variables.

To use dummy variables we must choose one category of the variable to serve as a reference category and then add as many dummy variables as there are possible values of the variable, minus the reference category. Each category is coded as either 0 or 1. In the example above, if you choose the male category as the reference category, you will have one dummy variable for the female category. That dummy variable would be assigned the value of 1 for females and 0 for males. We can also use dummy coding with categorical independent variables that have more than two categories.

ETHICAL DILEMMA

The telephone company offers a variety of services. A business research firm is hired to determine the level of customer satisfaction by target audience with its land-based telephone service, its wireless service, and its Internet services. Terry Brown, the firm's lead researcher, uses Pearson's correlation to calculate the relationships in the survey data. When checking the results before preparing the first draft of the executive summary, Terry's assistant notices that she has included the outliers in some calculations and not in others. Does this inconsistency affect the validity of the research? What should Terry's assistant do?

REVIEW QUESTIONS

1. What is the value of a correlation coefficient in measuring relationships between variables?
2. What is the difference between the statistical techniques of correlation and regression?
3. Explain the relationship between explained and unexplained variance in multiple regression.

DISCUSSION AND APPLICATION QUESTIONS

1. Why would a business researcher use multiple regression instead of bivariate regression?
2. Why is it important to understand multicollinearity when using multiple regression?
3. *SPSS Application:* With the customer database, use X_{17} "satisfaction," as the dependent variable and X_1 to X_{12} as independent variables. Split your sample by X_{28} "competitor," and run a multiple regression to determine the predictive capability for all twelve metric independent variables.
4. *SPSS Application:* Do the same as in question 3, but now select the stepwise option. Which independent variables are included in the final regression model? How does R^2 differ from what you found in question 3?
5. *SPSS Application:* Calculate the median and modal responses for the restaurant selection factors (X_{13}–X_{16}). Compare the responses of male and female customers. Are the rankings the same? If not, how do they differ and how would Phil use this information in preparing his business plan?

INTERNET EXERCISES

1. Use the Google and Yahoo! search engines. Type in the key words "multiple regression." Prepare a brief report of what you found and how the search results differed.

2. The Federal Reserve Bank of St. Louis has a database called FRED (Federal Reserve Economic Data). Go to their Web site, http://research.stlouisfed.org/fred/abotfred.html, and report what you find. Review the variables they provide information for and select a variable to be used as a dependent variable in a multiple regression model. Now look at the variables again and select several variables to use as the multiple independent variables to predict the dependent variable you chose. Prepare a brief report summarizing your logic in selecting the variables.

3. Go to http://www.statpac.com/surveys/statistical-significance.htm. Prepare a report on the concept of statistical significance. Distinguish between one-tailed and two-tailed tests of significance based on the information provided.

4. Go to www.surveysystem.com/correlation.htm. Prepare a brief report on the discussion of correlation.

NOTE

1. The coefficient of determination can also indicate how much of the variation in the dependent variable can be explained by a group of independent variables. This is explained further later in the chapter as part of multiple regression.

SUGGESTED READINGS

Cohen, J., S. West, L. Aiken, and P. Cohen. *Applied Multiple Regression/Correlation Analysis for the Behavioral Sciences*. 3rd ed. Hillsdale, NJ: Erlbaum, 2002.

Hair, J.F., B. Black, B. Babin, and R. Anderson. *Multivariate Data Analysis*. 7th ed. Upper Saddle River, NJ: Prentice Hall, 2010.

Johnson, R.A., and D. Wichern. *Applied Multivariate Statistical Analysis*. 5th ed. Upper Saddle River, NJ: Prentice Hall, 2002.

Neter, J., M.H. Kutner, W. Wassermann, and C.J. Nachtsheim. *Applied Linear Regression Models*. 3rd ed. Chicago: Irwin, 1996.

15 Other Multivariate Techniques

LEARNING OUTCOMES

1. Explain the difference between dependence and interdependence techniques
2. Understand how to use factor analysis to simplify data analysis
3. Demonstrate the usefulness of cluster analysis
4. Understand when and how to use discriminant analysis

Research projects sometimes include **data reduction** or simplification in their objectives. In such cases, we use statistical techniques that do not designate variables as either dependent or independent. Rather, they analyze only the dependent variables or only the independent variables. The two techniques appropriate in these situations are factor analysis and cluster analysis. The first technique we cover in this chapter is factor analysis. It is used for data summarization. The second technique discussed, cluster analysis, can be used to identify homogeneous subgroups of the total sample.

In the previous chapter, we showed you how to assess predictive capability using regression analysis with a single metric dependent variable and one or more metric independent variables. We did not, however, examine how to assess predictive capability when there is a single nonmetric dependent variable and several metric independent variables. The appropriate statistical technique in this situation is discriminant analysis. This is the third technique we discuss in this chapter.

The statistical techniques of multiple regression and discriminant analysis are referred to as dependence techniques. That is because the variables are divided into independent and dependent sets for analysis purposes. Sometimes we want to look at only one set of variables at a time to simplify or better understand them.

In such a case we analyze only the independent variables or only the dependent variables, instead of both sets at the same time. When we use a statistical technique with only one set of variables at a time, it is referred to as an interdependence technique. Factor analysis and cluster analysis are interdependence techniques. The Business Research Dashboard tells you how these and other multivariate statistical techniques are being used by many organizations to improve their decision making.

EXPLORATORY FACTOR ANALYSIS

Factor analysis is a multivariate statistical technique that can summarize the information from a large number of variables into a much smaller number of variables or factors. It is often referred to as exploratory factor analysis, or EFA, because the technique explores data patterns to identify the factors. By identifying latent (not easily identifiable) relationships and combining variables into a smaller number of factors, exploratory factor analysis simplifies our understanding of the data. When you use exploratory factor analysis the variables are not divided into dependent and independent categories. Instead, all variables are analyzed together to identify underlying patterns or factors. The technique can be used to factor analyze either independent or dependent variables considered separately.

Let's begin our discussion of exploratory factor analysis with an intuitive example. McDonald's has over 30,000 restaurants worldwide, while Burger King has only about 12,000. Burger King would like to close that gap and has set as a goal of opening 500 new restaurants each year worldwide. To do that they believe a survey to determine restaurant selection factors for McDonald's customers versus Burger King customers would help develop a marketing strategy to gain market share from McDonald's and attract customers to the new restaurants. Burger King surveyed 1,000 current and potential fast food customers and asked them to rate Burger King and McDonald's on six selection factors—taste, portion size, freshness, friendliness of employees, courtesy, and competence. The ratings of six customers who answered the survey are shown in Exhibit 15.1 (p. 388). Customers who gave lower ratings on friendliness also gave lower ratings on competence and courtesy. Likewise, when you examine the ratings of taste, portion size, and freshness, you can see the ratings are quite high on all three variables. From a visual inspection of the ratings, therefore, the six measures can be combined into two composite factors called food and employees. (See Exhibit 15.2, p. 388.)

As demonstrated by the above example, factor analysis enables us to examine the underlying relationships for a large number of variables and combine them into a smaller set of composite factors. Factor analysis is a statistical technique that develops linear combinations of variables that summarize the original variables based on their underlying patterns (latent relationships). For the above example, it was easy to visually see the relationships because we had only six respondents and six variables. But with larger numbers of variables and respondents we clearly would need a computer to use exploratory factor analysis.

■————**Business Research Dashboard**————■
Giving Credit Where Credit Is Due

Who decides whether you can afford to buy a new home or new car? These days, it's more likely to be a "what" than a "who"—a computer program based on mathematical figures that provides a score rating you as credit worthy or a credit risk. More and more, lenders, merchants, and even many insurers consider a customer's credit score a critical tool for predicting whether they'll make money on that customer. The scores are based on complex and closely guarded mathematical assumptions developed by Fair Isaac Corporation, based in San Rafael, California, and calculated using multivariate statistical methods. In fact, the company leads the industry so completely that credit scores are frequently referred to as FICO scores, after the company's initials.

What exactly is credit scoring? It's a three-digit number derived in part from a borrower's credit history. The FICO formula was developed by comparing past and current financial information provided by the country's three major credit bureaus—Equifax, Experian, and Trans Union—on a large sampling of consumers and then using that information to make predictions about future behavior. This information helps determine whether the borrower's tendencies match those of borrowers who default on debt, declare bankruptcy, or end up in other types of financial trouble.

The secret to an individual's FICO score isn't any single piece of information but how the different variables interact. According to the company's Web site (http://www.fairisaac.com), the consumer's payment history and debt load account for, respectively, 35 percent and 30 percent of the score. The other 35 percent is determined by how long the consumer has had credit, how actively the consumer is looking for new credit, and the types of credit the consumer uses. On the FICO scale, the higher the score the better. A low score of 300 indicates that a consumer is a poor credit risk, while a high score of 850 represents a model borrower. According to the company, the median score is approximately 720.

So how do you find out what many lenders already know about your FICO rating? After receiving political and consumer pressure, the company launched http://www.myfico.com, a Web site that gives consumers access to their personal FICO scores. For a fee of $12.95, a consumer gets thirty days of online access to her or his FICO report. According to the company, more than 1.5 million consumers have paid for the service, which it operates as a joint venture with Equifax. In addition to their scores, consumers who buy the basic service get a copy of their Equifax credit report and a general explanation of the factors that might be contributing to lower credit scores. Future upgrades to the site include an online calculator that will let consumers see how seven key variables could affect their FICO score. For example, according to a prototype of the service, a consumer with a 707 score could raise it by as much as twenty points by paying down $750 on $2,230 in credit-card balances.

The multivariate statistical methods being used by Fair Isaac to develop its scoring models are being incorporated by many businesses as well as other organizations, like the Internal Revenue Service, which uses them to identify which companies and individuals to audit. Keep in mind that in today's business environment, it's just as important to understand the relationship among variables as it is to gather the information in the first place. Thus, the importance of multivariate statistical methods used to understand relationships has increased dramatically in recent years.

Source: Ruth Simon, "Numbers Game: Looking to Improve Your 'Credit Score'?" *Wall Street Journal* (March 19, 2002), A1; *Morning Advocate* (September 30, 2001), 4I; "FICO," Fair Isaac Corporation, http://www.fico.com/en/Pages/default.aspx, accessed July 2010.

Exhibit 15.1

Ratings of Fast Food Restaurants

Respondent	Taste	Portion size	Freshness	Friendly	Courteous	Competent
#1	9	8	7	4	3	4
#2	8	7	8	4	5	3
#3	7	8	9	3	4	3
#4	8	9	7	4	4	3
#5	7	8	7	3	3	3
#6	9	7	8	5	4	5

Exhibit 15.2 **Factor Analysis of Restaurant Selection Factors**

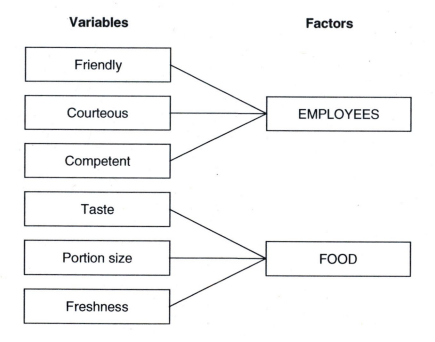

DERIVING FACTORS

A **factor** is a linear combination of the original variables. The first factor derived is the combination of variables that accounts for more of the variance in the data as a whole than any other linear combination of the original variables. The second factor accounts for the most residual (leftover or remaining) variance after the first factor has been extracted. Each subsequent factor accounts for less variance than the earlier ones but is still the best in terms of accounting for the largest amount of the residual variance.

To derive factors the analyst must first answer two questions:

1. What kind of factor model should be used?
2. How should the initial factor solution be rotated to make it easier to interpret?

There are two basic factor models. One is referred to as principal component analysis and the other is common factor analysis. **Principal component analysis** uses all the variance in the data set, while **common factor analysis** is based on only the common variance.

Factor Analysis Models

To help you understand the difference between the two factor analysis models, let's clarify what we mean by variance. Recall that **variance** describes the variability in the distribution of the data. In statistical analysis, each variable is assumed to have a total variance equal to 1. The total variance can be divided into three types—common, unique, and error—as shown in Exhibit 15.3. The **common variance** is that portion of the total variance that is shared by all the original variables in the analysis, or the portion of the variance for which all the variables covary together. The **unique variance** is that portion of the total variance that is specific or unique to one variable. **Error variance** is the portion of the variance that is the result of, for example,

Exhibit 15.3 **Types of Variance in Factor Analysis**

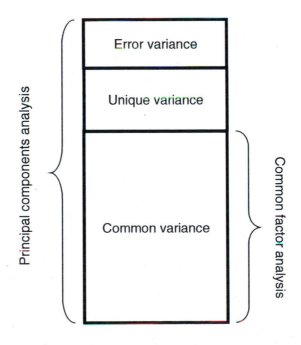

a measurement or data collection error. Principal component analysis uses all three kinds of variance to derive factor solutions. Common factor analysis uses only the common variance to derive factors.

Principal component analysis utilizes the entire variation in the set of variables being analyzed. The procedure reduces the original set of variables to a smaller set of composite variables, called principal components. Each principal component is formed by linearly combining the original variables. The objective is to explain as much of the original variance in the data set as possible by a few principal components. As an example of principal component analysis, let's consider the twelve perceptions variables from the Samouel's customer survey. If we were to run a principal component factor analysis program, we would expect the twelve variables to be reduced to three or perhaps four components, which together explain 70 percent or more of the variance in the original variables. Each of the new components would represent a separate composite factor.

Common factor analysis utilizes only the common variance to derive a factor solution. The objective is to identify underlying (latent) dimensions, referred to as common factors. If there are subsets of the original variables that are measuring the same underlying construct, the new common dimensions will be meaningful and interpretable. That is, we will be able to describe the original variables in terms of their common underlying dimensions. Common factor analysis is frequently used in the development of multi-item scales to see if the individual constructs are truly unidimensional (represent a single construct).

Principal component analysis and common factor analysis are both available in most popular statistical packages. If the business researcher knows that the unique and error variances are a relatively small portion of the total variance and wants to reduce the original set of variables to a smaller set of composite variables, then principal component analysis is typically used. In contrast, if little is known about the unique and error variance and the researcher wants to examine the original variables in terms of their common underlying dimensions, then common factor analysis is used.

The initial factors derived using principal component analysis are made up of mostly common variance and a much smaller portion of unique and error variance. Also, principal component factor solutions tend to be more stable. For these reasons, principal component analysis is the most commonly used approach in business research, so we will focus on only that method. There are several other analytical and computational differences between principal component analysis and exploratory factor analysis which are, however, beyond the scope of this book.[1]

Factor Analysis Rotation

The initial solution in a principal component analysis is unrotated. The unrotated solution produces factors that are independent (uncorrelated), but they are often difficult to interpret. For this reason, the researcher rotates the factors to get another view of their structure. There are two options for factor rotation—either

Exhibit 15.4 **Orthogonal and Oblique Rotation of Factors**

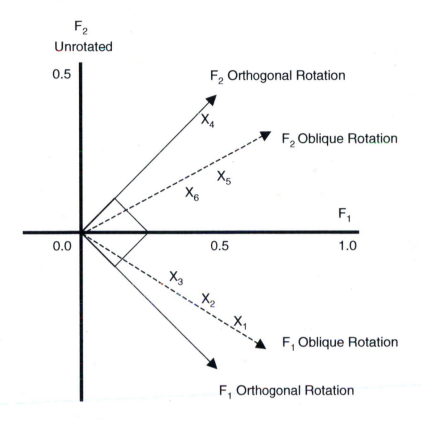

an orthogonal rotation or an oblique rotation. When you choose an **orthogonal solution**, the factors are rotated so they are independent of one another and the correlation between them is 0. An **oblique solution** permits the derived factors to be correlated with one another.

Factor rotation provides the researcher with different views of the same data. It is similar to the process you follow when you rotate a small object like a diamond in your hand to find the best viewing angle—that is, the one that allows you to understand it the best. In factor analysis, the term "simple structure" is used to describe factor analysis results in which each original variable has a high loading on only one factor and relatively low loadings on the other derived factors. A **factor loading** represents the correlation between an original variable and a derived factor. There is no guarantee that a given data set can produce simple structure. From a measurement perspective, however, results consistent with simple structure provide some evidence of convergent and discriminant validity. Simple structure makes it clear that an original variable is highly related to only one latent factor. One of the key reasons for factor rotation is to examine whether simple structure can be obtained.

Orthogonal and oblique rotated factors are illustrated in Exhibit 15.4. The vertical line represents unrotated factor 2. The horizontal line is unrotated factor 1. The unrotated factors are shown at a 90-degree angle, meaning they are uncorrelated. When we rotate factors, we show them moving in a clockwise direction. The factors are rotated until they more closely intersect with the variables that load on them. When we rotate the axes together and keep the 90-degree angle, that is an orthogonal rotation (shown as a solid line). When we rotate each axis individually and let the two axes form an oblique angle (less than 90 degrees), that is an oblique rotation (shown as a dashed line). If our research objective is to have uncorrelated factors, then we would use an orthogonal rotation if, for example, we wanted to use factor scores in a subsequent regression model. On the other hand, if we want to represent the factor structure that most closely portrays the relationship between the variables, then we would use an oblique rotation. In the real world factors are almost always correlated, but to meet the statistical assumptions of our research problem, we may choose to use an orthogonal rotation and represent the factors as uncorrelated.

An orthogonal rotation is by far the most commonly used approach in business research, so we will focus on only that method. There are several different options for deriving an orthogonal solution, but we will use the Varimax option since it, too, is the most widely used. To summarize our decisions, we will use principal component factor analysis that is orthogonally rotated based on the Varimax procedure.[2]

NUMBER OF FACTORS

Researchers use exploratory factor analysis in an attempt to summarize the information in many variables using only a few factors. Thus, a key issue involves how many factors are needed to effectively represent the variables. Our restaurant example derived only two factors, but most situations involve several factors. Deciding on how many factors to retain is a complex decision because most factor analysis problems can have more than one possible solution. That is, a three-factor and a four-factor solution may be comparable, and judgment is required to select the better one. We will discuss two of the most widely used methods to decide the number of factors to retain, the latent root and percentage of variance criteria.[3] These two methods are used along with the ability to interpret and name the factors in deciding how many factors to retain.

The most widely used method to decide the number of factors is the **latent root criterion**. The latent root is a measure of the amount of variance a particular factor represents. This criterion states that with principal component analysis, factors that have a latent root (also called an eigenvalue) of 1 or higher are retained. Factors with a latent root of less than 1 are considered insignificant and not retained. Each original variable has a variance of 1. Therefore, if you factor analyze a set of twelve variables, the total variance is 12. Since any single factor you retain must have a latent root of 1 or more, each factor you keep will represent at least 8.3 percent of the total variance (12/1 = 8.3 percent).

The latent root criterion is the default option in most statistical software programs. But the analyst needs to understand that it is calculated based on the unrotated solu-

Exhibit 15.5

Example of Varimax-Rotated Principal Components Factor Matrix

Variables	Loadings			Communality
	Factor 1	Factor 2	Factor 3	
X_1, "friendly"	.93	.19	.09	.91
X_2, "courteous"	.89	.27	.18	.90
X_3, "competent"	.76	−.21	.27	.70
X_4, "taste"	.11	.76	.31	.69
X_5, "portion size"	.03	.67	.44	.65
X_6, "freshness"	.19	.81	.24	.75
				Total
Sum of squares (eigenvalue)	2.32	1.83	.45	4.60
Percent of trace*	38.7	30.7	.075	76.97

*Trace = 6.0 (number of variables analyzed).

tion. After rotation some of the variance from earlier factors is shifted to later factors that then have a larger latent root. Thus, if the initial factor solution has four factors based on the latent root criterion, the analyst will need to also request a five-factor solution to evaluate as well. This is because after rotation the fifth factor may have an eigenvalue of 1 or higher. Also, rotating more factors may facilitate interpretation of the factors.

A second criterion to use in deciding how many factors to retain is the percentage of the variance in the original data that is explained by all factors considered together. A factor analysis software package (such as SPSS or SAS) will tell you the percentage of variation explained by each factor, as well as the total variance explained by all factors. An illustration of the factor loadings and variance extracted is shown in Exhibit 15.5. It is a three-factor solution for our six fast food variables. In this example, the first two factors are definitely good. When added together they explain a total of 69.4 percent (38.7 + 30.7 = 69.4 percent) of the variability in the six original variables, and their latent root is above 1.0. Since the third factor explains only .075 percent of the variance and has a latent root of only 0.45, it will not be retained. In fact, you would have to run the factor analysis again and use either the default criterion of retaining only factors with latent roots greater than 1.0, or requesting only two factors so you could eliminate the third factor.

Most analysts stop factoring when additional factors no longer make sense because the variance they explain often contains a large amount of error. The rule of thumb for this criterion is that a factor solution should account for a minimum of 60 percent of the total variance. But each situation may vary depending on the research objectives, and both less variance or more variance accounted for could be justified. In some situations, adding an additional factor to reach the 60 percent criterion cannot be justified because no variables load on the factor (i.e., loading > .30). Thus, the added factor is referred to as uninterpretable, and the factor solution is unacceptable.

In most situations, the number of factors retained is based on the size of the latent root, the percentage of variance extracted, and the ability to logically name the resulting factors. Specifically, the business researcher retains only factors that meet the minimum latent root criterion of 1, but the total variance accounted for by all the factors should be more than 60 percent, and the rotated factors should be able to be assigned a logical name. In applying these three considerations, for example, the researcher most often would select the five-factor solution if all factors have a latent root of 1 or higher. But a four-factor solution may be chosen instead of a five-factor solution even if the fifth factor has a latent root of 1. In such a case the four-factor solution must account for a minimum of 60 percent of the total variance, and the logic for naming the factors must be more easily supportable and theoretically sound than with five factors. The ultimate goal is to derive a set of factors that is theoretically meaningful, relatively easy to interpret, and accounts for as much of the original variance as possible.

There is additional information in Exhibit 15.5 you will need to understand. The numbers in the columns under each factor (and beside each of the six variables) are referred to as factor loadings. The number at the bottom of each column of factor loadings is the sum of squared factor loadings, also referred to as an eigenvalue. To obtain this number, you simply square each factor loading for a particular factor and add them together. The sum of squared factor loadings indicates the relative importance of each factor in accounting for the variance in the set of variables being analyzed. Note the sum of squares for factors 1, 2, and 3 are 2.32, 1.83, and .45, respectively. The percentage of **trace** for each of the three factors is also shown at the bottom of the table. The trace is the total amount of variance in a factor analysis. In this case the trace is 6 (six variables = trace of 6). To get the percentage of trace you divide a factor's sum of squared loadings by the trace. For example, for factor 1, 2.32 divided by 6 equals 38.7 percent.

At the far right of the factor matrix is the column of communalities. It represents the row sum of squared factor loadings. To get the communality you square each of the factor loadings for a variable (variable X_1 = .93 + .19 + .09 squared = .91). The **communality** tells us how much of the variance in a particular variable is accounted for by the factor solution (all the factors combined). Large communalities indicate a large amount of the original variance in a particular variable has been accounted for by the factor solution. For example, a commonality of .91 for X_1, "friendly" indicates the factor solution accounted for more variance in that variable than it did for variable X_5, "portion size," which had a communality of only .65.

INTERPRETING FACTORS

To interpret a factor matrix we examine the factor loadings. Factor loadings are the correlations between each of the original variables and the newly extracted factors. Each factor loading is a measure of the relative importance of a particular variable in representing that factor. Similar to correlation coefficients, factor loadings can vary from +1.0 to −1.0. If variable X_1, "friendly" is closely associated with factor 1, the factor loading will be high. The factor analysis software will execute the statistical analysis and calculate factor loadings between each newly created factor and each of the original variables. An example of the results of this statistical analysis is provided in Exhibit 15.5. Variables X_1, X_2, and X_3 have high loadings on factor 1. Similarly, variables X_4, X_5, and X_6 have high loadings on factor 2. A business researcher would use the pattern of loadings to name each of the factors. But before the pattern for these variables could be interpreted, the factor solution must be run again to request a two-factor solution.

We next assign a name to the resulting factors. To do so, the researcher examines the variables that have the highest loadings on each factor. What we are looking for is a common, underlying meaning among the variables that have high loadings on a given factor. We also prefer that there be no variables loading on a factor that are not related to the other variables with high loadings. In our example the three variables "friendly" (X_1), "courteous" (X_2), and "competent" (X_3) all loaded on the same factor, and we named this factor "employees," because the three variables are related to a customer's experience with the restaurant's employees. Similarly, the perceptions "taste" (X_4), "portion size" (X_5), and "freshness" (X_6) have high loadings on the same factor, so we named factor 2 "food" because the three variables all deal with the restaurant's food. In this example, both our factors were "pure" in that each variable had a high loading on one factor and a much lower loading on the other factors. Unfortunately, in practice we often find a variable will have relatively higher loadings on more than one factor, a situation referred to as a **cross loading**. When this happens it does not mean the factor solution is wrong or that we cannot use it. Rather, we prefer for a variable to load on only one factor because it is easier to interpret, assuming all the variables loading on a particular factor are in some way related. When variables load on more than one factor, however, it does complicate the naming of factors. Indeed, a typical procedure when cross loadings are found is to eliminate the variable from the analysis.

The process of naming factors is subjective. It combines logic and judgment with an assessment of the variables that have high loadings on each factor. Because of its subjective approach we must be cautious in developing names to represent factors to be sure the names do not misrepresent the underlying meaning of the factors.

AN EXAMPLE OF FACTOR ANALYSIS

Phil Samouel would like to know if he could simplify his understanding of the perceptions of the restaurants by reducing the number of variables to fewer than twelve. That is, can he represent the twelve original perceptions variables (X_1–X_{12}) with a smaller number of meaningful factors? The null hypothesis is that the twelve perceptions variables cannot be represented by a smaller set of meaningful factors. The twelve perceptions variables as measured in the customer survey are shown in Exhibit 15.6.

Let's look first at the information in Exhibit 15.7. We can check the means and sample sizes to make sure the data is correctly analyzed. For example, if the sample size is not 200, then you may have analyzed the wrong data set, or some respondents may have been eliminated because of missing data.

Exhibit 15.6

Twelve Perception Variables from Restaurant Customer Questionnaire

Listed below is a set of characteristics that could be used to describe Samouel's Greek Cuisine/Gino's Italian Ristorante. Using a scale from 1 to 7, with 7 being "strongly agree" and 1 being "strongly disagree," to what extent do you agree or disagree that Samouel's/Gino's has:

		Strongly Disagree						Strongly Agree
1.	Excellent food quality	1	2	3	4	5	6	7
2.	Attractive interior	1	2	3	4	5	6	7
3.	Generous portions	1	2	3	4	5	6	7
4.	Excellent food taste	1	2	3	4	5	6	7
5.	Good value for the money	1	2	3	4	5	6	7
6.	Friendly employees	1	2	3	4	5	6	7
7.	Appears clean and neat	1	2	3	4	5	6	7
8.	Fun place to go	1	2	3	4	5	6	7
9.	Wide variety of menu items	1	2	3	4	5	6	7
10.	Reasonable prices	1	2	3	4	5	6	7
11.	Courteous employees	1	2	3	4	5	6	7
12.	Competent employees	1	2	3	4	5	6	7

Exhibit 15.7

Descriptive Statistics for Customer Questionnaire

Variables	Mean	Analysis N
X_1, "excellent food quality"	5.53	200
X_2, "attractive interior"	4.70	200
X_3, "generous portions"	3.89	200
X_4, "excellent food taste"	5.45	200
X_5, "good value for the money"	4.33	200
X_6, "friendly employees"	3.66	200
X_7, "appears clean and neat"	4.11	200
X_8, "fun place to go"	3.39	200
X_9, "wide variety of menu items"	5.51	200
X_{10}, "reasonable prices"	4.06	200
X_{11}, "courteous employees"	2.40	200
X_{12}, "competent employees"	2.19	200

Now look at Exhibit 15.8. The names of the twelve variables analyzed (X_1–X_{12}) are shown in the left column. Note that the order of the variables is not from one to twelve. Instead, the sequence is based on the sizes of the individual variable loadings on the factors. That is, the largest loadings are at the top of the column, and they get smaller as you go toward the bottom. To make it easier to interpret the factor solution, we do not show factor loadings under .30 in the factor matrix. This is called an **easy-read matrix** because it does not show the smaller, less-significant factor loadings. In the popular software packages, this is an option you should select. You should realize that the loadings for all the variables are still computed. They are simply not shown. It is easier to pick out any problems, or to interpret the results, once this option has been selected.

Exhibit 15.8

Rotated Easy-Read Factor Solution for Customer Survey Perceptions

Variables	Components (factors)			
	1	2	3	4
X_4, "excellent food taste"	.912			
X_9, "wide variety of menu items"	.901			
X_1, "excellent food quality"	.883			
X_6, "friendly employees"		.892		
X_{11}, "courteous employees"		.850		
X_{12}, "competent employees"		.800		
X_8, "fun place to go"			.869	
X_2, "attractive interior"			.854	
X_7, "appears clean and neat"			.751	
X_3, "generous portions"				.896
X_5, "good value for the money"				.775
X_{10}, "reasonable prices"				.754

Extraction method: principal component analysis; rotation method: Varimax.

Total Variance Explained

Component	Rotation sums of squared loadings		
	Total	Percent of Variance	Cumulative Percent
1	2.543	21.188	21.188
2	2.251	18.758	39.946
3	2.100	17.498	57.444
4	2.060	17.170	74.614

To the right of the variable labels are columns of numbers representing the factor loadings for a four factor solution. We see only three numbers for each of the factors. This is because all the other factor loadings are under .30 and are therefore not shown in this easy-read factor matrix. As you recall, our preference is for a simple (pure) solution, in which each original variable loads on only one factor, and that is what happened in our example. But in many cases this does not happen. Instead, one or more variables will load on two factors.

Before trying to name the factors, let's decide if four factors are enough or if we need more. Our objective here is to have as few factors as possible and yet account for a reasonable amount of the information contained in the twelve original variables. We now look at the bottom part of Exhibit 15.8. It shows that four factors accounted for 74.614 percent of the variance in the original twelve variables. This is more than the minimum amount of variance we should account for (60 percent), and we have reduced the number of original variables by about two thirds, from twelve to four, so let's see if our factors seem logical.

To determine if our factors are logical and theoretically meaningful, look at the original variables combined as new factors. Factor 1 is made up of X_4, "excellent food taste," X_9, "wide variety of menu items," and X_1, "excellent food quality." Factor 2 is made up of X_6, "friendly employees," X_{11}, "courteous employees," and X_{12}, "competent employees." Factor 3 is made up of X_8, "fun place to go," X_2, "attractive

---

■————DATA ANALYSIS————■
Using SPSS to Develop a Factor Solution for the Customer Survey

For this analysis, we use all 200 respondents and do not split the sample. This is because we are looking for common patterns across all the restaurant customers. The SPSS click-through sequence is: ANALYZE → DIMENSION REDUCTION → FACTOR, which leads to a dialogue box where you select variables X_1 to X_{12}. After you move these variables into the Variables box, look at the alternatives on the right. Click first on the Descriptives box and then on the Univariate Descriptives box, and then click Continue. Next click on the Extraction box. We will use the default method of Principal components and the Extract default of Eigenvalues over 1, but unclick the Unrotated factor solution under Display and then click on Continue. Next go to the Rotation box where the default is None. Since we will rotate the initial factor solution, you click on Varimax as your rotational choice (this removes the default of None) and then on Continue. Finally, go to the Options box and click on Sorted by size, and then change the Suppress absolute values less than from .10 to .3, and click on Continue. The last two choices make the output easier to read because we eliminate information we will not use. We will not be calculating scores at this point, so we can click on OK to run the program. The results should be the same as in Exhibits 15.7 and 15.8.

---

interior," and X_7, "appears clean and neat," while Factor 4 consists of X_3, "generous portions, X_5, "good value for the money," and X_{10}, "reasonable prices." To analyze the logic of the combinations we look at the variables with the highest loadings (largest absolute sizes). That is why only the loadings of .30 or higher are shown in Exhibit 15.8. Factor 1 is related to "food," factor 2 is related to "employees," and factor 3 is related to "atmosphere." Factor 4 consists of the food portion and pricing variables. It is somewhat more complex to interpret but still logical. We have labeled it a "value" factor. The logic of this name is that customers who perceive the food portions to be somewhat larger also believe the prices are relatively more reasonable (positive correlation between the variables). Overall, customers believe the food portions are acceptable but not necessarily good ("generous portions" mean = 3.89 on a seven-point scale). For the pricing variables the means are slightly higher but still not very favorable ("good value for the money" mean = 4.33 and "reasonable prices" mean = 4.06). Thus, there is definitely room for improvement in customers' perceived value for their money.

The factor analysis of the twelve perceptions variables resulted in a four-factor solution. The four factors account for an acceptable amount of variance (above 60 percent) and display logic in the combinations of the original twelve variables. With this four-factor solution, instead of having to think about twelve variables we can now think about only four variables: "food," "employees," "atmosphere," and "value."

There is one final topic to cover on the interpretation of a factor matrix. In our example all the factor loadings are positive. Since factor loadings are the same as correlation coefficients, they can have either a positive (+) or a negative (−) sign. It is not unusual to have some variables with positive loadings and others with negative loadings on the same factor. If a variable has a loading with a negative sign, it means it is negatively related to that factor. Since factors are orthogonally independent, a negative loading for a variable on the first factor does not have any relationship to the other factors in the solution.

The simplification and reduction of the original twelve variables to four factors could be an end in itself. In other words, we could conclude that, by reducing the twelve variables to only four factors, we had accomplished our research objective. In some instances, however, we may wish to use the new factors as independent variables in a regression or discriminant analysis. The new research objective, then, would be to see if the four factor variables could accurately predict a single dependent variable, such as satisfaction or likelihood to recommend the restaurant to a friend.

CLUSTER ANALYSIS

Cluster analysis is an interdependence multivariate technique. **Cluster analysis** enables us to combine objects (e.g., individuals, brands, stores) into groups so that objects in each of the groups are similar to one another and different from objects in all other groups. In cluster analysis objects are combined so there will be high internal (within clusters) homogeneity as well as high external (between clusters) heterogeneity. That is, cluster analysis identifies natural groupings using several variables. But none of the variables is considered to be a dependent or independent variable. If it is successful, the objects in the clusters will be close together and the objects in different clusters will be far apart.

To better explain the process of cluster analysis, let's use an intuitive example. Sam's Club is interested in identifying customers who, when shopping, are dominated or driven by low prices and bargains. To do so, it conducts a survey of individuals within a five-mile radius of ten of its stores. On its questionnaire it asks questions like, How often do you use coupons from the newspaper? How often do you use the Valpak coupons sent to you in the mail? How often do you shop at stores that advertise low prices? and so on. The survey also collects demographic information such as age, income, education, and so forth. After the data has been collected, the questions relating to frequency of use of coupons and shopping based on sale offers and low prices are submitted to a cluster analysis. The cluster analysis procedure identifies groups of individuals more highly motivated by coupon offers and low prices. Instead of using arbitrary approaches like the mean or median, cluster analysis identifies the natural groupings where individuals in each cluster are the most similar. Sam's Club can thus identify one or more household segments that are most likely to shop at its stores for bargains. Once the price-driven segments have been identified, Sam's Club's advertising, products, and services can be tailored to appeal to them.

Exhibit 15.9 identifies three potential clusters for Sam's Club. Cluster 1 contains households that seldom shop for bargains or use coupons, cluster 2 includes households that are occasional bargain hunters, and cluster 3 has households that frequently shop based on low prices and the use of coupons. Note that clusters 1 and 3 are very different (no overlap), while clusters 2 and 3 are somewhat similar (large overlap). By examining the characteristics associated with each of the clusters, Sam's management can decide which clusters to target and how best to reach them through their marketing communications. In this case, Sam's Club would definitely target cluster 3 and possibly cluster 2.

Exhibit 15.9   **Three Clusters of Shopper Types**

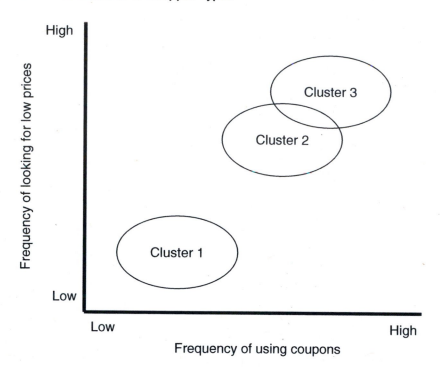

Cluster analysis is useful for the business researcher in many different situations. For example, a business that has collected survey data is often faced with a large number of observations where patterns are difficult to identify unless smaller, more homogeneous groups are identified. The researcher could use cluster analysis to identify, for example, groups of highly committed, loyal employees. Other possible applications include identifying good credit risks versus bad credit risks, highly satisfied versus highly dissatisfied employees, and so on. Cluster analysis can be used to perform this task on the basis of objective criteria instead of arbitrary ones, like the mean or median.

DERIVING CLUSTERS

Clusters can be developed from scatter plots. But this is a time-consuming, trial-and-error process that quickly becomes tedious as the sample size increases. Fortunately, software packages are available for this purpose and can be used to efficiently execute the clustering process. The mathematics underlying the various clustering procedures is beyond the scope of this book. But all the procedures are based on the concept of starting with some boundaries around an initial set of cluster seeds (individual respondents that are far apart) and adjusting the boundaries until the distances within

Exhibit 15.10 **Between- and Within- Cluster Variation**

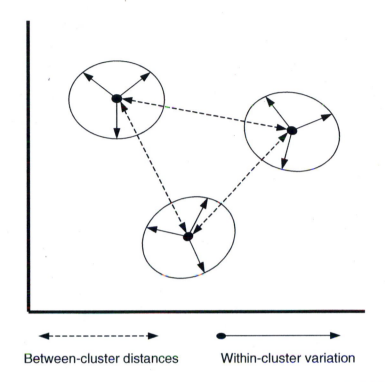

Between-cluster distances   Within-cluster variation

cluster boundaries (within cluster variation) are as small as possible relative to the average distances between clusters. Exhibit 15.10 shows between- and within-cluster variation. The general approach of all cluster programs is similar, therefore, and involves measuring the similarity (or differences) between objects based on a distance measure.

Cluster analysis involves three separate phases. The first phase divides the total sample into smaller subgroups. The second phase verifies the groups are statistically different and theoretically meaningful. The third phase then profiles the clusters by describing the characteristics of each cluster in terms of demographics, psychographics, or other relevant characteristics.

PHASE I

During the first phase we must answer three questions: How do we measure the distances between the objects we are clustering? What procedure will be used to group similar objects into clusters? How many clusters will we derive? Unfortunately, there are many different answers to these questions, and, depending on the circumstances, more than one of them could be correct. We therefore give you some general guidelines and refer you to other sources for the underlying details.[4]

The distances between the objects we are clustering can be measured in several ways. The most commonly used measure is Euclidean distance. Other options include squared Euclidean distances, the sum of the absolute differences, and Mahalanobis distance. Many statisticians recommend Mahalanobis as the best measure, but few statistical packages include this option. Squared Euclidean distances have the fewest weaknesses of the remaining measures, so we recommend it as the best. Before running the cluster program we suggest you identify and remove outliers where appropriate since cluster procedures are very sensitive to outliers. We also recommend you standardize the variables included in the cluster analysis if they are measured on scales with different units of measurement. For example, if you are using two variables to develop clusters, with one variable being "satisfaction" measured on a seven-point scale and the other variable being "amount purchased" measured on a 100-point scale, you must standardize the data before doing the cluster analysis. Otherwise, "amount purchased" will be weighted more heavily because the range of possible responses is much larger.

A second question you must answer in Phase I is what procedure will be used to group objects that are similar. Many approaches are available, but they can all be classified in two types—hierarchical and nonhierarchical. Both approaches attempt to maximize the differences (distances) between clusters relative to the variation within the clusters, as shown in Exhibit 15.10.

Hierarchical Clustering

A **hierarchical clustering** procedure develops a hierarchy, or treelike format. This can be done using either a build-up or a divisive approach. The **build-up approach**, also referred to as agglomerative, starts with all the objects (respondents) as separate clusters and combines them one at a time until there is a single cluster representing all the objects. The **divisive approach** starts with all objects as a single cluster and then takes away one object at a time until each object is a separate cluster. We discuss only the agglomerative approach since it is the most widely used.

Exhibit 15.11 illustrates the build-up (agglomerative) approach for a sample of five objects. The illustration is referred to as a dendogram, or tree graph. Note that objects 4 and 5 combine to form the first cluster (vertical lines indicate where two objects combine). Objects 2 and 3 combine next to form the second cluster. Object 1 combines with the previously formed cluster of objects 2 and 3. The final stage is when objects 1, 2, and 3 combine with objects 4 and 5 to form a single cluster.

The popular statistical software packages include many different options for calculating agglomerative clusters. Examples of these options include between-groups linkage, within-groups linkage, nearest neighbor, furthest neighbor, centroid, median, and Ward's. Each of these options calculates the distances between clusters differently, has strengths and weaknesses, and often produces different results. An examination of each method is beyond the scope of this book.[5] The Ward's method is popular and, more than other methods, tends to result in clusters with approximately the same

Exhibit 15.11   **Dendogram for Hierarchical Cluster Analysis**

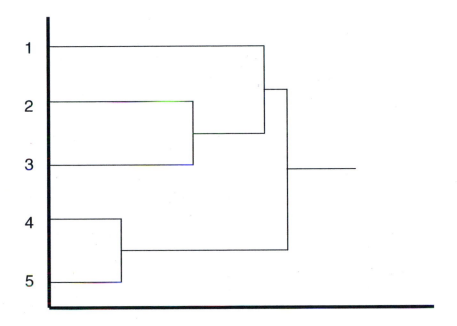

number of objects. We therefore recommend you use it first and then perhaps try the other approaches and compare the results.

Nonhierarchical Clustering

Nonhierarchical clustering procedures, referred to as *k*-means clustering, do not involve the treelike process of hierarchical clustering. Instead, one or more cluster seeds (initial starting points) are selected, and objects within a prespecified distance from the cluster seeds are considered to be in a particular cluster. A cluster seed can be either a single object (respondent) that is chosen to be the center of a new cluster or several objects that together represent an initial seed point.

Several different procedures can be used to execute nonhierarchical clustering. They differ depending on the number of cluster seeds initially selected, the sequence in which the cluster seeds are selected, and whether a single object can be reassigned to another cluster formed later once it has been assigned to an earlier-formed cluster. Indeed, one advantage of some nonhierarchical clustering procedures is that objects can be removed from an early-formed cluster and reassigned to another cluster formed later in the sequence. This is not possible with hierarchical procedures. Reassignment of objects can be a disadvantage, however, since it requires more computing capability and with large sample sizes may be time consuming on a personal computer. But the most significant disadvantage of nonhierarchical clustering is the lack of an objective, theoretically based method for identifying initial cluster seeds. Because of this, hierarchical procedures are more widely used, and we focus on them in the rest of our discussion.

A final question to be answered in Phase I is, How many clusters should be retained? Sometimes the researcher may know ahead of time that two, three, or some other number of clusters is desired. Other times there may be theoretical considerations that suggest the appropriate number of clusters. Still other times the researcher may examine the extent to which error variances are reduced when moving from fewer clusters to more clusters. Error variances are very large with one cluster but drop substantially when you go to a two-cluster solution. As you move from two clusters to three, four, and so on, the error variances continue dropping but not as quickly. Since fewer clusters are easier to evaluate, we recommend you run two, three, and four cluster solutions and select the one that is most logical and more closely meets your research objectives.

PHASE II

After you have determined the number of clusters to retain you must verify that the groups are in fact statistically different and theoretically meaningful. This process involves running statistical tests of the differences between the means of the clusters you have chosen. If one or more of the means of the variables used in the cluster analysis is statistically significant, then you would examine the logic of the differences in the group means for their underlying meaning. For example, recall that Sam's Club was interested in identifying individuals who would respond to coupons and low-price offers. If Sam's Club executes a two-cluster solution and examines the means, management would hope to find one cluster that frequently uses coupons and responds to low price offers and another group that may be less responsive to such appeals. If the groups show this logic and are statistically different, then the two group solution has been validated, and we can name one group "price sensitive" and the other "non–price sensitive," or something similar.

PHASE III

The third phase in cluster analysis examines the demographic and other characteristics of the individuals in each cluster and attempts to explain why the objects have been grouped as they are. For example, we would anticipate the "price sensitive" group identified above would perhaps have lower incomes or get more pleasure out of shopping for bargains. In contrast, the "non–price sensitive" group would likely have higher incomes and get less pleasure out of shopping around for the best deal. This process is sometimes referred to as profiling clusters. As in the Sam's Club example, profiling other cluster analysis results may allow a business researcher to identify, for example, employees most likely to be promoted quickly, stocks most likely to exceed the Dow Jones Industrial Average, or manufacturing units most likely to go on strike.

AN EXAMPLE OF CLUSTER ANALYSIS

Phil Samouel is trying to decide whether to use different business approaches with different customers. From a business research perspective, this implies a research question asking whether there are different subgroups (segments) of restaurant customers who exhibit distinctly different restaurant perceptions. In discussing the problem with his consultant, he notes that variables X_1 to X_{12} are customers' perceptions of the restaurant, and they are measured metrically. The task is to determine if there are subgroups or clusters of the 200 respondents that are distinctly different. We could cluster using all twelve perception variables. But using a smaller number of variables will provide an example that is easier to understand. It will also focus on a single concept instead of several related but different concepts represented by the twelve perceptions variables (recall that in our factor analysis we identified four different factors).

In selecting which perceptions variables to analyze, we would look for variables that are logically related. We could also consider the results of our factor analysis in the previous section. Of the twelve variables, the three food variables (taste, variety, and quality) are related, as are the three employee variables (friendly, courteous, and competent). Let's work with the three employee variables —X_6, X_{11}, and X_{12}. The research objective then is to try to identify clusters of respondents that have distinctly different perceptions of the restaurant employees. The null hypothesis is that different clusters do not exist based on the customer survey perceptions variables for restaurant employees.

Example: Phase I

Phil's business consultant has recommended that the cluster analysis approach be Ward's method and measurement using squared Euclidean distances. These recommendations are based on his previous work with a similar research question. The next step is to decide the number of clusters to retain in the solution.

When, for example, customer perceptions of employees are examined as a single group, there is typically a lot of error associated with the group because you are combining a lot of variability together. When you separate the single group into two groups, the error is reduced substantially and continues to grow smaller as more groups (clusters) are identified. The reduction in error is measured by an error coefficient. Exhibit 15.12 shows the error coefficients associated with the clustering of the employee variables from the restaurant customer survey. The numbers in this column show the extent to which error is reduced by going from one cluster to two clusters, from two clusters to three clusters, and so on. Comparing the coefficients for the one- and two-cluster solutions, you see a big drop (difference) in the error coefficient. Each time you move up the column the drop (difference) in the numbers gets smaller. In comparing the sizes of the coefficients, you are looking for the point where the difference between the coefficients gets substantially smaller. Small drops in the error coefficient do not justify going to a larger number of clusters.

Exhibit 15.12

Error Coefficients for Cluster Solutions

Error coefficients	Error reduction
Four clusters = 208.213	3–4 clusters = 49.791
Three clusters = 258.004	2–3 clusters = 55.733
Two clusters = 313.737	1–2 clusters = 360.993

Staying with Exhibit 15.12, if the difference in the sizes of the error coefficients between a three-cluster solution and a four-cluster solution is small, your error has not been reduced very much. In our cluster analysis of employee variables, the change is rather small from three clusters, 258.004, to four-clusters, 208.213, a difference of only 49.791 (258.004 − 208.213 = 49.791). The difference between the numbers as you go from three to four clusters is getting smaller, and a four-cluster solution is much more difficult to interpret. For this cluster solution, therefore, we definitely would choose three clusters over four. Note that your results may differ slightly depending on which version of the software you are using, but the approach remains the same.

Another option is to decide between two clusters and three clusters. When you move from two clusters to three, there is a drop in the error coefficient of 55.733 (313.737 − 258.004 = 55.733). Similarly, when two clusters are formed from one, there is a drop of 360.993 (674.730 − 313.737 = 360.993). Certainly two clusters could be used because you reduce your error a huge amount by going from one to two clusters, and two clusters may be easier to understand than three. In this example we could use either a two-cluster or a three-cluster solution. The decision to use a three-cluster solution would have to be based on what would be most useful for planning a new business strategy. That is, if there is business logic in using the three-group solution, then the drop in error variance is sufficient for examining the three-group cluster solution.

Example: Phase II

Phil and his business consultant have talked and agreed that, based on other studies and their judgment, they will initially examine a two-cluster solution. In Phase II we must verify that the two groups are statistically different and theoretically meaningful.

Exhibit 15.13 shows the sample sizes for each cluster (N) and the means of each variable for each cluster. For example, the sample size of cluster 1 is 113, and that of cluster 2 is 87. Moreover, the mean for X_6 in cluster 1 is 4.55, whereas in cluster 2 the mean is 2.49. The means for X_{11} and X_{12} have a similar pattern—they are higher in cluster 1 than in cluster 2. To see if the differences between the group means are statistically significant, we go to the ANOVA section of the table. The differences in the means of the clusters for all the employee variables are highly significant (.000). Thus, we reject the null hypothesis of no differences.

We compare the means of the variables for each of the groups to understand the clusters. Respondents in cluster 1 perceive employees to be much more friendly

■————DATA ANALYSIS————■
**Using SPSS to Identify Clusters for Selected
Customer Survey Perceptions Variables**

For this example we analyze the total sample because we are looking for subgroups among all the restaurant customers. The SPSS click-through sequence is: ANALYZE → CLASSIFY → HIERARCHICAL CLUSTER. This will take you to a dialogue box where you select and move variables X_6, X_{11}, and X_{12} into the Variables box. Now look at the other options to the right. We will use all the defaults shown in the dialogue box as well as the defaults for the Statistics options. Unclick the plots options to simplify your printout. Next click on the Method box and select Ward's under Cluster Method (it is the last one, and you must scroll down). Squared Euclidean Distances is the default under Measure, and we will use it. At this point we will not need the Save option, so click on OK to run the program.

When the program finishes, look for a table called "Agglomeration Schedule." There are lots of numbers in it, but we use only the numbers in the "Coefficients" column (middle of table). At the bottom of the agglomeration schedule table find the numbers in the "Coefficients" column. The number at the bottom will be the largest. As you move up the column, the numbers (error coefficients) get smaller. For example, the bottom number is 674.730 and the one right above it is 313.737. The other numbers are shown in Exhibit 15.12. *Note:* your numbers may be slightly different depending on your version of the software. Also, your groups 1 and 2 may be reversed from what is shown in the exhibit because the group numbers are randomly assigned.

Exhibit 15.13

Characteristics of Two-Group Cluster Solution

Descriptives Variables	Groups	N	Mean
X_6, "friendly employees"	1	113	4.55
	2	87	2.49
	Total	200	3.66
X_{11}, "courteous employees"	1	113	2.93
	2	87	1.71
	Total	200	2.40
X_{12}, "competent employees"	1	113	2.74
	2	87	1.46
	Total	200	2.19

ANOVA Variables	Comparison	F	Sig.
X_6, "friendly employees"	Between groups	396.013	.000
X_{11}, "courteous employees"	Between groups	134.430	.000
X_{12}, "competent employees"	Between groups	155.435	.000

(cluster 1 mean = 4.55 versus cluster 2 = 2.49) as well as more courteous (cluster 1 mean = 2.93 versus cluster 2 = 1.71) and more competent (cluster 1 mean = 2.74 versus cluster 2 = 1.46). Thus, cluster 1 has much more favorable perceptions of the restaurant employees than does cluster 2. But interestingly, overall on a seven-point scale (7 = very favorable), employees have a lot of room for improvement (for two of the three variables the means are well below the midpoint of 4 on the seven-point scale).

In Phase II we were able to identify distinctly different clusters. Moreover, the cluster solutions are theoretically meaningful because we can say that cluster 1 has significantly more favorable perceptions of employees than does cluster 2. Thus, we can now move on to Phase III so Phil can make use of these findings in his business plan.

Example: Phase III

Phase III of cluster analysis involves profiling the demographic characteristics of the clusters. You can run a one-way ANOVA between the two clusters to compare the demographic profiles.

Exhibit 15.14 displays the means of the demographic variables for each of the clusters, and the ANOVA section shows the statistical tests of the differences. There are no statistical differences between the groups on gender (.975). There are, however, significant differences on age and competitor, while income is significant only at the .097 level. Recall that perceptions of cluster 2 were much less favorable than those of cluster 1. Thus, older, higher income customers perceive employees much less favorably than do younger, lower income customers. Similarly, cluster 2 is mostly Samouel's customers, while cluster 1 is mostly Gino's customers (Samouel's coded = 0 and Gino's coded = 1). In interpreting the means of the cluster demographic variables, note that the older group is in their upper forties (mean = 48.11) and has an average annual income of $100,000 (mean = 100.10). To make these interpretations you must examine how these variables were coded, as is shown on the questionnaire in Chapter 10.

The two-group cluster solution could be the end of our analysis. Or we could go on to examine the three-group solution. But we could also use the clusters we identified in a subsequent type of analysis, such as a multiple discriminant analysis.

MULTIPLE DISCRIMINANT ANALYSIS

Recall from Chapter 12 that the selection of the appropriate statistical technique is based on several considerations, including the way your variables are measured. Business researchers can easily find themselves confronted with a research problem that involves a nonmetric dependent variable and several metric independent variables. For example, a business researcher may wish to predict employees who are likely to search for another job versus those who are not likely to do so, or similar nonmetric categories using relevant metric independent variables. Similarly, a researcher may wish to predict which customers are likely to purchase a particular product versus those who are unlikely to purchase it, or to predict viewers versus nonviewers of a television commercial, or satisfied versus dissatisfied employees. **Discriminant analysis** is a statistical procedure that can be used to predict which group an individual is likely to belong to using two or more metric independent variables.

■——DATA ANALYSIS——■

Using SPSS to Compare Demographic Group Means of Cluster Solutions

The SPSS click-through sequence is: ANALYZE → COMPARE MEANS → ONE-WAY ANOVA. Next you remove variables X_6, X_{11}, and X_{12} from the Variables box, move variables X_{25}, X_{26}, X_{27}, and X_{28} in, and leave the Cluster Membership variable in the Factor box. Click on the Options box and then on Descriptives. We use defaults for all other options, so click the OK box to get the output. The results will be the same as in Exhibit 15.14.

Exhibit 15.14

Demographic Profiles of Two-Cluster Solution

Descriptives Variables	Groups	N	Mean
X_{25}, "gender"	1	113	.47
	2	87	.47
	Total	200	.47
X_{26}, "age"	1	113	35.27
	2	87	48.11
	Total	200	40.86
X_{27}, "income"	1	113	80.15
	2	87	100.10
	Total	200	3.48
X_{28}, "competitor"	1	113	.79
	2	87	.13
	Total	200	.50

ANOVA Variables	Comparison	F	Sig.
X_{25}, "gender"	Between groups	.018	.975
X_{26}, "age"	Between groups	38.034	.000
X_{27}, "income"	Between groups	13.913	.097
X_{28}, "competitor"	Between groups	117.356	.000

As with factor analysis and cluster analysis, we use an intuitive example to help you understand discriminant analysis. Recall our survey of 1,000 McDonald's and Burger King customers discussed in the factor analysis section of this chapter. Burger King would like to know if its customers have different perceptions from those of McDonald's customers. Two of the perceptions variables measured on the survey were "fun place to go" and "food taste." The results of comparing the two customer groups could be plotted on a two-dimensional graph as in Exhibit 15.15.

The scatter plot of the data from the survey shows two groups, one containing primarily Burger King customers and the other containing primarily McDonald's customers. The McDonald's plot is larger because it has more customers than Burger King. From this example, it appears that taste is more important to Burger King customers and less important to McDonald's customers. In contrast, being a fun place for kids is more

Exhibit 15.15 **Two Dimensional Discriminant Analysis Plot of Restaurant Customers**

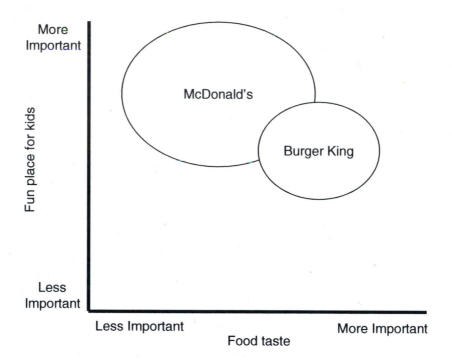

important to McDonald's customers than to Burger King customers. The two areas overlap, but not by much. To have high predictive capability, there must be minimal overlap between the groups examined in a discriminant analysis. The plot indicates the customers of Burger King and those of McDonald's are fundamentally different in terms of what is important in selecting a restaurant. Thus, Burger King will have difficulty attracting McDonald's customers unless it becomes more like McDonald's.

Multiple discriminant analysis is the appropriate statistical technique for testing the null hypothesis that the means of the independent variables of two or more groups are the same. The technique uses several metric independent variables to predict a single nonmetric dependent variable. The dependent variable can have two, three, four, or more categories. Discriminant analysis examines group differences by finding a linear combination of the independent variables—the discriminant function— that identifies differences between the group means. Thus, discriminant analysis is a statistical tool that develops linear combinations of independent variables to predict group membership as defined by the dependent variable.

To explain the analytical approach used in discriminant analysis, we will use our survey of Burger King and McDonald's customers. The dependent variable, Z, is measured with a nominal scale (i.e., customers of Burger King versus those of McDonald's), and the independent variables, "fun place for kids" and "food taste," are metric variables. The statistical objective is to predict whether an individual is a Burger King or McDonald's customer using the survey information. To do so, the researcher must find a linear combination of the independent variables that identifies statistically significant differences between the group means.

Discriminant scores (Z scores) are determined empirically by a linear function. That is, the computer analyzes the independent variables, develops a linear function, and uses it to predict in which group a survey respondent belongs. The Z score is calculated for each respondent using the following equation:

$$Z = W_1X_1 + W_2X_2 + \ldots + W_nX_n$$

Where

Z = discriminant score for each respondent
W_n = discriminant weight for the nth variable
X_n = respondent's value on the nth independent variable

Discriminant weights (W_n) are estimates of the predictive power of each independent variable. The discriminant analysis software package computes the weights so they are the optimal size for predicting the groups. Each independent variable has its own weight. The size of the weights is determined by the variance structure of the independent variables. Independent variables that are good predictors are assigned larger weights. Variables that do not predict well are given small weights.

An illustration of a two-group discriminant analysis is shown in Exhibit 15.16. Assume you have two groups, A and B, and two variables, X_1 and X_2, for each respondent in the two groups. We could plot in the scatter diagram the association of variables X_1 with X_2 for each group. Group identity is shown by circles in group A and by stars in group B. The resulting ellipses enclose some specified proportion of the points for each group, such as 95 percent. If a straight line is drawn through the two points where the ellipses intersect and then projected to a new axis, Z, we can say that the overlap between the univariate distributions of A' and B' is smaller than

Exhibit 15.16   **A Two-Group Discriminant Function**

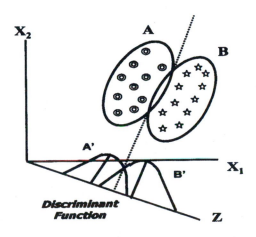

would be obtained by any other line drawn through the ellipses representing the scatter plots. The new Z axis is the discriminant function that represents a linear composite of the two independent variables.

The discriminant function in a discriminant analysis is similar to a regression equation. Recall that a regression equation uses a weighted combination of values for selected metric independent variables to predict an object's value on a continuously scaled dependent variable (Y). In discriminant analysis, the discriminant function uses a weighted combination of the independent variable values to classify an object (typically a respondent) into one of the dependent variable groups. That is, it assigns the object a value that identifies it as being in one of the dependent variable groups. The discriminant function is thus a weighted sum of values (Z) calculated for the individual independent variables.

How is the Z score used to identify group membership? The researcher must specify a cutoff score. Objects with discriminant scores larger than the cutoff score are assigned to one group, and objects with discriminant scores smaller than the cutoff score are assigned to the other dependent variable group. It there are two groups, there is only one cutoff score. But when there are three groups, there must be two cutoff scores. If, for example, the cutoff score is .567, then any respondent with a Z score below that would be assigned to one group, and any respondent with a Z score above it would be assigned to the other group. Following the same procedure, each respondent in the analysis is classified into one dependent variable group or the other, depending on its values on the individual independent variables and their weights.

Unless there is absolutely no overlap between the dependent variable groups, we are bound to make errors of classification. The larger the overlap, the more classification errors are made. The concepts of a cutoff score and discriminant function prediction are illustrated in Exhibit 15.17. In the top illustration (a) the discriminant function predicts well because there is very little overlap. In the bottom illustration (b) the discriminant function predicts poorly because there is a large amount of overlap. The cutoff score is in the middle, and therefore the discriminant function has an equal likelihood of predicting a respondent is in the wrong group. But if the cutoff score is moved to the right or left on the Z axis, it changes the likelihood of predicting which group a respondent is placed in. For example, if the cutoff score is moved to the right, the researcher could achieve 100 percent prediction accuracy for group A and substantially lower prediction accuracy for group B.

The business researcher must decide where to place the cutoff score based on the costs of misclassifying a particular respondent. If the costs of misclassification are equal, the cutoff score line is drawn in the middle. If they are unequal, then the cutoff score that results in the lowest cost of misclassification is chosen.

To clarify the nature of the discriminant function, let's refer again to our fast food example. But this time let's further assume that we have added a third variable, "friendliness of employees." Assume the discriminant function estimates the weights as shown in the following equation:

$$Z = W_1X_1 + W_2X_2 + W_3X_3$$
$$Z = .66X_1 + .37X_2 + .12X_3$$

Exhibit 15.17   **Discriminant Functions Z Axis and Cutoff Scores**

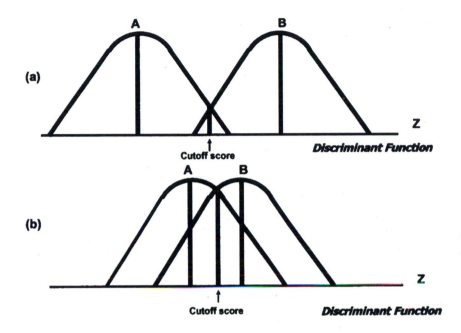

These results show that X_1, "food taste," is the most important variable in discriminating between customers of Burger King and those of McDonald's. X_2, "fun place for kids," with a coefficient of .37, also has good predictive power. In contrast, X_3, "friendliness of employees," with a weight of .12, has little predictive power.

The first step in discriminant analysis is to determine if the function is statistically significant. In a large sample size, we could find a statistically significant function that does not predict well. Therefore, if we find a statistically significant function we must test it further to see if it will correctly classify objects (individuals) into groups. In our example, the objective is to correctly classify respondents into Burger King and McDonald's customer groups. The null hypothesis is that no differences exist between the groups and therefore there is no predictive power.

The results of using a discriminant function to predict group membership are displayed in a table referred to as a classification (prediction) matrix. Exhibit 15.18 is the classification matrix for our fast food example. It shows the estimated function correctly classified customers of Burger King 80 percent of the time and incorrectly classified them 20 percent of the time. In contrast, the discriminant function correctly classified McDonald's customers 95 percent of the time and incorrectly classified them only 5 percent of the time. Overall the predictive accuracy was 87.5 percent. This predictive accuracy is much higher than would be expected by chance (two groups = 50 percent).

The overall predictive accuracy of an estimated discriminant function is called the hit ratio. The **hit ratio** is the percentage of objects (respondents) correctly classified by the discriminant function. In our preceding example it is 87.5 percent, which is very

Exhibit 15.18

Classification Matrix for Burger King and McDonald's Customers ($N = 400$)

	Burger King	McDonald's	Total
	Predicted group		
BK	160 (80%)	40 (20%)	200
	Actual group		
McD	10 (5%)	190 (95%)	200

Note: Overall prediction accuracy (hit ratio) = 87.5% (160 + 190 = 350/400).

high. But what is considered an acceptable or good hit ratio? Is predictive accuracy of 70 percent good? To answer this question you must determine the percentage of objects that could be correctly predicted by chance (without using a discriminant function). When you have two groups and the sample sizes are equal, the chance probability is 50 percent. Similarly, when you have three groups and the sample sizes are equal, the chance probability is 33 percent. This is because you could arbitrarily place all objects into one group without using a discriminant function, and your predictive accuracy, for example, for the two-group situation is 50 percent.

When your group sample sizes are unequal, the chance probability is based on the largest group. For example, if you have a sample size of 100, with 60 objects in one group and 40 in the other group, your chance probability is 60 percent. This is because you could place all objects in the group defined by the sample size of 60 and your predictive accuracy would be 60 percent.

To answer the question of what the classification accuracy should be relative to chance, we offer the following guidelines. The classification accuracy should be at least 25 percent larger than by chance. For example, if chance predictive accuracy is 50 percent, we recommend 62.5 percent. Similarly, if chance predictive accuracy is 33 percent, we recommend 41.5 percent. In the final analysis, the decision must be based on the cost versus the value of the predicted information. If the costs associated with predicting at 60 percent (chance predictive accuracy = 50 percent) are small relative to the value, then you should use discriminant analysis. If the costs are high, then do not use it.[6]

Before we show you an example of discriminant analysis, several issues need to be clarified. First, we assume the sample sizes of the two or more groups are comparable in size. Second, the sample sizes of the groups should be at least five times the number of independent variables. That is, if your discriminant function has five independent variables, then the smallest sample size of any single group should be twenty-five. Finally, the variance of the variables across the groups is assumed to be equal. In practice this last assumption is often violated, however, and fortunately the technique is robust, and this does not create many problems.

AN EXAMPLE OF DISCRIMINANT ANALYSIS

Phil Samouel would like to know whether his customers perceive his restaurant differently from how Gino's customers perceive that restaurant. Discriminant analysis can be used to answer that question. The nonmetric dependent variable is X_{28}, "competitor." This variable is coded 0 = Samouel's customer interviews and 1 = Gino's customer interviews. The metric independent variables could be the twelve restaurant perceptions variables. But to simplify the research question let's look at only the three food variables (X_1, X_4, and X_9) and the three employee variables (X_6, X_{11}, and X_{12}). The null hypothesis is that there are no differences in customer perceptions of the two restaurants on the food and employee variables.

The objective is to determine if perceptions of Samouel's customers, as measured by the six perception variables, are different from those of Gino's customers. That is, can the food and employee perception variables predict whether respondents are customers of a particular restaurant? Wilks' lambda is a statistic that evaluates whether the discriminant function has identified a statistical difference between two or more groups. In our example the Wilks' lambda is highly significant (.000), as shown in Exhibit 15.19. Since this statistic is significant, we next look at the classification results in Exhibit 15.19. Looking at the bottom of the table, we see that the overall predictive ability of the discriminant function is 83.0 percent. Without the discriminant function we could predict with only 50 percent accuracy (our sample sizes are Samouel's = 100 and Gino's = 100, so if we said all respondents were Samouel's, we would predict with 50 percent accuracy). Therefore, this is an excellent hit ratio (predictive capability). Based on these findings we can reject the null hypothesis that the group means are the same on the food and employee variables.

The discriminant function is slightly more accurate in predicting Gino's customers (86 percent) than it is Samouel's (80 percent). The way to interpret the table is to conclude the discriminant function accurately predicted Samouel's customers 80 percent of the time, and 20 percent of the time the function predicted a Samouel's customer was a

---

Exhibit 15.19

Discriminant Analysis of Customer Surveys

Wilks' lambda

Test of function(s)	Wilks' lambda	Sig.
1	.541	.000

Classification results*

		X_{28}, "competitor"	Predicted group membership Samouel's	Gino's	Total
Original group	Count	Samouel's	80	20	100
		Gino's	14	86	100
	Percent	Samouel's	80.0	20.0	100.0
		Gino's	14.0	86.0	100.0

*83.0 percent of original grouped cases correctly classified.

```
■————DATA ANALYSIS————■
Using SPSS to Execute a Discriminant Analysis Using the Customer Surveys

Using SPSS, the click-through sequence is: ANALYZE → CLASSIFY → DISCRIMINANT.
This takes you to a dialogue box where you select the variables. First highlight variable
X₂₈ and move it to the Grouping Variable box at the top. Now click on the Define Range
box just below it so you can specify the minimum and maximum numbers for the grouping
variable. For our example, the minimum is 0 = Samouel's and the maximum is 1 = Gino's.
Place these numbers in the box and click Continue. Next highlight and move variables X₁,
X₄, X₆, X₉, X₁₁, and X₁₂ into the Independents box. Now click on the Statistics tab on the
right and then click on Means, univariate ANOVAS, and Continue. Enter is the Method
default and we will use it. Click on Classify and use the default, All Group Equal (recall
that Phil interviewed 100 of his customers and 100 of Gino's customers). If you did not
know whether your group sizes were equal, then you should check the Compute from Group
Sizes option. Now click on Summary Table and Continue. None of the options under Save
are used, so click on OK to run the discriminant analysis. The results will be the same as
in Exhibits 15.19 to 15.21.
```

Gino's customer. Similarly, 86 percent of the time the discriminant function accurately predicted a Gino's customer, and 14 percent of the time it predicted a Gino's customer was a Samouel's customer.

Since we were able to develop a highly predictive discriminant function, we are now interested in finding out which independent variables have the most predictive power. To do this we examine the information in Exhibits 15.20 and 15.21. First, Exhibit 15.20 shows which perceptions variables are significantly different on a univariate basis. We see that all the variables except X_9 are highly statistically significant and are likely to be good predictors. Variable X_9 is not significant and therefore unlikely to be a good predictor. Thus, the perceptions relative to the two restaurants are very different on a univariate basis, with the exception of one variable (X_9).

We now want to examine the independent variables from a multivariate perspective. To do so we can look at either the standardized canonical discriminant function coefficients or the structure matrix correlations. Business researchers typically use the structure matrix correlations because they are considered more accurate, so we will use them too. (See Exhibit 15.21.) We must first identify the numbers (correlations) in the "Function" column that are considered significant. Just as in factor analysis, the numbers represent the correlation between the individual variables and the linear combination of all the independent variables. The cutoff level is determined in a manner similar to that of a factor loading. All variables .30 or higher are considered to be helpful in predicting group membership.

The order of the loadings in Exhibit 15.21 is from largest to smallest (not their order in the database). Similar to the univariate results, the variable with the smallest loading (X_9) is the one that was not significant on a univariate basis. The question at this point is whether to consider variables X_1 and X_4 as significant predictors.

Exhibit 15.20

Tests of Equality of Group Means

Variables	F	Sig.
X_1, "excellent food quality"	10.954	.001
X_4, "excellent food taste"	11.951	.001
X_6, "friendly employees"	119.366	.000
X_9, "wide variety of menu items"	.420	.518
X_{11}, "courteous employees"	54.821	.000
X_{12}, "competent employees"	105.073	.000

Exhibit 15.21

Structure Matrix for Restaurant Perceptions Variables

Variables*	Function 1
X_6, "friendly employees"	.843
X_{12}, "competent employees"	.791
X_{11}, "courteous employees"	.571
X_4, "excellent food taste"	.267
X_1, "excellent food quality"	.255
X_9, "wide variety of menu items"	.050

  *Variables ordered by absolute size of correlation within function.

According to our rule of thumb they are not considered helpful because they have loadings smaller than .30. But on a univariate basis they were highly significant (.001), so we may be experiencing a problem with multicollinearity. Another way to assess this would be to run a stepwise discriminant analysis to determine if they enter the equation and improve predictive accuracy. We could also run the discriminant analysis without these variables and see if the predictive capability of the function is lower. What we can conclude at this point is that customer perceptions of employees are very important in differentiating between the two restaurants, while perceptions of food are relatively less important, and menu variety is not important at all. Phil Samouel definitely needs to develop a plan for improving the employee area of his business.

As noted earlier, the predictive outcome of the discriminant function was moderately high, with a hit ratio of 83.0 percent. Interpretation of the discriminant function is based on the group means, as shown in Exhibit 15.22. Using our rule of thumb for significant loadings (.30), we note that variables X_6, X_{11}, and X_{12} are all significant predictors. For all three variables the perceptions of Gino's customers are more favorable than those of Samouel's customers (larger means indicate more favorable perceptions). This suggests that Gino's either hires much better employees or trains them better than Phil Samouel does. Thus, customer perceptions of employees are significantly different between the two restaurants and are good predictors of which respondents eat at a particular restaurant. The findings suggest Phil Samouel needs to

Exhibit 15.22

Means of Independent Variables for Restaurants

Variables	Mean	
	Samouel's	Gino's
X_1, "excellent food quality"*	5.24	5.81
X_4, "excellent food taste"*	5.16	5.73
X_6, "friendly employees"*	2.89	4.42
X_9, "wide variety of menu items"	5.45	5.56
X_{11}, "courteous employees"*	1.96	2.84
X_{12}, "competent employees"*	1.62	2.75

*Significant < .05 on a univariate basis.

Functions at Group Centroids

X_{28}, "Competitor"	Function 1
Samouel's	−.916
Gino's	.916

Note: Canonical discriminant functions evaluated at group means.

evaluate his employees and devise a method for improving their performance. This could be particularly important since, although Gino's is rated better on employees, the restaurant is still not rated very favorably (two of three variables are considerably below the midpoint of the seven-point scale).

One final approach to examining group differences is the centroid. In discriminant analysis a Z score is calculated for each respondent. The **centroid** is the mean of all the respondent Z scores in a particular group. A two-group discriminant analysis has two centroids, and a three-group analysis has three centroids. The centroids for our restaurant example are shown in Exhibit 15.22. Note that the Samouel's centroid is −.916, while the Gino's centroid is .916. This is an overall summary measure that indicates that Gino's is much more favorably perceived than is Samouel's.

STEPWISE DISCRIMINANT ANALYSIS

Like multiple regression analysis, discriminant analysis can be applied using a stepwise approach to select significant independent variables. We can input the entire set of independent variables in the discriminant function. Then we can let the discriminant function select a smaller set of independent variables that, it is hoped, discriminates well between the groups. The smaller set of independent variables is possible because of intercorrelations or redundancies among the independent variables. But, as in regression analysis, we must be cautious of multicollinearity among the independent variables. The popular statistical software programs have an option for the stepwise approach.

Summary

Explain the Difference Between Dependence and Interdependence Techniques

There are two broad types of multivariate statistical techniques. One type is referred to as dependence techniques. These techniques are used when one (or more) of the variables is identified as the dependent variable and the other variables are independent variables. Interdependence techniques are those where you analyze only one set of variables and do not identify any of them as independent or dependent. In this book we discuss three dependence techniques—multiple regression, ANOVA, and discriminant analysis. Two interdependence techniques are covered—factor analysis and cluster analysis.

Understand How to Use Factor Analysis to Simplify Data Analysis

Factor analysis is an interdependence technique. It is most often used to summarize and reduce the independent variables. But you can also use it to simplify the dependent set of variables. Factor analysis examines the underlying correlations among the variables and finds those that are similar. It then combines the large set of variables using a linear approach into a smaller set of factors that have common relationships.

Demonstrate the Usefulness of Cluster Analysis

Cluster analysis is also an interdependence multivariate technique. Cluster analysis enables us to combine objects (e.g., customers, brands, products) into groups so that objects in each group are similar to one another and different from objects in all other groups. Cluster analysis combines objects so there will be high internal (within clusters) homogeneity as well as high external (between clusters) heterogeneity. That is, cluster analysis identifies natural groupings using several variables without designating any of the variables as a dependent variable. If it is successful, the objects in the clusters will be close together, and the objects in different clusters will be far apart.

Understand When and How to Use Discriminant Analysis

Multiple discriminant analysis uses several metric independent variables to predict a single nonmetric dependent variable. The dependent variable can have two, three, four, or more categories. From a statistical perspective, this involves assessing group differences based on finding a linear combination of independent variables—the discriminant function—that identifies differences between the group means. Thus, discriminant analysis is a statistical tool for determining linear combinations of independent variables that predict group membership defined by the dependent variable.

ETHICAL DILEMMA

A state lottery commission has conducted a cluster analysis to gain a better understanding of public attitudes in the state toward the lottery and gambling. The commission plans to use the data to design marketing programs aimed at increasing support and participation in the weekly lottery drawings. The research identified five distinct clusters of citizens. Not surprisingly, the largest cluster (22 percent) was opposed to the lottery and had a low understanding of the economic impact the lottery had on the state. The smallest cluster (13 percent) was made up of people who loved the lottery. This group also had the best understanding of the lottery's impact on their state. The other three groups fell somewhere in between in both attitude and knowledge—qualified support (25 percent), neutral (27 percent), and nongamblers, who see some benefit for the state (13 percent).

Before the marketing team begins designing the communications strategy for each audience, the group considers issuing a news release to announce the research findings, focusing on the fact that a majority of citizens are in favor of the lottery in hopes of making a positive impression on the state's legislature. Only one of the lottery commissioners is uncomfortable with the plan because he feels they are overstating the results. What do you think? Is the marketing team misrepresenting the data to the public?

REVIEW QUESTIONS

1. What is the difference between dependence and interdependence techniques?
2. What is factor analysis and when would a business researcher use it?
3. How does the researcher decide how many factors to retain?
4. How does cluster analysis differ from factor analysis?
5. Explain the three phases of cluster analysis.
6. Why would researchers use discriminant analysis instead of regression analysis?

DISCUSSION AND THINKING ACTIVITIES

1. Describe a research problem that would benefit from a factor analysis. What are the variables, and what would you hope to achieve?
2. How could a researcher use cluster analysis to improve the validity of a research problem? Give an example to clarify your answer.
3. Describe a research problem that would require the use of discriminant analysis. Why would discriminant analysis be used instead of regression?
4. *SPSS Application:* Run a factor analysis using the twelve perception variables from the employee survey database. Prepare a brief report on your findings.
5. *SPSS Application:* Run a cluster analysis using the three organizational commitment variables (X_{13}, X_{14}, and X_{15}) from the employee survey database. Prepare a brief report on your findings.

6. *SPSS Application:* Run a stepwise discriminant analysis using the twelve perception variables from the customer survey database. Prepare a brief report on your findings.
7. *SPSS Application:* Run a cluster analysis using the three variables related to customer perceptions of employees from the customer survey database. Develop a three-cluster solution instead of the two-cluster solutions reported in the chapter. Prepare a brief report on your findings.

INTERNET EXERCISES

1. Use the key words "multivariate" and "multivariate data analysis" with the Google and Bing search engines (http://www.google.com and http://www.bing.com). Prepare a brief report on what you found and how the searches differed.
2. Use your favorite Internet search engine. Type in the key words "factor analysis," "cluster analysis," and "discriminant analysis." Prepare a brief report on the similarities and differences you found. Identify one interesting site and click through to it. Include a description of what you found.

NOTES

1. For more information, see J. Hair, B. Black, B. Babin, and R. Anderson, *Multivariate Data Analysis,* 7th ed. Upper Saddle River, NJ: Prentice-Hall, 2010. Hereafter Hair et al. (2010).

2. Those who wish more information on factor models and rotation approaches should refer to Hair et al. (2010).

3. An explanation of other approaches can be found in Hair et al. (2010).

4. For example, Hair et al. (2010).

5. We refer you to Hair et al. (2010) for additional explanation.

6. For more information on this topic, see Hair et al. (2010).

Part V

Communicating the Results

16 Reporting and Presenting Research

LEARNING OUTCOMES

1. Convey the importance of effective communication to research success
2. Describe the elements of a research proposal
3. Provide an overview of effective research reports
4. Summarize effective ways to deliver a research presentation

Good research is made useful by effectively communicating its purpose, methodology, results, and implications. The purpose of research is to answer specific research questions and thereby enable better decision making. Methodology is a detailed account of the research design and the project's implementation. The results and implications summarize the major findings and conclusions as they relate to the study's objectives.

Researchers use three formal communication approaches. They are the research proposal, the written research report, and the oral presentation. Occasionally, a project may skip one of these steps, for example the oral presentation. On other occasions, however, more than one presentation or report may be required. In any case, these three mechanisms provide opportunities to make the project useful. Certainly there have been occasions when the research was correctly executed though the results were ignored because they were presented poorly. If the research is to be useful in addressing the question that initiated it, careful attention must be given to these crucial communication opportunities.

This chapter describes proposals, reports, and presentations. The final form and content of these communication tools will vary depending on the type of project and the extent of involvement required of the researcher. But the examples here provide a basic framework. The different elements of each of the three communication tools are explained and illustrated using a project performed for Samouel's restaurant. In so doing, the characteristics of effective communication in each stage are described. Chapter 2 includes the research proposal for Samouel's restaurant. A sample report to Phil Samouel covering the primary research questions identified in the proposal is available on the book's Web site, at www.mesharpe-student.com.

WRITTEN AND ORAL COMMUNICATIONS

The primary role of the researcher is to place the decision maker in the best position to make an informed decision. The report and presentation should clearly highlight the key findings affecting organizational decision making. However, not all decision makers process information in the same way. Therefore, the researcher must consider the level of sophistication of the audience in preparing both written and oral communications.

AUDIENCE SOPHISTICATION

The researcher must present the results as simply as possible without being misleading. Consider the following potential audiences: business professors, engineers, scientists, managers for AT&T, and an entrepreneur—a former car salesman—wishing to establish his own car dealership. The researcher would likely use different communication styles for each audience. However, the basic format of communication would not change a great deal among these audiences.

Scientists, engineers, and professors are relatively sophisticated audiences. For these audiences, the researcher places more emphasis on the technical aspects of the research methods since these audiences are likely to have greater interest in this information and an ability to understand these topics. Likewise, a scientist is probably familiar with basic research techniques. But care must be taken to define key business terms that may be unfamiliar even to a technical audience. Overall, a slightly higher level of sophistication can be used when communicating with these groups.

For both the managers and the local automobile entrepreneur, the report would likely place less emphasis on the technical aspects. Details of any statistical tests, for example, would be placed in a technical appendix. Moreover, any statistical analysis would be reported in a more elementary way. These two audiences, however, are likely to be much more familiar with basic business terminology.

Remember, decision makers are less likely to act on results they do not understand. Consequently, the researcher should gear written and oral communications to the level of the least sophisticated potential user in the audience. This is sometimes referred to as the **least common denominator principle**.

WRITTEN COMMUNICATION

"Just the facts" is a phrase that implies getting to the important points quickly. "Just the facts" is a good orientation for writing business research documents. The writer must remember that the primary purpose of the document is not to entertain or impress the audience with literary eloquence but to assist in decision making. The Business Research Dashboard provides a manager's view of the typical internal research report.

■————Business Research Dashboard————■
MBAs Overdo It Again

Managers often struggle to get the most essential information from a research report. Consider the following managerial views:

"First line supervisors are intimidated by the blather and complicated, convoluted, thick reports circulated by the young MBAs on the staff." What this supervisor didn't know was that the president of the division had confessed the same thing to me on a flight to Los Angeles. He had suggested the reports from some of his own staff people—the ones with the graduate degrees—were a little intimidating and had sent him to the dictionary more than once. Not possessing a business degree himself, he felt a little out of his depth and was loath to talk directly to them about the reports and perhaps show his ignorance. The report authors with MBAs had fallen prey to the seductive idea that "the boss will be impressed that the authors had really done a lot of homework if they included sophisticated words in their reports and made them look physically impressive" (Hull 1995, 8–9).

Research reports are more useful if they simply address the following points:

1. Where are we now? Describe the situation that gave rise to the research.
2. Where are we headed? Stay on course and make sure everything in the report is fulfilling its purpose.
3. How do we propose to get there? Describe the analytical results that help accomplish the report's purpose.
4. How will we know when we have arrived? Make sure the "answers" (or end result) are easy to find and not hidden in the body of the text.

Source: William W. Hull, "Writing Reports for Top Management," *Supervision,* 56 (February 1995), 8–13.

Guidelines for Technical Writing

Research proposals and reports are typically considered technical writing. The following simple guidelines can greatly improve the quality of a technical report.

1. Front-End Loading. The writer should realize that the first few pages of the report are the most read pages. Therefore, the researcher should strive to pack as much content as possible into the first few pages. The key findings, implications, and recommendations, if requested, should appear in the first pages of the document, usually referred to as an executive summary.

2. KISS—Keep It Short and Simple. One of the best guides to technical writing is to be short and to the point. Follow these guidelines:

- Shorter sentences are better than longer sentences.
- Shorter words are better than longer words.
- Summarize information in tables or charts when possible.
- Use few prepositions (e.g., of, for, to, in, from).
- Use as little statistical jargon as possible.

3. Have Empathy. Remember readers have varying abilities to understand technical information. Not everyone can gain meaning from technical details in the document. Respect the reader's time by eliminating unnecessary information. Technical details can be included in an appendix, where they will not distract the less sophisticated reader.

4. Goal Orientation. Remember the document has a clear goal. It is designed to accomplish an important purpose for the business. All writing should be framed in the context of providing that information. It should be clear to the reader how the purpose will be accomplished.

5. Edit, Edit, Edit! Eliminate anything not necessary for clearly communicating the project's purpose.

6. Be Graceful in Ignorance. Avoid topics that the research findings do not address. Furthermore, any limitations or shortcomings of the study must be spelled out clearly. Not only is this the ethical approach but it is also better for the researcher to disclose any limitations rather having them discovered later by the decision maker.

7. Organization. Clearly organize the report's sections. Use a lot of headings and subheadings. These aid the reader tremendously. Also, include a listing of charts, figures, and tables to assist the reader in finding information in the report. The headings and subheadings provide an outline for the table of contents.

RESEARCH PROPOSALS

Research proposals are written during Phase I of the research process. Recall that proposals help ensure effective communication between the researcher and the decision maker. They describe the reasons for the study, including listing and explaining the research questions, a detailed description of the study design and tools to be used (research design), and a summary of the potential results. Finally, the research proposal includes a clear statement of the time schedule and proposed budget for the project.

Chapter 2 contains examples of research proposals. One of the proposals is the result of an interview between a professional business researcher and Phil Samouel, owner of Samouel's Greek Cuisine. The researcher used several creative problem-solving techniques to identify and refine the following research questions:

1. Are employees being managed to maximize their productivity as well as commitment to the success of the restaurant?
2. What are the best approaches to attract new customers and to retain existing customers?

The interview process creates a common understanding of the business situation faced by Samouel's. It is important, however, to commit this understanding to writing. By doing so, it is more likely the research will produce results that will be useful for

Exhibit 16.1

The Sections and Content of a Research Proposal

Section	Description
Background information	Describes the relevant business situation and the scope of the study. This includes an overview of related background material and previous research. The scope includes a statement of how the results are to be interpreted. For example, does the decision maker want operating recommendations from the researcher, such as strategies to improve Samouel's restaurant operations, or just a summary of research results? Some decision makers want the researcher to answer only the specific research questions, leaving the overall substantive interpretation to the decision maker.
Problem statement and research questions	Clearly defines the research problem. Lists and describes research questions to be addressed. If specific hypotheses can be developed, they should be listed and explained briefly.
Research strategy and methods	Describes how the study will be conducted. Referring back to the basic research process detailed in Chapter 2, this section describes the processes listed in Phases II and III. That is, it describes the research design to be used, the variables that must be measured, the data-collection approach, sample, how data will be collected, and the statistical techniques that will be used to analyze the data.
Final report outline	Outlines the final report. It lists the key sections of the final report along with a brief description of the expected contents. This is where dummy (or pro-forma) tables can be used to illustrate the type of quantitative results the researcher expects to find.
Budget and schedule	Provides a breakdown of the expected costs of performing the research project, including the researcher's fee and conditions of billing. It lists a time frame within which the research is to be conducted. This statement may also contain a brief description of the qualifications of the researcher.
Qualifications	Lists the qualifications of project consultants and the research firm.

decision making. This is because the decision maker, in this case Phil Samouel, will review and sign the proposal describing the research and its deliverables before the project gets underway. In other words, the proposal documents that the researcher and decision maker are "on the same page." The key sections of the proposal are described in Exhibit 16.1.

THE WRITTEN RESEARCH REPORT

The written report is the tangible result of a research project. For ongoing research, reports are often generated automatically through a company's information system. Although the content of such reports is similar to that of the type of report of interest here, this chapter focuses on reports written for one-time research projects. The format of all **research reports** is similar. In some ways, they simply build on the research proposal by describing what happened instead of what will happen.

AN OUTLINE OF AN APPLIED BUSINESS RESEARCH REPORT

Recall that business research can be described as either basic or applied. The content and style of the final report will vary slightly depending on which type of research is being performed. We first describe the outline for an applied business project. This type of report commonly results from projects completed by a business research consultant for a decision maker, like, for example, Phil Samouel. We discuss subsequently how the sections of the report might vary between applied and basic research projects.

Title Page

The **title page** lists the title of the project, the principal decision maker for whom the research is being performed, the date and names, affiliations, and contact information of the primary investigator(s). A title should be short but still descriptive of the research performed.

Executive Summary

Beyond any doubt, the **executive summary** is the most read portion of a research report. Remember, businesspeople are busy, so they want the key information summarized in an easy-to-read and concise format. In fact, many decision makers read only this section. It should thus be a brief, stand-alone overview of the entire report clearly emphasizing the key findings. The contents of the executive summary include:

1. a statement of the purpose and key research questions;
2. a brief description of the research design and related details;
3. a summary of statistical results of testing research questions and hypotheses;
4. a written interpretation of the findings framed as answers to the research questions; and,
5. if requested, a list of practical business implications derived from the research.

Executive summaries should be short. Two pages are acceptable, but a one-page executive summary is preferable. It's important that the primary and most interesting findings be formatted to attract attention, as a bulleted list, for example. The executive summary is also the opportunity to "sell" the report. It should try to convince the client that the project accomplished its purpose, and it should entice him or her to read further into the report.

Table of Contents

A **table of contents** makes the document more useful. It should list the headings and subheadings by page number. The location of all exhibits, tables, and figures should also be listed by their titles.

Introduction

The **introduction** is similar to that written for the proposal. It describes the purpose of the study in detail, including a list of research questions and hypotheses, along with explanations of each. It also contains background material detailing how the study came to be conducted, and includes a reference to the original proposal. The introduction prepares the reader for the information to come.

Research Methods

The **research methods** section, like the proposal, describes the way the study was conducted. It explains the sampling process and sample characteristics and the procedures used to gather data, including a description of the measures. In addition, this section may include a brief statistical overview of findings, presenting frequency distributions and descriptive variables such as means and standard deviations for all variables. This section may also refer to appendixes at the end of the document. The appendixes usually contain an actual copy of the data-collection instruments, such as a questionnaire and tables containing the frequencies and descriptive statistics. This is a good way to provide the user with contextual data that may be interesting but does not specifically address a research question.

Results

In the **results** section, the findings addressing the research questions and hypotheses are presented. The choice of data analysis techniques is explained, and details of the results are presented. Quantitative results are presented in tables and charts. Several examples of appropriate tables and charts for specific statistical approaches are shown in this book. Managers generally appreciate results presented graphically. Exhibits 16.2 and 16.3 illustrate the use of two versatile charts to present different types of results.

The famous pie chart is particularly useful in showing tabulated percentages for nominal or ordinal variables. This particular pie chart displays the percentage of Samouel's restaurant employees likely to search for another job. The pie slices vary according to the percentage of employees in each category. From the information provided in the frequency chart, we can see a high likelihood of searching. Indeed, a majority of employees are at least somewhat likely to search for a new job (29 + 11 +16 = 56 percent). This finding is something that Phil Samouel needs to address in developing a new business plan for his restaurant.

Exhibit 16.3 shows how bar charts can be used to display cross tabulation results. The charts cross the variable "intention to search" with gender and work type. In the "likely to search" categories, males are much more likely to search, as are the part-time employees of Samouel's. This situation clearly deserves Phil Samouel's attention.

Pie and bar charts can be useful in portraying other results. For example, bar charts can be used to depict means or standardized regression weights. Both types of charts are easily constructed using computer software. Virtually all spreadsheet packages

Exhibit 16.2

Displaying Results Using a Pie Chart

$X_{16,}$ "intention to search for another job"	Frequency	Percent	Valid percent	Cumulative percent
Extremely unlikely	4	6.3	6.3	6.3
Very unlikely	10	15.9	15.9	22.2
Somewhat unlikely	10	15.9	15.9	38.1
Neither—about 50-50	4	6.3	6.3	44.4
Somewhat likely	18	28.6	28.6	73.0
Very likely	7	11.1	11.1	84.1
Extremely likely	10	15.9	15.9	100.0
Total	63	100.0	100.0	

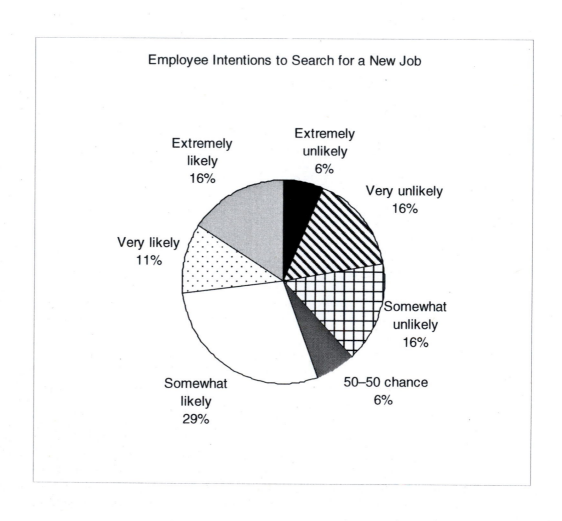

Employee Intentions to Search for a New Job

Exhibit 16.3

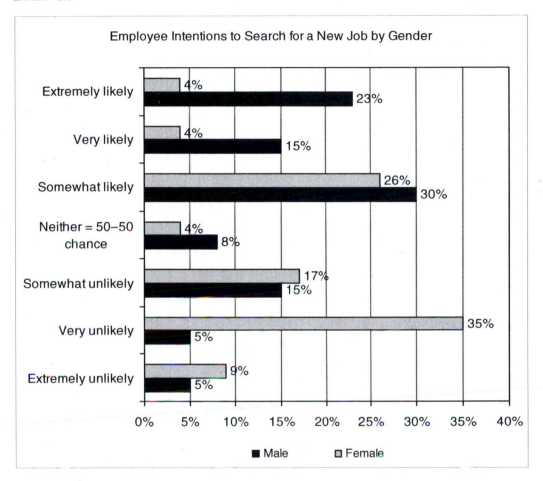

Employee Intentions to Search for a New Job by Gender

Category	Female	Male
Extremely likely	4%	23%
Very likely	4%	15%
Somewhat likely	26%	30%
Neither = 50–50 chance	4%	8%
Somewhat unlikely	17%	15%
Very unlikely	35%	5%
Extremely unlikely	9%	5%

■ Male   □ Female

have a click-through sequence for creating pie and bar charts, as well as other types of charts. Statistical packages like SAS, SPSS, and Excel can be used to construct some charts.

For some research results, the researcher can make use of an appendix. The report itself should be as free of clutter as possible. While all statistical analyses should be documented, not all of it needs to be included in the body of the report. Statistical results that cannot be presented in a simple, straightforward fashion should be placed in an appendix.

The main emphasis in the results section is to report on the research questions and hypotheses. But the researcher may wish to include a section summarizing other, unanticipated results discovered during the study. Some may seem particularly relevant and worthy of highlighting and perhaps suggest ideas for a follow-up study. Such results should be considered exploratory since they do not address the initial research questions or hypotheses.

Recommendations and Conclusions

The concluding section of the report begins by summarizing the results in everyday language. Using bulleted text to highlight key results addressing specific research questions is recommended. Any logical implications that emerge from the results are also discussed. If requested, a list of recommendations is provided. Recommendations may include suggestions for further research building on the current results. The **recommendations and conclusions** section also contains a discussion of the limitations of the research. No study is perfect. But the decision maker needs to be able to assess the confidence that can be placed in the results in light of a full accounting of the project's weaknesses.

Appendix

The **appendix** contains the questionnaire and detailed statistical analyses. Another important component of the appendix is a reference list. A **reference list** provides a complete description of the sources cited in the report. There are several different styles for reference lists.

The Business Research Dashboard summarizes the reflections of a senior executive in the marketing research industry.

An Outline of a Basic Research Report

Basic research is presented in much the same way as applied research. A basic research report has the same sections as that for applied research. The executive summary is sometimes replaced, however, with an abstract. The abstract is shorter than an executive summary. Abstracts are 100 to 150 words in length, describe the general study purpose, and give a broad overview of the study's results.

A **basic research report** is usually more theoretical than an applied business report. Therefore, a more thorough presentation of existing topical literature is presented. This literature is used to develop hypotheses, which are generally placed at the end of the literature review. "Conceptual Background" or "Theoretical Framework" is often used as the title of a special section focusing on how the research issues have been conceptualized. That is, the relationships among the various elements being examined are displayed visually in a chart or conceptual model, and the text of the report describes and explains the hypothesized relationships.

The research methods and results sections differ little from that in an applied research report. One exception in the style of reports is based on the intended audience. The primary audience for basic research reports is other researchers! Therefore, the writing can be more technical and present more detail about statistical and analytical issues. For example, a basic research report usually includes tables with more detailed information, while an applied research report relies more on charts. Because the presumption is that the audience for a basic research report is more sophisticated, the casual reader will sometimes find basic research reports esoteric and difficult to read.

■————Business Research Dashboard————■
Reflections on Decision-Based Research
Ronald L. Tatham, Ph.D., Chairman and CEO (retired), Burke, Inc.

The key to our mission at Burke, Inc., is embodied in the phrase "Applying Knowledge—Improving Decisions." This phrase gains its true meaning when you accept that for every manager in every organization the true job description is: "to make and implement decisions that increase the value of the organization." Typical job descriptions enumerate tasks, skills, or areas of management control . . . all of which should be supportive of the real job of "making and implementing decisions." A clear job description starts by describing the nature of the decisions that are to be made by the job holder. For a business researcher the appropriate job description starts with: "to make and implement research decisions that improve the organization's business decisions."

Everything in an organization revolves around decision making and at a practical level this requires you to wear two hats: one as a skilled research designer and the second as a consultant. I want to be clear in my meaning when I use the term "consultant." You are using your skills to help other managers think through their issues until they can articulate a decision and the basis on which they would make that decision. Often a manager will say to a researcher, "What I want to know is _____ (you fill in the blank)." The researcher's job is to trace that request back to a decision. What will this person do with the information? What decision is to be made? What are the alternative potential solutions within the decision? On what basis would that decision be made? What knowledge does the manager need to be most comfortable making the decision? If the decision were to be based on this knowledge . . . can it be implemented? As a business researcher, this requires tact and perseverance. Many times the manager requesting research has never thought in terms of a true decision and needs someone to pose alternatives to cause the decision to jell. I assure you, based on over thirty years of dealing with these issues, that when you pursue this line of discussion the request from the manager changes in over 50 percent of the instances. A thorough discussion of both the decision and of the necessity of prespecifying how the decision would be made very often changes a manager's perspective.

Without a specified decision and a specified basis for making the decision you have unfocused management and unfocused research. You may find yourself in the position of presenting research results only to hear a manager say, "You have given me a lot of good information and I learned a lot about the market." By my definition this is a poor outcome. The criterion for a successful research presentation is very simple. You always want to hear the key managers saying, "Thanks for a thorough presentation. We now know what decision we are going to make on this issue. Let's move ahead to the next steps to get it done!"

The implications and conclusions section is similar to that of the applied research report. However a basic research report may focus more on theoretical results. For example, it may discuss the implications for others studying the same issue. Since it is a basic research report, the implications will not pertain to any specific business but rather to businesses or industries in general. A basic research report may also provide relevant ideas for future basic research on related topics. These studies are suggested as follow-ups to the present effort. In this way, basic researchers develop a theoretical body of knowledge about important topics.

Finally, the basic research report contains appendixes and a reference list. There is less reliance on appendixes to present statistical results, however, since much of this material is included in the body of the report. A typical outline for a basic research report follows:

- Title page
- Abstract
- Introduction
- Conceptual background
- Research methods
- Results
- Limitations
- Implications and conclusions
- Reference list
- Appendixes

Examples of basic business research reports can be found in any of the leading academic journals in each business discipline.

ORAL PRESENTATIONS

Decision makers often require the researcher to make a formal presentation when the report is finished. Researchers should enthusiastically welcome this opportunity. The presentation provides an opportunity to follow up on the report. Thus, the researcher can clarify any material that may be difficult to understand in written form. The presentation is also interactive. This means members of the audience may and often do ask questions. In answering these questions, the researcher has another chance to communicate important findings. Put simply, the presentation is the best opportunity to "sell" the research and gain the enthusiasm of the decision makers.

CONSIDERING THE AUDIENCE

Just as in the written presentation, the researcher should consider the varying abilities of managers to understand the content of the presentation. It is a good idea to find out ahead of time which individuals will attend the presentation. Sometimes the presentation will be delivered only to the decision maker who requested the research. More commonly, however, others will be involved. The decision maker may invite any employee who might be affected by decisions that will be made. This might include superiors and subordinates. In some situations, line personnel or employees with little technical experience may attend. It is not unusual to present before eight to twelve key employees in a boardroom setting. Each person may have different concerns. A line manager may be most concerned with how a decision might affect production schedules. An accountant is likely to be interested in the impact on company profits and expenses. A manager may be most interested in the effect the decisions will have on his or her subordinates. Communication is enhanced when the presenter can tailor the presentation to the audience.

Audiences almost always ask questions or raise issues during the presentation. In fact, it may be a bad sign if the audience fails to interact with the presenter. Were audience members bored, confused? Questions and comments should be encouraged. It is good practice to try to anticipate questions and prepare a response before the presentation. Remember, researchers have an ethical obligation to make sure the research is useful. If the key players involved understand the research, it is more likely to be useful.

In preparing an oral presentation, use your creative skills. Creative tools can be useful in designing effective presentation themes, identifying the assumptions and misconceptions of potential audience members, and developing a list of questions that may be asked. Creativity is especially needed in developing a title that is both catchy and informative.

PRESENTATION FORMAT

There are many useful approaches for delivering a business research presentation. Avoid a strictly oral presentation. But even more important, do not merely read the report to the audience. Reading a report rarely makes a positive impact, and it can have the appearance of a lack of familiarity with the project. It may also be insulting since audience members are capable of reading the material themselves. PowerPoint slides and other visual aids are helpful to both the presenter and the audience. They cue the audience to important pieces of information as well as help to hold their attention. They also remind the presenter of the flow of the presentation and ensure important points are not forgotten.

PRESENTATION DOS AND DON'TS

The following "top-ten" list gives advice for preparing an effective presentation:[1]

1. Prepare Your Own Slides. Presentation software is easy to use, and anyone who does business research presentations should gain some competency with this important tool. Remember, as the presenter, you'll be blamed for any shortcomings in the visual aids. Do you want to trust the visuals to someone else? Moreover, by preparing your own presentation visuals, you maximize your familiarity with the material.

2. Create an Effective Title. Use the title to communicate. It should be short but insightful. This applies to both the overall presentation title and the titles of the individual slides. Suppose a researcher is presenting results about the effectiveness of salaried versus commission-based salespeople on customer satisfaction. The slide could be entitled either "Statistical Results" or "Commissions Lead to Satisfaction." Which is more effective?

3. Avoid Clutter in Your Visuals. Use a simple font. Titles can be as large as thirty-two to forty points in size. Bulleted lists are effective at twenty-four to twenty-eight points. Avoid fonts smaller than eighteen points for any important text. Limit the number of lines of text on any particular slide to six and the number of words to about thirty.

4. Use Simple Backgrounds That Produce High Contrast. Elaborate backgrounds may be decorative, but they can also be distracting. Use either a dark background with light letters or a white background with dark letters.

5. Vary the Slide Layouts. Slides do not always have to have clip art on the right and text on the left. If there is no picture that pairs well with a slide's content, do not use any. Take advantage of the white space in charts to drop in a meaningful short summary of the chart's findings.

6. Arrive Early. Presenters sometimes make presentations in a familiar room with familiar equipment. But more often, presentations are in an unfamiliar location with unfamiliar equipment. Particularly in this situation, arrive early enough to test the presentation. For example, different versions of the same software may not always work exactly the same. Animation or transitions between slides may work differently or not at all. Allow enough time to make any last-minute changes to ensure the presentation looks and functions as intended.

7. Use the Time Allotted. Make good use of the entire time allotted for the presentation. Businesspeople normally allow between twenty and sixty minutes for a presentation. While it varies from person to person, a rule of thumb is that the presentation will last two to three times the number of slides. Plan on using the entire time while still allowing time for questions. Plan ahead for material that can be skipped should the presentation begin to run behind. Stay until all questions have been answered.

8. Use Humor When Possible. Cartoons and funny phrases are usually acceptable. They help win the audience over and break the monotony of what might otherwise be very dry material. The humor should always be in good taste. If there is any doubt about the appropriateness of a particular piece of humor, leave it out.

9. Invite Audience Participation. Ask questions of the audience. For example, if the research involves employee reactions to a new company policy, invite one of the key decision makers to guess at how a typical employee responded to a key question about the policy. This keeps their interest up and helps them become part of the presentation. Remember to always respond favorably to their answers to your questions. The wrong response could demean the audience.

10. Do Sweat the Small Stuff. Presenters are part of the research package, so they must appear credible and professional. Pay attention to the details, including your dress and mannerisms during the presentation. Dress appropriately and remember it is usually better to overdress than to underdress. Like it or not, people will base their judgments of you and your work on your appearance. This may not always mean wearing a business suit. If you are making a presentation to decision makers on a retreat in Tahiti, a suit may not make the best impression. However, anything less formal to the same decision makers in a London office building would be very risky. Also, do not use distracting mannerisms and phrases. Try to limit the use of "you know," for example. If this is a concern, have someone watch you do a presentation and count the number of times you use such phrases. You may also want to videotape yourself to identify distracting mannerisms. Usually awareness of distractions is the best way to reduce them.

Some researchers are uncomfortable making presentations. Also, junior analysts or entry-level researchers are seldom called upon to make presentations. As the researcher advances, however, this changes. The Business Research Dashboard gives advice to those who may be apprehensive about delivering a presentation.

■————Business Research Dashboard————■
Presentation Anxiety? Have No Fear with This Cure-All

Giving an oral research presentation entails public speaking. Oral presentations frighten many people. Speaking about an innocuous topic or giving a classroom presentation is hard enough. A research presentation reflects the researcher's professional competence as well as the competence of any colleagues who were involved in the research. Thus, there is considerable pressure to make a good presentation. If you are afraid, consider this advice:

1. You will make a mistake during the presentation! But, even the best presenter will make mistakes. They are not fatal. Part of the apprehension may go away when you realize that mistakes are inevitable and that reasonable people expect them occasionally.
2. Study your material. One of the best ways to deal with nervousness is to be extremely familiar with the material. Discussing it becomes second nature at some point. It's as easy as dinnertime conversation. So, make sure you know all the details of the research. Find an audience to discuss the research with ahead of the presentation. Rehearsing the presentation relieves anxiety among some presenters. But having the confidence that you will be able to make some intelligent comment no matter what occurs is a good way of fighting presentation fear.
3. Practice your presentation out loud. Go in a room by yourself, perhaps stand in front of a mirror, and give your presentation. Good speakers modulate the tone of their voice, emphasizing key words and phrases and alternating the pace of their delivery. When you cannot speak out loud, then mentally rehearse the presentation.
4. Take advantage of opportunities to do public speaking. Eventually you'll become quite comfortable standing in front of an audience of faces staring up at you.
5. Laugh. Use humor when it is appropriate, and you have confidence that others will laugh with you. If you are unsure, don't use it, because a punch line that doesn't deliver will only increase apprehension.
6. Be confident. The reason you are giving a presentation is because you probably know something the audience doesn't. Therefore, you have an advantage. You can tell them something worthwhile. Expect to do a good presentation and you usually will.

Source: Steve Kaye, "It's Showtime! How to Give Effective Presentations," *Supervision*, 60 (March 1998), 8–10.

SUMMARY

CONVEY THE IMPORTANCE OF EFFECTIVE COMMUNICATION TO RESEARCH SUCCESS

Communication is essential to avoid wasting all the effort that went into the research. The research proposal, report, and presentation provide the means for the researcher to communicate the purpose, methodology, results, and implications of the research. If they are done poorly, it is less likely the research will be used to aid decision making. Reports and presentations "sell" the research project. This means they try to convince the users the information is useful and helpful.

DESCRIBE THE ELEMENTS OF A RESEARCH PROPOSAL

The research proposal is used to maximize the chances the decision maker and researcher will have the same understanding of the research purpose(s) and types of information to be produced prior to beginning the study. Proposals contain an introduction, a list of the research questions, a description of the research methods, a proposed outline of the final research report, including dummy tables, and a description of the time and financial resources required to complete the research project.

PROVIDE AN OVERVIEW OF EFFECTIVE RESEARCH REPORTS

There are many ways to increase the effectiveness of research reports. Executive summaries precede the body of a research report. They are in effect a mini report in themselves. They include the following sections: (1) a statement of the research purpose; (2) a brief description of the research design and implementation; (3) a summary of results derived from testing research questions and hypotheses; (4) a written interpretation of the findings framed as answers to the research questions; and (5) if requested, a list of practical business implications derived from the research. Given that the executive summary is often the only part of the report read in detail, great attention must be paid to making sure it communicates effectively. In preparing reports, the researcher must be sensitive to the audience. Do not overwhelm readers with technical jargon unless they have an everyday working knowledge of such terms. Finally, research reports are not a work of fiction and should present the facts in a concise way.

SUMMARIZE EFFECTIVE WAYS TO DELIVER A RESEARCH PRESENTATION

As in the report, effective communication in an oral presentation is essential. Careful consideration of the expected audience ensures the presenter provides the most important results and anticipates questions and objections. Ten suggestions are provided for making an effective presentation. Some of the more important ones include using visual aids, inviting audience participation, and being creative in developing effective presentation titles and content.

REVIEW QUESTIONS

1. List and briefly describe the three communication mechanisms used by business researchers. Is one mechanism better than the others?
2. List and briefly describe the elements of a research proposal.
3. What is an executive summary? Why is it so important? How long should it be?

4. What is the least common denominator principle and how would it apply when making a presentation to a group of military officers and enlisted people?
5. Explain the role of humor in a formal presentation.

DISCUSSION AND THINKING ACTIVITIES

1. Find an academic research report. Just about any article from *Academy of Management Review*, *Journal of Management*, *Journal of Marketing*, *Journal of Business Research*, or *Journal of Retailing*, among others, will do. Read the abstract. Try rewriting it as if it were being presented to a group of line managers, none of whom has a business or technical college degree.
2. A sample research report available on the Web site for this book (www.mesharpe-student.com) shows the results of examining only two research questions for an employee study. Develop a list of at least three more employee research questions and tell why they need to be examined. Similarly, the customer survey results examined only three research questions. Develop a list of at least three more customer research questions and tell why they need to be examined.
3. Use data analysis software and examine the research questions you developed in question 2. Prepare a brief report summarizing your findings and recommendations.
4. Using the SPSS customer data set accompanying this book, compute a cross-tabulation of the selection factors "prices" (X_{13}) and "employees" (X_{14}) by "restaurant" (X_{28}). In other words, do Gino's and Samouel's customers rate prices and employees as equally important? Present the results graphically using bar charts as shown in the chapter. Prepare the bar charts using a presentation software package.
5. Prepare a twenty-minute presentation for Phil Samouel to present the results shown in the sample research report on the Web site for this book (www.mesharpe-student.com). Assume he will be there along with his financial manager, floor manager, chef, and a member of the wait staff. Be sure to anticipate questions.

INTERNET ACTIVITIES

1. Access the Web site for this book (www.mesharpe-student.com). Locate the "Presentation for Samouel's." Critique the presentation for possible areas of improvement.
2. Go to http://www.edwardtufte.com and read the story "PowerPoint Does Rocket Science—And Better Techniques for Technical Reports," http://www.edwardtufte.com/bboard/q-and-a-fetch-msg?msg_id=0001yB). (If the URL has moved, try Googling "PowerPoint Does Rocket Science" to find the story.) The story presents an analysis of the role of PowerPoint in the Challenger accident. What does this story suggest about using PowerPoint to present

research findings? Could PowerPoint have been used more effectively, or should an alternative be used to communicate results?

3. Using a search engine of your choice, input the key words "research reporting." Prepare a brief report summarizing what you found when you followed the links to three to five of the results.

NOTE

1. Steve Kaye, "It's Showtime! How to Give Effective Presentations," *Supervision*, 60 (March 1999), 8–10; John Wareham, "From the Podium," *Across the Board*, 38 (March/April 2001), 67–69.

Glossary

Access complications arise from cost implications, lack of familiarity with parties providing the data, or methods used to summarize and draw conclusions about the data.

Aided questions are those that provide the respondent with a stimulus that jogs the memory.

Algorithm is a list of computer commands used to solve a problem.

Alternative-forms reliability is employed when a researcher develops two equivalent forms of a construct, and the same respondent is measured at two different times using equivalent alternative constructs. The measure of reliability is the correlation between the responses to the two versions of the construct.

Alternative hypothesis, as opposed to the null hypothesis, states there is a difference between two groups being compared.

Analytical phase is the stage in which data is analyzed.

ANOVA stands for analysis of variance; tests whether the means of two or more groups are statistically different on a single metric dependent variable.

Appendix is the section of a research report that contains the questionnaire and detailed statistical analyses.

Applied business research is concerned with solving a particular problem faced by an organization or individual.

Automatic Interaction Detection (AID) software considers possible relationships in pairs of quantified data in a data set.

Average summated score is the summated score divided by the number of variables.

Balanced scale refers to an equal number of favorable and unfavorable categories.

Bar chart is a vertical or horizontal display of a data distribution.

Basic business research is concerned with understanding a business related phenomenon as it relates to an entire industry or business in general.

Basic research report is a report that is usually more theoretical than an applied business report.

Behavioral intention scale is used by business researchers use to assess how likely customers are to demonstrate some type of behavior.

Behavioral learning theory provides managers with normative decision rules related to the amount and timing of employee compensation.

Bivariate regression is a type of regression that has a single metric dependent variable and a single metric independent variable.

Bivariate statistical test observes significant differences when two variables are used.

Box and whiskers plot is a visual display of the distribution's location, spread, shape, tail length, and outliers.

Branching questions in interviews or questionnaires direct respondents to questions relevant to their situation and ensure questions are answered in the proper sequence.

Build-up approach, also referred to as agglomerative, is a hierarchical clustering procedure that starts with all the objects (respondents) as separate clusters and combines them one at a time until there is a single cluster representing all the objects.

Business ethics is the application of moral principles and ethical standards to human actions in an exchange process.

Business research is a truth-seeking function that gathers, analyzes, interprets and reports information so that business decision makers become more effective.

Business researcher seeks to provide answers to specific business questions.

Business research process is a basic three-phase roadmap providing directions for conducting a research project; it includes formulation, execution and analytical phases.

Card reader is a device that scans data stored on a punched card.

Case study involves collecting in-depth information about a specific event or activity of a particular customer, group of people, firm or industry.

Categorical scale is a nominally measured opinion scale that has two or more response categories.

Causality describes a change in X (the cause) making a change in Y (the effect).

Causal research design is used to determine if a change in one event results in a change in another event.

Census refers to the collection of data from all members of a population under investigation.

Central tendency measures are the mean, median and mode; they are measures used to describe the distribution of data.

Centroid is the mean of all the respondent Z-scores in a particular group.

Chi-square is a statistical test used to assess differences between groups using nominal or ordinal data.

Classification (prediction) matrix is a table that displays predicted group membership results from the discriminant analysis results.

Classification question seeks information of a personal nature from a respondent in an interview or a questionnaire.

Closed question requires a respondent to choose from a number of predetermined answers.

Cluster analysis is a multivariate statistical approach that combines objects (e.g., individuals, brands, stores) into groups so that objects within each of the groups are similar to each other and different from objects in all other groups.

Cluster sampling is a technique in which the entire population of interest is divided into groups, or clusters, and a random sample of these clusters is selected. Within the selected cluster, all members are sampled.

Coding is the process of assigning meaningful numerical values to data for the purpose of analysis.

Coding units are words or images that have codes assigned to them.

Coefficient alpha, also referred to as **Cronbach's alpha**, is a measure of scale reliability that helps researchers assess how well several items together measure a construct.

Common factor analysis is a factor model that is based on only the common variance.

Common variance is the portion of the total variance of a variable that is shared with all the other variables in the analysis; the portion of the variance that covaries among all the variables.

Communality represents the amount of variance in a single variable that is explained by the factors extracted in a factor analysis; can be found by summing the squared factor loadings across all extracted factors for the variable (across the row of the factor pattern).

Comparative analysis involves evaluating the accuracy of secondary data by looking at the same data from multiple sources or by evaluating trends to see if there is any questionable data at a particular time.

Concept is an abstraction or idea formed on the basis of a perception of a phenomenon.

Conceptual framework is the section of a literature review that describes a model.

Conceptualization is the process of developing a model that represents relationships among constructs.

Conceptual model is a diagram showing relationships among constructs that displays the hypotheses to be tested.

Concurrent validity involves establishing that two measures of the same construct are related.

Conjoint analysis is a technique that enables researchers to determine the preferences that individuals have for various products and services, and which product features are valued the most.

Constant sum scale requires respondents to divide a constant sum over several categories to indicate, for example, the relative importance of specified attributes.

Construct is a combination of questions or statements representing a characteristic or concept.

Construct validity is an assessment of whether or not the questions or statements used to measure a construct (concept) successfully represent the domain of the construct.

Content analysis refers to categorization and analysis of existing written or visual materials to answer a research question.

Content validity, also called **face validity**, involves a systematic but subjective assessment of a scale's ability to measure a concept.

Context effect refers to a survey question's relative position influencing the response to other questions.

Convenience sample is a nonrandom selection of readily available, relevant survey participants.

Convergent validity is the relationship between two or more scales designed to measure the same construct.

Cost saving occurs when data already collected and compiled into a suitable format is provided to a third party for considerably less than the original cost.

Covariation is when one variable consistently and systematically changes relative to another variable.

Credibility is the assessment of the extent to which the conclusions that have been drawn are logical, believable, and justified by the data.

Criterion validity assesses whether a construct predicts an objective outcome it should predict.

Critical approaches actively seek to change social and economic circumstances. Researchers in the critical paradigm seek to undertake research that is "emancipatory" to enable people to free themselves, through self-reflection, from all forms of domination.

Cross-sectional analysis provides a snapshot of business elements at a given time.

Cross-tabulation is a frequency distribution of responses on two or more sets of variables.

Curvilinear relationship. See **Nonlinear relationship**.

Customer churn is the annual turnover rate of customers.

Customer commitment is the degree to which customers identify with the values of a firm.

Customer share is the proportion of resources a customer spends with one firm in a given competitor set.

Data display is the organization of information in a way that facilitates drawing conclusions.

Data editing is the process of inspecting data for completeness and consistency.

Data mining refers to electronically searching data warehouses for information used to improve organizational performance or solve a problem.

Data reduction involves selecting, simplifying, and transforming data to make it more manageable and understandable.

Data transformation is the process of changing the original form of data to a new form.

Data triangulation refers to collecting data from several different sources at different times and comparing it.

Data warehouses store and catalog company information in an electronic format.

Deductive reasoning involves going from a general case to a specific instance.

Dendogram is a tree graph that shows the history of how grouping was done in a hierarchical cluster analysis.

Dependence techniques are statistical tools in which variables are divided into independent and dependent sets and analyzed together to test dependence.

Dependent variable is a phenomenon a business researcher wishes to understand, explain, and predict.

Depth, or in-depth interview is an unstructured one-on-one discussion session between a trained interviewer and a participant.

Descriptive research is statistical information that characterizes what exists with respect to a research topic.

Descriptive theory explains relationships between descriptive variables.

Directional hypothesis is a hypothesis that includes information about whether the two variables are positively or negatively related.

Discriminant analysis is a statistical procedure that can be used to predict which group an individual is likely to belong to using two or more metric independent variables.

Discriminant function is a linear combination of independent variables used to predict group membership; its form is $Z = W_1X_1 + W_2X_2 + \ldots W_nX_n$.

Discriminant scores (Z-scores) are values calculated by inserting the appropriate values for an observation into the discriminant function and used to assign an observation to a group.

Discriminant validity is the extent to which a construct does not correlate with measures of other constructs.

Discriminant weights are estimates of the predictive power of each independent variable.

Dispersion measures describe the tendency for sample responses to depart from central tendency.

Disproportionately stratified sampling involves choosing elements from each stratum in a sampling frame according to its relative importance or the relative variability of the elements in a stratum; the sample size from each stratum is determined independently without considering the size of the stratum relative to the overall sample size.

Divisive approach is a hierarchical clustering procedure that starts with all objects as a single cluster and then takes away one object at a time until each object is a separate cluster.

Double-barreled question includes two or more issues and thus makes interpretation difficult and often impossible.

Double-headed arrows indicate bidirectional relationships and represent correlations or covariances between constructs that are neither predictive nor causal.

Drawing conclusions involves deciding what the identified themes and patterns mean and how they help to answer the research questions.

Dummy variable has two or more distinct levels which are coded 0 and 1; dummy coded variables enable us to use independent variables not measured using interval or ratio scales to predict the dependent variable.

Easy-read matrix displays only factor loadings that reach some pre-specified minimum size, usually at least .30 or larger.

Edited data has been inspected for completeness and consistency.

Eigenvalue represents the amount of variance in a data set that is represented by a single factor. It can be found by summing the squared factor loadings for a factor.

Electronic communication includes e-mail and technologies such as video conferencing and Skype.

Elements are common sets of characteristics.

Endogenous variables are constructs that are considered to be dependent in a conceptual model; any construct with an arrow pointing to it.

Error terms are included in the conceptual model to represent the amount of variance not explained by the hypothesized relationships between the variables (or constructs).

Error variance is the portion of the variance that is the result of a measurement or data collection error.

Ethics checklist is a list of questions useful for guiding decision making.

Ethnographic researcher interprets behavior through observation of actual life experiences.

Ethnography is the qualitative description of human sociocultural phenomena based on field observation.

Euclidean distance is a commonly used measure representing the distances between objects in a cluster analysis.

Execution phase is when the researcher actively gathers information from appropriate sources. The information is then checked for errors, coded, and stored in a way that allows it to be analyzed quickly and conveniently.

Executive summary is a stand-alone, very brief overview of the entire research report that clearly emphasizes the most important findings.

Exogeneous variables are constructs that are always only independent variables; any construct with an arrow pointing to it.

Experiment is a causal design in which a researcher controls a potential cause (experimental variable) and observes any corresponding change in hypothesized effects.

Exploratory research is conducted when the researcher has little information on a particular problem or opportunity; it is designed to discover new relationships, patterns, themes, and ideas.

Extended fieldwork involves collecting data over an extended period and is likely to improve both discovery and interpretation.

External peer review is an examination of research conclusions by other experts, including those both familiar with the research as well as disinterested parties; it is used to improve the trustworthiness of interpretations and conclusions.

External source refers to secondary data obtained from outside a company.

Face validity. *See* **Content validity**.

Factor is a mathematical, linear combination of the original variables of the form $F_1 = \lambda_1 X_1 + \lambda_2 X_2 + \ldots + \lambda_p X_p + e1$.

Factor analysis is a multivariate statistical technique that can summarize the information from a large number of measured variables into a smaller number of latent variables, or factors.

Factor loading is the correlation between a factor and an individual variable.

Factor rotation is a different but mathematically equivalent representation of the linear combination that makes up a factor.

Factor scores are composite scores that calculate a value for each factor for each respondent based upon factor analysis results.

Factorial design is an experimental design that controls the levels of two or more experimental treatments at the same time.

Field experiment is an experiment in which the manipulation of the causal variable takes place in a natural setting, such as a relevant business context, which emphasizes external validity.

Field-generated data is qualitative data gathered from interviews or focus groups in the field and consists of words and phrases in textual format.

Focus groups involve semistructured interviews that use an exploratory research approach and are considered a type of qualitative research.

Follow-up test is a statistical test to identify significance between three or more group means.

Forced-choice scale survey respondents are forced to make a choice in responding to a question.

Formulation phase involves defining the substance and process of the research.

Found data is qualitative data taken from existing sources like newspaper articles, speeches, diaries, advertisements, Internet sources, and audio and video records.

F-ratio is a statistic that assesses the statistical significance of the overall regression model; it is the ratio of the explained variance to the unexplained (residual) variance.

Frequency distribution examines data one variable at a time and provides counts of the different responses for the various values of the variable.

Funnel approach is when an interviewer moves from general to specific questions.

Geographic information system (GIS) can create, within a few minutes, numerous maps that overlay information from census data inventories on top of satellite photo imagery.

Graphic ratings scale is one that provides measurement on a continuum in the form of a line with anchors that are numbered and named.

Grounded theory refers to the development of theory based on extensive contact with the research context.

Hermeneutics explains human behavior based on an analysis of stories people tell about themselves.

Hierarchical clustering (break-down or divisive) is a clustering approach that begins with the initial assumption that every observation belongs to one cluster and then proceeds by separating the "furthest clusters" to result in two, then three, four and more clusters; the process continues until all observations represent a separate cluster.

Hierarchical clustering (build-up or agglomerative) is a clustering approach that begins with the initial assumption that every observation represents a separate cluster and then proceeds by combining the two closest observations (objects) to make a single new cluster, continuing the process until all observations are members of one cluster.

Histogram represents a vertical display of a distribution of responses.

Hit ratio is the proportion of observations classified correctly by discriminant analysis.

Hypothesis is a formal statement of an unproven supposition or proposition that tentatively explains certain facts or phenomena.

Hypothesis test is a systematic procedure followed to accept or reject hypotheses about proposed patterns or relationships.

Independent variable is a measurable characteristic that influences or explains a dependent variable.

In-depth interview is an unstructured, one-on-one discussion session between a trained interviewer and a participant.

Inductive reasoning is the process of identifying patterns in a large amount of data.

Inferential statistics are identified characteristics from a sample used to make estimates about the population.

Information-only business is one that exchanges information or information-related services such as distribution and storage for a fee.

Interaction effects refers to the combined effects of two independent variables.

Interdependence techniques are statistical tools in which the variables are not divided into independent and dependent sets; only independent or dependent variables are analyzed by themselves.

Internal consistency reliability is used to assess a summated scale where several statements (items) are summed to form a total score for a construct.

Internal source refers to secondary data obtained from within a company.

Interpretivism is a research philosophy that asserts that all access to reality is socially constructed. Interpretive researchers attempt to understand phenomena through meanings assigned to them by individuals rather than seeking an objective, bias-free reality.

Inter-rater reliability refers to multiple raters' evaluating the categorization of qualitative data to determine if the separate raters are consistent in their categorization.

Interval data can be obtained when scales have constant units of measurement so differences in any two adjacent points are equal, and almost any mathematical procedure, such as a mean or standard deviation can be calculated with them.

Interval scale numerically rates objects or events so that the distances between numbers on the scale are equal.

Interview involves a researcher directly questioning a respondent for the purpose of obtaining data.

Interviewer-completed method involves direct contact with respondents via face-to-face or telephone interviews.

Interview guide specifies for an interviewer the topics, questions, sequence of questions, and wording of the questions.

Intranet is an Internet-like network linking computers in a single organization.

Introduction is the portion of a research report that describes the purpose of the report and lists the research questions and hypotheses.

Issue is something that if altered will close the gap between the actual and desired states.

Judgment sample, sometimes referred to as a **purposive sample**, involves selecting relevant elements in a sample for a specific research purpose.

Kiosk survey is a type of self-completion interview; the self-contained kiosk is located in a high-traffic area, and individuals sign on to obtain information and submit survey information.

KISS stands for "keep it short and simple."

Kurtosis is a measure of a distribution's peakedness (or flatness).

Laboratory experiments involve the manipulation of the causal variable, which takes place in an artificial setting to emphasize internal validity.

Lack of familiarity, in connection with using secondary data, refers to an absence of knowledge of the initial motivation and processes followed when data was first collected and represents a potential weakness of using such data.

Latent root criteria occur when the number of factors extracted (computed) during a factor analysis is equal to the number of principal components with a latent root (eigenvalue) equal to or greater than 1.0.

Law-like generalizations are expectations of what will happen under specified circumstances that allow predictions of reality.

Leading question leads a respondent to a socially desirable or otherwise anticipated answer.

Least common denominator principle applies when written and oral communication is designed for the level of the least-sophisticated potential user in the audience.

Least squares is a mathematical technique that ensures the straight line computed in a regression model is the one that will best represent the relationship between the independent and dependent variables.

Likert scale is a measure of attitudes or opinions using a single scale to assess how strongly individuals agree or disagree with a particular statement; other adjectives, such as "favorable" or "unfavorable," or "positive" or "negative," can also be used with a Likert scale.

Linear relationship is a straight line association between two or more variables.

Literature review typically has two broad objectives: (1) to develop and expand research ideas and (2) to ensure familiarity with recent developments and a complete understanding of the relevant topics.

Logistic regression is a special type of regression that can have a nonmetric dependent variable.

Longitudinal analysis involves comparing findings across time to identify trends or seasonal patterns.

Longitudinal studies provide data describing events over time.

Mail survey is a survey delivered to a respondent via regular mail, fax or overnight delivery.

Main effects refers to the effects of two independent variables.

Manipulation is intentionally altering a causal (experimental) variable over different levels or conditions.

MANOVA is similar to ANOVA, but it can examine group differences across two or more metric dependent variables at the same time.

Market responsibility refers to a concern for ensuring products are ones consumers actually need and that their prices are fair.

Mean is the arithmetic average and one of the most commonly used measures of central tendency.

Measure of dispersion describes the tendency of a sample response to depart from the central tendency.

Measured variables represent the actual observations (raw data) and are referred to as indicator variables.

Measurement involves assigning numbers to a variable according to certain rules.

Measures of central tendency locate the center of the distribution as well as other useful information.

Median is the value in the middle of a distribution.

Member checking is when researchers ask key informants in their study to read their results and verify or offer alternative interpretations of their data.

Memoing is a process wherein qualitative researchers write their initial conclusions and observations, sometimes after every focus group, interview, or observational event.

Method triangulation involves conducting research using several different methods, sometimes both qualitative and quantitative approaches, and comparing the findings.

Metric scale is concerned with quantitative measurement.

Missing data refers to survey responses that are missing, typically because of data collection or data entry problems.

Mode is the measure of central tendency that identifies the value that occurs most often in a sample distribution.

Moderator encourages discussion in a focus group and keeps the group on track; a good moderator is a key to a successful focus group.

Multicollinearity is the correlation between the independent variables.

Multi-item scale consists of a number of closely related individual statements (items or indicators) whose responses are combined into a composite score or summated rating used to measure a concept.

Multiple regression is a type of regression that has a single metric dependent variable and several metric independent variables.

Multi-stage cluster sampling is a form of cluster sampling where primary clusters are first randomly selected, and then from the primary clusters a second set of clusters is randomly selected from which to collect data.

Multivariate test involves using statistical methods to analyze multiple variables at the same time.

Networking refers to computers linked to one another through various servers.

New insights can arise when secondary data and the conclusions drawn from the data are reexamined.

Nominal data is data that is placed in categories that have no arithmetic properties.

Nondirectional hypothesis postulates a difference or relationship but does not indicate a direction for the differences or relationship. Using such a hypothesis, we can thus postulate a significant relationship between two groups or two variables but not whether the relationship is positive or negative.

Non-forced choice involves a scale that has a mid-point that can be considered to be neutral or no opinion.

Non-hierarchical clustering is a clustering approach in which observations within a pre-specified distance from the cluster seeds are considered to be in a particular cluster; the observations can then be reassigned to different clusters in an effort to improve group distinctiveness.

Nonlinear relationship is often referred to as curvilinear, it is best described by a curve instead of a straight line.

Nonmetric scale is a scale that collects nominal or ordinal data.

Nonparametric statistical procedures are used when the researcher cannot assume a normal distribtution.

Nonprobability sampling is the inclusion or exclusion of elements in a sample according to the discretion of the researcher.

Normal distribution describes the expected distribution of sample means as well as many other chance occurrences.

Normative decision rule explains what a person is expected to do when faced with a situation described by a theory.

Null hypothesis states there is no relationship between two variables or constructs.

Numerical scale has numbers as response options rather than verbal descriptions.

N-way ANOVA is used when several independent variables are included in the test.

Oblique rotation is a factor rotation technique that allows factors to be correlated with each other.

Observational data is information collected by systematically recording observations of people, events, or objects.

Observation guide is used to record observed data. It indicates what the observer is to look for and provides a place to record the information.

Off-the-shelf data is readily available information compiled and sold by content provision companies.

One sample t-test assesses whether the observed differences between two sample means are significant.

One-shot research project addresses a single issue at a specific time.

One-tailed test is used when you can predict the direction of your hypothesized relationship (positive or negative).

One-way ANOVA involves a single non-metric independent variable and a single metric dependent variable.

Open-ended question is one with no constraints on a respondent in terms of the form of the response.

Opening questions are designed to establish rapport with respondents by gaining their attention and stimulating their interest in the topic.

Order bias is a situation where a question posed early in a survey influences how respondents answer the later questions.

Ordinal data is data that has categories that have the arithmetic property of more and less. However, intervals between categories in the scale are not equal.

Ordinal scale is a ranking scale that places objects into a predetermined category ordered from less to more according to a criterion such as preference, age, income group, importance, and so forth.

Organizational learning refers to the internalization of both external and internal information used as an input to decision making.

Organizational memory is a formal system that records all important events in a database.

Orthogonal rotation is a factor rotation technique that produces factors that are independent of each other (the correlation between any two factors is zero).

Outer model displays the relationships between the theoretical latent constructs and the indicator variables (rectangles).

Outlier is a data point for a respondent that is distinctly different from the values of the other respondents.

Outside research consultant is a researcher not employed by a firm seeking such expertise.

Paired-comparison scale is a type of categorical scale that includes a set of traits, product characteristics, or features that are paired against one another.

Panel is a fixed sample created for the purpose of regularly collecting data.

parametric tests are statistical tests used when the researcher can assume a normal distribution.

Parsimony states that a simpler solution is better than a more difficult one. Parsimonious research makes use of the simplest approach that satisfactorily addresses the research questions.

Participant feedback is information or responses provided by respondents when they are asked a question.

Pattern matching refers to data being used to predict or suggest a particular outcome, as well as evaluating the actual results to determine if they fit the predicted pattern.

Pearson correlation is a correlational measure that assumes interval or ratio (metric) data, a linear relationship and a normal distribution.

Personal interview is an interview that involves direct face-to-face contact with a respondent.

Phenomenology is a qualitative research method that studies lived experience and meaning.

Pie chart displays relative proportions of survey responses.

Placebo is an inert substance used in place of another being tested for effectiveness.

Population, also known as a **universe**, is the total number of elements sharing a set of characteristics relevant to the research project.

Population parameters are the characteristics of a population.

Position bias is a situation where one question is positioned before another one on a questionnaire and tends to influence the response to the later question.

Positivism is a research philosophy that views reality as something that can be objectively ascertained and described through research.

Postal survey is a survey delivered to respondents via regular post, fax, or overnight delivery.

Postpositivism is a research philosophy that posits that there is an objective reality but acknowledges that it is difficult to describe or analyze that reality without sociocultural and psychological lenses filtering interpretation; a modern revision of positivism.

Practical significance is a relationship between two or more variables that is meaningful, not just statistically significant.

Predictive validity assesses the ability of a construct measured at a particular time to predict another criterion at a future time.

Pretest is when evaluating the likely accuracy and consistency of responses to a questionnaire using a small sample of respondents with characteristics similar to the target population.

Primary data is information collected for the purpose of completing the current research project.

Principal component analysis is a factor model that uses all the variance in the data set.

Probability sampling refers to selecting sampling elements randomly, so that results will generalize to the population of interest.

Probing refers to a researcher's delving deeply into a response to identify any hidden reasons for a particular behavior.

Projective interviewing is where the researcher presents a survey respondent with an ambiguous stimulus.

Proportionately stratified sampling refers to the number of elements chosen from each stratum in a sampling frame being proportionate to the size of a particular stratum relative to an overall sample size.

Proxy is a variable that represents a single component of a larger concept; taken together several proxies are said to measure a concept. Proxies are also referred to in business research as indicator or manifest variables because they indirectly measure constructs.

Push poll is a short phone call used to spread negative and often false information about a candidate or issue under the guise of a poll.

Qualitative data is textual or visual information collected and categorized by researchers to address a research topic.

Qualitative research reliability is the degree of consistency in the assignment of similar words, phrases, or other kinds of data to the same pattern or theme by different researchers.

Quality research topic is one addressing gaps in existing knowledge that inhibit informed decision making.

Quantitative data is data to which numbers are assigned to represent specified characteristics. Its numeric form lends itself to statistical analysis.

Quantitative data collection involves gathering numerical data using structured questionnaires or observation guides.

Questionnaire is a prepared set of questions (or measures) used by respondents or interviewers to record answers (data).

Questionnaire administration is the method used to administer a questionnaire to respondents, such as telephone, personal interview, mail, Internet and so on.

Questionnaire design is the process of designing a questionnaire (survey instrument) to collect data in a survey.

Questionnaire sections refers to a three-part sequence of a questionnaire: questions in the initial section are referred to as opening questions; the middle section has questions directed specifically at the topics addressed by the research objectives; and the final section includes classification questions that help the researcher to better understand the results.

Quota sampling, like stratified random sampling, has the objective of the total sample proportionally representing groups in the target population. It differs from stratified sampling in that the selection of elements is done on a convenience rather than random basis.

Range is the simplest measure of dispersion.

Rank order scale is an ordinal scale that asks respondents to rank a set of objects or characteristics in terms of preference, similarity, importance, or similar adjectives.

Rating scale typically involves the use of statements on a questionnaire accompanied by precoded categories, one of which is selected by the respondent to indicate the extent of their agreement or disagreement with a given statement.

Ratio data. *See* **Interval data.**

Rational decision making is based on explanation and prediction.

Ratio scale provides the highest level of measurement. A distinguishing characteristic of a ratio scale is that it possesses a unique origin or zero point, which makes it possible to compute ratios of points on the scale.

Recommendations and conclusions is the section of a research report that summarizes the results and implications of the research, and puts forth suggestions for further research building on the current results.

Reference list is the section of a research report that provides a complete description of the sources cited.

Regression coefficient is a numerical value for the independent variable(s) that tells us how much of the variance in the dependent variable is explained by a particular independent variable, also referred to as a regression weight.

Regression sum of squares is the explained variance in the regression equation.

Related samples are data from the same group that compares two related variables, such as comparing the average number of Cokes® consumed each day by a group of females with the average number of cups of coffee consumed each day by the same group of females.

Relationship is a meaningful link believed to exist between two variables or constructs.

Relationship marketing emphasizes long-term interactions between a business and its stakeholders.

Relationship presence assesses whether a systematic relationship exists between two or more variables.

Reliability is associated with the term "consistency." A survey instrument is reliable if its repeated use results in consistent responses from samples with similar demographic characteristics.

Replicable means that a researcher could obtain the same results using identical procedures to the original researcher.

Representative means that a sample mirrors the characteristics of its associated population and thus minimizes sampling error.

Research is a discerning pursuit of the truth.

Research brief is an overview of the sponsor's (company or individual) initial perceptions of a problem or opportunity and may be presented in writing or orally.

Research design provides the basic directions or "recipe" for carrying out the project.

Researcher triangulation involves comparing the methods, analyses, and interpretations of different researchers on the same topic.

Research methods is the section of a research report that describes the research methods used in conducting the research.

Research proposal is a written document that describes the reasons for a research study, lists the research questions, provides an overview of the study design and tools, a summary of the potential results, and a proposed time schedule and budget.

Research question poses an issue of interest to the researcher and is related to the specific decision faced by the company or other research sponsor.

Research report is the written, tangible result of a research project.

Research topic question is designed to provide information related to the research topic.

Residual is the unexplained or error variance in a regression model.

Residual sum of squares is the unexplained variance in the regression equation.

Respondent fatigue refers to a respondent gets tired while responding due to the length or difficulty in completing the questionnaire.

Respondents are the human participants in business research.

Results is the section of a research report where the findings addressing the research questions and hypotheses are presented.

Rotated factor matrix is the matrix of numbers in a factor analysis showing the rotated factor loadings.

Sample is a relatively small subset of a population.

Sample frame is a comprehensive list of the elements from which a sample is drawn.

Sample statistics are the characteristics computed from a sample.

Sampling interval is the number of population elements between each unit selected for a sample.

Sampling unit is the elements or objects available for selection during the sampling process.

Scale is a measurement tool consisting of one or more items to measure variables or constructs.

Scatter diagrams, also referred to as scattergrams, are visual plots of the values of two variables for all the observations in the sample.

Scattergram. See **Scatter diagram**.

Science seeks to explain the world as it really is.

Scientific method is the method researchers use in the pursuit of knowledge.

Screening questions, sometimes referred to as **filtering questions**, are a type of opening question used on a questionnaire for ensuring respondents included in a study meet the predetermined criteria of the target population.

Secondary data is data used for research that was not gathered directly and purposefully for the project under consideration.

Self-completion methods are associated with collecting quantitative survey data and include postal surveys, Internet or other electronic surveys, drop-off and pickup surveys, and similar approaches.

Semantic differential scale is a type of metric scale used to measure attitudes.

Semistructured interview allows researchers the freedom to exercise their own initiative in following up an interviewee's answer to a question.

Simple random sampling is a straightforward method of sampling that assigns each element of the target population an equal probability of being selected.

Simple structure is the term used to refer to factor analysis results in which each variable loads highly on only one factor. This represents what is referred to as a pure factor solution.

Single-headed arrows indicate unidirectional relationships between two theoretical constructs or between a theoretical construct and its measured variables.

Skewness measures the departure from a symmetrical (or balanced) distribution.

Skipping question directs respondents to the appropriate section of a questionnaire.

Snowball sample, also called a **referral sample**, is one where the initial respondents are typically chosen using probability methods. The researcher uses the initial respondents to help identify other respondents in a target population. This process continues until the required sample size has been reached.

Social responsibility involves a concern for the way actions affect society or groups of people, including employees, customers, and the community.

Sorting scale asks respondents to indicate their beliefs or opinions by arranging objects (items) on the basis of perceived similarity or some other attribute.

Split-half reliability, a type of internal consistency reliability, refers to a researcher's randomly dividing a group of scale items in half and correlating the two sets of items.

Standard deviation describes the spread or variability of the sample distribution values from the mean and is perhaps the most valuable index of dispersion.

Standard error of the mean is the standard deviation of the sampling distribution of the mean.

Standardization is a method of adjusting for different units of measure across variables.

Standardized coefficients are regression coefficients that are standardized, referred to as beta weights.

Stickiness refers to how much it costs to transfer a given unit of information to an information seeker.

Statistical Package for the Social Sciences (SPSS) is an easy-to-use statistical software package that provides point and click access to statistical procedures like those discussed in this text.

Statistical significance is a relationship between two or more variables that is true and not due to random events or error.

Stem and leaf displays are diagnostic tools closely related to histograms that show actual data values that can be inspected directly.

Stepwise multiple regression is when each independent variable is considered for inclusion in the regression model and the order in which they are entered is based on the one that contributes the most toward predicting the dependent variable; only variables that contribute significantly are entered into the regression model.

Strategic and tactical decisions involve choosing between major alternative directions for an organization.

Stratified sampling is partitioning the sampling frame into relatively homogeneous subgroups that are distinct and nonoverlapping, called strata.

Strength of association is the magnitude or extent to which two or more variables are related.

Structured interview is one in which the interviewer follows a sequence of predetermined, open-ended questions.

Summated ratings scale is used to measure attitudes or opinions; it often consists of a five-point or seven-point scale to assess the strength of agreement about a group of statements.

Summated scores are what results when the scores of several individual items (questions) are added together and the mean is calculated. They can be used instead of factor scores to represent several items combined.

Survey is a procedure used to collect primary data from individuals.

Symptoms are signals that a change may be needed to avoid further problems or to take advantage of an important opportunity.

Systematic sampling is a process that involves randomly selecting an initial starting point on a list and thereafter selecting every nth element in the sampling frame.

Table of contents lists the heading and subheadings of the research report by page number.

Target population is the complete group of objects or elements relevant to the research project.

Telephone interview is an interview that is completed over the phone, rather than face-to-face.

Test market is an experiment that evaluates a new product or promotional campaign under real market conditions.

Test-retest reliability is obtained through repeated measurement of the same respondent or group of respondents using the same measurement device and under similar conditions.

Theoretical constructs are latent, nonmeasured composite or component variables.

Theory is a set of systematically related statements, including some law-like generalizations that can be tested empirically.

Theory-based decisions are decisions based on theoretical rationale.

Theory triangulation refers to using multiple theories and perspectives to interpret and explain data.

Title page is the page listing the title of the research project, the principal decision maker the report is being prepared for, the date, and names of contact individuals for the primary investigators.

Tolerance is a measure of the multicollinearity among the independent variables; small values (<.10) indicate multicollinearity is a problem; the opposite of variance inflation factor (VIF; see below).

Total sum of squares is the total variance in a regression model.

Trace is the total amount of variance in a factor analysis.

Translational equivalence means text can be translated from one language to another and back into the original language with no distortion in meaning.

Trust is an overriding issue in business ethics that involves believing an individual or organization will be honest and fair.

T-test assesses whether the observed differences between two sample means are significant.

Two-tailed test is used if you cannot predict the direction of your hypothesized relationship.

Two-way ANOVA involves two or more non-metric independent variables and a single metric dependent variable; also called a factorial design.

Type I error, referred to as alpha (α), occurs when the sample results lead to rejection of the null hypothesis when it is true.

Type II error occurs when, based on the sample results, the null hypothesis is not rejected when it is in fact false.

Unaided questions are those that do not provide the respondent with a stimulus that jogs the memory.

Unbalanced scale has an unequal number of favorable and unfavorable categories.

Unique variance is the portion of the total variance in a variable that is specific or unique to that variable.

Univariate test is statistical test of significance using one variable.

Universe, also known as a **population**, is the total number of elements sharing a set of characteristics.

Unobtrusive refers to a respondent's being unaware of his or her participation in a research project.

Unstandardized coefficients are regression coefficients (weights) that are not standardized.

Unstructured interview is an interview that is conducted without the use of an interview sequence; the researcher elicits information through a free and open discussion of the topic of interest.

Validity is accurate measurement of a concept or construct.

Variable is an observable, measurable characteristic in a conceptual model.

Variance is a measure of the variation or dispersion of data.

Verification involves checking and rechecking data to ensure initial conclusions are realistic, supportable, and valid.

VIF stands for the variance inflation factor and it measure multicollinearity among the independent variables; the maximum acceptable VIF is 5.0 and any higher number indicates multicollinearity is a problem; the opposite of tolerance.

Web-hosted Internet survey are typically created and hosted by an independent research company on its own server.

Wilk's lambda (Λ) is the statistic that evaluates whether the discriminant function has identified a statistical difference between two or more groups.

Index

Italic page references indicate charts, graphs, and boxed text.

ABI/Inform, 97
Absolute magnitudes, 306
Abstract concepts, 211
Access complications of secondary
    business data, 122–123
Access Japan, 19
Access to data, 84
Access to participants in research
    barriers to, 71–73
    cover letter to, sample, 72, *72*
    guidelines for obtaining, 73, *73*
    issues in obtaining, 69–71, *70*
    overview, 69, 75–76
Accounting business research, 7–8
Accuracy. *See* Validity
Administering questionnaires, *249*,
    268
Advertising. *See also* Marketing
    content analysis in, 190
    direct marketing campaigns, 200,
        201
    Interactive Advertising Bureau
        and, *120, 168*
    mobile phone, *154*
    sales relationship and, 33–34
Agree-disagree scales, 297, 301,
    301
AID, 15
Aided questions, 263–264
Algorithms, 14
AllBusiness.com, *127*
Alpha (α) errors, 324–325
Alternative hypotheses, 136–137,
    323
Amway, 283, *284–286*
Analysis of variance. *See* ANOVA
Analytical phase (phase III), *28*, 32

ANOVA (analysis of variance)
    F distribution and, 337
    factors and, 336
    follow-up tests and, 339–340, *339*
    group means and, 336–343, *338,*
        339, 343
    N-way, 336, 341
    null hypotheses and, 338, 340
    one-way, 336
    overview, 325, 327, 345–346
    quality control issue and, 343, *344*
    two-way, 336, 340–343, *341*
    use of, 336
    variation between groups and,
        337–339
    variation within groups and,
        337–339
Appendix of research report, 434, *435*
Apple (technology firm), 148
Applied business research, 6, *7*, 33
Arthur Andersen, 8, 67
Assessment. *See also* Data analysis;
    Reliability; Validity
    credibility, 286–289
    of scales, criteria for
        overview, 232–233, *233*
        reliability, 233–238, *233*
        validity, 233, 238–240
Associative techniques. *See*
    Correlation analysis; Regression
    analysis
Assumptions. *See* Hypotheses
AT&T, *103*
Audience and oral presentations,
    426, 436–437
Automatic Interaction Detection
    (AID), 15

Average summated score, 298–299,
    299

Balanced scales, 231
Bank of Credit and Commerce
    International bankruptcy, 67
Bank theft, *179*
Bar charts, 306, *307, 433*
Bar codes, *202*
Barings bankruptcy, 67
Basic business research, 6, *7*
Basic research report, 434–436. *See
    also* Research reports
Behavioral intention scales, 222
Behavioral learning theory, 34–35
Bell shaped curve, 308–310, *309*, 353
Best Buy, *103*
Beta (β) errors, 324–325
Beta coefficient, 366, 379
Bias
    from inconsistent interviewing
        practices, 191
    measurement, 126
    order, 265
    position, 265
    response, 264–265, *264*
    sampling, 169
Bidirectional relationships, 139
Biometric IDs, *179*
Bivariate correlation analysis, 358
Bivariate regression analysis,
    361–363, *364, 365, 382*
Bivariate statistical tests, 325,
    330–335, *331, 332, 333*, 345
Blank responses, 295–297, 317
Bloomberg Professional, 119,
    122–123

Bond markets, 111
Books as sources of literature reviews, 97
Branching questions in questionnaire, 261
Budweiser beer taste test, 331, *331*
Burger King, 386, *388*, 409–414, *410, 414*
Burke, Inc., *236*
Business decision makers. *See* Decision makers
Business ethics, 53. *See also* Ethics in business research
Business pragmatics, 40, 49–50
Business research. *See also* Business research process; Ethics in business research
accounting, 7–8
applied, 6, *7*, 33
basic, 6, *7*
businesses benefitted by, 9
communicating, 425–426, 439–440
decision making in, 8, 19
defining, 4–5
elements of, 5–6
in entrepreneurial adventure, 7, *8*
finance, 7
formal, 5
frequency distribution in, 302
function of, 5–6, 8, 23, 247
global, conducting, *21*
globalization and, 10
historical perspective, 3–4, 22–23
informal, 5–6
information-only businesses and, 8–9
literature reviews in, 92
manufacturing, 7
marketing, 7
measurement in, 209–214
multi-item scales in, 235, *236*
need for, determining, 28
outsourcing, 19
overview, 3, 22–23
problems, 30
research proposals and, 41
theory and, 33–37
tools of, 8
trends impacting
information revolution, 12–18, 23
international research, 10–11
market freedom, expanding, 9–10

Business research
trends impacting *(continued)*
overview, 9, 23
relationship marketing, 11–12
truth and, 4–5
Business research process. *See also* Research proposals; Research reports; Theory
basic project, 27, *28*
data analysis in, 32
data collection in, 31
defining, 27
overview, 17, 49–50
phases
analytical (phase III), *28*, 32, 49
execution (phase II), *28*, 31–32, 49
formulation (phase I), 28–31, *28*, 49
overview, 27, *28*, 49
research problem in, 28–30, *29*
research question in, 37, 83, 85–89
research reports in, 32
sameness of, 8
sampling in, 164
scientific method, 37–40, *38*, 49
Business researchers
ethics in business research and
after research, 57–64
before research, 55–57
during research, 57–64
overview, 55, 74–75
in-house, 20
information revolution and, *17–18*
out-of-house, 19
purpose of, 4–5, 23
relationships with
decision makers, 57, 426
managers, 19–20
participants, 58–64
role of, 19, 426
topics studied by, 6–9, *8*, 320
Business scandals, 52
Business school ranking surveys, 121
Business-to-business survey, 41, *44*
Buying behavior, *120, 202*

Card reader, 12–13
Case studies, 196. *See also* Gino's Italian Ristorante case study; Samouel's Greek Cuisine case study
Cashpoint fraud, *179*
Casual Fridays, 39, *39*
Categorical independent variables, 336

Categorical scales, 227–228
Causal research design, 153–155, *154*
Causality, 153–155
Causation, 362
Cause-and-effect relationships, 153–155
Census, 163
Central tendency measures, 310–311, *312*, 318
Characteristics. *See* Variables
Charts. *See* Graphics
Chi square (X^2) statistical test, 325, 330–333, *331*, 346
Children's Health Foundation, 41, *42–44*
Classification questions in questionnaire, 261–262
Client and ethics in business research, 64–65, *65*, 75
Close-ended questions, 255–256
Cluster analysis
between-cluster variation and, 400–401, *401*
deriving clusters, 400–404, *401*
example of, 405–408, *406, 407, 409*
hierarchical clustering and, 402–403, *403*
nonhierarchical clustering and, 403–404
overview, 399, 419
phases of
I, 401–404, 405–406, *406*
II, 404, 406–408, *407*
III, 404, 408, *409*
Sam's Club and, 399–400, *400*, 404
software, 402
two-group cluster solution and, 408, *409*
use of, 385, 419
within-cluster variation and, 400–401, *401*
Cluster sampling, 173–174, *174*
Coca-Cola, 6
Coding data, 32, 282, 297–298
Coding units, 282
Coefficients
alpha, 235, *235, 237*
beta, 366
correlation, 350–352, *351*, 355
of determination (r^2), 353
error, 405–406, *406*
multiple, of determination, 368
regression, 365–366

Coefficients (*continued*)
rho correlation, 219, 356, *356, 357, 358, 358*
standardized, 366
unstandardized, 366
Coercion issues, 58–60
Common factor analysis, 390
Common variance, 389–390
Communalities, *393*, 394
Communications. *See also* Oral presentations; Research proposals; Research reports
electronic, 13
oral, 426, 439–440
research, 425–426
written, 426–428
Company policy, developing, 194, *194*
Comparative analysis, 120
Comparative scales. *See* Nonmetric scales
Competition, 33
Competitive advantage, 33, 253
Competitive markets, 10
Complex concepts, 211
Concepts. *See also* Constructs
abstract, 211
complex, 211
customer interaction, 210
defining, 209–210
measuring, 214–215
proxy variables for, 211, *212*
Conceptual models, 139–144, *140, 141, 143, 144*, 321, *322*
Conceptualization
defining, 133
inner model and, 139
outer model and, 139
tasks of
constructs, identifying, 134–138
diagrams, preparing, 139–144, 140, 141, 143, 144
hypotheses and relationships, specifying, 135–138
overview, 133, 157
variables, identifying, 134–138
Conclusions
drawing and verifying, 286–287
section of research report, 434
Concurrent validity, 240
Conference proceedings as sources of literature reviews, 97–98
Confirmation of expectations construct, 234, *234*
Consistency. *See* Reliability

Constant sum scales, 229
Constructs. *See also* Concepts; Variables
in conceptual model, 139–144, *140, 141, 143*
confirmation of expectations, 234, *234*
in hypothesized relationships, 321
identifying in conceptualization, 134–138
job satisfaction, 7, 238
measuring, 210, 214–215
reliability of, 233–238
restaurant satisfaction, 241, *241*
SERVPERF, 124
SERVQUAL, 124
theoretical, 139
validity of, 238–239
Consultants, outside and in-house research, 19–20
Content analysis, 189–190
Content validity, 238
Context effect, 265
Contingency tables, 331–332, *332*
Continuous scales. *See* Metric scales
Convenience sampling, 175
Convergent validity, 239
Correction factor, *180*
Correlation analysis
bivariate, 358
coefficient of determination and, 353
coefficients, 350–352, *351*, 355
measurement of scales and, 355–356
multivariate, 358–359
null hypotheses and, 353–354
overview, 352–353, 381–382
Pearson correlation, 352–356, *354, 355*
Samouel's Greek Cuisine and, 354–356, *354, 355, 357*
Spearman rank order, 219, 356, *356, 357, 358, 358*
univariate, 358
Cost saving in data collection, 110–111
Covariation, 350–352, *352*
Craigslist, *90*
Credibility, 286–289
Credit scoring, *387*
Criterion validity, 239–240
Critical theory, 278
CRM system, 113
Cronbach's alpha, 235, *235*, 237, *237*

Cross-sectional analysis, 121
Cross-sectional studies, 113–114, 149–150, *151*, 158
Cross-tabulation, 330–333, *333*
Curvilinear relationship between variables, 349, 381
Customer churn, 12
Customer commitment, 12
Customer interaction concept, 210
Customer interaction, measuring, 210
Customer loyalty, 12
Customer relationship management (CRM) system, 113
Customer satisfaction surveys, 303–305, *304, 305, 306*, 322, 335, *335, 336*
Customer share, 12
CYA (cover your ass) principle, 195

Data
accessibility, 84
coding, 32, 282, 297–298
editing survey, 295–296
editor, 297–298
entering, 297–298
field-generated, 278, 291
found, 278, 291
interval, 326
knowledge and, 320
manipulation check and, 295–296
missing, 295–297, 317
nominal, 326, 353
observational, 186–188, 197, 204–205
off-the-shelf, 14
ordinal, 326, 353
preparing, 32, 295–299, 317
ratio, 326
transformation, 298
Data analysis. *See also* Descriptive statistics
in business research process, 32
with descriptive statistics, 299–315
from multiple sources, 286
nominal scales and, 216
in qualitative research, 32, 281–287, *283, 288*, 289, *290*, 291
in quantitative research, 295–299, 317
software, 287, *288*
statistical techniques and, 358–360
Data collection
in business research process, 31
cost saving in, 110–111

Data collection *(continued)*
  in descriptive research design, 149
  errors, 31–32
  extended fieldwork, 289
  forms, 31
  Internet and household, 126
  primary business
    overview, 185–186, 187,
      204–205
    qualitative, 186–196, 187,
      204–205
    quantitative, 197–205
  in qualitative research
    analyzing, 32, 281–287, 283,
      288, 291
    coding, 32
    content analysis, 189–190
    ethnographic research, 188–189
    interviews, 190–196
    managing, 278–280
    observation, 186–188
    online, 278, 280
    overview, 186, 187, 204–205
  in quantitative research
    analyzing, 32
    coding, 32
    interview-completed surveys,
      197, 203, *203*, 206
    observation, 197, 204
    overview, 197–198, *198*,
      204–205
    self-completion surveys,
      197–202, 206
    technology and, 198, *199*
  questionnaires and, 269–270
  for Samouel's Greek Cuisine, *204*
  secondary business, 113–114
  selecting best, *204*
  time saving in, 110
Data display, 283, *284–286*
Data management, 278, 280, 291
Data mining, 14–15, *16*
Data reduction, 283, *284–286*
Data triangulation, 289
Data warehouses, 13–14, 298–299,
  300
Debriefing issues, 62
Decision Analyst, Inc., *153*
Decision makers
  ethics in business research and,
    64, 75
  relationship with business
    researchers and, 57, 426
Decision making, strategic and
  tactical, 3, 8, 19
Deductive reasoning, 276

Deloitte and Touche, 67
Deloitte Touche Tohmatsu, 8
Dependence techniques, 385, 419.
    See also ANOVA; Discriminant
    analysis; Multiple regression
    analysis
Dependent variables, 134, 143, 321,
  359–360, 362, 366–367, 385
Depth interviews, 145, 194–195, *196*
Descriptive research design
  cross-sectional, 149–150, *151*
  data analysis in, 149
  errors in, 150
  examples of, 149
  longitudinal, 149–153, *151, 152,*
    153
  use of, 148–149, 155, 158
Descriptive statistics
  bar charts, 306, *307, 433*
  basis of, 150
  central tendency measures,
    310–311, *312*, 318
  dispersion measures, 309,
    312–315, *315*, 318
  frequency distribution, 300–302,
    301, 302, 303, 304
  Gino's Italian Ristorante and,
    301–304, *304, 305, 306, 317*
  histograms, 302–305, *303, 304,*
    305
  Nightingale and, *308*
  normal distribution, 308–310, *309,*
    353
  overview, 299, 317–318
  pie charts, 306, *307*, 308, *308*, 431,
    432
  Samouel's Greek Cuisine and,
    301–304, *304, 305, 306, 317*
Descriptive theory, 35
Design of research. *See* Research
  design
Deviation, standard, 177, 308,
  313–314
Diagrams, preparing, 139–144, *140,*
  141, 143, 144
Digit telephone dialing, random,
  169
Digital money payment systems, *88*
Dining out expenditures, measuring,
  213
Direct marketing campaigns, 200,
  201
Direction (variable relationship),
  349–350
Directional hypothesis, 137
Disclosure issues, 61–62

Discriminant analysis. *See also*
    Multiple discriminant analysis
  example of, 415–418, *415, 416,*
    417, 418
  Gino's Italian Ristorante and,
    415–418, *415, 416, 418*
  overview, 408, 418
  Samouel's Greek Cuisine and,
    415–418, *415, 416, 418*
  stepwise, 418
  use of, 385, 419
  Wilks' lambda and, 415
Discriminant scores (Z scores),
  411–413, *413*, 418
Discriminant validity, 239
Dispersion measures, 309, 312–315,
  315, 318
Disproportionately stratified
  sampling, 172
Dissertations as sources of literature
  reviews, 98
Distortion, 127
Double-barreled questions, avoiding,
  264
Drawing conclusions, 286–287
Dummy variables, 362, 377–378,
  379, 382–383

E-mail, 13
Easy-read matrix, 396–397, *397*
Editing survey data, 295–296
Editor, data, 297–298
Eigenvalue, 394
Electronic communications, 13
Electronic databases as sources of
  literature reviews, 98
Electronic search engines, 114, *115,*
  116, *118*
Electronic surveys, 200, 202
Elements, 164
Employee loyalty, 12
Employee survey, *322*, 353–355, *354*
Employee turnover, 12
Employment trends in United States,
  115
Enron, 8
Entering data, 297–298
Error terms, 139, 142, 143, 362
Error variance, 389–390
Errors
  alpha(α), 324–325
  beta (β), 324–325
  coefficients, 405–406, *406*
  data collection, 31–32
  in descriptive research design, 150
  in nonprobability sampling, 164

Errors *(continued)*
  in probability sampling, 164
  standard, 309
  standard error of the mean, 314
  Type I and II, 323–325
Ethics checklist, 68–69
Ethics in business research
  access to participants and, 69–73,
    70, 72, 73, 75–76
  business researchers and
    after research, 57–64
    before research, 55–57
    during research, 57–64
    overview, 55, 74–75
  business scandals and, 52
  client and, 64–65, *65,* 75
  content analysis and, 189–190
  decision makers and, 64, 75
  defining, 52–53, 74
  dilemmas in, 53–55, *55,* 57
  experimental designs
    coercion issues, 58–60
    debriefing, 62
    disclosure, 61–62
    freedom from harm, 60–61
    Human Resource Review
      Committee, 62, 64
    overview, 58
    privacy, 58, *59,* 61, 66
    scenarios, *63,* 64
  organizational culture and, 55, *56*
  overview, 52, 74–76
  participants and, 65–66, 75
  relevance of, 53–55, *54,* 74
  Samouel's Greek Cuisine and, *74*
  scenarios, *63,* 64
  secondary business data and, 127
  standards for research and, global,
    68
  trust and, 52–53
  unethical actions and, implications
    of, 66–69, 75
Ethnographic research, 188–189,
  289
Euclidean distance, 402
European Agency for Safety and
  Health at Work, 53
European Commission, *155–156*
European Society for Opinion
  and Marketing Research
  (ESOMAR), 67, *68*
European Union, 113, *155–156*
Execution phase (phase II), *28,*
  31–32
Executive summary of research
  report, 430

Experimental research design,
    ethical
  coercion issues, 58–60
  debriefing issues, 62
  disclosure issues, 61–62
  freedom from harm issues, 60–61
  Human Resource Review
    Committee, 62, 64
  overview, 58
  privacy issues, 58, *59,* 61, 66
  scenarios, *63,* 64
Explained variance, 364
Exploratory factor analysis
  deriving factors, 388–392
  example of, 386, *388*
  models, 389–390, *389*
  number of factors, 392–394
  overview, 386
  rotation, 390–392, *391*
  use of, 386
  variance in, 389–390, *389*
Exploratory research design,
  147–148, 155
Extended fieldwork, 289
External peer review, 289
External source, 112, *113*

F distribution, 337
F ratio, 337, 364–365
F test, 337
Face-to-face interviews, 190. *See
  also* Interviews
Face validity, 238
Factor analysis
  common, 390
  credit scoring and, *387*
  easy-read matrix and, 396–397, *397*
  example of, 395–399
  exploratory
    deriving factors, 388–392
    example, 386, *388*
    models, 389–390, 389
    number of factors, 392–394,
      393
    overview, 386
    rotation, 390–392, 391
    use of, 386
    variance in, 389–390, 389
  Gino's Italian Ristorante and, *396*
  interpreting factors, 394–399
  overview, 386, 419
  Samouel's Greek Cuisine and,
    395–399, *396, 397, 398*
  simple structure in, 391
  software, 393
  use of, 385

Factor loadings, *393,* 394
Factorial design, 340–343
Factors, 336
Faithful participants in research, 66
Family wealth, measuring total,
  213–214
Fast food survey, 386, 388, 409–414,
  410, 414
Federal Reserve System report,
  112–113
FedEx, 13
Feedback from participants in
  research, 190, 268
FICO scores, *387*
Field-generated data, 278, 291
FIFA World Cup football games
  (2010), 176
Filtering questions in questionnaire,
  260, 296
Finance business research, 7
Focus groups, 145, 191–193, *193,
  196*
Follow-up tests, 339–340, *339*
Forced-choice scales, 231–232
Format
  of oral presentations, 437
  of research reports, 429
  of secondary business data,
    112–113, *113*
Formulation phase (phase I), 28–31,
  28
Found data, 278, 291
Framing questions, avoiding, 264,
  264
Free markets, 10
Freedom from harm issues, 60–61
Frequency distribution, 300–302,
  301, 302, 303, 304
Front-end loading, 427
Funnel approach, 261

Gap (clothing chain), 30
Gates, Bill, 316, *316*
Gender, measuring, 213
General Electric, 4
General Mills, 280, *281*
Geographic information system
  (GIS), 14
Gino's Italian Ristorante case study
  customer satisfaction surveys,
    303–305, *304, 305, 306,* 322,
    335, *335, 336*
  descriptive statistics and, 301–304,
    304, 305, 306, 317
  discriminant analysis and,
    415–418, *415, 416, 418*

Gino's Italian Ristorante case study
(*continued*)
factor analysis and, *396*
frequency distribution and,
301–302, *301, 302, 304*
group means test and, 335, *336,*
337–340, *338, 339, 355*
overview, 20, 23
questionnaires and, *250–252, 269*
regression analysis and, 363–366,
364, 365, 370–374, *371, 372*
scales and, 222
testing hypotheses in quantitative
research and, *338,* 340–343,
341, 342, 343
GIS, 14
Global market, 10
Global positioning system (GPS),
15–16, *17,* 188
Global research, conducting, *21*
Globalization, 10
GMAT, 240
Google, 8, *36,* 99, 116, *116,* 148, 278
Google Scholar, 96–97, 99
Gorkovsky Avtomobilny Zavod
(GAZ), 10
Government reports as sources of
literature reviews, 98
GPS, 15–16, *17,* 188
Graduate Management Admission
Test (GMAT), 240
Grant Thornton International, 8
Graphic ratings scales, 225–226
Graphics
bar charts, 306, *307, 433*
frequency distribution, 300–302,
301, 302, 303, 304
histograms, 302–305, *303, 304, 305*
normal distribution, 308–310, *309,*
383
pie charts, 306, *307,* 308, *308,* 431,
432
use of, 299
Graphs. *See* Graphics
Grounded theory, 276–277, 290
Group means
ANOVA and, 336–343, *338, 339,*
343
SPSS in comparing, *380, 409*
testing differences in, 334–335,
335, 336
testing equality of, 416, *417*
Grouping objects, 401–404, *403*

Harrison Global, *324*
Hermeneutics, 277–278, *279–280*

Hierarchical clustering, 402–403,
403
Hierarchy of effects theory,
104–105, *105*
Histograms, 302–305, *303, 304,*
305
Hitachi, *179*
Honesty, 66
Human Resource Review
Committee, 62, 64
Hypotheses. *See also* Null
hypotheses; Testing hypotheses
in quantitative research
alternative, 136–137, 323
business examples, 37, *38*
defining, 37, 135
developing, 135–136, 158
directional, 137
literature reviews and, 95
nondirectional, 137
in qualitative research, 145–146,
276
in quantitative research, 145–146
relationships and, specifying,
135–138
research question and, 37, *38,* 39,
39, 95
support of, 40
testing, 138, 158
theory and, 33, 39, *39*

IBM, *103*
Ideas, research, 85–89
IMF, 111–112
In-depth interviews, 145, 194–195,
196
In-house business research, 20
Independent samples, 334
Independent variables, 134, 321,
362, 366–367, 374, 385
Index. *See* Scales
Indicator variables, 139
Inductive reasoning, 275–276
Industry reports as sources of
literature reviews, 98
Inferential statistics, 321–323
Information age, 12, 110. *See also*
Technology
Information-only businesses, 8–9
Inner model, 139
Instructions for questionnaire, 266,
267
Inter-rater reliability, 287
Interaction effects, 340
Interactive Advertising Bureau
(IAB), *120, 168*

Interdependence techniques, 386,
419. *See also* Cluster analysis;
Factor analysis
Internal consistency reliability, 235
Internal source, 112, *113*
International Business Research, 19
International Monetary Fund (IMF),
111–112
International organizations, 98,
111–112
International research, 10–11
Internet
billing and payment methods, *88*
growth of, 121
household data collections and, 126
questionnaires and, 266
search engines, 114, *115,* 116, *118*
secondary business data on, 114,
116, *116, 117–118*
as source of literature reviews, 99
as source of secondary business
data, 30–31, 113, *116,*
117–118, 121, 127, *129*
surveys, 200, 202
theory and, 35, *36*
women's usage of, 180, *181*
world market and, 10
Interpretivism, 277
Interval data, 326
Interval scales, 219–220, 362
Interview-assisted instructions, 266
Interview guide, 248
Interviewer-completed surveys, 197,
203, *203,* 206
Interviews
case studies, 196
computer-assisted, 297
content analysis in interpreting
text, 190
defining, 190
depth or in-depth, 145, 194–195,
196
face-to-face, 190
overview, 190, 205–206
probing technique in, 190
projective techniques, 195–196,
197
semistructured, 191–193, *193, 196*
structured, 191
telephone, 190
unstructured, 194, *194*
Intranets, 13
Introduction section of research
report, 431
Intuition-based decision rules,
36–37, *37*

iPhone, 148
iPod, 148
Issues (change potential to close gap between actual and desired), 103, *104*

Japanese Camera and Imaging Products Association, 114, 116
Job satisfaction construct, 7, 238
Job stress survey, 60
Johns Hopkins University, 62
Journals as sources of literature reviews, 97–98
JSTOR (electronic database), 97
Judgment sampling, 175

Kaiser Permanente, 155
KDD, 14–15
Keynes, John Maynard, 89
Kieskeurig, 8
Kiosk survey, 202
KISS (Keep It Short and Simple) principle, 427
Knowledge and data, 320
Knowledge discovery in databases (KDD), 14–15
Kurtosis, 315

Lack of familiarity with secondary business data, 123
Laphroaig scotch taste test, 331–332, *332*
Latent root criterion, 392–393
Law-like generalizations, 33
Leading questions, avoiding, 264, *264*
Least common denominator principle, 426
Least squares method, 362, 366
Likert scales, 221–222, 298
Linear relationship between variables, 349, 381
Literature reviews
  in business research, 92
  contributions of, 93–96
  defining, 107
  functions of, 29–30, 92
  hypothesis and, 95
  interpretation of findings and, 96
  methodology and, 95–96
  overview, 107
  planning, 99–100, *100*, 107
  preparing, 89–93, *93*, *101*
  quantity needed for research, 92
  research problem and, 93–94
  research question and, 95, 102–105, 108

Literature reviews *(continued)*
  sources
    balance of, 92–93
    books, 97
    conference proceedings, 97–98
    dissertations, 98
    electronic databases, 98
    government reports, 98
    industry reports, 98
    Internet searches, 99
    journals, 97–98
    locating, *103*
    overview, 96–97, 107
    textbooks, 97
    theses, 98
  stages of, 90–91
  writing, 100–102, *102*, 107
Longitudinal analysis, 120-121
Longitudinal studies, 149–153, *151*, *152*, *153*, 158
Loyalty, customer, 12

Macy's, 33
Mahalanobis distance, 402
Maiden Group PLC, *154*
Mail surveys, 199–200, *201*
Main effects, 340
Managers
  marketing, 7
  relationship with business researchers, 19–20
Manipulation check, 295–296
MANOVA, 343
Manufacturing business research, 7
Market freedom, expanding, 9–10
Market Research Online Communities (MROCs), 280, *281*
Market responsibility, 53
Marketing. *See also* Advertising
  business research, 7
  direct, 200, *201*
  hierarchy of effects theory and, 104, *105*
  relationship, 11–12
  as topic for business researcher, 7
Marketing Research Association (MRA), 52–53
Mathematical theory, *36*
Maxwell House, *197*
Mcallan scotch taste test, 331–332, *332*
McDonald's, 12, 386, *388*, 409–414, *410*, *414*
Médecins Sans Frontières, 123

Mean
  defining, 310. *See also* Group means
  overview, 310–311
  sample size for, estimating, 177, *178*
  standard error of, 314
Measured variables, 139, 142–143, *143*
Measurement. *See also* Scales
  bias, 126
  in business research, 209–214
  of central tendency, 310–311, *312*, 318
  as common occurrence, 209
  of concepts, 210, 214–215
  of constructs, 210, 214–215
  of customer interaction, 210
  defining, 214, 243
  difficulties, 211
  dining out expenditures, 213
  of dispersion, 309, 312–315, *315*, 318
  distance between objects, 401–402
  family wealth, total, 213–214
  gender, 213
  levels of, 214–215
  overview, 209, 241–244
  of product complexity, 225, *226*
  proxy variables and, 211, *212*
  scale of, 325–326, *326*, 355–356
  validity, 126
Media consumption patterns survey, *120*
Median, 311
Member checking, 289
Memoing process, 286
Message framing check, *213*
Method triangulation, 289
Methodology, 431
Metric scales, 222–226
Missing data, 295–297, 317
Mobile phone advertising, *154*
Mode, 311
Moderator of focus group, 191–193
Moen, 189
Multi-item scales, 230, 233–235, *234*, *236*
Multicollinearity, 374–377, *375*, *376*, 382
Multiple coefficient of determination, 368
Multiple discriminant analysis
  example of, 409–414, *410*, *413*, *414*
  overview, 408
  use of, 385

Multiple group hypothesis testing, 330–335, *331, 332, 333*

Multiple regression analysis
advanced topics in, 377–380
example of, 369–374, *370, 371, 372*
multicollinearity and, 374–377, *375, 376,* 382
overview, 366–367, 382
statistical versus practical significance and, 368–369

Multistage sampling, 174

Multivariate analysis of variance (MANOVA), 343

Multivariate correlation analysis, 358–359

Multivariate techniques, 385–386, *386,* 418

Multivariate tests, 325, 330–335, *331, 332, 333,* 345

Music in department stores survey, 150, *151*

N-way ANOVA, 336, 341
Netflix, 58, *59*
Networking, 13
New insights, 122
NGOs, 111–112, 123
Nightingale, Florence, *308*
Nike, *154*
Nominal data, 326, 353
Nominal scales, 215–216
Nondirectional hypothesis, 137
Nongovernmental organizations (NGOs), 111–112, 123
Nonhierarchical clustering, 403–404
Nonlinear relationship between variables, 349, 381
Nonmetric scales, 222, 227–229
Nonparametric statistical technique, 326–327
Nonprobability sampling
convenience sampling, 175
defining, 167
errors and, 164
judgment sampling, 175
overview, 174–175, 182–183
in qualitative research, 163
quota sampling, 175–176
snowball sampling, 176
Normal distribution, 308–310, *309,* 353
Normative decision rules, 34
Null hypotheses
alternative hypotheses versus, 136–137

Null hypotheses *(continued)*
ANOVA and, 338, 340
correlation analysis and, 353–354
defining, 136–137, 323
multiple group hypothesis testing and, 330, 332
population parameter and, 323
predictive power and, 413
significance and, 330, 338, 346
two-way ANOVA and, 340
Numerical labels for scales, 232
Numerical scales, 222–224, *224*

Objectives of research, 85–89, *88,* 103, *104*
Objectivity, 146
Oblique rotation of factors, *391,* 391–392
Observation, 186–188, 197, 204–205
Observation guide, 248
Occupational Safety and Health Administration (OSHA), 53
Off-the-shelf data, 14
Older worker employment survey, *155–156*
One-sample *t* test, 328–329, *329*
One-shot research projects, 5
One Stop (convenience store business), 85
One-tailed test, 372–373
One-way ANOVA, 336
Online billing and payment methods, *88*
Open-ended questions, 255–256, 297
Opening questions in questionnaire, 260
Oral communications, 426, 439–440. *See also* Oral presentations
Oral presentations
audience and, 426, 436–437
format, 437
guidelines, 437–439, *439*
least common denominator principle and, 426
overview, 426, 439–440
with PowerPoint, 437
Order bias, 265
Ordinal data, 326, 353
Ordinal scales, 216, 218–219
Organizational behavior, 287, *288*
Organizational commitment, 12
Organizational culture, 55, *56*
Organizational learning, 14–15
Organizational memory, 14
Orthogonal rotation of factors, 391–392, *391*

OSHA, 53
Outer model, 139
Outliers, 310, 315–316, *316,* 318
Outside research consultants, 19
Outsourcing business research, 19

Paired-comparison scales, 227–228
Panel surveys, 151–153, *153*
Parametric statistical technique, 326–327
Parmalat, 8
Parsimony principle, 40
Participants in research. *See also* Access to participants in research
business researchers and, relationship with, 58–64
coercion issues and, 58–60
debriefing issues and, 62
disclosure issues and, 61–62
ethics in business research and, 65–66, 75
faithful, 66
feedback from, 190, 268
freedom from harm issues and, 60–61
honesty and, 66
Pepsi Challenge, 59
privacy issues and, 58, *59,* 61, 66
voluntary, 65–66
Pattern matching, 125
Pearson chi square test, 333
Pearson correlation, 352–356, *354, 355*
Peer review, 289
Pepsi, 6
Pepsi Challenge, 6, 59
Percentage of variance in original data, 393
Pfizer, 15, *16*
Phenomenology, 277
Pie charts, 306, *307,* 308, *308,* 431, *432*
Placebo, 62
Policy makers, 122
Population
defining, 164, 327
large, sampling from, 176–177, *178*
parameters, 321–323, 345
small, sampling from, 179–180
target, 165–166, *167,* 182, 254
Position bias, 265
Positivism, 277
Postal surveys, 199–200, *201*
Postpositivism, 277
PowerPoint presentations, 437

Practical significance, 355, 368–369, 372

Predictive power, 413

Predictive validity, 240

Premier cigarettes ethical dilemma, 57

Presence (variable relationship), 349

Presenting research, 425–426, 439–440. *See also* Oral communication; Research reports

Pretesting questionnaires, 267–268

Price Waterhouse, 67

Primary business data
  collection methods
    editing and, 296
    overview, 185–186, 187, 204–205
    qualitative, 186–196, 187, 204–205
    quantitative, 197–205
  overview, 185, 204–206
  skills for collecting, 185

Principal component analysis, 390

Privacy issues, 58, *59*, 61, 66

Probability sampling
  cluster sampling, 173–174, *174*
  defining, 167
  errors and, 164
  multistage sampling, 174
  overview, 168, 182–183
  in quantitative research, 163
  simple random sampling, 169, *170*
  stratified sampling, 171–173
  systematic sampling, 169–171, *171*

Probing technique in interviews, 190

Product complexity, measuring, 225, *226*

Productivity survey, worker, 287, *288*

Professional and Emerald, 123

Professional associations, 97–98

Projective techniques, 195–196, *197*

Proportionately stratified sampling, 172

Proportions of responses, 306

Proposals. *See* Research proposals

Proxy variables, 211, *212*

Public speaking. *See* Oral presentations

Purchasing behavior, *120, 202*

Purposive sampling, 175

Push polls, 61

Qualitative data collection
  analyzing, 32, 281–287, *283, 288, 289, 290,* 291

Qualitative data collection *(continued)*
  coding, 32
  content analysis, 189–190
  ethnographic research, 188–189
  interviews, 190–196
  managing, 278, 280
  observation, 186–188
  online, 278, 280, *281*
  overview, 186, *187,* 204–205

Qualitative research. *See also* Qualitative data collection
  approaches, 276–278, 290–291
  conclusions of, drawing and verifying, 286–287
  credibility, assessing, 287–289, *290*
  critical theory and, 278
  criticisms of, 275
  data analysis in, 281–287, *283, 288,* 289, *290,* 291
  data management in, 278, 280, 291
  defining, 275–276
  exploratory research design and, 148
  grounded theory and, 276–277, 290
  hermeneutics and, 277–278, *279–280*
  hypotheses development in, 145–146, 276
  inductive reasoning and, 275–276
  nonprobability sampling in, 163
  overview, 275, 290–291
  positivism and, 277
  postpositivism and, 277
  quantitative research versus, 145–147, *145*
  reliability and, 287
  in Samouel's Greek Cuisine, *289*
  sample size in, 164
  unstructured interviews and, 194
  using, 276

Quality control issue, 343, *344*

Quantitative data collection
  analyzing, 32
  coding, 32
  interview-completed surveys, 197, 203, *203,* 206
  observation, 197, 204
  overview, 197–198, *198,* 204–205
  self-completion surveys, 197–202, 206
  technology and, 198, *199*

Quantitative research. *See also* Descriptive statistics; Quantitative data collection; Testing Hypotheses in quantitative research

Quantitative research *(continued)*
  data analysis in, 295–299, 317
  descriptive statistics, 299
  hypotheses development in, 145–146
  outliers and, 310, 315–316, *316,* 318
  overview, 294, 317–318
  probability sampling in, 163
  qualitative research versus, 145–147, *145*
  sample size in, 164
  testing hypotheses in, 299

Questionnaires
  administering, *249,* 268
  aided questions in, 263–264
  branching questions in, 261
  classification questions in, 261–262
  closed-ended versus open-ended questions in, 255–256
  context effect and, 265
  data collection and, 269–270
  defining, 247–248
  design of
    as art or science, 248, *248*
    branching questions, 261
    clarification of concepts, *249,* 254
    classification questions, 261–262
    good questions, preparing and presenting, 262–266
    initial considerations, 249, 252–254
    instructions, preparing clear, 266, *267*
    opening questions, 260
    overview, 248–249, *249,* 269
    pretesting, *249,* 267–268
    question types, format, and sequence, *249,* 254–262, 270
    research topic questions, 260–261
    sections, 256, 257–259, 270
    sources on, *248*
  double-barreled questions in, 264
  filtering questions in, 260, 296
  funnel approach and, 261
  Gino's Italian Ristorante and, *250–252, 269*
  Internet and, 266
  interview guide and, 248
  leading questions in, 264, *264*
  observation guide and, 248

Questionnaires *(continued)*
order bias and, 265
overview, 247, 269–270
respondent fatigue and, 262
Samouel's Greek Cuisine and, *250–252, 269*
screening questions in, 260, 296
self-completed, 198–202
as self-completion surveys, 198–199, *203*
skipping questions in, 260
unaided questions in, 263
Quirk's Marketing Research Review, 198, *199*
Quota sampling, 175–176

r^2 (coefficient of determination), 353
R^2 (multiple coefficient of determination), 368
Random sampling, simple, 169, *170*
Range, 313
Rank order scales, 228
Rating scales, 219–220
Ratio data, 326
Ratio scales, 220–221, 362
Rational decision making, 35–36
Reading research report, 437
Recommendations section of research report, 434
Reference list in research report, 434
Referral sample, 176
Regression analysis
bivariate, 361–363, *364, 365,* 382
coefficients, 365–366
dummy variables in, 377–378, *379,* 382–383
explained variance and, 364
F ratio and, 364
Gino's Italian Ristorante and, 363–366, *364, 365,* 370–374, *371, 372*
least squares method and, 362
multiple
advanced topics in, 377–380
example of, 369–374, *370, 371, 372*
multicollinearity and, 374–377, *375, 376,* 382
overview, 366–367, 382
statistical versus practical significance and, 368–369
one-tailed test and, 372–373
overview, 361, 381–382
Samouel's Greek Cuisine and, 361, *361,* 363–366, *364, 365,* 369–374, *370, 371, 372*

Regression analysis *(continued)*
sums of squares and, 364–365
two-tailed test and, 372–373
unexplained variance and, 364
Related samples, 334
Relationship marketing, 11–12
Relationships between variables, 348–350, 381
Relative magnitudes, 306
Reliability
alternative forms, 235
caution on, 237–238
coefficient alpha and, 235, *235*
of constructs, 233–238
defining, 233–234
inter-rater, 287
internal consistency, 235
overview, 232–233
qualitative research and, 287
split-half, 235
test-retest, 234
validity versus, 244
Replicable research, 6
Reports. *See* Oral presentations; Research reports
Representative sampling, 165
Research. *See also* Business research
background information and, 94–95
communications, 425–426
decision making in, 3, 8
defining, 3–4
international, 10–11
objectives, 85–89, *88,* 103, *104*
one-shot projects, 5
replicable, 6
skill sets and, 84
technology and, 12
Research-based theory, 36, *37*
Research brief, 430
Research design. *See also* Descriptive research design
basic
overview, 144–145, 158
qualitative versus quantitative, 145–147, *145*
conceptualization and
constructs, identifying, 134
diagrams, preparing, 139–144, *140, 141, 143, 144*
hypotheses and relationships, specifying, 135–138
inner model, 139
outer model, 139
overview, 133, 157
variables, identifying, 134

Research design *(continued)*
in evaluating secondary business data, 124–125, *125*
overview, 133, 157–158
with Samouel's Greek Cuisine, *156–157*
selecting best, 144–145, 154, *154–155*
types of
causal, 153–155, 154
descriptive, 148–153, 151, 152, 153, 155
exploratory, 147–148, 155
overview, 147, 158
using, 154
Research ideas, 85–89
Research methods section of research report, 431
Research problem
in business research process, 28–30, *29*
defining, 28–29, 81, 83, 93–94
evaluating, 84, *85*
literature reviews and, 93–94
overview, 81, 106–108
research question and, 83, 85–89, 106
research topic and, 82–84, *83,* 106
Research proposals
benefits of, 41
in business research, 41
for business-to-business survey, 41, *44*
for Children's Health Foundation, 41, *42–44*
defining, 41
function of, 41, 428
overview, 40–41, 50, 428
purpose of, 425, 428
research question and, 428
for Samouel's Greek Cuisine, *46–48,* 428–429
structure of, 41–42, *42–44,* 45, 429, *429,* 440
Research question
in business research process, 37, 83, 85–89
causal research design and, 155
confirming with literature review, 102–105
descriptive research design and, 155
examples, 103, *104*
exploratory research design and, 155
formulating, 88, *88, 104*

Research question *(continued)*
hypothesis and, 37, *38*, 39, *39*, 95
literature reviews and, 95,
102–105, 108
objectives of research and, 85–89,
88, 103, *104*
research problem and, 83, 85–89,
106
research proposals and, 428
for Samouel's Greek Cuisine,
105–106
theory and, 104–105
Research reports
basic, 434–436
in business research process, 32
editing, 428
empathy and, 428
format of, 429
front-end loading and, 427
function of, 32
guidelines, 427–428
KISS principle and, 427
manager's view of, 426, *427*
organized, 428
orientation and, 428
purpose of, 429
reading, 437
structure of
appendix, 434, *435*
conclusion, 434
executive summary, 430
introduction, 431
overview, 430, 440
recommendations, 434
reference list, 434
research methods, 431
results, 431, *432*, 433, *433*
table of contents, 430
title page, 430
topics not addressed in, avoiding,
428
Research standards, global, *68*
Research topic
overview, 106
questions in questionnaire, 260–261
refining, 86–89
research problem and, 82–84, *83*,
106
risk profile of, 94–95, *95*
sources of, 85–86
theory and, 82, 89
Researcher triangulation, 289
Researchers, 3. *See also* Business
researchers
Respondent fatigue in
questionnaires, 262

Respondents. *See* Participants in
research
Response bias, 264–265, *264*
Restaurant satisfaction construct,
241, *241*
Results section of research report,
431, *432*, 433, *433*
Reuters, 123
Rho correlation coefficient, 219,
356, *356*, *357*, 358, *358*
R.J. Reynolds (RJR), 57
RJR, 57
ROWE (results-only work
environment) research, *103*

Sales-advertising relationship, 33–34
Samouel's Greek Cuisine case study
business decision from theory-
based generalization, 34, *34*
business plan research, 20, *21–22*
correlation analysis and, 354–356,
354, *355*, *357*
customer satisfaction surveys,
303–305, *304*, *305*, *306*, 322,
335, *335*, *336*, 341–343, *342*,
343
data collection method for, *204*
descriptive statistics and, 301–304,
304, *305*, *306*, *317*
discriminant analysis and,
415–418, *415*, *416*, *418*
employee survey, *322*, 353–355, *354*
ethical considerations, *74*
factor analysis and, 395–399, *396*,
397, *398*
frequency distribution and,
301–302, *301*, *302*, *304*
group means test and, 335, *335*,
336, 337–340, *338*, *339*
histograms and, 302–305, *303*,
304, *305*
multicollinearity and, 374–377,
375, *376*
overview, 20, 23
qualitative research in, *289*
questionnaires and, *250–252*, *269*
regression analysis and, 361, *361*,
363–366, *364*, *365*, 369–374,
370, *371*, *372*
research design with, *156–157*
research proposal, *46–48*
research question for, *105–106*
sampling for, 164–165, 170–174,
170, *171*, *172–173*, *174*, *182*
scales and, 216, *217–218*,
219–220, 225, 237, *237*

Samouel's Greek Cuisine case study
(continued)
secondary business data with, *128*
summated and average summated
scores and, *299*
testing hypotheses in quantitative
research and, 321–322, *322*,
340–343, *341*, *342*, *343*,
344–345
theory, *45*
two-way ANOVA and, 340–343,
341, *342*
univariate tests and, 328–329, *329*
Sample, 163
Sample plan, implementing,
180–181
Sample size, 164, 176–180, *178*,
180, 183, 296
Sample statistics, 321–323, 345
Sample surveys, 149
Sampling
bias, 169
in business research process, 164
convenience, 175
disproportionately stratified, 172
independent sample and, 334
judgment, 175
nonprobability, 163, 174–176
overview, 163, 182–183
probability, 163, 168–174
process
nonprobability sampling,
174–176
overview, 165
probability sampling, 168–174
sampling frame, choosing,
166–167
sampling method, selecting,
167, *168*
target population, defining,
165–166
proportionately stratified, 172
purposive, 175
quota, 175–176
related sample and, 334
representative, 165
for Samouel's Greek Cuisine,
164–165, 170–174, *170*, *171*,
172–173, *174*, *182*
sample plan, implementing,
180–181
sample size, determining, 176–180,
178, *180*
selecting best method of, 177, *179*
simple random, 169, *170*
systematic, 169–171, *171*

Sampling frame, choosing, 166–167, 182
Sampling interval, 169–170
Sampling methods, selecting, 167, *168*, 183
Sampling unit, 165–166
Sam's Club, 399–400, *400*, 404
Samuel Adams beer taste test, 331, *331*
SAS software, 339
Satellite technology, 15–16
Scale of measurement, 325–326, *326*, 355–356
Scales. *See also* Measurement
  agree-disagree, 297, 301, *301*
  assessing, criteria for
    overview, 232–233, 233
    reliability, 233–238, 233
    validity, 233, 238–240
  balanced, 231
  behavioral intention, 222
  categorical, 227–228
  categories of, 230–232
  constant sum, 229
  defining, 212
  developing
    practical decisions for, 230–232
    steps in, 240–241
  forced-choice, 231–232
  Gino's Italian Ristorante and, 222
  graphic ratings, 225–226
  interval, 219–220, 362
  Likert, 221–222, 298
  metric, 222–226
  multi-item, 230, 233–235, *234*, *236*
  nominal, 215–216
  nonmetric, 222, 227–229
  numerical, 223–224, *224*
  numerical labels for, 232
  ordinal, 216, 218–219
  overview, 215, 243–244
  paired-comparison, 227–228
  rank order, 228
  rating, 219–220
  ratio, 220–221, 362
  resources, *242–243*
  Samouel's Greek Cuisine and, 216, *217–218*, 219–220, 225, 237, *237*
  semantic differential, 224–225, *226*
  sorting, 228
  summated ratings, 221–222
  unbalanced, 231
  unlabeled, 232
  verbal labels for, 232
Scandals, business, 52

Scanning devices, 202, *202*
Scatter diagram, 351, *352*
Scattergram, 351, *352*
Scheffé follow-up test, 337
Science, 4, 40, 49–50, 146
Scientific method, 37–40, *38*, 49
Screening questions in questionnaire, 260, 296
Seasonal trends survey, 149, 151, *151*, *152*
Second Life (digital environment), 29
Secondary business data
  access complications with, 122–123
  advantages of, 119, *119*, 129
  collecting, 113–114
  defining, 111
  disadvantages of, *119*, 122–124, 129
  ethical issues related to using, 127, 130
  evaluating
    comparative analysis, 120
    cross-sectional analysis, 121
    data collection methods, 125–127, 125
    longitudinal analysis, 120–121
    overview, 124, *125*, 130
    purpose of, 121–122
    research design, 124–125, 125
    source, 124, *125*
  external, 112, *113*
  format, 112–113, *113*
  internal, 112, *113*, 114
  on Internet, 114, 116, *116*, *117–118*
  lack of familiarity with, 123
  locating, 114, *115*, 116, *116*
  overview, 110, 128–130
  policy makers and, 122
  reexamining, 122
  with Samouel's Greek Cuisine, *128*
  sources
    caution about, *116*
    contextual issues and, 121
    cross-sectional analysis and, 121
    Internet, 30–31, 116, 117–118, 121, 127, 129
    locating, 114, *115*, 116
    overview, 111–114, 113, 129
  types of, 111–114, *113*
Sections of questionnaire, 256, *257–259*, 270
Secure Customer Index, *236*

Self-completion instructions, 266
Self-completion surveys, 197–202, 206
Semantic differential scales, 224–225, *226*
Semistructured interviews, 191–193, *193*, *196*
SERVPERF construct, 124
SERVQUAL construct, 124
Share of customers, 12
Siemens, 147
Significance
  of correlation coefficient, 350–352, *351*
  null hypotheses and, 330, 338, 346
  practical, 355, 368–369, 372
  statistical, 355, 368–369, 372
Simmons Market Research Bureau, *120*
Simple random sampling, 169, *170*
Simple structure in factor analysis, 391
Single group hypothesis testing, 327–329
Skewness, 314
Skill sets, 84, 185, 191–192
Skipping questions in questionnaire, 260
Skoda (Czech car), 10
Snowball sampling, 176
Social responsibilities, 53
Soda survey, 6
Sorting scales, 228
Spearman rank order correlation, 219, 356, *356*, *357*, 358, *358*
Split-half reliability, 235
SPSS software
  ANOVA follow-up tests and, 339
  bivariate regression analysis and, *364*
  cluster identification for customer survey perception variables, *407*
  correlation coefficient significance and, 350
  Cronbach's alpha and, 237, *237*
  equal variance and, 339
  group means and, *409*
  missing data and, 296
  simple random sampling and, 169, *170*
  Spearman rho correlation and, *356*
  t test and, 335
  testing hypotheses in quantitative research and, 321
  two-tailed test and, 373

Squared Euclidean distances, 402
SSI LITe eSamples, *166*
Standard deviation, 177, 308, 313–314
Standard error, 309
Standard error of the mean, 314
Standard normal distribution, 309
Standardization, 366
Standardized coefficients, 366
Statistical Office of the European Commission, 113
Statistical power, 325
Statistical significance, 355, 368–369, 372
Statistical techniques. *See also* Descriptive statistics; Inferential statistics; Sample statistics
  application of, appropriate, 337, *337*
  classification of, 359, *359*
  data analysis and, 358–360
  defining, 360, *360*
  inferential, 321–323
  nonparametric, 326–327
  parametric, 326–327
  selecting, 325–327, 345
Stepwise discriminant analysis, 418
Stickiness, defining, 9
Stock markets, 111, 121
Strategic decision making, 3, 8, 19
Stratified sampling, 171–172
Strength of association (variable relationship), 350
Structured interviews, 191
Studies. *See* Case studies; Surveys and studies
Subjectivity, 146
Subjects. *See* Participants in research
Sum of absolute differences, 402
Sum of squared factor loadings, *393*, 394
Summated ratings scales, 221–222
Summated score, 298–299, *299*
Sums of squares, 364–365
Survey Sampling International (SSI), 165, *166*
Surveys and studies. *See also* Questionnaires
  beer taste, 331, *331*
  business school rankings, 121
  business-to-business, 41, *44*
  buying behavior, *120, 202*
  casual Fridays, 39, *39*
  customer satisfaction, 303–305, *304, 305, 306,* 322, 335, *335, 336*

Surveys and studies *(continued)*
  editing, 295–296
  electronic, 200, 202
  employee, *322,* 353–355, *354*
  fast food, 386, *388,* 409–414, *410, 414*
  interview-completed, 197, 203, *203,* 206
  job stress, 60
  kiosk, 202
  mail, 199–200, 201
  media consumption patterns, *120*
  methods of, frequency of usage of, 198, *198*
  music in department stores, 150, *151*
  older worker employment, *155–156*
  panel, 151–153, *153*
  postal, 199–200, *201*
  productivity of worker, 287, *288*
  sample, 149
  scotch, 331–332, *332*
  seasonal trends, 149, 151, *151, 152*
  self-completion, 197–202, 206
  soda, 6
  Web-hosted Internet, 200, 202
SurveySpot panel, *166*
Symptoms (signals for change), 103, *104*
Systematic sampling, 169–171, *171*

t test, 325, 327, 328, *329,* 334–335, *335,* 337, 345–346, 365–366
Table of contents of research report, 430
Tactical decision making, 3, 8, 19
Target population, 165–166, *167,* 182, 254
Taylor, Frederick, 4
Technical writing guidelines, 427–428. *See also* Research proposals; Research reports
Technology. *See also* Internet
  business researcher-participant relationship and, 58
  business researchers and, *17–18*
  card reader, 12–13
  data warehouses, 13–14
  digital money payment systems, *88*
  electronic communications, 13
  electronic search engines, 114, *115,* 116, *118*
  focus groups and, 193
  global positioning system, 15–16, *17,* 188
  knowledge, testing, *18*
  networking, 13

Technology *(continued)*
  office restructure and, *103*
  organizational learning, 14–15
  overview, 12–13, 23
  quantitative data collection and, 198, *199*
  research and, 12
  satellite, 15–16
  scanning devices, 202, *202*
  USB stick, 13
  videoconferencing, 13
  voice over IP, 13
  wireless, 94
Telephone interviews, 190. *See also* Interviews
Tesco, *29,* 121
Test-retest reliability, 234
Testing hypotheses in quantitative research
  ANOVA and, 336–343, *341, 344*
  bivariate tests, 325, 330–335, *331, 332, 333*
  chi square tests, 325, 330–333, *331,* 346
  F distribution, 337
  Gino's Italian Ristorante, *338,* 340–343, *341, 342, 343*
  hypothesis testing and, 325–329
  hypothesized relationships and, understanding, 321–325, *322, 344–345,* 345
  MANOVA and, 343
  multiple group hypothesis testing and, 330–335, *331, 332, 333,* 345
  multivariate tests, 325, 330–335, *331, 332, 333,* 345
  overview, 320–321, 345–346
  Samouel's Greek Cuisine and, 321–322, *322, 338,* 340–343, *341, 342, 343, 344–345*
  single group hypothesis testing and, 327–329, *329*
  SPSS software and, 321
  t test, 325, 327, 328, *329,* 334–335, *335,* 337, 346
  univariate tests, 325, 327–329, *329,* 345
Textbooks as sources of literature reviews, 97
Theoretical constructs, 139
Theory
  behavioral learning, 34–35
  benefits of, 36–37, *37*
  in business research process, 33–35, 39, *39,* 49, 88–89

Theory *(continued)*
  competition, 33
  critical, 278
  defining, 33, 49, 104
  descriptive, 35
  grounded, 276–277, 290
  hierarchy of effects, 104–105, *105*
  hypothesis and, 33, 39, *39*
  Internet and, 35, *36*
  law-like generalizations and, 33
  mathematical, *36*
  overview, 49
  practicality of, 35–37
  rational decision making and,
      35–36
  research-based, 36, *37*
  research question and, 104–105
  research topic and, 82, 89
  in Samouel's Greek Cuisine, *45*
Theory-based decision rules, *37*
Theory triangulation, 289
Theses as sources of literature
    reviews, 98
3M, 189
Title page of research report, 430
Total variance, 389–390
Toyota, 5
Transformation of data, 298
Translational equivalence, 10–11, *11*
Treatment (level of factors), 336
Triangulation, 289
Trust, 52–53
Trustworthiness, 287. *See also*
    Credibility; Validity
Truth-seeking, 3–5
Two-group cluster solution, 408, *409*
Two-tailed test, 372–373
Two-way ANOVA, 336, 340–343,
    341
Type I and II errors, 323–325

U.K. Office for National Statistics,
    123
Unaided questions, 263
Unbalanced scales, 231
Unethical actions, implications of,
    66–69
Unexplained variance, 364
Unidirectional relationships, 139
Unique variance, 389
United Nations, 123
Univariate correlation analysis, 358
Univariate statistical tests, 325,
    327–329, *329*, 345

Universe (group of knowledgeable
    people), 164. *See also*
    Population
Unlabeled scales, 232
Unobtrusive approach, 121–22, 188
Unstandardized coefficients, 366
Unstructured interviews, 194, *194*
UPS, 13
U.S. Census Bureau, 14, 98, 123
U.S. Department of Commerce, 98
U.S. Department of Labor, *115*
U.S. Federal Reserve, 120
USB stick, 13

Validity
  concurrent, 240
  of constructs, 238–239
  content, 238
  convergent, 239
  credibility and, 286–287
  criterion, 239–240
  defining, 238
  discriminant, 239
  face, 238
  measurement, 126
  overview, 232–233, 238
  predictive, 240
  reliability versus, 244
Variables. *See also* Correlation
    analysis; Regression analysis
  categorical independent, 336
  concrete, 211, 213–214
  covariation and, 350–352, *352*
  curvilinear relationship between,
      349, 381
  customer survey perceptions, *407*
  dependent, 134, 143, 321, 359–360,
      362, 366–367, 385
  direction and, 349–350
  dummy, 362, 377–378, *379*,
      382–383
  identifying in conceptualization,
      134–138
  independent, 134, 321, 362,
      366–367, 374, 385
  indicator, 139
  linear relationship between, 349,
      381
  to measure customer interaction, 210
  measured, 139, 142–143, *143*
  in measuring constructs, 210
  metric dependent, 359–360
  nonlinear relationship between,
      349, 381

Variables *(continued)*
  nonmetric dependent, 359–360
  number of, statistical technique
      selection and, 325
  presence and, 349
  proxy, 211, *212*
  relationships between, 348–350,
      381
  strength of association and, 350
  types of, 134
Variance. *See also* ANOVA;
    MANOVA
  common, 389–390
  defining, 313, 389
  dispersion measurement and, 313
  error, 389–390
  error term and, 143
  explained, 364
  in exploratory factor analysis,
      389–390, *389*
  percentage of, in original data, 393
  total, 389–390
  unexplained, 364
  unique, 389
Variation between groups, 337–339,
    400–401, *401*
Variation within groups, 337–339,
    400–401, *401*
Varimax option, 392, *393*
Verbal labels for scales, 232
Verification of qualitative research,
    286–287
Verifying conclusions, 286–287
Videoconferencing, 13
Voice over IP (VoIP), 13
Volga (Russian car), 10
Voluntary participants in research,
    65–66

Web-hosted Internet survey, 200,
    202
Wilks' lambda, 415
Worker productivity survey, 287,
    288
World Bank, 111–112, 120
World market, 10
Written communications, 426–428.
    See also Research proposals;
    Research reports

Yahoo!, 8, 148

Z distribution, 309–310
Z scores, 411–413, *413*, 418

About the Authors

Joseph F. Hair Jr. is director of doctoral programs in the Coles College of Business at Kennesaw State University (KSU), Kennesaw, Georgia. He has authored or coauthored over forty books, including *Marketing*, 11th ed. (Cengage, 2009); *Multivariate Data Analysis*, 7th ed. (Prentice Hall, 2010); *Research Methods for Business* (Wiley, 2007); *Marketing Research*, 4th ed. (McGraw-Hill/Irwin, 2009); and *Sales Management* (Houghton Mifflin, 2009). He has also published numerous articles in professional journals such as the *Journal of Marketing Research*, *Journal of the Academy of Marketing Science*, *Journal of Business*, *Journal of Advertising Research*, *Journal of Business Research*, *International Marketing Management*, *Journal of Marketing Theory and Practice*, *European Business Review*, *Journal of Personal Selling and Sales Management*, *Industrial Marketing Management*, *Journal of Experimental Education*, *Business Horizons*, *Journal of Retailing*, *Marketing Education Review*, *Journal of Marketing Education*, *Multivariate Behavioral Research*, and others.

Dr. Hair is a distinguished fellow of the Academy of Marketing Science and of the Society for Marketing Advances. He has also served as president of the following organizations: the Academy of Marketing Science, Society for Marketing Advances, Southern Marketing Association, Association for Healthcare Research, Southwestern Marketing Association, and American Institute for Decision Sciences, Southeast Section. He has been program chairperson and proceedings editor for several scholarly associations.

He was recognized as the KSU Coles College Foundation Distinguished Professor in 2009 and received the Berkman Lifetime Service Achievement Award from the Academy of Marketing Science. Professor Hair was also recognized as the Aronoff Distinguished Professor in 2008 and as Innovative Marketer of the Year in 2007 by the Marketing Management Association. In 2004 he received the Academy of Marketing Science Outstanding Marketing Teaching Excellence Award.

Mary Wolfinbarger Celsi is associate dean for accreditation and professor of marketing at California State University, Long Beach (CSULB). She earned a BS in English from Vanderbilt University and a master's in business and public administration and a PhD in marketing at the University of California, Irvine. Her specialties include Internet marketing, marketing research, and internal marketing. She has been teaching at CSULB since 1990. Dr. Celsi has expertise in both quantitative and qualitative research methodologies.

Dr. Celsi has coauthored articles about consumer behavior and the Internet. Her interest in e-commerce and technology extends to the classroom: she developed and taught the first Internet marketing course at CSULB in 1999. She has also written articles on the impact of technology and e-commerce on the classroom and on the business school curriculum.

Dr. Celsi has collaborated in research on the topic of internal marketing, conducting studies at several Fortune 500 companies. The Marketing Science Institute awarded Dr. Celsi two grants to study internal marketing. She has published articles in the *Journal of Marketing, Journal of Consumer Research, Journal of Retailing, Journal of the Academy of Marketing Science, California Management Review, Journal of Business Research*, and *Earthquake Spectra*.

Arthur H. Money holds a PhD in mathematical statistics from the University of Cape Town, South Africa. He is professor emeritus at the Henley Business School at the University of Reading, Henley-on-Thames, Oxfordshire, U.K. He is actively involved in doctoral programs, master's programs, and staff development programs in the United Kingdom, Ireland, United States, Sweden, Norway, and South Africa.

Dr. Money has been a member of the South African Statistical Association and the Operations Research Society of South Africa, which he served as president. He has served on the Executive Committee of the European Doctoral Programmes Association in Management and Business Administration and on the Steering Committee of the European Doctoral School on Knowledge and Management.

He has authored or coauthored journal articles in the following areas: mathematical statistics, operations research, finance, information systems, marketing, and human relations. He is a coauthor of twelve books. He has also been listed in *Who's Who in the World* since 1997 and was listed in *Barron's 500* (Millennium Edition). Finally, he has the distinction of being the first holder of the honorary degree of master of the college (honoris causa) at Henley Management College.

Phillip Samouel was educated in the United Kingdom, gaining a BA first class honors in social science and two master's, one in economics and the other in management science from, respectively, the London School of Economics and Imperial College London. He earned his PhD in business administration from Henley Management College/Brunel University in 1995 and recently received an honorary PhD from the Academy of National Economy, Moscow.

His career has included successful endeavors in both academia and the commercial world. Between 1974 and 1984 he built Sammy George Fashion Ltd., a garment manufacturer in London, with its own label, London Lady. Since 1984 he has been running a successful farming enterprise, Ladyland Farm: "The Living Classroom," which is also an education center delivering aspects of the U.K. Science National Curriculum to over 35,000 children a year.

Dr. Samouel was on the faculty of Kingston University, London, where he has been head of the Department of Strategy, Marketing, and Entrepreneurship, director of the Business School, and most recently dean of faculty and a member of the university's executive committee. He has served on the Executive Committee of the European Doctoral Programmes Association in Management and Business Administration and on the Steering Committee of the European Doctoral School on Knowledge and Management.

Michael J. Page is the vice president for academic affairs and the dean of business and the McCallum Graduate School, Bentley University, Waltham, Massachusetts. Prior to his appointment at Bentley University, Dr. Page held senior positions at the Graduate School of Business of the University of Cape Town, South Africa, and at the Rotterdam School of Management, Erasmus University, Netherlands. His international experience spans the globe, with successful engagements and strategic alliances on every continent. An advocate of diversity and inclusion, he has assisted companies and institutions in developing learning paradigms that maximize human capital performance.

Dr. Page's business and management education experience covers all forms of tertiary education, from undergraduate to executive development of both an open and customized nature. The majority of his teaching and research experience is in finance and statistics. He held the Len Abrahamse Chair in Finance while at the University of Cape Town, was a trustee professor at Erasmus University, and currently has a joint professorial appointment in finance and management at Bentley University.

Throughout his twenty-year career as an academic, Dr. Page has maintained his applied focus, with significant commercial consulting and leadership experience, including extensive involvement with all aspects of business school life in the state and private sectors. Directorship positions at two internationally recognized business schools have involved managing commercial operations run independently of their parent universities.